OXFORD ST
IN
MODERN LEGAL

GENERAL EDITOR

A. W. Brian Simpson
Professor of Law, University of Michigan

A History of Water Rights at Common Law

JOSHUA GETZLER

OXFORD
UNIVERSITY PRESS

OXFORD
UNIVERSITY PRESS
Great Clarendon Street, Oxford OX2 6DP

Oxford University Press is a department of the University of Oxford.
It furthers the University's objective of excellence in research, scholarship,
and education by publishing worldwide in

Oxford New York

Auckland Bangkok Buenos Aires Cape Town Chennai
Dar es Salaam Delhi Hong Kong Istanbul Karachi Kolkata
Kuala Lumpur Madrid Melbourne Mexico City Mumbai Nairobi
São Paulo Shanghai Singapore Taipei Tokyo Toronto

Oxford is a registered trade mark of Oxford University Press
in the UK and in certain other countries

Published in the United States
by Oxford University Press Inc., New York

First published 2004

Published new as paper back, 2006

British Library Cataloguing in Publication Data
Data available

Library of Congress Cataloging in Publication Data
Data available

ISBN 978-0-19-920760-2

3 5 7 9 10 8 6 4

Typeset by SPI Publisher Services, Pondicherry, India
Printed in Great Britain
on acid-free paper by
Biddles Ltd., King's Lynn

To my parents

General Editor's Preface

This book provides the first comprehensive study of the evolution of the English common law relating to rights to water. The resource itself is of course vital to agricultural and industrial development, and indeed to life itself, and, notwithstanding the popular feeling that in England and Wales it never stops raining, competition over access to water has a continuous history since the dawn of the common law itself. Yet until the late nineteenth century, long after the peak of the agricultural and industrial revolutions, and long after the rapid urbanization which went with them, the common law courts had not managed to produce a settled and coherent body of water law, and no form of comprehensive legislative code existed to supply the deficiency. On the face of things this is a very surprising fact. If, as some argue, a clear allocation of rights to resources, coupled with an effective body of contract law, is a prerequisite to economic progress, development, and increasing accumulation of wealth, how did the English Industrial Revolution contrive to occur?

Dr. Getzler bases his views on this and other wider questions on a meticulous and highly original analysis of the case law and on the writings of Bracton, Coke, Hale, Blackstone, and Gale, and of the theoretical underpinnings of the common law doctrines as to natural rights, servitudes, claims based on prior appropriation, on prescription, and on custom. But Dr. Getzler's book is not simply important as a study of the history of water law, viewed as an autonomous body of legal doctrine. It also provides the basis upon which it becomes possible to assess the validity of theories which link the evolution of bodies of private law to the conception of economic efficiency. In addition to this water law has a peculiar conceptual history. It first developed in a world dominated by the structure provided by the world of the forms of action, being uneasily located in the interstices of procedure. The characteristic theoretical poverty of the indigenous law was, to a considerable degree, eventually offset by borrowings from ancient Roman and more modern continental civil law, and from other sources, to produce, in the late Victorian period, a coherent and developed jurisprudence. In the process of doctrinal development fundamental ideas about the nature and basis for property rights competed with each other. What place should be given to the first in time? Should the use of water be subjected to communitarian ideas, or should Blackstone's despotic dominion reign uncontrolled, as it did in *Mayor of Bradford* v. *Pickles*,[1] the subject of

[1] [1895] A.C. 587 (H.L.).

another study in this series?[2] Was the regulation of access to water beyond the ability of the common law, and better left to legislative control? Or could a combination between property law and contract law settle the problem of competition for the use of a limited resource? These and other issues are explored in this book.

And more general ones too. To what extent is this process to be understood as internal to the common law, and to what extent was legal development in this branch of the law the product of philosophical, political, and economic ideas external to the system? Is doctrinal legal development driven primarily by specifically legal considerations, or does doctrine merely reflect the pressure of external forces on the process of adjudication?

While providing a meticulous and detailed analysis of the legal materials Dr. Getzler addresses these and other wider issues in the explanation of the evolution of private law, and his book is both a contribution to legal history and an important and fascinating contribution to legal theory. It is a pleasure to welcome it to the series.

A.W. Brian Simpson

[2] M. Taggart, *Private Property and Abuse of Rights in Victorian England: The Story of Edward Pickles and the Bradford Water Supply* (Oxford, 2002).

Preface

As I was completing this book, water supplies to my home and to my office were cut off for a few days in the middle of the cool English summer. My family enjoyed the rude transformation of our life caused by this disruption, and it brought home to me how crucially important an orderly water supply is for nearly everything we do.

Water law is a chief institutional component of our water supply; yet water law comprises a particularly obscure part of English land law, a dark area within a system scarcely marked by rationality at its best. Water rights are difficult because they emerge from the borderlands between servitudes, nuisance law, trespass, and the various actions for possession. Medieval lawyers' thinking became trapped among these categories, preventing a confident statement of the juristic basis of rights to water. In the formative seventeenth century judges inserted Romanist and Bractonian concepts of natural rights and servitudes into the common-law categories of trespass and nuisance; but the fit was uneasy. Blackstone in the 1760s recast servitude and easement law with the addition of new theories of incorporeal property and rights by occupancy. After him, the jurisprudence of water remained unsettled for close on one hundred years. A coherent modern law of riparian and ground water rights emerged only after a transplant of American and civilian doctrine in the 1850s. Thus there was no rationalized body of water law throughout the long span of England's agrarian reform and industrialization. The underlying problem addressed in this book is to explain how economic development in England, which was heavily dependent on water resources from the early thirteenth century, could have taken place in the absence of definite property rights in those resources. Economic science instructs us today that clarity of property rights is an essential pre-condition of economic growth. The history of the common law of water during early industrialization tells a different story.

This book derives from my Oxford D.Phil. thesis. At Oxford I was able to learn from many fine lawyers and historians, building on foundations laid by my teachers in Australia in the 1980s. It is a pleasure now to thank those who helped me over many years of study in Oxford. David Ibbetson, the supervisor of my doctoral dissertation, was painstaking in details and unsparingly generous in insights, learning, criticism, and enthusiasm. Brian Simpson and Gerry Rubin examined the thesis and suggested many improvements. Brian's work on the history of property doctrine in particular has been a seminal influence, and he has helped me reshape the book with an acute eye. Stuart Anderson and Bernard Rudden helped me define my earlier ideas, and Avner Offer and Jane Stapleton gave me essential guidance throughout. Clare Dalton kindly shared with me her work on tort liability in the nineteenth century. Ron Harris's investigations of industrialization and corporate form demonstrated to me the rewards of combining legal and economic history, and his friendship has been a secure rock for many years now. Much-appreciated help was given by Bob Allen, Peter Birks, Brian Bix, Susan Bright, Lynette Costello, John Dewar, Jeffrey Hackney, Charles Donahue, Charles Feinstein, Jim Harris, Andrew Hildreth, Morton Horwitz, Tessa Jarvis, Fiona Jenkins Gerard Kahn, Sandy Kedar, Rande Kostal, Michael Lobban, Janet Loengard, Andrea Loux, Mark McGaw, Anne MacKenzie, Ezra Marcus, Alain Pottage, David Omissi, Maurice Scott, Philip Torr, and Katherine Turner. The Bodleian Law Library at Oxford was a fine work-place with ever-helpful staff. I am grateful to the fellows and heads of three Oxford colleges for support. Balliol College provided help for the first two years of doctoral work and afforded me the intense community I had hoped to find in Oxford. I was then awarded a Commonwealth Scholarship at Nuffield College, which brought me good fellowship and intellectual stimulation in equal measure. St Hugh's College, my academic home for many years now, provided me with fine surroundings for the last stages of writing, and allowed me a term of sabbatical leave early in my teaching career to develop my dissertation. At St Hugh's, Edward Burn, Andrew Burrows, Adrian Moore, David Robertson, Ann Smart, Lionel Smith, and Derek Wood were superb counter-parties to conversations about law and much else. I am particularly fortunate to have Mike Macnair as my colleague. He has afforded me the great benefit of his legal expertise, and also deepened my understanding of the history of law in the course of much fruitful conversation. Another free term for writing was provided by the British Academy's Research Leave Award Scheme. The late Paul Bourke arranged a productive summer stay at the Department of History of the Research School of Social Sciences at the Australian National University where I first studied law and history. The law faculties of the Hebrew University of Jerusalem and Tel Aviv University were fascinating workplaces, and for this I particularly thank Oren Gross, Alon Harel, Assaf Likhovski, Ariel Porat, and Alex Stein. For a lively and stimulating visit to the University of Chicago I thank especially Lisa Bernstein, Richard Epstein, Philip Hamburger, and Richard Helmholz. Richard Hart and John Louth were patient editors, and I am also grateful to Kate Elliott and the production editors at the Press, and to two anonymous readers for their acute comments before publication. The Oxford Law Faculty funded various stages of the project, and Lisa Gourd gave priceless help in the preparation of the proof manuscript.

On a more personal note, Ezra, Abigail, Israel, and Dvorah Getzler offered me every support during my years sequestered in doctoral research. My daughters Naomi and Esther have taken a selective view of my water law project; they enjoy aquatic activities very much but it is still a little early for them to be studying any law. My final debts are greatest of all. Lucia Zedner has taught me what is most valuable and important. My parents Manny and Rochelle have always given me the strongest encouragement as a student, at home in Australia and in distant England, and I dedicate the book to them.

JSG
Oxford
March 2003

Acknowledgements

Selected extracts are reprinted by kind permission of the publisher from Henry de Bracton, *De Legibus et Consuetudinibus Angliae* (*On the Laws and Customs of England*), *Volumes II and III*, translated and with revisions and notes by Samuel E. Thorne, Cambridge, Mass.: Harvard University Press: Copyright 1968, 1977 by the President and Fellows of Harvard College.

Contents

Table of Cases

Anonymous Year Book Cases

Table of Statutes

Regnal Years

Adapted from J. H. Baker, *An Introduction to English Legal History* (4th edn., London, 2002) xliii–xliv

House of Normandy

Will. 1	25 December 1066
Will. 2	26 September 1087
Hen. 1	5 August 1100
Stephen	26 December 1135

Angevins (*House of Plantagenet*)

Hen. 2	19 December 1154
Ric. 1	3 September 1189
John	27 May 1199

Plantagenets (*continued*)

Hen. 3	28 October 1216
Edw. 1	20 November 1272
Edw. 2	8 July 1307
Edw. 3	25 January 1327
Ric. 2	22 June 1377

House of Lancaster

Hen. 4	30 September 1399
Hen. 5	21 March 1413
Hen. 6	1 September 1422

House of York

Edw. 4	4 March 1461
Edw. 5	9 April 1483
Ric. 3	26 June 1483

House of Tudor

Hen. 7	22 August 1485

Hen. 8	22 April 1509
Edw. 6	28 January 1547
Mary 1	19 July 1553
Phil. & Mary	25 July 1554
Eliz. 1	17 November 1558

House of Stuart

Jac. 1	24 March 1603
Car. 1	27 March 1625
[Interregnum]	1649–1660
Car. 2	30 January 1649 [*de jure*]
Jac. 2	6 February 1685
Will. & Mary	13 February 1689
Will. 3	28 December 1694
Anne	8 March 1702

House of Hanover

Geo. 1	1 August 1714
Geo. 2	11 June 1727
Geo. 3	25 October 1760
Geo. 4	29 January 1820
Will. 4	26 June 1830
Vict.	20 June 1837

House of Saxe-Coburg and Gotha

Edw. 7	22 January 1901

House of Windsor

Geo. 5	6 May 1910
Edw. 8	20 January 1936
Geo. 6	11 December 1936
Eliz. 2	6 February 1952

For calendar years the abbreviations CE (Common Era) and BCE (Before Common Era) are used rather than AD and BC.

Abbreviations

COURTS AND JURISDICTIONS

C.A.	Court of Appeal
Ch.	Chancery
Ch. Ap.	Chancery Appeals
C.P.	Common Pleas
Ex.	Exchequer
Ex. Ch.	Exchequer Chamber
H.L.	House of Lords
K.B.	King's Bench
L.C.	Lord Chancellor (Chancery, first instance and appeal)
M.R.	Master of the Rolls (Chancery)
N.P.	Nisi Prius
P.C.	Privy Council
Q.B.	Queen's Bench
V.C.	Vice-Chancellor (Chancery)

Nominate reports are given in the standard abbreviated form only. English Report (E.R.) citations are generally added to nominate citations.

SOURCES

Bl.Comm.	Blackstone, Sir William, *Commentaries on the Law of England* 4 vols. (1st edn., Oxford, 1765–9; 15th edn., by E. Christian, 1809)
Bracton	Bracton, Henry de, *De Legibus et Consuetudinibus Angliae*, 4 vols. (ed. G.E. Woodbine, translated S.E. Thorne, Cambridge, Mass., 1977)
C.	*Codex Justinianus* (ed. P. Krueger, Berlin, 1877)
Co.Litt.	Coke, Sir Edward, *The First Part of the Institutes of the Laws of England, or, A Commentary on Littleton* (1628; ed. F. Hargrave and C. Butler, 19th edn., London, 1832)
D.	*Digest of Justinian* (ed. T. Mommsen and P. Krueger, translation ed. A. Watson, 4 Vols., Philadelphia, Penn., 1985)

F.N.B.	Fitzherbert, A., *The New Natura Brevium* (*La Nouel Natura Breuium*) (1534; 9th edn., London, 1794)
G.Inst.	Gaius, *Institutiones Iuris Civilis, The Institutes of Gaius* (ed. and translated by F. de Zulueta, Oxford, 1946)
Glanvill	Henry de Glanvill, *Tractatus de Legibus et Consuetudinibus regni Anglie qui Glanvilla vocatur* (*The treatise on the laws and customs of the realm of England commonly called Glanvill* (*c.*1187–9), (G.D.G. Hall (ed. and trans.), London, 1965)
HEL	F. Pollock and F. W. Maitland, *The History of English Law Before the Time of Edward I*, 2 vols. (1895, 2nd edn., Cambridge, 1898, reprinted 1968)
H.L.R.O.	House of Lords Record Office
Inst.	*Justinian's Institutes* (ed. P. Krueger, translated P.B.H. Birks and G. McLeod, London, 1987)
Littleton	Littleton, T., *Les Tenures* (London, *c.*1481, ed. E. Wambaugh, Washington, DC, 1903)
NPDEL	*The New Palgrave Dictionary of Economics and the Law*, 3 vols. (P. Newman (ed.), London, 1998)
P.R.O.	Public Record Office
Reg. Omn. Brev.	*Registrum Omnium Brevium* (London, 1531, reprinted 1634, 1687)
Roll. Abdgt.	Rolle, H., *Un Abridgment des Plusieurs Cases et Resolutions del Common Ley* 2 vols. (ed. Sir M. Hale, London, 1668)
Viner's Abdgt.	Viner, C., *A General Abridgement of Law and Equity*, 23 vols. (Aldershot, 1741–53; 2nd edn., 1794)

Spellings in modern form are given for most primary sources, but with some exceptions, e.g. Blackstone's spelling of 'assise' is preserved, 'assize' is used elsewhere.

Introduction

Though the Water running in the Fountain be every ones, yet who can doubt, but that in the Pitcher is his only who drew it out? His *labour* hath taken it out of the hands of Nature, where it was common, and belong'd equally to all her Children, and *hath* thereby appropriated it to himself. . . .

Nor was this *appropriation* of any parcel of *Land*, by improving it, any prejudice to any other Man, since there was still enough, and as good left; and more than the yet unprovided could use. So that in effect, there was never the less left for others because of his enclosure for himself. For he that leaves as much as another can make use of, does as good as take nothing at all. No Body could think himself injur'd by the drinking of another Man, though he took a good Draught, who had a whole River of the same Water left him to quench his thirst. And the Case of Land and Water, where there is enough of both, is perfectly the same.[1]

THE SIGNIFICANCE OF RIPARIAN DOCTRINE

John Locke used the example of water to illustrate his moral theory of property rights, which was part of his wider political doctrine of representative government. By contrast, in today's world private property in goods such as land and water is commonly justified by the theory that clearly defined, assignable, and enforceable legal titles to appropriable goods are a critical feature of productive market economies. The efficiency theory of property will be put to the test in this book through an investigation of the legal history of a key resource of England's Industrial Revolution, namely flowing water.

Water resources were central to England's precocious economic development in the thirteenth and sixteenth centuries, and then again in the industrial, transport, and urban revolutions of the late eighteenth and early nineteenth centuries. Each of these periods saw much legal conflict over water rights, typically between domestic, agricultural, and manufacturing interests competing for access to flowing water. From 1750 the common-law courts developed a large but unstable body of legal doctrine, specifying strong property rights in flowing water attached to riparian possession, and also limited rights to surface and underground waters. The new water doctrines were built from Roman law and Roman-derived civil-law concepts of common goods and the natural rights of ownership, together with the

[1] J. Locke, *Second Treatise of Government* ss. 29 and 33, in *Two Treatises of Government* (P. Laslett (ed.), Cambridge, 1960) 331, 333.

English sources of Bracton and Blackstone, part-civilians themselves. Water law is one of the most Romanesque parts of English law, demonstrating the extent to which common and civilian law have commingled. Water law stands as a refutation of the still-common belief that English and European law parted ways irreversibly in the twelfth century.

A large body of common-law water and land-use doctrine had developed in medieval times, combining native feudal and cosmopolitan Institutionalist influences. Natural-right and prescriptive theories of water rights extant before 1700 were challenged and eventually supplanted around 1800 by Blackstone's occupancy theory of entitlement. Over the next fifty years there emerged a modified theory of rights to natural flow, whereby riparian owners could use water for the reasonable needs of their land, or could exceed reasonable use by grant or prescription giving an expanded right against neighbours.

The long instability of riparian doctrine stemmed from the nature of its subject matter. Flowing water cannot be possessed in a tangible fashion like land, only quasi-possessed or appropriated by user. The common-law theory of title based on a hierarchy of seisin or possession required some apparent user—a matter of evidence—in order to establish an actionable right. The requirement of established use to ground seisin was emphasized by the rise to dominance of the trespass on the case form of action, which characteristically focused on indirect or non-invasive damage. Hence water rights defended by action on the case came to appear as possessory interests based on current usage, rather than titles or claims to a resource regardless of levels of use; and the legal system found it particularly difficult to evolve doctrines describing and balancing such use-claims. Added to this is the issue of balancing the interests of multiple yet rivalrous users: 'Problems concerned with the sharing of water supplies and the joint utilization of river systems are inherently unsuited to adjudicative solution, involving as they do a complex interplay of diverse interests' concluded Lon Fuller in a sociological analysis of western American water law.[2]

[2] L. L. Fuller, 'Irrigation and Tyranny' (1965) 17 Stanford Law Review 1021, 1042. Other American jurists noted the difficulties of legal control of water: 'in our western states, where there was abundant opportunity for free judicial development, judicial law making proved inadequate to adjust water rights': Roscoe Pound, 'Law in Books and Law in Action' (1910) 44 American Law Review 12, 23. The inherent uncertainty in specification of water rights has been explained by various intellectual strategies, e.g. (i). economic analysis: see R. N. Johnson, M. Gisser, and M. Werner, 'The Definition of a Surface Water Right and Transferability' (1981) 24 Journal of Law and Economics 273; C. M. Rose, 'Energy and Efficiency in the Realignment of Common-Law Water Rights' (1990) 19 Journal of Legal Studies 261; (ii). philosophical scrutiny: see R. A. Epstein, 'On the Optimal Mix of Private and Common Property' (1994) 11 Social Philosophy and Policy 17, 27–37; (iii). comparative analysis: see J. M. Ramseyer, 'Water Law in Imperial Japan: Public Goods, Private Claims, and Legal Convergence' (1989) 18 Journal of Legal Studies 51; J.-L. Rosenthal, *The Fruits of Revolution. Property Rights, Litigation, and French Agriculture,*

The evolution of the common law of water rights in England was characterized by the ready adaptation of old legal ideas to modern uses. It will therefore be necessary to examine the development of the categories of disseisin, trespass, and nuisance; the principle of *sic utere tuo ut alienum non laedas* ('so use your own property as not to harm that of another'), or forbearance between owners as a source of rights; praedial servitudes and the doctrine of appurtenancy; the inter-relationships of prescription, seisin, and title; the distinction between *injuria* and damage; and the shifting line between fact and law in pleading and adjudication. The common law of water use will be traced through the detail of courtroom debate, showing how lawyers sought to establish solid social rules governing an ephemeral element of nature.

THE ECONOMIC CONSEQUENCES OF THE LAW

There has been considerable writing in recent years about riparian rights and associated developments of property, tort, and nuisance law, much of it of a speculative nature. Authors working in the post-realist traditions of law-and-economics and critical legal scholarship have sought to identify social and economic needs and ideologies driving the evolution of private-law doctrine. If a general criticism can be made of these interpretations, they do not take into account the power of formal, conceptual, and procedural arguments in the English common law which shape legal policy and practice.[3] The history of property-use doctrines reveals a strong continuity of legal ideas across the centuries, with the lawyers in court displaying a remarkable resistance to utilitarian and economic ideology.

If formalism and legalism are indeed the keys to understanding the history of property use, then the reader may wish to know whether the legal history described in this study impacts on the well-known question of the relationship between the common law and economic development. Common-law

1700–1860 (Cambridge, 1992); and (iv). historical method: M. J. Horwitz, *The Transformation of American Law 1780–1860* (Cambridge, Mass., 1977); R. G. Bone, 'Normative Theory and Legal Doctrine in American Nuisance Law: 1850 to 1920' (1986) 59 South California Law Review 1101; W. W. Fisher III, *The Law of the Land: An Intellectual History of American Property Doctrine, 1776–1940* (MS., Harvard Law School, 1990); T. Steinberg, *Nature Incorporated: Industrialization and the Waters of New England* (New York, 1991). This study follows the historical method, with glances at other approaches; various recent theories are reviewed in the conclusion to this book.

[3] An exception to this blanket charge is C. Dalton, 'Losing History: Tort Liability in the Nineteenth Century and the Case of *Rylands v Fletcher*' (Unpublished MS. 1987, on file with author and at Bodleian Law Library). Also of high interest is M. Taggart's recent study *Private Property and Abuse of Rights in Victorian England: The Story of Edward Pickles and the Bradford Water Supply* (Oxford, 2002), which shares many themes with this book.

reasoning has often been regarded as more than a self-referential system of professional thought about legal rights and actions; it has also been portrayed as a crucial device for resource allocation and risk-spreading during the heroic period of economic modernization. Economic models of the common law have, however, found some surprisingly variant expressions, dividing roughly into two camps.

One school of interpretation, tracing back to Max Weber, Karl Renner, and Frederic William Maitland, holds that the common law between 1750 and 1850 was dual in its effects, both beneficial and backward. According to this view, the common law provided a complex, imperfect, and costly system of rights and actions; yet this same professionalized legal system, gradually reformed from within by the courts and from without by the legislature, provided regular legal procedures and definite property and contract rights, and so served the English economy adequately well as the nation moved into the modern industrial age.[4] The dualist model has become the fashionable wisdom of many economists and economic historians on the occasions when they turn their attention to the history of law.[5] In a further twist, American legal historians such as Morton Horwitz[6] and Lawrence

[4] M. Weber, *Economy and Society: An Outline of Interpretive Sociology*, 3 vols. (*Wirtschaft und Gesellschaft*, Tübingen, 1921–2; G. Roth and C. Wittich (eds.), New York, 1968, Berkeley, Calif., 1978), i, 311–38; ii, 641–900; M. Weber, 'The Development of Bureaucracy and its Relation to Law', extract from *Economy and Society*, reprinted in *Max Weber: Selections in Translation* (W. R. Runciman (ed.), Cambridge, 1978) 341–54; F. W. Maitland, 'Trust and Corporation', in F. W. Maitland, *Collected Papers*, 3 vols. (H. A. L. Fisher (ed.), Cambridge, 1911) iii, 321–404; F. W. Maitland, 'Introduction' to O. Gierke, *Political Theories of the Middle Ages* (Cambridge, 1900) pp. vii, ix–xii, xviii–xxxv; K. Renner, *The Institutions of Private Law and their Social Functions* (O. Kahn-Freund (ed.), London, 1949), ch. II, 81–250, and O. Kahn-Freund, 'Introduction', ibid., 1–43. For similar views propounded by modern legal historians, see P. S. Atiyah, *The Rise and Fall of Freedom of Contract* (Oxford, 1979) passim; W. R. Cornish and G. de N. Clark, *Law and Society in England 1750–1950* (London, 1989), 123–36, 166–72; G. R. Rubin and D. Sugarman, 'Towards a New History of Law and Material Society in England, 1750–1914', in G. R. Rubin and D. Sugarman (eds.), *Law, Economy and Society in England, 1750–1914: Essays in the History of the English Law* (Abingdon, 1984) 1–123.

[5] R. M. Hartwell, *The Industrial Revolution and Economic Growth* (London, 1971) 244–61; P. Mathias, *The First Industrial Revolution* (2nd edn., London, 1983) 10, 33–6, 80; D. S. Landes, *The Unbound Prometheus* (Cambridge, 1969) 198–9; D. C. North, *Structure and Change in Economic History* (New York, 1981) 147–70; and, *Institutions, Institutional Change and Economic Performance* (Cambridge, 1990) 92–104, 125–30; P. K. O'Brien, 'Central Government and the Economy, 1688–1815', in R. Floud and D. N. McCloskey (eds.), *The Economic History of Britain Since 1700, Vol. 1 1700–1860* (2nd edn., Cambridge, 1994) 205–41. For critical analysis of this model of law and the economy, see P. A. David, 'Why Are Institutions the "Carriers of History"? Notes on Path-Dependence and the Evolution of Conventions, Organizations and Institutions' (Working paper, Stanford Institute for Theoretical Economics, 1992); J. Getzler, 'Theories of Property and Economic Development' (1996) 26 Journal of Interdisciplinary History 639; R. Harris, *Industrializing English Law: Entrepreneurship and Business Organization, 1720–1844* (Cambridge, 2000) 3–11; and 'Government and the Economy' in R. Floud and P. Johnson (eds.), *The Cambridge Economic History of Modern Britain* (Cambridge, 2004) i, 204–37.

[6] Horwitz, *The Transformation of American Law 1780–1860*.

Friedman[7] have portrayed judge-made common law as an instrument of class power which promoted redistribution and subsidy to the rich in the course of industrialization, thus promoting capital accumulation and capitalist technological innovation at the expense of equity. Their model can be characterized as a further variant of the Weberian dualist theme, whereby law is accorded an even stronger role in influencing and guiding economic development.

Opposed to the dualist view is a functionalist model of the relationship of law and economy, which reverses the direction of causation. This model asserts that law does not generally determine or affect economic life, but rather follows in the wake of strong social and economic imperatives. Legal rules and procedures are called into existence primarily by the needs of entrepreneurs; legal methods, institutions, and precedents are moulded by evolutionary selection. If the law stands in the way of economic agents, then they will bargain around the law, or else litigate or agitate to change the law in order to suit their interests. The law is interesting and important as an epiphenomenon, a complex reflection of economic interests and social ideology; but legal rules themselves are not leading forces in the allocation of rights, duties, and resources. The functionalist view has been propounded by economic analysts of law ranging from Marx[8] to modern neo-classical theorists such as Ronald Coase and his followers.[9] Their approach in effect minimizes the causal importance of law-making in English (and American) history. The functionalist model does not readily allow that judicial determination of rights, whether in local litigations or in major appellate decisions and statutory law-making, can be an active force radically redistributing

[7] L. Friedman, *A History of American Law* (2nd edn., New York, 1985); see also W. Nelson, *Americanization of the Common Law. The Impact of Legal Change on Massachusetts Society, 1760–1830* (Cambridge, Mass., 1975); J. W. Hurst, *Law and Economic Growth* (Cambridge, Mass., 1964); H. N. Scheiber, 'Law and the Imperatives of Progress: Private Rights and Public Values in American Legal History', in J. R. Pennock and J. W. Chapman (eds.), *Ethics, Economics, and the Law* (London, 1982) 24 Nomos 303–20.

[8] H. Collins, *Marxism and Law* (Oxford, 1982); D. Harvey, *The Limits to Capital* (Oxford, 1982) 330–72.

[9] R. H. Coase, 'The Problem of Social Cost' (1960) 3 Journal of Law and Economics 1; *The Firm, the Market and the Law* (Chicago, Ill., 1988); and 'The Institutional Structure of Production', in R. H. Coase, *Essays on Economics and Economists* (Chicago, Ill., 1994) 3–14; R. A. Posner, *Economic Analysis of Law* (5th edn., New York, 1998) 271–81. For historical applications of the theory, see A. J. Field, 'Do Legal Systems Matter?' (1991) 28 Explorations in Economic History 1; G. T. Schwartz, 'Tort Law and the Economy in Nineteenth-Century America: A Reinterpretation' (1981) 90 Yale Law Journal 1721; J. F. Brenner, 'Nuisance Law and the Industrial Revolution' (1973) 3 Journal of Legal Studies 403; R. C. Ellickson, 'Property in Land' (1993) 102 Yale Law Journal 1315. For functionalist interpretations of non-European legal history, see S. Levmore, 'Rethinking Comparative Law: Variety and Uniformity in Ancient and Modern Tort Law' (1986) 61 Tulane Law Review 235; J. M. Ramseyer, 'Water Law in Imperial Japan: Public Goods, Private Claims, and Legal Convergence' (1989) 18 Journal of Legal Studies 51; R. C. Ellickson and C. DiA. Thorland, 'Ancient Land Law: Mesopotamia, Egypt and Israel' (1995) 71 Chicago-Kent Law Review 321.

resources and entitlements; rather law is seen as reinforcing existing distributions of wealth and power.[10]

DOCTRINAL AND EMPIRICAL CASE-STUDIES

These two broad theses of the relationship of law and economy—the dualist and the functionalist—have dominated modern scholarship. Few writers have addressed the issue of causation in the English legal-economic past by the case method.[11] Water law provides an apt case to study. The medieval economy relied heavily on water power, and much litigation and law-making about water rights ensued. Then, in the circumstances of industrializing England, the medieval doctrines were adapted and simplified as judges sought legal solutions to new economic problems and unprecedented levels of litigation. Blackstone's *Commentaries* were an early source of structuring ideas. Then American and civilian doctrine was borrowed to create a coherent body of water law in the later nineteenth century, though the courts continued to struggle with difficult issues such as drainage rights, the status of artificial and underground waters, and the severability and assignability of appurtenant water entitlements.

The confrontation of new economic and social practices with ancient laws after 1750 revealed the limits of the common law as an effective means of governance. This ultimately led to a shift in rule-making from the courts to Parliament in many of the most important and alive areas of property law, such as enclosure, entails, securities and charges, eminent domain, easements, ratings assessments, safety, and pollution.[12] Significant redefinition and reallocation of property entitlements took place through the private bill

[10] This description over-simplifies Coase's vision of the role of property rights in economic life. His theory famously has two parts: if transaction costs are low, the formal existence and initial assignment of property rights will be irrelevant to efficiency outcomes, as parties will invent and trade rights as suits them best; but if transaction costs are high, the assignment of property rights or their absence will have a grave impact on efficiency. For Coase and the new institutionalist economists, the analysis of transaction costs therefore becomes the proper focus of economic inquiry, and this inquiry dissolves into analysis of the nature of bargaining and economic rationality: see T. Eggertsson, *Economic Behaviour and Institutions* (Cambridge, 1990); North, *Institutions*.

[11] With the notable exceptions of Atiyah, *Rise and Fall of Freedom of Contract*; R. W. Kostal, *Law and English Railway Capitalism 1825–1875* (Oxford, 1994); A. W. B. Simpson, *Leading Cases in the Common Law* (Oxford, 1995); Harris, *Industrializing English Law*.

[12] A. W. B. Simpson, *A History of the Land Law* (2nd edn., Oxford, 1986) 270–91, 'Legal Liability for Bursting Reservoirs: The Historical Context of *Rylands v. Fletcher*' (1984) 13 Journal of Legal Studies 209, 252–64, revised version of same: 'Bursting Reservoirs and Victorian Tort Law: *Rylands and Horrocks v. Fletcher* (1868)' in A. W. B. Simpson, *Leading Cases in the Common Law* (Oxford, 1995) 195, 218–26; F. Clifford, *A History of Private Bill Legislation*, 2 vols. (1885) i, 1–12, 33–42, 249–55; ii, 36–198; Kostal, *Law and English Railway Capitalism*, 110–43.

mechanism, which was perhaps the major form of law-making between 1750 and 1850, and which remains little understood to this day. Water rights were one field of law-making, however, where the articulate contribution of the common lawyers remained important.

The lengthy courtroom debates over fine points of water law and underlying issues of property, contract, and tort often shrouded economic problems that were hardly to be resolved by legal reason. Yet with the exception of a handful of extraordinary judges such as Bramwell B.,[13] those problems were resolved with near-blindness to economic models or theories, and instead were regarded as purely legal issues of precedent and conceptual coherence, or at best as pragmatic questions of fact-finding and interest-balancing. The rules and principles which finally emerged from the appellate courts were not always understood or followed in the lower courts; and the economic impact of rulings was seldom considered or perceived. The history of riparian rights demonstrates that English property-use doctrine remained intractably legalistic and casuistical, and resistant to political and economic calculation. The legal system of the world's first modernizing industrial economy was able to resist fundamental rationalization and reform until the close of the nineteenth century—though it will be seen that the pursuit of economic efficiency did finally have an oblique role in the elaboration of modern doctrine.

Before continuing, some disclaimers: this study will be preoccupied with law-making by elite judges and jurists. There were important arenas of law-making beyond the common law courts; but little will here be said about local litigations and the private bill procedure, though they undoubtedly had a major part to play in regulating land and water use. Law-making of a sort also appears in the negotiated arrangements recorded in the archives of the water companies and other undertakings, another rich source. The history of legal doctrine embodied in case reports will be preceded by an investigation of the social and economic conditions that led to legal conflict over water use.[14]

[13] Atiyah, *The Rise and Fall of Freedom of Contract*, 374–80; Dalton, *Losing History*, 87–95; 'Baron Bramwell at the End of the Twentieth Century' (Symposium) (1994) 38 American Journal of Legal History 241–373; R. Kostal, *Law and English Railway Capitalism*, 315–18; C. Fairfield, *Some Account of George William Wilshere Baron Bramwell of Hever and his Opinions. A Memoir of Lord Bramwell* (London, 1898) esp. 79–93, 302–66. Fairfield describes Lord Bramwell's active participation in debates over railway rates, tithes, trade union rights, the Victorian water supply question, limited liability, employer torts, and other issues of contemporary political economy and law.

[14] Cf. R. A. Posner, 'The Material Basis of Jurisprudence', in R. A. Posner, *Overcoming Law* (Cambridge, Mass., 1995) 33–80; Simpson, *Leading Cases in the Common Law*; B. Rudden, *The New River: A Legal History* (Oxford, 1985).

1. *The Exploitation of Water in Historical Perspective*

LANDSCAPE AND INDUSTRY

Popular imagery of the English landscape in the modern age has been shaped by the poetry and art of the Romantics. They celebrated England's beautiful wildernesses and its park-like landscapes as bequeathed by the Agrarian Revolution; and they mourned the hastening extinction of this environment by the violent force of coal and steam.[1] For Blake, 'mountains green' and 'pleasant pastures' give way to 'clouded hills . . . dark Satanic mills', lines received into English culture as a visionary criticism of industrialism.[2] Wordsworth portrays the demonic impact of industry upon the land in 'The Excursion' of 1814.

—An inventive Age
Has wrought, if not with speed of magic, yet
To most strange issues . . .
Industrious to destroy! With fruitless pains . . .
The earth has lent
Her waters, Air her breezes . . .
. . . Meanwhile, at social Industry's command,
How quick, how vast an increase!
. . . Here a huge town, continuous and compact
O'er which the smoke of unremitting fires
Hangs permanent, and plentiful as wreaths
Of vapour glittering in the morning sun.[3]

The imagery of the poets is compelling; the reality of the Industrial Revolution was less dramatic. The transformation in techniques for controlling and reordering the natural environment known as industrialization was not launched by the steam-powered factories and forges of Manchester and Leeds, in all their Promethean grandeur and menace. More important by far

[1] See generally J. Barrell, *The Dark Side of the Landscape* (Cambridge, 1980); A. Clayre, *Nature and Industrialization* (Oxford, 1977); R. Williams, *The Country and the City* (London, 1973); W. G. Hoskins, *The Making of the English Landscape* (Harmondsworth, 1970); K. Thomas, *Man and the Natural World. Changing Attitudes in England 1500–1800* (Harmondsworth, 1984); S. Schama, *Landscape and Memory* (London, 1995).

[2] William Blake, Preface to 'Milton', in *The Complete Poems* (W. H. Stevenson (ed.), London, 1972) 488–9.

[3] William Wordsworth, 'The Excursion', bk. VII, lines 87–127, in *Poetical Works* (T. Hutchinson (ed.), E. de Selincourt (rev.), Oxford, 1936) 682–3.

were the gentle watermills of Lancashire, Derbyshire, and Yorkshire's West Riding. It was falling water which first freed manufacture from dependence on human or animal muscle power, and it was the efficient harnessing of water power after 1760 which began modern England's expansion of machine production, making it the first industrial nation. Coal and steam power belong to the later nineteenth century, when the classical Industrial Revolution was already long complete.[4]

This chapter investigates the economic history of water use and introduces the characteristic problems of private water law. It examines how water power became the technological foundation of industrialization, and why this process climaxed in late eighteenth-century England. Our story begins two millennia before the British Industrial Revolution, for it was the Roman law that first addressed the problem of water rights, and we must see why the Romans came to invent their elaborate system of water rights which provided the basis for much later law; and how later European societies with different technological bases created new forms of water law.

WATER USE IN THE ANCIENT WORLD—THE 'HYDRAULIC SOCIETY' HYPOTHESIS

Water-lifting screws, wheels, levers, and other irrigation devices moved by animal or human muscle were well-known in the ancient Mediterranean and the Near and Far East. Elaborate irrigation and water-supply systems with dams, aqueducts, and accompanying administration leave traces as far back as 4000 BCE. Marx and Engels fastened on the irrigation needs of the ancient Near East to propound a model of the 'Asiatic mode of production', refined by the German Marxist Wittfogel as the 'hydraulic society'. This entailed a despotic, slave-owning and centralized set of social institutions, called into being by the imperative need to build and maintain large-scale irrigation networks.[5] According to Engels, 'However great the number of despotic governments which arose and fell in India and Persia, each was fully aware

[4] G. N. von Tunzelmann, *Steam Power and British Industrialization to 1860* (Oxford, 1978) 283–98.

[5] K. Marx, *Pre-Capitalist Economic Foundations* (J. Cohen (ed. and trans.), London, 1964); E. Gellner, 'The Economic Interpretation of History', in J. Eatwell, M. Milgate, and P. Newman (eds.), *The New Palgrave: A Dictionary of Economics* (London, 1987) ii, 47–51; K. Butzer, *Early Hydraulic Civilization in Egypt* (Chicago, Ill., 1976); K. A. Wittfogel, 'The Theory of Oriental Society', reprinted in M. H. Fried (ed.), *Readings in Anthropology* (2nd edn., New York, 1968) ii, 180 and *Oriental Despotism. A Comparative Study of Total Power* (New Haven, Conn., 1957); J. N. Postgate, *Early Mesopotamia: Society and Economy at the Dawn of History* (London, 1992); N. Smith, *A History of Dams* (1st edn., London, 1971; American edn., Secaucus, NJ, 1972); R. C. Ellickson and C. DiA. Thorland, 'Ancient Land Law: Mesopotamia, Egypt and Israel' (1995) 71 Chicago-Kent Law Review 321.

that its first duty was the general maintenance of irrigation throughout the valleys, without which no agriculture was possible'.[6] Historians today doubt the economic determinism of this model, and have shown that a more pluralistic order existed in the ancient Near East, involving considerable individual property holdings and private and local communal initiatives in water management.[7] This, however, is not to deny the powerful role of a highly regulated Statist system of irrigation and water supply in the making of those civilizations. Thus in southern Mesopotamia, where the Euphrates was prone to flood and where uncontrolled irrigation led to pollution of the soil, risk-spreading and prevention of over-use of common goods were achieved by concentrating riparian lands and irrigation works within the state ownership of palace and temple. Close control of private use of irrigation is demonstrated in the Code of Hammurapi (*circa* 1750 BCE), which states:

> If a man has opened up his channel for irrigation, and has been negligent and allowed the water to wash away a neighbour's field, he shall pay grain equivalent to (the crops of) his neighbours.[8]

> If a man has released the water and allowed the water to wash away the works [i.e. furrows and soil preparation] on a neighbour's field, he shall pay ten *gur* of grain per *bur*.[9]

There thus seems to have been a negligence standard for flooding fields, and a strict liability for some sorts of flood damage.[10] Little is known of the land and water institutions of Ancient Egypt, the other classical hydraulic society of the Near East; but again a strong state control of water and other property rights is indicated by the evidence. The hydraulic thesis can be inverted: where a strong state existed, water supply could be extended.[11]

[6] F. Engels, *Anti-Dühring* (London, 1878), quoted in Gellner, 'Economic Interpretation of History', 50.

[7] Mediterranean evidence refuting the Marxist hydraulic society thesis is marshalled in P. Horden and N. Purcell, *The Corrupting Sea: A Study of Mediterranean History* (Oxford, 2000) 147–57. Wittfogel's version of the hydraulic society thesis had a second life in the 1960s, as he developed an anti-Communist theory of totalitarianism based on state economic power. Wittfogel's revamped thesis found adherents and enemies in debates over corporate power in the arid western states of America. For example, Lon L. Fuller stressed the possibility of consensual community control of water resources, as in the south-east of California where Fuller was raised in the early twentieth century; he launched a fervent attack on Wittfogel in 'Irrigation and Tyranny' (1965) 17 Stanford Law Review 1021; see further D. Worster, *Rivers of Empire: Water, Aridity, and the Growth of the American West* (New York, 1985) 22–60.

[8] Art. 55, in Postgate, *Early Mesopotamia*, 182.

[9] Art. 56, ibid.

[10] See further Ellickson and Thorland, 'Ancient Land Law', 346–50.

[11] Butzer, *Early Hydraulic Civilization*; cf. M. Silver, *Economic Structures of the Ancient Near East* (London, 1983) 57–117; J. Diamond, *Guns, Germs and Steel: The Fates of Human Societies* (New York, 1997) 282–4.

Two millennia later, the Roman state also on occasion used public law to protect its water supply. The *Lex Quinctia* of 9 BCE, passed by the *comitia tributa* at the time of Augustus, is an example:

Whoever, after the passing of this Act shall knowingly and maliciously have holed or fractured or shall have procured the holing or fracturing of the underground conduits, the covered channels, the arches, pipes, tubes, reservoirs, or pools of the public waters, which are or shall be brought to the city, or shall have interfered with them, so as to prevent those waters or any of them from coming, descending, flowing, reaching or being brought to the city of Rome or, within the city of Rome and in the places continuous with the city where there are or shall be houses, so as to prevent the waters rising, being distributed, being divided or being brought into reservoirs and pools in those gardens, properties and places to the owners, possessors or usufructaries of which gardens, properties, or places water has been or shall have been granted or attributed, he is to be condemned to pay 100,000 sestertii to the Roman people.[12]

However, the Romans diverged from the public command controls of other Near Eastern civilizations. The Romans controlled irrigation rights and water supply by making an office of curators of the water supply, dating from the time of Augustus and Agrippa and described by Frontinus, the imperial curator in 97–98 CE. But adjoining this the civil law erected a web of individual property rights over water, delegating to users the legal power to regulate water access.[13] The *Lex Quinctia* even frames public access rights in terms of vested individual claims:

It is not the intent of this law to revoke the right of persons to take or draw water from these springs, mains, conduits, or arches to whom the curators of the water supply have given or shall give such right, except that it is permitted with wheel, water regulator, or other mechanical contrivance, and provided that they dig no well and bore no aperture into it.[14]

It was generally the private law that maintained the water systems that served the populace of the Roman cities and the farms which fed them. The civic hydraulic systems which provided water for drinking, farming, and bathing came to be a defining quality of Roman civilization, and water supply lay close to the centre of Roman consciousness, as Pliny noted:

If we take into careful consideration the abundant supplies of water in public buildings, baths, pools, open channels, private houses, gardens and country estates near the

[12] *Lex Quinctia de Aquaeductibus* (translation given by P. Birks); A. C. Chester, P. R. Coleman-Norton, and F. C. Bourne (eds.), *Ancient Roman Statutes* (Austin, Tex., 1961) 119–20.

[13] J. Getzler, 'Roman Ideas of Landownership', in J. Dewar and S. Bright (eds.), *Law and Land: Themes and Perspectives* (Oxford, 1998) 81–106; J. L. Westcoat, 'Toward a Modern Map of Roman Water Law' (1997) 18 Urban Geography 100.

[14] *Lex Quinctia de Aquaeductibus* art. 9; *Ancient Roman Statutes*, 120.

city, if we consider the distances traversed by the water before it arrives; the raising of arches, the tunnelling of mountains and the building of level routes across deep valleys, we shall readily admit that there has never been anything more remarkable in the whole world.[15]

Frontinus could proudly state: 'With such an array of indispensable vast enterprises carrying so many waters, compare the superfluous pyramids, or the useless though famous works of the Greeks'.[16]

WATER FOR POWER IN THE ANCIENT WORLD

A Technically Simple Society?

Water as a source of motive power, rather than for transportation or consumptive use, was little known or exploited in the ancient world. The *noria* or water-pump turned by the stream itself was known from earliest times, but the water wheel as a power source turned by the flowing stream for other industrial uses such as corn-milling, rather than as an irrigation pump for propelling water, was known in the West only at the close of the Roman republican era.[17] There is no archaeological evidence of industrial use of

[15] Pliny, *Natural History* (H. Rackham (trans.), Cambridge, Mass., 1986) 36.24. See further O. F. Robinson, *Ancient Rome: City Planning and Administration* (London, 1992) 83–129.

[16] Sextus Julius Frontinus (c.35–104 CE), *De Aquis Urbis Romae* (c.97 CE), 16, cited in Robinson, *Ancient Rome*, 99; and in C. Herschel, *The Two Books of the Water Supply of the City of Rome of Sextus Julius Frontinus* (Boston, Mass., 1879) 75–83, 130–280. Frontinus gave a fascinating account of public water organization in ancient Rome. He indicated that baths and fulling mills (not corn mills) were the main consumers of water after domestic use. Life leases were granted for enhanced supply; there was no general privilege of alienability or succession; fresh grant or renewal had to be sought by successors. The ban on assignment was taken very seriously. Illicit irrigation could lead to land confiscation; pollution with malice was heavily fined. Excess water-drawing required sovereign grant; and the water commissioners had discretionary powers to maintain water supply including powers of eminent domain. See further C. Bruun, *The Water Supply of Ancient Rome: A Study in Imperial Administration* (Helsinki, 1991); A. Trevor-Hodge, *Roman Aqueducts and Water Supply* (London, 1992; 2nd edn., London, 2002).

[17] The first reference to a water wheel is found in the *Pneumatica* of Philo of Byzantium around 200 BCE, but the manuscript source is suspected to be a medieval Arabic interpolation. The first plausible mention of water-powered devices is by Strabo (c.65 BCE), who wrote of a '*hydraleta*' at the palace of Mithridates in the *Geographia.* Lucretius at the same time wrote of 'rivers which turn wheels and buckets' (*De Rerum Natura*)—though both authors may have been describing the *noria* rather than the watermill. Less ambiguous references to both the *noria* and the vertical undershot watermill are found in Vitruvius's great treatise *De Architectura* of c.25 BCE (*On Architecture*, 2 vols., (F. Granger (ed. and trans., London, 1934)). There is a verse by Antipater describing water nymphs turning the millwheel early in the morning so that the domestic slave-women may sleep in. See further T. S. Reynolds, *Stronger than One Hundred Men: A History of the Vertical Water Wheel* (Baltimore, Md., 1983), 14–30. A mine of information is to be found in the great antiquarian work by R. Bennett and J. Elton, *History of Cornmilling* 4 vols. (London, 1898–1904, reprinted East Ardsley, 1973).

vertical water mills until the third and fifth centuries.[18] The horizontal water wheel was possibly older; it was a simpler machine requiring no gearing, and was apt to be built by grain millers with limited starting capital and small local operations.[19] The horizontal wheel used only 10 to 15 per cent of the water energy available from the stream; the undershot vertical used perhaps 22 per cent and the overshot vertical wheel up to 70 per cent of available energy.[20] The overshot wheel was the most sophisticated and powerful, and also the most expensive wheel to build, as it generally required a dam and mill-race or channel, excavation and construction to site the wheel and machinery in the proper place under the water flow, and gearing to bring the power into a horizontal plane. There were sixteen overshot wheels at the large Roman settlement at Barbegal near Arles, each of which might have had an energy output of two-and-a-half horsepower.[21] Water power in the ancient world seems to have been used almost exclusively for milling grain, though there are hints of usage for sawing of wood and stone, and for other industrial processes.[22] The dominance of flour production in early water-powered industry from the Romans to the early Industrial Revolution bequeaths the word 'mill' (*molendinum*, from *molare*, to grind) to denote any powered factory, whether involving grinding or not.[23]

Economic historians have long puzzled over the apparent technological simplicity of the Roman and Hellenistic world, indicated partly by the paucity of invention, but mainly by the non-diffusion of available technologies such as water-milling. The Graeco-Roman macro-invention of the water-powered wheel was not matched by accompanying micro-inventions refining and perfecting its operation until medieval and modern times. There was little innovative use of water power in substitution for muscle-power before 400 CE, even where considerable efficiency savings were possible. The Digest of Justinian is full of mention of uses of water for irrigation, manufacturing, and consumption, but almost never for power.[24] Other classical sources maintain a similar silence. Roman legal sources hint that ingrained social attitudes placed restraints on the exploitation of economic resources such as water. In the Digest, navigation and irrigation are given absolute priority

[18] J. G. Landels, *Engineering in the Ancient World* (London, 1978) 18.

[19] The first evidence of the horizontal mill comes from Jutland in the early Christian era. Some scholars have characterized this type of water wheel as a separate development from the *noria* and the overshot wheel: see Reynolds, *Stronger than One Hundred Men*, 18–25.

[20] Ibid., 11, 14, 106–7.

[21] Landels, *Engineering in the Ancient World*, 21–2.

[22] Ausonius' *Mosella* of *c*.370 CE describes water-powered sawing on a tributary of the Moselle, but this may be an interpolation: see Reynolds, *Stronger than One Hundred Men*, 31.

[23] P. Mantoux, *The Industrial Revolution in the Eighteenth Century* (Paris, 1905; M. Vernon (ed. and trans.), 1928) 229; Bennett and Elton, *History of Cornmilling*, ii, 107–8, 117–18.

[24] For example Ulpian (D.39.2.24.) lists injuries caused to buildings and land by obstruction of water flow solely in terms of undermining of foundations.

over other consumptive uses.[25] Classical Roman law developed highly sophisticated doctrines governing rights to rural and urban water supply, indicating a favouring of agricultural and domestic production over all other activities. This bias would have inhibited the building of weirs, channels, and mill races necessary for hydro-industries. Only in the *Codex Justinianus*, issued in 538 CE, is there any mention of water supply to corn mills and the imperative of protecting water supply from interference. Such provisions date from no earlier than the fourth and fifth centuries.[26]

The usual explanation for Roman backwardness in the field of power technology is the abundance of cheap slave and forced labour, which removed any incentive for owners and rulers to substitute machinery and inanimate power in the production process. This is a factor-pricing theory of technological innovation, arguing that an abundant and cheap factor such as labour supply will inhibit the pursuit of savings in the costs of production elsewhere. Relative factor pricing can, however, provide only a very incomplete or approximate explanation for long-term patterns of technical change. Even if animate motive power was relatively cheap, replacement of slaves and animals with natural resources and capital would still have advanced the production frontier, and should have been attractive to the rational or maximizing economic mind.[27] In other words, a strong factor endowment such as cheap labour inputs should not exclude efficient substitution by other factors such as technology. Some further explanation of the Roman lack of technological achievement is necessary, for the means certainly were available for the Romans to profit from a reduction of slave use and an increase in mechanical hydraulic power. The scarcity of suitable water falls in the dry Mediterranean is often invoked as a further factor-price reason for Rome's backward power technology. However, the absence of regular watercourses in Mediterranean lands was often remedied by civil works enhancing the urban water supply; capital and labour could enlarge inadequate water resource endowments. Many or most mills resorted to the artificial source of aqueduct waters rather than natural streams to turn the wheel.[28] It was likely that there was an enormous unused capacity of water energy available from the Roman hydraulic system, yet no concerted effort was made to harness that energy. Tacitus relates that, in the year 39 or 40 CE, a victory

[25] On irrigation: D.8.3.17. (Papirus Justus, Antoninus and Verus); D.43.20.1.11.–15., 19.–20. (Ulpian); D.43.20.3.pr, 2. (Pomponius); cf. D.43.20.1.16. (Ulpian). On navigation and fishing: D.39.2.24.; D.43.12.1.; D.43.14.1.pr.; D.43.14.7. (Ulpian); D.39.3.10.2. (Labeo); D.43.12.2. (Pomponius); D.43.12.16. (Ulpian, Labeo); and see G. J. MacGrady, 'The Navigability Concept in the Civil and Common Law' (1975) 3 Florida State University Law Review 511.

[26] *Codex Justinianus* (534 CE) (P. Kruger (ed.), Berlin, 1877) 11.43.1–10; cf. Bennett and Elton, *History of Cornmilling*, ii, 41–2.

[27] J. Mokyr, *The Lever of Riches. Technological Creativity and Economic Progress* (New York, 1990) 19–30, 151–5, 193–200.

[28] Reynolds, *Stronger than One Hundred Men*, 31–45.

celebration by Caligula involved the commandeering of all the city's mill animals to carry his war booty, and this caused an immediate bread shortage. The well-watered city of Rome at the peak of its wealth and power evidently relied little on water energy to mill its grain. Moreover, the Romans did not develop water power in regions such as Britain and Gaul, where there were plenty of suitable natural water falls.

Culturalist Explanations of Technological Stagnation

The unorthodox Marxist historian M. I. Finley found an explanation for the technological stagnation of Roman civilization in the cultural rather than economic effects of slavery. He argued that the significance of slavery lay not in the cheap factor pricing of labour as a direct cause, but rather in the impact of slave-holding on aristocratic Roman culture and entrepreneurial behaviour. Masters, who did not labour and regarded their labourers as objects of property, had little or no incentive to seek efficiency savings. The patrician class therefore took little interest in engineering productivity increases.[29] As Marc Bloch earlier observed, '[w]hen classes become closed to one another; when the richer and more powerful classes cease to communicate with those ranged beneath them on the economic ladder, it can happen that the governing elements, by this very circumstance, come to consider everything that has to do with the material aspects of work unworthy of their attention'.[30] In steeply polarized ancient societies wealth was typically sought in order to enhance conspicuous consumption and so win public esteem, not to demonstrate entrepreneurial skill. The favoured means of enrichment for the Roman upper classes were primarily rentier-investment in land managed by bailiffs, and then public careers which yielded tax incomes, tributes, war plunder, and other emoluments. Wealth-making farm and estate management, manufacture, and trade were not high priorities. A great tradition of public enterprise was dedicated to bettering the condition of the populace through lavish civic works, colonization, and wars of plunder and conquest—but not through the organization of production for the market. The ancients thus followed settled canons of economic irrationality—the pursuit of satisfaction rather than the maximization of production and consumption—combined with an ethos of civic participation which encouraged progress in the public sphere, but which almost extinguished private innovation.

[29] M. I. Finley, 'Technical Innovation and Economic Progress in the Ancient World' (1965) 18 Economic History Review 29, reprinted in M. I. Finley, *Economy and Society in Ancient Greece* (London, 1981) 176–95; and see M. I. Finley, *The Ancient Economy* (London, 1973) passim; Mokyr, *Lever of Riches*, esp. 151–92.

[30] M. Bloch, 'Technical Change as a Problem of Collective Psychology', in *Land and Work in Mediaeval Europe: Selected Papers by Marc Bloch* (J. E. Anderson (ed. and trans.), London, 1967) 124–35, esp. at 135.

Science and invention were admired as pure philosophy and aesthetics, and were not pursued in a spirit of applied innovation. If increased mastery of the natural world was sought, it was to improve the range and quality of consumption goods, not to increase the quantity of production through enhanced capital goods and production techniques. Only in the later empire, with increasing labour shortages, is evidence left of extensive water- or animal-powered mechanization of production and the cultivation of manufactures.[31]

MEDIEVAL WATER USE AND POWER TECHNOLOGY

Medieval societies were less able to produce the public goods of civil peace, centralized law and adminstration, urban water supply, roads, and secure long-distance trade. But in contrast to the ancient world, Europeans between 500 and 1500 CE were fertile both in technical invention and technological innovation. Again, a factor-pricing theory might be invoked to solve this riddle: medieval people were confined within decentralized political and social units, and therefore had sharper incentives to increase their well-being through improvement of local production processes. The absence of sources of wealth in public life and urban trade, combined with magnified labour prices, gave the spur to harnessing of inanimate water power together with the implementation of other technologies such as improved use of animal power in agriculture and wind power in shipping.

The decline of slavery caused by the demise of the Roman military state was the driving force behind medieval technological virtuosity. Servile labour was feeble and expensive, and depended on a ready supply of captives won by war and plunder. The decline of Rome's military advantages against its neighbours choked off the supply of slaves in the later empire. With scarcity of servile labour, it became profitable to relax coercions of domestic servants, and allow them increasing customary rights to set up their own households and farms, and to pay rents rather than labour services to their lord. *Servus* ceased to be the word for a slave and became the word for a serf, both bound and protected by feudal custom. Another cause of this profound transformation of labour was the Church's prohibition on the enslavement of fellow Christians in the course of Europe's internecine wars. Bloch summed up the emergence of a feudal world from a servile one as follows: 'the servile

[31] Mokyr, *Lever of Riches*; A. H. M. Jones, *The Roman Economy. Studies in Ancient Economic and Administrative History* (P. A. Brunt (ed.), Oxford, 1974) 1–60; Reynolds, *Stronger than One Hundred Men*, 30–46; K. D. White, *Greek and Roman Technology* (Ithaca, NY, 1984); cf Horden and Purcell, *The Corrupting Sea*, 237–57, which forwards a hypothesis of pervasive grassroots use and manipulation of hydraulic technologies in late antiquity, arguing from literary sources where the archaeological evidence is weak.

masses of former times dwindled in number as slaves were transformed into tenants without any new entrants being recruited to make up this constant drain'.[32]

The replacement of slaves by tenants and the ensuing curbs on coercion made labour more expensive, and thus automatically increased the marginal return to investment and innovation elsewhere in the production process. Bloch offers a straightforward factor-pricing explanation for the adoption of inanimate power technologies (such as watermills) from the tenth century onwards. His basic idea was that 'an invention rarely spreads until it is strongly felt to be a social necessity';[33] he argued that labour scarcity drove the intensification of water-driven industry, but this in turn encouraged a new ethos that sought constant savings in the cost of labour.[34] But an alternative cause of change, perhaps more important than any simple shift in factor-pricing, was the cultural transformation in the relationship of lords and labourers evoked by the ending of both paganism and slavery. According to this model, it is not the case that 'necessity' or material circumstances can directly cause technological, economic, and social change; priority must be given to shifts in mentalities.[35] Lynn White Jr. has sketched one version of a 'culturalist' explanation for the technical revolution of the Middle Ages. The Judaeo-Christian tradition, he argued, destroyed the pagan animist world view, and replaced it with a belief that man, under God, must master and control the natural world. The monastic tradition taught that work was a prayer, and that orderly productive labour was an act of sanctification. The monasteries set up elaborate mills and factories and forced the pace of technological innovation by their own practice and example. Monastic enterprise thus intensified the Christian regard for work and, ironically for an other-worldly movement, materially advanced the harnessing of nature to satisfy human wants.[36]

[32] See further M. Bloch, *Feudal Society* (L. A. Manyon (ed. and trans.), London, 1965) i, 163 ff. Cf. E. A. R. Brown, 'The Tyranny of a Construct: Feudalism and Historians of Medieval Europe' (1974) 79 American Historical Review 1063; S. F. C. Milsom, *The Legal Framework of English Feudalism* (Cambridge, 1976); S. M. G. Reynolds, *Fiefs and Vassals: The Medieval Evidence Reinterpreted* (Oxford, 1994) esp. 1–74, 323–95; J. Hudson, *Land, Law, and Lordship in Anglo-Norman England* (Oxford, 1994) esp. 15–62.

[33] M. Bloch, 'The Advent and Triumph of the Watermill', in *Land and Work in Mediaeval Europe*, 136, at 146. This essay of 1935 is a classic of *Annales*-school and French historiography.

[34] M. Bloch, 'Mediaeval "Inventions"', in *Land and Work in Mediaeval Europe*, 169, at 180–2.

[35] For criticisms of the necessity theory of innovation see Mokyr, *Lever of Riches*.

[36] L. White, Jr., *Medieval Technology and Social Change* (Oxford, 1962) 79–134. White's influence has been pervasive: see B. Hall, 'Lynn White's *Medieval Technology and Social Change* After Thirty Years' in R. Fox (ed.), *Technological Change: Methods and Themes in the History of Technology* (Amsterdam, 1996) 85–102; F. and J. Gies, *Cathedral, Forge, and Waterwheel: Technology and Invention in the Middle Ages* (New York, 1994); Reynolds, *Stronger than One Hundred Men*, 109–14, and Mokyr, *Lever of Riches*, 151–208. Other historians have argued that medieval society was not technically precocious compared to other societies: M. M. Postan,

The utilization of water for power in the Middle Ages took place in a social world far distant from classical civilization: rural, religious, and fragmented into many intersecting jurisdictions.[37] The decline of urban economies reduced the scale and concentration of demands for milling and water supply, but correspondingly created needs for milling in every autonomous community. There is much evidence of widespread hand-milling of grain which occupied a fair amount of the time of the early medieval peasant household—perhaps two hours in every day for the womenfolk. Mechanized solutions were developed for household and industrial tasks where water and animal power was available to substitute for human labour. By the late tenth and eleventh centuries the innovations of the cam and the crank were added to the geared vertical wheel, allowing translation of rotary into reciprocating lateral motion. Water wheels were then used to drive fulling hammers for the preparation of woollen cloth. Techniques for mechanized sawing, crushing, grinding, polishing, drawing, turning, stamping, and blowing of furnaces soon followed, producing laundering, hemp, wrought iron, tanning bark, ground ore, beer mash and other processed foods, paper pulp, turned and finished wood and stone, polished gems, pigments, coins, wires, nails, and a plethora of other industrial goods, all in addition to the ubiquitous flour-milling.[38]

In the Domesday Book of 1086, there appear 5,624 listings of mills in the kingdom, serving some 3,000 communities. There was one mill for every fifty households in England, and certain streams had a density of one to three mills in every mile.[39] The Domesday returns show that the industrialization of milling has taken firm root: for example two mills are shown paying rents to the seigneur in the form of blooming irons. Water-powered industry was further advanced by the expanding monasteries, which built mills for an array of uses, often on an imposing scale.[40] Manorial returns and accounts suggest a medieval industrial revolution centred on the application of inanimate water power and animal power to production processes.[41]

The social impact of the medieval power revolution was profound and long-lasting. The medieval wool cloth industry moved location in the

'Why Was Science Backward in the Middle Ages', in M. M. Postan, *Essays on Medieval Agriculture and General Problems of Medieval Economy* (Cambridge, 1973) 81; R. Holt, 'Medieval Technology and the Historians: The Evidence of the Mill', in Fox (ed.), *Technological Change*, 103–21.

[37] Bloch, 'Advent and Triumph of the Watermill', 136 ff., especially 143–6, 149–53; R. Holt, 'Whose Were the Profits of Corn Milling? An Aspect of the Changing Relationship Between the Abbots of Glastonbury and Their Tenants 1086–1350' (1987) 116 Past and Present 3.

[38] White, *Medieval Technology*, 79–84.

[39] Reynolds, *Stronger Than A Hundred Men*, 52. An exhaustive analysis of the Domesday returns is given in Bennett and Elton, *History of Cornmilling*, ii, 101–80.

[40] Ibid., 51–4, 109–14.

[41] Bloch, 'Advent and Triumph of the Watermill'; White, *Medieval Technology*; Mokyr, *Lever of Riches*, 31–56; J. Gimpel, *The Medieval Machine: The Industrial Revolution of the Middle Ages* (2nd edn., London, 1988, reprinted 1992) 1–24.

thirteenth century from the south and east of England to the north and west, to take best advantage of water power for fulling. Clothing and other production departed from the precincts of the home to the workshop-mill, and industry changed to become a typically rural rather than urban activity. The heightened capital needs and changed geography of the mechanized trades pulled these away from guild and borough control.[42] It is during this period of rapid industrial change that Bracton's treatise on the laws of England in the 1220s and 1230s gives the first extensive treatment of water rights in English law, an imposing theoretical edifice which is given detailed treatment in the next chapter.

Feudal Milling Monopolies

Bloch drew attention to the legally-enforced rent-extracting monopolies attached to mill sites, which were types of feudal rights known as *banalités* or soke-services.[43] Seigneurs (both secular lords and monasteries) could claim a manorial monopoly over certain forms of local production by setting up the capital equipment and then insisting that all tenants exclusively use that equipment. The corn mill was the pre-eminent form of manorial monopoly in England; but soke-rights could also extend to the bread oven, the wine press, the brewery, the dye-pan, the breeding bull or boar, and the fulling mill. Bloch argued that these seigneurial charges removed the relative efficiency or cost-advantage of water power as against simpler industrial methods using animal or human power.[44] However, later scholars have suggested that the manorial and monastic monopolies helped disseminate more capital-intensive uses of water power. Soke services provided lords with the fiscal means to set up machinery with high sunk costs, as the monopoly rents helped them recoup their outlays. Most of the mills leaving historical traces were seigneurial, often monastic, because only large-scale owners could fund and run them.[45] The seigneurial monopolies of mill-suit were aggressively defended in the lords' courts; and sometimes lords claimed to

[42] E. M. Carus-Wilson, 'An Industrial Revolution of the Thirteenth Century' (1941) 11 Economic History Review 1, reprinted in E. M. Carus-Wilson (ed.), *Essays in Economic History* (London, 1954) i, 41–60.

[43] Bloch, 'Advent and Triumph of the Watermill', 136–68. For a dense antiquarian treatment, see R. Bennett and J. Elton, 'Feudal Laws and Customs' in *History of Cornmilling*, iii (London, 1900).

[44] Bloch, 'Advent and Triumph of the Watermill', 152–60.

[45] Ibid., 151. For examples of the importance of mills within the seigneurial and monastic economies of the late Middle Ages, see R. Holt, *The Mills of Medieval England* (Oxford, 1988); J. H. Tillotson (ed.), *Monastery and Society in the Late Middle Ages. Selected Account Rolls from Selby Abbey, Yorkshire, 1398–1537* (Woodbridge, 1988) passim. The spread of the mill was seen across Europe: R. Lamond, 'An Early Fulling Mill' (1947) 17 Economic History Review 150, showing tithes and toll from a mill being assigned in Rouen as early as 1060; J. Muendel, 'The "French" Mill in Medieval Tuscany' (1984) 10 Journal of Medieval History 215.

control all possible uses of a local watercourse, in effect claiming complete seigneurial control of water flow in the manor. Carus-Wilson writes that '[e]ven before the introduction of the fulling mill, the lord claimed the right to dispose of the watercourse as he pleased for fulling and dyeing, reserving it wholly to himself, or leasing it out, often as a monopoly, to others.... So profitable were such monopolies that frequently when some measure of freedom was granted to tenants the lord expressly reserved the right to maintain them in his hands'.[46]

F. W. Maitland associated the various forms of mill-soke with the feudal customs of folding:

> [W]e speak chiefly of the lowly 'free men' and sokemen of the eastern counties. Besides having their commendation and their soke, the lord very often has what is known as their *consuetudo* or their *consuetudines*.... In all probability the word when thus employed... points to payments and renders to be made in money and in kind and to services of an agricultural character. Of such services only one stands out prominently..., it is fold-soke, *soca faldae*. The man must not have a fold of his own; his sheep must lie in the lord's fold. It is manure that the lord wants; the demand for manure has played a large part in the history of the human race. Often enough this is the one *consuetudo*, the one definite service, that the lord gets out of his free men.... From the nature of this one *consuetudo* and from the prominence that is given to it, we may guess the character of the other *consuetudines*. Suit to the lord's mill would be analogous to suit to his fold. Of 'mill-soke' we read nothing, but often enough a surprisingly large part of the total value of a manor is ascribed to its mill, and we may argue that the lord has not invested capital in a costly undertaking without making sure of a return.[47]

In the numerous free or lordless villages existing at the time of the Domesday census, 'the ownership of a mill is divided up into so many shares that we are tempted to think that this mill has been erected at the cost of the vill'. For example, a free villager holding a tiny manor in Suffolk comprising twenty-four acres of land and one-and-a-half acres of meadow also held 'a fourth part of the mill in every third year'.[48] Maitland surmised that 'he [took] his turn with his neighbours in the enjoyment of the revenue of the mill'.[49] R. Holt has shown how lords often allowed freemen to control or compete with the feudal monopolies.[50] But these free mills became rarities with the increase of feudal power between the twelfth and fourteenth centuries. Lords (often monasteries) demanded that their monopolies over corn-milling, food production, and fulling be observed, and this led to widespread evasion, strenuous attempts at enforcement, and substantial litigation in local and rural courts. Guilds and boroughs for their part tried to legislate against

[46] Carus-Wilson, 'Industrial Revolution of the Thirteenth Century', 53.

[47] F. W. Maitland, *Domesday Book and Beyond* (Cambridge, 1897, 2nd edn. with a foreword by J. C. Holt, Cambridge, 1987) 76–7.

[48] *Domesday Book* ii, 404b, cited in Maitland, *Domesday Book and Beyond*, 144.

[49] Maitland, *Domesday Book and Beyond*, 144.

[50] R. Holt, 'Whose Were the Profits of Cornmilling?'.

these swelling feudal monopolies which undermined urban trades; but with little success. Manorial milling and fulling rights remained highly profitable to lords, and long resisted commutation to money payments. These hard-pressing impositions became a major grievance for urban and rural workers; and many lords' mills and bakehouses were destroyed in the Peasants' Revolt of 1381 and other popular insurrections.

The story of medieval milling suggests that where ruling classes have a palpable economic interest in expansion of productive activity, then increased investment and protection of that activity will follow. The French were so wedded to the banal mills as a component of the seigneurial system that these were encouraged by law in Quebec from the seventeenth century onwards, resulting in a rapid expansion of watermill enterprise.[51] As Bloch observed more generally, 'these seignorial undertakings were not unlike some of our great present-day commercial enterprises. First of all they saw themselves constrained by the shortage of manpower to bring about this great improvement in human equipment; then they harshly imposed the system on all around them. Thus technical progress resulted from two constraining forces; and this, we may be quite sure, is not the only example'.[52]

Early Legislative Control of Water Use

The intensive use of water power in England before 1500 interfered with other water uses, especially river transport and fishing. A series of statutes and royal writs were issued requiring that causeways and dams interfering with navigation or fishing should be removed as presumptive public nuisances,[53] as in the twenty-second chapter of Magna Charta: 'all weirs from henceforth shall be utterly put down through Thames and Medway, and through all England, except by the sea coasts'.[54]

The source of the king's power over rivers was unclear. The Crown claimed this as prerogative, but the power of conservancy was often delegated, and

[51] Reynolds, *Stronger than One Hundred Men*, 154.

[52] Bloch, 'Advent and Triumph of the Watermill', 160.

[53] See 1 Hen. 4, c. 12 (1399); 13 Edw. 1, c. 47 (Statute of Westminster II, 1285); 13 Rich. 2, c. 19, c. 47 (1389–40); 17 Rich. 2, c. 9 (1393–4); 1 Hen. 4, c. 12 (1399); 4 Hen, 4, c. 11 (1402); 1 Hen. 5, c. 2 (1413); 2 Hen. 6, c. 19 (1423); 3 Hen. 6, c. 5 (1424); 12 Edw. 4, c. 7 (1472); 9 1 Eliz. c. 17 (1558–9); 21 Jac. 1, c. 32 (1623–4). Weirs catching fish and obstructing navigation dating from before 1350 or the reign of Edward I were legalized by 25 Edw. 3, st. 4, c. 4 (1350–2). The king's regulatory authority was vested partly in the Commissioners of Sewers, as described in Anon., *The Laws of Sewers* (London, 1726, 2nd edn., London, 1732); and *The Reading of Robert Callis upon the Statute of Sewers, 23 Hen. VIII c. 5* (London, 1622; 4th edn. by W. J. Broderip, London, 1824). See also Sir Matthew Hale, *De Jure Maris* (*c.*1670) in F. Hargrave (ed.), *A Collection of Tracts Relative to the Law of England* (London, 1787); reprinted in S. A. Moore, *A History of the Foreshore* (3rd edn., London, 1888) 370–413; H. J. W. Coulson and U. A. Forbes, *The Law Relating to Waters, Sea, Tidal and Inland and Land Drainage* (6th edn. by S. R. Hobday, London, 1952) 537, 552–4.

[54] 9 Hen. 3 (Magna Charta, 1224–5), c. 22.

magnates pressed franchises and feudal monopolies against the Crown's exclusive rights. Legislation governing rights to river use was rarely the subject of litigation or enforcement, however, and common law doctrines basically governed private parties' conflicts over water until the later nineteenth century.

THE MODERN AGE OF WATER POWER

By 1700, before the so-called 'take-off' of industrialization, there were between 10,000 and 20,000 watermills in Britain. Up to five watermills for every mile of usable stream could be found near large industrial towns such as Sheffield. Fitzherbert and Camden record that in the sixteenth and seventeenth centuries there was extensive building of dams, weirs, and power canals or leats for water supply and hydro-power.[55] This strong water-powered industrial base was multiplied many times in the late eighteenth century as textiles, mining, and metals trades achieved breakthroughs in technology and organization amounting to an 'industrial revolution'. Hydro-powered factory production of textiles was the 'glamour industry' of the early Industrial Revolution, though if a longer view is taken it was the mining and metals industries, with hydro-powered hauling, draining, crushing, and high-pressure smelting which led the technological transformation of aggregate productivity of the economy between 1760 and 1830.[56]

During this 'Age of Water Power'[57] the water wheel provided the great bulk of industrial power in Britain until at least the first decades of the nineteenth century; and its dominance would have lasted longer had Britain

[55] Reynolds, *Stronger than One Hundred Men*, 122–7 and ff.

[56] For survey and analysis of the Industrial Revolution: Mantoux, *Industrial Revolution*; D. S. Landes, *The Unbound Prometheus* (Cambridge, 1969) 1–123; R. M. Hartwell, *The Industrial Revolution and Economic Growth* (London, 1971); R. Floud and D. N. McCloskey (eds.), *The Economic History of Britain Since 1700, Vol. 1 1700–1860* (Cambridge, 1st edn., 1981; 2nd edn., 1994); J. Mokyr (ed.), *The Economics of the Industrial Revolution* (London, 1985); and (ed.), *The British Industrial Revolution: An Economic Perspective* (Boulder, Col., 1993); D. Cannadine, 'The Present and the Past in the English Industrial Revolution 1880–1980' (1984) 103 Past and Present 131; E. A. Wrigley, *People, Cities and Wealth. The Transformation of Traditional Society* (Oxford, 1987); R. M. Hartwell, 'Was There an Industrial Revolution?' (1990) 14 Social Science History 567; J. Hoppit, 'Counting the Industrial Revolution' (1990) 43 Economic History Review 173; P. K. O'Brien and R. Quinault (eds.), *The Industrial Revolution and British Society* (Cambridge, 1993); M. Berg and P. Hudson, 'Rehabilitating the Industrial Revolution' (1992) 45 Economic History Review 24; J. Hoppit and E. A. Wrigley (eds.), *The Industrial Revolution in Britain* 2 Vols. (Oxford, 1994); M. Berg, *The Age of Manufactures 1700–1820: Industry, Innovation, and Work in Britain* (2nd edn., London, 1994); M. J. Daunton, *Progress and Poverty. An Economic and Social History of Britain 1700–1850* (Oxford, 1995); R. Floud and P. Johnson (eds.), *The Cambridge Economic History of Modern Britain* (Cambridge, 2004) i.

[57] A. E. Musson, *The Growth of British Industry* (London, 1978) 142.

been as well endowed with water energy as the United States, France, and alpine Europe. The availability of swift-moving streams and valleys amenable to damming for hydro-power worked to shift industry from the south-east to the north-west of mainland Britain. The steady power of the water wheel was especially suited to woollen manufacture. In 1850 one-third of power in the wool industry still came from water; and in 1838 cotton manufacture still relied on water for over one-quarter of its power. Outside Lancashire the figure may have exceeded 40 per cent of power use (see Table 1.1).[58] Cotton manufacturers turned to steam-power rapidly, but other industries remained dependent on water for most of their power needs until the end of the nineteenth century.[59] Even where coal energy was employed, it was very common to use a steam engine to pump water to a wheel in order to drive the machinery smoothly with traditional water technology.[60]

The dominance of water power was observed by many contemporaries, including John Robison writing on 'Mechanics' in 1797: 'Water is the more common power, and indeed the best, as being the most common and equable'.[61] As early as one hundred years before, the engineer John Mortimer could observe that 'Water is . . . maintained with least cost, and being the most advantageous hath gained the Preheminence [*sic*]'.[62]

All new forms of inanimate power, including hydro-power, were heavily supplemented by traditional muscle-driven methods for most of the history of the emergent industrial economy. Marx's vision of industrialism as the rise of centralized factories powered by water and steam was still an exceptional form of production until his death in 1883.[63] Outside textiles and heavy metals and mining, handicraft labour continued to dominate most sectors almost until 1900, though the water- and steam-powered sectors had a growing impact on staple exports and the organization of industry.[64]

[58] R. B. Gordon, '"Factory Discipline" during Industrialization in New England and Great Britain: A Geological Interpretation' (1983) 36 Economic History Review 240; D. Greenberg, 'Reassessing the Power Patterns of the Industrial Revolution: An Anglo-American Comparison' (1982) 87 American Historical Review 1237 and 'Energy, Power, and Perceptions of Social Change in the Early Nineteenth Century' (1990) 95 American Historical Review 693; Mokyr, *Lever of Riches*, 90–2; Reynolds, *Stronger than One Hundred Men*, 266–320 and ff.; von Tunzelmann, *Steam Power and British Industrialization*, 125–41, 175–225; Musson, *Growth of British Industry*; R. L. Hills, *Power in the Industrial Revolution* (Manchester, 1970); Landes, *The Unbound Prometheus*, 65, 95–9, 104; H. J. Habakkuk, *American and British Technology in the Nineteenth Century: The Search for Labour Saving Inventions* (Cambridge, 1962); P. N. Wilson, 'Water Power and the Industrial Revolution' (1954) 6 Water Power 8; J. Shaw, *Water Power in Scotland, 1550–1870* (Edinburgh, 1984); Daunton, *Progress and Poverty*, 190–2.

[59] Von Tunzelmann, *Steam Power and British Industrialization*, 175 ff.

[60] Reynolds, *Stronger than One Hundred Men*, 322–3.

[61] Quoted in ibid., 152. [62] Ibid.

[63] N. Rosenberg, 'Marx as a Student of Technology', in N. Rosenberg, *Inside the Black Box. Technology and Economics* (Cambridge, 1982) 34–51; Berg, *Age of Manufactures*, 235–54.

[64] Ibid.; R. Samuel, 'Workshop of the World: Steampower and Hand-Technology in Mid-Victorian Britain' (1977) 3 History Workshop 6; L. A. Clarkson, *Proto-Industrialization: The*

Table 1.1 *Water and Steam Power in 1835*

	No. of mills	Steam h.p.	Water h.p.
Northern region	934	26,513	6,094
Scotland	125	3,200	2,480
Midlands	54	438	*c.*1,200
Total	1,113	30,151	*c.*9,774

Source: E. Baines, *History of the Cotton Manufacture in Great Britain* (London, 1835; 2nd edn., London, 1966) 386–92; S.D. Chapman, *The Cotton Industry in the Industrial Revolution* (2nd edn., London, 1987), reprinted in L.A. Clarkson (ed.), *The Industrial Revolution: A Compendium* (Basingstoke, 1990) 11.

Reasons for the incomplete diffusion of water-power technologies were influenced by expense and work-force resistance. The purchase of legal rights to water was a significant initial cost. Water supplies could be exhausted unless boosted by expensive weirs, leets, and sluices. Water sources were vulnerable to seasonal interruptions such as drying in summer and freezing in winter. Factories arranged around a common power source could be difficult to set up if workers adhered to 'proto-industrial' practices of domestic outwork and handicrafts and were reluctant to submit to the new factory discipline. There could be half-way houses where artisans would share the costs and use of a water-powered fulling or spinning mill, without submitting to in-house factory discipline and surrender of their producer's independence; putting-out systems long co-existed with centralized manufactures.[65] Sufficient capital for the first fixed investments in mill-wheels, mill-houses, and factory equipment could be lacking. Similar influences explain why water-powered mills remained the most prominent form of manufactory until around 1870, long after the coming of steam engines. Compared to the ancient and well-developed craft of water power, early steam technology was unreliable; and it entailed expenses not only in initial fixed-capital investment, but also in running costs of coal and maintenance of a labour-force sufficiently skilled to keep the machines operative. G. von Tunzelmann

First Phase of Industrialization (Basingstoke, 1985), reprinted in L. A. Clarkson (ed.), *The Industrial Revolution: A Compendium* (Basingstoke, 1990) 149–210; J. de Vries, 'The Industrial Revolution and the Industrious Revolution' (1994) 54 Journal of Economic History 249; W. Mager, 'Proto-Industrialization and Proto-Industry; The Uses and Drawbacks of Two Concepts' (1993) 8 Continuity and Change 181.

[65] S. Pollard, *The Genesis of Modern Management. A Study of the Industrial Revolution in Great Britain* (London, 1965; reissued Aldershot, 1993) 30–47, 89–96, 160–208; Berg, *Age of Manufactures*, 217 and *The Machinery Question and the Making of Political Economy, 1815–1848* (Cambridge, 1980); S. A. Marglin, 'What Do Bosses Do?' (1974) 6 Review of Radical Political Economy 60, reprinted in A. Gorz (ed.), *The Division of Labour: The Labour Process and Class Struggle in Modern Capitalism* (Hassocks, 1976); G. Clark, 'Factory Discipline' (1994) 54 Journal of Economic History 128; de Vries, 'Industrial Revolution'.

has shown that over the 1840s and 1850s, water power declined only 9 per cent in textiles and 14 per cent in Britain as a whole.[66] Steam power complemented rather than substituted for water, and it was the combination of the two that permitted a vast extension of the production frontier.

The rise of steam has also been described as part of a secular shift from an advanced organic economy based on natural flows of resources to a mineral fuel economy based on practically limitless resource stocks.[67] Just as water power reached the highest intensity of use in the early nineteenth century due to demand for new sources of inanimate power, so with coal: resource endowment did not set the pattern and pace of industrialization, but rather focused the directions that might be chosen by entrepreneurs and innovators responding to evolving demands in the economy.[68]

The Arkwrights and the New Industrialism

The first large-scale application of water power in the textile spinning process was made by Richard Arkwright and his partners at Cromford, Derbyshire, in 1771–2. There were a number of important precursors to their enterprise. The medieval fulling mills for woollens and linen had begun the water-driven mechanization of textile production; and a further precedent was set with the installation of water power for silk-throwing by Thomas Cotchett on the River Derwent in Derby in 1702. These innovations were intensively developed in the large Derby Silk Mill set up in 1717–18 by John and Thomas Lombe.[69] Mantoux describes this as the first real factory in England; it astonished Defoe, who described it at some length in his *Tour of Great Britain*.[70] It was built at a purported cost of £30,000, and was six storeys high and 500 feet wide, containing a large number of complex machines powered centrally from a large water wheel. The Derby Silk Mill ran successfully for generations, and imitations were built at Congleton, Macclesfield, Sheffield, Stockport, and Watford.[71]

The early silk-spinning factories pioneered water-powered machine methods which were then applied to cotton production. The first water-powered cotton-spinning machines were built in 1742 by Lewis Paul and Edward Cave on the river Nene at Northampton, an enterprise which survived until 1755. The breakthrough in power-factory organization was made

[66] Von Tunzelmann, *Steam Power and British Industrialization*, 125–41, 156–73, 232–5.

[67] E. A. Wrigley, *Continuity, Chance and Change. The Character of the Industrial Revolution in England* (Cambridge, 1988).

[68] Mokyr, *Lever of Riches*, 159–65; N. Rosenberg, *Perspectives on Technology* (Cambridge, 1976); Berg, *Age of Manufactures*, 172–8.

[69] Ibid., 211–12.

[70] D. Defoe, *A Tour Through the Whole Island of Great Britain*, 2 vols. (1724–6, G. D. H. Cole and D. C. Browning (eds.) London, 1962) ii, 156–7; Mantoux, *Industrial Revolution*, 198–9.

[71] Ibid., 193–224; Berg, *Age of Manufactures*, 219–21.

by Richard Arkwright, the archetypal entrepreneur of the Industrial Revolution. Arkwright's skills lay not in original invention, despite his legendary status as the inventor of the water frame or water-powered spinning machine;[72] but rather in realizing the application of technological innovations through his superior skills in co-ordinating management, labour, credit, and material supplies within the organizational framework of large, centralized, highly disciplined factories; and also through careful cultivation of mass consumer markets for his factory product.[73] Looking back from 1835, Andrew Ure wrote that Arkwright's main challenge was 'above all, in training human beings to renounce their desultory habits of work, and to identify themselves with the unvarying regularity of the complex automaton. To devise and adminster a successful code of factory discipline, suited to the necessities of factory diligence, was the Herculean enterprise, the noble achievement of Arkwright.'[74] Arkwright set up his manufacturing enterprise with Jedediah Strutt and four other partners in 1768. After early experiments with horse-powered spinning, the enterprise shifted to Cromford near Matlock in the Peak District of Derbyshire. For a £14 annual rent Arkwright took a twenty-one year lease in 1771 on land with a natural stream, with a further sixty-three year option, and built a fully mechanized cotton factory there.[75] Looking back in 1790, Arkwright stated that he had chosen Cromford as 'a place affording a remarkable fine Stream of Water, And [it was situated] in a Country very full of inhabitants vast numbers of whom & small Children are constantly Employed in the Works'.[76] Labour was cheap and compliant in this isolated part of Britain. There was no local history of machine-breaking by organized tradesmen and artisans, and this may have been the major attraction of the site. Both water and labour proved to be in

[72] For Arkwright's fights over patents and technological innovation, see *Arkwright's Patent* (1775), *Arkwright* v. *Mordaunt* (1781, K.B.), *Arkwright* v. *Nightingale* (1785, K.B.), and *R* v. *Arkwright* (1785, K.B.), in T. Webster, *Reports and Notes of Cases on Letters Patent for Inventions* (London, 1844) 56–75; R. S. Fitton, *The Arkwrights: Spinnners of Fortune* (Manchester, 1989) 91–145; Mantoux, *Industrial Revolution*, 226–51; more generally, C. MacLeod, *Inventing the Industrial Revolution: The English Patent System, 1660–1800* (Cambridge, 1988) 58–74; J. Hewish, 'From Cromford to Chancery Lane: New Light on the Arkwright Patent Trials' (1987) 28 Technology and Culture 80; C. Wellington, 'Sir Richard Arkwright—Premier Crook in the Industrial Revolution' (1993) 20 International Journal of Social Economics 37.

[73] Mantoux, *Industrial Revolution*, 238–76; Fitton, *The Arkwrights*, 146–81; G. Unwin, *Samuel Oldknow and the Arkwrights* (London, 1924, reprint edn., Manchester, 1968); Pollard, *Genesis of Modern Management*, 91–2, 183–4, 191–9; S. D. Chapman, *The Cotton Industry in the Industrial Revolution* (2nd edn., London, 1987), reprinted in Clarkson (ed.), *The Industrial Revolution: A Compendium*, 1–64; S. D. Chapman, *The Early Factory Masters: The Transition to the Factory System in the Midlands Textile Industry* (London, 1967, reissued Aldershot, 1992). Cf. Berg, *Age of Manufactures*, 230, denying the novelty of Arkwright's factory techniques, seeing them as outgrowths of silk-throwing and other existing proto-industrial and handicraft methods.

[74] A. Ure, *The Philosophy of Manufactures; or, An Exposition of the Scientific, Moral and Commercial Economy of the Factory System of Great Britain* (London, 1835) 15.

[75] Fitton, *The Arkwrights*, 22–32.

[76] Arkwright to John Lee, 1790, Arkwright Family Papers, quoted in Fitton, *The Arkwrights*, 28.

much shorter supply than Arkwright had hoped. He had to spend large capital sums in order to establish his work-force in a purpose-built village, to buy water rights from hostile neighbours, and to build leets and canals to bring water to his mill. It was also expensive to bring in raw materials and send out the finished product to distant consumer markets. Chapman argues that the main attraction of Cromford for Arkwright was its very isolation, which gave him the freedom to build his manufactory away from the deadening hand of established local governments, guilds, and magnates. At Cromford, Arkwright and his son Richard could find their place in the world through industrialism as self-made men, magnates in their own right. Entrepreneurship was soon abandoned for the higher calling of social recognition: after their initial successes, the Arkwrights were content to take monopoly profits from their patent, and then lend money out to more active entrepreneurs. It was men such as the Strutts of Derby and the Oldknows of Wirksworth who continued the technological and industrial innovations in textiles that the Arkwrights had begun, closely imitating Arkwright's enterprises but on a larger scale.[77]

The Genesis of the Factory: Water Power and Monopoly

Whatever his reputation as a technology creator, Arkwright must be given his credit for virtually inventing the modern, centrally-powered textile factory. Until recently the genesis of the factory has been traced to the imperatives of the water-frame, the underpinning technology of Arkwright's enterprise. The model is one of linear causation—new technology required new power sources which necessitated the centralized workplace—but this causation is not securely established. The parallel inventions of the spinning jenny and the mule, which could substitute for the water-frame, did not necessarily require inanimate power, and were well suited to artisanal and domestic production outside the factory, or in workshops involving centralized manufacture without factory discipline under capitalist direction. Arkwright's original model of the spinning frame was designed to be suitable for domestic outwork use. However, the highly elaborate design he submitted for patent was a re-working of James Hargreaves' invention in the form of a large power tool, done so partly in order to put the invention beyond the reach of artisans and thereby guarantee a more effective industrial monopoly to the patentee.[78] The design of manufacturing technology around water

[77] Chapman, *Early Factory Masters*, 62–76; Derwent Valley Mills Partnership, *The Derwent Valley Mills and their Communities* (Derby, 2001).

[78] On the Arkwright patent, see R. Arkwright, 'A State of Facts Respecting the Case of Mr. Richard Arkwright... Cotton Manufacturer' (London, 1782), and J. Chippindale, 'Petition [of the Manchester Committee of Trade against the Arkwright patent]' (9 February 1782) (Seligman Folio 1782E St29, Columbia University Rare Book and Manuscript Library); Mokyr, *Lever of Riches*, 247–58; the references in n. 72 above.

power was thus guided by the search for monopoly profit, and was only marginally intended as a device to replace labour and increase output.[79]

The orthodox economic view, recently defended by Landes and Mokyr, is that the new power technologies exemplified by Arkwright's water-frame did indeed dictate the rise of the factory system. Increased fixed capital investment and the division of labour entrusted the worker with responsibility for expensive plant and circulating inventory capital. Traditional self-disciplining labour practices had to be eliminated in order to maintain the uninterrupted flow of materials through the capital-intensive production process; discipline ensured that interdependent labour and capital would fully be employed. Factory discipline therefore was mandated by co-ordination problems posed by the new intensity of capital and the heightened division of labour.[80] Other interpreters have, however, reversed the causation of the relationship between technological innovation and labour discipline. Marglin argues that capitalists were seeking to seize control of the production process in order to intensify the coercive supervision of labour and extract maximum value from the worker. Bosses therefore designed their production technology around the imperative of coercive factory discipline. Thus the centrally-powered industrial factory—typically the water-driven textile mill—was not summoned into being by technology, but was an instrument of social and economic power in the struggle between the classes.[81] Marglin's model is in direct descent from those of Adam Smith and Karl Marx, who argued that the rise of large-scale manufacture with its finer division of labour allowed the gradation of skills, which then permitted substitution of machines and further de-skilling. The result was that the labourer worked not to the rhythm of his craft but to the motion of the machine. Capital goods owned by the boss dictated the labour process, reversing the position where labour hired capital for a fixed rent and thereby retained flexible choice over the intensity of effort and profit, as in the earlier handicraft and workshop industrialism.[82]

The debate between orthodox and Marxist economic views of the factory has taken new directions in recent scholarship, with arguments downplaying the causal role of new technologies such as water power and emphasizing

[79] MacLeod, *Inventing the Industrial Revolution*, 75–96, 115–81.

[80] J. Mokyr, 'Introduction' to *The British Industrial Revolution*, 110–18 and, 'Knowledge, Technology, and Economic Growth During the Industrial Revolution', in B. van Ark, S. K. Kuipers, and G. Kuper (eds.), *Productivity, Technology and Economic* Growth (The Hague, 2000); D. S. Landes, 'What Do Bosses Really Do?' (1986) 46 Journal of Economic History 585; Pollard, *Genesis of Modern Management*, 1–24, 160–91.

[81] Marglin, 'What Do Bosses Do?'. For a still grimmer analysis see D. Melossi and M. Pavarini, *The Prison and the Factory: Origins of the Penitentiary System* (London, 1981) 1–47.

[82] Compare Karl Marx's view that 'th[e] workshop, the product of the division of labour in manufacture, produced in its turn—machines' (*Capital* i, quoted in Berg, *Age of Manufactures*, 255).

instead relationships within labour, capital, and consumer markets. Thus the seasonality of labour may have been one factor deciding for central factory organization and discipline. In early textile industry short-term circulating capital may have been the predominant capital base, so that industrialization was determined by the availability of credit. And finally, early capitalism, especially in the textiles trades, depended on the cultivation of new demand for consumer market goods. Although workers' living standards did not rise, and possibly fell in the early phases of the Industrial Revolution to 1830, a new consumerist ethos emerged which transformed the motivational spring of work. Labour came to be viewed by the worker not as an artisan's calling, but as a cost sacrificed to win income for consumption at leisure; and this may have favoured the cultivation of centrally-organized factory production.[83]

Gregory Clark in a striking revisionist interpretation has recently argued that factory discipline cannot be explained entirely by co-ordination problems determined by technology, but can be shown to be coercive of worker effort. This suggests that labour markets in the early water-powered textiles trades were not fully competitive, in that uncoerced voluntary agreements to work for financial reward cannot explain the intensity and discipline of work imposed by the factory system. The explanation provided by Clark is that, *pace* Marx, it was not simply the capitalist ownership of technology itself that imposed factory discipline. Rather, the workers volunteered for servitude in the centralized factory because high incomes and consumer desires often proved more attractive to them than the traditional producer culture. The 'slavery' was in that sense a freely chosen course; the capitalist was 'hired' by the labourer in order to coerce and hence enrich the labourer himself.[84] Clark estimates that factory discipline in capital intensive trades during the nineteenth century pushed up worker effort by 33 per cent. This result was achieved by coercions, but it did not involve significant redistributions of profit away from the work-force; hence it was not classical Marxist exploitation. Owners were required to pay their labour force an over-the-market wage premium of 56 to 66 per cent. Workers bargained to accept factory discipline in return for higher pay, because they lacked the self-discipline to work regularly in response to pure financial incentives. Arkwright grasped this point by imposing the most severe disciplines in his textile mills, with punishments far in excess of damage and interruption caused by

[83] S. Pollard, 'Fixed Capital in the Industrial Revolution in Britain' (1964) 24 Journal of Economic History 299 and *Genesis of Modern Management*; R. Harris, *Industrializing English Law: Entrepreneurship and Business Organization 1720–1844* (Cambridge, 2000) 114–17; K. L. Sokoloff and D. Dollar, 'Agricultural Seasonality and the Organization of Manufacturing in Early Industrial Economies: The Contrast between England and the United States' (1997) 57 Journal of Economic History 288; de Vries, 'Industrial Revolution'; Daunton, *Progress and Poverty*, 173–90.

[84] Clark, 'Factory Discipline', 131.

infractions.[85] His new factory discipline was not mandated only by his innovations in centralized hydro-power technology, but also by labour's complex attitude to the work/consumption trade-off.[86]

The centralized water-powered factory may therefore be seen as a redistributive and disciplinary organization, rather than as the natural organizational form for technological industrialism. This insight may be joined to recent cliometric work which denies any sharp aggregate impact of the Industrial Revolution on productivity, and which minimizes the effects of the leading sectors—textiles, iron, coal—on the overall economy.[87] Other historians have gone further and argue that industrialization was entirely dispensable, and that it was agriculture, mercantile shipping, insurance, finance, and trade services, rather than value-added production, which were always the mainstay of the expanding English economy. Industrialization, in this view, was a deviation, a passing phase in the life of the core mercantile economy.[88] Another interpretation still identifies the dynamic sector of the English economy in the domestic, artisanal, and handicraft industries, linked with factory industry to produce an effective 'network capitalism', an 'industrious revolution'. Centralized factory production was therefore not the essence of economic transformation; the strength of the English economy lay rather in the *mittelstand* firm, highly productive though light in capital use, conservative in technology, and unsupported by government. The legal history of industrial enterprise from 1780, the heyday of the Age of Water Power, suggests that the early industrialists used traditional or archaic forms of business enterprise to carry forward new forms of production, tending to confirm the *mittelstand* theory.[89]

[85] Cf. Ure, *Philosophy of Manufactures*.

[86] For a nuanced review of the debate, see Daunton, *Progress and Poverty*, 173–90.

[87] C. K. Harley, 'Reassessing the Industrial Revolution: A Macro View', in Mokyr (ed.), *The British Industrial Revolution*, 171–226; N. F. R. Crafts, *British Economic Growth During the Industrial Revolution* (Oxford, 1985); N. F. R. Crafts and C. K. Harley, 'Output Growth and the Industrial Revolution: A Restatement of the Crafts-Harley View' (1992) 45 Economic History Review 703.

[88] P. J. Cain and A. G. Hopkins, 'Gentlemanly Capitalism and British Expansion Overseas' (1986) 39 Economic History Review 501 and (1987) 40 Economic History Review 1; and *British Imperialism: Innovation and Expansion, 1688–1914* (London, 1993); S. D. Chapman, *Merchant Enterprise in Britain: From the Industrial Revolution to World War One* (London, 1992); M. J. Daunton, 'Gentlemanly Capitalism and British Industry 1820–1914' (1989) 122 Past and Present 119; W. D. Rubinstein, 'Gentlemanly Capitalism and British Industry 1820–1914' (1991) 132 Past and Present 150 and *Capitalism, Culture and Decline in Britain, 1750–1990* (London, 1993).

[89] Berg, *Age of Manufactures*, 208–54; cf. P. O'Brien, 'Central Government and the Economy, 1688–1815', in Floud and McCloskey (eds.), *Economic History of Britain*, 205–41; P. O'Brien, T. Griffiths, and P. Hunt, 'Political Components of the Industrial Revolution: Parliament and the English Cotton Textile Industry, 1660–1774' (1991) 44 Economic History Review 395; Harris, *Industrializing English Law*, and 'Government and the Economy', in Floud and Johnson (eds.), *Cambridge Economic History of Modern Britain* (Cambridge, 2004) i, 204–37.

WATER SUPPLY, WATER RIGHTS, AND INDUSTRIAL LOCATION

Derbyshire, where the Arkwrights began, was close to frame-knitting areas, providing ready local markets for factory-made yarn. The water supply at Cromford flowed from a lead mine sough (channel) mingling with hot spring water from Matlock. These underground waters were hoped by the factory masters to be immune from seasonal variation and freezing in winter. Nearly all mill sites closer to population centres and trade routes had already been occupied in previous centuries of industrial development.[90] The secluded Cromford mill proved to be a success, employing 300 workers and thousands of spinning machines by 1779, and providing a base for Arkwright and Strutt's textile empires.[91] Other textile entrepreneurs based their early operations in Derbyshire: Lombe the silk king, and also Paul, Hargreaves, and Cartwright. However beneficial the network economies of Derbyshire proved to be in the pioneering phase, the region was soon found to be inadequate and most of the textile industry had moved to Lancashire by the end of the 1790s.[92]

The all-important water privileges attached to the land at Cromford were carefully specified in Arkwright's original lease, which granted him legal rights to:

> All that River Stream or Brook called Bonsall Brook Situate and being within the Liberty of Cromford . . . together with the Stream of Water Issuing and running from Cromford Sough in Cromford . . . into the said Bonsall Brook with full Liberty and power . . . to divert Turn and carry the said Brook Stream and Water down the South Side of the High Way in Cromford . . . and under or over the said Highway And also all that piece or parcel of Ground situate . . . between the said Bonsall Brook and the intended new Cutt and extending the length from the Turnpike road leading to Matlock Bath to a Garden in the Possession of James Cooper . . . Together with a full and free Liberty Power and Authority . . . to Erect and Build one or more Mill or Mills for Spinning Winding or throwing Silk Worsted Linen Cotton or Other Materials and also such and so many Waterwheels Warehouses Shops Smithies and other Buildings Banks and Dams Gails Shuttles and other Conveniences as they should think proper for the effectual Working of the said Mills.[93]

The lease also stipulated that Arkwright's textile mill was not 'to prejudice the corn-mill in the possession of Mr. Baxter, by taking away or diminishing the quantity of water . . . used or necessary for working . . . the cornmill'. Baxter's mill-site dated back to the thirteenth century; and nearby was a

[90] S. D. Chapman, 'The Cost of Power in the Industrial Revolution in England: The Case of the Textile Industry' (1971) 1 Midland History 8; Reynolds, *Stronger than One Hundred Men*, 122–4.

[91] Mantoux, *Industrial Revolution*, 229–39; Fitton, *The Arkwrights*, 146–223.

[92] Berg, *Age of Manufactures*, 98–115, 213–34; P. Hudson (ed.), *Regions and Industries. A Perspective on the Industrial Revolution in Britain* (Cambridge, 1989).

[93] Lease document in Arkwright Family Papers, quoted in Fitton, *The Arkwrights*, 28.

lead smelter that had occupied a portion of available water power to blow its bellows.[94] The ambiguous statement in the lease describing pre-existing water rights—protecting waters either 'used' or 'necessary'—reflected a degree of uncertainty about the nature of legal entitlements to riparian waters.

That new manufacturers had to fit in with a much older pattern of local industries and share in finite water resources is demonstrated by conflicts over water rights that broke out in 1776 over Arkwright's appropriation of water from the Bonsall Brook and the Cromford Moor Sough when he expanded his factory operations. By varying the flow and levels of the waters he managed to flood the local lead mines, and the miners retaliated by pulling down the factory's flood gates. Arkwright responded by covering over his watercourses and installing an eight horsepower steam engine to raise water to his works. The miners backed by the Sough proprietors continued to oppose the Arkwright waterworks, and in 1781 an arbitrator determined that Arkwright had no 'proofs or evidence' of his claims to water supply.[95]

The search for water power soon led to a fresh dispute with the Duke of Rutland when Arkwright and his nephew and heir Richard opened operations in Bakewell. Rutland was lord of the manor of Bakewell, and in 1783 he began to complain that the Arkwrights' activities had interrupted water supplies to his ancient corn mill and had damaged his trout fishing. The parties quarrelled for three-and-a-half years without formally going to law. However, legalism coloured their argument from the outset, as may be seen in the lengthy document where Rutland first presented his grievances:

> Whereas the said Charles Duke of Rutland is Lord of the Manor of Bakewell.... And whereas the said Charles Duke of Rutland and his Ancestors have for time immemorial been seized and possessed of a certain ancient Corn Mill situate... within the said manor of Bakewell and turned and worked by the said River Wye... at which Mill the tenants of the said Duke of Rutland... have of ancient right and custom been used to have their Corn Ground paying the customary Toll.... And the said Richard Arkwright the elder and Richard Arkwright the younger both or one of them have erected upon them the said piece of ground called Lumford a Cotton Mill and have likewise without the leave or licence of the said Duke or of John Duke of Rutland his late Grandfather deceased made erected built and set up Divers Wares Sluices Dams and other Obstructions upon and about the said River Wye within the said Manors of Ashford and Bakewell and have made great Dams Pools or Reservoirs in the Grounds called Great and Little Lumford and have diverted the Waters of the said River Wye from its ancient course thro' the said Ground called Lumford into the said Pools for the purpose of impounding the Water and for the turning the Wheels and Engines of the said Cotton Mill and have thereby prevented and obstructed the Water of the said River from flowing in its ancient and usual course to the aforesaid Corn Mill Of the

[94] For other typical leases of mill sites with water rights, see ibid., 76–7.
[95] Chapman, *Early Factory Masters*, 64–9.

said Duke of Rutland Whereby the same is obstructed and injured and the fishery of the said Duke is affected and prejudiced And whereas the said Richard Arkwright hath also cut through the ancient Mill dam of the said Corn Mill and hath taken up and carried away the Stone Gravel and Soil from the Commons and Waste grounds belonging to the said Duke of Rutland within the said Manor of Bakewell for the making of the said Dams and Mounds.[96]

Fitton has suggested that the Arkwrights had appropriated the Wye waters without approaching the duke because they feared his permission would have been refused. The harm to the lord's corn mill cited in Rutland's claim was only a legal pretext; the duke likely resented the overall rise of modern industrialism in his manors. Hence the Arkwrights acted without permission to change land and water use around them, then offering the adjacent landowner *ex post* compensation. The final settlement of December 1786 accorded the duke a nominal rent of £10 a year for a forty-two year lease of the waters of a portion of the Wye, together with a right to maintain sluices, dams, and bridges, provided that the ancient corn mill was not affected, and provided also that the duke could stipulate at any time that the watercourse of the river be restored to its original state. The settlement seems to have been designed to uphold the duke's underlying right to the waters as a component of his dignity as a feudal lord and to maintain his overall control of land-use, not in order to farm an economic rent from the Arkwrights' activities. Aristocratic landowners such as Rutland might manage their properties with non-commercial 'old property' sensibilities, as where they installed expensive drainage systems, enclosures, hunting runs, and garden landscapes, sometimes with elaborate ornamental lakes and water works.[97] The rental agreement in this case expressly allowed Rutland to control the extent of industrialization on his estates, and thus brought him into a loose kind of partnership or truce with the Arkwrights. The resolution of this conflict between land and capital demonstrates how bargaining could result in a new allocation of property rights in water, without there being any clear pre-existing idea of the legal rights of the parties. The purpose of the bargain was to create a mechanism for co-operation and for aligning the differing objectives of the parties, not to divide the profits of an economic enterprise.[98] More generally, rents for water supply were static and unresponsive to new uses, and so took a long time to adjust to shifts in the marginal costs of power, which varied widely with geography and the availability of coal. Hence the cost of water privileges did not commonly reflect their true

[96] Arkwright MSS. at Chatsworth, 69, quoted in Fitton, *The Arkwrights*, 55–6.

[97] J. Getzler, 'Judges and Hunters: Law and Economic Conflict in the English Countryside, 1800–1860' in C. Brooks and M. Lobban (eds.), *Communities and Courts in Britain, 1150–1900* (London, 1997) 199–228.

[98] Cf. R. C. Ellickson, *Order Without Law: How Neighbours Settle Disputes* (Cambridge, Mass., 1991).

economic or productive value; there was no efficient market in water power to set such a value.[99] There was therefore an element of arbitrariness in the rents extracted from industrialists by landowners.

Arkwright and his partners, the advance guard of hydro-industrialists, soon had to contend with newcomers seeking to use waters in the Derby area. In 1768 George White leased land in Matlock 'to build Mills and Erect Water-Wheels upon a parcel of Land adjoining to the River Derwent called Masson'; and in 1769 other industrialists took a lease 'to Erect Water-Wheels & other machines on the East side of River Derwent . . . near Matlock Bridge for the purpose of Unwatering Mines'. In 1771 a paper mill was built on a leasehold at Matlock, with the lords of the manor guaranteeing water supplies to the mill for twenty-one years. Hundreds of entrepreneurs were soon purchasing leases and erecting water mills along similar lines throughout Derbyshire and Lancashire. In 1780 Arkwright commisioned steam engines from Watt and Boulton to lift water up to his water wheel at Cromford after local lead miners 'lett down his water so that it cannot move', following precedents set by Smeaton and others from the 1760s.[100]

In this Age of Water Power, industrialists could find themselves sued by existing users of mill-streams, or would sue later entrants who disturbed their own newly-established uses. Two situations typically produced conflict. An upstream user might dam back a stream to store the water, or to slow, accelerate, or divert the stream so as better to meet the needs of his enterprise. For example, the water needs of a large mill might require that water be saved overnight in order to provide a good fall during daytime operation. Such manipulations of the stream often interfered with the working of lower mills. The second generic type of conflict arose where a downstream user penned back the water by a weir and thus reduced the fall available to an upstream miller. A commentator in 1819 summed up the problem thus:

> Upon most rivers in this country all the falls of water are fully occupied, and at every mill there is a weir, which pens up the water as high as the mill above can suffer it to stand without inconvenience. Each miller is anxious to obtain the greatest possible fall, and he can at any time augment the fall, by raising the surface of his weir; but as this may produce an inconvenience to the mill above . . . it is a constant source of dispute and litigation.[101]

In these conditions of competition for hydro-resources, the Arkwrights and other industrialists were forced to devote much effort and money to purchasing ancient corn mills as well as fresh mill sites, in order to acquire the

[99] See von Tunzelmann, *Steam Power and British Industrialization*, 132–41, who gives estimates of water rent values from the scanty pre-1860 evidence.

[100] R. S. Fitton and A. P. Wadsworth, *The Strutts and the Arkwrights 1758–1830. A Study of the Early Factory System* (Manchester, 1958), 80.

[101] 'Water', *The Rees Cyclopedia*, xxxviii (London, 1819), quoted in Reynolds, *Stronger than One Hundred Men*, 268.

appendant water rights ready for conversion to industrial uses.[102] It was common practice for the early industrialists to buy inadequately watered sites and then to install steam engines in order to pump sufficient water into the mill races.[103]

A technical development exacerbating the possibilities for conflict over resources was the construction of damming systems on a new scale, designed to secure the necessary water supplies for industry. It was common practice to invest heavily in works such as weirs, leets, and canals and thereby transform meagre water supplies into mighty prime movers; thus could capital augment land resources. Arkwright built a thirty-foot high dam on the Irwell near Manchester; and on the river Wye he dammed back a lake with an area of twenty-four acres. Elaborate dams were erected in the late eighteenth century in Derby and Gloucestershire, at Stockport and New Lanark, and at many other locations, often initiated by the Arkwright family. From the 1780s, hundreds of entrepreneurs were following the Arkwrights' example and building ever-larger mills and dams. Strutt built notable mills at Milford and Belper on the Derwent in the 1780s, together with dams and weirs on a scale sufficient to supply multiple water wheels. Oldknow built a large works at Stockport, and early employed steam power on a large scale to supplement his considerable water power. In 1837 the first dam over 100 feet high was built near Bolton, powering dozens of mills in the valley.[104] For one especially revealing example, at the enormous Catrine Cotton Works on the river Ayr £4,000 was spent in acquiring the water privileges; £4,500 on the mill wheels; and fully £8,000 on the canal and sluice system.[105]

Technical developments in wheel construction also increased calls on hydro-power; heightened efficiency thus led to increased rather than diminished overall energy use. By 1795 Strutt, one of Arkwright's original partners and an industrial magnate in his own right, was building mill-wheels forty feet long and eighteen feet in diameter, or forty-eight feet long with a twelve-foot diameter. Such wheels made of oak could cost £630 or more. By 1811, iron wheels of fifteen feet length and twenty-one-and-a-half foot diameters were in place.[106] Innovation and improvements in the construction of blades and ventilated water buckets, and in new breast-shot wheel designs,

[102] Thus Arkwright bought a corn mill at Tutbury in 1781 and invested £820 to build a new cotton mill: Hills, *Power in the Industrial Revolution*, 105–6. Constant haggling over water privileges crops up in many archival sources. eg. Letter of George Worthington to Samuel Oldknow, Altrincham, 14 February 1787 (Ms Coll Arkwright–Oldknow, Rare Book and Manuscript Library, Columbia University).

[103] Fitton, *The Arkwrights*, 57.

[104] Unwin, *Samuel Oldknow and the Arkwrights*, 123; Reynolds, *Stronger than One Hundred Men*, 273; and see generally Smith, *History of Dams*, 170–91.

[105] Von Tunzelmann, *Steam Power and British Industrialization*, 131.

[106] Fitton and Wadsworth, *The Strutts and the Arkwrights*, 207.

continued throughout the nineteenth century. John Smeaton's high breast-shot wheel utilized the directed impulse of the stream together with the weight of the water against the blades, and this increased power efficiencies to double that of the standard undershot wheel, to 60 per cent to 70 per cent of available raw water energy.[107] Arkwright's mill at Shudehill, Manchester, was capable of converting 6,000 gallons per minute over a thirty-foot fall into 54½ horse power driving 4,000 cotton spindles—an energy efficiency of 73 per cent.[108] Further leaps forward came with use of iron wheels and the accumulation of scientific knowledge of mechanics and hydrodynamics permitting quantitative accuracy in the design of suspension wheels, ever-lighter axles, high-tensile arms, rim transmission gears, and sheet-iron blades and buckets. Water wheels grew in size to over sixty feet in diameter. Their iron construction made them durable for the first time and doubled their power efficiency again to over 80 per cent by the 1860s. A new trade of millwrights learnt their skills by executing this novel work. These early metalworkers helped lay the foundations for the engineering and metallurgy trades, skills which kept British manufacturing technology in the first rank until the rise of American and German engineering some generations later.[109]

Accompanying wheel and machinery improvements between 1750 and 1850 there were vast investments in river-widening, wells, weirs, dams, sluices, bridges, leets, and mill-races, allowing engineers to bring a steady and controlled water-stream to mills and mines miles away from water sources.[110] Mathematical calculation turned dam construction into a science, with the crude gravity dam replaced by composite and masonry dams of sophisticated design. Longer mill-leats or power canals with well-governed sluices focused water-streams into jets yielding maximum fall and impact. Finally, in the 1840s the Fourneyron water turbine began to supplant the vertical water wheel. The old idea of the turbine was redesigned with mathematical rigour to pass a high fall of water through an enclosed chamber, so to deliver high efficiency in all types of water conditions.[111] This invention surpassed the most modern breasted wheel designs. Turbines did not become quite as prevalent in Britain, with its low pressure falls, as they did in Europe and America where they became the dominant water-power technology from the 1880s. It was the development of electricity generation, whether coal-fired or hydro-driven, which finally superseded traditional mechanical hydro-power in Britain between 1880 and 1900.[112]

[107] Reynolds, *Stronger than One Hundred Men*, 281–3.

[108] Calculations from von Tunzelmann, *Steam Power and British Industrialization*, 128.

[109] Berg, *Age of Manufactures*, 255–79.

[110] Reynolds, *Stronger than One Hundred Men*, 196–320; Fitton and Wadsworth, *The Strutts and the Arkwrights*, 221–3.

[111] Reynolds, *Stronger than One Hundred Men*, 338–49.

[112] G. N. von Tunzelmann, 'Technology in the Early Nineteenth Century' in Floud and McCloskey (eds.), *Economic History of Britain*, 271, 286–8.

The long train of innovations listed above—the micro-inventions that continuously refined the ancient macro-invention of the water wheel—helped preserve hydropower as a leading technology in the face of growing competition from the steam engine.[113] There was a great race for water sites and water supplies throughout the nineteenth-century Industrial Revolution, and this provides the essential historical context for the development of modern riparian law—the law of rights to flowing streams.

OTHER USES OF WATER IN THE INDUSTRIAL AGE

In his 1835 *History of the Cotton Manufacture* E. Baines observed how networks of interdependent industry clustered along the major watercourses around cotton manufactures:

> In the early part of their course, these streams and streamlets furnish water-power adequate to turn many hundred mills; they afford the element of water, indispensable for scouring, bleaching, printing, dyeing, and other processes of manufacture, and when collected in their larger channels, or employed to feed canals, they supply a superior inland navigation, so important for the transit of raw materials and merchandise.[114]

Water was not only an energy source for the Industrial Revolution; it was also a crucial raw material for production and urbanization. Water was necessary for brewing and food manufacture; and especially for manufacturing processes requiring washing and draining such as the textiles, dyeing, printing, chemical and mining industries. Moreover, water resources were essential to the transport revolutions of the same period: it was the construction of an intricate inland navigation system of improved river-channels in the 1730s and man-made canals from the 1780s which enabled the heavy raw materials of the emergent mineral-based economy and its finished products to be moved across regional spatial barriers. Water thereby contributed to the creation of a vast internal free-trade area, lessening the need for small-scale autochthonous production as an insurance against dearth, and helping to develop regional comparative advantages in agriculture and industry with the benefits of economies of scope, scale, and specialization.[115] The building of the canal system was a major exercise in

[113] Reynolds, *Stronger than One Hundred Men*, 266–71; von Tunzelmann, *Steam Power and British Industrialization*, 125–41.

[114] E. Baines, *History of the Cotton Manufacture* (London, 1835; 2nd edn., London, 1966) 86; and see Hills, *Power in the Industrial Revolution*, 94–5.

[115] Mantoux, *Industrial Revolution*, 93–139; Berg, *Age of Manufactures*, 106–14; P. Deane, *The First Industrial Revolution* (2nd edn., Cambridge, 1979) 72–86; T. S. Ashton, *The Industrial Revolution 1760–1830* (London, 1948, reprinted 1969) 81–4; J. R. Ward, *The Finance of Canal Building in Eighteenth-Century England* (Oxford, 1974); G. Turnbull, 'Canals, Coal and Regional

capital formation, and involved the construction of large reservoirs and river diversions to supply the canals and locks. Investment in waterways served as an important outlet for investment capital which helped stabilize the eighteenth-century British economy by maintaining turnover, demand, and profit rates. The rise of the canal system hastened the development of large business organizations such as joint stock companies incorporated by private Act of Parliament.[116]

In wet British conditions, irrigation was rarely necessary. More importantly for agricultural productivity, from 1700 there were major innovations in the draining of farm estates or removal of water from sodden land. Farmers fought not over who should have the right to receive water for their estates (as in the dry Mediterranean lands governed by Roman law), but rather over who should have the right to eject unwanted water onto their neighbours' lands. Effective drainage of estates was one of the leading motives for enclosure of the commons, or the gathering of fragmented feudal claims over land together into consolidated estates in order to permit large-scale and capital-intensive farming. The ensuing productivity increases in agriculture were an essential pre-condition for industrialization and urbanization.[117]

Water resources were also crucial in urban housing developments necessitated by the expanding population of industrial England. The Victorian cities descended into epidemic and mass mortality unless amply serviced with water for drinking and drainage.[118] Much of local government's energies and capital was devoted to this problem, and scores of local and personal Acts of Parliament were passed establishing local government corporations and highly regulated private utilities for the purposes of sanitation and water supply, with powers to raise capital, to appropriate land and water rights, and to build major reservoirs, pools, sewers, and drains as required. So

Growth during the Industrial Revolution' (1987) 40 Economic History Review 537; G. R. Hawke and J. P. P. Higgins, 'Transport and Social Overhead Capital', in Floud and McCloskey (eds.), *Economic History of Britain*, 227–52; Daunton, *Progress and Poverty*, 239–42, 288–93, 307–14.

[116] A. B. DuBois, *The English Business Company After the Bubble Act 1720–1800* (New York, 1938) passim; B. C. Hunt, *The Development of the Business Corporation in England 1800–1867* (Cambridge, Mass., 1936) passim; Ward, *The Finance of Canal Building*; Harris, *Industrializing English Law*, 85–100. The story was continued with the railway boom: see R. W. Kostal, *Law and English Railway Capitalism 1825–1875* (Oxford, 1994) 11–143.

[117] Berg, *Age of Manufactures*, 77–97; R. C. Allen, *Enclosure and the Yeoman: The Agricultural Development of the South Midlands, 1450–1850* (Oxford, 1992); G. Clark, 'Agriculture and the Industrial Revolution, 1700–1850' in Mokyr (ed.), *The British Industrial Revolution*, 227–66.

[118] J.-P. Goubert, *The Conquest of Water: The Advent of Health in the Industrial Age* (Oxford, 1989); B. Rudden, *The New River: A Legal History* (Oxford, 1985) 150–66; J. A. Hassan, 'The Growth and Impact of the British Water Industry in the Nineteenth Century' (1985) 38 Economic History Review 531 and *A History of Water in Modern England and Wales* (Manchester, 1998); F. B. Smith, *The People's Health, 1830–1910* (corrected edn. 1990; reissued edn., Aldershot, 1993).

important was this aspect of urban organization that the usual inhibitions about public enterprise and state control were weakened.[119]

LEGAL CONFLICT OVER WATER RIGHTS

The significance of water power and water resources in modern Britain's economic life was reflected in two surges of litigation concerning riparian and other water rights, one in the early seventeenth and one in the nineteenth century. Both phases closely follow on from the peak periods of expansion of industrial water use. By the late eighteenth century mills were crowding densely along the stretches of rivers and streams in the three major industrial regions of Britain, namely in Birmingham, Nottingham, Sheffield, and North Derbyshire; in Glasgow, New Lanark, Paisley, and the Clyde Valley; and above all in Southern Lancashire, around Manchester, Bolton, Blackburn, Bury, and Oldham. Water for power bestowed a potent comparative advantage upon those areas, at least until the more widespread diffusion of steam technologies.

Emergent modern industry retained strong links to agriculture and handicrafts, and was predominantly rural in location compared to pre-modern manufacture which typically was sited in urban areas. Industrial location was determined by social institutions and incentives as much as by physical or geographical advantages. Berg has observed how legal provision of welfare to the poor through common rights, protected tenures, and Poor Law relief underpinned industrial growth; hence local variations in land-holding systems could be significant.[120] Social institutions may have over-determined the response of a local economy to factor endowments and technology, but nonetheless the natural distribution of endowments such as water resources played some role in directing the regionalization of industry. We can remember that Arkwright cited the ready availability of compliant female and child labour—an institutional factor—together with the stable water supply as equal reasons for building his first textile factory at Cromford. At

[119] P. Schwartz, 'John Stuart Mill and Laissez Faire: London Water' (1966) 33 Economica 71; J. Prest, *Liberty and Locality: Parliament, Permissive Legislation, and Ratepayers' Democracies in the Nineteenth Century* (Oxford, 1990); J. Foreman-Peck and R. Millward, *Public and Private Ownership of British Industry 1820–1900* (Oxford, 1994); M. Taggart, *Private Property and Abuse of Rights in Victorian England: The Story of Edward Pickles and the Bradford Water Supply* (Oxford, 2002) 5–22, 75 ff.; W. R. Cornish and G. de N. Clark, *Law and Society in England 1750–1950* (London, 1989) 158–66; R. Harris, 'Government and the Economy', in Floud and Johnson (eds.), *The Cambridge Economic History of Modern Britain*, 13–15; and see references to the private bill procedure in Introduction, n. 12, above. The complex history of London's water supply is described in Rudden, *The New River*, n. 118 above.

[120] Berg, *Age of Manufactures*, 93–4.

Cromford there was not only an ample water and labour supply, but the legal opportunities to bargain effectively for the use of these factors. Comparative advantage was thus a union of natural endowments and the social institutions permitting their effective utilization; and here the analysis of legal institutions clearly has a role.[121]

The ready availability of water supplies in the North of England could eliminate regional variation as well as cause it. Access to sea transportation had once favoured entrepôt towns as sites of manufacture; but ports such as Liverpool were soon linked by canal and waterway to new industrial centres in the rural hinterland, and population growth and urbanization in sparsely populated areas followed swiftly as large workforces congregated to form factory towns.[122] Dispersal of factories through the countryside did not long prevent overcrowding of water resources: densities of thirteen mills for every two miles of river, or even two hundred mills for each six miles of river, were recorded.[123] Baines noted that '[o]n the river Irwell, from the first mill near Bacup, to Prestolee, near Bolton, there is about 900 feet of fall available for mills, 800 of which is occupied. On this river and its branches it is computed that there are no less than three hundred mills'.[124] By 1800 an energy crisis was commencing as all possible mill sites in the country were occupied, driving up the value of water privileges pending the development of steam power. England's energy crisis came approximately fifty years before that of rival industrializing regions—alpine Europe and New England—which enjoyed superior natural water endowments.

England's scarcities of flowing water provoked acute competition to capture the available resources, a rivalry that commonly spilled into the courts.[125] The engineer John Sutcliffe in 1816 pointed to the growing legal problems:

> In consequence of so many water mills, the country is never free from litigations and vexatious law suits, respecting erecting, repairing, or raising mill-weirs, by which the peace and harmony of neighbours and friends are often destroyed.... Some years ago, the annual expense of water cases and arbitrations, in consequence of them, in the counties of York and Lancaster, were estimated at £10,000, and should trade revive, it is probable in a few years they will exceed this sum.[126]

[121] Cf. D. C. North, *Institutions, Institutional Change and Economic Performance* (Cambridge, 1990).

[122] Mantoux, *Industrial Revolution*, 251–76.

[123] Reynolds, *Stronger than One Hundred Men*, 267–8.

[124] Baines, *History of the Cotton Manufacture*, 86.

[125] Reynolds, *Stronger than One Hundred Men*, 266–76; P. Mathias, 'The Industrial Revolution: Concept and Reality', in P. Mathias and J. A. Davies (eds.), *The First Industrial Revolutions* (Oxford, 1989) 4–24; cf. Gordon, 'Cost and Use of Water Power', 240–3, 259.

[126] J. Sutcliffe, *Treatise on Canals and Reservoirs, and the Best Mode of Designing and Executing Them* (Rochdale, 1816).

Two types of conflict commonly arose: upstream interference with the flow to lower mills and downstream damming-back of water causing flooding of the upstream mill. In many cases there may have been a non-legal custom that a lower miller had to guarantee his own water supply no matter what interferences were imposed from above. The *Rees Cyclopedia* in 1819 stated that this was the case where a storage dam was built upstream, and added: 'The same question arises when any mill is altered or enlarged, so as to consume the water faster than the river brings it down, for such a mill can only work for short intervals, and must then stop that the water may accumulate in the dam until there is sufficient supply to set to work again.'[127] An example of the uncertain customs governing these issues was given by the Quarry Bank Mill built by Samuel Greg on the Bollin in Styal. This was the first large mill on the river, but in 1815 the solicitor of a new downstream mill wrote to complain of Greg's enlarged water use:

It is quite impossible that Mr. Greg could be in perfect ignorance of this complaint. Mr. Greg has for years past so impounded the water that in dry seasons Mr Neild's mill has been stopped every day until noon.... If Mr. Greg will make an offer of compensation, or will meet Mr. Neild to confer on the subject, Mr. Greg will find that Mr. Neild is not untractable or unreasonable.[128]

There is no record that Greg offered compensation to his downstream neighbour. However, Greg did offer compensation to an upstream owner who demanded that Greg lower his weir in order to allow an ancient ford to be used; Greg built a new bridge for that owner and thereby won his permission to enlarge the dam further. Examples of such informal dispute and negotiation over water rights could be multiplied. Often parties kept out of legal conflict by forward planning to avoid confrontations over water access. For example Strutt concentrated much of his enterprise at Belper on the Derwent precisely because he could accumulate ownership rights to all the river banks and thereby free himself of objections by rival water users. He was able to build a fourteen-acre weir at that site, in contrast to his Milford works where elaborate damming was restrained by rival users.[129]

That resource developers dependent on water supply laboured under a regime of legal conflict and uncertainty is abundantly suggested by their incessant legal claims, litigations, and Parliamentary contests over water rights. At least 200 cases concerning water rights are reported between 1770 and 1870; many hundreds more eluded the central records, for example at the preliminary circuit trials of Nisi Prius and in actions before local courts. Conflicts over flowing water could be fought by industrialists

[127] *Rees Cyclopedia* (1819), 104.
[128] Quoted in ibid., 108–9.
[129] Hills, *Power in the Industrial Revolution*, 108–14.

and landowners outside the courts, but very much in the shadow of the law.[130] Moreover, there were numerous contested proceedings for the passing of private legislative bills in the committees of the Lords and Commons which closely resembled courtroom litigation. One prominent example involved the proceedings on the Cromford Canal Acts, where a canal company sought to appropriate land and water in order to provide cheap navigation for coal and heavy goods to Derbyshire, and used a parliamentary bill to overcome fierce opposition from local millowners and landowners fearing loss of resources and damaging competition.[131]

Judges were called upon to frame elaborate rules for the allocation and securing of water rights as a form of wealth, and they showed acute awareness of the economic importance of the subject. In the 1866 case of *Nuttal* v. *Bracewell*, for example, Martin B wrote:

> The application and use of flowing water to work machinery is as old as the law. Corn mills have existed from time immemorial, and it appears, from old legal authorities, that fulling and other mills worked by water for the purpose of manufacture are of a very ancient date. Until the last century, steam as a power was, if known, not much in use; and until it was introduced, water power was very generally used, and it is still the cheapest when available. . . . So also, water was and is very frequently conveyed from the natural stream . . . for the purposes of irrigation. And it is not too much to say, that the value of actual or supposed water rights of this character throughout England may be estimated by hundreds of thousands, perhaps millions.[132]

When the House of Lords finally addressed riparian issues in *Chasemore* v. *Richards* in 1859,[133] Lord Wensleydale found the subject to be 'of the greatest importance. . . . No case that has occurred in my time has been so worthy of the most careful consideration',[134] whilst Lord Kingsdown held water rights to be 'one of the most important questions that ever came under the consideration of a court of justice'.[135]

[130] See above, the text accompanying nn. 96–98 (Rutland negotiations with Arkwright). The Arkwrights were constantly involved in negotiations with neighbours over water rights; see R. Arkwright, *Correspondence with Sir Christopher and Sir M. M. Sykes re water rights, etc., at West Beck and Wansford Mills* (Hull University Library, P.P. 345–6, 1789–1822); R. Arkwright, *Deeds and papers related to mill at Bakewell* (East Sussex Record Office, Cavendish private records, Ark. 1–97). Samuel Oldknow similarly engaged in protracted negotiations with the Peak-Forest Canal Company between 1784 and 1797 over water rights at Stockport without ending up in court: see George Worthington-Oldknow Correspondence (Arkwright–Oldknow Collection, Columbia University Rare Book and Manuscript Library).

[131] *Arkwright* v. *Gell* (1839) 5 M. & W. 203; 151 E.R. 87 (Ex.); *House of Commons Journals*, xliv (1789) 280, 376, 410, 422; *House of Lords Journals* xxxviii (1789) 437, 443–59, 460, 470, 475, 497, 502–3, 514, 574, 577–86; xxxix (1790) 356–62, 392–3, 401; *House of Lords Petitions* (1789) LP 281/21–4, 29, 40–1; and *House of Lords Committee Book* xxxiii (1789) 175–6, 183–92, 197–234 (H.L.R.O.). The legal conflict is discussed further below in Ch. 5.

[132] (1866) L.R. 2 Ex. 1, 9 (Ex.).

[133] (1859) 7 H.L.C. 349; 11 E.R. 140 (H.L.).

[134] 7 H.L.C. 349, 380; 11 E.R. 140, 152.

[135] 7 H.L.C. 349, 390; 11 E.R. 140, 156.

THE DOCTRINAL HISTORY OF WATER RIGHTS

The judges may have taken water law seriously, but they had the greatest difficulty in deciding what the law was. The regime of riparian water rights in England from its origins in the early common law to the 1870s presents a striking complexity and confusion of common-law entitlements accorded to property owners. There is little support here for the theory that clear and distinct property rights and their efficient legal protection were an essential precondition of the Industrial Revolution, or even that the existence of property rights significantly contributed to increases in productivity.

Riparian doctrine was shaped most immediately by an inherent feature of its subject matter: that flowing water is a thing in constant state of change which may be diverted, abstracted, or polluted by competing users, and hence destroyed. So a running stream cannot be appropriated or possessed in the way that land as a stable, immutable object of property is capable of possession.[136] Robert Callis captured this idea in 1622:

> But that there should be a property fixed in running waters, I cannot be drawn to that opinion; for the civil law saith ... *quod aqua profluens non manet in certo loco, sed procul f[l]uit extra ditionem ejus cujus flumen est ut ad mare tandem perveniat* [that running water does not flow in a defined place, yet removes in many streams until at length it reaches the sea]; for in my opinion, it should be strange the law of property should be fixed upon such uncertainties as to be altered into *meum, tuum, suum*, before these words can be spoken, and to be changed in every twinkling of an eye, and to be more uncertain in the proprietor than a chameleon of his colors.[137]

This quality of instability creates difficulties of legal characterization, for underlying the law's intricate structure of property rights corporeal and incorporeal, of tenures, estates, and trusts, lay an abiding principle of physical possession (or rights to the fruits of possession) as the foundation of right.[138] No such firm anchor was available to describe riparian ownership, for the riparian proprietor does not 'possess' water flow, in the sense of appropriating or controlling or occupying a stream to the exclusion of all other persons. Other non-corporeal appurtenant property rights, such as

[136] See *Challenor* v. *Thomas* (1608) 1 Brownl. 142; 123 E.R. 718 (C.P.) (interference with water flow is not an invasion of possession); *Brown* v. *Best* (1747) 1 Wils. K.B. 174, 176; 95 E.R. 557, 559 (K.B.) per Dennison J ('And a watercourse is a quite distinct thing from the land'); *Magistrates of Linlithgow* v. *Elphinstone* (1768) 3 Kames' Decisions (S.C.S.) 331, 331–2 ('A river, which is in perpetual motion, is not naturally susceptible of appropriation').

[137] *The Reading of Robert Callis upon the Statute of Sewers, 23 Hen. VIII c. 5* (1622) 78–9 (4th edn. by W. J. Broderip, London, 1824) 97. The civilian material is possibly of glossator or commentator provenance; it is not classical. Thanks are due to Michael Macnair for help with this text.

[138] O. W. Holmes Jr., *The Common Law* (Boston, Mass., 1881; M. De Howe (ed.), Boston, Mass., 1963) 192–4; W. S. Holdsworth, *An Historical Introduction to the Land Law* (Oxford, 1927) 121–31, 176–88; and see Ch. 2, below.

covenants touching and running with land, and rights of air, light, support, and way can broadly be conceived as servitudes over land—a mode of enjoying one's own land through non-possessory control of neighbouring land: *iura in re aliena* or 'rights in a stranger's property' in the terminology of civilian law.[139] By contrast the use of water privileges need not be entwined with the enjoyment of adjoining land, but might be claimed as an incident of value in itself; for example, as the common property of a number of individuals, or of a collectivity; or as *res communes*—collective goods available for the enjoyment of all, with legal restraints placed on rival or exclusive uses.

The nineteenth-century courts commonly described water rights as naturally connected to land or a concomitant of ownership of riparian land, in the sense that ownership or occupation of abutting land was both necessary and sufficient to afford a right to appropriate the benefit of a running stream. However, with the diversification of industrial and urban water uses in the nineteenth century, enjoyment of water could be divorced from association with neighbouring land, and thus shown to be distinct from incidents of landownership such as light and air. Multiplication of legitimate users inevitably led to heightened conflict over appropriation of finite available water. The courts finally adhered to a natural incident theory of riparian rights, based on a discretionary standard of reasonable usage of natural flow, which limited the class of legitimate users to riverbank owners and balanced the requirements of competing users. This position emerged slowly and fitfully; a large number of theories were considered, adopted, and rejected before the modern principles were settled around 1860.[140]

Many factors internal to the legal system made for the long instability of riparian doctrine. These included the complexities of the disseisin and trespass forms of tort action for the protection of possessory and non-possessory interests in property; contending doctrine and policy regarding the principles of prescription and adverse possession; the slow and confused development of the law of easements and natural property rights and of modern doctrines of private nuisance law; the complexities of Roman law principles which were erected as a model or starting point for the evolution of many of the English land-use rules; and, finally, changes in pleading practice and legal process which concentrated discretionary power to determine fact in the hands of the judges at the expense of juries.

Ultimately the common law's capacity to govern water entitlements proved inadequate, and an ad hoc regime of private (and later public) statute was erected to perform the task. But the common law served as the background or baseline for the statutory re-ordering of rights: private bill pro-

[139] Getzler, 'Roman Ideas of Landownership', 101–5.

[140] Lord Blackburn noted that the modern natural-right doctrine 'can hardly be considered as settled law in England before the case of *Mason* v. *Hill* in 1833': *Orr Ewing* v. *Colquhoun* (1877) 2 App. Cas. 839, 854 (H.L.(Sc.)).

ceedings in Parliament invoked common-law principle; and the courts looked through common-law spectacles as they strove to interpret and apply the many hundreds of private and public Acts issuing from Parliament.[141] Hence a close study of the judge-made law of water as a private good must precede discussion of statutory allocation of water as a public good amongst individual property owners, commercial actors, and urban users.

In dealing with the historical common law, we must cast our net back far in our search for origins, to Bracton and the medieval inheritance of Romanist jurisprudence. The doctrines generated by the central courts and the ideas of the jurists who commented on their decisions will take centre stage. Local courts were also of considerable importance in mediating conflict between land and water users in the course of industrialization; but the norms applied in those courts, with their strong magisterial and jury discretions, are far more inscrutable.

[141] A telling example was *R.* v. *Directors of the Bristol Dock Company* (1810) 12 East 429; 104 E.R. 167 (K.B.), where a statute (Bristol Dock Act 43 Geo.3, c.140, s.107) gave a general right to compensation for damage to property caused by dock works. When a brewery sued the dock company for polluting water used by the brewery, compensation was denied on the basis that this was merely a common nuisance interfering with the general public's water supply, and not a private nuisance to an existing property right in water. According to the court, the legislation could not be presumed to have impliedly expanded private rights at common law: 'These persons have no more claim to compensation under the Act than every inhabitant of Bristol would have who had been used to dip a pail into the river for water for the use of his house' (Le Blanc J, 12 East 429, 432, 104 E.R. 167, 169). The fact that this interpretation left common-law rights entirely untouched and so rendered the Act redundant was not discussed. Cases could be multiplied, eg. *Broadbent* v. *The Imperial Gas Co.* (1856) 7 De G., M. & G. 436; 44 E.R. 170 (Ch. L.C.); *Attorney-General* v. *Council of Borough of Birmingham* (1858) 4 Kay and Johnson 528, 70 E.R. 220 (V.C.); cf. injunctions against utilities: *Attorney-General* v. *Sheffield Gas Consumers Company* (1853) 3 D. G. M. & G. 304; 43 E.R. 119 (Ch, L.C.). See further A. W. B. Simpson, 'Victorian Law and the Industrial Spirit' (Selden Society Lecture, London, 1995) 21–5, and Taggart, *Private Property and Abuse of Rights*, 96–106, which trace mid-Victorian judicial policies regarding legislative takings of private property.

2. *Servitude Doctrine in Early Law*

Water rights in England developed first through the application of title and nuisance actions to land-use disputes, and then by the adaptation of Roman-law doctrine as lawyers categorized the results of such litigation. This chapter analyses the medieval law of proprietary incidents emerging from these two juristic sources.

THE FORMS OF ACTION

The classical Roman formulary system invented legal concepts through case development of remedies by adjudicators and rationalization of the forms of remedy by the jurists.[1] These concepts were appropriated by nearly all national legal systems in Europe as they constructed their own codes and languages of law.[2] In the sweep of European legal history, the peculiarity of the English was to launch their own formulary system of case law in the twelfth century, administered by the officials of a powerful monarch whose jurisdiction combined feudal with national authority.[3] The distinct writs or forms of action were defined by pleading requirements that served to state the type of legal claim and remedy sought, and to identify the essential facts which grounded the action and which were to be decided by

[1] F. Schulz, *Principles of Roman Law* (M. Wolff (trans.), Oxford, 1936), *History of Roman Legal Science* (Oxford, 1946) 99–140, and *Classical Roman Law* (Oxford, 1951) 11–70; W. W. Buckland, *A Textbook of Roman Law from Augustus to Justinian* (3rd edn., revised P. G. Stein, Cambridge, 1963) 14–45; W. Kunkel, *An Introduction to Roman Legal and Constitutional History* (J. M. Kelly (trans.), Oxford, 1966) 84–124; P. G. Stein, *Regulae Iuris: From Juristic Rules to Legal Maxims* (Edinburgh, 1966) and 'The Development of the Institutional System', in P. G. Stein and A. D. E. Lewis (eds.), *Studies in Justinian's Institutes in Memory of J. A. C. Thomas* (London, 1983) 151; F. Horak, *Rationes decidendi: Entscheidungsbegründungen bei den älteren römischen Juristen bis Labeo* (Aalen, 1969) i; H. F. Jolowicz and B. Nicholas, *Historical Introduction to the Study of Roman Law* (3rd edn., Cambridge, 1972) 374–94, 405–20; A. A. Schiller, *Roman Law: Mechanisms of Development* (New York, 1978) 269–441; F. Wieacker, *Römische Rechtsgeschichte* (Munich, 1988) i, 531–662; B. Frier, *The Rise of the Roman Jurists* (Princeton, NJ, 1985).

[2] R. C. van Caenegem, *An Historical Introduction to Private Law* (D. Johnston (trans.), Cambridge, 1992); P. G. Stein, *Roman Law in European History* (Cambridge, 1999); F. Wieacker, *A History of Private Law in Europe: with Particular Reference to Germany* (T. Weir (trans.), R. Zimmermann (introd.), Oxford, 1995).

[3] R. C. van Caenegem, *The Birth of the English Common Law* (2nd edn., Cambridge, 1985) 85–110. M. Lupoi, in *The Origins of the European Legal Order* (Cambridge, 2000) 1–4 ff, stresses that the pre-Conquest English writ system shared the same customary and civilian influences as the early medieval *ius commune* of Europe, with the 'unbridgeable gulf' between the legal orders opening only from the late eleventh century.

the jury.[4] The intense focus on writs rather than rights helped ensure that any reception of Roman institutional learning into the common law would be limited and slow. Medieval lawyers were chiefly concerned to fit their clients' cases within the simplest and most effective actions, avoiding the procedural hurdles of more archaic and cumbersome writs—or alternatively to deny that the opponent could properly use a writ of action to advance a claim. The early learning of the forms of action was an oral tradition maintained by a professional consensus as to what counted as a correct curial procedure. Such orality ensured conservatism, an inertia that carried over as the tradition was recorded gradually and unsystematically in the Year Books. It took centuries for the common-law rules to be organized into works such as Fitzherbert's *Natura Brevium* of 1534, supplemented by the great abridgements which exhaustively listed the appropriate writs for different cases.[5] These works are raw descriptions of legal actions, not analyses of rights. The result of this formulaic path of legal evolution was that rights of land and water use were not directly based on concepts such as possession, grant, custom, prescription, common right, and natural right. Such ideas were present, but submerged within professional argument over forms of pleading, proof and remedy.

Actions for Rights and Wrongs

The early forms of action may be divided between claims asserting rights on the one hand and actions for the remedying of wrongs on the other.[6] In the first category the plaintiff claimed some interest by a demand of right projected into the future—for example a real right to an asset or a proprietary right to descending land. In the second category the plaintiff sought protection of his interests from some past wrong, by bringing a plaint alleging an injury to the person or to property or an incident of possession,

[4] S. F. C. Milsom, 'Law and Fact in Legal Development', and 'Reason in the Development of the Common Law', both in S. F. C. Milsom, *Studies in the History of the Common Law* (London, 1985) at 171 and 149.

[5] H. S. Maine, *Early Law and Custom* (London, 1891) 389; F. W. Maitland, *The Forms of Action at Common Law* (1st edn., 1909), A. H. Chaytor and S. J. Whittaker (eds.), (Cambridge, 1965) 52 n. 1 and see 1–11, 78; F. Pollock and F. W. Maitland, *The History of English Law Before the Time of Edward I* (*HEL*) (1895, 2nd edn., Cambridge, 1898, reprinted 1968) i, ch. V; ii, ch. IX; S. F. C. Milsom, *Historical Foundations of the Common Law* (2nd edn., London, 1981) 37–81; cf. R. C. Palmer, *English Law in the Age of the Black Death* (Chapel Hill, NC, 1993), who argues for a more conscious policy of Crown lawyers working governmentally through court and chancery to develop improved legal actions, 'exhibiting a government intent on using the law to control society' (at 5).

[6] This argument is developed more fully in J. Getzler, 'Patterns of Fusion', in P. B. H. Birks (ed.), *The Classification of Obligations* (Oxford, 1997) 157–92. D. J. Ibbetson, *A Historical Introduction to the Law of Obligations* (Oxford, 1999), 1–23, notes that the actions of debt, covenant or trespass could each encompass claims based on either entitlement or harm: '[t]his ambiguity was never quite resolved'.

or some wrongful breach of obligation. A writ directed to the prospective vindication and maintenance of proprietary rights was generally more formal, ceremonial, and unwieldy than a writ remedying an executed invasion of interest, a past infliction of loss.[7]

Actions both for rights and for wrongs involved assertion of a plaintiff's economic or other interests, such as protection of personality and bodily integrity; but there was a crucial theoretical distinction between right-assertion and wrong-remedying in the eyes of the medieval law. A continuing proprietary right defined the status of its holder in medieval society, whether as lord of a manor with seigneurial jurisdiction or as tenant with customary familial claim to landholding by free or unfree tenure. Property rights in this sense had a public, governmental, or constitutional aspect as well as a private resource-allocation function.[8] The real actions were not simply writs for the recovery or claiming of property, but claims of permanent rights within a feudal jurisdiction. By contrast, an action for some past wrong formally had no continuing implications for the distribution of status and power in society: the public interest in remedying wrongs was rather to remove the threat to public peace posed by individuals seeking compensation, restitution, or revenge against the wrongdoer through self-help or private enforcement.

The early common law's broad categories of right (concerned with property and status in the feudal hierarchy—distributive justice) and wrong (concerned with harms, breach of the peace—corrective justice) were combined over a period of centuries as a function of the decline of feudal governance and the rise of central state power under the Crown. Royal justice gradually developed from a limited system of regulation and policing—even judicial review—of decentralized feudal jurisdictions into a general legal system. The common law more or less came to fill the space of judicial power in society, distributing and enforcing individual rights and correlative duties which were directly ordained from a single point of sovereignty. This large process of transformation—from local, customary norms towards centralized definition and allocation of property rights—was once seen as an aspect of a broad-fronted bid for exclusive power by the English state. According to the revisionist interpretation offered by S. F. C. Milsom, the transformation was not engineered by the intentional agency of an expansive royal government of Parliament and courts, but was driven by the centripetal pressure of litigants seeking individual justice where best they could find it.[9] But the results were the same, however the process is characterized.

[7] J. H. Baker, *An Introduction to English Legal History* (4th edn., London, 2002) 57–64.

[8] Cf. Pollock and Maitland, *HEL*, ii, 1–6.

[9] Milsom, *Historical Foundations*, 99–165, *Legal Framework of English Feudalism* (Cambridge, 1976), and 'The Real Actions', introduction to Pollock and Maitland, *HEL*, i, pp. xxvii–xlix. Maitland also noted the slow and partial centralization of English justice,

The motivations for erecting a common law system of rights may be elusive, but the doctrinal path to such a system can be observed more clearly. Actions for executed wrongs—notably novel disseisin and trespass—were adapted into swift means of vindicating the continuing proprietary rights of owners seeking undisturbed enjoyment of their land, through the technique of upholding superior rights to possession against intruders. Property rights (rights of seisin and tenure) in the localized feudal system were thereby subsumed within a centrally-administered system of ranked possessory rights protected by remedies (actions for wrongs) in the royal courts. The emergence of a system of relative title was complete by the early thirteenth century, and was plain to Bracton who could write: '[O]ne may have a firm seisin against some persons, as against non-lords, at once, and a tenuous and weak seisin against true lords, and thus a free tenement against some and not against others.'[10] The circumlocutory doctrine of title as a hierarchy of relative rights to possession gave rise to a tangle of fictions and presumptions complicating legal procedures. But beyond procedural inconveniences, the absence of any developed, explicit theory of ownership comparable to Roman *dominium* bred conceptual problems which impeded rational specification of rights of title, enjoyment and user of landed property.

Romanism in Early English Property Actions

The formal concept of *dominium* as absolute ownership was derived from classical Roman learning by later civilians, and denoted the fullest possible private ownership involving rights of use, enjoyment, and disposal. It was ownership free of inherent limitations in time or space, or of controls by others, such rights being balanced only by the external restrictions and power

describing the intended purpose of the Assize of Novel Disseisin as a police action rather than a control or abrogation of feudalism: see Maitland, *Forms of Action*, 10–11, 21–4. R. C. Palmer, in 'The Origins of Property in England' (1985) 3 Law and History Review 1, 1–12, suggests that the very early common law, existing within a working feudal structure of government, knew concepts only of personal obligation and personal wrong; prospective property rights developed out of regular bureaucratic enforcement of personal claims by the central courts, a symptom and cause of the decline of feudal jurisdictions. For recent continuations of the debate see J. Biancalana, 'For Want of Justice: Legal Reforms of Henry II' (1988) 88 Columbia Law Review 433; P. Brand, '"Multis Vigiliis Excogitatam et Inventam": Henry II and the Creation of the English Common Law' and 'The Origins of English Land Law: Milsom and After', in P. Brand *The Making of the Common Law* (London, 1993) at 77 and 203; D. J. Seipp, 'The Concept of Property in Early Common Law' (1994) 12 Law and History Review 29; J. Hudson, *Land, Law, and Lordship in Anglo-Norman England* (Oxford, 1994) 253–81 and 'Anglo-Norman Land Law and the Origins of Property', in G. Garnett and J. Hudson (eds.), *Law and Government in Medieval England and Normandy. Essays in Honour of Sir James Holt* (Cambridge, 1994) 198–222.

[10] Henry de Bracton, *De Legibus et Consuetudinibus Angliae* 4 vols. (G. E. Woodbine (ed.), S. E. Thorne (trans.), Cambridge, Mass., 1977) (cited as *Bracton*, with vol. number indicated by lower case Roman numerals) f. 159–160b, iii, 13–14; f. 208b, iii, 131.

of the impersonal state standing above all owners.[11] This was an abstract model of ownership alien to the feudal land law of England. Nonetheless a heavily Romanesque conceptualization of the possessory assizes and real actions was offered in the early thirteenth-century treatise *De Legibus et Consuetudinibus Angliae* compiled under the name of Bracton. *De Legibus* may have been written as early as the 1220s by a number of authors and redactors, and its account of the law often contradicts both itself and the evidence of thirteenth-century practice.[12] *De Legibus* is nonetheless a critical source for the law of its time, as well as a live authority for the common law down to the late nineteenth century, and the treatise must be given detailed attention.

De Legibus presents a detailed description of procedures and remedies creating rights of individual property, an analysis relying heavily on the categories and language of possession and ownership found in Justinian's *Institutes* and *Digest* and in the work of later civilians and canonists.[13] There are difficulties, however, in employing Bracton to assess the Roman content of the early possessory actions in practice. Maitland noted that the Roman possessory interdicts, as transmitted to medieval law through the Canonists' *actio spolii*, provided precedents for novel disseisin and the possessory writs; but the old English and Norman possessory assizes 'have many features which are not Roman and not Canonical. Roman law may have afforded suggestions but hardly models'.[14] There was no close fit between English

[11] B. Nicholas, *An Introduction to Roman Law* (3rd edn., Oxford, 1962) 153–7; P. B. H. Birks, 'The Roman Law Concept of *Dominium* and the Idea of Absolute Ownership' [1985] Acta Juridica 1; Jolowicz and Nicholas, *Historical Introduction*, 140–2, 152–5; Buckland, *Textbook*, 185–8, *Main Institutions of Roman Private Law* (London, 1931) 93–102, and *Elementary Principles of the Roman Private Law* (Cambridge, 1912) 60–4.

[12] J. L. Barton, *Roman Law in England* (London, 1971) Ius Romanum Medii Aevi, V, 13a: 13–25, 95–97, 'Bracton as Civilian' (1968) 42 Tulane Law Review 555, 'The Mystery of Bracton' (1994) 14 Journal of Legal History 1; D. W. Sutherland, *The Assize of Novel Disseisin* (Oxford, 1973) 34–5; D. J. Seipp, 'Bracton, the Year Books, and the "Transformation of Elementary Legal Ideas" in the Early Common Law' (1989) 7 Law and History Review 175.

[13] On Romanism in Bracton and the early common law see F. W. Maitland, 'Introduction' to *Bracton and Azo* (Selden Society, viii, 1894) pp. ix–xxxiii; Seipp, 'Bracton', 'The Reception of Roman and Civil Law in the Common Law Courts Before 1600' (1993) 13 Oxford Journal of Legal Studies 388, and 'Roman Legal Categories in the Early Common Law', in T. G. Watkin (ed.), *Legal Record and Historical Reality* (London, 1989) 9–36; Sutherland, *Novel Disseisin*, 20–42 (royal judges were aware of Roman concepts as they developed the assize); S. E. Thorne, 'Introduction' to Bracton, *De Legibus* i, pp. xxxiii–xxxvi, 'Henry de Bracton, 1268–1968', in S. E. Thorne, *Essays in English Legal History* (London, 1985) 75–92, and 'The Text of Bracton's *De Legibus Angliae*', 93–110; Milsom, *Historical Foundations*, 41–2, 120, 150; Barton, *Roman Law in England*, 13–25, 95–7; C. Donahue, 'Ius Commune in England' (1992) 66 Tulane Law Review 1745, 1758–60; R. H. Helmholz, 'Magna Carta and the Ius Commune' (1999) 66 University of Chicago Law Review 297; R. H. Helmholz, *The Ius Commune in England: Four Studies* (Oxford, 2001).

[14] *Forms of Action*, 27, 43; cf. Sutherland, *Novel Disseisin*, 20–42; M. Cheney, '*Possessio/proprietas* in Ecclesiastical Courts in Mid-Twelfth-Century England', in Garnett and Hudson (eds.), *Law and Government*, 245–54.

practice and Bracton's Romanist description: fundamentally, the petty assizes operated on a concept of relativity of claims which blurred the line between seisin and title. The assizes therefore resembled the early Roman possessory interdicts rather than the developed classical law that distinguished sharply between right to bring action for restoration of possession and the ultimate right of ownership.[15]

The mature Roman doctrine of ownership was made up of a number of basic ideas, including the following:[16]

1. Possession at its simplest involves the fact of physical occupation.[17]
2. A mental and a physical element—*animus* and *corpus*—together go to constitute possession.[18]
3. Ownership may be asserted without possession.[19]
4. Possession may be defended without title, by interdict protecting the last immediate possession.[20]
5. Ownership must be proved as an absolute right, that is, beyond disproof by an opponent's evidence of rival title.[21]
6. Original acquisition (such as occupation) is a direct source of ownership; derivative ownership of a *res* already owned must derive from a *causa* or source of title, for example contractual transfer accompanying delivery.[22] Thus both contract or private agreement and conveyance as a public, apparent act are required to constitute ownership by grant.[23]

Bracton's description of the writs of right and the petty assizes drew on many of these ideas, but the actions could not easily be reduced to

[15] The thesis that the earliest Roman property law was based on relative possessory rights is set out in M. Kaser, *Eigentum und Besitz im älteren römischen Recht* (2nd edn., Cologne, 1956) *Roman Private Law* (R. Dannenbring (trans.), based on the tenth revised German edition, 3rd edn., Pretoria, 1980) 110–19, and 'The Concept of Roman Ownership' [1964] Tydskrif vir Hedendaagse Romeins-Hollandse Reg 5, 8–13; cf. Buckland, *Main Institutions*, 93–4, 121–2 and ff., and *Textbook*, 186–8; Jolowicz and Nicholas, *Historical Introduction*, 145–55. For the origins of the classical distinction between possession and ownership see ibid., 272 ff.; G. Diosdi, *Ownership in Ancient and Preclassical Roman Law* (Budapest, 1970) 121–36.

[16] See further J. Getzler, 'Roman Ideas of Landownership', in J. Dewar and S. Bright (eds.), *Land Law: Themes and Perspectives* (Oxford, 1998) 81, 94–100.

[17] D.41.2.1.pr. (Paul, Labeo); D.41.2.3.21. (Paul); Nicholas, *Introduction*, 111 (*possessio* is 'sitting in power'); J. A. C. Thomas, *Institutes of Justinian. Text and Commentary* (London, 1975) 94–6 ('physical sovereignty'); Buckland, *Main Institutions*, 104 ('possession is ... having effective control of a thing ... *possessio* is a question of fact').

[18] D.41.2.3.1., 6., 7.; D.41.2.8. (Paul); D.41.2.44.2.–4. (Papinian); for interpretations of physical acts as evidence of determining possessory intention see D.41.2.3.1. (Paul); D.41.2.17.1. (Ulpian); D.41.10.1.pr. (Ulpian); D.8.6.9. (Javolenus) (similar rule for servitudes).

[19] D.41.2.12.1.; D.41.2.35. (Ulpian); cf. Inst.4.15.4., 4a., 8.

[20] Inst.4.15.4a.; D.41.2.17.pr. (Ulpian); D.41.2.53. (Venuleius); D.43.17.2. (Paul).

[21] Cf. J. L. Barton, '*Animus* and *possessio nomine alieno*', in P. B. H. Birks (ed.), *New Perspectives in the Roman Law of Property* (Oxford, 1989) 43–60.

[22] D.41.1.20.pr. (Ulpian); D.41.1.31. (Paul); D.7.6.5. (Ulpian) (usufruct).

[23] Inst.2.1.40.; Buckland, *Main Institutions*, 104–12; R. Evans-Jones and G. D. MacCormack, '*Iusta causa traditionis*' and W. M. Gordon, 'The Importance of the *iusta causa* of *traditio*', both in Birks (ed.), *Roman Law of Property*, at 99 and 123.

these principles, for claimants were not required to show or vindicate an ultimate real title, nor was property claimed independently of some right to possession. Bracton's project was to describe rights to protected possession, seisin, and succession within a system of centrally regulated feudal custom.[24]

De Legibus was therefore written not as an accurate handbook of legal practice, but as a scholarly treatise on a grand scale, resorting to Justinian for an abstract vocabulary with which to analyse the emergent native actions. What Maitland took to be a developed, distinctly English jurisprudence of property in the mid-thirteenth century as portrayed by Bracton might instead be described as a most rudimentary native system, first assembled in the late twelfth century, and then re-arranged around a borrowed Roman conceptual framework.[25] Novel disseisin, which is likely to have drawn from the formal model of the Roman interdicts protecting possession,[26] played a varied role within the English feudal system as a police action, a tort process, and also as an extension of royal supervision of manorial courts. The feudal dimensions of the possessory and proprietary actions must be grasped if Bracton's account of land use and water rights is to be placed in its proper context.

Nuisance, Water Rights, and the Forms of Action

The medieval law of water rights was subsumed within the various categories of action dealing with the wrong of nuisance or *nocumentum*.[27] Nuisance early came to mean those actions addressing the wrongful disturbance of enjoyment of property where there was no trenching on title, no dispossession of the landholder, nor 'direct' physical or trespassory injury to the land. Perhaps the bulk of nuisance actions up to the fifteenth century

[24] For Bracton's discussion see f. 3, 8–9b, 13b, 38b–52, especially 39–39b (analysis of possession), 102–103b, 159b–160b, 161b–181b and ff. (tractate on Assize of Novel Disseisin), in Thorne edition, ii, 24, 37, 42–3, 56–7, 121–57, 292–5, iii, 13–4, 18–64 ff.

[25] S. F. C. Milsom, 'F. W. Maitland', in Milsom, *Studies*, 261, 275–7. The recording and centralization of local and customary legal systems with the aid of Roman legal concepts was a European movement from the end of the eleventh century to the sixteenth: M. Bloch, *Feudal Society* (L. A. Manyon (ed. and trans.), London, 1961) 109–20.

[26] Inst.4.15.

[27] This summary draws on J. Loengard, 'The Assize of Nuisance: Origins of an Action at Common Law' [1978] Cambridge Law Journal 144 and 'Free Tenements and Bad Neighbours: The Assizes of Novel Disseisin and Nuisance in the King's Courts before the Statute of Merton (1236)' (unpublished doctoral dissertation, Columbia University, 1970); Baker, *Introduction to English Legal History*, 401–35; J. H. Baker and S. F. C. Milsom, *Sources of English Legal History. Private Law to 1750* (London, 1986) chs. 2, 12–15, 23; C. H. S. Fifoot, *History and Sources of the Common Law: Tort and Contract* (London, 1949) chs. 1, 3–5, 8–9; S. F. C. Milsom, 'Legal Introduction' to *Novae Narrationes* (E. Shanks and S. F. C. Milsom (eds.), Selden Society, lxxx, 1963) pp. xcvi–civ; Ibbetson, *Law of Obligations*, 97–106. I am grateful to Janet Loengard for much advice and information on the early nuisance actions.

were brought by viscontiel writs, returnable in the county courts or in other local courts.[28] Viscontiel actions were available for a very wide range of nuisances to land. Where there were interferences with a house or urban land, such as blocking of light and air, or stinks and noises, a writ might be obtained by plaint that a neighbour's house or wall or privy or trade was causing a wrongful harm, and typically seeking the remedy of abatement or removal of the nuisance. Rural economic interests were also protected by this broad jurisdiction, for example fisheries, piggeries, and sheep and cattle folds. Also embraced were rights of way and their extensions such as bridges, ferries, and highways. Another category of rights were charters and franchises representing grants of governmental power, such as markets and fairs, parks, warrens, gaols, and gallows. However, the great bulk of viscontiel nuisance actions involved the protection of water rights attached to mills, including dykes, watercourses, walls of rivers and marshes, and weirs.[29]

In the royal courts remedies were made available for nuisances, or harms to land, by extending the categories of real right, disseisin, and trespass in order to create jurisdiction. Royal remedies coexisted with the viscontiel and local actions from an early date, but applied to a narrower range of generally more serious nuisances, inflicted on freehold land only.

In the twelfth and thirteenth centuries *praecipe* writs provided a 'real' action to the freeholder for damage to the incidents of his property, as well as for assertion of right or title to the freehold. Maitland writes that these writs 'stand mid-way between the indubitably possessory assizes and the

[28] Such as the hundred, or the borough or manorial court: Baker, *Introduction to English Legal History*, 424–6; Milsom, *Novae Narrationes*, pp. xcvi–civ; for examples of viscontiel and other local writs see *Early Registers of Writs* (E. de Haas and G. D. G. Hall (eds.), Selden Society, lxxxvii, 1970) writs 32, 85, 259–61; H. M. Chew and W. Kellaway (eds.), *The London Assize of Nuisance, 1301–1431* (London, 1973) pp. ix–xxvi; Sutherland, *Novel Disseisin*, 61–4 and ff.

[29] *The Early Curia Regis Rolls* (C. T. Flower (ed.), Selden Society, lxii, 1943) ch. 18: 'Nuisances', 325–34. This long list of protected interests can apply only to the viscontiel nuisance actions, as the Assizes of Novel Disseisin and Nuisance never had so wide a jurisdiction: see Loengard, 'Assize of Nuisance', 147 ff. A mnemonic device listing the various nuisances appears in many of the registers of writs: 'Fossatum, stagnum, sepe que vi diversi cursus aquarum poscunt assiam; mercatum, feria bancum. Fabrica, furca, porta, domus, virgultum, gurges, molendinum, murus, ovile et pons, traduntur haec vicecomitibus.'; [Dykes, ponds, hedges, roads, various watercourses, can be dealt with by assise; Markets and fairs in the Bench. Forges, forks (?gallows), gates (watergates or tolls), houses, shrubbery, weirs, walls, (suit of) mill, walls, sheepfolds (or free fold); And bridges (or bridge-tolls) are sent to the sheriffs]: *Reg. Omn. Brev.* (1634), 199r. FNB (1730 edn.) at 428–9 gives a simpler version: *Fos, stag, sepe, vi, diversi cursus aquarum, Poscunt assisam, mercatum, feria, bancum, Fab, fur, porta, domus, vir, gur, mo, murus, ovile, Et pons, tradantur haec vicecomitibus*'. Cf. *Early Registers of Writs*, 260–1 (*regulae* on the assize and viscontiel writs); A. K. Kiralfy, *The Action on the Case* (London, 1951) 55–6; and Milsom, in 'Introduction' to *Novae Narrationes*, pp. xcvii–xcvii, who suggests that the list of nuisances embraced houses, mills, weirs, ovens, privies, bridges, walls, doors, workshops, plantations, sheepfolds, and gallows, though he finds many of the terms in the writs obscure. Thanks go to Mike Macnair for translations and expert help with these texts.

indubitably proprietary writ of right'.[30] The initiating writ for recovery of land was the *quod reddat*; the main writ for recovery or defence of incidents was known as *quod permittat*, by which the defendant could be ordered positively to remove a nuisance interfering with the plaintiff's enjoyment of property, or negatively to permit the plaintiff the untrammelled enjoyment of his appurtenant or incidental property rights.[31] These were cumbersome real actions, taking a variety of forms depending on the type of nuisance at issue and the nature of the parties' interests, whether undivided freehold or something lesser.[32] They were generally modelled on the pattern of the writ of right, requiring solemn and extensive enquiries into past evidences of title. Milsom argues that *quod permittat* for drawing water existed more in formularies than in actual litigation in the royal courts, a result he found surprising.[33]

The assize of novel disseisin, created in the reign of Henry II around 1166, provided a simple and widely employed remedial procedure for dispossessions. An assize could require the lord of a tenement to redress wrongful recent interferences with a plaintiff freeholder's possession of the tenement, rather than trying and establishing title directly.[34] Novel disseisin could be used to protect from dispossession not only freehold titles but also a range of appurtenant freehold rights, such as water use, where there had been some invasion of the plaintiff's tenement or other acts sufficient to invoke the jurisdiction. This may have been an emulation, conscious or not, of the Roman employment of possessory interdicts to protect usufruct and use incidents of immovable property.[35] Glanvill understood the dimensions of nuisance under the new assize of novel disseisin as a disseisin of a useful element of possession of a free estate, such as access to water for a miller or common for pasture.[36] The action was brought before royal justices and a

[30] Respectively, the *quod permittat prosternere* and *quod permittat habere* forms: Maitland, *Forms of Action*, 46.

[31] Pollock and Maitland, *HEL*, ii. 63.

[32] Loengard, 'Assize of Nuisance', 147; cf. *Anon.* (C. P., Mich. c.1495), in *Reports of Cases by John Caryll Vol. 1* (J. H. Baker (ed.), *Selden Society*, cxv, 1999) 292; *The Danby Claim* (Hil. 1497), ibid., 322–8; *Crykdale* v. *Bishop of Salisbury* (C. P., Mich. 1511), ibid., 621–5.

[33] Milsom, 'Introduction' to *Novae Narrationes*, p. lxxxviii, citing *Reg. Omn. Brev.*, f. 155 r. and A. Fitzherbert, *The New Natura Brevium* (1534; 9th edn., London, 1794) f. 124a.

[34] Baker, *Introduction to English Legal History*, 229–37; note that sometimes a fully constituted seisin might not necessarily be insisted upon before allowing an assize to try the title: *Roger of Wigwig* v. *Prior of Much Wenlock* (C. P., 1283), Case 1283.10 in *The Earliest English Law Reports Vol. I* (P. A. Brand (ed.), Selden Society, cxl, 1996) 142–3 (trying title to a water mill).

[35] Loengard, 'Assize of Nuisance', 161–5; cf. D.43.16.3.15.–16; D.43.17.3.2.

[36] Henry de Glanvill, *Tractatus de Legibus et Consuetudinibus regni Anglie qui Glanvilla vocatur* (*The treatise on the laws and customs of the realm of England commonly called Glanvill*) (c.1187–9), bk. XII, c. 11–4, bk. XIII, c. 32–7; G. D. G. Hall (ed. and trans.), (London, 1965) 142–3, 167–8; to similar effect: Fleta, *Commentarius Iuris Anglicani* (c.1290) ('*Fleta*'), (H. G. Richardson and G. O. Sayles (eds. and trans.), Selden Society, lxxxix, 1972) Vol. 3, bk. IV, c. 1, 2, 5, 18, 19, 26, 27, at pp. 42–53, 56–9, 92–6, 110–14; Fifoot, *History and Sources*, 4–7, 11–5. Later examples of a novel disseisin writ encompassing appurtenances are given in: *De Ashby* v. *De Langton and*

local jury.[37] Verdicts under this procedure might carefully set out the details of the parties' respective rights and duties regarding the nuisance, as in a 1213 assize of novel disseisin for diversion of water from a mill, where the nuisance to the mill was abated by specifying rights of the parties to the water flow for particular times and places along the stream, and assigning duties for the maintenance and repair of the watercourse.[38]

Disseisin and Nuisance Forms of Action

In the early thirteenth century, Bracton writes of the assize of novel disseisin being supplemented by a further remedy—the assize of nuisance brought by the *questus est* writ.[39] This action may have been a later development of novel disseisin, but it seems to have originated from the same legislation of Henry II which had created the novel disseisin action. Later judges might insist that the action be used in preference to local jurisdiction to cure nuisances, as in a 1284 case involving cutting down of trees:

Moreover, I will prove to you that such a trespass cannot be amended by virtue of such a [leet] presentment. Where a bank has been wrongfully raised or a fishpond or watercourse diverted or something like that, a certain remedy is available in the king's court of the nature of a novel disseisin, that is the writ 'why he levied or knocked down a wall, bank or pond to the nuisance etc.' Each writ has a certain rationale which is that the king's court supposes that each man's tenancy is good until the reverse is proved and that no-one ought to answer for his free tenement without the king's writ.[40]

Peverel Y. B. Mich, 14 Edw. 2, (1320), in *Year Books of Edward II* (S. J. Stoljar and L. J. Downer (eds.), Selden Society, civ, 1988) Case 36, 127–35; *Anon.* C. P. Roll (1472) Pas. 12 Edw. IV, rot. 43, in *Select Cases in the Exchequer Chamber, Vol. 2* (M. Hemmant (ed.), Selden Society, lxiv, 1948) 25–8; and see 'Dicta by Mr Justice Townshend' (C.P., 1490), in *Reports of Cases by John Caryll Vol. 1*, 41; *The Danby Claim* (Hil. 1497), ibid., 322–8; 'Huntley's Reading on Marlborough' (1499), in *The Notebook of Sir John Port* (J. H. Baker (ed.), Selden Society, cii, 1986) Case 96, 175, all discussing use of assize remedies rather than real actions for recovery of profits, commons, franchises, and liberties.

[37] *Bracton*, f. 233–233b, iii, 192–3.

[38] See Flower (ed.), *Curia Regis Rolls*, 326–8; Case 554, 'Concord in the king's court', (York, 1184), in *English Law Suits from William I to Richard I, Vol. II* (R. C. van Caenegem (ed.), Selden Society, cvii, 1991) 606. Affirmative duties of maintenance were commonly ordered in the early common law as a pre-condition for the enjoyment of appurtenant property rights; examples include repair of ways, water-courses, and dykes. See *Case of Repair of Bridges, Highways, &c* (1609) 13 Co. Rep. 33; 77 E.R. 1442 (K.B.), with exhaustive notes of the preceding case law; cf. Kiralfy, *Action on the Case*, 35–40.

[39] *Bracton*, f. 233–235, iii, 192–8.

[40] *Simon of Ruston* v. *Richard of Skeyton* (C.P., 1284), Case 1284.11 in *The Earliest English Law Reports Vol. I*, 169–70 at 170; see further Loengard, 'Assize of Nuisance', 163–6; Baker, *Introduction to English Legal History*, 422–35; Milsom, 'Introduction' to Pollock and Maitland, *HEL*, i, pp. xlii–xliii (suggesting that it was originally a remedy against lords refusing their tenants rightful pasture); cf. Fifoot, *History and Sources*, 9; H. G. Richardson and G. O. Sayles, *Law and Legislation* (London, 1966) 109; Flower (ed.), *Curia Regis Rolls*, 325–34; Chew and

Evidence suggests that very early use of the two assizes did not make careful distinction between the possessory and nuisance forms, with novel disseisin sometimes doing duty as an action for nuisance in the absence of dispossession or wrongful act on P's land. The assize of nuisance may originally have been a specific legislative remedy for pure cases of recent harm to tenements without disseisin. However, that assize was held by the thirteenth century to be distinguished from novel disseisin purely according to the *locus* of the harmful act: direct invasion was disseisin; indirect interference from without the tenement was nuisance.[41]

The Form of Action for Defence of Servitudes and User

Bracton's treatise drew an analogy between seisin—the full right of possession of land—and enjoyment of servitudes, the lesser rights of use and amenity free from nuisance by neighbours:

> We have explained... how the *dominium* of corporeal things is acquired and the acquisition of possession; the kind of remedy available to one ejected from his tenement and how possession may be restored to him, [or] freedom and quiet enjoyment if his possession is disturbed. Now we must show how one is restored who has been wrongfully ejected from things appurtenant to a free tenement, for rights are appurtenant to a free tenement just as corporeal things are: rights, or servitudes, depending upon how they are regarded. Rights may be called liberties from the point of view of the tenements to which they are owed, servitudes from that of the tenements which owe them.[42]

Appurtenant rights of seisin and rights of servitude exercised over another's land were thus portrayed as analogous or identical.

Kellaway (eds.), *London Assize of Nuisance*, pp. xii–xx, D. R. Coquillette, 'Mosses from an Old Manse: Another Look At Some Historic Property Cases About the Environment' (1979) 64 Cornell Law Review 761, 766–9.

[41] Loengard, 'Assize of Nuisance', 163–6; cf. *Royal Writs in England from the Conquest to Glanvill* (R. C. van Caenegem (ed.), Selden Society, lxxvii, 1959) 283–90, 444–64. Two cases from 1235 requiring direct injury or dispossession to permit a Novel Disseisin action are *Anon.* P.R.O. Just. 1/1173 m. 2 and Just. 1/80 m. 12; see also *de Gonceby* v. *le Power* (1290) Plac. Abb. 284a; Y.B. 20 & 21 Edw. 1 (Rolls S.) 414 (1293), in Fifoot, *History and Sources*, 21.

Milsom's analysis of the early possessory assizes (stated in the 'Introduction' to Pollock and Maitland, *HEL*, ii, pp. xxvii–xlix; *Historical Foundations*, 99–151, and *The Legal Framework of English Feudalism* (Cambridge, 1976) 1–102) does not account for the aggressive enforcement of nuisance claims by royal justices, material which suggests that from the outset the petty assizes were directly concerned with establishing norms for the protection of enjoyment of title from neighbours' aggression, independently of local feudal custom. Milsom hints (*Legal Framework* at 13, 22–5; 'Introduction' at pp. xlii–xliii) that he sees the assize of nuisance as directed chiefly at interfering lords; but this supposition is overwhelmed by evidence of a more general jurisdiction for the action. See further Loengard, 'Assize of Nuisance', passim, especially 144–9, 163–6; Biancalana, 'For Want of Justice', 481, analysing *Glanvill*, bk. IX, c. 11–13, Hall (ed.), 114–15.

[42] *Bracton*, f. 220b, iii, 162.

Bracton's discussion of the correct form of action to defend possessory rights clearly distinguished between the assize of novel disseisin, centred on the notion of a physical dispossession taking place on the plaintiff-freeholder's land itself, and the assize of nuisance involving interference from without. He explained the distinction by the example of interference with riparian ownership, as where one flooded a neighbour's tenement adjoining a stream, or diverted such tenement's supply of water:

With respect to a pond and weir constructed or destroyed to another's wrongful nuisance, we must see whether it was constructed entirely on the plaintiff's tenement, when he has a tenement on both sides of the stream. If so it will be the disseisin of a free tenement rather than an assize of nuisance. If it was constructed wholly on the defendant's tenement, it will there be an assize of nuisance rather than of free tenement, since it is wholly on the other's land.[43]

Where the injury was caused by an act partly on both the plaintiff's (P's) and the defendant's (D's) lands, for example by stopping a watercourse owned equally by riparian owners on opposite banks of the stream, novel disseisin was inadequate 'to abate the *injuria* completely ... [for] ... an assize of novel disseisin of a free tenement ... does not include the assize of nuisance, what is done in the property of another'.[44] Bracton recommended that rather than bringing both types of actions, the plaintiff could here proceed by the nuisance remedy as pragmatically covering both the nuisance and the disseisin aspects of the injury.[45] Elsewhere he describes nuisance as a particular example of dispossession:

A nuisance ... does not differ substantially from a disseisin, and ought therefore to be removed by the assize, when it was wrongful, at the costs of him who erected the obstruction, if it is on his own land; if on another's an assize of novel disseisin of a free tenement lies for him on whose land the work was erected, and, according as the assize of novel disseisin includes nuisance, because every disseisin is harmful (*nocet*), by it the nuisance may be removed and damages restored to the plaintiff, both for the disseisin of his tenement and for the nuisance, which would not be true if the suit were concerned only with the nuisance.[46]

[43] *Bracton*, f. 234b, iii, 197, and see f. 235, iii, 198, discussing diversion of a watercourse; f. 232b, iii, 191. Cf. *Araz* v. *Bosant* (1232), in F. W. Maitland (ed.), *Bracton's Note Book* pl. 701 (Cambridge, 1887) ii, 538, a water diversion case which is brought as nuisance ('ad nocumentum liberi tenementi ...') and *de Beaumes* v. *Blakeman* (1238, K.B.) *Bracton's Note Book* pl. 1254, iii, 267, an assize of disseisin for interrupting the flow of water to a mill-pond; see also pl. 469, 494, 578, 786, 1037, 1081, 1253, 1255, 1282, 1953. One source speaks of freeholders being 'seised of a certain piece of water' ('*un homme seisi de certeyn ewe*'), but this doubtless means seisin of water-covered land: 'Cases from the Severnake Manuscript', Case 2, c.1400, in *Readings and Moots at the Inns of Court Vol. II* (S. E. Thorne and J. H. Baker (eds.), Selden Society, cv, 1997) 2.

[44] *Bracton*, f. 234b, iii, 397.

[45] Ibid. Likewise when a single act caused many disseisins and nuisances to many tenements and incorporeal rights, all actions might be combined in one assize of nuisance: f. 234b–235, iii, 197–8.

[46] *Bracton*, f. 232, iii, 190.

The idea of nuisance as a lesser form of dispossession was also suggested by the remedies available. A person disseised was required to take a writ of novel disseisin (or pursue a real action if sufficient time had passed since the disseisin), and not threaten the peace by attempting self-help to recover the land.[47] In the case of a nuisance interfering with a servitude or natural right such as an interference with a watercourse, self-help was also curtailed:

What is thus done may at once be undone and demolished, even without a writ, if action is taken while the deed is still fresh; after time has passed, however, a writ will be necessary.... And so if the right to conduct water is granted... and it is diverted, partially or completely, to the nuisance [of his free tenement].[48]

Bracton gives as an example of these principles a case *coram rege* in 1247–8 involving a presumptuous resort to self-help to restore diverted water, in usurpation of the authority of the judge to decide seisin by the assize of nuisance; the self-help was undone by order of the court.[49]

Bracton's Exposition of the Assize of Nuisance

The Real Form of the Nuisance Action

Bracton gives the following example of the form of a real writ for the remedying of nuisance to free tenements, including interferences with water rights:

'The king to the sheriff, greeting. Such a one has complained to us that such a one has wrongfully and without judgement constructed a certain wall ("bank",... "pond", "weir", "mill"...) in such a vill *to the nuisance of his free tenement*.... Therefore we order you to hear that plea and cause him to be justly dealt with therein. etc.'

[Similarly a writ may be drawn as to the foregoing in the reverse way: 'why one wrongfully cast down such things to the nuisance of his free tenement etc.' Also 'why he raised a pond,'... [or] 'why he diverted a water-course', and the like.][50]

The act amounting to nuisance could be positive, such as building or demolishing a structure so as to interfere with the flow of water; or negative, such as failing to stop up, scour, or repair a watercourse as required by a servitude. An otherwise legal act done on one's property, such as repairing or varying a watercourse on one's land, would become a nuisance if it 'exceeds due measure'.[51]

[47] *Bracton*, f. 103, ii, 294; f. 161–165, iii, 18–30; f. 179b, iii, 58; f. 204–204b, iii, 120–1; f. 210–210b; iii, 135–6; f. 233, iii, 192; *Crakehall* v. *Anon.* (1313) Y.B. Trin. 6 Edw. 2 (Selden Society, xxxvi, 76); Maitland, *Forms of Action*, 28–9; Fifoot, *History and Sources*, 9.

[48] *Bracton*, f. 231b, iii, 189; and see f. 233–233b, iii, 192–4.

[49] *Bracton*, f. 234b, iii, 196–7.

[50] *Bracton*, f. 233, iii, 192 (emphasis added).

[51] *Bracton*, f. 232b, iii, 191.

The Doctrine of Appurtenance

The nuisance form of action emphasized the praedial nature of the protected rights as appurtenances to property.

It ... says 'to the nuisance of the free tenement ...'. Hence the plaintiff must have a free tenement, for no one may acquire a servitude attached to an estate or land unless he has an estate and a free tenement, nor may anyone be subject to a servitude unless he who has an estate and a free tenement.[52]

Two explanations may be given for the requirement that the plaintiff have a freehold. First, the origins of the action in the assize of novel disseisin led to the position that nuisance was conceived as a lesser form of dispossession of free tenement, inflicted on a freeholder who ought to have a swift and effective remedy. Outside this fact matrix the assize was unavailable, as where the freeholder had transferred the estate to a feoffee after the commission of the nuisance; the feoffee would then have to bring a writ of nuisance in *quod permittat* form to enforce his title to untrammelled enjoyment and have the interference abated.[53] Secondly, Bracton was copying Roman models of servitude action brought by the owner of a dominant tenement to restrain interferences from a servient tenement; in that system, both natural and acquired praedial rights were conceived as servitudes over neighbours' lands. Thus an assertion of natural rights of possession could take the form of an action of 'counter-servitude' by *actio negatoria*, denying the existence of a neighbour's right to trench on one's enjoyment of property.[54] The Roman precedent might also explain why the common law required that the defendant in a nuisance assize also be a neighbour with a freehold, rather than just anyone who interfered with the possession or enjoyment of a freehold.[55] Bracton's tendency to copy the *Digest* texts indiscriminately is also suggested by his inclusion of personal usufructary rights to water in his discussion of nuisance, contradicting his stated appurtenance principle: 'A water-course is sometimes owed and granted to lands, sometimes to persons; if to lands, it is not extinguished with the death of the person; if to persons it dies with them, and thus does not pass to a successor.'[56] It is not made clear

[52] *Bracton*, f. 234, iii, 195; see also f. 7b, ii, 39; f. 220c, iii, 163; cf. Inst.2.3.3.; text at n. 122.

[53] 'Reading of John Grene', c.1490/1, in *Readings and Moots at the Inns of Court Vol. II*, 199; cf. Case 127 per Frowyk, and Case 127, in Inner Temple Cases, 1490–9 in MS. Hargrave 87, ibid., 288, 292.

[54] A. Rodger, *Owners and Neighbours in Roman Law* (Oxford, 1972) 1–5, 38 ff., 89–113, discussing *inter alia* Inst.4.6.2.; D.8.2.3.,9., 10. (Marcellus), 15.,17. (Ulpian), D.8.2.9., D.8.5.2., D.8.5.8.5.–6. (Ulpian); D.8.2.16. (Paul); cf. Buckland, *Textbook*, 264.

[55] Bracton f. 167b, iii, 33; f. 234, iii, 195, following Inst. 2.3.3; Baker, *Introduction to English Legal History*, 422–6; Fifoot, *History and Sources*, 93–6; Coquillette, 'Mosses from an Old Manse', 768, 773–5; W. S. Holdsworth, *A History of English Law* 13 vols. (London, 1922–52) iii, 11; see e.g. Y.B. Mich. 11 Hen. 4 f. 25 pl. 48; *Right's Case* (1455) Y.B. Trin. 33 Hen. 6, f. 26, pl. 10, in Baker and Milsom, *Sources of English Legal History*, 584–5.

[56] *Bracton*, f. 233, iii, 193, cf. D.43.20.1.43. (Ulpian).

whether this personal right to a watercourse was purely contractual or had some proprietary aspect.

Real and Personal Remedies

The mixed *in rem* and *in personam* quality of the nuisance action for servitudes was also suggested by the remedial consequences of the writ. There was a 'penalty for the delict', a damages liability, personal to the perpetrator of the nuisance and no others; and there was a right to abatement of the nuisance and full restitution (restoration of the original condition of the property), akin to a real recovery of the property as an integral thing, which right could be enforced against any successor or heir to the tenement on which the nuisance took place.[57] Thus the assize was at once 'penal, personal and restitutory'.[58] This was an application of Bracton's general bipartite distinction between personal and real remedies, faithfully following the plan of Justinian's *Institutes*.[59]

The problem of fitting the English materials around the real–personal distinction[60] was revealed by Bracton's extensive resort to the categories of mixed or hybrid actions, also derived from the *Institutes*.[61] Real actions are there said to be generally restorative, whilst personal, especially delictual, actions are penal in operation. Actions could also be both real and personal; or both restorative and penal.[62] Bracton seems to classify servitude actions as mixed in each sense: they were 'in part recuperatory, they lie against any who can restore, whether the possessor is he who despoiled or another; in so far as they are penal they lie only against those who committed the wrong'.[63] The personal dimension of remedy could nonetheless be very harsh in a case of lengthy disseisin or nuisance disrupting the enjoyment of a servitude. Maitland noted 'the severity of [the common] law against *bona fide* possessors holding under faulty titles', for a plaintiff could treat the wrongful dispossession of rights 'as one long continued trespass, and sue [the defendant] in an action for mesne profits in which he could recover not only compensation for

[57] *Bracton*, f. 234, iii, 195–6, following Inst.2.1.29., D.41.1.7.10. (Gaius). The mixed penal/personal and restitutory/real nature of the nuisance action is further discussed in f. 235b–236b, iii, 199–201.

[58] *Bracton*, f. 235b, iii, 199.

[59] *Bracton*, f. 159, iii, 13, following Inst.4.6.1.; and see D.44.7.3.pr. (Paul); D.44.7.25.pr. (Ulpian); cf. D.44.7.53.pr. (Modestinus), suggesting that the *in rem/personam* distinction was an exegetical guide to the actions only, with no substantive implications.

[60] Maitland, *Forms of Action*, 7–8, 61–3, 73–8.

[61] Inst.4.6.16.–20.

[62] Inst.4.6.17., 18., 20. Thus in Roman, as in English law, many actions are *in rem* in effect but *in personam* in form, in that the judicial order is for the making of a payment which effects restitution: see e.g. the *vindicatio* procedure and other obligations to surrender possession (e.g. D.44.7.28. (Papinian); D.44.7.52. (Modestinus)); contractual obligations to deliver (D.44.7.1.1.–2. (Gaius)); cf. the trespass to goods actions of the common law.

[63] *Bracton*, f. 202, ii, 291.

damage done to the land, but compensation for loss of enjoyment'.[64] Bracton indicated that some discretion was given to the court to alleviate this remedial severity. In the case of infringed water rights, there could be an order regarding 'waters diverted, that they be re-directed and restored to their proper state', allowing the successor of a tortfeasor to restore rights as from time of judgment rather than returning to the status quo ante, thus avoiding possibly massive disruption to the successor's extant proprietary expectations.[65]

Seisin and Title

Bracton's categories of real actions for claiming incorporeal rights and corporeal things were further divided according to whether possession or title was sought, and by whom; and here too his doctrine was suffused with Romanism:

> Of actions *in rem*, some are founded on the possession, others on the property, for there is the possession of a thing and the *proprietas*. Of civil actions *in rem* [on the property, some are for the recovery of a corporeal thing], as *rei vindicatio*, when one alleges that some corporeal thing belongs to him, . . . [others for the recovery of an incorporeal thing], one being *confessoria*, the other *negatoria*. The *actio confessoria* is that in which you allege that you have a right to go over your neighbour's land or to draw water on it and the like without his permission. It is called an action *in rem* because you are claiming your incorporeal *res* . . . and confessory because it is framed in affirmative words. The *actio negatoria* is one which the lord of an estate institutes against you, one who customarily crosses his land, alleging that you have no right to do so. This is said to be an action *in rem* because by it the owner of the estate vindicates his liberty. Actions of this sort do not lie for the ownership of a thing but of a right, [as] praedial servitudes.[66]

The assizes of novel disseisin and mort d'ancestor were included in a separate classification of possessory actions by which title was tried: 'Of actions *in rem* [on the possession] some are for recovering possession, some for obtaining possession, some for retaining possession. . . . Sometimes actions are for the recovery of the possession and the property at the same time . . . '.[67]

Bracton's Analysis of *Injuria* and *Damnum*

Bracton seemed to take damage or loss as an essential but not sufficient element of the action for nuisance or interference with servitudes. A partial as

[64] Maitland, *Forms of Action*, 77–8. Maitland's comment was made in the context of the ejectment actions.

[65] *Bracton*, f. 234, iii, 195; f. 236–236b, iii, 200–1.

[66] *Bracton*, f. 103, ii, 294; cf. f. 234, iii, 195.

[67] *Bracton*, f. 103–103b, ii, 294–5; cf. Inst.4.15.2.–8., detailing the possessory interdicts as modes of asserting title as an alternative to *vindicatio*.

well as a total interference with right or enjoyment causing loss could ground an action, but the *damnum* in all cases had to be accompanied by *injuria*, or legally-recognized harm:

A nuisance may be rightful or wrongful, wrongful where one on his own land wrongfully does something prohibited by law, contrary to law or a constitution. If he cannot be prohibited by law from doing it, though he creates a nuisance and causes damage it will not be wrongful, for each may do on his own property [whatever he wishes if] wrongful damage does not accrue to a neighbour, as where one erects a mill on his own land and takes from his neighbour his own suit and that of others; he does his neighbour damage but no *injuria* [*damnum et non iniuria*] since he is not prohibited by law or a constitution from having or erecting a mill.[68]

...

It is clear that some nuisances are wrongful and harmful, others harmful and not wrongful. Hence when a plaint of nuisance is made, we must ask what harm is done and see whether it is harmful and wrongful. If so, it must be removed; if not wrongful though harmful, it must be upheld.[69]

The test for distinguishing actionable harms from *damna sine injuria* was not given by Bracton.[70] Nor does Bracton overtly discuss the converse problem, whether an invasion of rights not causing harm (*injuria sine damno*) is actionable. His general theory of actionable wrong was entirely circular: *iniuria autem dici poterit omne id quod non iure fit* (an injury may be said to be anything done without right).[71] Injury without damage may have been actionable in cases of disseisin of incorporeal rights, as well as corporeal things, because invasion of the possession of an appurtenant right was itself a presumptive harm through denial of future use of the right, and a threat to the continuing title by adverse possession, even if there was no present damage caused by the invasion. These justifications may be gleaned from the following passage:

As rights and servitudes may be taken away by disseisin, so that he cannot use, so wrongful nuisances may be committed in the appurtenances of things appurtenant, so that he cannot use the aforesaid servitudes... and, according as the assize of novel disseisin includes nuisance, because every disseisin is harmful (*nocet*), by it the nuisance may be removed and damages restored to the plaintiff, both for the disseisin

[68] *Bracton*, f. 221, iii, 163–4.

[69] *Bracton*, f. 231b, iii, 189; see also f. 45b–46, ii, 140–1; f. 92b, ii, 267, f. 221–221b, iii, 164; f. 234–234b, iii, 195–6; f. 235–235b, iii, 198–9 (on rival markets and nuisance); Pollock and Maitland, *HEL*, ii, 534. Ibbetson, *Law of Obligations*, 100 n. 16 follows Thorne, 'Introduction' to *Bracton*, i, 402 in suggesting that the latter discussion of nuisance to markets in f. 235–235b is an interpolation.

[70] J. H. Baker, 'Introduction' to *Spelman's Reports, Vol. 2* (J. H. Baker (ed.), Selden Society, xciv, 1978) 221–2; Pollock and Maitland, *HEL*, ii, 534; cf. Barton, 'Bracton as Civilian', 561–4, suggesting that *iniuria* in the sense of contempt or indignity was a strong element in Bracton's concept of actionable injury.

[71] *Bracton*, f. 45b, ii, 140; also f. 155, ii, 437; cf. Inst.4.4.pr.; D.47.10.1.pr. (Ulpian).

of his tenement and for the nuisance, which would not be true if the suit were concerned only with the nuisance.[72]

The relationship between *injuria* and *damnum* presents another face of the uneasy interplay within private law between actions based on right (*injuria* equating with right invasion) and actions for wrongs (*damnum* equating with temporal harm). The judges for long varied over whether property rights ought to be maintained by trespassory actions in the absence of harm.

The Forms of Action after Bracton

By the fourteenth century the Bractonian distinction between the assizes for disseisin and nuisance based on *locus* was being abandoned, and the assize of nuisance was used to remedy injuries to land use where the wrongful act had been committed wholly on the plaintiff's land, a common example being diversion of water from a corn mill.[73] The conception of nuisance as a species of disseisin, rather than solely a wrong or injury to the proprietary incidents of landholding, was thereby undermined by the pressures of procedural convenience.

The assize of nuisance into the fourteenth century was still restricted in subject matter, confined in practice to cases of interference with ditches, dykes, and hedges, obstruction of ways, diversion of water, and interference with mills and mill dams.[74] These cases may have attracted attention as serious economic wrongs to essential rural interests, such as drainage and irrigation for farming and milling with water power. Other, less important nuisances were left to the local jurisdictions. Litigants could win the advantages of royal judicial procedures by the removal of these lesser actions to Common Pleas from the county court by writ of *pone*,[75] by the limited expansion of the operation of the assize of nuisance to new areas by the Statute of Westminster II of 1285,[76] and after 1382 by the creation of an action 'in the nature of an assize', available at Westminster or in local courts and substituting for the viscontiel nuisance action, at plaintiffs' election.[77]

[72] *Bracton*, f. 232, iii, 190.

[73] Fifoot, *History and Sources*, 10–11; and see *Smeterborn* v. *Holt* (1348) Y.B. Hil. 21 Edw. 3, f. 2, pl. 5 (interference with way to a water mill); Y.B. Lib. Ass. 32 Edw. 3, f. 194 pl. 2 (1359) (diversion of a watercourse from a mill), in Fifoot, *History and Sources*, 22–3. The old distinction between novel disseisin by act on P's land and nuisance by wrongful act off the land was sometimes revived, however: see Y.B. Lib. Ass. 9 Edw. 3, f. 23 pl. 19 (1336).

[74] Loengard, 'Assize of Nuisance', 165.

[75] Baker, *Introduction to English Legal History*, 422–4.

[76] See 13 Edw. 1 c. 24 (*in consimili casu*); c. 25 (assize of novel disseisin).

[77] 6 Rich. 2 sess. I (1382) c. 3 (viscontiel writs)—in effect, another extension of the Assize of Nuisance action of the common law to overlay or replace local court remedies; see Baker, *Introduction to English Legal History*, 423–4.

The Rise of Trespass

The real actions for vindicating proprietary rights, and the assizes of novel disseisin and nuisance for protecting possession or the incidents of possession, co-existed through the thirteenth and fourteenth centuries, and began to converge in character and operation. The writs of right were replaced by the writs of entry sur disseisin in *praecipe* form,[78] and these latter forms of 'real' action came to focus on the rightfulness of the defendant's recent possession (or the rightfulness of the transactions by which he had come into possession) rather than the long pedigree and legitimacy of the plaintiff's title. The assize of novel disseisin conversely came to try the rightfulness of transmission of titles, a procedure more in the nature of a proprietary enquiry which extended the original concerns of this remedy with wrongful forcible or physical disseisins.[79] By 1400 novel disseisin and writs of entry as 'droitural' or right-centred actions had all but driven out the competing earlier real actions for title;[80] but this transformation of possessory procedures into formal droitural actions conversely undermined their effectiveness as a means of speedy justice. The assize of nuisance was also hampered by its nature as an action confined to protecting proprietary rights of freeholders against action by other freeholders; and many types of nuisance to land were excluded.[81] From the fourteenth century onwards, problems of dispossession and nuisance were addressed in the royal courts by the development of still simpler remedies derived from the writs of trespass, namely trespass *quare clausum fregit* and *vi et armis* for physical invasion of land; trespass on the case for injuries to land without invasion or direct force; ejectment for recovery of possession and the trying of freehold as well as lesser titles.[82]

The development of trespassory remedies for ejectment as oblique actions for title came chiefly after Bracton.[83] He was ambivalent about the use of trespass actions for the defence of freehold titles and appurtenances: he states that either a trespass action or a disseisin action could be brought for interference with a common boundary, wall, or bank between neighbouring tenements. However, he suggests that only a disseisin action was available if the boundary was destroyed or completely altered, as such invasion amounted to a full dispossession of tenement going beyond the limits of the

[78] A. W. B. Simpson, *A History of the Land Law* (2nd edn., Oxford, 1986) 34–6; Sir William Blackstone, *Commentaries on the Law of England* 4 vols. (1st edn., Oxford, 1765–9; E. Christian (ed.), 15th edn., Oxford, 1809) (*Bl.Comm.*) iii, ch. 10, 179–96.

[79] Baker, *Introduction to English Legal History*, 234–7; Maitland, *Forms of Action*, 41–6.

[80] The real actions were still the only remedy in certain instances: see Baker, *Introduction to English Legal History*, 422–4.

[81] See the text accompanying nn. 27–41 above.

[82] Baker, *Introduction to English Legal History*, 301–3, 424–6; Maitland, *Forms of Action*, 47–50, 53–60.

[83] Ibid., 47–8, 56–61; *Britton* (F. M. Nichols (ed.), Oxford, 1865) bk. V, c. 14–15, f. 264–267b, ii, 296–307; cf. *Bracton*, f. 317b–318 ff., iii, 21–22 ff.

trespass action: 'Trespass, however, does not include disseisin, but . . . disseisin includes both. . . . [H]e who does a greater thing does a lesser, but not conversely.'[84] The rise of the action of trespass on the case for nuisance as the dominant remedy in this field belongs to a later period, and will be elaborated below.

BRACTON, ROMAN LAW, AND THE SUBSTANTIVE NATURE OF WATER RIGHTS

The forms of action described how remedies defended rights, not when the rights arose, nor why. It was Roman jurisprudence that provided the substantive core of land- and water-use doctrines for the English law. These doctrines had to be naturalized within the English writ system, and here Bracton played the major role. His treatise offers the first attempt to formulate principles of user-rights within the common law,[85] analysing the assize of nuisance using Roman concepts of praedial servitude and natural right.[86] To understand the importance of this analysis we must set Bracton's work into a wider setting of civilian concepts of property.

Ownership and Incorporeal Rights: Some Institutionalist Distinctions

Bracton discussed private property using both the feudal language of lord and tenant and Romanist terminology of possession and ownership ('*dominum proprietatis*').[87] First, he adopted wholesale the fundamental Roman jurisprudential categories.[88] There was private law 'which pertains primarily to the welfare of individuals and secondarily to the *res publica*'; and public law which had the converse concerns.[89] The private law was deduced from natural law, the *jus gentium* of all peoples, and the civil laws and customs of particular polities.[90] Within the private law there were three main categories: persons; things (or *res*); and actions by which persons secured their things.

[84] *Bracton*, f. 207–207b, iii, 127–8; see also f. 210b, iii, 136–7.

[85] T. E. Lauer, 'The Common Law Background of the Riparian Doctrine' (1963) 28 Missouri Law Review 60, 64–72, and E. F. Murphy, 'English Water Law Doctrines Before 1400' (1957) 1 American Journal of Legal History 103, 103–9. (Both Lauer's and Murphy's discussions of Bracton are more than a little impressionistic.) Other medieval treatments of nuisance and natural rights are considerably less developed than Bracton's; see *Glanvill*, bk. IX, c. 11–13; bk. XIII, c. 32–37, Hall (ed.), 113–15, 167–9; *Britton*, bk. I, c. 30, ss. 1–3, f. 71b–72, i, 179–80; bk. II, c. 2, s. 1, f. 84b, i, 213; bk. II, c. 30–32, f. 153b–157, i, 397–408; *Fleta*, bk. III, c. 1, 1–2.

[86] *Bracton*, f. 232, iii, 189–90.

[87] *Bracton*, f. 208b, iii, 131.

[88] Similar adoptions of Romanism may be seen in *Britton*, bk. II, c. 2, ss. 1–8, f. 84b–86b, i, 213–20; *Fleta*, bk. III, c. 1, 2 at 1–5.

[89] Inst.1.1.4. [90] Bracton, f. 3b, ii, 25–6; cf. Inst.1.2.pr.–1.

A primary distinction was drawn between things capable of ownership and things not capable. Things capable of ownership could fall 'within our patrimony',[91] that is, all types of private property, including unowned *res nullius, humani iuris* such as wild animals once captured and whilst in possession.[92] Things outside the patrimonial category were entirely beyond individual appropriation and alienation, including *res communes* and *res nullius, divini iuris*.[93] Some things, however, were 'neither within nor without our patrimony, as rights and servitudes, a usufruct... or a right to conduct water over another man's land and similar arrangements'. The explanation for this third exceptional category was the non-alienability of praedial rights, a result of the appurtenance rule, colourfully described by Bracton:

> Servitudes are said not to be owned because they cannot be aliened by themselves apart from the land. Praedial servitudes cannot be thought of as having an existence of their own, and thus are taken not to exist, or to be extinguished, when regarded separately, for a sleeve is taken no longer to exist as such when [not] attached to a garment.... Nevertheless, these servitudes are not thought of as things unowned, since [for them] possessors have an exception and those who do not possess an action.[94]

In sum, for Bracton there were: things susceptible to appropriation and transfer; things that were appropriated only as appurtenant rights and not transferable; and things neither transferable nor capable of appropriation. It is striking that he did not, in order to describe incorporeal rights over land, use the characteristic Roman dual concept of *res* as both a thing and a right over a thing.[95]

Bracton's second division of ownership was between corporeal things and incorporeal things, 'such as rights... which can neither be seen nor touched, as a right of way over another's land,... to... conduct water over it and other such, which cannot be possessed only *quasi*-possessed'.[96] Ownership of corporeal, physical things could be fragmented by the constitution of incorporeal rights, which were themselves rights of property or 'free tenements' issuing from the *corpus* and vested in individuals or groups of individuals.[97]

[91] Cf. Inst.2.1.pr.

[92] *Bracton*, f. 8–9, ii, 41–3; cf. Inst.2.1.12.; D.41.1.1.,3. (Gaius); D.41.10.2. (Paul).

[93] *Bracton*, f. 7b–8b, 14, ii, 39–41, 57–8; f. 207–207b, iii, 127–8: 'Some tenements are divine, some human. The human... are privately owned or common.'; f. 208, iii, 130: 'Those things which are among the possessions of God... belong to no man, nor may they be possessed by man, nor transferred to another... nor recovered as a free tenement.' Cf. Inst.1.8.1.pr.; Inst.2.1.1.,4.,7.–10.; D.1.8.1.–2. (Marcianus); D.1.8.5. (Gaius).

[94] *Bracton*, f. 7b, ii, 39.

[95] On the dual concept of the *res* as a thing and a valuable right to a thing, see Inst.2.2.pr.–2.; Birks, '*Dominium*', 4–7, 14, 25–7; Nicholas, *Introduction*, 98–107; F. de Zulueta, *The Institutes of Gaius, Part 2, Commentary* (Oxford, 1953) 56–7.

[96] Ibid.; and f. 10b, ii, 48.; cf. Inst.2.2.2., 2.4.pr.; D.7.1.1.,4. (Paul); D.7.1.2. (Celsus); D.7.1.3.2. (Gaius); D.8.2.32.1. (Julian); D.41.2.3.pr. (Paul).

[97] *Bracton*, f. 207–208b; iii, 128–32.

'Incorporeal things, as rights, cannot be partitioned though they are common.'[98] Bracton followed the classical position of the Digest that use-rights over one's own land were natural rights inherent in the holding of the land itself, rather than separate incorporeal rights, 'since no-one may have a servitude on his own land'.[99]

A third classification of things distinguished between individual property and the different forms of communal or public goods: *res communes*, *res publicae*, and *res universitatis*; or common, state, and corporate goods, all described by Bracton in near-identical terms to the *Institutes* which carefully recognized the important role of public goods in the universe of property rights.[100] Bracton also followed the *Institutes* to hold that running water is a common good: 'The things which are naturally everybody's are air, flowing water, the sea, and the sea shore.'[101] Moreover, by the *ius gentium* rivers and river banks were public goods 'that belong to all people, that is, which are for the use of mankind alone', adding that 'this is to be understood of permanent rivers, for streams that do not flow uninterruptedly may be privately owned'.[102] These Justinianic and Bractonian formulations are perhaps the key texts in the long history of water rights; they are cited continually in judgments and treatises for the next 600 years, and warrant some exegesis.

Common Ownership Contrasted with *Res Communes* Ideas

The defining quality of the type of *res nullius* known as *humani iuris* is that it can become privately owned, that is, unlike the *res nullius, divini iuris*, and *res communes* forms, it is susceptible to appropriation by individuals as their exclusive property. Some Roman texts state that public goods are capable of appropriation, blurring the line between communal and unowned goods; but this is against the main classical tradition of classification.[103] The earlier

[98] *Bracton*, f. 208; iii, 129; cf. D.8.3.24. (Pomponius); D.8.3.33.1. (Africanus); D.8.4.5. (Javolenus); for alternative rules allowing sharing of servitudes: D.8.3.2.1.–2. (Neratius); D.39.3.17. (Paul); D.43.20.1.2. (Pomponius); D.43.20.4.–5. (Julian).

[99] *Bracton*, f. 208; f. 220c, iii, 130; 162; cf. D.7.6.5.pr. (Ulpian); D.8.2.26. (Paul); D.8.6.1. (Gaius).

[100] *Bracton*, f. 7b–8, ii, 39–40; f. 207; iii, 128; see also f. 170 b, iii, 40; f. 180a–181, iii, 60–1; f. 207b–208, iii, 128; f. 208b–211, iii, 130–7; f. 406b–407, iv, 265.; cf. Inst.2.1.,2.,4.–6.,11.

[101] Inst.2.1.1.; D.1.8.2.pr.–1. (Marcianus).

[102] *Bracton*, f. 8–8b, ii, 40–1; cf. Inst.2.1.2.,4.–5.; D.1.8.4.–5., D.41.1.65.1.,2. (Paul); D.8.3.3. (Ulpian); D.43.8.3.pr.–1. (Scaevola), 4. (Celsus); D.43.12.1.3. (Ulpian). Paul alone treats the river banks as well as the waters as public property: D.41.1.65.1.; 43.12.3.pr.; Buckland, *Textbook*, 185.

[103] See e.g. D.41.1.14.pr. (Neratius):

> 'What a man erects on the seashore are public, not in the sense that they belong to the community as such but that they are initially provided by nature and have hitherto become no one's property. Their state is not dissimilar to that of fish and wild animals which, once caught, undoubtedly become the property of those into whose power they have come.'

Institutes of Gaius[104] describe the two classes of things 'subject either to divine right or to human' as 'the leading division of things', rather than the private/non-private division. After Gaius discusses the various divine categories in some detail, the non-divine are brusquely dealt with:

Now what is subject to divine right cannot belong to anyone, whereas what is subject to human right belongs in general to someone, though it may belong to no one.... Things subject to human right are either public or private. Public things are regarded as belonging to no individual, but as being the property of the corporate body. Private things are those belonging to individuals.[105]

It may be that this text reflects the early origins of property in sacralized communal ownership, with private appropriation emerging as a delegation of property-holding powers to individuals.[106]

Bracton, unsurprisingly, does not directly confront the place of Romanist communal property ideas in his own world of feudal titles. The Romanist categories of common and corporate goods were sometimes described by Bracton as extensions of simple co-ownership ideas, sometimes as fully public goods:

Some tenements are neither sacred nor holy but public, that is, the property of some *universitas* or commune, the property of all the [citizens] and not of any private or individual man....

Some tenements are privately owned, the property of an individual by himself, without a parcener or one joined to him, others are not held alone but with another joined to him or a parcener:... or conversely, who are not called parceners because their rights and the property do not admit of division....

The word 'common' means 'together with others' or 'with others in one', that is 'together'. A common tenement is not the property of any one by himself, nor is [any] separate part, but his with others as a whole in common.

A thing may be held in common with others, not by one without the others, and not admit of division, with or without the consent of the parties.... A tenement may also be common among several who are not parceners, with respect to some use, it will not

Cf D.41.1.50. (Pomponius) (administrative control of building on the seashore). The problems of distinguishing common and public property exercised the glossators and commentators: see R. Perruso, 'The Development of the Doctrine of *Res Communes* in Medieval and Early Modern Europe' (2002) 70 Tijdschrift voor rechtsgeschiedenis (Legal History Review) 69. These issues have not gone away in modern times: see J. W. Harris, 'Private and Non-Private Property' (1995) 111 Law Quarterly Review 421.

[104] Gaius, *Institutiones Iuris Civilis* (F. de Zulueta (trans.), Oxford, 1946, reprinted 1991) (henceforth G.Inst.). The Justinianic law is imbued with or founded upon Gaius's conceptions, though the Gaian text was re-discovered only in 1816: see P. B. H. Birks and G. McLeod, 'Introduction' to *Justinian's Institutes* (London, 1987) 16–18; T. Honoré, *Gaius* (London, 1962).

[105] G.Inst.2.9.–11.

[106] See E. Durkheim, 'The Nature and Origins of Property', from E. Durkheim, *Professional Ethics and Civic Morals* (C. Brookfield (trans.), London, 1957), reprinted in S. Lukes and A. T. Scull (eds.), *Durkheim and the Law (Selected Writings of Durkheim on Law)* (Oxford, 1983) 158–91.

be the property of any one by himself nor common to specified persons, but the property of a *universitas*. . . .

There is also a tenement which is . . . common to a greater extent, that is, which is not the property of any individual person by himself, nor in common, nor the property of a *universitas* by itself, but the common property of all, as the king's highway, the shore of the sea. . . . [107]

An assize remedy was readily available for interference with an individual's interest in a common, or in commonly-held property rights.[108] Bracton does not identify a private action to sue for special damage caused by a public nuisance;[109] elsewhere he suggests means to assert a personal right to enjoy access to *res communes* without interference.[110] In Bracton, as in Roman law, the solution lay in formulating specific heads of individual rights of access to public goods, not in a general right to such goods.[111]

Natural Water Rights as 'Servitudes Imposed by Law'

In addition to the communal property rights in public flowing waters and rivers just noted, Bracton included among the 'servitudes imposed by law' a number of natural water rights attached as common incidents of riparian ownership. In the main these incidents were lifted directly from the Digest's elaborate series of rights protected by interdict: for example, rights to draw water from a spring, well, or pond to no more than the level used in the last year;[112] or rights to prevent neighbours diminishing or altering a stream to one's disadvantage:

[U]nder the guise of re-establishment one cannot make anything worse, nor higher or wider, deeper or longer. Nor may one so scour a watercourse that the water flows otherwise than it used to flow. [He is liable] if he is convicted by the assize of having diverted water, or having done something or introduced something by which the flow of water is lowered or raised, or made less frequent or swifter, or by which it is in any way diminished, or of altering the channel of a stream to the disadvantage of a neighbour. Not only is he who diverts liable but he who refuses to allow the water to flow in another way, when he has no right. He is liable who does something deceitfully by which the water flows more readily otherwise than it used to flow or

[107] *Bracton*, f. 207–208, iii, 128–30.

[108] *Bracton*, f. 231–231b, iii, 188–9; cf. D.43.7.1. (Pomponius).

[109] Cf. *Bracton*, f. 234, iii, 195–6.

[110] *Bracton*, f. 232b–233b, iii, 191–3, f.234–234b, iii, 196. Cf. *K.* v. *M.*, *The Case of the Queen's Forester* (1520) Y.B. Hen. 8 fo 8 (C.P.), in *Year Books of Henry VIII, 12–14 Hen. VIII 1520–1523* (J. H. Baker (ed.), Selden Society, cix, 2002), 42–6 at 45 per Brudenell CJ:

'For one may have right in something and yet have no property: as in a common fountain in a town, or stocks, or a pillory, or the common street in a town, for everyone in the town has a right in something and yet have no property'.

[111] Cf. D.43.8.2.9. (Ulpian).

[112] *Bracton*, f. 233, iii, 192–3; cf. D.43.12.1.1., D.43.13.1.pr.–1.,3.–5.,11.–13., D.43.20.1.1.–37. (Ulpian), D.43.12.1.2. (Pomponius); D.43.22.1.1.–11. (Ulpian).

less readily, as where he constructs a ditch on his own land, or so reconstructs or scours a watercourse that he exceeds due measure and by which he draws off his neighbour's water completely or in part, In all these cases, the whole will be restored to its former condition by the assize.[113]

Servitudes as Praedial Rights over Another's Property

Bracton opens his discussion of the law of praedial servitudes with a rhetorical flourish: '[t]he rights one may have in another's property are infinite'. This is a Roman or civilian idea, here given very broad and unrestricted scope. For example, there was no rule in *De Legibus* against grant of servitudes *in faciendo* requiring positive acts, such as feudal labour services or levies of produce; the Roman prohibition on such positive real obligations was simply overlooked.[114] Bracton describes these real rights in another's property as 'servitudes' because they 'subject . . . one piece of land to another'. They were incorporeal appurtenant rights guaranteeing full enjoyment and possession of one's land, constituted by grant or long use giving one person control over others' property.[115]

The Distinction Between Servitudes and Natural Rights, and the Unity of Remedy

Nuisance was the appropriate form of action for defending servitude rights, as well as for repelling general interferences with property enjoyment. Bracton moved from the idea that there were unlimited varieties of servitude rights to hold that there were limitless ways to breach such rights: 'The nuisances which destroy servitudes completely or, at the least, keep them from being used effectively, are infinite.'[116] Bracton described all proprietary interests which fell to be protected from interferences by the action for nuisance as 'servitudes', without discriminating between differing types of rights defended by that action.[117] This meant that the Roman concept of servitude was often used beyond the Justinianic sense of a *ius* or landowner's right over another's land created by grant or prescription. For Bracton

[113] *Bracton*, f. 234b, iii, 196; cf. D.43.12.1.1., D.43.13.1.pr.–1.,3.,5.–7.,9., D.43.14.1.pr. (Ulpian).

[114] Cf. D.8.1.15.1. (Pomponius); D.8.5.6.2 (Gallus, Ulpian). See further Buckland, *Textbook*, 259–60; Jolowicz and Nicholas, *Historical Introduction*, 282; Birks, 'Dominium', 19–20; F. Schulz, *Classical Roman Law* (London, 1951) 383–5. Compare the anomalous duty imposed to keep a supporting wall in repair: D.8.2.33. (Paul); D.8.5.6.2.; D.8.5.8. (Ulpian), described by Buckland as 'a piece of ancient custom not resting on any theory': *Main Institutions*, 155.

[115] *Bracton*, f. 10b–11, ii, 48–9; f. 220c–221, iii, 162–3.

[116] *Bracton*, f. 231 b, iii, 189.

[117] Compare Bracton's discussion of rights of common unattached to land ownership: f. 222–222b, iii, 166.

servitudes also meant rights to the ordinary enjoyment and amenity of land free of interference by neighbours, a broad concept of *servitus* including the 'natural rights' of property and possession. To take first his discussion of water rights as servitudes created by grant:

One may have this servitude, that is, the right of conducting water from another's land and over another's land to his own land in order to irrigate his field, or to provide some other benefit; he ought not then to be completely prevented from conducting it, or kept from conducting it conveniently or in the proper way, according to the constitution of the servitude, as where, he ought to conduct it at all times, ... [a]nd so if he does not permit him to conduct it in the quantity due, [or] to scour the channel, by which the flow of water is impeded.... In all these cases a disseisin is done the neighbour and he is protected [by the writ 'why he diverted a 'watercourse to the nuisance of his free tenement,'].[118]

Apart from such servitudes constituted by grant, there could be water rights independent of grant, also 'servitudes':

[Just as a servitude] is sometimes constituted by man, sometimes by acquiescence and use, so it is sometimes imposed by law, neither by man or use, that is, no one can do anything on his own land by which damage or nuisance accrues to a neighbour ... that is, that he not raise the level of his pond so high that his neighbour's tenement is flooded, [or] dig a ditch on his own land whereby he diverts his neighbour's water, so that he cannot return to his original channel, completely or in part, [or] do anything on his own land by which his neighbour may not use a servitude imposed or granted, or may use it only in a less convenient way; [as] in place, time, number or kind, quality or quantity.[119]

...

And so ... a servitude is imposed on another's land by law, not by man ... by which one is prohibited from doing on his own land what may damage a neighbour.

...

The servitude that one may have a water course through another's land is imposed by man. And as there is a constitution of man, there is also a constitution of law, that one may not do anything wrongfully on his own land by which his neighbour may be damaged, that is, that he not make a pond (or raise its level or lower it) ... nor a house, bridge, pond, weir, sluice or mill by which his neighbour is wrongfully damaged.[120]

Bracton's mixed concepts of servitude and natural right are so obviously drawn from Roman property doctrine that an excursus into the Justinianic texts is appropriate.

[118] *Bracton*, f. 232, iii, 188–9; cf. Inst.2.3.pr.; D.8.3.1., 5. (Ulpian) (*aquae ductus*); Inst.2.3.2.; D.8.3.30. (Paul, Alfenus) (*aquae haustus*).

[119] *Bracton*, f. 221–221b, iii, 163–4. This is the crucial 'natural right' passage later cited in C. J. Gale, *A Treatise on the Law of Easements* (1st edn., London, 1839) 130–1; (3rd edn., London, 1862) 190 (see below, Ch. 6, the text accompanying n. 22).

[120] *Bracton*, f. 232–232b, iii, 189–91.

Roman Servitude Doctrine

Servitudes as Proprietary Land-use Rights

Real (not personal) servitudes (*servitutes*) were described in Roman law as praedial rights, '[t]he rights which belong to urban and rustic estates (*praediorum urbanorum et rusticorum*)'.[121] Praedial servitudes may be defined as incorporeal rights *in rem* that give some benefit to a dominant estate, by restraining use of servient neighbouring land in some specific way, and binding all owners including assignees and successors of the servient land.

The Praedial Doctrine

The reason these rights are called servitudes belonging to land is that they cannot exist independently of land. Nobody can acquire a servitude of urban or rustic land unless he has land nor can one without land bear the liability implicit in a servitude.[122]

The praedial doctrine has two parts: for there to be a servitude there must be servient land burdened by a restriction and there must be dominant land correspondingly benefited by the restriction. This dual doctrine had many implications, for example there could be no servitude over one's own property as there was no servient tenement to be burdened;[123] 'praedial servitudes are extinguished by merger if the same person becomes owner of both estates', for the same reason;[124] the servitude could only benefit the dominant tenement directly as land; and could not benefit activities that happened to be conducted on the land,[125] nor benefit non-owners or adjacent, non-contiguous lands,[126] so that water drawn under a right of *aquae haustus* could not be sold for industrial use.[127] The praedial doctrine also meant that the servitude right was appurtenant to ownership of particular land, and could not take effect as a right *in personam*, for example servitudes could not be partitioned and exercised by persons not being co-owners of a property right.[128]

The rustic praedial servitudes were originally conceived not as personal rights, nor as abstract *res incorporales* or rights over land, but as a *corpus* or

[121] Inst.2.2.3.; G.Inst.2.14.–14a.

[122] Inst.2.3.3.; see also G.Inst.2.29.; D.8.1.8.pr. (Paul); D.8.1.15.pr. (Pomponius), D.8.1.19. (Labeo); D.8.2.30. (Paul); D.8.2.32. (Julian); D.8.3.5.1. (Ulpian).

[123] D.7.6.5.pr. (Ulpian); D.8.2.26. (Paul); D.8.6.1. (Gaius).

[124] D.8.6.1. (Gaius).

[125] D.8.1.8.pr. (Paul); D.8.3.5.1. (Ulpian); D.8.3.3.4. (Pomponius); D.8.3.6. (Paul); D.8.4.13.pr. (Ulpian).

[126] Buckland (*Textbook*, 263; *Main Institutions*, 155) has perceived a possible variation of this rule in D.20.1.2. (Papinian), allowing the enjoyment of a rustic servitude to be pledged to a landed neigbour in security or part-payment of a debt, the pledge allowing sale of the right.

[127] D.8.3.24. (Ulpian); D.8.3.5.1. (Pomponius).

[128] D.8.1.17. (Pomponius); see also D.8.4.5. (Javolenus); D.43.20.4. (Julian); D.41.2.43. (Marcian); Buckland, *Textbook*, 261–2.

physical thing, owned and occupied separately from the land or soil itself. These rights could be described as an ownership of the defined way or watercourse (or minerals or produce), being a physical part of the land—an ownership concurrent with the land itself. Hence the rustic servitudes were transferred by the same means as land, at first as *res mancipi* conveyed by a symbolic physical delivery;[129] in later law by *cessio in iure* and *traditio*.[130]

The full list of mancipatible rustic servitudes includes rights of way and *aquae ductus* as well as various profits or rights to take elements of the land;[131] all these rustic servitudes exemplify the physical or material origin of such ancient rights in agricultural usage. The urban servitudes governing the use of buildings in towns developed later; these rights, being divorced from the activities of the agricultural economy, were seen to be more disembodied or intangible rights, and hence were not *res mancipi* but were real rights transferred by *cessio in iure*.[132] By the time of the classical lawyers, the older rustic servitudes were also losing their physical quality and were conceived of as intangible *iura*, remaining within the class of *res mancipi* as an historical anomaly only.[133]

Traces of the older corporeal conception may be seen in the idea that servitude rights were transferred formally by a metaphoric 'delivery' of possession or *quasi*-possession;[134] and also in the rule that servitudes might survive the alienation[135] or abandonment[136] of a servient (or dominant) tenement to bind (or benefit) the next owner, as if the servitude maintained a physical existence in the land. However, upon merger of a dominant and servient estate, servitudes were extinguished and did not revive upon separation of the estates, because of the strong principle that servitudes as *iura*

[129] G.Inst.2.14a., 28., 29.; Jolowicz and Nicholas, *Historical Introduction*, 158 ff.; Kaser, 'Roman Ownership', 7–8; Buckland, *Textbook*, 261–6; Birks, *Dominium*, 8–9. For a balanced criticism of the orthodoxy that servitudes originated as a form of corporeal ownership rather than as an independent class of incorporeal rights, see Diosdi, *Ownership in Ancient and Preclassical Roman Law*, 107–16.

[130] Buckland, *Textbook*, 264; D.8.3.30. (Paul, Alfenus); D. 39.3.11.pr. (Paul); D. Daube, 'Slightly Different' (1961) 12 Iura 81, 97–101.

[131] G.Inst.2.14.; D.8.3.1.1. (Ulpian); D.8.3.3. (Ulpian); D.8.3.30. (Paul). There are occasional references to *aquaeductus* as an urban servitude when appurtenant to houses: Buckland, *Textbook*, 262–3; D.6.2.11.1. (Ulpian); D.8.2.18. (Pomponius).

[132] Personal servitudes such as usufruct or personal rights of way were originally non-assignable rights of user or enjoyment, enforceable only against the *dominus* of the burdened land. The personal enjoyment of these rights could be transferred contractually; and then as the rights became more proprietary, there could be transfer by *quasi-traditio* or informal delivery. See W. W. Buckland, 'The Conception of Servitudes in Roman Law' (1928) 44 Law Quarterly Review 426 and 'The Protection of Servitudes in Roman Law' (1930) 46 Law Quarterly Review 447; K. Kagan, 'The Nature of Servitudes and the Association of Usufruct with Them' (1947) 22 Tulane Law Review 94.

[133] D.8.1.14.pr. (Paul); D.8.5.4. (Ulpian); D.8.1.20. (Javolenus); Jolowicz and Nicholas, *Historical Introduction*, 426–7.

[134] D.8.1.20. (Javolenus); D.8.3.14. (Pomponius); D.39.3.11.pr. (Paul), on *aquae ductus* as a physical right incompatible with the co-existence of a right of way along the same route.

[135] D.8.6.13. (Marcellus).

[136] Buckland, 'Conception of Servitudes'.

could not exist in one's own land: in this instance the abstract incorporeal quality of servitudes was more important than their physical, tangible qualities.[137] According to Buckland:

> A servitude is a burden on the land rather than on the ownership. It is an independent *ius* which must be thought of rather as parallel to ownership than as a burden on it. If we reflect on the fact that the earliest servitudes were *res mancipi*, capable of *usucapio* and pledge, the idea that they were thought of as physical things, actual visible tracks and channels, will account for those rules which may look anomalous in classical law.[138]

Servitudes Asserted by in Rem *Actions*

The residual physicality of servitudes may help explain why *in rem* or real actions came to be regarded as the proper procedure for claiming these rights.[139] Servitudes were rights *in rem* because they were rights of property attached to and running with land;[140] rights which all persons were bound to respect independently of contractual or personal relations.[141]

Ius *and* Ius in Re Aliena

The right of usufruct was eventually assimilated to the category of servitudes as a 'personal servitude'.[142] The creation of this unified law of servitudes can be seen as a move to generalize all rights over land amounting to less than full ownership as burdens upon, or fractions of, the ownership of another's land.[143] The later civilians beginning with Donellus made this plain, using the general concept of *iura in re aliena*, incorporeal rights in the property of another, to describe the unified category of personal and praedial servitudes. *Dominium* was then re-defined as the sum of the bundle of abstract rights over land—not simply the ultimate right of the owner to claim title to a thing. The impulse behind this new conceptualization of property rights was not solely analytic. Humanist jurists believed that *dominium* as absolute owner-

137 Buckland, *Textbook*, 260. 138 Ibid., 268.

139 Inst.4.6.1.–2. 140 D.41.1.20.1. (Ulpian).

141 D.8.5.10.1. (Ulpian); see also D.8.5.4., D.8.5.18. (Julian). The classical forms of action for asserting usufruct and servitude rights by *vindicatio* seeking real restitution through the personal sanction of a pecuniary condemnation are discussed in Buckland, 'Protection of Servitudes'; Birks, '*Dominium*', 3–7, 14, 25–6; Diosdi, *Ownership in Ancient and Preclassical Roman Law*, 107 ff. Buckland suggests that *iura in rem*, for the purposes of real procedure, were treated fictitiously as if they were a type of *dominium*: *Elementary Principles*, 61; *Main Institutions*, 160. Developments of the law after Justinian are traced in Kagan, 'Nature of Servitudes'; R. Feenstra, '*Dominium* and *ius in re aliena*: The Origins of a Civil Law Distinction', in Birks, *New Perspectives in the Roman Law of Property*, 111–22.

142 D.8.1.1. (Marcian). Buckland states that *usufructus* is described as a servitude only six times, and suggests that this description was a late classical or Justinianic idea interpolated into Digest texts; *Textbook*, 268.

143 D.7.1.4. (Paul). Cf. definition of usufruct in Inst.2.4.pr. and D.7.1.1. (Paul); see Buckland, *Textbook*, 259; Buckland, *Elementary Principles*, 92–114.

ship, summing all possible fractional rights in land, was the more modern institution, preferable to a concept of *dominium* as the superior right amongst many possible rights over land, a concept too reminiscent of feudal lordship and inequality of status amongst right-holders.[144] These later categorizations were not, however, part of classical or Digest law. Both usufruct and servitude were thus seen simply as *iura*—abstract incorporeal rights entitling the holder to engage in certain uses of, or activities upon, the land of another; rights which co-existed with the *dominus*'s ultimate right which was likewise a *ius* over the land. The special ultimate character of *dominium* was expressed in the rule that a *dominus* could not have a separate right of usufruct or servitude over his own land.[145]

Diosdi[146] suggests it was not the case that sophisticated concepts of *iura* were developed as extensions of a more primitive concept of ownership as lawfully protected possession and control. Rather the reverse case held:

> The creation of the notion of *dominium* was also dependent on the previous formation of the category of *servitus* and the appearance of the institution of *usus fructus*. A statue is only finished when the chisel of the sculptor has removed the superfluous marble. Likewise, the abstract notion of ownership can only be created after everything not belonging to ownership, has been stripped off. The classical Roman notion of ownership... is characterized by an utter disregard of those external appearances which represent the very idea of ownership to the layman. Thus *dominium* is not only clearly separated from possession, but also from the use of the thing and from enjoyment of its fruits.[147]

Bracton's Adoption of Specific Roman Water Doctrines

Bracton's use of the Roman conceptual apparatus is exemplified in the case of water rights. At least five servitudes of grant were itemized, in close concordance with the elaborate servitude law of the Digest: going to take water from a spring, well, or pond (that is, rights of access to a water

[144] Feenstra, '*Dominium* and *ius in re aliena*', and J. W. Cairns, 'Craig, Cujas, and the Definition of *feodum*: Is a Feu a Usufruct?', in Birks (ed.), *New Perspectives in the Roman Law of Property*, 76–84; P. Stein, 'Donellus and the Origins of the Modern Civil Law', in J. A. Ankum (ed.), *Mélanges Félix Wubbe* (Fribourg, 1993) 439; Stein, *Roman Law in European History*, 82; J. P. Dawson, 'The Codification of the French Customs' (1940) 39 Michigan Law Review 780; J. Q. Whitman, 'The Seigneurs Descend to the Rank of Creditors' (1994) 6 Yale Journal of Law and the Humanities 249; on the issues concerning *dominium* and relativity of titles, see Buckland, *Textbook*, 186–8; Diosdi, *Ownership in Ancient and Preclassical Roman Law*, 131–6, 180–5; Birks, '*Dominium*', 25–31.

[145] D.7.6.5.pr. (Ulpian); D.8.2.26. (Paul); D.8.6.1. (Gaius); see further Buckland, 'Conception of Servitudes'.

[146] Diosdi, *Ownership in Ancient and Preclassical Roman Law*, 131–6.

[147] Ibid., 133. Kaser offers a differing general theory of the history of Roman ownership, whereby *dominium* emerges from actions defending relative rights to physical possession; see Jolowicz and Nicholas, *Historical Introduction*, 144–55.

source);[148] driving cattle to water;[149] common of fishery in another's waters;[150] drawing water;[151] conducting or channelling water to one's land from another's land, at times and in quantities stipulated by the grant.[152]

The Natural Source Doctrine

Bracton also adopted the Roman doctrine that natural and permanent water sources only—that is, perpetual springs and running streams, and not cisterns or artificial reservoirs and channels—could be the subject of appurtenant rights of property, whether as servitudes or natural rights imposed by law.

> If one does something to prevent another from going to a spring, a lake, a well [or] a fish-pond or from drawing from a spring, such persons may fall into the assize [of nuisance]. . . . But this is not so in the case of a cistern because a cistern does not have a perpetual source nor running water, since it is filled by rains, and so a lake, a fish pond or a well sometimes do not have running water.[153]

The doctrine rests on a notion that property rights must be capable of indefinite duration as part of the natural world, and not be dependent on man-made contingencies. Yet rights in permanent man-made reservoirs and water-courses were possible forms of servitude (such as *aquae ductus*); the line between a water right with an artificial or a natural source was not easy to draw, and so the doctrine of natural source could not be rigorous.

Standards of Reasonableness in the Exercise of Rights

Reasonable Extensions of Right

Echoing the Roman law, Bracton held that there were rights implied into the grant of the servitude to do whatever acts were reasonable to enjoy a servitude effectively. It was nuisance to 'destroy servitudes completely or, at the least, keep them from being used effectively'.[154] For example, to deny the use of a convenient path for a right of way, or else to deny full access to land for a right of pasturage, were each nuisances:

[148] *Bracton*, f. 233, iii, 192; cf. D.43.22.1.1., 2., 5. (Ulpian); other sources for *aquae haustus* include: Inst.2.3.2.; D.8.2.28., D.8.3.9. (interpolated) (Paul); D.8.3.30. (Paul, Alfenus); D.43.20.1.7.,8.,38. (Ulpian).

[149] *Bracton*, f. 233, iii, 192; cf. D.43.22.1.1. (Ulpian).

[150] *Bracton*, f. 233b, iii, 194.; cf. D.43.14.7. (Ulpian).

[151] *Bracton*, f. 233, iii, 192–3; cf. D. 43.22.1.1. 2. 8. 9. (Ulpian).

[152] *Bracton*, f. 233, iii, 192–3; cf. Inst.2.3.pr.; D.8.3.1. (Ulpian); D.43.22.1.1. (Ulpian); D.43.20.2. (Pomponius), D.43.20.5.pr. (Julian).

[153] *Bracton*, f. 233, iii, 192–3; cf. D.8.2.28. (Paul); D.8.3.9. (Paul, interpolated); D.8.4.2., D.43.20.1.7.–8., 39.; D.43.22.1.4. (Ulpian).

[154] *Bracton*, f. 231b, iii, 189.

[a]nd so in connexion with a water course, as where the right of conducting water is granted and the grantor does not permit him to conduct it at all, or only with difficulty, because... what he ought to conduct continuously he only permits him to conduct at certain hours, or what he ought to conduct completely he only permits him to conduct in part.[155]

Also protected were the 'appurtenances of appurtenances', the auxiliary rights attached to servitudes as was reasonable and necessary for their enjoyment.[156] Bracton included the rights to have convenient access to a watercourse; and rights to repair, restore, and cleanse a water channel to its former state, but not to increase its capacity.[157] The justifying idea here was that stability and workability of private rights was to be upheld in the public interest. Interferences with the exercise of servitude rights were 'disseisins' comparable to full dispossessions: 'It will be an obvious disseisin when he does not permit him to exercise his right in any way, or not conveniently or not in the proper manner';[158] and such disseisins were to be removed because the owner has 'suffered the wrong [done to] what is his, and because of the common welfare, lest he be prevented for long from making use of his right, or using it advantageously'.[159] Bracton added in another passage: 'A nuisance may be wrongful and harmful to one or several private persons with respect to their private welfare. It may also be against the common welfare, which must always and in every case be preferred to the private.'[160]

Reasonable Restraints of Right

Again reiterating Roman doctrine, Bracton held that the various rights to reasonable exercise of one's servitude were mirrored by corresponding restraints on unreasonable exercise: 'One may have and use a servitude in another's property unless he is prevented for some proper reason. If he exceeds due measure, he may be expelled at once but not after the lapse of time, unless with an investigation of the reason.'[161] Where a servitude of common was exceeded, two remedies were available against the wrongdoer, namely 'novel disseisin... since he thus appropriates the lord's tenement against his will, as though he had no common at all and had attempted to

[155] *Bracton*, f. 221b, iii, 164–5; f. 231b, iii, 188–9.

[156] *Bracton*, f. 232, iii, 190.

[157] *Bracton*, f. 221b, iii, 164; f. 232, iii, 190; f. 233, iii, 193 and f. 234–234b, iii, 196; cf. D.7.6.1.1.–4., D.8.3.3., D.11.7.12.pr. (Ulpian); D.8.3.30., D.18.1.40.1. (Paul); D.8.3.20.pr., D.8.4.11.1., D.8.6.17. (Pomponius); D.43.8.2., D.43.8.11., D.43.11.1.2., D.43.13.1.pr., D.43.21.–22. (Ulpian).

[158] *Bracton*, f. 221b, iii, 165. For a later example see *Bishop of London* v. *Richard de Stogerton* (C.P.40/435, m. 250, Trin. 1369), in *Select Cases of Trespass from the King's Courts 1307–1399 Vol. II* (M. S. Arnold (ed.), Selden Society, ciii, 1987) 281.

[159] *Bracton*, f. 221–221b, iii, 164.

[160] *Bracton*, f. 234, iii, 196.

[161] *Bracton*, f. 221b, iii, 165; cf. D.8.1.9. (Celsus); D.8.3.5.1. (Ulpian); D.8.3.6., D.8.6.18.pr. (Paul); D.8.3.15. (Pomponius).

put in his beasts by force against the will of the lord, and also another remedy, that by another writ the excess be reduced to proper number and due measure'.[162] This latter remedy was the writ of admeasurement, initiating an inquiry by the sheriff and the assembled hundred in order to establish reasonable exercise of the right of common—a communal control of individual servitude rights. A wide range of matters might be the subject of the inquest: the terms of the original grant, the established mode of user, the competing rights of others, the physical capacity of the servient pasture or land, and the needs of the dominant land to which the right was appurtenant. Finally, an order to reduce over-use or over-stocking of the pasture could be made.[163] Actions protecting and regulating the water servitudes were likely to have proceeded on similar lines to those for the communal regulation of commons;[164] indeed Bracton often discusses water rights expressly as a species of common.[165]

Bracton articulated the nature of admeasurement in describing the regulation of estovers, a large and important class of commons in the medieval rural economy. Estovers were rights to benefits apart from food, such as 'wood . . . for building, fencing, burning and other necessary things, much or little, according to the constitution of the servitude'; also 'right of digging, mowing and cutting, and servitudes of every other kind'. Bracton discussed the control of estovers allowing takings of wood or other profits in terms of reasonable proportionality of user to the appurtenant tenement:

> [D]ue measure must be observed, that the estovers be reasonable according to the size of the wood or waste in which the servitude is constituted, according as it is large or small. The size of the tenement to which the servitude is owed [must also be considered, that the estovers] neither exceed due measure nor are reduced below it, that everything remain in proper proportion. If one of them attempts to exceed or withhold due measure, that is, he to whom the servitude belongs, by taking more than reason permits or than is permissible, and thus commits waste and destruction, let the lord whose land it is obtain admeasurement or sue for trespass or disseisin. And so if it is reduced or withheld completely by the lord, let him to whom the servitude is owed sue by writ, that he be permitted to use fully or at least to proper advantage. . . .[166]

[162] *Bracton*, f. 229, iii, 183.

[163] *Bracton*, f. 229–230, iii, 183–5; similar writs are reproduced in Glanvill and Fleta; see references at n. 85 above.

[164] See Pollock and Maitland, *HEL*, i, 362–6, and W. O. Ault, *Private Jurisdiction in England* (New Haven, Conn., 1923), on communal regulation of the manorial fields and annual redistribution of virgates by the manorial court.

[165] See e.g. *Bracton*, f. 231b, iii, 189. Roman doctrine controlling the exercise of appurtenant water rights is stated in D.8.3.5.1. (Ulpian); D.8.3.20.3.–4. (Pomponius); D.8.3.17. (Papirus Justus, Antoninus, Verus); D.39.3.11.pr., D.39.3.17.1. (Paul).

[166] *Bracton*, f. 231, iii, 188; see also f. 233b, iii, 194 on admeasurement of a common of fishery. Cf. D.8.2.1.pr., 38., 39. (Paul).

Where there was a dispute over estovers between commoners taking from the same land, a jury was to make inquest by writ of trespass, or else the parties were 'compelled to partition by a judgement *de communi dividundo*'.[167] According to Bracton, it was wrong to say that the jurors could not view and make inquest into servitude rights because they were 'incorporeal, and thus invisible and intangible'. The demandant could 'make a view of the tenement to the jurors', for:

the bodies may be seen, that is, the tenements in which the rights are constituted, and also the tenements to which they are said to be appurtenant, in order to ascertain in what places and within what limits they are contained, as is done every day with respect to common of pasture [claimed] by writ of right and the writ *quo jure*.[168]

The admeasurement actions for commons are examples of local administrative controls enforcing standards of reasonableness in the day-to-day enjoyment of servitudes. Admeasurement as a communal and discretionary method of deciding rights may be contrasted with the process of adjudication between rights of competing individuals through application of rules in a court of law.[169]

Immediately after discussing the actions for commons, Bracton commences his exposition of the servitude rights to conduct water to one's land. Though the relevant forms of action here are the assizes of novel disseisin and nuisance,[170] their function as described by Bracton mirrors the admeasurement actions for the reasonable, proportional exercise of commons. The same principles of regulation were thus applied to all forms of common, including water rights.

Constitution of Rights of Grant by Livery and Use

In Roman law an initial use of an incorporeal right over another's property was sufficient to constitute the right as property and delimit its extent, following the act of grant.[171] The English doctrine of livery of seisin produced an analogous theory, with some important differences.

167 *Bracton*, f. 231–231b, iii, 188.

168 *Bracton*, f. 236, iii, 200; f. 376–379, iv, 179–88, on viewing of corporeal and incorporeal rights.

169 The judicial procedures of the Assize of Novel Disseisin also had some features of communal inquest by sherriff and jurors (see *Bracton*, f. 179–180b, iii, 57–60); but this was more a factual inquest rather than a communal adjudication and regulation of entitlements as with the writs examined here. On the role of jurors and recognitors as fact-finders and arbitrators in medieval law see Maitland, *Forms of Action*, 14–19, 26–8, 34–5; Pollock and Maitland, *HEL*, i, 138–49; J. P. Dawson, *The Oracles of the Law* (Ann Arbor, Mich., 1968) 118–29; M. Macnair, 'Vicinage and the Antecedents of the Jury' (1999) 17 Law and History Review 537.

170 See *Bracton*, f. 232, iii, 188–9.

171 On constitution or incorporeal rights by user: C.2.3.20.; D.41.2.30.5. (Paul); on forms of grant: Inst.2.3.4.; D.7.6.1.1. (Ulpian); D.8.1.5., D.8.4.16. (Gaius); D.8.2.34.–35. (Julian).

In order to constitute a right to a thing by transfer, it was necessary to obtain full seisin—physically to possess the thing with intention to possess, drawing here from the complex of Roman ideas of possession as a 'legal fact' composed of the elements of *corpore* and *animo*.[172] The relative strength or rank of the property right would then be determined by the rightfulness or wrongfulness of the possession: 'Some possession is bare, some clothed by a vestment: bare, as where one has no right in a thing, not the slightest spark of right, only a bare physical entry; clothed, [as where one's possession is clothed] by right, title or time.'[173] Livery was a voluntary, willed vesting of right and title with seisin, involving a public withdrawal from possession of a tenement on the part of the grantor, and immediate entry into possession or full seisin by the grantee, demonstrated by a ceremonial entry and viewing of the house or estate.[174] Transfer without livery, for example by homage or execution of an instrument of grant, was incomplete and did not constitute a full transfer. Bracton summed up livery as 'the transfer of a corporeal thing...from one person to a second; a voluntary transference from one's own hand or another's.... In one sense, livery is nothing other than an induction into possession'.[175] A complex series of rules existed to facilitate livery, permitting transfers by third-party, ratification, usucapions to expand flawed seisins, and the like.[176] Bracton learnt from classical Roman law a general respect for freedom of contract and for freedom to dispose of one's property; he asserts 'nothing is more consonant with natural equity than that effect be given to the intention of an owner wishing to transfer his property to another';[177] and in discussing contracts for burdened titles, Bracton states: 'Each person who contracts knows or ought to know what and what sort of thing it is that he takes free or servile, burdened or not, bound or not, as to all of which he must examine and inquire diligently since ignorance does not excuse him and contracting parties are permitted to deceive each other.'[178] Bracton's regard for contractual intentions as a determinant of property rights did not, however, dominate his property doctrine; intention to grant and to possess was balanced by requirements of conveyance and physical

[172] *Bracton*, f. 38b–39, ii, 121–4. The terms possession and seisin are used interchangeably by Bracton: see Pollock and Maitland, *HEL*, ii, 29 ff. In the fifteenth century these concepts were split by the development of ejectment and trespass actions which protected the *possession* of the leasehold tenant, whilst the non-occupying freehold lord retained the *seisin* without possession.

[173] *Bracton*, f. 39, ii, 122.

[174] *Bracton*, f. 40, ii, 125; cf. classical Roman concept of transfer of derivative ownership as abandonment and occupation, rather than translation: Buckland, *Main Institutions*, 112.

[175] *Bracton*, f. 39b, ii, 124. The grantor's subjective intention to transfer was inferred by the objective manifestation of outward acts: *Bracton*, f. 50b, ii, 158.

[176] The rules of livery are set out in *Bracton*, f. 39b–45b, ii, 124–40; see further Pollock and Maitland, *HEL*, ii, 80–106.

[177] *Bracton*, f. 39b–40, ii, 125; cf. D.41.1.9.3. (Gaius).

[178] *Bracton*, f. 48b, ii, 147–8; cf. D.4.4.6.4., D.50.17.19. (Ulpian). The rule is originally from Gaius.

control as requisites of legal seisin. Livery was never reduced to a purely symbolic, legally abstracted form of delivery (as in Roman conveyance), but retained a factual kernel of intentional, physical, apparent control, granted as by formal investiture. However, actual use of the tenement was not required in addition to the constitutive act of livery: 'a simple entry with the *affectus possidendi* and the donor's consent suffices.... For one may have a free tenement by livery though he does not immediately use or take the issues.'[179] 'Issues' meant the profits or fruits of possession, and to appropriate the issues was the strongest evidence of an assertion of rightful possession.[180] Conversely, use by itself, in the absence of grant or prescription (that is, *causa*) was never a formal livery; there had to be grant as well as possession.[181]

The function of user as an *indicium* of livery and seisin was further blurred by the idea that once possession had been acquired, 'though the donee at once has a free tenement, nevertheless, in order to make his possession evident... he must use his seisin'.[182] Here a distinction was drawn between substantive and evidential requirements for title: '[U]se and issues do not much affect a gift, [They are often of value as evidence of possession and, like livery, may be called the vestments of gifts]'.[183] Ceremonial, formal seisin by some symbolic livery sufficed to create a protected possession; but proof of seisin might require evidence of user, of genuine possession in fact.

Rules for the Constitution of Incorporeal Rights

The mode of constitution and acquisition of incorporeal, appurtenant rights was said to be similar to that for corporeal property, with one major difference (borrowed from post-classical Roman law):

> an incorporeal thing does not admit of livery, as the right itself which inheres in a thing or a body, because [rights] cannot be possessed, only *quasi*-possessed. They therefore do not admit of livery, only *quasi*-livery, nor are they acquired or retained except by acquiescence or use.[184]
>
> [I]ncorporeal things cannot be possessed or be the subjects of usucapion or be transferred apart from some corporeal thing, since they do not admit of delivery by themselves. They therefore are said to be *quasi*-possessed [and] can be transferred or *quasi*-transferred by acquiescence and use.[185]

179 *Bracton*, f. 40, ii, 125.
180 See Pollock and Maitland, *HEL*, ii, 83–90, on how livery might operate in practice.
181 Ibid.
182 *Bracton*, f. 49, ii, 149–50.
183 *Bracton*, f. 40, ii, 125.
184 *Bracton*, f. 39b, ii, 124; cf. D.8.1.17. (Pomponius); D.8.1.20. (Javolenus); D.8.2.20.pr. (Paul); D.8.3.1.2., D.8.3.5.pr. (Ulpian); D.41.1.59. (Callistratus); Buckland, *Textbook*, 260–6.
185 *Bracton*, f. 38b, ii, 121; and see also f. 223, 226b, iii, 168–9, 177. See further L. O. Pike, 'Feoffment and Livery of Incorporeal Hereditaments' (1889) 5 Law Quarterly Review 324.

Quasi-livery and *quasi*-possession were explained thus:

Corporeal things are acquired *animo* and *corpore*, by livery; incorporeal things, as rights and servitudes, when they are in a definite place simply by the view of the taker or his procurator or the will and intention to possess, because rights do not admit of livery.[186]

[F]or livery a view of the place in which the rights are constituted and the mutual consent of the contracting parties and the *animus possidendi* suffice, and the donee, solely through will and intention, is in *quasi*-possession, and though he does not immediately use he always uses or *quasi*-uses until by non-use, that is, by force, negligence or long acquiescence, he loses seisin.[187]

Bracton expressly states that use here was not an essential element of seisin: 'Possession of a corporeal thing may be acquired without use, and similarly the *quasi*-possession of an incorporeal thing may be acquired without use.'[188] But at the same time, use by the grantee had an evidential function, much more important than in the case of transfer of corporeal things. Without some use there could not be seisin constituting the property right to its fullest extent:

Rights, being incorporeal, cannot be seen or touched, and thus do not admit of delivery as corporeal things do. The gift must therefore be effected by the intention of the contracting parties, simply by the intention and will to transfer and accept and the view of the corporeal thing in which these rights inhere, and in that way, by means of a legal fiction, they are *quasi*-possessed; he who is thus in possession by a legal fiction always *quasi*-uses until he is disseised by force or without force by non-use. . . .

[T]he *quasi*-possession of an incorporeal thing may be acquired without use. But when use has been made of an incorporeal thing, by such use possession is retained, and what before was fictitious is made real; when one has made use of such a right he can transfer to another both the right and the use, which he could not do before such use.[189]

This doctrine is unfolded in Bracton's discussion of 'the most celebrated servitude . . . the right of pasturing . . . called common of pasture'.[190] 'Common' was the general legal term for any right appurtenant to one's own property 'held together with another in another's property'.[191] There were many species of common apart from the leading example of pasturage, including mining rights; 'reasonable estovers' as described above,[192]

[186] *Bracton*, f. 221b–222, iii, 166–7.

[187] *Bracton*, f. 223, iii, 168; cf. Roman *quasi*-possession doctrine, above, n. 134.

[188] *Bracton*, f. 53, ii, 159.

[189] Ibid.; and see Pollock and Maitland, *HEL*, ii, 135–40, on the operation of fictitious seisin; J. Biancalana, 'Actions of Covenant 1200–1330' (2002) 20 Law and History Review 1, 5–38, esp. 27ff.

[190] *Bracton*, f. 222, iii, 166.

[191] Cf. Bracton's comparison of common to *res communes*, the text accompanying nn. 101–111 above.

[192] The text accompanying nn. 165–168 above.

namely rights to cut turf, heather and wood for the benefit of one's tenement; '[s]imilarly a right of hunting and fishing, drinking and drawing water and many others, infinite in number, with their appurtenances'.[193] These property interests were distinct from rights to take resources not attached to any estate, such as herbage and profits-à-prendre which Bracton labelled '*quasi*-personal interests'.[194] Discussing the common of pasture, Bracton writes:

We must see how one must use a right granted him as to retain possession and as evidence of his right. And first of servitudes, as where one is granted the right of pasturing cattle in another's land. Let him, as soon as possible, drive in his beasts, one or several; by that he will retain his seisin.... And when he has so used it in fact, he transmits that right and use to his heirs and assigns which, without use, he could do before, and thenceforward he can transfer that right to strangers, with use and seisin, which he could not do before, without use. And let what was said of the right of pasturing apply as well to rights of way, of driving cattle, of conducting water, and to all other servitudes, which are infinite; it does not matter.[195]

In another passage Bracton states:

If a neighbour imposes this servitude on his land, that his neighbour may pasture his cattle therein, that servitude is binding. He may thus [make] his land, originally free, servient to his neighbour's, [simply] by such constitution and the mutual agreement of both parties, provided the taker has his view and assents. Since rights of this kind do not admit of livery, he is at once in seisin, though he does not immediately put in his beasts, and is always taken to use until he loses his seisin by non-use, that is, until he has been disseised in whole or in part, so that he cannot put in his beasts [at all], or... cannot use the servitude conveniently or in the proper way. He must then be aided by the assize, whether he has used or not, since, solely by the constitution, he is in *quasi*-possession, because rights are *quasi*-possessed. Possession of a servitude is thus acquired before use, [but it cannot be transferred to another without use, unless the constitution of the servitude provided that it may remain to him and his heirs or to whom he wishes to give or assign, or unless one says that he may transfer it [before use] with the tenement to which the servitude is appurtenant...,] but it is never retained except by true use, that is, when he has put in all his beasts, one or more, though he does not put in all, or all the kinds, of beasts he could put in by the constitution.[196]

The doctrine, in sum, states that grant of the incorporeal right vests the right in possession without use—a *quasi* or fictitious possession; but the right is not fully constituted as a hereditable or assignable proprietary interest in possession until there has been a 'true use'.

[193] *Bracton*, f. 231b, iii, 189.

[194] *Bracton*, f. 222–222b, iii, 166–7; f. 231–232, iii, 187–9; see further Milsom, 'Introduction' to *Novae Narrationes*, pp. lxvii–xc.

[195] *Bracton*, f. 53b, ii, 160–1.

[196] *Bracton*, f. 222, iii, 165–6.

Prescription

Livery and user gave rise to seisin of corporeities by acts of patent possession. In Bracton's doctrine, by contrast, prescription as a positive acquisition of seisin by long user could be applied to incorporeal rights only. He states: 'seisin of a servitude may be acquired and retained without any formal constitution, by acquiescence or long use'; and this general rule extended to all servitudes, including 'the right to pasture in another's property, [or] the right to cultivate it, to go over it, to draw water from it, to fish in it, to conduct water over it, to hunt on it, and there may be an infinite number of other rights. . . .'[197]

Roman Prescription Precedents

Bracton's prescription doctrine drew from Roman analogues whereby a user of sufficient length might establish a servitude, or at least a use-right protected by interdict. Roman sources give the following:[198]

> If a man has obtained a right to channel water by long use and, as it were, by long possession, he is not required to lead evidence to establish the legal title on which his right to the water is founded, for example, to show that it rests on a legacy or on some other ground. He is entitled to an *actio utilis* to establish that he has had the use of the water, say, for so many years, and that this was not obtained by force, stealth, or *precarium*. . . . [Judges] normally uphold aqueducts to which antiquity of use gives some authority, even where their legal right to exist is not proved.[199]

An action could be brought 'against anyone at all who prevents one from channeling the water, as is the case with servitudes in general'.[200] There was also the interdictal protection of established usages of daily and summer water.[201] Moreover there was a general principle of servitude acquisition by long user:

> [W]here it is discovered that no servitude has been imposed, the person who has for a long time acted as though there were a servitude and has done so neither by force nor *precarium* nor secretly, he is regarded as having a servitude imposed quasi-legally by reason of prolonged custom.[202]

[197] *Bracton*, f. 222, iii, 166.

[198] On the civilian conceptions of *usucapio* generally see D. Johnston, *Prescription and Limitation* (Edinburgh, 1999) 3–15; J. Getzler, 'Roman and English Prescription for Incorporeal Property', in J. Getzler (ed.), *Rationalizing Property, Equity and Trusts: Essays in Honour of Edward Burn* (London, 2003) 281–323.

[199] D.8.5.10.pr. (Ulpian); D.39.3.26. (Scaevola); see also D.43.19.5.3. (Ulpian).

[200] D.8.5.10.1. (Ulpian); D.43.19.1.pr.–4. (Ulpian).

[201] D.8.5.10.pr. (Ulpian); D.39.3.26. (Scaevola); D.39.3.1.23. (Ulpian, Labeo); D.39.3.2.pr. (Paul); D.43.19.2. (Ulpian); D.43.20.3.4. (Pomponius); C.3.34.1.–2.,7.; C.7.33.12.4.

[202] D.39.3.1.23. (Ulpian).

Usucapio

The various modes of servitude acquisition by long user were outside the chief Roman prescription doctrine of *usucapio*.[203] *Usucapio* was centrally a doctrine for the perfection of purported transfers of *dominium* possessed by an owner in good faith,[204] and hence was of inherently limited application in creating incorporeal rights over land. Earlier forms of acquisitive prescription involving presumed grant once applied equally to *res incorporales* and land,[205] but the *lex Scribonia* of *c*.60 BCE formally ended *usucapio* for servitudes in Roman civil law,[206] unless the servitude was usucapted with land.[207] The prohibition probably embodied a policy of protecting the *dominus* from too ready a loss of use-rights over land, for as the agricultural community of the Roman state grew to an impersonal size, it became difficult to maintain face-to-face relations with one's neighbours and so maintain immediate knowledge of activities affecting one's own land use.[208] There were also formal juristic reasons for the rule against positive prescription, as described by Paul:

> Rustic praedial servitudes, even though attached to corporeal property, are nevertheless incorporeal and so are never acquired by usucapion. Or the reason may be that the nature of these servitudes is such as not to engender clear and continuous possession. For no one can make use of a right of way in so continuous and uninterrupted a manner that his possession of it will be held to be unbroken. The same rule applies to urban servitudes as well.[209]

Despite these limitations associated with *usucapio*, Bracton was to raid the Roman doctrine for many of his leading concepts of prescription for servitudes. The main features of *usucapio* must therefore be noted. There had to be a period of uninterrupted use of a thing capable of ownership; good faith by the possessor, or belief that the taking of the thing was not an interference with another's right at the time of the taking (a question of fact which was *prima facie* presumed);[210] and finally, there had to be a real *iusta causa*, a legitimate ground of right, or acquisition by a transaction which would ordinarily have been a legitimate basis of acquisition by transfer, such as a

[203] From *usu capere*, to acquire by use.

[204] Inst.2.6.pr.; D.41.3.1. (Gaius); D.41.3.3. (Modestinus); D.41.10.5.1.pr.–1. (Neratius).

[205] D.41.3.4.28(29). (Paul); Buckland, *Main Institutions*, 157–8.

[206] D.8.1.14.pr., D.41.3.4.28(29). (Paul).

[207] D.8.2.32.1. (Julian); D.41.3.10.1. (Ulpian); D.41.3.23.pr. (Javolenus).

[208] Inst.2.6.pr.; Buckland, *Main Institutions*, 121–2.

[209] D.8.1.14.pr.; D.41.2.3.pr.–1., D.41.3.4.26(27). (Paul); D.8.2.32.1. (Julian); D.41.2.45.pr. (Papinian); D.41.3.25. (Licinus Rufinus); D.41.3.9. (Gaius).

[210] 'Usucapion is a matter of law, while the question whether a person is a possessor in good faith or in bad faith is a matter of fact': D.41.1.48.1. (Paul); D.41.10.5.1. (Neratius); D.41.4.2.15. (Paul). The good faith requirement was a subjective refinement of the earlier objective rule against theft: Jolowicz and Nicholas, *Historical Introduction*, 154; Buckland, *Main Institutions*, 122–3.

sale, legacy, or gift.[211] Conversely there could be no *usucapio* if the thing was taken by force or was stolen.[212] These requirements were demanding and extensive, and protected owners from too-ready a loss of *dominium* to later holders, under flawed transactions beyond the true owner's control.

It may be that *usucapio* began as a mode of acquisition derivatively based on some constitution, grant, conveyance, or other conventional root of title, and was not based on user directly creating an original title. A long user might have operated as a legal fact pointing to some further legal fact constituting the right, typically grant or transfer of another's right. Following the lapse of prescriptive time, the claimant of the right was relieved from having to give factual proof of the legitimate origin of his title; the long enjoyment was taken as presumptive evidence of a rightful derivation of ownership. It was then left to the opponent of the right to disprove the title by showing an absence of legitimate origin. The development of the rule that *usucapio* could be complete without possible evidence of constitution or grant was a later refinement, abstracting from the original function of *usucapio* as a simplification of proof of title. Thus over time the juristic source of prescriptive titles, in derivative transfer by presumed grant, was concealed.

Extinctive Prescription

In place of acquisitive *usucapio* for servitudes, Roman law developed a doctrine of extinctive prescription known as *usucapio libertatis*, akin to the classical *longi temporis praescriptio* for provincial land.[213] *Usucapio libertatis* freed land of burdens where a non-continuous servitude such as *aquae ductus* or way was not used, or where a continuous servitude such as light or support was interrupted by adverse user, thus demonstrating through acquiescence an intention of the dominant owner to surrender the right.[214]

Bracton's Doctrine of Prescription for Servitudes

Bracton's discussion of pasturage elaborated on the various modes of acquisition by livery, possession, and prescription, which applied to all forms of commons and servitudes including water rights.

[211] Inst.2.6.7.–11.; Buckland, *Textbook*, 242–8 (on putative and real *causa*). The classical law excluded putative *causa* or subjective belief in a valid source of right in the absence of a real but flawed transaction. Generally the flaw vitiating the transfer would be seen as an error of fact, for 'an error of law never benefits the possessor in the matter of usucapion': D.41.3.31.pr. (Paul); D.41.3.17. (Marcellus).

[212] Inst.2.6.2.–3.

[213] Inst.2.6.pr.,7.; D.8.5.10.pr., D.39.3.1.23. (Ulpian); Buckland, *Textbook*, 250–2.

[214] D.8.2.6. (Gaius); D.8.2.32.pr.–1. (Julian); D.8.6.9.,12. (Celsus); D.8.2.5; D.8.6.7.,10.,25., D.8.6.12.2., D.8.6.18.2., D.41.2.3.4.–7.,11.,21.–22., D.41.3.2. (Paul); D.41.2.17.1., D.41.10.1.pr. (Ulpian); D.41.2.44.2.–4., D.41.2.49.2. (Papinian); D.8.6.16., D.41.2.27. (Proculus); D.8.6.19.pr., D.41.2.31 (Pomponius); D.41.2.2., D.41.2.13.1. (Ulpian); D.41.10.5.1. (Neratius).

Common [of pasture] is acquired in many ways, for example, through the *causa* of gift, as where one gives land with the appurtenances, with common of pasture etc. Through the *causa* of purchase and sale, as where one buys common in another's land that it may be appurtenant to his tenement, though it is of another's fee... through... a service certain. Through the *causa* of vicinage, as where one [intercommons] with his neighbour and his neighbour with him. Through a constitution [made] by the lords of the estate, [or] without a constitution, by long use, with peaceful possession, continuous and uninterrupted, [through the knowledge and acquiescence of lords...] which is taken ['*pro traditione accipiuntur*' or '*accipitur*'] for livery, provided it is not by force, stealth or at will. ...[215]

Bracton thus adapted the Roman concepts of *causa* and long user from *usucapio* in order to describe the prescriptive acquisition of incorporeal rights, notwithstanding the Roman prohibition on *usucapio* for servitudes.

After listing the various *causae* of grant, long user is described as a fact substituting for grant, rather than as a type of grant itself. Bracton is ambiguous as to whether a lost grant is supposed actually to have been made. The long use of an incorporeal right is a *causa* in itself, or legal fact constituting full (*quasi*-)seisin in that right. The effect of user on incorporeal rights could also be negative or extinctive; for example, in the case of a grantee entering into a common, 'though he does not immediately use he always uses or *quasi*-uses until by non-use, that is by force, negligence or long acquiescence, he loses seisin, as where... the grantee is completely excluded'.[216] This doctrine of non-use resembled *longi temporis praescriptio* and (as in Roman law) was distinct from original acquisition upon abandonment.[217]

When Bracton stated that a servitude 'is never *retained* except by true use'[218] this may refer to prescriptive extinction of an incorporeal right—that is, loss of the right, a failure to maintain it—rather than failure to acquire the full seisin and right by a constitutive use. Such an interpretation constructs a categorical distinction between use for the acquisition and use for the retention of rights. However, this neat ordering of Bracton's doctrine cannot always be borne out by the text. For example, Bracton's general discussion of the theory of possession states that 'natural possession', and the civil action to defend such possession, would be lost by a grantee:

though he is in possession, though he has not been ejected, if he is prevented from using and enjoying, or cannot use conveniently or in the usual way.... The same is true whenever one's property, whether he is in possession or not, is abridged without his consent, by building upon it, plowing or sowing it, diverting its water, reaping or digging it, or by doing any other similar act.[219]

215 *Bracton*, f. 222b, iii, 166–7.

216 *Bracton*, f. 223, iii, 168; and see also f. 223–223b, iii, 168–70.

217 Inst.2.6.7., 2.1.47.; D.41.7.1. (Ulpian); D.41.3.4.26(27)., D.41.7.2.pr.–1. (Paul); D.41.7.5.1. (Pomponius).

218 *Bracton*, f. 222, iii, 165–6 (emphasis supplied).

219 *Bracton*, f. 51b, ii, 155–6.

And elsewhere, incorporeal prescription is discussed in quite different terms as a result of laches or limitation of actions:

A servitude in the estate of a neighbour, as where one has common of pasture and the right to pasture in another's estate, is not always owed through consent and the constitutions of lords, but through the negligence and dissimulation of a neighbour, simply because of use. Such seisin derives its strength from time rather than right, and thus it will be altogether absurd for possession to remain with him [that is, the neighbour with a legal title to the land in question], though it has once been acquired by an assize, unless he shows his right.[220]

Bracton's analysis does not cohere; in different passages he can be found saying the following:

1. Continuous use of incorporeal rights may amount to a *causa* substituting for positive grant;
2. Continuous use of incorporeal rights may be a substantive condition for maintaining legally protected possession;
3. Continuous use is an evidential condition for bringing actions to defend possession;
4. Non-use for a period of time (long or short not specified) results in substantive extinction of the right by prescription; and
5. Non-use for a period of time (long or short not specified) results in procedural barring of the right by laches or limitation.

Modern Analysis of Bractonian Prescription

F. W. Maitland

Bracton's contradictory doctrines of incorporeal prescription deeply influenced English property law and left a residue of problems into modern times. Maitland in his 1895 analysis of medieval prescription law identified the prime source of confusion in the relationship between legislative limitation of proprietary actions for land and possessory rights to servitudes founded on long or immemorial use. Maitland writes:[221]

Seisin itself is protected, seisin of the incorporeal thing. We can see this best if we consider the modes in which the ownership of such a thing can be acquired. It can be acquired by inheritance; it can be acquired by conveyance, though . . . the grantee has never got full and secure ownership until he has got possession, actual exploited possession; it can also be acquired by long-continued user. Of the effects of long-continued user Bracton speaks somewhat obscurely; his romanesque terms, *usucapio* and the like, perplex his doctrine.[222] (When Bracton is speaking of this matter, it is not always easy to say whether he is dealing with the acquisition of good right or with the acquisition of protected seisin. He has a, to us, misleading habit of calling the short

[220] *Bracton*, f. 229b, iii, 185.
[221] Pollock and Maitland, *HEL*, ii, 140–1.
[222] *Bracton*, f. 51b, 52, ii, 156–8.

period which protects the disseisor against the self-help of the disseisee... 'longum tempus,' 'longum intervallum,' etc.) We must, however, draw a marked line between land and incorporeal things. Our medieval law knows no acquisitive prescription for land; all it knows is a limitation of actions. This principle seems to be implicit in the form which every demand for land by proprietary action must take. The claimant must allege that he or some ancestor of his was seised as of right; he must deduce his title from a seisin that was rightful. He must not indeed plead 'higher up' than a certain limiting period. In Bracton's day he must allege a seisin as of right on this side of Henry II.'s coronation. That date will leave him a hundred years or thereabouts. He will have to tender a champion prepared to swear to this rightful seisin, as one who either saw it, or was enjoined to bear witness of it by a dying father. Thus a limit is set to the action.[223]

Maitland here isolates three differing notions of user affecting property rights in the law of Bracton's time. First, there was the relatively short limitation period on the possessory actions by petty assize. Secondly, there is an 'evidentiary' limitation on proprietary actions, set by the formal requirement that rightful seisin should be capable of having been witnessed within the last two generations, viz. that a demandant's champion could formally, if fictitiously, swear to the existence of the controverted right by personal knowledge or else by the sacrosanct hearsay of his father. Glanvill records some ambivalence as to whether a champion who was no witness could blatantly be hired to do battle, and in 1220 it is recorded that a champion was convicted for hiring himself and lost his foot. In 1275 the Statute of Westminster I, c. 41 acknowledged the practice of hire and abolished the form of oath swearing upon one's own father's knowledge; but otherwise leaving the common-law limitation period based on a past generation's witness untouched.[224]

The preservation of the notion of direct witness through a father's sacred command supplied a human measure of title or long use, based on the possibility of direct verification without resort to hearsay evidence. Time before this point was known as 'time immemorial', in the sense of occurrences literally outside living memory.[225] This contrasts with a legislative definition of time immemorial as beyond a specified point of legal memory.

[223] Citing *Bracton*, f. 373; *Bracton's Note Book* pl. 1217, iii, 230.

[224] *Glanvill*, bk. II, c. 3, Hall (ed.), 22–6; 3 Edw. 1 (Statute of Westminster I, 1275) c. 41: 'Since it seldom happens that the demandant's champion is not forsworn in making oath that he or his father saw the seisin of his lord or ancestor and his father commanded him to *deraign*, it is provided tht the demandant's champion be not bound to swear this; but be the oath kept in all other points.' See further J. B. Thayer, *A Preliminary Treatise on Evidence at the Common Law* (London, 1898) 39–46; J. W. Salmond, 'The History of the Law of Prescription', in J. W. Salmond, *Essays in Jurisprudence and Legal History* (London, 1891) 73–120, at 81–7. The *quo warranto* controversy of the reign of Edward I echoes this point; see M. T. Clanchy, *From Memory to Written Record: England 1066–1307* (2nd edn., Oxford, 1993) 35–43.

[225] Y.B. 20 & 21 Edw. 1 (Rolls S.) 414 (1293); H. Rolle, *Un Abridgment des Plusiers Cases del Common Ley* (1688) (*Roll. Abdgt.*), ii, 268; Salmond, 'History of the Law of Prescription', 81–3; Simpson, *History of the Land Law*, 109–10.

This period of legal memory was set by the lengthy limitation times for the real or proprietary actions, introduced to replace the vagaries of customary or historical memory. The cut-off date for this period was originally set at the time of the Norman Conquest, as the ultimate historical fount of all titles. Later the time was set at Richard I's coronation. The Statute of Merton 1236 then fixed time of memory for the writ of right at the commencement of the reign of Henry II in 1154, some eighty-two years before, with a shorter limitation for mort d'ancestor and writs of entry, being the last return of King John from Ireland.

These various dates were conceived as more than simple statutory limitation periods; they were statutory definitions of what shall be taken to be time of memory at law, superseding the conception derived from the rule against hearsay. Bracton, writing perhaps in the reign of Henry III after the new limitations have been introduced, expressly states that the limitation statute is supposed to clarify the limits of direct evidence at common law:

> A writ of right, like other writs, is limited within a certain time, for it does not exceed the time of King Henry [II, that is, 1154].... The reason is because no one can prove anything beyond that time, since he cannot speak of his own sight, nor of the sight of his father, who enjoined him to be a witness if he could hear speak of it. And hence, if any one should speak of the time of King Henry the Elder, he may lose through failure of proof.[226]

In the case of a writ of entry, Bracton similarly states that the legislative limitation is to ensure that no one should exceed the time of testimony 'within their sight and hearing', again a stylized hearsay rule in the sense of not exceeding the legislative limitation.[227] Thus the second and third concepts of limitation—the period of long possession guaranteeing seisin, and the lengthy limitation period barring proprietary actions—are both described conventionally as 'time beyond which the memory of man does not run' or 'time immemorial'.[228] The much shorter novel disseisin limitation periods are distinct because of the special nature of the action, and are not part of the limitation rules regarding proof and the limits of memory.

Maitland continued his analysis: 'Mere lapse of time may serve as a shield for the tenant, but it can not serve as a sword for the demandant.'[229] Thus there was limitation of titles by the passing of time in adverse possession barring rival titles, yet no positive title by long use:

[226] *Bracton*, f. 373 a, iv, 170; see also f. 437 b, iv, 359. [227] *Bracton*, f. 318a, iv, 21–2.

[228] For the history of the limitation periods and their impact on the law of title, see further Ch. 5, below; Pollock and Maitland, *HEL*, ii, 51–2, 81, 141; Salmond, 'History of the Law of Prescription', 86–90; Simpson, *History of the Land Law*, 150–5, 267–9. At 150–1 Simpson notes: 'Around these statutes arose an extraordinarily complex body of law . . . a massive body of subtle doctrine'.

[229] Pollock and Maitland, *HEL*, ii, 141.

But further, we may doubt whether for land there is any extinctive prescription. The man who can not allege a seisin on this side of Henry II.'s day has lost every action for the land; but it does not follow that his right is extinct. Hereafter it may prove its vitality, if this man, having obtained seisin under some new and defeasible title, is 'remitted' to the oldest title he has. . . . [A]t a later time 'it is commonly said that a right can not die'[230] and this we may well believe to be an old, as well as a common, saying.[231]

The avoidance of true extinctive prescription in medieval English law may be ascribed to its feudal context. Legal and social status, as well as economic wealth, were formally determined by one's proprietary or tenurial rights within the feudal ladder; hence such rights were not readily to be extinguished by prescription.[232] By contrast, the Roman property right in land was more properly an economic or commercial right, with status being determined by another set of legal rights and doctrines; and a variety of modes of prescription were freely made available to clear titles and facilitate trade in land, without adverse affect on individual and family status.

In the sphere of incorporeal rights, which were outside or supplementary to the standard tenurial arrangements, the communal agricultural institutions of English feudal society may suggest some reasons why land could readily be affected by prescriptive servitudes at common law, again diverging sharply from the Roman system. Maitland noted that prescription proper was unavailable for land itself; but incorporeal things could be acquired by prescription or by long-continued user. Maitland's analysis of the doctrine of prescription for incorporeities repays careful attention:

In particular we may see this in the case of rights of common. There is an action by which the landowner calls upon the person who asserts such rights to prove his title, the action *Quo iure clamat communam*[233] . . . a thoroughly proprietary action. Now one of the usual answers to this action is a prescriptive claim—'I and those whom I represent have commoned here—always—from before the Norman Conquest—from time immemorial.' In most cases the Norman Conquest is mentioned. Behind the great resettlement of the land one must not go; on the other hand one can, to all seeming, be required to allege a continuous seisin ever since that remote event.[234]

This is a proprietary action; but it is fairly evident that a man can acquire a legally protected possession of an incorporeal thing on much easier terms. We put this case:- For some time past a man openly and peaceably, and as though asserting a right, has been turning his beasts out on my land; he may have been doing it for so long a time that I can no longer bring an assize against him as against one who has been disseising me of my land; still he can not assert a user that goes back nearly as far as the Conqueror's days. The question is whether this man is protected against my self-help. May I bar out his beasts from the pasture or seize them if they are there? To this

[230] *Littleton*, s. 478. [231] Pollock and Maitland, *HEL*, ii, 141.
[232] Cf. Simpson, *History of the Land Law*, 150–5.
[233] *Bracton*, f. 229b, iii, 184; *Note Book*, i, 185.
[234] Pollock and Maitland, *HEL*, ii, 142–3.

question the answer that Bracton gives is that against self-help this man is protected. My proper course is to bring against him some more or less proprietary action. Possibly ... the *Quo iure*, and then there may be a grand assize. It is very possible that this man should one day 'recover the common' in an assize and the next day be made a defendant in a proprietary action which will deprive him of the common for good and all.[235] The idea of a purely possessory protection for those who are enjoying 'incorporeal things,' but who can not yet say that those things are their own, is one that can not be easily managed. We seem to have before us a pasture right that is only half a right, an incorporeal right that exists and yet does not exist. But the lawyers of the thirteenth century made a strenuous endeavour to pursue this idea through all speculative difficulties. (We have been dealing with a case which ... Holmes[236] rightly treated as a good test of the so-called 'possession of rights,' and we believe that, if this test is applied to Bracton's age, the result is that an user which falls far short of establishing an indefeasible right obtains a possessory protection.)[237]

Maitland identified a tension in Bracton between a doctrine whereby user establishes an immediate right to protected continuing possession of servitudes and a doctrine of long user which hardens possessory rights into property rights, either by barring of rival claims or by positive constitution, the law is not entirely clear which.

J. W. Salmond

Maitland did not attempt further to resolve or explain these contending conceptions of incorporeal prescription. This gap is noteworthy, as Maitland was certainly aware of J. W. Salmond's fine essay on 'The History of the Law of Prescription' which was published in 1891.[238] Salmond there provided an analytical model of Bracton's prescription doctrine and its relationship with later medieval law. The analysis rested on three premisses: first, that prescription doctrine was based on an evidential presumption that the fact of possession was evidence of right; secondly, that conversely the fact of not possessing was evidence of absence of right; and thirdly that long possession (or non-possession) increased the power of these evidential presumptions so that they eventually became conclusive, or immune to rebuttal by direct contrary evidence. An irrebuttable presumption of right led to direct prescription; a rebuttable presumption made for indirect prescription, as the fact of long possession was then taken as evidence of some other disprovable fact forming the true legal root of the title or protected seisin. At English law there was no positive prescription for corporeal things; instead one pleaded descent of title from the rightful seisin of an ancestor stretching back to

[235] *Bracton*, f. 230, iii, 185 ff.; f. 52b, ii, 158.

[236] O. W. Holmes Jr., *The Common Law* (Boston, Mass., 1881; M. De Howe (ed.), Boston, Mass., 1963) 241, 384.

[237] Pollock and Maitland, *HEL*, ii, 142–3.

[238] See e.g. citation of Salmond, 'History of the Law of Prescription', in Pollock and Maitland, *HEL*, ii, at 141 n. 4.

beyond the current limitation period. The reason for this was in part because a line of protected seisins of land could readily be given direct proof, rendering presumptions from the fact of long possession unnecessary; but a deeper reason was that title to land was 'of common right', a title taking effect by operation of the general custom of the common law. By contrast, most (not all) incorporeal rights, including many contractual agreements, were conceived of as being 'against common right'. These were 'specialties' or rights conferred under private law created by deed, prescription, or custom.[239] Prescription proper was a specialty akin to a customary right for particular individuals, proved by usage from time immemorial. Prescription proper thus was not a principle of limitation protecting seisin, but a branch of custom law.

Salmond explained how the theory of prescriptions as specialties or singular customs disappeared from the modern law, probably in the seventeenth century:

A custom continues to be regarded as embodying a rule of special law, superseding in its particular sphere the common law. For example, when the [owner of an estate] claimed a right of way by reason of immemorial user of it by him and his ancestors, he

[239] Charters relating to warranty of title make a separate subject; see J. G. H. Hudson, *Land, Law, and Lordship in Anglo-Norman England* (Oxford, 1994) 57, 70–77; P. R. Hyams, 'The Charter as a Source for the Early Common Law' (1991) 12 Journal of Legal History 173. A specialty in its widest meaning was a local or private law outside and derogating from the common law; only later did specialty come to connote a formal obligation such as a debt or covenant embodied in a deed. This is touched upon by *Glanvill's* treatment of covenant and charter (bk. X, Hall (ed.), 116–32, esp. at 124, 132), which states that 'it is not the custom for the court of the lord king to protect or warrant private agreements of this kind concerning the giving or receiving of things... nor does it even concern itself with such contracts as can be considered to be like private agreements'. Ibbetson, *Law of Obligations*, 17–23, in a close reading of *Glanvill* emphasizes the procedural or probative aspect of specialty. Recent scholarship on specialty has focused chiefly on explaining how deed requirements came to be applied to the action of covenant around 1300, whether through application of civilian formality requirements by analogy to lease covenants (e.g. D. J. Ibbetson, 'Words and Deeds: The Action of Covenant in the Reign of Edward I' (1986) 4 Law and History Review 71 and *Law of Obligations*, 24–30); or as a graft from county court procedure (R. C. Palmer, *The County Courts of Medieval England, 1150–1350* (Princeton, NJ, 1982) 198–215, and 'Covenant, Justicies Writs, and Reasonable Showings' (1987) 31 American Journal of Legal History 97; cf. J. S. Beckerman, 'Procedural Innovation and Institutional Change in Medieval English Manorial Courts' (1992) 10 Law and History Review 197, 219–26); or as an apt method of proof of private will or intention to be bound in conscience (J. Barton, 'The Medieval Contract', in J. Barton (ed.), *Towards a General Law of Contract* (Berlin, 1990), 15–37; [P. Philbin], 'Proving the Will of Another: The Specialty Requirement in Covenant' (1992) 105 Harvard Law Review 2001). Palmer, *English Law in the Age of the Black Death*, 64–5, suggests that mid-fourteenth-century use of a specialty covenant was generally non-litigious, and amounted to a formal method to put into effect the final concord for land transactions. This analysis returns specialty transactions to their earliest character as creators of private or special law, privilege, or jurisdiction. Elements of a substantive view of specialty are discussed further in A. W. B. Simpson, *A History of the Common Law of Contract: The Rise of the Action of Assumpsit* (Oxford, 1975) 15–25; Palmer, *County Courts of Medieval England*, 263–96; J. Biancalana, 'Medieval County Courts: A Review Essay' (1983) 52 University of Cincinnati Law Review 994, 1015–16 and 'Actions of Covenant 1200–1330'.

was according to the original theory, setting up and relying upon a rule of special law, which *ipso jure* conferred upon him the right claimed; just as if he had relied on a private Act of Parliament conferring the right upon him. But, according to the modern theory, he is regarded as setting up, not a rule of law, but a title (to wit, that of long possession), which gives him the right at common law. According to the modern theory, there exists a rule of common law, to the effect that the immemorial possessor of an easement acquires a right thereto, and a claimant, in proving immemorial possession, is regarded as bringing himself within the supposed rule. The radical distinction that thus came to be recognised between prescription and custom has been well expressed in the following words: 'Prescription seems to us to be the making of a right; custom the making of a law.... Prescription is creative of a right which gets its sanction from law; custom is creative of a law which gives its sanction to rights.'[240]

The change of theory of prescription was a natural result of their quality of singularity: most laws were general, conferring rights on a claimant who could show facts bringing himself within a norm-creating rule; it was anomalous to have laws directly conferring rights on a particular individual; hence 'by a natural process of assimilation to the ordinary form, immemorial user came to be regarded as a title bringing the claimant within a supposed rule of the common law'. The same change overtook the concept of contract as a specialty, as Salmond explains: 'We no longer regard a special agreement as the source of a rule of special law excluding the common law. To say that a rent charge is against common right, has now no real meaning for us. We have come to regard agreements as titles operating at common law.'[241]

This abandonment of specialties as a category of analysis in modern law helped conceal the reasons for a fundamental rule of common-law prescription: that there cannot be a title to corporeal things made by prescription, and that only incorporeal hereditaments are things claimable by prescription. We have noticed that this rule of English law contrasts with Roman and civil law where the reverse rule held, that is, that incorporeities being things incapable of apparent possession cannot be claimed by positive prescription or *usucapio*. Salmond's explanation for the contrary English rule was as follows:

Now, it is true, as a matter of fact, that the division between things claimable by prescription and things not so claimable, is largely coincident with that between incorporeal and corporeal hereditaments. As a matter of principle, however, these divisions have nothing to do with each other. The true rule on this point is that matters against common right are claimable by prescription, while matters of common right are not so claimable. 'Every prescription is against common right.'[242]

[240] Salmond, 'History of the Law of Prescription', 97, quoting J. H. B. Browne, *The Law of Usages and Customs* (London, 1875) 14; see also Pollock and Maitland, *HEL*, i, 177–8.

[241] Salmond, 'History of the Law of Prescription', 98.

[242] *Robert Gray's Case* (1560) 8 Co. Rep. 125b; 77 E.R. 663, 664.

This rule follows directly from the origin of prescription as already set forth. If a right is recognised by the common law, it cannot be regarded as also conferred by an inconsistent special law, and, therefore, cannot be claimed by either of those titles that originated as sources of special law, *i.e.* by grant or by prescription. If, on the other hand, a right is not recognised by the common law, if it is *contra jus commune*, it must be claimed by special law, that is, either under a custom, or by the titles of grant or prescription.[243]

This doctrine explains Coke's dictum: 'a custome cannot be alledged generally within the kingdome of *England*, for that is common law.'[244]

In the early forms of action for property, the law required that seisin of the claimant or his ancestor at some recent time be shown, as the basis of a claim at petty assize and as an element of a claim of right in a higher action for proprietary title. Bracton tended to confuse this lesser requirement of proof of recent possession with the greater requirement of seisin since time immemorial (more accurately *quasi*-seisin), where a title to an incorporeal thing was claimed by prescription against common right.[245] Bracton really had no discrete concept of title by positive prescription whatsoever, only concepts of long possession as bestowing a protected seisin, as Salmond writes:

Bracton tells us, indeed, that rights of common and other servitudes may be acquired by long possession. He gives us no indication . . . as to how long this possession requires to be, or any detailed information as to this branch of the law. . . . [T]o him prescription was merely a part of that chaos of special customs into which it was no business of his to introduce order. At first sight, however, Bracton may be thought to say very much more about positive prescription then he really does. He speaks frequently about the effect of lapse of time in creating rights, but what he is really treating of is the acquisition, not of ownership, but of possession. By what means possession or seisin was lost and gained, was in the early law of property an extremely important subject. It was the rule that possession could be retained *animo solo*; until, therefore, an ejected possessor had actually or constructively acquiesced in his ejectment, he was not regarded by law as having lost possession, nor was the ejector regarded as having gained it. If, however, the person ejected delayed re-entering upon the ejector for a certain period, he was presumed by the law to have acquiesced in his ejectment. He, therefore, lost possession, and the ejector gained it, and could be removed only by action, *per breve et judicium*. These principles applied not only to the possession of corporeal things, but also to the quasi-possession or user of incorporeal things.[246]

Bracton's discussion of prescription for incorporeal things is not, then, truly about acquisition of a title by long use, but about acquisition of seisin. The proper analogy is not with *usucapio*, but with common-law seisin of corporeal things, as Bracton writes:

243 Salmond, 'History of the Law of Prescription', 98–9.

244 Co. Litt. 110b; cf. H. E. Salt, 'The Local Ambit of a Custom', in G. G. Alexander (ed.), *Cambridge Legal Essays* (Cambridge, 1926) 279, 282–4.

245 Salmond, 'History of the Law of Prescription', 107–8.

246 Ibid.

And when a long and peaceable and continuous possession has intervened, they (the possessors) begin to possess against all the world, and to have a freehold, so much so that they cannot be ejected without a writ and a judgment, for just as time is a mode of creating and destroying an obligation, so it is a mode of acquiring possession.

. . .

It has been discussed in what way a person acquires possession of a corporeal thing by time without delivery, with or without use; now we must discuss in what way possession of an incorporeal thing is acquired, as possession of a right, such as a servitude, by sufferance (which is equivalent to consent) and long and peaceful enjoyment, without grant or express consent. For sufferance is taken for consent, and the possession of a right is acquired through use, as if the lord of the property, having a free estate, has, through sufferance, when present and cognisant of the fact, allowed his neighbours to enjoy on his estate a servitude . . . for a long time peaceably and without interruption, from such an enjoyment and sufferance there is a presumption of consent and of willingness, and so possession is acquired by the lapse of time, so that any one so using it cannot be ejected without a writ and a judgment.[247]

Bracton's concept of *longa et continua possessio* was extremely variable: it could be barely four days if the disseisee was present and took no action to make re-entry; it could range up to three years if the disseisee was absent on pilgrimage to the Holy Land. Upon lapse of this period, there must be resort to a petty assize for novel disseisin or a higher action to recover lost possession: the lapse of time gives the disseisor a protected seisin in his turn.

Bracton and the early authorities have very little to say about the requisite long user for acquiring protected possession of an incorporeal thing; for Bracton it was probably a period of time indicating acquiescence in the taking, a period measured according to the discretion of the court. In the Year Book of Edward I, it is stated that ten years' enjoyment suffices to create a legally-protected possession of a profit: 'If she had been seised of that profit for ten years, think you that she were disturbed she would not have the Novel Disseisin? She certainly would.'[248] When the possessory actions become more droitural in character, so that a title can be pleaded in bar to an action, 'this whole branch of the law falls into desuetude'.[249] Later interpreters, working with an entirely different set of concepts, confuse the protection of possession upon lapse of time, as found in Bracton and the Year Books, with the vesting of title by long user on a Roman model of *usucapio*.[250] On this matter, Salmond concludes:

The rules found in Bracton, therefore, as to the acquisition of rights by lapse of time, do not refer to prescription in the sense in which the term is understood in English

[247] *Bracton*, f. 52a, iii, 156–7.

[248] Y.B. 21 & 22 Edw. 1. 422 (1294); and see Statute of Westminster II (1285), 13 Edw. 1., c. 46 (commons).

[249] Salmond, 'History of the Law of Prescription', 110.

[250] E.g. K. E. Digby, *An Introduction to the History of the Law of Real Property with Original Authorities* (1st edn., London, 1875) 149.

law. They constitute part of the ancient law of possession, and are quite unconnected with those rules as to immemorial user whose history we have been considering.[251]

The confusion within medieval doctrines of prescription is noted in Littleton's *Tenures* (1481, written in the 1450s), in the discussion there of custom as a source of rights:

And note that no custom is to be allowed, but such custom as hath been used by title of prescription, that is to say, from time out of mind. But divers opinions have been of time out of mind, &c., and of title of prescription, which is all one in the law. For some have said, that time out of mind should be said from time of limitation in a writ of right; that is to say, from the time of King Richard the First after the Conquest, as is given by the statute of Westminster the First.... And in so much that it is given by the said statute, that in a writ of right none shall be heard to demand of the seisin of his ancestors of longer time than of the time of King Richard aforesaid, therefore this is proved, that continuance of possession, or other customs and usages used from the same time [Littleton: *puis le dit temps*; Coke's translation gives 'after the same time'], is the title of prescription, &c. And this is certain. And others have said, that well and truth it is, that seisin and continuance from [Coke: 'after'] the limitation, &c., is a title of prescription, as is aforesaid, and by the cause aforesaid. But they have said, that there is also another title of prescription, that was at the common law before any statute of limitation of writs, &c., and that it was, where a custom, or usage, or other thing, hath been used, for time whereof the mind of man runneth not to the contrary. And they have said, that this is proved by the pleading, where a man will plead a title of prescription of custom. He shall say, that such custom hath been used from time whereof the mind of man runneth not to the contrary, that is as much to say, when such a matter is pleaded, that no man then alive hath heard any proof of the contrary; nor hath no knowledge of the contrary; and insomuch that such title of prescription was at the common law, and not put out by statute, *ergo*, it abideth as it was at the common law.... [252]

If the nature of prescription was obscure to Littleton in the fifteenth century, then the relationship between prescription and possession as sources of incorporeal rights was only further complicated when parliaments and courts recast the limitation periods for real actions from the sixteenth century onwards. This part of the story will be examined later.

THE LATER MEDIEVAL LAW: FROM BRACTON TO COKE

The Exclusion of Romanism from Legal Reasoning

Between Bracton and Coke the law of water and land use became still more technical and abstruse. Legal analysis was expressed almost entirely in terms

[251] Salmond, 'History of the Law of Prescription', 110.

[252] T. Littleton, *The Tenures* s. 170, translation (following *Co.Litt.*) from E. Wambaugh, *Littleton's Tenures in English* (Washington, DC, 1903) 81–2.

of debate over the correct selection of writ or of words of pleading.[253] Much of the law lies in manuscript form outside the Year Books and hence had a lesser influence on later law-makers.[254]

One reason for the rebarbative technicality of Year Book-era law may be the decline of Romanism as a source of lucid structuring ideas. The counters of the late-medieval Court of Common Pleas had little use for Roman jurisprudence in the public exercise of their craft; and there was professional jealousy towards the competing conciliar and ecclesiastical courts that explicitly used civilian and canon law principles. In addition to these rivalries, the period after 1500 saw a general rise of nationalism in legal and political thought in England, joining a European trend as national schools of law turned away from the idea of a universal Continental system of Roman and Canonist jurisprudence and began a humanist project of rationalizing local custom.[255] In this intellectual climate Roman influence was not excluded from English law: it might come from Bracton[256] or else from Canonists, Glossators, and Commentators.[257] Moreover, law-makers could not ignore

[253] *Rickhill* v. *Two Parsons of Bromaye* (1400) Y.B. Mich. 2 Hen. 4, f. 11, pl. 48; in Fifoot, *History and Sources*, 83–4, and the text accompanying nn. 282–286 below; *Prior of Southwark's case* (1498) Y.B. Trin. 13 Hen. 7, f. 26, pl. 4, S.C.; *Prior of Christ Church, Canterbury* v. *Hore* (C.P., Trin. 1493) CP40/922, m.244d, in *Reports of Cases by John Caryll Vol. 1*, 175–7; *Sly* v. *Mordant* (c.1580) 1 Leon. 247; 74 E.R. 225 (K.B.); *Gile's Case* (1586) Godb. 58; 78 E.R. 36 (K.B.); *Luttrel's Case* (1601) 4 Co. Rep. 84b; 76 E.R. 1063 (K.B.).

[254] Baker, 'Introduction' to *Spelman's Reports Vol. 2*, 220–36.

[255] The literature on the Reception and the reactive rise of national schools of jurisprudence is immense; for synoptic treatments see H. D. Hazeltine, 'The Renaissance and the Laws of Europe', in Alexander (ed.), *Cambridge Legal Essays*, 139–71; J. Q. Whitman, *The Legacy of Roman Law in the German Romantic Era: Historical Vision and Legal Change* (Princeton, NJ, 1990) and 'Why Did the Revolutionary Lawyers Confuse Custom and Reason?' (1991) 58 University of Chicago Law Review 1321; P. Stein, *Roman Law in European History* (Cambridge, 1999); T. G. Watkin, *An Historical Introduction to Modern Civil Law* (Aldershot, 1999) 81–149. The English dimension is examined in J. W. Cairns, 'Blackstone, An English Institutist: Legal Literature and the Rise of the Nation State' (1984) 4 Oxford Journal of Legal Studies 318; D. J. Seipp, 'The Structure of English Common Law in the Seventeenth Century', in W. M. Gordon and T. D. Fergus (eds.), *Legal History in the Making* (London, 1989) 61–83; Seipp, 'Reception of Roman and Civil Law'.

[256] Baker, *Introduction to English Legal History*, 27–9; Barton, *Roman Law in England*, 13–25, 95–7; C. Güterbock, *Bracton and His Relation to English Law: A Contribution to the History of the Roman Law in the Middle Ages* (Berlin, 1862, B. Coxe (trans.), Philadelphia, Penn., 1866); D. T. Oliver, 'Roman Law in Modern Cases in English Courts', in Alexander (ed.), *Cambridge Legal Essays*, 243; T. F. T. Plucknett, 'The Relations Between Roman Law and English Common Law Down to the Sixteenth Century: A General Survey' (1939) 3 University of Toronto Law Journal 24, 351; F. Pringsheim, 'The Inner Relationship Between English and Roman Law' (1933–5) 5 Cambridge Law Journal 347; Seipp, 'Bracton'; D. E. C. Yale, '"Of No Mean Authority": Some Later Uses of Bracton', in M. S. Arnold, T. A. Green, S. A. Scully, and S. D. White (eds.), *On the Laws and Customs of England* (Chapel Hill, NC, 1981) 383.

[257] And later, from the great natural-law jurists who transformed Roman ideas into a new philosophical cast: Hazeltine, 'Renaissance and the Laws of Europe', 151 ff.; Stein, *Roman Law in European History*, 1–8 and *Roman Law and English Jurisprudence Yesterday and Today* (Cambridge, 1969); R. H. Helmholz, 'Continental Law and Common Law: Historical Strangers or Companions?' [1990] Duke Law Journal 1207; H. F. Jolowicz, 'Some English Civilians' (1949) 2 Current Legal Problems 139; D. J. Ibbetson, 'Natural Law and Common Law' (2001) 5 Edinburgh Law Review 4.

the existence of well-developed Roman precedents as they developed areas such as bailment, trespass, and covenant.[258] Often the borrowing was overt; for example Callis could write in 1622: 'In my conceit the civil law makes prettier and neater distinctions of these [the property in running waters] than our common law doth; for there it is said, That *naturali ratione quaedam sunt communia ut aer, aqua profluens, mare et littora maris* (the things which are by reason of nature everybody's are air, flowing water, the sea, and the sea-shore).'[259] An important later borrowing was Holt CJ's use of Roman civil fault standards in *Coggs* v. *Barnard* in 1703.[260] It was not unusual, however, for common lawyers to borrow directly from the civilians without openly avowing their intellectual debts.

The feudal land law which dominated the legal world of Littleton and Coke had an ambivalent relationship with Roman models.[261] There is little explicit Roman doctrine or Institutionist arrangement in Coke's *Institutes*, the most influential common law text until well after the time of Blackstone. Yet Coke and his contemporaries accepted Bracton with all its inherent Romanism as good common-law authority.[262] The late-medieval common-lawyers were certainly aware of the Roman models and made use of them[263] but were shy to admit their influence for ideological reasons. Publicly they associated a purely English common law with the cause of Parliamentary rule and constitutional monarchy, and they denigrated Roman law for its affinity with the princely and bureaucratic absolutism of Europe.[264] Natural-law traditions of resistance to authority and sacrosanct individual rights were

[258] Ibbetson, *Law of Obligations*, 159, 164–8; J. S. Beckerman, 'Adding Insult to *Inuria*: Affronts to Honor and the Origins of Trespass', in Arnold, Green, Scully, and White (eds.), *Laws and Customs of England*, 159. The influence of the Lex Aquilia on early modern English tort doctrine is particularly striking.

[259] *The Reading of Robert Callis upon the Statute of Sewers, 23 Hen. VIII c. 5* (1622) 78–9; (4th edn. by W. J. Broderip, London, 1824) 97. The citation is from Justinian's *Institutes* and *Digest*; see e.g. Inst.2.1.1.; D.1.8.2.pr., 1. (Marcian); D.1.8.2., 4.–6. (Marcian); D.1.8.1., 5. (Gaius); D.41.1.14.–15. (Neratius), D.41.1.50. (Pomponius); D.43.7.1. (Ulpian); D.43.8.1. (Paul), D.43.8.2. (Ulpian), D.43.8.3. (Celsus), D.43.8.4. (Scaevola), D.43.8.5. (Paul), D.43.8.6. (Julian), D.43.8.7. (Ulpian); D.43.12.1. (Ulpian); D.43.12.3. (Paul); D.43.13.1.; D.43.14.1.; D.43.15.1. (Ulpian).

[260] See D. J. Ibbetson, '"The Law of Business Rome": Foundations of the Anglo-American Tort of Negligence' [1999] Current Legal Problems 74; J. Getzler, 'Duty of Care', in P. B. H. Birks and A. Pretto (eds.), *Breach of Trust* (Oxford, 2002) 41–74; M. Graziadei, 'Changing Images of the Law in XIX Century English Legal Thought (The Continental Impulse)', in M. Reimann (ed.), *The Reception of Continental Ideas in the Common Law World 1820–1920* (Berlin, 1993) 115, 135–41.

[261] Sir Edward Coke, *The First Part of the Institutes of the Laws of England, or, A Commentary on Littleton* (F. Hargrave and C. Butler (eds.), 19th edn., London, 1832) (*Co. Litt.*).

[262] Yale, 'Later Uses of Bracton', 383.

[263] Helmholz, 'Continental Law and Common Law', 1214–15; D. J. Ibbetson, 'Common Law and *Ius Commune*' (Selden Society Lecture, 2001).

[264] H. F. Jolowicz, 'Political Implications of Roman Law' (1947) 22 Tulane Law Review 62; J. C. A. Pocock, *The Ancient Constitution and the Feudal Law* (Cambridge, 1957, 2nd edn., 1987) 3–29.

associated with the common law, which was opposed to the centralized institutions of prerogative and church courts. Such political antipathies, together with the strong educational traditions of the Inns of Court,[265] help to account for the absence of any overt adoption of Roman law in Tudor and Stuart England comparable to the Reception in Continental countries.

The Rise of the Action on the Case for Nuisance

The most significant doctrinal development of English land-use law after Bracton was the expansion of the action of trespass on the case (commonly contracted to 'action on the case') as the practical procedure for remedying torts to land. The turn to personal remedies helped produce a useful nuisance action for litigants, but remedy-driven reform also obscured the nature of use-rights attached to land possession. It is hard to see any significant conceptual advance, beyond the Romanist analysis of rights given in Bracton, until the end of the sixteenth century or later. Simpson notes that in the late-medieval period, the common law barely assimilated Bracton's work: '[t]he distinction between natural rights, local customary rights, and easements was not at all clearly formulated.... Even in Coke's time the subject of easements was only scantily explored, and it is hardly mentioned in Coke's commentary on Littleton.'[266]

The genealogy of the action on the case for nuisance, the modern action for remedying injury to proprietary incidents, lay (like much of the common law) in the king's jurisdiction to remedy wrongs and so keep the peace: that is, to suppress 'trespasses' in the broadest sense of wrongdoing. The development of the action on the case as a catch-all remedy may be traced from three sources within the general trespassory jurisdiction. First, the action on the case procedure was a convenient substitute for the assize of nuisance, the concomitant writ to the novel disseisin jurisdiction policing the possession of land. Secondly, the action on the case developed as a variation of pleading and procedure in standard actions for trespass *vi et armis* and *quare clausum fregit*, or forcible and invasive trespasses. Thirdly, the action on the case provided a means of giving private redress for special damage caused by common nuisances injurious to the public, where such nuisances were subject to administrative or criminal remedies through presentment and indictment before the royal courts. The assize of nuisance precursor has been discussed; we next turn to the other main sources, trespass and common nuisance.

[265] F. W. Maitland, *English Law and the Renaissance* (Cambridge, 1901); J. H. Baker, *The Legal Profession and The Common Law. Historical Essays* (London, 1986) 7–24, 45–124, 461–76 and 'The Third University of England: The Inns of Court and the Common-Law Tradition' (Selden Society lecture, 1990); Brand, *Making of the Common Law*, 1–20, 57–76, 77–102.

[266] Simpson, *History of Common Law of Contract*, 114–15.

Trespass to Land and Trespass on the Case for Nuisance

The 'private' or 'personal' lineage of trespass on the case through general or common trespass begins in the fourteenth century.[267] Plaintiffs began to bring common trespass actions (pleading force or invasion) for nuisances which formally fell outside the assize remedy—for example, nuisances causing harm independent of freehold ownership; or executed nuisances where damage had been caused but the interference had been abated; or other lesser nuisances which hitherto had been the province of feudal or local courts. Common-law jurisdiction could be invoked by a general trespass writ, which fictitiously alleged the use of force and arms by the defendant even where he had interfered with the plaintiff's interests without any 'direct' physical invasion or proximity, for example through acts performed outside the plaintiff's land; or through non-feasance or dereliction of duty. Assize of nuisance, by contrast, strictly lay only for misfeasance, on the analogy of novel disseisin.[268] The defence of rights to watercourses featured prominently in these developments.[269] The action on the case expanded to absorb these nuisance actions masquerading as trespasses, as the formal requirement of declaring forcible injury was discarded, and parties were allowed to plead their 'case'—the facts of damage grounding a claim for remedy, stated for the

[267] On the development of trespass on the case from general trespass see Maitland, *Forms of Action*, 65–72; S. F. C. Milsom, 'Not Doing is No Trespass: A View of the Boundaries of Case', in *Studies*, 91, and 'Trespass from Henry III to Edward III', in *Studies*, 1; Baker, 'Introduction' to *Spelman's Reports Vol. 2*, ch. VII, 220–55; Baker and Milsom, *Sources of English Legal History*, 297–357, 581–622; Kiralfy, *Action on the Case*, 2–17, 19–54; and Fifoot, *History and Sources*, 44–101; H. G. Richardson and G. O. Sayles, 'The Writ of Trespass' (Selden Society, lx, 1941) ch. VIII, pp. cviii–cxxxiv; *Year Books of Richard II: 6 Richard II* (ed. S. E. Thorne, introd. by C. Donahue Jr., Ames Foundation, Cambridge, Mass., 1996), 42–6, 55–6, 149–52; Palmer, *English Law in the Age of the Black Death*, 217–93; Ibbetson, *Law of Obligations*, 39–70, 95–125, 153–68.

[268] *Rickhill* v. *Two Parsons of Bromaye* (1400) Y.B. Mich. 2 Hen. 4, f. 11, pl. 48, below; Y.B. Mich. 11 Hen. 4 f. 25 pl. 48; Y.B. Trin. 11 Hen. 4 f. 82 pl. 28; Bacon, 'Reading at Serjeant's Inn' (1602), in Baker and Milsom, *Sources of English Legal History*, 431, 434; see further Kiralfy, *Action on the Case*, 56; C. Viner, *General Abridgement of Law and Equity* 23 vols. (Aldershot, 1741–53; 2nd edn., 1794) (*Viner's Abdgt.*) XVI, 25–47 ('Nusance'); *Select Cases of Trespass from the King's Courts 1307–1399 Vol. I* (M. S. Arnold (ed.), Selden Society, c, 1984) pp. lxxii–lxxiii.

[269] Defendants tried to block the expansion of trespass remedies to cover nuisances, e.g. *Thomas de Lowth* v. *Abbot of Lesnes* (1317), ibid., 348, case 31.1, where the pleading of trespass was challenged because polluting and blocking of a watercourse had taken place on the defendant's land; Arnold (ed.), *Select Cases of Trespass Vol. I*, lxx–lxxxiii, 348–65, presents numerous fourteenth-century cases where trespass writs are seemingly accepted as apt means to remedy interferences to watercourses causing flooding, pollution, and interruption of domestic, farm, and mill water supplies; note especially cases dealing with economic harm to mill operations caused by water diversion: *Prior of Hatfield Peverel* v. *Roger de Willingdale* (1364), ibid., 352–3, case 32.2, and *John Little* v. *Andrew atte Brooke* (1380) ibid., 353–4, case 32.3; *Abbott of Beeleigh* v. *Thomas de Maldon (Nos. 1/2)* (1386) ibid., 358–60, cases 32.5/6. See generally Ibbetson, *Law of Obligations*, 98–103; Baker, 'Introduction' to *Spelman's Reports Vol. 2*, 232–4, especially cases listed at 234, nn. 1, 3; Baker, *Introduction to English Legal History*, 424–6; Kiralfy, *Action on the Case*, 56–60; *Viner's Abdgt.*, xvi, 25–8, 36; xxii, 525–8.

attention of a local jury.[270] Henceforth, specification in a *per quod* clause of some damage or loss of profit, caused by a stated wrongful act by the defendant inflicting harm upon the plaintiff or his property, sufficed to bring an action in case, provided that no other real or assize remedy for the special loss was available.[271]

The emergence of the action on the case in the fourteenth century allowed gradual exclusion of the fictitious *vi et armis* action as an alternative tort unnecessarily complementing nuisance. A case of 1402 is reported by Brooke stating: 'If a man *stops a water-course in his own soil to the nusance of his* [the plaintiff's] *franktenement*, he to whom the nusance is done shall not have *trespass vi & armis* of the act done in his [the defendant's] own franktenement.'[272] The eventual position was that harmful acts outside the plaintiff's land could be brought either by assize of nuisance or by the action on the case for nuisance, as was appropriate. Fictitious trespass *vi et armis*, where the wrongful act is patently done without forcible invasion, was thus superseded.[273] In later medieval law, where nuisance actions are brought in the form of 'trespass' *simpliciter*, this is likely to be trespass on the case, with the nomen of trespass used in the generic sense of a damages action for a wrong, to distinguish it from assize remedies.[274]

Action on the case and nuisance were separated above all by the requirement that where the plaintiff, P, had a freehold estate the assize action for nuisance against a defendant, D, was mandatory.[275] Conversely where P did not have a freehold estate, the action on the case was the only available remedy for nuisances to the tenement. Thus Fitzherbert: 'And if a man levy a nusance unto the house of another who hath therein an estate but for term of years, then he shall not have an assize of nusance, but an action upon the case

[270] Kiralfy, *Action on the Case*, 2. It is unlikely that the desire to avoid wager of law was a strong factor in the turn to action on the case. The original assize of nuisance was a jury action as a petty assize. In the trespass jurisdiction the royal courts tended in any event to refuse wager of law in cases involving matters of common knowledge, including matters touching on land or wrong-doing; nuisance as a subset of trespass partook of both. Especially before 1300 the compurgation procedures may have been employed within the trespassory and nuisance jurisdictions of the manorial courts, but this does not affect the major point. Macnair, 'Vicinage' at 552, observes that by the fourteenth century the theory was emerges that [w]ager of law is only appropriate to secret transactions'; see also Milsom, 'Sale of Goods in the Fifteenth Century', in *Studies*, 105 at 113–14.

[271] Kiralfy, *Action on the Case*, 12–14, 61.

[272] Br. Trespass, pl. 78 cites 3 H. 4. 5; *Viner's Abdgt.*, xxii, 525, entry B.1; and see Y.B. 21 Lib. Ass. f. 74 pl. 1 at f. 75; Y.B. Mich. 48 Edw. 3 f. 27 pl. 13 (1375). Cf. Case 83, 122–3; C.R.Roll 570/ m.69d (Mich. 1358), in *Select Cases in the Court of King's Bench Vol. 7* (G. O. Sayles (ed.), Selden Society, lxxxviii, 1971) Case 22, 141–4 (action for trespass, claiming that abatement of a nuisance involving demolition of weir was collusive and itself a trespass; here trespass is the form of action for the defence).

[273] Kiralfy, *Action on the Case*, 57–8; Ibbetson, *Law of Obligations*, 102–3.

[274] Ibid., 16.

[275] See e.g. *Hornedon* v. *Paine* Trin. 15 Eliz.; *Viner's Abdgt.*, xxii, 525 entry B.2 in marg.; Kiralfy, *Action on the Case*, 56.

against him, because he hath no freehold: but yet it seemeth, he may enter and abate the nusance.'[276] Sir John Port's notes on debates at the Inner Temple *c.*1494 record:

If something is put up which is a nuisance to the person, but not to the freehold, no assize of nuisance lies on that account, but an action on the case.

Thus a dunghill causing a stink would be an offence to the person only, unless it was left so long as to harm the freehold, or if it leaked into a well. Port continues:

[*Vavasour*] In an assize of nuisance the person who is the freehold tenant of the land where the nuisance is committed must be named, for even if a stranger creates a nuisance the assize must still be brought against the stranger and the freehold tenant. Likewise if tenant for years causes a nuisance. If, however, a nuisance is caused to the tenant for years, he shall not have an assize of nuisance but an action on the case; whereas the freeholder in that case shall have an assize of nuisance and recover no damages.[277]

Freeholder plaintiffs began to evade the rules for choice of action by pleading colourably that their damage was within the categories of the action on the case, even where a freehold assize remedy for nuisance was available. The action on the case was desired by parties in order to win the benefit of speedy jury trial, and then to have the convenient, readily executed remedy of trespassory damages including consequential loss. Common examples were actions on the case brought by mill owners for lost profits caused by diversion of water from their freehold mills by neighbours.[278] The emphasis placed by the pleadings on special damage to a possessor's enjoyment of land served to give such actions on the case the necessary 'personal' character distinguishing it from the 'proprietary' assizes.[279] Trespass on the case for nuisance in this form emerged by the end of the fifteenth century as the most important and popular action for defending water rights[280] and other incidents of landed property.[281]

In the important 1400 case of *Rickhill* v. *Two Parsons of Bromaye*[282] the plaintiffs (who numbered two judges and a recorder—no ignorance of the law here) sued by writ of trespass for disturbance of a way across D's land, the title of which was by prescription from time immemorial in a *que estate*. The court discussed whether the trespass writ should have been laid *contra pacem* or *sur*

276 Fitzherbert, *N.B.* 185.

277 Vavasour J in moot, Entry on 'Nusance', in *Notebook of Sir John Port*, Note 64, c.1494, 117–18, and Baker and Milsom, *Sources of English Legal History*, 583–4.

278 *Viner's Abdgt.*, xvi, 26–34.

279 On the primacy of damage in the action on the case see Kiralfy, *Action on the Case*, 12–14.

280 Baker, *Introduction to English Legal History*, 425–6.

281 See Fifoot, *History and Sources*, 93–7.

282 Y.B. Mich. 2 Hen. 4, f. 11, pl. 48 (1400); in Fifoot, *History and Sources*, 83 and Baker and Milsom, *Sources of English Legal History*, 581.

nostre case, with argument given that a non-forceful interference with a way properly lay in trespass on the case. Thirning CJ then queried whether a general trespass action was appropriate for a 'trespass' (that is, a wrong) to 'something incident or pertaining to freehold'. Markham J elaborated:

> If a man puts up a hedge or ditch across my way, I shall have an assize of nuisance for it, and not this writ. . . . If you have common of pasture on my land, and I cause all my land to be ploughed up so that your beasts cannot be pastured, shall you there have a good writ of trespass upon your case (*matier*)? (As if to say, no.). But I know full well that you shall have a good assize. And it may well be that the way which you claim, and in which you allege the nuisance, is not so advantageous to you as it was, by reason of such ploughing; but it seems to me that such an action as this is not maintainable for it.[283]

The reply from Rede, counsel for P, used the example of water rights: 'If a watercourse runs to your mill, and I make part of this water to take another course into my own soil so that your mill—which used to grind ten [MSS. two] quarters a day—will no longer grind one quarter a day, you shall have such a writ.'[284] Markham J rejected the argument: 'You shall not [have the trespass on the case writ]; but you shall have the assize. Likewise, if you have reasonable estovers in my wood, and I fell all the timber so that you cannot have them, you shall have the assize and no other remedy.'[285] P's writ of trespass was accordingly abated, as the assize of nuisance could have been brought. Beneath the technicality of the argument, the substantive point is a conventional one: that interferences with a freehold not involving physical invasion or force are appropriate for the more 'proprietary' assize of nuisance rather than the 'personal' trespass action of case, because the proper focus here is the attack on enjoyment of integral possession of the freehold, and not harm to economic rights or infliction of economic loss caused by the wrongful act. The interference with the freehold possession may cause the economic loss, but the medieval law insisted on a direct, proprietary remedy of the interference with freehold use-rights; it did not allow a personal damages action to be brought solely for loss of income-rights from the property, without the larger freehold action. The point was made again in later fifteenth century cases, such as the *Prior of St. Nedeport's Case* of 1443,[286] where the owner of an existing ancient mill sued in trespass on the case for losses caused by erection of a new mill reducing his business and profits. The court seems to acknowledge that an ancient claim to mill suit was actionable, but could not decide whether the interference was an attack on

[283] Ibid., 582; Fifoot, *History and Sources*, 84.

[284] Baker and Milsom, *Sources of English Legal History*, 582–3.

[285] Ibid., 583.

[286] (1443) Y.B. 22 Hen. 6, f. 14., pl. 23; in Fifoot, *History and Sources*, 96–7; see also *Right's Case* (1455) Y.B. Trin. 33 Hen. 6, f. 26, pl. 10, in Baker and Milsom, *Sources of English Legal History*, 584–5.

the freehold necessitating an assize, or simply a wrongful economic interference justifying trespass on the case remedy. On traversal the writ was abandoned.

In the fifteenth century, assize of nuisance was generally the correct writ for remedying diversion of water flowing to a freehold.[287] From around 1500, however, plaintiffs increasingly sought to bring actions for trespass on the case for the damage caused by interferences with water flow, even if the harm was done to a freehold. The courts treated these pleadings with ambivalence, with Common Pleas and King's Bench sometimes allowing, often rejecting the trespassory action.[288] Traditionally-minded judges such as Dyer CJ of the Court of Common Pleas did not wish to lose property cases to the King's Bench trespass jurisdiction, but the use of actions on the case to try disturbances to title was more than he could stomach.[289] In the much-reported case of *Yevance* v. *Holcomb* in 1566, the judges of Common Pleas continued to insist that where the assize was available to remedy nuisance between freeholders, there could be no trespassory action on the case;[290] even thirty years later King's Bench could hold to same effect.[291] However, an anonymous 1522 case suggests a wider operation of the action on the case was gestating. In that case P, a freeholder, 'brought an *Accion sur le cas* against S. for this, whereas the river [of] S. had run through such a vill, he had set up a mill so that the river ran into the meadows and flooded the land'. The court allowed the action on the case to be brought rather than assize of nuisance, after the following exchange:

Rowe: It seems that here he should have had an assize of nuisance, and not an *Accion sur le cas*. Likewise if you stop a conduit, I shall have an assize of nuisance.
Pollard, J.: There is a distinction between the case where he stops all your way so that you cannot pass, for there you shall have an assize of nuisance, and where he stops part so that you can pass, albeit narrowly, for there you shall have an *Accion sur votre case*. And so there is a distinction between restraining part [of the stream water] and restraining the whole.[292]

[287] e.g. *Duke of Exeter* v. *Hengescote* (1473) C.P. 40/848, m. 508, cited in Baker and Milsom, *Sources of English Legal History*, 586 n. 1.

[288] *Gilbert* v. *Francke* (1472) C.P. 40/844, m. 126; *Debenham* v. *Bateman* (1491) K. B. 27/921, m. 75; *Lord De Grey's Case* (1505) Y.B. Mich. 21 Hen. 7. f. 30 pl. 5; *Scrop* v. *Leverthorp* (1507) K.B. 27/983, m. 70; *Bishop of Exeter* v. *Ackelod* (1518) C.P. 40/848, m. 321; *Beaumont* v. *Benet* (1519–25) C.P. 40/1024, m. 345; all cited in Baker and Milsom, *Sources of English Legal History*, 586–7.

[289] J. H. Baker, 'Introduction' to *Dyer's Reports* (J. H. Baker (ed.), Selden Society cix, 1993) i, pp. xxvi–xxvii.

[290] (1566) 2 Dyer 250b; 73 E.R. 553; 3 Leon 13; 74 E.R. 509; 4 Leon. 167, 224; 74 E.R. 799, 835–6 (C.P.); Baker and Milsom, *Sources of English Legal History*, 587–8.

[291] *Beswick* [*Heswick*] v. *Cunden No. 2* (1596) Cro. Eliz. 520; 78 E.R. 768 (K.B.); *Viner's Abdgt.* xvi, 36, N.2.5.

[292] Y. B. Easter, 14 Hen. 8, f. 31, pl. 8 (1522), in Baker and Milsom, *Sources of English Legal History*, 587, S.C. as *Yarford* v. *Holyman* in *Year Books of Henry VIII, 12–14 Hen. VIII, 1520–23* (J. H. Baker (ed.), Selden Society, cxix, 2002) 193; *Right's Case* (1455) Y.B. Trin. 33 Hen. 6 f. 26 pl. 10, in ibid., 584–5; Fifoot, *History and Sources*, 97; Kiralfy, *Action on the Case*, 56.

This allowance of trespass on the case for a partial interference with freehold water rights suggests that this action was appropriate where the damage was of a more consequential and economic nature (as in cutting back water to a mill and reducing its power), rather than a patent interference with the amenities of property possession (as in physically interfering with a conduit or completely cutting water off from a tenement). In other words, a total interruption of water flow to a tenement resembled an interference with possession or property, not merely loss of profits or enjoyment; and hence it was appropriate to bring the more formal, more proprietary assize action. But this was a flimsy distinction of degree that was difficult to maintain. Doubts on this score remained for a while: in 1565 the judges of King's Bench could not decide whether trespass on the case for loss of profits or rather assize of nuisance lay following the diversion of part only of a stream customarily flowing to a freehold corn mill.[293] But shortly afterwards, in the King's Bench at least, the distinction based on full or part interference broke down: in a 1569 decision: 'in assize of nusance *pro diversione majoris partis cursus aquae*, the plaintiff recovered judgment';[294] and in 1601 in *Luttrel's Case*, 'it was resolved ... it was not possible to shew how much water runs to mills, and the quantity of the water is not material, forasmuch as the defendant, by the breaking of the bank, diverted the water which ran to the said mills'.[295] In *Bradshawe* v. *Nicholson*, decided that same year, the Exchequer Chamber held that non-feasance by a tenant causing water damage to a tenant's shop below could sustain an action on the case, though a right to be free of rain-water in particular might have to be prescribed for. What is interesting about this case is that three judges rejected Walmsley J's argument that 'this action on the case is in the nature of an assize of nuisance, which does not lie for non-feasance ... and because no prescription is alleged why the defendant should be bound to repair [to prevent flooding] as against the plaintiff'.[296]

[293] *Anon.* (1565) 2 Dyer 248b; 73 E.R. 549 (K.B.); *Hoskins* v. *Robins* (1671) 2 Wms. Saund. 324; 85 E.R. 1123 (K.B.); *Russell* v. *Handford* (1583) 1 Leon. 273; 74 E.R. 248; *Webb* v. *Paternoster* (1620) Palm. 71, 81 E.R. 983; Poph 151; 79 E.R. 1250.

[294] *Wyke* v. *Serle* Mich. 12 & 13 Eliz. (1569), cited in 2 Dyer 248b; 73 E.R. 549 (K.B.): S.C. cited as *Wikes and Searle* in *Luttrel's Case* (1601) 4 Co. Rep. 89a; 76 E.R. 1063 (K.B.); *Viner's Abdgt.*, xxii, 525, B.2 in marg.; *Anon.* (1587) H.L.S. MS. 16, f. 401v, pl. 71 (Q.B.), in Baker and Milsom, *Sources of English Legal History*, 588; *Sly* v. *Mordant* (c.1580) 1 Leon. 247; 74 E.R. 225 (K.B.) (freeholders allowed to bring an action on the case where way to house was obstructed or land was flooded by a blocked watercourse, despite objections that assize should be brought); to like effect *Aston's Case* (1586, K.B.) and *Villet* v. *Pankhurst* (1586, K.B.), noted in 2 Dyer 250b (marginal note of Treby C.J. (1688 edn.), in J. Vaillant (ed.), 1794, Dublin), 73 E.R. 553–4 (K.B.).

[295] (1601) 4 Co. Rep. 84b, 89a.; 76 E.R. 1063, 1070 (K.B.); *Viner's Abdgt.* xxii, 526, C.3.

[296] *Bradshawe* v. *Nicholson* (1601) HLS MS. 2076, fo. 66, B.L. MS. Add. 25203, fol. 266v; YLS MS. G. R29.14 fol. 118, in Baker and Milsom, *Sources of English Legal History*, 609.

Public or Common Nuisance and the Action on the Case

The king's jurisdiction to maintain the peace and welfare of the realm gave rise to a jurisdiction to suppress common nuisances hurtful to the public. Much of this jurisdiction included controls of water such as prevention of flooding, escapes, pollution, and interference with watercourses, sewers, ponds, and navigation channels. Public nuisances could involve other misfeasance, for example blocking a drain or watercourse, breaking a dam or dyke; or else non-feasance, such as failing to perform an appendant or customary duty to repair a sea-wall or dyke, or to scour a watercourse. The king's jurisdiction to police nuisances was first applied in sheriffs' tourns, but came to be exercised in court leet, a jurisdiction held in the name of the king and applying to all residents of a locale, but operated by local lord and jurymen. Court leet was in large part a criminal jurisdiction, and was separate from the personal and territorial jurisdictions of the manorial lord in court baron and court customary. These manorial courts dispensed justice to free and unfree tenants, dealing with both personal and real actions. The common-law courts stood as an adjacent or superior recourse for tenants seeking justice directly from the king as feudal overlord; this direct recourse to the Crown was a distinctive feature of English tenurialism.[297]

The common law came to permit private individuals to recover damages for special loss to their holdings over and above that suffered by the general public, caused by breach of negative and positive public-nuisance duties, for example where a dam was broken flooding an individual's close or cutting water off from his mill; or where a sea-wall was not repaired to the damage of a particular tenement. These actions were another strand in the ancestry of the action on the case outside general trespass, as courts allowed an injured

[297] *Glanvill*, bk. IX, c. 11, Hall (ed.), 113–4; cf. Chew and Kellaway (eds.), *London Assize of Nuisance*, pp. xxvi–xxx; F. J. C. Hearnshaw, *Leet Jurisdiction in England* (Southampton, 1908) 43–78; Case 133 (Abbot of Abingdon's Court, 1088), in *English Law Suits from William I to Richard I, Vol. I* (R. C. van Caenegem (ed.), Selden Society, cvi, 1990), 90; *Leet Jurisdiction in the City of Norwich During the 13th and 14th Centuries* (W. Hudson (ed.), Selden Society, v, 1891) 8, 9, 24, 39; *John Spelman's Reading on Quo Warranto delivered in Gray's Inn (Lent 1519)* (J. H. Baker (ed.), Selden Society, cxiii, 1997) 15–25; J. Comyns, *Digest of the Laws of England* (5th edn., A. Hammond (ed.), London, 1822) iv, 841–5. For public nuisance before the royal courts see *Select Cases in the Court of King's Bench Vol. 6* (G. O. Sayles (ed.), Selden Society, lxxxii, 1965) C.R.Roll 391/m.15 (Easter, 1358); Case 109 per Frowyk, Inner Temple Cases, 1490–99 in MS. Hargrave 87, in *Readings and Moots at the Inns of Court Vol. II*, 278–9; *Anon.* (C.P., Trin. 1505), in *Reports of Cases by John Caryll Vol. 2* (J. H. Baker (ed.), *Selden Society*, cxvi, 2000), Case 323, 460–2. On the relationship of the English Crown to all tenants, see F. W. Maitland, *Domesday Book and Beyond* (Cambridge, 1897) 150–72; J. C. Holt, '1086', and 'Politics and Property in Early Medieval England', both in Holt, *Colonial England 1066–1215* (London, 1997) 31, 113; G. Garnett, 'The Origins of the Crown', in J. Hudson (ed.), *The History of English Law: Centenary Essays on 'Pollock and Maitland'* (Proceedings of the British Academy 89, Oxford, 1996) 171.

plaintiff to bring a formed writ 'conceived on his case'.[298] Another form of nuisance, partaking of both public and private actions, was described as 'common nuisance', that is where injury is inflicted on the enjoyment of rights of common or property owned in common.[299]

A large body of case law eventually produced a test for determining when a private person could recover through a personal action for particular harms resulting from public or common nuisances. Thus in 1535 Fitzherbert J permitted a private action for special damage from a public nuisance such as digging up or stopping a highway, offering this definition of the jurisdiction:

[E]ach nuisance done in the King's highway is punishable in the Leet and not by an action [on the case], unless it be where one man has suffered greater hurt or inconvenience than the generality have . . . [H]e shall have this action *pour ce special matiere*: but if he had not suffered greater damage than all others suffered, then he would not have the action.[300]

A classical version of the test for availability of the action was given in *William's Case* of 1592:

A man shall not have an action on the case for a nuisance done in the highway, for it is a common nuisance, and then it is not reasonable that a particular person should have the action; for by the same reason every one might have an action, and then he would be punished 100 times for one and the same cause. But if any particular person afterwards by the nuisance done has more particular damage than any other there for that particular injury, he shall have a particular action on the case: and for common nuisances, which are equal to all the King's liege people, the common law has appointed other Courts for the correction and reforming of them, *scil.* tourns, leets, &c.[301]

Apart from the rules that there had to be special damage and no alternative remedy, the court could decide whether the defendant's conduct was justified

[298] Milsom, 'Trespass From Henry III to Edward III', 52–8; Baker, *Introduction to English Legal History*, 62–3; Palmer, *English Law in the Age of the Black Death*, 283–93. This was a late fourteenth-century development; see e.g. *Prior of Drax* v. *John Devall* (C.P. 40/448, m. 99, Mich. 1372), in Arnold (ed.), *Select Cases of Trespass Vol. I*, 458, where riparian owners could be sued for damages for failing to maintain the banks of streams and the free flow of water; by contrast, in the same period failure to repair a river wall was sometimes held to be a public duty, not actionable as trespass on the case: see Y.B. Trin. 45 Edw 3 (1372) f. 17 pl. 6, discussed in Ibbetson, *Law of Obligations*, 55. The action on the case is here well established by the sixteenth century, e.g. *Anon.* (1589) 2 Leon. 184; 74 E.R. 462 (K.B.).

[299] *Viner's Abdgt.*, xvi, 19–24 ('Nusance'—common); *Westbury* v. *Powell*, cited in *Fineux* v. *Hovenden* (1599) Cro. Eliz. 664, 665; 78 E.R. 902, 903; cf. *Dewell* v *Saunders* (1618) Cro. Jac. 490; 79 E.R. 419; *Cope* v. *Marshall* (1757) 2 Wilson King's Bench 51; 95 E.R. 680 (K.B.).

[300] Y.B. 27 Hen. 8, f. 27, pl. 10 (1535); Fifoot, *History and Sources*, 98; *Fineux* v. *Hovenden* (1599) Cro. Eliz. 664; 78 E.R. 902.

[301] (1592) 5 Co. Rep. 72b, 73a; 77 E.R. 163, 164–5 (K.B.); *Co.Litt.* 56a; see Baker and Milsom, *Sources of English Legal History*, at 571, 581–610, charting the continuous development of trespass on the case for nuisance to the 1600s.

by the balance of utilities.[302] The law regulating public and common nuisance actions was digested in copious detail by Comyns, Coke, Viner, and Blackstone;[303] Blackstone's summary of these actions will be reviewed in a later chapter.

Water as Public Property Defended by Mixed Nuisance Actions

The chief heads of public and common nuisance touching on water rights were: flooding or escapes;[304] interference with public water-works such as dykes, river-banks, and sea-walls;[305] interference with flow of watercourses;[306] pollution of watercourses;[307] failure to maintain sea-walls, dykes, and other water-works;[308] and interference with navigation and fishing rights, a jurisdiction given shape by Hale in his late seventeenth-century treatise *De Jure Maris*.[309] The general principles of public nuisance were well known to Bracton who wrote:

> there may be a wrongful nuisance because of the common and public welfare, as where one having lands on both sides of a stream builds a fishery or pond, when his land is in every way free and under no obligation to neighbouring land, below or above; by so doing, though he causes damage to his neighbours, he commits no *injuria*; but nevertheless, what must be upheld [because of the private] may be demolished because of the public welfare, which is preferred to the private.[310]

[302] *Rankett's Case* (1605); *Anon.* (1618) both in *Roll. Abdgt.*, ii, 139, 137 ('Nusans' F2, B1–3).

[303] E.g. *Co.Litt.*, 56a; 2 Inst. 406; Comyns, *Digest*, i, 418–24; iii, 13; iv, 679, 841–5; *Viner's Abdgt.*, xiv, 394–5 ('Indictment'—nuisance); xvi, 19–47 ('Nusance'); xxii, 525–8 ('Water-Courses'). See also J. R. Spencer, 'Public Nuisance—A Critical Examination' (1989) 48 Cambridge Law Journal 55, 56–73.

[304] e.g. *R.* v. *Rosewall* (1699) 2 Salk. 459; 91 E.R. 397 (K.B.).

[305] *Public Works in Mediaeval Law*, (C. T. Flower (ed.), Selden Society, Vol. 1, xxxii, 1915) 58–60, 257, 260, 292–5, 303–5, 309–10; (Vol. 2, XL, 1923), pp. xxiii–xxix, 40–3, 186–93. There was also a quantity of medieval legislation which attempted to police interferences with waterways; see Ch. 1, the text accompanying nn. 53–54.

[306] *Public Works in Mediaeval Law*, i, 154–66, 184–6, 297–8; ii, 88, 106–8, 112–14, 276–306, 360–1; *Viner's Abdgt.*, xv, 398–400 ('Mill', entry C); xvi, 36 ('Nusance', entry O). There was also a criminal jurisdiction for riotous conduct disturbing watercourses: *R.* v. *Colson* (1604) 3 Mod. 72; 87 E.R. 47. (K.B.).

[307] *Viner's Abdgt.*, xvi, 36, ('Nusance', entry O).

[308] Milsom, 'Trespass From Henry III to Edward III', 54–8; Kiralfy, *Action on the Case*, 10, 23; *Bernardeston* v. *Heighlynge* (1342–4) C.P. 40/330, m. 304 (Pas. 1342) (C.P.); K. B. 27/338, m. 41d & Y.B. Trin. 18 Edw. 3 f.23 pl. 6 (Mich. 1344) (k.b.); abstracted in Y.B. 16 Edw. III. Rolls I, 259 and Selden Society, xxxii, 309, and as *B* v. *K*, in *Keighly's Case* (1609) 10 Co. Rep. 139b; 77 E.R. 1137.

[309] Sir Matthew Hale, *De Jure Maris* (c.1670), discussed in Ch. 4, the text accompanying nn. 127–138; *Viner's Abdgt.* xiv, 394–5; xvi, 19–24, 41–7; see e.g. *Hind* v. *Manfield* (1614) Noy. 103; 74 E.R. 1068 (K.B.) (£200 fine for diverting water and weakening the current of the river Thames to the detriment of barge traffic and the rights of the Crown); *Royal Fishery of the Banne Case* (1611) Dav. 55; 80 E.R. 540 (K.B.).

[310] *Bracton*, f. 232b, iii, 191; also f. 234, iii, 196.

What is novel after Bracton is the creation of a private remedy for damage from public nuisance, solidified by the issue of new writs in the mid-fourteenth century[311] and eventually incorporated into actions on the case.[312]

Why did the common law leave this mixed public–private nuisance jurisdiction relatively undeveloped? One explanation is that in the earlier decentralized system of landholding, supporting an agricultural economy of open fields and commons, individuals seeking access to communal resources could resort to local legal and administrative institutions safeguarding common rights, such as the court leet. In this system there was no definite split between public and private property, nor sharp division of public and private remedies. By the sixteenth and seventeenth centuries, however, when local institutions had begun their long decline and statute and common law began to cover the field of property law, private property rights were seen to be conceptually distinct from public rights to common resources. The courts now insisted that public and private remedies be kept separate: there appeared new and exacting requirements that private nuisance actions show special damage; and conversely, an indictable public nuisance had to clearly extend beyond harm to individuals or groups and affect the whole community.[313] Public and private nuisance remedies often coincided in practice, but they were perceived to work within jurisdictions that did not touch; they were not seen as two aspects of the same action. A graphic example of this turn in legal thought is provided much later by *R.* v. *Stanton* in 1679.[314] A statute provided for criminal indictment on cutting the banks of a public river and triple damages to injured individuals, amounting to a special statutory nuisance regime; yet outside this statutory remedy it was held that a concurrent private action for general trespass damages remained. Pollexfen as counsel successfully argued that: 'There may be damages to the party grieved, and yet an indictment too, as in case of forcible entry, the remedy of the party at common law is not taken away by affirmative statutes. An *indictment* and *action* will lie for a nuisance, though in a private man's soil; and so for trespass *vi et armis* in a private man's house both action and indictment lie.'

The relationship of public and private rights in cases of nuisance and injury to land attains a high importance in the eighteenth century, as Parliament and the courts develop the principles of eminent domain, statutory author-

[311] Y.B. Trin. 18 Edw. 3 f. 23 pl. 6 (1344); Kiralfy, *Action on the Case*, 10, 35–40.

[312] Cf. *Right's Case* (1455) Y.B. Trin. 33 Hen. 6, f. 26, pl. 10, in Baker and Milsom, *Sources of English Legal History*, 584–5; Fifoot, *History and Sources*, 89, 95–6.

[313] See e.g. *R.* v. *Jenner* (1686) Comb. 41; 90 E.R. 331 (K.B.) (public nuisance indictment for turning a watercourse, apparently to the injury of riparian neighbours, was quashed 'because it was in the nature of an action on the case').

[314] (1679) 2 Show K.B. 30; 89 E.R. 773 (K.B.).

ization of tort, and 'statute tort' or breach of statutory duty.[315] But that is a large theme, lying outside the story of the rise of the private law remedy of action on the case for nuisance.

Dominance of Action on the Case for Nuisance

After 1400 the action on the case gradually expanded to become the dominant action for asserting proprietary incidents including water rights. This development, promoted chiefly in the Court of King's Bench, was marked by hesitations indicating a residual belief in the separation of personal and proprietary remedies. The final unifying steps, as we have seen, came sometime around 1600, when the courts began to allow the action on the case to be brought in defence of rights of possession even where the assize of nuisance or some real action would have been available to remedy the freeholder's loss.[316] In 1596 the Court of King's Bench held that a freeholder seeking remedy to nuisance 'might have an action upon the case, or an assize, at his election. And Popham [CJ] said, he had seen it so in experience divers times'.[317] However, the 1601 case of *Cantrel* v. *Church* showed that the courts had not completely embraced this position, and still had lingering doubts. The report of the case by Croke might suggest that the judges were unanimous in allowing a free election between the actions;[318] but the judges were probably more ambivalent over this point. Baker and Milsom adduce a manuscript report of the case[319] showing division over whether there was generally an election between trespass on the case and other actions. The judges of King's Bench would have allowed the action on the case even if the plaintiff's pleadings left room for an action under the assize of nuisance; the judges of Common Pleas in the Exchequer Chamber were less sure, holding that they would allow the action on the case where there was ambiguity over availability of the assize, but also implying that there was not to be a straightforward election between the remedies where it appeared that an assize lay.

If we cannot tell precisely what *Cantrel* v. *Church* decided, it is clear that from 1601 the action on the case dominates the reported litigations for water

[315] *Tenant* v. *Goldwin* (1704) 2 Ld. Raym. 1089; 92 E.R. 222; 3 Ld. Raym. 324; 92 E.R. 712; 6 Mod. 311; 87 E.R. 1051 (K.B.); Kiralfy, *Action on the Case*, 133–5.

[316] See cases cited in nn. 292–294, above, and *Leverett* v. *Townsend* (1590) Cro. Eliz. 198; 78 E.R. 454 (K.B.); *Alston* v. *Pamphyn* (1596) Cro. Eliz. 466; 78 E.R. 719 (K.B.).; cf. *Beswick (Heswick)* v. *Cunden No. 2* (1596) Cro. Eliz. 520; 78 E.R. 768 (K.B.).

[317] *Alston* v. *Pamphyn* (1596) Cro. Eliz. 466; 78 E.R. 719 (K.B.).

[318] (1601) Cro. Eliz. 845, 78 E.R. 1072; Noy 37; 74 E.R. 1007; (Exch. Ch.); Fifoot, *History and Sources*, 94–5, 98–9; cf. D. J. Ibbetson, 'Sixteenth Century Contract Law: *Slade's Case* in Context' (1984) 4 Oxford Journal of Legal Studies 295, 296–303 f. Ibbetson, *Law of Obligations*, 103–4.

[319] Baker and Milsom, *Sources of English Legal History*, 588–91, citing LI MS. Misc. 492, f. 224v.

rights. The older actions were henceforth effectively redundant.[320] This process was accelerated by the 1608 case of *Challenor* v. *Thomas*.[321] Here an action for ejectment was brought on behalf of the owner by his putative lessee D, who claimed under a lease '*de quodam rivulo & aquae cursu*'. The right to the waterflow was doubtless being claimed as a possessory interest using the trespass remedy of ejectment, in an action initiated by the owner of the fee. King's Bench upheld P's writ of error, on grounds that no real or possessory remedy lay for flowing water, 'for *rivulus seu aquae cursus* doth not lie in demand, neither doth a praecipe lie of it; nor can livery of seisin be made of it, for *non moratur* [it does not delay] but is ever flowing;... for it is not constant to be put in possession of it'.[322] It was stated that land covered by water could be the subject of a possessory action,[323] '[b]ut if the land under the water or river do not pertain to the plaintiff, but the river only, then upon a disturbance his remedy is only by action upon the case, upon any diversion of it, and not otherwise'.[324] Thus riparian rights in a stream were generally to be enforced by trespass on the case; the only sphere where other actions were pertinent was the protection from direct interference of a body of water owned as an integral part of land. This oft-cited decision marks the point from which the action on the case took over completely. In 1649, Rolle CJ could state: 'The Plaintif may have an assize or an action upon the case at his election, although here be a disturbance of the Plaintifs freehold, although that the antient books say the contrary.'[325]

[320] Attempts to bar election were tried in the early seventeenth century but the dominance of trespass on the case over assize remedies is amply demonstrated in the case law collected in e.g. *Roll. Abdgt.*, i, 88–90; 104 ('Action sur Case', entry N 'Nusans'; entry L-ii, 'Case nemy Assise'); ii, 137–45 ('Nusans); *Viner's Abdgt.*, i, 1–2 ('Abatement', entry A); xvi, 24–43 ('Nusance'); xxii, 525–8 ('Water-Courses'). Viner states (xvi, 31, 'Nusance', entry I.2 in marg.):

> 'The diversity between a Quod permittat, or an Assise for a Nusance, and an Action upon the Case for the Nusance is, That a Quod permittat and a Writ of Assise are to abate the Nusance; but an Action on the Case is only to recover Damages; therefore, tho' the Nusance be removed, the Plaintiff is intitled to his damages which accrued before.'

Most of the nuisance actions for water rights of the early modern period, discussed in the next ch., are brought as actions on the case, without an action to enforce the real remedy of abatement. See also Kiralfy, *Action on the Case*, 55–9, 65– 9.

[321] (1608) 1 Brownl. & Golds. 142; 123 E.R. 718 (K.B.); also Godb. 157 pl. 213; Poph. 167; Yelv. 143; *Viner's Abdgt.*, xxii, 526, entry B.3.

[322] (1608) Yelv. 143; 80 E.R. 96 (K.B.).

[323] See *Throckmerton* v. *Tracy* (1555) 1 Plow. 145; 75 E.R. 222 (C.P.) and *Co.Litt.* 4a–b, for a similar point.

[324] (1608) 1 Brownl. & Golds. 142; 123 E.R. 718; Yelv. 143.

[325] *Ayre* v. *Pyncomb* (1649) Style 164; 82 E.R. 614 (K.B.) (NB. Fifoot transcribes this case incorrectly in *History and Sources*, 95). See further *Anon.* (1702) 3 Salk 248; 91 E.R. 805 (K.B.); *A Briefe Declaration for What Manner of Speciall Nuisance Concerning Private Dwelling Houses, A Man May Have His Remedy by Assise, or Other Action as the Case Requires, Unfolded in the Argument, and Opinions of Four Famous Sages of the Common Law* (1639); Baker, 'Introduction' to *Spelman's Reports Vol. 2*, 232–6.

The Nature of Water Incidents—A Confusion of Theories

The *Prior of Southwark's Case* of 1498[326] raised the issue of distinguishing trespass *vi et armis* from case where water flowing to riparian tenements was polluted upstream. The discussion also touched on the substantive nature of water rights, and illustrated the limits of Year Book thought compared to the richness of Bractonian jurisprudence.

In the *Prior of Southwark's Case*, trespass on the case was brought by P who was seised (through tenants) of houses 'and of certain gardens in Southwark in right of their houses from time whereof the memory of man does not run',

and that they . . . for the same time have had a water-course or stream running into a ditch of the river Thames near to the said houses and gardens and running between all the said houses and gardens, to dye their clothes, to water their beasts, to bake and to brew, and for other easements; and that the defendant had made a lime-pit for calf-skins and sheep-skins so close to the stream that a corruption of the said lime-pit had corrupted the said stream, wherefore the tenants had left the said houses.[327]

The damage grounding the action on the case was the harm to water use incident to the tenements, and the ensuing loss of P's tenants and rents.[328] The court agreed that P's declaration incorrectly stated that D had made the injurious pit on P's land, which plainly would have made for trespass *quare vi et armis*. P was permitted to amend the writ making clear that the pit was on D's land and had caused injury from outside P's tenement, so making an action on the case. But what was the nature of the right claimed to be injured? On one view, P's water rights might be natural rights in a stream flowing past his tenement. Yet P's pleadings claim a list of particular uses of the water as separate prescriptive 'easements': each and every user of the water enjoyed 'from time whereof etc.' was said to give rise to a distinct amenity-right in the water. D claimed against this that P must allege his riparian right as owner of the land covered in water, or at least as owner in common with specified neighbours.

Brian CJ's summation of the issues of the case reveals some three conceptual bases of water right, all mentioned in the one sentence in the Year Book source:

I put the case that I and a stranger are *tenants in common of a stream*, and I have *houses adjoining* for which I have an *easement of such water*, as in the case here, and my

[326] (1498) Y.B. Trin. 13 Hen. 7, f. 26, pl. 4.; Fifoot, *History and Sources*, 87; S.C. *Prior of Christ Church, Canterbury* v. *Hore* in *Reports of Cases by John Caryll Vol. 1*, 175–7.

[327] Ibid.

[328] For loss of tenants and rents as a damage grounding the action on the case see also Y.B. Mich. 9 Hen. 7, f.7, pl. 4 (1493); Kiralfy, *Action on the Case*, 13.

companion commits such a nuisance as this and corrupts the water; shall I not have an action sur mon case against him? I think so: for *this nuisance is done to my soil*, since he has no rights in the houses to which the nuisance is done.[329]

It is not clear what this means. Was the infringed water right incident or appendant to possession of riparian land? Was it incident to possession of the stream-bed or of the stream itself? Was it a natural or common right attaching to possession of riparian soil? Or was the right appurtenant to posssession of houses as a praedial easement, an incorporeal right arising from grant? Medieval lawyers were confused on all of these points, and answers were not developed until the seventeenth century, when there was a fresh lease of creativity in the law of property and tort.

Injury and Damage

Baker suggests that in the Year Book period of the late fifteenth and sixteenth centuries it was a general principle that for a wrong to be actionable it had to cause damage.[330] This theme was reiterated in the forms of pleadings, and in statements by lawyers such as Littleton to the effect that causes of action were grounded on damage; for example, 'If a man has damage, it is right that he should be compensated.'[331] On the other hand, Bracton's countervailing concept of *damnum absque injuria* was also well accepted, barring recovery for certain types of damage, particularly in cases of economic loss caused by market competition. The judges explicitly recognized this policy, as in a case before Court of King's Bench in 1502–3:

[W]here a man has damage and also wrong, it is right that he should have an action. But damage alone is not a cause of action. Thus [where] an innkeeper or other victualler comes and dwells next to another [innkeeper] and therby more of the customers resort to him than to the others, it is a damage to the other but no wrong, for he cannot compel men to buy vituals from him rather than from the other. But if a man prescribes for himself and all his tenants to grind at a mill without toll, and the miller takes toll from the tenants, the lord shall have an action of trespass on his case, for this is a wrong to the lord.[332]

We have seen how Bracton linked injury and damage by asserting that a trespassory invasion of legal right necessarily implied damage, as where there

[329] Translation by Fifoot, *History and Sources* 87 (emphases added). The version in Caryll's *Reports*, at 175–7, gives '*moy sole*' in the last clause, which Baker suggests could be translated as 'me alone'; the sense is not really changed.

[330] Baker, 'Introduction' to *Spelman's Reports Vol. 2*, 220–4; and see Kiralfy, *Action on the Case*, 12–17.

[331] *The Thorns Case* (1466) Y.B. Mich. 6 Edw. 4, f. 7, pl. 18 per Littleton J, translated by Baker, 'Introduction' to *Spelman's Reports Vol. 2*, 221; Fifoot, *History and Sources*, 195–7.

[332] *Prior of Christchurch, Canterbury* v. *Bendysshe* (K.B., Mich. 1502/3), Case 11 in *Spelman's Reports, Vol. 1*, (J. H. Baker (ed.), Selden Society, xciii, 1976) 8, 9, per Rede, Tremayle JJ and Fyneux CJ.

was trespass *quare clausum fregit* or *vi et armis*. This was wholly circular reasoning as the damage implied from the fact of trespass depended on the law recognizing a prior protected right, yet the damage was also the gist of the action creating the right.[333] How, then, could actionable interference with land and its appurtenances be defined without circularity? Coquillette has argued that the law of the Year Books treated actionable wrongs to land generally as interferences with the 'natural rights' of the property owner or possessor. Such 'natural rights' arose solely through the operation of the property law and did not depend on an express grant or prescription. Furthermore, they could not be taken away by express grant or prescription.[334] Coquillette cites a large number of authorities to find a policy of protection of normal residential use or enjoyment of property together with any established economic use of the land going beyond the normal type of use.[335] Any damage to simple enjoyment could support a finding of legal injury.[336] But Coquillette concedes that the so-called 'natural right' test he divines in the Year Books was at best an inconclusive guide: 'no amount of harm gave rise to actionable damages unless the injury was of a type legally recognized as giving a right of action'.[337] We return to the trap of circular reasoning whereby damage is actionable if it be actionable damage.

Baker makes similar findings in this area, stating: 'the right to clean air, undiverted and unpolluted water, light, and quiet, seems to have been incident to house ownership in general', and did not require annexation through prescription.[338] He concludes that the law of the Year Book period lacked a coherent abstract principle describing or defining the relationship between damage and legal injury—and was not looking for one, any more than modern tort law owns a coherent theory for when duties of care is imposed to prevent damage: 'today, as in 1500, the lawyer's approach is to look at the precedents and to seek the "policy" of the law'.[339] Kiralfy interprets the Year Book law as expressing contradictory desires, both to provide remedy for any damage suffered and to proceed slowly, by precedent and analogy, in the invention of rights and remedies. The rise of the action on the case can be seen as an attempt to reconcile these contradictory purposes.[340]

The late medieval and early modern common-law theory of injury to land was shaped by the forms of action as much as, or more than, by substantive precedents and policies. Under the triumphant action on the case writ, property-use rights were defended by trespassory tort actions rather than

[333] See the text accompanying nn. 68–72 above.

[334] *Fowler* v. *Sanders* (1617) Cro. Jac. 446; 79 E.R. 382 (K.B.).

[335] Coquillette, 'Mosses from an Old Manse', 769–71, nn. 40–46.

[336] Ibid., 770–1.

[337] Ibid., 771.

[338] Baker, 'Introduction' to *Spelman's Reports Vol. 2*, 235, following G. Traherne's 'Reading on Forest Law' (Lincoln's Inn, 1520).

[339] Baker, n. 338 above, 221–2.

[340] Kiralfy, *Action on the Case*, 1–17.

proprietary claims. Damage was the *sine qua non* of action, and damages compensation the pre-eminent form of remedy; but damage might be imported if there was any type of infringement or injury to a right of grant or prescription such as an easement.[341] Trespass on the case was to lie especially in those instances where an infringed interest would otherwise go unprotected.[342] Where natural rights to common resources were asserted special damage might have to be shown, since by common-law theory a landholder's interest in the untroubled enjoyment of his land was the very definition of the interest protected by natural right. The law could not decide whether the right of a riparian owner to water flow was to be characterized as a natural right inherent in ownership, or else as an easement resting on grant, prescription, or custom—an issue left blurred by Bracton's eclectic use of the Roman categories of servitude and *usucapio* in describing the rights of amenity incident to land-ownership.

The lawyers' focus on the appropriate use of common trespass, trespass on the case, and nuisance distracted attention from the substantive nature of property rights being defended by the various tort actions. It was left to the modern courts to reconstruct the field of land-use and riparian rights, and to address the issues of policy and doctrine left unresolved by the medieval law.

[341] See *Ashby* v. *White* (1703) 6 Mod. 45; 87 E.R. 810; 2 Ld. Raym. 938; 92 E.R. 126; 3 Ld. Raym. 320; 92 E.R. 711; Holt K.B. 524; 90 E.R. 1188 (K.B.) per Holt CJ; see Ch. 3, the text accompanying nn. 120–129.

[342] Baker, 'Introduction' to *Spelman's Reports Vol. 2*, 233–5; Y. B. Easter, 14 Hen. 8, f. 31, pl. 8 (1522) per Brooke J: '*Accion sur le cas* lies where there is no other action provided for a wrong', in Fifoot, *History and Sources*, 97; *Westbury* v. *Powell*, reference in *Fineux* v. *Hovenden* (1599) Cro. Eliz. 664; 78 E.R. 902 (K.B.); *Ashby* v. *White* (1703), cited in n. 341 above.

3. *The Common Law of Riparian Rights 1580–1750*

ANCIENT USE

The Romanist and natural-right conceptions of water law outlined by Bracton were not nativized within the English common law, though their presence was always felt. Instead in the fifteenth and sixteenth centuries a peculiarly common-law principle of entitlement took root, namely that a riparian owner asserting right to unimpeded flow of water must, in the absence of express grant from neighbours, plead ancient use ('from time immemorial') of the flow as evidence of a presumed grant constituting the right. Where the water use was for a particular purpose, such as powering a mill wheel, it might be necessary additionally to plead '*antiquum molendinum*': that there was an ancient mill, and that use of water by that particular mill was legitimated by immemorial custom or grant.[1]

It was not always easy to distinguish the prescriptive and natural-right principles, for a natural flow of water to a tenement could be characterized as an immemorial flow protected by prescription; and conversely an immemorially long user might be described as natural. There are also few signs of the older theory that a reasonable level of user is an entitlement of common right universally attached to riparian tenements; and that any extraordinary user surpassing common right will take effect as a specialty right established by grant or prescription.

The 1583 case of *Russell* v. *Handford*[2] is a convenient starting point for the post-medieval law. In this action on the case, the plaintiff, P, pleaded that he was seised in fee of an ancient mill (*molendinum ab antiquo fuit erectum*) and that the defendant, D, had erected a new mill diverting the flow of water to P's mill. D argued that ancient erection and use of a mill was not a sufficient pleading to raise a prescriptive right: that for a prescription there must, according to the well-known formula, be enjoyment from 'time out of mind' or 'time whereof the memory of man runneth not to the contrary'.[3] In support of his declaration, P offered two theories of riparian right by user. First, it was argued that there need be no ancient use but merely some prior appropriation of water flow, such that '[i]f I have a mill and another levies another mill there, and the miller hinders the water to run to my mill, or doth any such nusance, an action lyeth without any prescription'. Secondly, it was

[1] *Luttrel's Case* (1601) 4 Co. Rep. 84b; 76 E.R. 1063; *Co.Litt.* 114b.
[2] (1583) 1 Leon. 273; 74 E.R. 248 (K.B.).
[3] *Co.Litt.* 110a, 113a–115b.

suggested that prescription operated as local feudal custom, binding the tenants of a manor or borough by 'privity of custom and prescription', analogous to the obligation of a newly-admitted tenant to grind corn at his lord's customary mill. The court did not pronounce on these arguments, narrowly holding that P had pleaded use 'time out of mind, &c.' sufficiently by use of the words *ab antiquo*, so that the case could be resolved on orthodox grounds of prescription by long user. It was agreed that the party claiming prescriptive right must be seised in fee at law, in order to claim the descending benefit of the prescription as an ancient title attached to the freehold.[4] However, seisin in fact, or actual entry and possession, was not required in order to assert a prescriptive title, implying that such a prescription subsisted even when unexercised by the person prescribing. A century later this point was settled: in *Scoble* v. *Skelton*[5] it was held that if a claimant has seisin in law, he may prescribe through the possession and enjoyment of his servants without himself having factual possession.[6]

Prescription doctrine determined when a right existed; a further question was whether there had been actionable infringement of the extant right. In actions for trespass on the case, the courts commonly required present proof of damage or wrongful loss, since actual harm to possession was more patently at issue in this form of writ than defence of property or title against invasion. For example, in *Moore* v. *Browne*[7] it was decided that an owner claiming damages for trespass on the case for an occasional diversion of water from a stream on his land had to plead that he was actually seised in fee at the time of diversion, as well as at the time of action, in order to prove actionable damage to his interests. Since the case went against P due to the bad pleading of seisin, the court did not need to specify the juristic source of a riparian owner's interest. Certainly there was no resort to the Bractonian concept of natural rights to water flow to a riparian tenement or mill, being a 'servitude' imposed by law.

Moore v. *Browne* also decided that an intermittent drawing of water from a spring by a pipe could found an action on the case, as each use of the pipe was a fresh positive act of diversion. D claimed that by using the existing pipe she was merely continuing an existing nuisance begun by someone else, and not

[4] Cf. *Dent* v. *Oliver* (1604) Cro. Jac. 43; 79 E.R. 35 (K.B.); *Sands* v. *Trefuses* (1639) Cro. Car. (3 Cro.) 575; 79 E.R. 1094 (K.B.); *Yard* v. *Ford* (1671) 2 Wms. Saund. 172; 85 E.R. 922 (K.B.); *Coryton* v. *Lithebye* (1671) 2 Wms. Saund. 112; 85 E.R. 814 (K.B.); *Villiers* v. *Ball* (1689) 1 Show. K.B. 7; 89 E.R. 412 (K.B.).

[5] (1682) 2 Show. K.B. 195; 89 E.R. 886; Skin 36; 90 E.R. 18; 2 Mod. 318 (K.B.).

[6] Cf. acquisition of ownership through others in Roman law: D.41.1.10.pr.–2., D.41.1.32. (Gaius); D.41.1.54.4. (Pomponius); D.41.1.59. (Callistratus); D.41.2.13.1., 11.–13. (Ulpian); D.41.2.14. (Paul); D.41.2.25.1.; D.41.2.30.5. (Paul); D.41.2.31. (Pomponius); D.41.2.44.2.–3. (Papinian).

[7] (1572) 3 Dyer 319b–320a; 73 E.R. 723 (K.B.); Bendl. 215, 216 pl. 24.; *Viner's Abdgt.*, xxii. 525–6.

herself inflicting new damage, hence falling outside the action on the case which required a positive wrongful act; but the Court rejected this argument on the facts.[8] In *Brent* v. *Haddon* a similar issue arose, where it was held that a lessee who continued a nuisance begun by his lessor was guilty of a fresh nuisance by continuation. This factual determination trumped the doctrinal point that the original tortfeasor and the defendant were different persons.[9] A twist on this theme was afforded by *Smith* v. *Babb*,[10] where P sued D for diverting a continuous stream by his land causing flooding and damage. D took exception to the pleadings, 'because it is not alledged that the water had so run time out of mind'. Gawdy J did not take the objection: 'If the water hath run there but for one year, if the defendant hath diverted it, so as he hath drowned the plaintiffs land, the action will lye well enough.' These three cases probed yet again the hovering boundary between trespassory, personal actions correcting temporal damage inflicted by tortfeasor on victim (typically action on the case), and actions vindicating title or the proprietary right to enjoy a secure seisin forward across time, against all interferers (typically nuisance actions).

The sixteenth-century law's hazy definition of water rights requires some explanation in light of the dynamism of the English agrarian and manufacturing economy in this period, with its high incidence of water-powered industry. It may be that water power, used chiefly for corn-milling and for fulling and forging, was subject to seigneurial control through tenurial and franchise powers; and seigneurial claims to monopolist milling rights dovetailed well with a riparian doctrine based on prescription protecting only ancient or long-established mills. The converse result of the prescription doctrine was to deny protection to new, competing water uses.

Before 1600 the bulk of water disputes would have fallen to be decided in local courts outside the common law. Local decision-making would have

[8] See also *Beswick* v. *Cunden* (1592/5) Cro. Eliz. 402; 78 E.R. 646, 647 (K.B.): 'the case in 14 & 15 Eliz. Dyer, 319. is good law; for there the Lady Brown made a new nusance by every turning of the cock, for which she was punishable, although she made it not at the first'; also *Westbourne* v. *Mordaunt* (1590) Cro. Eliz. 402; 78 E.R. 447 (nuisance begun before P acquires title is actionable in trespass on the case for damage done later to property); *Anon.* (1577, Nottingham Borough Assizes), *Dyer's Reports* (J. H. Baker (ed.), Selden Society, cx, 1994) no. 210, vol. 2, 459; cf. *Beswick* v. *Cunden No. 2* (1596) Cro. Eliz. 520; 78 E.R. (K.B.). In *Penruddock's Case* (1598) 5 Co. Rep. 100b, 77 E.R. 210 (C.P.), it was stated that *quod permittat* lay to abate an existing nuisance, where notice was given to a new neighbour who continued a nuisance begun by his predecessor without any fresh act; by contrast action on the case for damages could be brought against the successor in the absence of fresh act or notice; see also *Rippon* v. *Bowles* (1615) 1 Rolle 221, 81 E.R. 446.

[9] (1619) Cro. Jac. 555; 79 E.R. 476 (K.B.). In *Brent* it was also stressed that the location of the injured land must be pleaded in order to erect a case action: see also *Viner's Abdgt.*, xvi, 26–31; xxii, 526–7; cf. *Rosewell* v. *Prior* (1701) 1 Ld. Raym. 1089, 1094; 91 E.R. 1375, 1570; S.C. 12 Mod.; 2 Salk. 460; Jac. 555 (K.B.), where similar rules are developed for ancient lights; and *Woolridge* v. *Cloberrie* (1606) 3 Salk. 117, 91 E.R. 726, on survivorship rules for a tort action for interference with a watercourse.

[10] (1588) 4 Leon. 193; 74 E.R. 815.

been at the discretion of court and jury, with scant reference to legal rules, though common-law entitlements as developed in the royal courts may have served as a base-line for claims. What is striking is a steep increase in common-law water litigations from around 1600, prompted by factors such as the increasing density of industry on watercourses, the general rise of business of the common-law courts, and also the burgeoning common-law hostility to traditional monopolies. The common law increasingly resorted to natural rights to promote effective solutions and at the same time to enhance jurisdiction. Much of this development was engineered by Sir Edward Coke.[11]

Luttrel's Case[12] of 1601 was reported elaborately by Coke as a leading decision. In this case, P pleaded that he was seised in fee of 'two ancient and ruinous fulling mills', to which 'a great part of the river ... did run; and also before, from time whereof the memory of man (&c.) was continually accustomed and used to run'. The flow of the river was directed to P's mills by an earthen bank, which also dated from time immemorial. P had recently pulled down the old mills and built two new corn mills on the same site, and thereby 'had gotten divers gains and profits' from milling for the local people. Following this change, D cut down the earthen bank, diverting water from P's new mills. P sued for interference with his prescriptive rights, declaring that the water 'did run, and ought and used to run, from its ancient and used course' to his new mills, and that its interruption caused P wholly to lose his profits. In his action on the case P claimed that the prescriptive right to water flow in the ancient watercourse was appurtenant to the ancient milling site, and was not affected by any change in the nature of the mills using the water. D then brought writ of error to Exchequer Chamber against P's verdict in King's Bench, objecting that by destroying the old mills and 'building ... new mills of a different nature', P 'had destroyed the prescription ... as if a man grants me a water-course to my fulling mills, I cannot ... convert them to corn mills, *nec e contra*'. The association of prescriptive right with an implied-in-fact grant for a definite purpose was elaborated by analogy with estovers or necessary takings of firewood for use by a house: 'if I grant to one estovers to burn in his hall, he cannot convert his hall into a kitchen or malt-house: *the same law of a prescription; for prescription in such a case shall be intended to commence by grant* ... '.[13] D offered an alternative analogy: that where there

[11] The debate over Coke's economic ideology was begun by D. O. Wagner, 'Coke and the Rise of Economic Liberalism' (1935–6) 6 Economic History Review Ser. 1, 30; D. O. Wagner, 'The Common Law and Free Enterprise: An Early Case of Monopoly' (1936–7) 7 Economic History Review Ser. 1, 217; and continued by W. L. Letwin, 'The English Common Law Concerning Monopolies' (1954) 21 University of Chicago Law Review 355; C. Hill, *Intellectual Origins of the English Revolution* (Oxford, 1965), 225–65, esp. 233–43; and J. I. Corré, 'The Argument, Decision, and Reports of *Darcy v. Allen*' (1996) 45 Emory Law Journal 1261.

[12] *Luttrel's Case, Cottel* v. *Luttrel* (1601) 4 Co. Rep. 84b, 86a; 76 E.R. 1063, 1065 (K.B.).

[13] 4 Co. Rep. 84b, 86a; 76 E.R. 1063, 1066 (emphasis added).

is a lord and tenant relationship by which the tenant holds under a requirement of service and repair to the lord's hall, the obligation could not be made more onerous by enlarging the hall, 'for the lord by his act cannot alter the nature of the tenure'. Applying this theory of right limited by ancient grant to the present case, D argued:

> it might be more beneficial to him who made the original grant, and to others who had his estate to have them fulling mills, than corn mills: for perhaps they have corn mills so near, that the building of corn mills would be prejudicial to them, and it would be against reason to extend a grant or prescription to [that] which is not within the purport or intention of the grant or prescription. ...[14]

In its reasons for judgment the court assumed that any right to water flow must be established by ancient use. The idea of natural rights inherent in riparian ownership was not affirmed or even mentioned. This did not, however, detract from P's case. P's prescriptive right was held to be good notwithstanding his variation of the mill, for:

> the mill is the substance, and thing to be demanded, and the addition of grist, or fulling, are but to shew the quality or nature of the mill, and therefore if the plaintiff had prescribed to have the said watercourse to his mill generally (as well he might) then the case would be without question, that he might alter the mill into what nature of mill he pleased, provided always that no prejudice should arise, either by diverting or stopping of the water, as it was before.[15]

The court held further that a prescriptive water privilege could be established by pleading an ancient course of water flowing past the riparian land, without further showing immemorial use by any mill in particular:

> [I]t should be intended that the [immemorial] grant to have the watercourse was before the building of the mills, for nobody will build a mill before he is sure to have water, and then the grant of a watercourse being generally to his mill, he may alter the quality of his mill at his pleasure.[16]

Riparian rights here are conceived as entitlements to exploit water flow, as a customary incident of riparian landownership. They are not seen as a privilege or special right attaching by prescription to long-established milling activity. Mill use was simply one means of establishing an expanded water right appurtenant to the riparian tenement. Expounding this point, the court stated:

[14] 4 Co. Rep. 84b, 86b; 76 E.R. 1063, 1066.

[15] 4 Co. Rep. 84b, 87a; 76 E.R. 1063, 1067. A like point was pursued with enormous erudition but to no conclusion in *Duke of Norfolk* v. *Myers* (1819) 4 Maddock 83, 56 E.R. 639 (Leach VC).

[16] 4 Co. Rep. 84b, 87a; 76 E.R. 1063, 1067 (particular mill); cf. *Countess of Rutland* v. *Bowler* (1622) Palm. 290; 81 E.R. 1087 (K.B.) (no mill use need be alleged); see further the text accompanying nn. 31–33 below.

[W]hen a man has anything appendant or appurtenant to an house or mill, the most perdurable part of it is the land in which the foundation is, and upon which the whole fabric of it consists and in respect thereof, by grant of all his lands, all his houses, mills, and woods will pass.[17]

Here it appears that water for a mill, like woods attached to land, is to be characterized as an integral part of seisin or possession of land. By so describing riparian rights as guaranteed access to the usual flow, the court took a long step towards re-defining water as a natural right attached to riparian tenements, a necessary appendant right of seisin, wholly independent of grant.

THE USE OF THE MAXIM *SIC UTERE TUO UT ALIENUM NON LAEDAS* TO EXPLAIN NATURAL RIGHTS

William Aldred's Case of 1610[18] contributed to a new theory of correlativity as the foundation of all natural appendant land-use rights, derived from the maxim *sic utere tuo ut alienum non laedas* ('so use your own property as not to harm that of another'). At the Norwich Assizes (Coke CJ and Williams J), Aldred (P) brought an action on the case for nuisance caused to his house by air pollution from his neighbour's (D's) hog-sty, and also blocking of his lights with a woodstack in his adjacent orchard. P claimed that his ancestors had had an estate in fee in the house with large windows since 'time whereof, &c.'; and that they 'have used to have for them and their tenants aforesaid divers wholesome and necessary easements and commodities, by reason of the open air and light, &c'.[19] P further pleaded that D, 'maliciously intending to deprive the plaintiff of the use and profit of his house, erected a swine stye . . . '.[20] The claim of malice was possibly formalistic, perhaps to ensure that the case fell within the trespass on the case writ; yet at trial it was not argued as an element of the action. The rights to open air and light were thereby claimed as appurtenances, or rights of implied grant rather than necessary natural rights. In the alternative they were claimed as necessary rights, in the form of a prescription presumed to have attached beneficial rights to possession.[21] D pleaded in arrest of the assize trial judgment 'that

[17] 4 Co. Rep. 84b, 87b; 76 E.R. 1063, 1068. Query whether this is Coke's doctrine rather than the court's. Cf. *Nicholas* v. *Chamberlain* (1606) Cro. Jac. 121; 79 E.R. 105 (K.B.) per Popham CJ who moots the possibility that artificial watercourses such as water-pipes are appendant rights that are fixtures to the house rather than to the subsoil or land itself.

[18] (1610) 9 Co. Rep. 57b; 77 E.R. 816 (K.B.); J. H. Baker and S. F. C. Milsom, *Sources of English Legal History. Private Law to 1750* (London, 1986) 599–601.

[19] 9 Co. Rep. 57b, 58a; 76 E.R. 816, 819–20.

[20] 9 Co. Rep. 57b, 58a, 59a; 77 E.R. 816, 817, 822.

[21] Cf. *Co.Litt.* 113a–114a, 122a–b, 140.

the building of the house for hogs was necessary for the sustenance of man: and one ought not to have so delicate a nose, that he cannot bear the smell of hogs; for *lex non favet delicatorum votis*'.[22] The assize jury awarded damages; D then sought arrest of judgment before a court comprising Coke CJ, Foster and Warburton JJ. P argued for a natural right to enjoy possession without air pollution, and the court upheld his claim.

P's right in *Aldred's Case* was cast in terms of natural necessity rather than prescription, and the 1587 King's Bench decision of *Bland* v. *Moseley*[23] was cited to illustrate the Court's approach. Coke's report notes the case as follows:

> It may be, that before time of memory the owner of the said piece of land has granted to the owner of the said house to have the said windows, without any stopping of them, and so the prescription may have a lawful beginning: and Wray Chief Justice, then said, that for stopping as well of the wholesome air as of light, an action lies, and damages shall be recovered for them, for both are necessary.... [A]nd if the stopping of the wholesome air, &c. gives cause of action, *a fortiori* an action lies in the case at Bar [i.e. *Aldred's Case*] for infecting and corrupting the air. And the building of a lime kiln is good and profitable; but if it be built so near a house, that when it burns the smoke thereof enters into the house, so that none can dwell there, an action lies for it. So if a man has a watercourse running in a ditch from the river to his house, for his necessary use; if a glover sets up a lime-pit for calve skins and sheep skins so near the said watercourse that the corruption of the limepit has corrupted it, for which cause the said tenants leave the said house, an action on the case lies for it ... and this stands with the rule of law and reason, *sc. Prohibetur ne quis faciat in suo quod nocere possit alieno: et sic utere tuo ut alienum non laedas.*[24]

The provenance of the *sic utere tuo* doctrine was not given, and it is indeed obscure; it does not appear in the Justinianic texts and was probably coined

[22] 9 Co. Rep. 57b, 59a, 77 E.R. 816, 817.

[23] (1587) Trin. 29 El. Tho.; 9 Co. Rep. 58a, 77 E.R. 817. In the report of *Bland* v. *Moseley* in K.B. 27/1302, m. 253 (K.B.) (Baker and Milsom, *Sources of English Legal History*, 597–9), *sic utere tuo* is adduced to the court by Coke as 'an old rule'. The *sic utere tuo* rule also appears as a general abuse of rights doctrine, e.g. *Mansor's Case* (1584) 4 Leon. 62, 74 E.R. 731 (K.B.) (restraint of unreasonable exercise of rights of covenant; cf. *Brown* v. *Tanner* (1825) 1 Carr. & Payne 651, 656, 171 E.R. 1354, 1356 per Carrington); *Edwards* v. *Halinder* (1594) 2 Leon. 93, pl. 116; 74 E.R 385; (Baker and Milsom, *Sources of English Legal History*, 606–8) per Godfrey (Ex.) (rupturing a floor with a heavy load so as to crush a neighbour's goods below is caught by the *sic utere tuo* rule, even if the damage was not foreseeable because of latent flaws in the structure). Another extension of this line of doctrine was given in *Pomfret* v. *Ricroft* (1669) 1 Wms. Saunders 321, 85 E.R. 454 (K.B.), where the grantor of a lease with e.g. a watercourse or a water pump was held to owe both a negative duty not to interfere with the water flow and a positive obligation to repair the same in order not to derogate from his grant; this case was controversial and both applied and attacked. Saunders noted (at 322; 455) that *sic utere tuo* could not logically be used to generate positive duties; Lord Campbell CJ made the same point in *Gott* v. *Gandy* (1852) 2 El. & Bl. 845; 118 E.R. 984; and see *Todd* v. *Flight* (1860) 9 C.B. N.S. 377; 142 E.R. 148 per Erle CJ.

[24] 9 Co.Rep. 58a, 59a; 77 E.R. 817, 821.

by late medieval lawyers as a useful maxim; it appears in English case law only in the late sixteenth century. An early use of the phrase is found in *Hales' Case* from 1569,[25] where Hales brought an action to stop a neighbour from building a new house blocking Hales' ancient lights. The neighbour pleaded a custom of London permitting such blockage. Mounson argued that denial of air and light was tantamount to disseisin of the freehold:

As, if I have a mill, and another will turn away the water running to the same, I may bring an assize against him. So, if I have a pipe which conveyeth water to my house through the ground of another, and he will cut my pipe, I shall have an action against him. In like manner who so stoppeth my light is the cause that no air can enter my house, without which no man can live....

The idea that reasonable give-and-take between neighbours controlled their rival use-rights was derived from the claim that each must respect the other's appropriations from the common of natural goods, presaging Lockean property theory by a hundred years:

And though light and air be common, yet of by any man's own act they be made private, they may not then be taken from him, and if they be he shall not be without remedy. This appearath by hawks and deer, which be *ferae naturae*, yet if by man's industry they are made tame, the owner will thereby gain property in them. But peradventure it will be said, the soil is his own, and it is *damnum absque injuria.* What then? Though it be his own, he must so use it that he hurt not his neighbour. As, if a man had a pond of water, and will suffer it to drown his neighbour's land, he shall have remedy against him.... You may perhaps say [that] there is plenty of light remaining: this notwithstanding, our action will lie very well for the taking away or imparing part thereof.

Wray in argument added that a custom must be reasonable: the London custom alleged 'is in effect as if a man should take my life from me, for these be the instruments to maintain and preserve man's life. And the law saith, *sic utere tuo ut alienum non laedas*. Therefore a custom against this precept is *malus usus*, and therefore *abolendus*'. Manwood spoke against the use of *sic utere tuo* to judge correlative rights of neighbours, for 'this [maxim] is not meant of things of pleasure but of things of profit', and partial blocking of light and air affected amenity of a dwelling only. A brief manuscript report gives Catlyn CJ finding for Hales on the basis of Ulpian's maxims of justice '*honeste vivere, alienum non laedere*, and *reddere cuique quod suum est*' (live honestly, hurt no-one, give each his due).[26] He also referred to the prior,

[25] *Hales' Case* (*c.*1569), possibly a moot case, reprinted in *A Briefe Declaration For What manner of speciall Nusance concerning private dwelling Houses, a man may have his remedy by Assise, or other Action on the Case requires* (1636), in Baker and Milsom, *Sources of English Legal History*, 592–7.

[26] Inst.1.1.3.; D.1.1.10. (Ulpian); Bracton f. 3–3b, ii, 24–5.

rather inconclusive nuisance authorities;[27] but the specific *sic utere tuo* theory was not broached.

In *Aldred's Case* the lawyers all accepted that natural appurtenant rights would only be recognized as necessary amenities for possession and habitation, and could not merely be 'things of delight', desirable and pleasant features such as prospect. The larger issue at stake was whether natural rights as regulated by the *sic utere tuo* principle operated to exclude any defence to the suit based on the supposed social utility of the land use which had given rise to the harm, except in cases where the interference could be regarded as so trivial as to count as part of the inevitable give and take of land ownership. In other words, would the court prevent any but neglible interferences with natural rights, or were socially useful or valuable interferences with neighbours to be tolerated? In *Jones* v. *Powell* (1629)[28] the judges differed on whether to apply a social balancing test or to give priority to natural rights over utility. In that case D burnt sea-coal in his brew-house to make beer. The fumes ruined the records and papers of his neighbour P, a court registrar, and injured his health. P won an action on the case before a jury, and D sought arrest of judgment before King's Bench. Whitelocke CJ found that brew-houses were necessary, whether manufacturing for public sale or private use; but the key question was whether burning sea-coal was an actionable nuisance. He held not, 'for this is the common and principal fuel of the realm', and without its use no-one could afford to brew, 'and then great prejudice would accrue to the common wealth. And what is necessary for the common wealth shall never be called a nuisance to any private person.' Balancing public good and private harm was a question of degree; hence a lime-pit could be suppressed by private action as less valuable to the public and more obnoxious to individuals. Dodderidge J also would have arrested the action on utilitarian grounds, discursing on the reduction of timber stocks in the country and the turn to coal for necessary fuel. He added that there could be no question of allowing an action if the coal-burning operation had preceded the dwelling house, so that the plaintiff had come to the nuisance. Jones J and Hyde CJ held that even a necessary action such as commercial burning of coal would be actionable at law if causing special prejudice; domestic property could be protected from new levels of industrial pollution, and immoderate pollution of homes was unlawful even if done in the course of a lawful trade. *Sic utere tuo* seems to have been cited to

[27] *Dalby* v. *Perch* (1330) Y.B. Trin. 4 Edw. 3 f. 36, pl. 26; *Prior of St. Nedeport's Case* (1443) Y.B. 22 Hen. 6, f. 14., pl. 23; Y.B. Mich. 11 Hen. 4 f. 82 pl. 28. Cf. *K.* v. *M.*, *The Case of the Queen's Forester* (1520) Y.B. Hen. 8 f. 8 (C.P.), in *Year Books of Henry VIII, 12–14 Hen. VIII 1520–1523* (J. H. Baker (ed.), Selden Society, cix, 2002) 42–6.

[28] *Jones* v. *Powell* (1629) Hut. 135; 123 E.R. 1155; Palm. 536; 81 E.R. 1208; 9 Co. Rep. 51a; 77 E.R. 806 (C.P.), SC. in Baker and Milsom, *Sources of English Legal History*, 601–6.

the court,[29] but the maxim was not expounded by the judges. The result of the case was inconclusive; the judges differed on how best to balance competing land uses in this instance, and so no judgment was entered (perhaps in deference to the opinion of Whitelocke CJ); so P finally won his action.

It has been argued that seventeenth-century nuisance law gave the courts a policy discretion to manipulate the *sic utere tuo* standard and so strike a social balance between useful modes of land use, leading eventually to highly malleable fault and negligence standards for torts to land.[30] The case of *Turberville* v. *Stamp* in 1697, dealing with escaping fire, is often cited as an example of how *sic utere tuo* language fitted well with modern negligence concepts. There Holt CJ stated:

> Every man must so use his own as not to injure another. The law is general; the fire which a man makes in the fields is as much his fire as his fire in his house . . . and he must at his peril take care that it does not, through his neglect, injure his neighbour: if he kindle it at a proper time and place, and the violence of the wind carry it into his neighbour's ground, . . . this is fit to be given in evidence. But now here it is found to be by his negligence. . . .[31]

The rise of a general flexible negligence standards is a slow process extending into the late nineteenth and early twentieth centuries, however; the seventeenth-century case law is rather more complex and hesitant in using discretionary standards to solve land-use conflicts.[32] The *sic utere tuo* principle, which tended to impose a strict liability for harms, was developed alongside a necessity test which qualified the existence of actionable appurtenant rights, and restricted the number of harms to land use which would attract legal sanction, thus departing from a strict liability standard.[33] Here jury discretion may have softened the operation of the rules.

[29] Palm. 536; 81 E.R. 1208 per Sjt. Berkley. For the profit/pleasure distinction see also *Hughes* v. *Keme* (1612) Yelv. 215; 80 E.R. 141 (K.B.); *Webb* v. *Paternoster* (1620) Palm. 71, 81 E.R. 983; *Roll. Abdgt.* ii, 143; 81 E.R. 713, 719 (K.B.).

[30] See J. F. Brenner, 'Nuisance Law and the Industrial Revolution' (1973) 3 Journal of Legal Studies 403; M. J. Horwitz, *The Transformation of American Law 1780–1860* (Cambridge, Mass., 1977) 63–108; D. Kretzmer, 'Transformation of Tort Liability in the Nineteenth Century: The Visible Hand' (1984) 4 Oxford Journal of Legal Studies 46; D. R. Coquillette, 'Mosses from an Old Manse: Another Look At Some Historic Property Cases About the Environment' (1979) 64 Cornell Law Review 761, 782; C. Dalton, *Losing History: Tort Liability in the Nineteenth Century and the Case of Rylands v Fletcher* (MS., 1987).

[31] (1697) 12 Mod. 151; 88 E.R. 1228 (K.B.); SC 1 Comyns 32, 34, 92 E.R. 944, 945.

[32] The doctrinal story is outlined in C. H. S. Fifoot, *History and Sources of the Common Law: Tort and Contract* (London, 1949) 154–213; D. J. Ibbetson, *A Historical Introduction to the Law of Obligations* (Oxford, 1999) 153–87.

[33] *Morley* v. *Pragnel* (1638) Cro. Car. 510; 79 E.R. 1039 (K.B.); *Roll. Abdgt.* i, 89, ii, 140–1; *Arnote* v. *Breame* (1704) 6 Mod. 245; 87 E.R. 992 (K.B.). The position was especially complex with regard to window-light, where there was (1) a natural right to the bare minimum of light for a house, provided the use of light preceded rival users; and (2) a right to a reasonable or expanded amenity of light if this were acquired by prescription: see *Bury* v. *Pope*, sc. *Page* (1588) Cro. Eliz. 118; 78 E.R. 375; 1 Leon. 168; 74 E.R. 155 (Ex. Ch.) (blocking P's windows was legal 'for it was [P's] folly to build his house so near to the other's land'); *Hughes* v. *Keme* (1612) Yelv. 215; 80

Ultimately, it is best to see *Aldred's Case* and the cases that immediately followed not as an intentional innovation in substantive doctrine, but rather as a moderate adjustment of legal categories. *Sic utere tuo* justifications for land-use entitlements represent a departure from the older view that all necessary rights are implied by prescription, or by grants presumed from the fact of possession following the principle that a grantor shall transfer the fullest rights of seisin. In the more modern view expressed in *Aldred*, the necessary rights are directly implied as natural elements of possession, without detouring into any version of implied grant theory. The effective result of the natural-right analysis may be the same as a presumed grant or prescription theory; but the language has crucially changed. The shift of legal categorization forced further doctrinal development as later lawyers re-interpreted the old authorities to fit into a natural-right structure.

PROTECTION OF IMMEMORIAL FLOW

The principle derived from *Luttrel's Case* was encapsulated by the usual form of pleading for water rights after 1600. This was to assert riparian right to an ancient watercourse by claiming *qui currere consuevisset et debuisset* ('that which customarily flowed and ought to flow'), without declaring that the water was for an ancient mill or any other established use. The plaintiff would henceforth state an established use of the water flow, whether ancient or modern, only in order to establish quantum of loss. There need no longer be proved an ancient use of the water as a sine qua non of action—only an ancient flow of that water.[34]

Uncertainty still surrounded the essentials of pleading.[35] In *Biccot* v. *Ward*, decided around 1620,[36] Hobart CJ recorded how King's Bench had caused a

E.R. 141 (K.B.) (conflict between immemorial use and custom allowing blockage of light by new buildings); *Rosewell* v. *Prior* (1701) 1 Ld. Raym. 1089, 1094; 91 E.R. 1375, 1570 (K.B.); *Tenant* v. *Goldwin* (1704) 6 Mod. 311; 87 E.R. 1051; 2 Ld. Raym. 1089; 92 E.R. 222; 3 Ld. Raym. 324; 92 E.R. 712 (K.B.); *Aldred's Case*, authorities collected in Note (B), 77 E.R. 816, 817–20. The same process of reasoning informs today's law, as in *Southwark London Borough Council* v. *Tanner* [2001] 1 A.C. 1, 20 per Lord Millett:

> The law of nuisance is concerned with balancing the conflicting interests of adjoining owners. It is often said to be encapsulated in the Latin maxim sic utere tuo ut alienum non laedas. This suggests a strict liability, but in practice the law seeks to protect the competing interests of both parties so far as it can. For this purpose it employs the control mechanism described by Lord Goff of Chieveley in *Cambridge Water Co* v. *Eastern Counties Leather Plc* [1994] 2 A.C. 264, 299 as 'the principle of reasonable user—the principle of give and take'.

34 *Countess of Rutland* v. *Bowler* (1622) Palm. 290; 81 E.R. 1087 (K.B.).

35 For a survey of the case law on requisite pleadings of possession see T. E. Lauer, 'The Common Law Background of the Riparian Doctrine' (1963) 28 Missouri Law Review 60, 81–5; A. J. Kedar, 'History of Anglo-American Law of Light' (Harvard LL.M thesis, 1990); *Aldred's Case* (1610) 9 Co. Rep. 57b; 77 E.R. 816 (K.B.) Note (B).

36 (c.1620) Hobart 193; 80 E.R. 340 (K.B.); *Viner's Abdgt.*, xxii, 527.

new writ to be issued where P, a millowner, had brought a meritorious but ill-declared action on the case, after D cut down his mill dam which was located on another's land. P had pleaded 'having an ancient water-course, or river coming to his mill', with a recent dam having been built to maintain the ancient banks of his watercourse. He brought an action on the case for cutting of the riverbank, which was neither part of his own land nor a servient tenement by grant or prescription. It was held that he ought to have laid the action for direct interference with the dam, which indirectly affected the watercourse and current which had flowed to the bank 'time out of mind'. The proprietary right to an ancient water flow had to be remedied by a direct trespass form of tort action. It was easy enough to go awry by incorrect legal identification of the salient facts.

By contrast, in the 1622 case of *Countess of Rutland* v. *Bowler*[37] pleading formalism was relaxed. The defendant claimed that action on the case for diversion of water was not permitted without alleging an ancient mill use. P's plea was nonetheless held good, on the basis that it sufficed to plead any present enjoyment of an ancient watercourse, such as a mill use, even if that mode of use was novel. An ancient mill, it was agreed, should attract protection; the same type of action could be brought if the land itself was shown to enjoy ancient water flow. Dodderidge J made it clear that proof of an ancient mill use could be dispensed with:

> If one erects a *new mill* on his freehold, and another *diverts the water-course* from this mill, tho' it passes by his land, yet if the water used to follow this course, action on the case lies against him; for he cannot use his land, or the water that passes by his land to the damage of another; and they say that has been several times adjudged.[38]

In two anonymous cases of 1638, involving diversion of water from a mill and from use for irrigation and cattle, it was similarly held that pleading an *antiquus aquaeductus* by which water 'was accustomed to flow and ought to flow' sufficed to found trespass on the case; there was no need to plead further a prescription based on use of flow or enjoyment time out of mind, as the allegation of ancient and customary flow 'compriseth in itself sufficient title, especially against a stranger who diverted it'. This decision probably does not mark a turn from prescriptive notions of right; the pattern of pleadings in this case and other cases of the early seventeenth-century

[37] (1622) Palm. 290; 81 E.R. 1087 (K.B.); *Viner's Abdgt.*, xv, 399–400.

[38] *Viner's Abdgt.*, xv, 399–400. Viner here gives an accurate rendition into English of the original text (Palm. 290), which states:

> in cest action ne besoigne, q soet auncient mill; car si erect un novel mill sur son freehold, & un auteur divert le course de water de cest mill, comt q pass p son tre; uncore si le water used sequer cest course, action sur le case gist vers luy; car ne poet user son terre, ou le water, q passe p son terre, al damage d'auteur: et diont, q issint ad estre plusors foits adjudge devat: et judgmt fuit enter p le plt.

King's Bench suggests that the notion of ancient, customary right was identical to a pleading of prescriptive right 'from time immemorial'.[39]

The shift from a prescriptive basis for property rights in water to natural rights was signalled in the brief report of the 1627 case of *Duncombe* v. *Sir Edward Randall*:

> In an action on the case between [P] and [D] for diversion and stopping of a river, it was agreed by the court that if one had antiently ponds which are replenisht by chanels out of a river, he cannot change the chanels, if any prejudice accrew to another by that. And yet the effect by prefluxions, is to have the ponds fed out of the river. But sic utere tuo ut ne laedas alieno.[40]

On a conservative interpretation, the case may have involved D exceeding the bounds of his prescriptive or ancient right to river-water for his ponds, to the detriment of another customary user. This could be seen as a simple breach of a defined prescriptive grant or entitlement. But the addition of the *sic utere tuo* maxim may indicate that in the eyes of the court, it was now the detriment caused by D's increased user to P's enjoyment of natural water flow to land which had founded the action—not breach of implied grant.

THE TRIUMPH OF NATURAL-RIGHT ANALYSIS

A natural-right basis of riparian doctrine was expressly adopted by King's Bench in the leading case of *Sury* v. *Pigot* of 1625.[41] P here brought an action upon the case for the stopping of his watercourse, pleading a standard prescription to found his right. P declared that he was possessed of a rectory and curtilage which had a pond or watering-place 'time out of mind . . . for the watering of the cattel of [P] and others, and for other necessary uses, and that a certain water-course had time out of mind flowed from Mildford Stream to this curtilage' to fill the pond. D had since built a dam on his land and diverted the stream, causing P special and continuing damage.[42] D argued for a non-suit on the ground that P's pleading of prescription was inadequate; and further mounted a defence that any right of water appended to P's tenement as a servitude against D's neighbouring land had been extinguished by the recent common possession of both lands by another

[39] Cf. *Co.Litt.* 110a–114b; A. W. B. Simpson, *A History of the Land Law* (2nd edn., Oxford, 1986) 110; see further Ch. 5.

[40] (1627–31) Hetley 33; 124 E.R. 320 (C.P.); *Viner's Abdgt.*, xxii, 525.

[41] (1625) Poph. 166; 79 E.R. 1263; 3 Bulst. 339; 81 E.R. 280 (K.B.). The importance of the decision is suggested by the numerous extant case reports: see e.g. Benloe 188, 73 E.R. 1046; Jones Rep. 145; 82 E.R. 77; Latch. 153; 82 E.R. 312; Noy. 84; 74 E.R. 1051; Palm. 444; 81 E.R. 1163; *Viner's Abdgt.* xxii, 525.

[42] A plea of *continuando* was necessary to quantify the sizeable damages sought for a protracted injury, in this case £20.

party (none other than the king), since a whole interest in the land was inconsistent with a particular right in one part of that land when divided from the other. The question for decision by the court was 'whether this unity of possession . . . hath extinguished the water-course'.[43]

Counsel for D characterized water rights as customary rights akin to easements, granted by one riparian owner to another: 'A way is but an easement, yet by the purchase of the land the way is extinguished, and also the watering-course is not only an easement, but a profit, or prender . . . '. There was no necessity nor local custom that the water right should revive after a unity of possession, nor should such revival be implied. By way of comparison, '[c]ommon appendant is destroyed by unity of possession, and yet it is a thing of common right, but a water-course being a thing against common right, *a fortiori* it shall be extinguished'. D further argued that there could be two types of prescriptive watercourse, one established by prescription as appurtenant to land, another as necessary to a prescriptive ancient mill:

> [T]his water-course hath its original out of the land, and this case cannot be compared to an ancient water-course running to a mill, for notwithstanding the unity it shall pass with the mill, for otherwise it shall not be *molendinum aquaticum*, so that the water there is a parcel of the thing, and so of necessity ought to pass with the thing, but here it doth not appear that it is a water-course of necessity, and for anything that appeareth, it may be filled with another water-course.[44]

Counsel for P conceded that 'it is repugnant for a man to have a way upon his own land' but argued that a watercourse was a different case, since unlike a way or other easement created by legal transaction, a watercourse 'hath a being and existence, notwithstanding the unity [of possession]' and therefore 'is not destroyed by the unity'. Support for this proposition was found in *Challenor's Case*,[45] where it was held that a possessory action of ejectment was allowed for the recovery of the soil or land of a watercourse (if not for the water flow itself), thus suggesting that a watercourse as a physical object was an incident of property legally separate from the ownership of the surrounding riparian tenements. Counsel for D rejected this extrapolation: 'I conceive that the water-course is not *stagnum* [a pond, being land capable of possession] but *servitium* [a servitude or incorporeal hereditament created by law], which is due from the one land to the other: it is but a liberty'. A watercourse could not be a right attached to riparian land unless it was a permissive way

[43] On unity of possession in Roman law and Bracton, see Ch. 2, the text accompanying nn. 122–30. Cf. *Sydowne* v. *Holme* (1635) Jones W 368; 82 E.R. 193; *Aldermen and Burgesses Bury St Edmund* v. *Evans* (1739) 2 Comyns 643, 92 E.R. 1249.

[44] Poph., 166, 169; 79 E.R. 1263, 1266.

[45] *Challenor* v. *Thomas* (1608) 1 Brownsl. & Golds. 142; 123 E.R. 718; S.C. *Chancellor* v. *Thomas* (1608) Yelv. 143; 80 E.R. 96 (K.B.); *Viner's Abdgt.*, xxii, 525.

for water or a right attached prescriptively to an ancient water mill which passed by necessity as 'parcel' of the mill.[46]

King's Bench allowed P's action, deciding that a riparian owner enjoyed a natural right to the flow of water to his tenement, and that such a right was not a servitude affected by a recent unity of possession. However, this new naturalist doctrine of water rights was not sharply distinguished from alternative riparian doctrines. The judges gave content to the opaque notion of natural right by an admixture of ideas of necessity, custom, and prescription. A water right could be seen to be 'natural' variously because the water had always flowed past the owner's land, or because the water had customarily been an incident of value to that land, or was a necessary incident to the enjoyment of the land.[47]

The judgments drew a modern-sounding distinction between matters of substantive law and matters of pleading and procedure. Whitlock CJ held that the right to flowing water was independent of grant or prescription:

> [T]he question here is of *aqua profluens*, and I conceive that there needs no prescription or custom in this case, for water hath its natural course . . . *natura sua descendit*, it may be called *usu captio*, or usage. . . . [T]he watercourse doth not begin by the consent of the parties, nor by prescription, but ex jurae naturae, and therefore shall not be extinguished by unity.[48]

In distinction to the natural water right, the cases of a way or a common were described as praedial servitudes attached to land 'by private writ, to wit, by grant or prescription'.[49] The reports have Whitlock CJ cite Bracton for this distinction;[50] but as has been seen, Bracton habitually merged within the category of servitudes both praedial rights 'imposed by man' through grant, and natural rights 'imposed by law'.[51] Bulstrode's report suggests that Whitlock was carefully trying to split Bracton's expansive concept of servitudes:

> There is a difference between a way, a common, and a water-course. Bracton lib.4 f.221, 222 calls them servitutes praediales, these which begin by private right, by prescription, by assent, as a way common, being a particular benefit, to take part of the profits of the land; this is extinct by unity, because the greater benefit shall drown

[46] Poph. 166, 167; 79 E.R. 1263, 1264.

[47] Cf. W. S. Holdsworth, *A History of English Law* (2nd edn., London, 1937) vii, 329–30.

[48] Poph. 166, 170; 79 E.R. 1263, 1267; Crew CJ to the same effect, at 172; 1268–9. Whitlock cited 'Brudnel in 12 H. 8' for this doctrine, which was probably a reference to a manuscript report of *K.* v. *M.*, *The Case of the Queen's Forester* (1520) Y. B. Hen. 8 f. 8 (C.P.), in *Year Books of Henry VIII, 12–14 Hen. VIII 1520–1523* (J. H. Baker (ed.), Selden Society, cix, 2002) 42–6 at 45 per Brudenell CJ, n. 27 above; Ch. 2 n. 110.

[49] *Sury* v. *Pigot*, Poph., 166, 170, 79 E.R., 1263, 1266–7.

[50] Ibid.: 'by the unity of possession the water-course is not extinguished, and yet I agree the cases of a way and common upon the differences which are put in Bracton lib. 4. 221. These are called *servitutes*, as *jus eundi, fodendi, hauriendi, &c. sunt servitutes quas praedia ex quibus exeunt aliis praediis debent, and are called servitutes praediales*, and this began by private writ . . .'.

[51] Ch. 2, above, the text accompanying nn. 117–20.

the less; a water-course doth not begin by prescription, nor yet by assent, but the same doth begin ex jure naturae, having taken this course naturally, and cannot be averted.[52]

It is this statement of the natural-right doctrine, as a category distinct from servitude law, that is digested in Viner's *Abridgement* of 1794 as the leading statement in English law on watercourses, and the statement was extensively cited and quoted in the nineteenth-century courts.[53]

Whitlock CJ further held that the right to air through a window of a house was another natural right apt to be defended by action on the case; but not window-light, which had to be prescribed for, even though it might be requisite for proper enjoyment of a house. Interference with the natural flow of water was thus isolated as a special natural right, attaching to land as land, independent of any use of, or buildings upon, the land: 'The course of a spring, is a natural course, and current, and to stop this, may be a nusans to the common-wealth [that is, a public nuisance], and a private wrong'.[54] Whitlock CJ also indicated that he wished to limit the common law's defence of existing property usages by prescription and grant, lest this encourage a tendency to monopoly or inflexibility in use of resources. He drew a careful distinction between rights of amenity attaching to land through natural right, rights through prescription by long-standing practice, and finally permissible activities carried out on land which could never, through right of nature or continued practice, attract legal protection from competing activities. The following example was given: 'If there be a school-master in a town, and another erect a new school in the same town, an action upon the case doth not lie against him, because schools are for the publick benefit, and every private man may have a school in his house'.[55]

Jones J came to similar conclusions, holding that a watercourse was a natural right 'being a thing which ariseth out of the land', drawing careful distinctions between rights attached to land by necessity, by grant, or by prescription, and rights recognized simply because they were part of the fabric of the land.

A man hath things out of another man's land, either by grant as a seigniory, rent, common, &c. and these are extinguished by unity &c. and the reason is, because one who hath interest as owner of the land, cannot have a particular interest in the same land also. Or by prescription, and those things are extinguished by unity of possession also, and not only for the first reason because he is owner of the land... but also because that by the unity the prescription fail.... But now for our case, it differs... for the prescription here is in another manner than is made for common, for it shall be pleaded either as appendant, or appurtenant, but *currere solebat* is only in this

[52] 3 Bulst. 339, 340; 81 E.R. 280, 281.

[53] *Viner's Abdgt.*, xxii, 525.

[54] Bulst., 339, 340; 81 E.R. 280, 281.

[55] Poph. 166, 170; 79 E.R. 1263, 1266; cf. *Case of Gloucester School* (1410) Y.B. Hil. 11 Hen 4, f. 47, pl. 21 per Hankford J, in Baker and Milsom (eds.), *Sources*, 613–14; *Jeffrey's Case* (*c.*1560) ibid., 592; the text accompanying nn. 103–4 below.

pleading, for here no interest is claimed, but in the other cases [of common] an interest is claimed: in this case the land remains as it was before, and therefore the unity will not extinguish it: and if such an unity by construction of law should extinguish water-courses, it would be too dangerous, for... suppose that the water-course after it hath been in the curtilage of the plaintiff, goes into another curtilage, is it reason that by this unity the second man [that is the plaintiff as owner of both curtilages] shall lose his water-course? without doubt it is unreasonable.[56]

A *res communes* or common right argument was offered by Crew CJ, who saw a watercourse as a 'thing natural', 'a linement out of which every man shall have a benefit', and also a 'matter of necessity'; and so was distinguished from non-natural appurtenant rights incident to land:

In our law every case hath its stand or fall from a particular reason or circumstance: for a warren and tythes they are not extinguished by unity, because they are things collateral to the land... of an inclosure; I conceive that by the unity the inclosure is destroyed, for the prescription was interrupted.... [A]nd for our case... is not like to the cases of common, or a way, because the water-course is a thing natural and therefore by unity it shall not be discharged.[57]

Dodderidge J gave two reasons for preserving a watercourse under a unified ownership: '1. For the necessity of the thing. 2. From the nature of the thing being a water-course, which is a thing running.'[58] He suggested that water rights revived upon division of a unified tenement, as did a right of common appendant; both were rights of necessity, for a common right was appendant to ancient arable and pastoral land 'which is necessary for the preservation of the commonwealth... as... there is a necessity of bread; so in our case there is a necessity of water'. But water rights were not only appendant rights of necessity like commons; there was also a right attached to riparian property arising '[f]rom the nature of water, which naturally descends, it is always current, *et aut invenit aut facit viam*, and shall such a thing be extinguished which hath its being from the creation?'.[59] Thus water was seen not as a transient servitude between tenements, but as a permanent part of the land and an inherent attribute of title. This riparian doctrine was distinguished from the necessity principle, as the right to a watercourse required for the working of a mill[60] or a dye-house[61] subsisted, even if that necessary use of the water was varied or abandoned: '[A] mill is a necessary thing, and if I purchase the land upon which the stream runs to this mill, and afterwards I alien the mill, the water-course remains.'[62]

56 Poph. 166, 171; 79 E.R. 1263, 1267–8.

57 Poph. 166, 172; 79 E.R. 1263, 1268–9.

58 Poph. 166, 172; 79 E.R. 1263, 1268.

59 Ibid.

60 Cf. *Luttrel's Case*, the text accompanying nn. 12–17 above.

61 Cf. *Moore* v. *Browne* (1572) 3 Dyer 319b–320a; 73 E.R. 723 (K.B.); the text accompanying nn. 7–8 above.

62 Citing *Luttrel's Case*; and see *Sury* v. *Pigot* in 3 Bulst. 339, 340–1; 81 E.R. 280, 281, where the necessity ground is emphasized.

To summarize, in *Sury* the judges preferred natural-right analysis to servitudes as the juristic basis of water rights, using the doctrine as an instrumental device to overcome the bar of the recent unity of possession of P's land with neighbouring tenements. The court carefully addressed the role of prescription as an alternative basis for the constitution of water rights. First, it was held unnecessary to plead ownership of a specific type of ancient messuage (such as an ancient rectory, park, or mill) to which water descended; it was only the flow of water which had to be immemorial, not the form of estate of the claimant's tenement. Secondly, a relatively informal plea of customary flow sufficed to import a prescription (for example, '*currere solebat & consuevit*').[63] Thirdly, no prescription need be made to establish an interest in the watercourse as land in possession; P need only claim an interest in land to which the water customarily flowed. The requisite interest in the land was not specified, but it appears to be a fee simple in possession. P could also claim on behalf of his customary tenants for interference with the prescriptive right, this 'being in an action on the case where damages only are to be recovered', that is, where injury to executed interests, rather than assertion of continuing rights, was at stake.

A further shift in the foundations of water law from prescription to natural rights can be identified in the 1639 case of *Sands* v. *Trefuses*.[64] Here the King's Bench held that there was no requirement that a plaintiff asserting right to an unimpeded water flow to his land must plead ancient or customary use, of either mill or watercourse, in order to establish a particular water right. Thus P could 'maintain his action on the case being lawfully in possession, and the stopping of the water is tortious, and a damage to his mill', it being immaterial that he did not show special title to the watercourse, or even show that he was in possession as tenant in fee simple. Simple possession of a riparian tenement and special damage to an existing use of water flow were the only prerequisites of action.[65] It may be doubted, however, whether this shift in the form of pleading can be equated with the adoption of a novel natural-right concept of water right, wholly independent of prescription. At this time, Coke in his gloss on Littleton was writing that appendant rights of common—rights of necessity attached to agricultural land—would be attached by a legally presumed prescription or grant without necessitating a special pleading of the right, in contrast to common

[63] Doderidge J, Poph. 166, 171; 79 E.R. 1263, 1268; cf. *Anon.* (1638) Cro. Car. 499; 79 E.R. 1031 (K.B.).

[64] (1639) Cro. Car. 575; 79 E.R. 1094 (K.B.); Lauer, 'Common Law Background', 88–9; C. M. Rose, 'Energy and Efficiency in the Realignment of Common Law Water Rights' (1990) 19 Journal of Legal Studies 261, 267–70.

[65] Cf. *Dent* v. *Oliver* (1604) Cro. Jac. 43; 79 E.R. 35, where King's Bench held that in an action on the case for disturbance of a fair toll, P need only plead seisin in fee of a manor together with a bare assertion of right to the market, without showing special title by prescription to such appurtenant right.

appurtenant where special pleading was required. This simplification of the pleading rules ensured that certain property rights would be presumed as inherent or necessary in all grants, an application of the principle that a grantor shall not derogate from his grant. Coke was not purporting to describe appendant commons as pure natural rights of possession, but as incidents 'of common right', complementing freehold titles. His doctrine does, however, lend itself to a natural-right analysis if the substructure of legal implications is ignored.[66]

Similar doctrines implying incidental ownership rights developed in the 1670s, allowing many other species of right of property enjoyment to be pleaded on the sole basis of possession, rather than by prescription attaching a right to a fee simple estate. Examples include rights of way;[67] and monopoly rights such as mill suits and tolls,[68] and exclusive markets and fairs.[69] This development encompassed rights incidental to property which evidently were not 'natural' or necessary physical concomitants of land ownership, but rather social entitlements created as servitudes appurtenant to ownership. This might suggest that by the late seventeenth century, an owner bringing an action on the case for damage to incidents to property, whether natural rights or servitudes, need only show possession of land, and then assert that such land ought to have appurtenant or appendant rights, without formally pleading the source of title to those rights. The usual procedure was that seisin in fee and special title arising from prescription would be assumed unless challenged. Pleading and argument could then proceed on factually contested issues of causation and damage, rather than issues of title; hence a source of rights beyond legal possession need not be stated.[70]

The simplifications of pleading reform of the late seventeenth century were used expansively by judges to promote new natural-right concepts, especially

[66] *Co.Litt.* 122a–b; see also *Bishop of Salisbury's Case* (1614) 10 Co.Rep. 59b, 77 E.R. 1013, 1015 (K.B.) Note (B). For thorough treatment see J. Williams, *Rights of Common and Other Prescriptive Rights* (London, 1880) 31–43, 168–85.

[67] *Blockley* v. *Slater* (1692) 1 Lutw. 119; 125 E.R. 63 (C.P.); *Warren* v. *Sainthill* (1689) 2 Vent. 185; 86 E.R. 383 (C.P.); *St John* v. *Moody* (1675) 3 Keb. 528, 531, 84 E.R. 860, 862; 2 Lev. 148, 83 E.R. 492; 1 Vent. 274; 86 E.R. 184 (K.B.); *Prothonotary Winford* v. *Wollaston* (1690) 3 Lev. 266, 83 E.R. 682 (C.P.).

[68] *Coryton* v. *Lithebye* (1671) 2 Wms. Saund. 112; 85 E.R. 814 at 818–9 (K.B.); *Smith* v. *Martin* (1672) 2 Wms. Saund. 400, 85 E.R. 1210.

[69] *Yard* v. *Ford* (1671) 2 Wms. Saund. 172; 85 E.R. 922 (K.B.), with Sjt. Saunders' notes; and see *Palmer* v. *Keblethwaite* 1 Show. K.B. 64; 89 E.R. 451 (K.B.) per Hoyle for P *in arg.*; *Eden* v. *Marche* citing *Rutland* v. *Bowler* (1622) Palm. 290; *Fletcher* v. *Palmer* (1663) 1 Lev. 122; 1 Sid. 167, 227; 83 E.R. 329 (K.B.).

[70] The seventeenth-century pleadings for nuisance to possession are summarized in Sjt. Saunders' and John and Edward Williams' annotations to *Coryton* v. *Lithebye* (1671) 2 Wms. Saund. 112; 85 E.R. 814 (K.B.); *Yard* v. *Ford* (1671) 2 Wms. Saund. 172; 85 E.R. 922 (K.B.); *Mellor* v. *Spateman* (1670) 1 Wms. Saund. 339; 85 E.R. 489 (K.B.), Note (2); see also *Bishop of Salisbury's Case* (1614) 10 Co.Rep. 59b, 77 E.R. 1013 (K.B.) Note (B); *Fentiman* v. *Smith* (1803) 4 East. 107; 102 E.R. 770 (K.B.); *Wickham* v. *Hawker* (1846) 7 M. & W. 63; 151 E.R. 679 (Ex.).

rights pertaining to the 'physical' concomitants of property enjoyment, such as access to water, light, and air. An example is found in the briefly reported but influential 1673 case of *Cox* v. *Matthews*.[71] It concerned an 'action for a nusance' for stopping of lights, where P failed to plead an 'ancient messuage' enjoying such lights. P's pleadings were held valid, with the court suggesting that a right to light subsisted even in a case where P's house was newly built. The result seems to have been stated in terms of a necessarily implied grant attaching to P's land upon separation from the land of D. Here the idea of a necessary implication to prevent derogation from grant stood as an analogy to natural right.

Hale CJ explained the result by the following comparison: 'If a man hath a water-course running through his ground, and erects a mill upon it, he may bring his action for diverting the stream, and not say *antiquum molendinum*.' This was a reworking of the rule stated in *Sands* v. *Trefuses* and presaged in *Luttrel*. He continued: '[U]pon the evidence it will appear, whether [D] hath ground through which the stream runs before [P], and that [D] used to turn the stream as he saw cause; for otherwise [D] cannot justify it, though the mill [of P] be newly erected.'[72] This ambiguous dictum might mean that D's defence to P's action for natural or customary flow is D's own established, inconsistent use of that water flow—though whether the competing use must be a rival ancient use, or a prescription displacing P's alleged prescription, or else a recent form of appropriation superseding P's customary right was left unclear. At any rate judges perceived that the ground had shifted. In a 1675 right of way case possession without a pleading of prescription sufficed: 'in truth, the greatest part of the enclosures in England have been within time of memory. . . . 'tis true, before 7 Jacobi [*quaere*, *Aldred's Case*], the usage has been in actions of this nature to prescribe, but not since'.[73]

The theory of property use-rights as prescriptions, based on immemorial custom, created pleading problems where P and D each claimed inconsistent prescriptive rights, as King's Bench explained in *Aldred's Case*: 'When a man has a lawful easement or profit, by prescription from time whereof, &c. another custom which is also from time whereof &c. cannot take it away, for one custom is as ancient as the other.' In a diversion case of 1690, it was indicated that D had to traverse the factual existence of P's prescription for water, if D wished to plead his own rival prescriptive right to the water.[74]

[71] (1673) 1 Ventr. 237; 86 E.R. 159 (K.B.); 3 Keble 133; 84 E.R. 636; *Viner's Abdgt.*, xv, 400.

[72] 1 Ventr. 237; 86 E.R. 159; to similar effect see 3 Keble 133; 84 E.R. 636.

[73] *St John* v. *Moody* (1675) 1 Vent. 274; 86 E.R. 184 (K.B.), citing also *Sands* v. *Trefuses* (1639) Cro. Car. (3 Cro.) 575; 79 E.R. 1094 (K.B.).

[74] 9 Co. Rep. 57b, 59a; 77 E.R. 816, 821; *Murgatroyd* v. *Law* (1690) Carth. 116; 90 E.R. 672 (K.B.). See also *Waring* v. *Griffith* (1758) 2 Kenyon 183, 96 E.R. 1149, S.C. 1 Burrow 440, 97 E.R. 392 (K.B.); *Morewood* v. *Wood* (1791) 4 Term Reports 157; 100 E.R. 948 (K.B.).

Many of these conceptual difficulties were reviewed in the case of *Palmer* v. *Keblethwaite* (1682–6).[75] In this protracted litigation, action on the case was brought by a millowner, P, for loss of profit upon diversion by D of an ancient watercourse from his 60-year-old corn mill. D argued that P had failed to plead a prescriptive right to an immemorial flow of water for the use of an ancient mill; and further that D had legitimately broken the dam which had previously supplied water to D's mill as well as to P's, claiming that he [D] had an untrammelled right as owner to remove the millpond from his land if he had no use for it. 'Upon these exceptions the case depended long.'[76] At first instance, King's Bench agreed that P was seised of the stream by virtue of his ownership of riparian land; and hence that 'an action had lain for diverting a stream, though no mill had been erected; and that therefore it need not be shewn to be an antient mill, as it must be where he prescribes to have a water-course, where the water is not his own'.[77] This seems to support a natural-right theory, whereby title to water flow is incidental to possession of land through which water has immemorially flowed (including where a stream naturally runs through the land). The court stated that 'the stream is his [P's] own'; hence proof of a particular ancient or prescriptive use of the flowing water was irrelevant.[78] But this position was not favoured at a later hearing. D's counsel seems to have persuaded the court to reject the idea that a prescriptive right to water could ever be founded on 'the nature of the land it self', on two grounds. First, the law required an ancient, prescriptive use to establish the proprietary right of enjoyment. In the absence of a prescriptive right, nobody could claim a protected access to water, following the analogy of window-light:

[75] The scattered reports of the action suggest that there were maybe three stages of litigation:
(1) Original judgment in a K.B. action: *Palms* v. *Heblethwait* (1682) Skin. 65; 90 E.R. 31 and *Palmes* v. *Keblethwayte* (1682) 2 Show. K.B. 243; 89 E.R. 916, (adjournatur, K.B.); *Palmis* v. *Heblethwait* (1682) 2 Show. K.B. 249, 89 E.R. 921 (special verdict on one count affirmed, K.B.); (1682/4) Skin. 175; 90 E.R. 81 (cur. adv. vult.).
(2) Original judgment, in a separate C.P. action: *Nulmes* v. *Hoblethwayte* (1683) 3 Lev. 133; 83 E.R. 615.
(3) Argument for demurrer on error from C.P.; argument; judgment affirmed by K.B.: *Heblethwaite* v. *Palmes* (1684/89) 3 Mod. 48; 87 E.R. 30; *Keblethwait* v. *Palmes* (1686) Comb. 9; 90 E.R. 311; *Palmer* v. *Keblethwaite* (1689) 1 Show. K.B. 64; 89 E.R. 451; *Heblethwait* v. *Palms* Carth. 84; 90 E.R. 653; Holt 5; 90 E.R. 901. See also *Viner's Abdgt.*, xv, 400; XXII, 527.

For the vagaries of reporting in early modern English law see L. W. Abbott, *Law Reporting in England, 1485–1585* (London, 1973); D. J. Ibbetson, 'Law Reporting in the 1590s', and W. H. Bryson, 'Law Reports in England from 1603 to 1660', both in C. Stebbings (ed.), *Law Reporting in England* (London, 1995), 73–88; and 113–22; M. Macnair, 'The Nature and Function of the Early Chancery Reports', ibid., 123–32; J. W. Wallace, *The Reporters, Arranged and Characterized with Incidental Remarks* (4th edn., Boston, Mass., 1882) 114 ff. We can assume that printed reports supplemented by the more widely copied and circulated manuscript reports influenced legal development to a greater degree than the more 'private' manuscript reports: weak authenticity undermined forensic authority.

[76] *Viner's Abdgt.*, xxii, 527. [77] (1682) Skin. 65; 90 E.R. 31.

[78] (1682) Skin. 65; 90 E.R. 31. (1682/4) Skin. 175; 90 E.R. 81.

[N]o man can prescribe to light *quatenus* such, because it is of common right to all men, and cannot be claimed but as affixed to a particular thing or purpose. A *water-course* may be claimed to several purposes, but *water* is of as universal use and benefit to mankind as *light*; and therefore no particular man hath a right to water, but as belonging to an ancient house, or running to an ancient mill, or for some other ancient use.[79]

A *res communes* concept of water and light was thus employed to deny any persons an action to maintain private use of these amenities. Secondly, it was argued that in the absence of a special use laid, such as pasturing, irrigation, or milling, there could be no conceivable damage or prejudice in law to the owner's riparian right; and an established use of the water flow rather than its natural extent was said to be the measure of right:

[P] said, he had the water *pro usu & commodo*, and sets not forth what use or profit, for it may be for watering his cattle, or flowing his ground, or other special use; so that by pulling down the dam, nothing is done in prejudice to that right, though there may not be sufficient to drive the mill.[80]

Against this pure ancient use theory, P's counsel proposed a theory based upon the natural right of an owner and occupier of the soil in the water flowing upon the soil, the extent of this right being set by the *sic utere tuo* principle. This meant that a mill use not interfering with others' uses was to be protected, no matter how recent the mill:

[P] went upon the right the owner hath in the soil, and to the water upon the soil; and said it was lawful for a man to use his own after what manner he pleased, so as not hurting his neighbour; and that he having lawfully erected a mill upon his own soil, the diverting part of the water-course is an injury which ought to be repaired in damages; and that here in this case no prescription is necessary.[81]

At this stage the court inclined to the idea that an interference with an existing use (but not, it seems, an ancient use) was necessary to establish actionable damage, and that interference with natural flow without more was insufficient.

At a still later hearing before King's Bench on error from Common Pleas, Pollexfen argued for P that where damage is inflicted on an owner's enjoyment of land, it was sufficient to show '*possession* against a *wrong doer*' without proving title by prescription: '[P] has a good cause of action; for it cannot be denied, but where an injury is done to another, and damages ensue, it is sufficient to maintain an action of trespass, or upon the case.'[82] Where wrongful damage was inflicted, use was to be pleaded 'only to inform the

[79] (1684/9) 3 Mod. 48, 49–50; 87 E.R. 30, 31. [80] Skin. 175; 90 E.R. 81.
[81] Skin. 175–6; 90 E.R. 81.
[82] 3 Mod. 48, 50; 87 E.R. 30, 32; cf. Comb. 9.; 90 E.R. 311; 1 Show K.B. 64; 89 E.R. 451, citing Bracton l.4 c.3, f. 221–222.

Court of the damages', or to 'aggravate the damages'.[83] Formal proof of right by prescription or grant was unnecessary, for the action on the case here operated like trespass to defend 'possession alone . . . against a wrongdoer'; '[i]n possessory actions the title need not be strictly made out, as in a prescription: Bract[on] cap. 43'.[84] By analogy 'where a man hath the possession, tho' he hath no property in the goods, he may have trespass';[85] '[t]his action is of the same nature with an action of trespass, and therefore good upon the possession only'.[86] Counsel for P cited a number of precedents dealing with incorporeal rights, stating:

> [a]ll which prove, that a prescription goes to the right, but a possession is sufficient to support an action against a *tort feasor*. . . . [W]here he prescribes for *a way*, he may set forth his estate without shewing how he came by it, because it is but a conveyance to the action, which is grounded upon the disturbance done to the possession.[87]

Following this doctrine, it was argued 'that this was only a possessory action and need say no more'.[88] The defence of water rights was thereby characterized as a branch of tort (remedy of executed wrongs to possession) rather than property (vindication of prospective rights).

In what amounted to an evasion of P's doctrinal arguments, King's Bench was content to find an implied prescription in P's plea that water had immemorially flowed to his mill, in order to found an actionable title to the water flow without more. 'The word "*solet*" [of P's pleadings] implies antiquity, and will amount to a prescription; and *solitus cursus aquae* running to a mill, make the mill to be ancient; for if it were newly erected, there cannot be *solitus cursus aquae* towards that mill.'[89] Holt CJ seems to have doubted this ratio, stating that there could be no action in the absence of a specific ancient use going to prove title: '[I]f the cause had been tried before him, the plaintiff should have proved his mill to be an antient mill, otherwise he should have been non-suit.'[90] At an earlier hearing of the case on error in King's Bench, Holt CJ had elaborated his approach: 'Suppose a watercourse run to my ground, and I have no use for it, and one, upon another ground, divert it before it come to mine, will an action lie? . . . must you not lay some

[83] See also *Richards* v. *Hill* (1695) 5 Mod. 206; 87 E.R. 611 (K.B.).

[84] Comb. 9; 90 E.R. 311.

[85] Carth. 84, 85; 90 E.R. 653.

[86] Carth. 84, 85; 90 E.R. 653, 655.

[87] 3 Mod. 48, 52; 87 E.R. 30, 33.

[88] 2 Show K.B. 243; 89 E.R. 916.

[89] 3 Mod. 48; 87 E.R. 30. Only Dolben J appears to support P's argument, citing *Hart* v. *Bisset* (1687), 'which was an action for stopping an usual an convenient way to his (the plaintiff's) land; and this declaration was held good, without shewing a title': Carth. 84, 85; 90 E.R. 653, 654; a similar rule is expressed in *Anon.* (1638) Cro. Car. 499; 79 E.R. 1031 (K.B.) and *Sury* v. *Pigot* (1625) Poph. 166; 79 E.R. 1263; 3 Bulst. 339; 81 E.R. 280 (K.B.), text accompanying nn. 41–63 above; but here the readiness to imply a pleading of prescription is taken a step further.

[90] Holt K.B. 5, 6; 90 E.R. 901; Carth. 84, 85; 90 E.R. 653, 654; cf. 3 Mod. 48, 52; 87 E.R. 30, 33: 'if the cause had been tried upon such a declaration, [P] ought to have proved his *prescription*, or else he must be nonsuited.'

use for it?'.[91] This might be taken as ruling that damage to a present use must be pleaded as the gist of the action on case; but in light of Holt CJ's judgment in the final hearing, this dictum should rather be interpreted as stating that there was no initial property-right in the water to defend, unless it were a right established by long user or prescription. This position aligns with Holt CJ's later opinion in *Ashby* v. *White*[92] asserting that actual loss was not required in order to bring an action defending property rights; but that some source of property right must be shown prior to any claim for injury to the right.

All the members of the final Court of King's Bench in *Palmer* v. *Keblethwaite* were indifferent to P's radical argument for a tort-to-possession theory of action for water rights; yet this theory does seem to underpin legal reasoning in many other water cases of the time. Ideas of natural right are in the ascendancy, but judges are not sure if the natural right is based on rights of seisin, *sic utere tuo*, ancient flow, ancient use or prescriptive grant. There is no hard-and-fast line between natural-right and prescription analyses based on use.

PLEADING AND SUBSTANCE IN THE LATE SEVENTEENTH CENTURY

Two entwined problems of water law may be isolated within the seventeenth-century debates: determining the nature of the legal interest in water use; and delimiting the extent of legal protection afforded to a recognized interest in water flow.

The Nature of the Interest

Water rights could be claimed by two methods, through prescriptive claims to flowing water aid against neighbours; and by asserting a possessory interest in riparian land with appurtenant water rights. The case law suggests widely varying pleading requirements supporting these two types of claim.

Maximalist Pleadings

At the strictest level of pleading, a fee simple ownership of land with an ancient watercourse, put to an ancient use, always had to be stated.[93] More

[91] 1 Show K.B. 64; 89 E.R. 451.

[92] *Ashby* v. *White* (1703) 6 Mod. 45; 87 E.R. 810; 2 Ld. Raym. 938; 92 E.R. 126; Holt K.B. 524; 90 E.R. 1188 (K.B.), discussed in the text accompanying nn. 119–129 below.

[93] For earlier precedents see *Russell* v. *Handford* (1583) 1 Leon. 273; 74 E.R. 248 (K.B.); *Scoble* v. *Skelton* (1682) 2 Show. K.B. 195; 89 E.R. 886; Skin. 36; 90 E.R. 18 (K.B.), where it was held that a bare plea of seisin in an estate was bad, as seisin *in fee* of a continuing estate must always be alleged to support a prescriptive claim.

commonly, it sufficed to demonstrate seisin in land served by an ancient flow of water, together with a present use of that water which was harmed by D's actions. For an example, in *Prickman* v. *Tripp*[94] there was no need to declare the origin and terminus of the water flow: 'having shewn, that the stream was used to run to the well; and [D] having diverted it when it was at the well, this is a tort, and it was not material from whence it comes'. In this case the court was willing to relax pleading requirements and presume the necessary factual indicia, in order to avoid having to set aside a completed verdict. The missing declarations (that the water had been used time out of mind, etc.) were characterized as matters of fact that were obvious from the tenor of the case or else assumed by the completed verdict. The water flow claimed by prescription need not be stated to have 'run from time whereof &c.' provided that prescription was indicated by the words '*aquae currere consueviset et debuit*'—the water customarily flowed and ought to have flowed.[95]

Minimalist Pleadings

Abbreviation of pleadings could be pushed much further. In some instances it sufficed to plead possession of land enjoying the flow of water harmed by D's actions, basing the claim on the tortious notion of wrongful harm to possession, with the plaintiff in possession not being required to plead seisin of a particular estate in order to establish his right. Protected interests in water flow could thus include that of a lessee (or lessor) suffering special damage whether the legal interest was vested or in possession;[96] or the individual commoner's right of use where the full right was vested in a communal or corporate body—an analogy commonly used to explain how proprietary incidents could be attached to a mere possessory interest.[97] For example, in *Jackson* v. *Savage* a pleading of simple possession of a house and messuage in the absence of a fee simple claim, with water customarily flowing across the messuage, sufficed to establish a water right without any prescription for the watercourse in a free tenement, 'this being a possessory action'.[98]

[94] (1693) Skin. 389; 90 E.R. 173; Comb. 231; 90 E.R. 447 (K.B.); *Viner's Abdgt.*, xxii, 527–8.

[95] Skin. 389; 90 E.R. 173.

[96] *Glynne* v. *Nichols* (1687–8) 2 Show. K.B. 507; 89 E.R. 1069; Comb. 43; 90 E.R. 333 (K.B.); *Villiers* v. *Ball* (1689) 1 Show. K.B. 7; 89 E.R. 412 (K.B.); *R.* v. *Inhabitants of the Hermitage* (1690) Carthew. 114; 90 E.R. 671 (K.B.); *Jackson* v. *Savage* (1692) Skin. 319; 90 E.R. 142 (K.B.); *Rosewell* v. *Prior* (1701) 1 Ld. Raym. 1089, 1094; 91 E.R. 1375, 1570 (K.B.) (notion of harm to a reversion); *Leveridge* v. *Hoskins* (1709) 11 Mod. 257; 88 E.R. 1025 (K.B.), discussed in the text accompanying nn. 117–118 below.

[97] *Mellor* v. *Spateman* (1670) 1 Wms. Saund. 339; 85 E.R. 489 (K.B.). Holt CJ discussed this case in *Ashby* v. *White* (1703) 2 Ld. Raym., 953; 92 E.R., 135:

> '[W]here the Corporation of Derby claim common by prescription, and though the inheritance of the common be in the body politic, yet the particular members enjoy the fruit and benefit of it, and put in their own cattle to feed on the common, and not the cattle belonging to the corporation.'

[98] (1692) Skin. 319; 90 E.R. 142 (K.B.); *Viner's Abdgt.*, xxii, 527.

The category of 'maximalist' cases preserved the triple requirements of (1) loss or damage, (2) inflicted on a prescriptive right to an ancient watercourse, flowing to (3) a tenement seised in fee. All three elements had to be shown to ground a claim.[99] By contrast, the 'minimalist' approach, even if narrowly characterized as a pragmatic relaxation of rules of pleading and proof, allowed lesser possessory interests to be brought to court for remedy.[100] In the eighteenth century there was a further abandonment of the requirement of ancient right attached to fee simple ownership, such that simple prior appropriation of water flow by a riparian owner grounded a legal claim to the uninterrupted flow.

The Extent of Protection—Damage or Title?

It has been shown how in the action of trespass on the case, the courts might require a pleading of present use of a prescriptive water flow in order to set the extent of special damage inflicted by D's acts of interference.[101] This requirement flowed from a theory of trespass on the case which aligns legal *injuria* with damage to a recognized use. It implies that an actionable water right derives from an established use of the natural stream, and that diversion of the stream is a wrong because it reduces the present utilities enjoyed by the riparian owner. As plaintiffs began to argue that any interference with the flow of water to a tenement was a tort, regardless of existing use of the water flow, a notion of *injuria sine damno* emerged whereby the tort action obliquely defended prospective title to water flow. This theory implied that property rights are to be upheld to the fullest extent compatible with like ownership of others (a variant of the *sic utere tuo* principle[102]). It also implied that a watercourse is of present benefit as a capital asset which may be utilized in the future, so that any invasion of natural flow diminishes a present right to future enjoyment.

The intractable issue was whether an actionable injury to water rights required damage, as in the actions falling within assize of nuisance and trespass on the case; or was rather an invasion of possession, a general

[99] See e.g. *Prickman* v. *Tripp* (1693) Skin. 389; 90 E.R. 173; Comb. 231; 90 E.R. 447 (K.B.); *Palmer* v. *Keblethwaite* (1682) Skin. 65; 90 E.R. 31 (K.B.) etc., and the text accompanying nn. 75–92 above.

[100] For a nineteenth-century discussion of this doctrine see *Frankum* v. *Earl of Falmouth* (1835) 6 C. & P. 529 (N.P.); 2 Ad. & E. 452; 111 E.R. 175 (K.B.); *Ward* v. *Robins* (1846) 15 M. & W. 237; 153 E.R. 837 (Ex.).

[101] See e.g. *Mellor* v. *Spateman*, n. 97 above, where it was held that for a case to be brought for injury to a commoner's right there must be special damage to an existing use. See the further discussion of public, common, and private nuisance in Ch. 2, the text accompanying nn. 297–315.

[102] *Sic utere tuo ut re non laedas alienum*, 'every man must so use his own, as not to damnify another' (i.e. another's property); *Tenant* v. *Goldwin* (1705) 2 Ld. Raym. 1089, 1092–3; 92 E.R. 222, 224 (K.B.) per Holt CJ.

trespass, to be remedied lest such invasion detract from seisin or title by adverse possession.

The difficulties of the courts in distinguishing between damage-centred and right-centred claims may be traced to the replacement of the *quod permittat* and assize remedies by the modern action on the case. The earlier remedies can be described as real actions triggered by a wrong (disseisin). The real remedy directly affected title (or continuing entitlement to the resource) through the enforcement of a particular pattern of rightful possession—for example, by an order to D to restore unimpeded possession or to abate or permit the abatement of a nuisance. Trespass on the case, by contrast, awarded damages only for the loss caused by nuisance, and hence only indirectly sanctioned the rightful pattern of possession. Category problems arose if the action on the case was to be used to vindicate title without showing executed damage or loss; or if a real assize remedy was sought where damage had been caused by a nuisance that only marred, but did not destroy, a servitude or natural right of enjoyment; or where there was a past act of nuisance since abated, and no longer causing disturbance to title; or where the interference was harmful but socially justified by market competition. In the 1410 *Case of Gloucester School* Hankford J held that a new school could be set up in competition with an existing school without actionable trespass on the case, even though the school was established since 'time immemorial' and claimed a local monopoly:

> *Damnum* may be *absque injuria*. For instance, if I have a mill and my neighbour sets up another mill, so that the profit from my mill is reduced, I shall have no action against him; and yet it is damaging to me.

Hankford J stated that the economic interest to be protected must comprise a title, a 'freehold and an inheritance', such as a franchise of market, and not simply some established business. Thus a miller's profits were not protected by title, though his water supply might be:

> In the case of a mill, as I said before, if my neighbour sets up a mill, and others who used to grind at my mill go to the other mill, so that my toll is reduced, I shall not for this reason have an action. If, however, a miller prevents the water from running to my mill, or commits some nuisance of that kind, I shall have such an action [against him] as the law gives.[103]

Similar difficulties inhered in the assize remedy, as aired in a reading at Inner Temple in the 1490s, probably referring to the *Gloucester School Case*:

> If someone sets up a water-mill, and another mill is set up on the same watercourse, and the second mill is a nuisance to the first, the person who had the first mill shall have an assize of nuisance. If, however, the old mill still works and has enough water,

[103] Y.B. Hil. 11 Hen 4, f. 47, pl. 21 per Hankford J, in Baker and Milsom (eds.), *Sources*, 613–14.

then even though he is damaged [by the competition] by the setting up of the second mill he shall not have an assize of nuisance, for it is *dampnum sine injuria.*[104]

General trespass to defend the possessory right to a water flow in the absence of damage could not readily be used as a catch-all remedy where diversion of the flow had occurred on D's or another's land;[105] for general trespass conventionally required direct force or invasion of P's interest.

These problems of categorization were aired in the 1677 case of *Kendrick* v. *Bartland.*[106] P brought an action for trespass on the case for diversion of water from his mill, pleading a *continuando*, that is an allegation of trespassory damage continuing from day to day for a particular period. D argued that the plea was bad as P had abated the nuisance on a day within the declared period, and was thus seeking damages for a time without legal injury.[107] P's pleadings were upheld:

> [T]he Court... took this difference between a *quod permittat* or an assize for a nuisance, and an action on the case for the same; for the end of a *quod permittat* or an assize was to abate the nuisance, but the end of an action on the case was to recover damages, therefore, though the nuisance was removed, [P] is intitled to his damages that accrued before; and it is usual in actions of this nature to lay the *continuando* for longer time than [P] can prove, but he shall have damages for what he can prove... he sustained before the abatement.[108]

The cryptically brief report of *Glynne* v. *Nichols*[109] from 1688 held that action could be brought to prevent diversion where there was neither a prescription nor a present usage shown, suggesting that trespass on the case can be used to prevent injury to title *sine damnum.* P here claimed remedy 'for diverting a water-course *in, par et trans messuage*' without more, asserting that the natural flow of water to his land was protected from diversion. D objected that P had laid no title to the watercourse, and 'that he does not say for what use, whether family, cattle, or field; and if it were not *useful* where it run, it cannot be actionable to divert it'[110]—the very

[104] *The Notebook of Sir John Port* (J. H. Baker (ed.), Selden Society, cii, 1986) Note 65, c.1494, 118.

[105] See *Leveridge* v. *Hoskins* (1709) 11 Mod. 257; 88 E.R. 1025 (K.B.), discussed in the text accompanying nn. 117–18 below.

[106] (1677) 2 Mod. 253; 86 E.R. 1056 (K.B.).

[107] Cf. *Prince* v. *Moulton* (1697) Carth. 387; 91 E.R. 1062 (K.B.) (trespass *continuando* pleaded for loss of 'total use and profit' of land for a whole year following flooding of harvest at close of year; plea held to state damage too widely as some use remained).

[108] 2 Mod. 253; 86 E.R. 1056. See also *Rosewell* v. *Prior* (1697) 12 Mod. 635; 88 E.R. 1570; 1 Ld. Raym. 713; 91 E.R. 1375 (K.B.) (on nature of nuisance, case, assise; nuisance as a defence to trespass for abatement; continuance of nuisance as repetition of injury). *Leveridge* v. *Hoskins* (1709) 11 Mod. 257; 88 E.R. 1025 (K.B.) suggests that the requirement of a *continuando* plea would be inferred from an allegation of damage consequent on a wrongful diversion, thus in effect abolishing the requirement: see the text accompanying nn. 117–18 below.

[109] (1687–8) 2 Show. K.B. 507; 89 E.R. 1069; Comb. 43; 90 E.R. 333 (K.B.).

[110] Ibid.

argument raised by Holt CJ in *Palmer* v. *Keblethwaite*.[111] The court, however, found that P's action was good in the absence of declared use.

Soon afterwards, in *Prickman* v. *Tripp*[112] in 1693, P pleaded that water flowed from a well to his house 'for the necessary use of his house'. The court took this plea as establishing the existence of a watercourse, which of itself sufficed to mount the action; the plea was not seen as identifying use requiring remedy for damage; the need to plead special damage (resulting from diversion of a spring) was not discussed.[113]

Similar issues were raised in a curious manner in *Richards* v. *Hill*.[114] P declared that he was seised of an ancient watercourse and mill, and that D's diversion of the water had prevented him grinding corn; but the plea was stated in bad Latin (*molare non potuit* instead of *molere*), so that D could argue that 'the hindrance of the grinding is designed to be the gist of the action, and therefore it ought to be shown to expressly, but here it is not shown intelligibly'. This technicality was met by the court's broad holding that an injury to prescriptive or possessory right without damage to any use was actionable. Holt CJ and King's Bench stated that 'where the act [of D diverting the water] implies a tort of itself, a *per quod* [i.e. a pleading of special damage] is not necessary to support the action, but only aggravates the damages'.[115] In 1701, the same court held, however, that where a nuisance by flooding was anticipated due to interference with a natural flow, the feared damage was not an injury justifying preventive abatement.[116]

In *Leveridge* v. *Hoskins*[117] of 1709, D objected that for special damage to support an action on the case, it must be shown 'that the diversion of the water was *consequential*' to D's wrongful action (diverting a river from a meadow by cutting a ditch), as such a consequential harm 'is the git [gist] of the action [on the case]'. The court ruled that consequential damage could simply be presumed after verdict; and that the action turned on the injury done to P's interests, rather than the quality of the physical act which caused the diversion and damage.[118] This decision preserved D's election to bring his action on the case regardless of where the damage was suffered or where the injurious act occurred. Consequential damage was thus assumed in order to invoke the convenient action on the case for what might be a wrong causing no temporal loss. Such broad application of the action on the case expanded

[111] See the text accompanying nn. 90–2 above.

[112] (1693) Skin. K.B. 389; 90 E.R. 173 (K.B.).

[113] See discussion in the text accompanying nn. 94–95 above.

[114] (1695) 1 Ld. Raym. 102; 91 E.R. 964; 5 Mod. 206; 87 E.R. 611 (K.B.); *Viner's Abdgt.*, xxii, 528.

[115] 1 Ld. Raym. 102; 91 E.R. 964.

[116] *R.* v. *Wharton* (1701) 12 Mod. 510; 88 E.R. 1483 (K.B.) per Holt CJ.

[117] (1709) 11 Mod. 257; 88 E.R. 1025 (K.B.).

[118] Compare the older Assize of Nuisance, where the act causing the nuisance was the gist of the action and determined the *locus*: Bracton f. 233, iii, 192.

its potential beyond its central function as a damage-centred remedy. Trespass on the case could now be used to defend incidental property rights as, in effect, titles to future enjoyment.

THE THEORY OF *INJURIA SINE DAMNO*

The relationship between trespass and harm generated constant headaches for the courts. There is a good example of the quandary in a late medieval case where a man broke into a neighbour's close in order to dig a trench expelling flood water, so preserving a common right of the villagers including the owner of the close. The Common Pleas could not decide whether he could be sued as a trespasser where his actions had in fact benefited his neighbour rather than harming him.[119] The concept of trespass to property involving *injuria sine damno* was given its classical expression outside the field of land use, in the great constitutional case of *Ashby* v. *White* in 1703.[120] The facts were that a borough official refused to record P's vote in a parliamentary poll, on the ground that P was outside the property franchise. P then brought action on the case for breach of his elector's right to register his voice in the choosing of burgesses for Parliament. Three out of four judges of King's Bench held that the action on the case did not lie. Gould J in the majority identified four main grounds for refusing remedy: first, that the borough officials had an unreviewable discretion in determining intricate electoral qualifications; secondly, that the courts could not interfere with matters within the realm of Parliamentary privilege and self-regulation, so that persons could find remedy only from Parliament; thirdly, that there was no damage to support the action: a 'privilege of voting is not a matter of property or profit, so that the hindrance of it is merely *damnum sine injuria*'; and finally, that the breach did not affect the plaintiff specially, but was a 'publick offence' or public nuisance, which could not be enjoined by a private individual.[121] Holt CJ forcefully dissented from all of these grounds, and his judgment in P's favour was upheld in the House of Lords—yet finally overturned by resolution of the House of Commons in the course of a major constitutional battle.[122] Outside the constitutional issues of privilege

[119] *Harecourt* v. *Spencer* (1519–21) Y.B. Trin. 12–13 Hen. 8 f. 1, in *Year Books of Henry VIII*, 7–13.

[120] (The *Aylesbury Voters* case) (1703) 6 Mod. 45; 87 E.R. 810; 2 Ld. Raym. 938; 92 E.R. 126; 3 Ld. Raym. 320; 92 E.R. 711; Holt K.B. 524; 90 E.R. 1188 (K.B.). The common-law authorities on *injuria sine damno* are collected in *Webb* v. *Portland Manufacturing Co.* (1838) 3 Sumn. 189; 3 Law Rep. 374; 29 Fed. Cas. 506 (No. 17,322) per Story J, in Ch. 6 below, the text accompanying nn. 35–39.

[121] Per Gould J, 2 Ld. Raym. 938, 942; 92 E.R. 126, 129.

[122] *Ashby* v. *White* (1703) 1 Brown. 62; 1 E.R. 417 (H.L.); and see note 1 E.R. 418–19 on the constitutional battle. Holt CJ was defending the Whig vote against the manipulations of a Tory-

and jurisdiction, there was much discussion in King's Bench of the common-law requirements of injury and damage in actions on the case for the defence of property rights; and Holt's dissent was later followed as an authoritative statement of common-law principle.[123]

Of the majority, Gould J stated: '[H]ere is no profit present, or possibility of future profit, so it is an *injuria sine damno*; and *damnum sine injuria*, . . . for both [damage and injury] must necessarily concur to maintain the action; for things must not only be done amiss, but it must redound to the prejudice of him that will bring his action for it.'[124] Powell J elaborated:

> [T]o maintain an action on the case, there must be either a real damage, or a possibility of real damage, and not merely a damage in opinion or consequence of law. . . . [A]n action upon the case lies for the owner of an ancient market, for erecting a new market near his; and yet perhaps the cattle that come to the old market might not be sold, and so no toll due; and consequently no real damage, but there is a possibility of real damage. But in our case there is no possibility of a damage.

Damage might have been shown, he held, if P had been put out of pocket in presenting himself to vote, or if he could have sold his property right to vote; but this was not the position. Moreover the existence of a public remedy excluded the operation of action on the case; a point illustrated by the water-rights case of *Westbury* v. *Powell*, 'where the inhabitants of Southwark had a watering place for their cattle by custom, which was stopped up; there any inhabitant might have an action, because there was no other remedy by presentment or the like: but if it had been a nusance presentable, no action would have lain'; the aggrieved parties would have to resort to a presentment for public nuisance.[125] It was further suggested that since jurisdiction for determining voting rights lay exclusively with Parliament, the common-law courts could not even recognize that a right existed until the jurisdiction was exercised.[126]

Against these arguments, Holt CJ asserted, first, that the right to vote was an incident of property and status and was therefore within the cognizance of the common law; and secondly that 'If the plaintiff has a right, he must of

dominated Country interest which then controlled a majority of the Commons; the House of Lords that supported Holt was controlled by the Whigs. See P. A. Hamburger, 'Revolution and Judicial Review: Chief Justice Holt's Opinion in City of London v. Wood' (1994) 94 Columbia Law Review 2091, 2143–5; G. N. Clark, *The Later Stuarts, 1660–1714* (Oxford, 1934) 244–6; E. N. Williams, *The Eighteenth Century Constitution 1688–1815: Documents and Commentary* (Cambridge, 1960) 221–32.

[123] See *Webb* v. *Portland Manufacturing Co.* (1838) 3 Sumn. 189; 3 Law Rep. 374; 29 Fed. Cas. 506 (No. 17,322) per Story J, discussed in Ch. 6 below, the text accompanying nn. 35–39, which provides a lengthy review of the case references.

[124] *Ashby* v. *White* (1703) 6 Mod. 45, 46; 87 E.R. 810, 810–11.

[125] *Westbury* v. *Powell*, cited in *Fineux* v. *Hovenden* (1599) Cro. Eliz. 664, 665; 78 E.R. 902, 903.

[126] *Ashby* v. *White* (1703) 6 Mod. 45, 49; 87 E.R. 810, 812–13.

necessity have a means to vindicate and maintain it, and a remedy if he is injured in the exercise or enjoyment of it; and indeed it is a vain thing to imagine a right without a remedy; for a want of right and want of remedy are reciprocal.'[127] On the doctrine of *injuria sine damno*, after reviewing the seventeenth-century authorities Holt concluded:

I think it impossible that there should be an injury without damage; injury in its nature imports damage, though it cost not the party injured a farthing; for damages do not consist in things pecuniary, but in a disturbance of right. . . . So if another ride in a path-way in my land, I may have an action, because it is an invasion of my property, and an injury to my right; and here [in the present case] the wrong being not *vi et armis*, so as to maintain trespass generally, the law in that case gives this remedy [of action on the case] . . .

The law consists not in particular instances, but in the reason that rules them; and if where a man is injured in one sort of right he has a good action, why shall he not have it in another?[128]

This judgment greatly influenced later developments of the law regarding wrongs to property incidents.[129] However the doctrine which Holt CJ extracted from the pleadings of the prior century—that injury imported damage, and that *injuria sine damno* to property was therefore remediable by the action on the case—gave no further guidance as to the circumstances in which a property right should be recognized by the law. Tests for identifying such rights were formulated only from the middle of the eighteenth century, as will be seen.

DIRECT AND INDIRECT CAUSATION: NEW CONCEPTUALIZATIONS OF TRESPASS AND CASE

In *Sury* v. *Pigot* the court held that trespass on the case was the proper writ of action for all instances of 'nusance', or interference with incidents of property by acts outside the claimant's land; and further that trespass *vi et armis* and

[127] *Ashby* v. *White* (1703) 2 Ld. Raym. 938, 955; 92 E.R. 126, 137; see also 6 Mod. 45, 53–4; 87 E.R. 810, 815–16. Holt CJ's fuller reasons were that the constitution vested parliamentary legislative power over persons and estates in the representatives of freeholders, cities, and boroughs, the right of freeholders and freemen to choose representatives was therefore valuable in itself. Parliament itself could not provide an effective remedy for breach of the right, as such breach might have corrupted the Parliament which would therefore be sitting as judge in its own cause. See 6 Mod. 45, 51–6; 87 E.R. 810, 814–17; 2 Ld. Raym. 938, 950–8; 92 E.R. 126, 134–9; Holt K.B. 524, 524–6; 90 E.R. 1188, 1188–9; 1 Salk. 19, 20–1; 91 E.R. 19, 19–20; Hamburger, 'Revolution and Judicial Review', at 2143–5.

[128] *Ashby* v. *White* (1703) Holt K.B. 524, 525; 90 E.R. 1188, 1189.

[129] See further *Webb* v. *Portland Manufacturing Co.* (1838) 3 Sumn. 189; 3 Law Rep. 374; 29 Fed. Cas. 506 (No. 17,322); *Williams* v. *Mostyn* (1838) 4 M. & W. 145: 150 E.R. 1379 (Ex.); *Embrey* v. *Owen* (1851) 6 Exch. 353, 368; 155 E.R. 579, 585 per Parke B. (Ex.).

contra pacem was appropriate only where the nuisance was combined with trespassory acts on the claimant's soil.[130] The court ignored counsel for the defendant's express invitation to enter into the legal metaphysics of *causa causans* and *causa causata* as a means of distinguishing immediate from indirect causation of damage as the determinant of the proper form of action.[131]

The question of the appropriate form of wrong action surfaced again in *Courtney* v. *Collet* in 1697.[132] There it was held that blocking a watercourse so as to flood another's land by some act outside his property was direct and not consequential damage, which could be remedied only by simple or direct trespass *vi et armis* or *quare clausum fregit* with aggravated damages, rather than an action of trespass on the case with consequential damages or trespass *vi et armis* for malfeasance. Further, a plea combining general trespass and an action on the case was held to be bad because the remedies were incompatible, trespass being the mandatory action for claiming or vindicating possession, whilst the action on the case brought money damages at the court's discretion. The wrongful act in *Courtney* was thus classified as invasion of land by flooding, rather than damage caused by interference with appurtenant rights to natural water flow.

The 1725 decision of the King's Bench in *Reynolds* v. *Clerke*[133] formed something like a resting point in the development of action on the case as the dominant framework of the law of civil wrongs. The case is famous above all for Fortescue J's pungent distinction between general trespass and action on the case as appropriate remedies:

> Trespass will not lie for procuring another to beat me. If a man throws a log into the highway and in that act it hits me, I may maintain trespass, because it is an immediate wrong; but if, as it lies there, I tumble over it and receive an injury, I must bring an action on the case; because it is prejudicial *in consequence*, (for which originally I could have no action at all).

This distinction between immediate and consequential harm was later picked up by Blackstone and enlarged into general principle.[134] It was a novel means of distinguishing trespass and the action on the case, and it was pitched at a very high level of abstraction. The older, more concrete test for distinguishing the forms of action saw trespass proper as direct invasion of land, or injury to property or persons caused by force; the action on the case was left as the appropriate residual category for all other wrongs that ought

[130] See e.g. Poph. 167, 169; 79 E.R. 1264, 1266 per Jones J.
[131] Poph. 167, 169; 79 E.R. 1264, 1266.
[132] (1697) 1 Ld. Raym. 272; 91 E.R. 1079 (K.B.).
[133] (1725) 1 Strange 634; 93 E.R. 747; 2 Ld. Raym. 1399; 92 E.R. 40 (K.B.); Fifoot, *History and Sources*, 201–2; *Viner's Abdgt.*, xxii, 524.
[134] *Bl.Comm.*, iii, 208–9; Ch. 4, the text accompanying nn. 147–148 below.

to have remedy. Trespass on the case therefore had the character of an inclusive, flexible remedy for many types of wrongful damage, rather than an exclusive category of indirect torts. Kiralfy in his study of the action on the case notes that the immediate–consequential harm distinction dates significantly from the early eighteenth century, though traces of the idea are found much earlier.[135] He states: '[t]o say that Case lay for indirect damage is simply a corollary of the obvious fact that general trespass lay for direct damage, and is not a definition of Case.'[136]

The abstract categories of immediate and consequential injury can be interpreted as attempts to find a more accurate or meaningful explanation of the distinction between trespass and the action on the case in their evidential operation. In the medieval common law, *quare clausum fregit*, *vi et armis*, and *contra pacem regis* pleadings of trespass could be stretched by fiction to cover injuries lying very far from the core cases of physical invasion or forcible injury. The new test cleared away those fictions and identified in direct injury (rather than in force or invasion or violent disturbance) the significant factor making for a trespass action. By so defining trespass, the nature of the action on the case as a residual remedy for wrongful damage was thrown into relief, and the substantive issues of relating damage to legally recognized injury could be confronted more surely.

Reynolds v. *Clerke* was a transitional case, presenting the older distinction between trespass and the action on the case, that is, between invasive wrongs and residual wrongs, alongside the new dichotomy between immediate and consequential harms. The facts of the litigation were that D erected a water spout in P's yard which caused damage to P's house. D claimed the act was legal as he had licence or liberty as tenant of an adjoining house freely to enter and use the yard, and further that his act was a necessary use of the yard. P brought a trespass action on the ground that D had exceeded the scope of the licence, and had therefore been an ordinary trespasser. D demurred, arguing that there was a prejudice caused by nuisance, to be remedied solely by action on the case: 'This is an action of trespass brought for a nuisance upon our own possession'.

Raymond CJ and the court supported P's argument that the licence had been exceeded, so making an actionable trespass; but the court explored D's arguments carefully, using water rights as illustrations:

Et per Fortescue Justice, trespass is a possessory action, and how does this invade the plaintiff's possession? The difference between trespass and case is that in trespass the

[135] A. K. Kiralfy, *The Action on the Case* (London, 1951) 16–17; see *Bullen* v. *Sheene* (1623) Godb. 343; 78 E.R. 202 (K.B.) per Doderidge J; *Slater's Case* (1708) Holt K.B. 22; 90 E.R. 910 (K.B.) per counsel; *Star* v. *Rookesby* (1710) 1 Salk. 335; 91 E.R. 295 (Q.B.); cf. *Leveridge* v. *Hoskins*, in the text accompanying nn. 117–118 above. Ibbetson, *Historical Introduction*, 158–60, suggests Roman and early medieval English presages of the new causation-based theory.

[136] Kiralfy, *Action on the Case*, 43–4.

plaintiff complains of an immediate wrong, and in case of a wrong that is the consequence of another act.
Et per Raymond [Chief] Justice, that distinction is perfectly right. I remember a case in B.R. [King's Bench] *Courtney* v. *Collett*, which was for the defendant's diverting his own watercourse in his own land, *per quod* the plaintiff's land was overflowed;... it was often debated whether this was an action of trespass or upon the case, and at last judgment was for the plaintiff, who had brought trespass only.
[At second hearing:] We must keep up the boundaries of actions, otherwise we shall introduce the utmost confusion. If the act in the first instance be unlawful, trespass will lie; but if the act is *prima facie* lawful (as it was in this case), and the prejudice to another is not immediate but consequential, it must be an action upon the case; and this is the distinction. The case I mentioned last time of *Courtney* v. *Collett* was a plain trespass, and the account I then gave of it from memory was mistaken. It was Hil.9 W.3 in B.R., trespass for taking fishes... he broke down the bank of the river, per quod the water issued and other fishes went away: after verdict for the plaintiff it was moved in arrest of judgment, that the latter part was case and not joinable with trespass; but the court said that, it not being laid to be a digging upon the plaintiff's ground, the action upon the case was the most proper. And I take that and this to be the same case; the defendant having a right to enter the yard and do the first act which is here complained of, I think this should have been an action upon the case and that trespass will not lie.... [T]his is only injurious in its consequence, for it is not pretended that the bare fixing of a spout was a cause of action without the falling of any water. The right of action does not accrue till the water actually descended, and therefore this should have been an action on the case.[137]

Where the injury alleged was the harmful diversion rather than augmentation of water flow to P's land (diversion generally being the standard issue regarding riparian rights), it became more difficult to fit such injury within the new conceptualization of trespass on the case as direct harm. Does it make sense to say that the harm to P's land in a water-diversion case is immediately caused by D's actions, so that those actions can be characterized as an interference with rights and therefore unlawful *per se?* Or is cutting water off from land merely prejudicial in consequence? The courts tended to prefer the second analysis.[138] However, here the older test distinguishing injurious acts on the plaintiff's land from acts without his land was the more precise guide, corresponding to the categories of general trespass and nuisance rather than to categories of immediate and consequential damage.

Another fundamental division that was better captured by the older forms of action was the distinction between, on the one hand, actionable invasions of right which need cause no temporal loss (the core action being trespass *quare clausum fregit*), and on the other, acts inflicting damage or loss as the gist of the wrong (action on the case where the act is legal *per se*). This crucial

[137] (1726) 1 Strange 634; 93 E.R. 747; Fifoot, *History and Sources*, 201–2.
[138] Kiralfy, *Action on the Case*, 57–8 on flooding cases and forms of action.

distinction, so important in Bracton's analysis, was not addressed by the new immediate-or-consequential injury test.

Thus in two respects—specifying the location and quality of the injurious act, and identifying the necessity of actual harm or loss—the test for the forms of action for wrongs set out in *Reynolds* v. *Clerke* made the analysis of water rights more difficult. The modern categorizations were more forced, and less sensitive to the significant issues. The judges had tried to give a rationalized test for distinguishing the forms of action, and had thereby undermined the serviceability of the pragmatic formulary system. The over-simplification of the learning of the forms of action helps to explain why new, more serviceable tests for water rights had to be developed in the eighteenth and nineteenth centuries: namely, titles by appropriation and short prescription; expansive doctrines of *sic utere tuo* establishing entitlement by natural right; and finally discretionary reasonableness standards of common riparian right. These doctrines were evolved under the influence of ideas from outside the formulary English common law. The learning of the actions had exhausted its capacity to give meaningful or workable solutions.

4. *Blackstone's and Hale's Doctrines of Land and Water Use*

INSTITUTIONALISTS AND THE DEVELOPMENT OF THE MODERN LAW

Eighteenth-century land- and water-use law was developed by treatise literature rather than judicial decision. Some subjects such as commons waste receive judicial attention. However, Viner's comprehensive *Abridgement*, published in 1741–53 and revised in 1794,[1] lists decisions dealing with water only from the seventeenth century or earlier.[2] This lacuna may be due partly to the irregular state of law reporting before the 1800s;[3] but it may also reflect a simple absence of litigation in the central courts.[4] Possible reasons for this include the stabilization of traditional water-using manufactures before textile industrialization and the acceleration of water exploitation late in the eighteenth century, resort to private legislation rather than common law to order land use at the time of the enclosure movement, a general diminution of litigation in all fields of law during this period, perhaps due to increased relative expense, and finally an indifference of common lawyers to the intellectual problems posed by land-use law. This is in marked contrast to the medieval law of Bracton's time and after, when commons and servitudes were treated with detailed seriousness. In the early seventeenth century, Sir Edward Coke (1552–1634) in his *Institutes* and *Reports* gives some treatment of incorporeal rights and prescriptions, especially in relation to commons and fisheries; but Coke's main concern is with tenures and estates: with title to land, not use of land.

[1] See J. H. Baker, *An Introduction to English Legal History* (4th edn., London, 2002) 184–6; see also his 'Records, Reports and the Origins of Case Law in England' in J. H. Baker (ed.), *Judicial Records, Law Reports and the Growth of Case Law* (London, 1989) 15–46.

[2] *Viner's Abdgt.* (2nd edn., London, 1794) xiv, 394–5 ('Indictment—(Q) Nusance'); xv, 399–400 ('Mill—(C) Actions. Diverting the Watercourse'); xvi, 19–47 ('Nusance'), xxii, 525–8 ('Water-Courses'). Almost all the law digested under these categories is from before 1700; moreover the Supplement to Viner's *Abridgement* of 1806 reveals almost no fresh case law on riparian rights or nuisance to watercourses.

[3] Baker, *Introduction to English Legal History*, 182–4; J. W. Wallace, *The Reporters, Arranged and Characterized with Incidental Remarks* (4th edn., Boston, Mass., 1882) 287–453.

[4] J. C. Oldham, *The Mansfield Manuscripts and the Growth of English Law in the Eighteenth Century*, 2 Vols. (Chapel Hill, NC, 1992) ii, 882–925, shows a trickle of nuisance cases in Lord Mansfield's court, with only two cases of obstruction of navigation, and none of obstruction of a watercourse. Oldham notes that Mansfield tended to have parties compromise and settle nuisance claims rather than go through to a judicial verdict: ibid., 882.

Sir Matthew Hale (1609–76)[5] and Sir William Blackstone (1723–80)[6] by contrast provided detailed and systematic treatments of the rights of enjoyment incidental to land ownership. A justifiable claim can be made that these writers, Blackstone in particular, laid the foundations for the nineteenth-century law of land and water use.[7] Here Blackstone, like Coke, was cited by the judges in leading cases as a direct authority in the search for right answers. This chapter reconstructs these modern institutionalists' schemes of property and water law, which in turn reveals much of their legal technique and ideology.

THE THEORY OF WATER RIGHTS IN BLACKSTONE'S *COMMENTARIES ON THE LAWS OF ENGLAND*

Blackstone's analysis of water law is scattered throughout the *Commentaries* and must be reassembled carefully. The essence of his water doctrine can be compassed in five points:

(1) Water is a type of corporeal right, a transient element available to the public but subject to a qualified individual property or title during use.
(2) The first appropriator of water wins title under a natural principle defending occupation.
(3) Title subsists only during time of use, as water can not be possessed or appropriated in the manner of land.
(4) The prior appropriation theory is distinct from theories of acquisition of incorporeal rights by prescriptive long user.
(5) Actions for wrongs, such as nuisance and trespass, are used to defend such water rights; and this raises the issue of identifying actionable damage.

Blackstone is an eclectic legal writer; there is no 'structure' in the *Commentaries* beyond the skeletal Civilian framework borrowed from Justinian and Hale's *Analysis of the Laws of England* (1713); the work is as much as a

[5] Sir Matthew Hale, *De Jure Maris* (*c.*1670), in Francis Hargrave (ed.), *Collection of Tracts Relative to the Law of England* (MS., 1787), reprinted in S. A. Moore, *A History of the Foreshore* (3rd edn., London, 1888) 370–413.

[6] Sir William Blackstone, *Commentaries on the Law of England* 4 vols. (1st edn., Oxford, 1765–9; 15th edn. by E. Christian, 1809) (cited in this ch. by volume number and page only, e.g. i, 1–2).

[7] See S. F. C. Milsom, 'The Nature of Blackstone's Achievement', in S. F. C. Milsom, *Studies in the History of the Common Law* (London, 1985) 197; cf. M. J. Lobban, *The Common Law and English Jurisprudence 1760–1850* (London, 1991) 17–47; cf. A. W. B. Simpson, 'The Rise and Fall of the Legal Treatise: Legal Principles and the Forms of Legal Literature', in A. W. B. Simpson, *Legal Theory and Legal History: Essays on the Common Law* (London, 1987) 273, 290–7, stressing the marginal role of Hale and Blackstone in the mainstream English common law.

polished *summa* of the medieval abridgements and of Coke as any work of rational civilian institutionalism.[8] Fleshing out Blackstone's loose institutionalist framework is a group of legal and philosophical ideas drawn from civil and common law, natural law, utilitarianism, and social contractarianism. These ideas must be expounded in some detail if Blackstone's property theory and water law is to be understood.

NATURAL LAW, POSITIVISM, AND PROPERTY THEORY

For Blackstone, property rights at law were a social and positive protection of the natural right to maintain first occupancy.[9] Blackstone viewed human. positive law as institutional arrangements necessary to maintain natural-law rights in the context of social life with all of its potential for hierarchy, oppression, and conflict. Organized societies evolved in order to guarantee natural wants and needs, beginning with the small unit of the self-sufficient family and ending with larger societies governed by municipal law. Society did not originate in any factual social contract made to put an end to anarchy and isolation. Nonetheless the idea of social contract had a useful explanatory or heuristic role:

> And this is what we mean by the original contract of society . . . that the community should guard the rights of every individual member, and that (in return for this protection) each individual should submit to the laws of the community; without

[8] He was also perhaps influenced by other extant treatises on the common law with a civilian or natural law framework, such as Thomas Wood's *Institute of the Laws of England* (London, 1720) and also possibly by Cowell and Gilbert. See Simpson, 'Legal Treatise', 281, 296–7 and 'Introduction' to Blackstone's *Commentaries* (Chicago, Ill., 1979) ii; J. W. Cairns, 'Blackstone, An English Institutist: Legal Literature and the Rise of the Nation State' (1984) 4 Oxford Journal of Legal Studies 318; M. Macnair, 'Sir Jeffrey Gilbert and his Treatises' (1994) 15 Journal of Legal History 252; R. B. Robinson, 'The Two Institutes of Thomas Wood: A Study in 18th Century Legal Scholarship' (1999) 35 American Journal of Legal History 432; A. Watson, 'The Structure of Blackstone's Commentaries' (1988) 97 Yale Law Journal 795. By contrast, Duncan Kennedy, in his article 'The Structure of Blackstone's Commentaries' (1979) 28 Buffalo Law Review 205, ignores the institutionalist and juristic qualities of Blackstone's treatise, preferring to trace jurisprudential contradictions in the *Commentaries* to the tensions and antinomies of political thought of 'liberal legal consciousness' in England and America; to similar effect see K. J. Vandevelde, 'The New Property of the 19th Century: The Development of the Modern Concept of Property' (1980) 29 Buffalo Law Review 325; C. M. Rose, 'Canons of Property Talk, or, Blackstone's Anxiety' (1998) 108 Yale Law Journal 601.

[9] See e.g. i, 7–8, 41–2, 57–8, ii, 38–40. See further J. M. Kelly, *A Short History of Western Legal Theory* (Oxford, 1992) 244–300; R. W. Gordon, 'Paradoxical Property', in J. Brewer and S. Staves (eds.), *Early Modern Conception of Property* (London, 1995) 95–110; R. P. Burns, 'Blackstone's Theory of the "Absolute" Rights of Property' (1985) 54 University of Cincinnati Law Review 67; F. G. Whelan, 'Property as Artifice: Hume and Blackstone', in J. R. Pennock and J. W. Chapman (eds.), *Property*, Nomos XXII (New York, 1980) 101; A. W. Alschuler, 'Rediscovering Blackstone' (1996) 145 University of Pennsylvania Law Review 1.

which submission of all it was impossible that protection could be certainly extended to any.[10]

Blackstone uses the idea of social contract pervasively in the *Commentaries* to justify particular laws, as well as to explain the legitimacy of law in society. By deploying ideas of 'implied contract' derived from the implicit social compact, particular legal coercions of the individual could be characterized as consensual submergence of the individual before the needs of the community,[11] a Hobbesian reconciliation of liberty and compulsion.

The Relationship of Common Law and Custom

According to Blackstone, municipal law was divided between unwritten customary and written statute law.[12] Statute law represented the will of Parliament and derived its authority from parliamentary sovereignty rather than customary acceptance. In the case of customary law or *leges non scripta*, the classical Roman model was followed:

their original institution and authority are not set down in writing, as acts of parliament are, but they receive their binding power, and the force of laws, by long and immemorial usage, and by their universal reception throughout the kingdom.

Blackstone saw the derivation of legal practices from immemorial custom as the essence of the common law. Unlike imperial Roman law, which was a product of authoritarian legislation by a princely government,[13] English customary law was:

one of the characteristic marks of English liberty [in] that our common law depends upon custom; which carries this internal evidence of freedom along with it, that it probably was introduced by the voluntary consent of the people.[14]

The unwritten customary law consisted of three parts: '*general customs*, or the common law properly so called; .... *particular customs* of certain parts of the kingdom; and likewise those *particular laws*, that are by custom

[10] i, 47–8.

[11] See e.g. the use of social contract theory to explain legally-imputed private contracts: iii, 159–65; or compulsory acquisitions: i, 139–40.

[12] Cf. *Co.Litt.* 110b.

[13] i, 72–3, quoting D.1.4.1.; C.1.14.12.; C.1.23.5. Blackstone execrates the text J.1.2.6.; D.1.3.3.2. (Ulpian) defining law as the will of the prince: 'It is no wonder from this specimen, that the civil law should have experienced such protection and patronage from all the despotic governments of Europe, and such opposition and detestation from the sturdy English barons': i, 72–3. Blackstone relentlessly criticizes Roman law for its method, procedure, irrelevance, and dangerous political content: see i, 4–6, 14–22, 32–3, 46, 59–61, 66–7, 79–84, 144, 234–5; ii, 328, 472; iii, 99–100, 355–6, 364–5, 378–84; but his admiration for Roman legal science is also made abundantly clear throughout the *Commentaries*: see i, 5, 29, 121–9; ii, 16, 35–6, 259–62, 404, 443 ff., 461 ff.

[14] i, 74.

observed only in certain courts and jurisdictions'.[15] Blackstone supposed that the general common law was woven out of a collection of particular customary law between the times of Alfred and Edward IV. Any remaining particular laws continued to have force only because it was a norm of the common law to permit such particular customs to subsist.[16] By becoming the common custom of the land, the common law emerged as the superior source and legitimation of all unwritten law (and maybe legislation also[17])—a primary rule for recognizing valid law.

Custom and Time Immemorial

Customs were founded by immemorial usage:

> [T]he maxims and customs [of the common law] are of higher antiquity than memory or history can reach; nothing being more difficult than to ascertain the precise beginning and first spring of an antient and long established custom. Whence it is that in our law the goodness of a custom depends upon it having been used time out of mind; or, in the solemnity of our legal phrase, time whereof the memory of man runneth not to the contrary. This it is that gives it it's weight and authority and of this nature are the maxims and customs which compose the common law, or *lex non scripta*, of this kingdom.[18]

The authority of 'that antient collection of unwritten maxims and customs, which is called the common law',[19] rested 'entirely upon general reception and usage':

> and the only method of proving, that this or that maxim is a rule of the common law, is, by shewing that it hath been *always* the custom to observe it.[20]

The judges discovered the customs of the common law by 'experience and study' and through knowledge of precedents; they were the 'depositaries of the law, the living oracles'.[21] In the process of defining law through customary acceptance of precedents, only law conformable to reason survived; unreasonable law would not have been accepted by past generations, so that if a general rule were clearly unreasonable and unjust it could be declared to be not law.[22] A rule that was not unjust but appeared to have no good reason was sound because 'the law will presume it to be well founded'; the customary acceptance and antiquity of a rule gave it legitimacy even if its reason could not be discerned—and even if the rule was inconvenient.[23] Thus 'reasonableness' in common law bears a special meaning of accepted custom not contrary to reason: it was by virtue of this ancient acceptance that common law embodied 'the perfection of reason, that... always intends to conform thereto, and that what is not reason is not law'.

[15] ii, 63. [16] i, 74–9. [17] i, 85–91. [18] i, 67. [19] i, 17.
[20] i, 68. [21] i, 69. [22] i, 68, 70. [23] i, 68–9.

Blackstone acknowledged that this theory was not unique to the common law; Roman law owned a similar principle:

Law comes into being without writing when a rule is approved by use. Long-standing custom founded on the consent of those who follow it is just like legislation.[24]

ABSOLUTE AND RELATIVE PROPERTY AND SOCIAL CONTRACT THEORY

Blackstone followed an institutionalist plan and divided the law between rights of persons and rights of things, and between private and public wrongs.[25] Personal rights were of two sorts, absolute and relative:

By the absolute *rights* of individuals we mean those which are so in the primary and strictest sense; such as would belong to their persons merely in a state of nature, and which every man is entitled to enjoy, whether out of society or in it.[26]

Relative rights of persons were those 'which are incident to them as members of society, and standing in various relations to each other'.[27] The three absolute rights were personal security, personal liberty, and private property. Moreover,

the principal aim of society is to protect individuals in the enjoyment of those absolute rights, which are vested in them by the immutable laws of nature, but which could not be preserved in peace without that mutual assistance and intercourse which is gained by the institution of friendly and social communities. Hence it follows, that the first and primary end of human laws is to maintain and regulate these *absolute* rights of individuals.[28]

Relative or social rights—the bulk of legal rights—were not natural rights, but ancillary positive rights 'posterior to the formation of states and societies', which guaranteed or superseded the absolute rights of the state of nature. Thus all actual rights in society were necessarily 'relative' according to Blackstone's definition, even if they had a source in natural absolute right. Blackstone acknowledged this positivity and relativity of rights, stating that society declared and enumerated the rights of persons as the social, and therefore relative, guarantee of the postulated absolute rights of the isolated individual. Relative rights were:

either that *residuum* of natural liberty, which is not required by the laws of society to be sacrificed in public convenience; or else those civil privileges, which society hath engaged to provide, in lieu of the natural liberties so given up by individuals.[29]

[24] Inst.1.2.9.; cf. D.1.3.32. (Julian); D.1.3.35. (Hermogenian); D.1.3.39. (Celsus); C.1.14.12.
[25] See iii, 1–3; 119–43. [26] i, 123–4. [27] i, 123.
[28] i, 123. [29] i, 129, and see i, 138, 140–4.

Blackstone here echoed in legalistic language the Lockean construct of a social contract setting up a framework of civil rights to protect the ideal of natural rights of 'life, liberty and property'.

Property as an Absolute Personal Right or Natural Right

Blackstone diluted his institutionalist split between property and persons by naming property as an 'absolute personal right'. 'The third absolute right inherent in every Englishman, is that of property: which consists in the free use, enjoyment, and disposal of all his acquisitions, without any control or diminution, save only by the laws of the land.'[30] Primarily this classification was not legalistic but political or ideological, aiming to elevate property to a paramount natural right. Blackstone's language of absolute property also suggests resort to Civilian ideas of ownership, as an absolute right comprising the *ius utendi fruendi abutendi* (rights to use, enjoy, dispose).[31]

The primacy of positive property rights was such that the only justification for collective action by the State was the securing of enjoyment of those rights, together with the other absolute rights of personal security and liberty.[32] In a famous passage Blackstone describes property in absolute terms as 'that sole and despotic dominion which one man claims and exercises over the external things of the world, in total exclusion of the right of any other individual in the universe';[33] and he seeks further to exclude common welfare as a ground for curbing the absolute property rights of the individual, using instead a fiction of implied consent to expropriation for social purposes.[34]

Blackstone's theories of law and property are relevant to our inquiry on two counts. First, he stresses the natural origins of the right of absolute property in occupation, giving the Roman idea of original acquisition a more philosophical expression.[35] Secondly, he relies extensively on social contract theory and notions of implied consent in order to explain the institutions of positive English property law. The dual themes of occupation and consent dominate Blackstone's discussion of land and water use.

[30] i, 138–9.

[31] Cf. ii, 1, where Blackstone discusses in Civilian language '*jura rerum*...the rights of dominion, or property'.

[32] i, 138.

[33] ii, 2.

[34] i, 139–40, ii, 2.

[35] See Ch. 2 above, the text accompanying nn. 11–24 (on possession and ownership in Roman law).

THE NATURAL BASIS OF PROPERTY TITLES IN USE AND OCCUPATION

The Distinction between Use and Title

Blackstone identified in all property regimes an inherent distinction between rights to the substance of goods and to the use of goods. Under primitive communism there was communal property in the substance but not in use, '[f]or, by the law of nature and reason, he, who first began to use it, acquired therein a kind of transient property, that lasted so long as he was using it, and no longer:[36] or, to speak with greater precision, the *right* of possession continued for the same time only that the *act* of possession lasted'.[37] Thus in a system without private property, a person could not be ejected from a piece of ground he was presently using or occupying; 'but the instant that he quitted the use or occupation of it, another might seise it, without injustice'.[38] When crowding and competition created the need for private property titles or a 'more permanent dominion', it became necessary 'to appropriate to individuals not the immediate use only, but the very *substance* of the thing to be used',[39] that is, a right of title allowing an exclusive control of the use of a thing, projected into the future.

Occupation as the Natural Source of Title

Blackstone asserted that occupation was the 'original and foundation' both of use-rights and title. In developed legal systems, the idea of ownership was commonly accepted to be possession justified by lawful acquisition from a predecessor in title:

> Pleased as we are by the possession, we seem afraid to look back to the means by which it was acquired, as if fearful of some defect in our title; or at best we rest satisfied with the decision of the laws in our favour, without examining the reason or authority upon which those laws have been built. We think it enough that our title is derived by the grant of the former proprietor... not caring to reflect that (accurately and strictly speaking) there is no foundation in nature or natural law, why a set of words upon parchment should convey the dominion of land.[40]

Blackstone was looking for a more abstract understanding of property from a point beyond the law, philosophically distanced from untutored wisdom.[41] Like many natural lawyers before him he began with Scriptural assertions of the basis of property and title:

[36] Samuel von Pufendorf, *De Jure Nature et Gentium* (Lund, 1672), *Of the Law of Nature and Nations* (with notes of J. Barbeyrac, B. Kennett (trans.), Oxford, 1710, enlarged edn., London, 1729) 1.4, c.4.

[37] ii, 3. [38] ii, 3–4. [39] ii, 4. [40] ii, 2.

[41] Ibid.; cf. Lobban, *Common Law and English Jurisprudence*, 27–33; M. J. Lobban, 'Blackstone and the Science of Law' (1987) 30 Historical Journal 311.

In the beginning of the world, we are informed by holy writ, the all-bountiful creator gave to man 'dominion over all the earth . . . '. This is the only true and solid foundation of man's dominion over external things, whatever airy metaphysical notions may have been started by fanciful writers upon this subject. The earth, therefore, and all things therein, are the general property of all mankind, exclusive of other beings, from the immediate gift of the creator. And, while the earth continued bare of inhabitants, it is reasonable to suppose, that all was in common among them, and that every one took from the public stock to his own use such things as his immediate necessaries required.[42]

For Blackstone, the divine ordinance established communal ownership with possessory use-rights, and not private property. Hence some additional historical or sociological argument was required to explain the evolution of the relative or social rights of individual property as title, replacing possessory use-rights. There were three reasons for the emergence of a paradigm of private ownership. First, conflicts over the allocation of scarce resources had to be contained. Natural primitive communism could not survive the emergence of closer settlement and agriculture; competitive appropriations of resources required regulation through private titles:

But when mankind increased in number, craft, and ambition, it became necessary to entertain conceptions of more permanent dominion. . . . Otherwise innumerable tumults must have arisen, and the good order of the world continually broken and disturbed, while a variety of persons were striving who should get the first occupation of the same thing, or disputing which of them had actually gained it.[43]

Secondly, there was a tendency in a more sophisticated society for goods to evolve into more permanent articles in constant use. Elaborate habitations were affixed to the soil; whilst:

moveables of every kind became sooner appropriated than the permanent substantial soil: partly because they were more susceptible of a long occupancy, which might be continued for months together without any sensible interruption, and at length by usage ripen into an established right.[44]

The final and principal reason for recognition of private property as continuous title was that labour invested in moveables naturally made for permanent ownership:

[F]ew [moveables] could be fit for use, till improved and meliorated by the bodily labour of the occupant: which bodily labour, bestowed upon any subject which before lay in common to all men, is universally allowed to give the fairest and most reasonable title to an exclusive property therein.[45]

Blackstone also employs the familiar argument of Locke that 'the right of occupancy itself . . . is founded on the personal labour of the occupant'; that

[42] ii, 3. [43] ii, 3. [44] ii, 5. [45] Ibid.

is, occupation was one method of mixing one's labour into a thing and thereby appropriating it.[46]

Blackstone elaborated these ideas through further historical and anthropological speculation. He writes that the need to secure food supply early led men 'to establish a permanent property in their flocks and herds'; and '[t]he support of these their cattle made the article of *water* also a very important point':[47]

And therefore the book of Genesis (the most venerable monument of antiquity, considered merely with a view to history) will furnish us with frequent instances of violent contentions concerning wells; the exclusive property of which appears to have been established in the first digger or occupant, even in such places where the ground and herbage remained yet in common. Thus we find Abraham, who was but a sojourner, asserting his right to a well in the country of Abimelech, and exacting an oath for his security, 'because he had digged that well.'[48] And Isaac, about ninety years afterwards, reclaimed this his father's property; and, after much contention with the Philistines, was suffered to enjoy it in peace.[49]

Blackstone's reading of scripture was not merely a decorous illustration of his property theory; this source helped him to construct a novel principle of title in water granted to the first appropriator.

The problems of overcrowding, competition, and depletion of resources likewise explained the historical establishment of private property in land as well as moveables. The benefits of improving labour were necessary to make a productive agriculture, for without a guarantee of secure reward there would be no investment of labour in land.[50] Blackstone drew here on the conventional four-stage social theory of the Enlightenment evoked by Henry Kames and Adam Smith, whereby hunting societies were followed by pastoral, agricultural, and finally commercial societies with organized States, governments, and laws.[51] In this schema, moveables and then immoveables attract private property rights as the economic basis of society grows more complex.

Blackstone's ideas may be summarized in modern economic terminology: private property titles are required in order to regulate competition, to promote capital-intensive production, and to protect the return on sunk labour and capital costs and guarantee monopoly profits. Later in the *Commentaries*, Blackstone mentions the need to define property rights for benefit of trade: 'property best answers the purposes of civil life, especially in

[46] Ibid. [47] ii, 5–6. [48] Genesis xxi, 30. [49] Genesis xxvi. 15. 18, &c.

[50] ii, 7–8.

[51] For further reference to eighteenth-century evolutionary theories of law and society see P. G. Stein, *Legal Evolution* (Cambridge, 1980) and 'The Four Stage Theory of the Development of Societies', in P. G. Stein, *The Character and Influence of the Roman Civil Law. Historical Essays* (London, 1988) 395–409.

commercial countries, when it's transfer and circulation are totally free and unrestrained'.[52] But for Blackstone, use and development of resources, and not exchange, were the primary reasons for the evolution of private property institutions.[53]

Explaining the Creation and Vesting of Titles

Blackstone next addressed the basis for creation of specific titles, asking 'how this property became actually vested: or what it is that gave a man an exclusive right to retain in a permanent manner that specific land, which before belonged generally to every body, but particularly to nobody'. The leading idea of occupancy or physical appropriation was again put to work. Blackstone was not entirely confident of the philosophical justifications for awarding a property title to the first occupier, and so fell back on conventionalist argument:

> [A]s we before observed that occupancy gave the right to the temporary *use* of the soil, so it is agreed upon all hands that occupancy gave also the original right to the permanent property in the *substance* of the earth itself: which excludes every one else but the owner from the use of it. There is indeed some difference among the writers on natural law, concerning the reason why occupancy should convey this right, and invest one with this absolute property: Grotius and Pufendorf insisting, that this right of occupancy is founded on a tacit and implied assent of all mankind, that the first occupant should become the owner; and Barbeyrac, Titius, Mr. Locke, and others, holding, that there is no such implied assent, neither is it necessary that there should be so; for that very act of occupancy, alone, being a degree of bodily labour, is, from a principle of natural justice, without any consent or compact, sufficient of itself to gain a title. A dispute that savours too much of nice and scholastic refinement! However, both sides agree in this, that occupancy is the thing by which the title was in fact originally gained; every man seising to his own continued use of such spots of ground as he found most agreeable to his own convenience, provided he found them unoccupied by anyone else.
>
> Property, both in land and moveables, being thus originally acquired by the first taker, which taking amounts to a declaration that he intends to appropriate the thing to his own use, it remains in him, by the principles of universal law, till such time as he does some other act which shews an intention to abandon it; for then it becomes, naturally speaking, *publici juris* once more, and is liable to be again appropriated by the next occupant.[54]

An intentionalist or will theory of occupation and appropriation is affirmed at a later point:

[52] ii, 288; Blackstone's position is clearly stated again at iii, 145.

[53] On gains through trade of property in more developed societies, and the necessity of promoting certainty of contract, see iii, 325–9.

[54] ii, 8–9; and see ii, 293.

Occupancy is the taking of possession of those things, which before belonged to nobody. This as we have seen, is the true ground and foundation of all property . . . which by the law of nature, unqualified by that of society, were common to all mankind. But when once it was agreed that every thing capable of ownership should have an owner, natural reason suggested, that he who could first declare his intention of appropriating any thing to his own use, and, in consequence of such intention, actually took it into possession, should thereby gain the absolute property of it; according to that rule of the law of nations, recognized by the laws of Rome *quod [enim] nullius est, id ratione naturali occupanti conceditur.*[55]

In an established society there was little unoccupied property remaining in the public domain, and so little property available for original appropriation, though all transfers of title or conveyances from a present owner to a new owner could be modelled as the new occupation of an abandoned good, creating a fresh title by appropriation.[56] An analogy may be drawn with the early classical law of Rome, which saw transfers of property by delivery as the constitution of a fresh *dominium* by occupation.[57]

THE TAXONOMY OF TITLE RIGHTS

Blackstone followed Coke in defining title as 'the means whereby the owner of lands hath the just possession of his property'.[58] A Romanized anatomy of the common-law relationships of possession and property right or title was then set out.

There were four ascending degrees of title emanating from the fact of possession. First was '*mere possession*', naked possession or actual occupation without any apparent right, as where a man takes possession wrongfully by disseisin. The rightful owner could terminate this possession by legal remedy, but the possessor had a secure title against third parties; and further:

till some act be done by the rightful owner to devest this possession and assert his title, such actual possession is, *prima facie*, evidence of a legal title in the possessor; and it may, by length of time, and negligence of him who hath the right, by degrees ripen into a perfect and defeasible title.[59]

This 'actual possession' correlated to the delivery of seisin necessary to constitute a title; 'at all events, without such actual possession no title can be completely good'.[60]

[55] ii, 258, incompletely citing D.41.1.3.pr. (Gaius): 'What belongs to no one becomes by natural reason the property of the first taker'; see further ii, 258–62.

[56] ii, 9; and see ii, 288, 293.

[57] W. W. Buckland, *Main Institutions of Roman Private Law* (London, 1931) 112.

[58] ii, 195; *Co.Litt*, 345. [59] ii, 196. [60] ii, 196.

Next was the '*right of possession*', where a person has lost the actual possession, but has a right to recover the possession 'by entering upon the disseisor, and turning him out of that occupancy which he has so illegally gained'. There were two rights of possession: 'an *apparent* right of possession, which may be defeated by proving a better; and an *actual* right of possession, which will stand the test against all opponents'. The actual right is a possessory claim in name, which bestows an effectively proprietary right within the common-law system of relative titles. Limitation of actions could convert an apparent into an actual right of possession, for where a person with an actual possessory right 'omits to bring this his possessory action, within a competent time, his adversary may imperceptibly gain an actual right of possession, in consequence of the other's negligence'.[61]

The next-highest title was the '*mere right of property*', where there was no right of possession at all (for example, due to limitation of the possessory actions); but the person out of possession had a real right or 'true ultimate property' and hence could bring a real action to recover the land.[62] Lastly there was the '*complete legal title*' where the right of property coincided with the right of possession and actual possession.[63]

This fourfold categorization of title gave a schematic picture of the relationships of the possessory and real actions for land in English law, aiming to explain the intricacies charted by Littleton and Coke to the layman.[64]

INCORPOREAL HEREDITAMENTS

Blackstone distinguished corporeal and incorporeal hereditaments, roughly following the Roman distinction between tangibles and intangibles.[65] Unlike the Romans, he did not classify water rights as incorporeal property,[66] but rather as a 'qualified property' in a public good, or else as part of corporeal land and tenements. Nonetheless, water rights do find some place within his discussion of incorporeal rights, and it is a classification of great importance in later water law.[67]

[61] ii, 197. [62] ii, 197–8. [63] ii, 199.

[64] Details of the historical actions for possession and title are further described in iii, ch. 10.

[65] ii, 17.

[66] Excepting common of fishery: ii, 39.

[67] Blackstone's originality is highlighted in R. A. Epstein, 'On the Optimal Mix of Private and Common Property' (1994) 11 Social Philosophy and Policy 17, extracted in R. A. Epstein (ed.), *Liberty, Property, and the Law, Vol. III: Private and Common Property* (New York, 2000) 357. Bentham's criticism of the common law of incorporeals is analysed in M. Sokol, 'Bentham and Blackstone on Incorporeal Hereditaments' (1994) 15 Journal of Legal History 287.

Definition of Incorporeal Property

Blackstone defined incorporeal hereditaments as follows:

An incorporeal hereditament is a right issuing out of a thing corporate (whether real or personal) or concerning, or annexed to, or exercisable within, the same.[68] It is not the thing corporate itself, which may consist in lands, houses, jewels, or the like; but something collateral thereto, as a rent issuing out of those lands or houses, or an office relating to those jewels. In short, as the logicians speak, corporeal hereditaments are the substance, which may be always seen, always handled: incorporeal hereditaments are but a sort of accidents, which inhere in and are supported by that substance; and may belong, or not belong to it, without any visible alteration therein. Their existence is merely in idea and abstracted contemplation; though their effects and profits may be frequently objects of our bodily senses. And indeed, if we would fix a clear notion of an incorporeal hereditament, we must be careful not to confound together the profits produced, and the thing, or hereditament, which produces them.[69]

Examples were an annuity producing money as a corporeal fruit, but which was itself incorporeal, 'a thing invisible, [which] has only a mental existence, and cannot be delivered from hand to hand'.[70] Similarly tithes gave rise to corporeal agricultural produce, 'yet they are indeed incorporeal hereditaments: for they, being merely a contingent springing right, collateral to or issuing out of lands, can never be the object of sense: that casual share of the annual increase is not, till severed, capable of being shewn to the eye, nor of being delivered into bodily possession'.[71] The inability to possess true incorporeal rights is stressed by Blackstone repeatedly:

[T]here could no common occupancy be had of incorporeal hereditaments, as of rents, tithes, advowsons, commons, or the like,[72] (because, with respect to them, there could be no actual entry made, or corporal seisin had . . .).[73]

There were ten principal sorts of incorporeal hereditaments: 'advowsons, tithes, commons, ways, offices, dignities, franchises, corodies or pensions, annuities, and rents'. *Aquae ductus*, *aquae haustus*, and the other traditional Roman praedial servitudes (apart from ways) prominently do not figure in this list. Advowsons, commons and franchises, in addition to ways, were the most important categories of incorporeal property in Blackstone's discussion.

The Nature of Incorporeal Rights—Advowsons

Advowsons were the right of presentation to a church, and Blackstone held that these rights 'completely illustrate the nature of an incorporeal hereditament':

[68] *Co.Litt.* 19, 20. [69] ii, 20. [70] Ibid. [71] ii, 21–2.
[72] *Co.Litt.* 41; *Holden* v. *Smallbrook* (1668) Vaugh. 187, 201; 124 E.R. 1030, 1037 (C.P.).
[73] ii, 260.

It is not itself the bodily possession of the church and it's appendages; but it is a right to give some other man a title to such bodily possession. The advowson is the object of neither the sight, nor the touch; and yet it perpetually exists in the mind's eye, and in contemplation of law. It cannot be delivered from man to man by any visible bodily transfer, nor can corporal possession be had of it.[74]

Because advowsons are incorporeal rights incapable of livery, they 'can therefore be only conveyed by operation of law, by verbal grant, either oral or written, which is a kind of invisible mental transfer'.[75] This statement was inaccurate, as Christian noted in his scholarly fifteenth edition of the *Commentaries*,[76] for before the Statute of Frauds a freehold interest in a corporeal hereditament (including its appendant incorporeal rights) could pass by informal contract with livery of seisin; but an incorporeal advowson by itself 'could never, in any age of the English law, pass by oral grant without deed';[77] Coke expressly held that 'grant is properly of things incorporeal, which cannot pass without deed'.[78] The deed requirement can be seen as substituting for a tangible livery of seisin of a corporeal thing, whereby a patent, formal act constitutes the property right; and also as the legal form for the creation of specialty rights, or rights supplementing the common-law appurtenances of property enjoyment. The doctrinal necessity for a constitutive deed or specialty helps to explain the origin of the doctrines of presumed and lost grant in the English law of prescription for incorporeal property, as is discussed in the next chapter.

Rights of Common

As for Bracton, for Blackstone the most important of the incorporeal hereditaments was the right of common. Blackstone divides this category into commons of pasture, piscary, turbary, and estovers. The case of common of pasture illustrates four types of incorporeal right emanating from land, classifications which are of general application.[79]

First, common could be *appendant* to arable land, as a universal right attached to such land because it was necessary to pasture animals in order to maintain the ploughing and manuring necessary for an effective agriculture: 'The law therefore annexed this right of common, as inseparably incident to the grant of the lands'.[80] Because appendant rights are necessary to enjoyment of the land, they are implied into grant by law as a 'common right', without requirement of pleading actual grant or prescription.[81] Coke by

[74] ii, 21.
[75] ii, 22; cf. *Co.Litt.* 335 b: incorporeal property 'doth not lie in livery, but in grant'.
[76] ii, 22 n. (1). [77] 2 *Wooddeson* 64.
[78] *Co.Litt.* 9; 335 b: 'It appeareth that an advowson doth not lie in livery, but in grant'.
[79] Blackstone's treatment builds on *Co.Litt.* 122a–b.
[80] ii, 33. [81] ii, 33–4.

contrast states that 'appendants are ever by prescription'; Hargraves reconciled this requirement by stating that appendancy of itself always implies prescription and grant. In other words, appendant rights are implied as integral to grant of common, as a necessary element of such grant.[82]

Next there was '[c]ommon *appurtenant*', which:

> ariseth from no connection of tenure, nor from any absolute necessity: but may be annexed to lands in other lordships, or extend to other beasts . . . which neither plough nor manure the ground. This not arising from any natural propriety or necessity, like common appendant, is therefore not of general right; but can only be claimed by immemorial usage and prescription[83] which the law esteems sufficient proof of a special grant or agreement for this purpose.[84]

Thus appurtenant rights are those desirable or convenient rights attached to land by actual (not implied) grant.[85] Common *because of vicinage*, or neighbourhood, was the permissive intercommoning of beasts on the fields of contiguous communities, and was a mere licence, revocable at election of either side.[86]

> Common *in gross*, or at large is such as is neither appendant nor appurtenant to land, but is annexed to a man's person; being granted to him and his heirs by deed; or it may be claimed by prescriptive right. . . . This is a separate inheritance, entirely distinct from any landed property, and may be vested in one who has not a foot of ground in the manor.[87]

Thus common in gross was a personal right to take benefits from another's land. The right of pasturable common was generally limited as to time and number of feeding animals. Sometimes the right was without stint, but there may have been a rule additionally limiting an unstinted right of pasturing to those animals which could be supported by the dominant land—an implication of a reasonableness test derived from the notion of appendancy or appurtenancy.[88]

Commons of piscary and of digging for turf or minerals were said to resemble the latter category of common of pasture, and were subject to the same regulations as for commons in gross. Common of estovers (or the Saxon 'bote') for the taking of wood for households was limited by an express test of necessity; '[t]hese botes or estovers must be reasonable ones'; that is, the appurtenancy principle again implied a proportionality test for takings.[89]

Blackstone concluded that the four types of right of common all derived from necessity, 'for the maintenance and carrying on of husbandry'. They

[82] *Co.Litt.*, 122a. [83] *Co.Litt.* 121–122. [84] ii, 33. [85] *Co.Litt.* 122a.
[86] ii, 33–4; *Co.Litt.* 122a. [87] ii, 34; *Co.Litt.* 122a. [88] *Co.Litt.* 122 a.
[89] Ibid.; and note Bractonian and Roman analogues: see Ch. 2 above, the text accompanying nn. 148–170 and passim.

were calculated to feed, fuel, repair, and fence the homes of agricultural tenants and to pasture their beasts; and the justification of necessity for those purposes implied limits of reasonableness controlling the extent of these rights.

Ways

The right of way was a private incorporeal right: it could be a licence annexed to a person by special permission; or a proprietary right by grant; or a right implied into a grant by necessity, as where land is sold without access except by an implied way. Moreover:

> [a] way may be also by prescription; as if all the inhabitants of such a hamlet, or all the owners and occupiers of such farm, have immemorially used to cross such a ground, for such a particular purpose: for this immemorial usage supposes an original grant, whereby a right of way thus appurtenant to land or houses may clearly be created.[90]

All the other incorporeal hereditaments, notably franchises, followed similar rules, with Blackstone reiterating that 'these may be held by prescription, which, as has frequently been said, presupposes a grant'.[91]

PRIOR APPROPRIATION, COMPETITION, AND MONOPOLY—THE CASE OF FRANCHISES

Blackstone's discussion of the legal acquisition and protection of the incorporeal rights of franchise, such as markets and fairs, raised important issues of competition and monopoly. Franchise rights were delegations of royal jurisdiction, granting control of government, trade, and other activities within a locale. The first person to establish a particular franchise by investing in an activity might be awarded a property right by express or implied grant, such that any competition injuring his flow of income was a nuisance to his franchise as a right of property. The question then arose whether a first appropriation of economic rights or other franchises should result in a monopolist income, legally protected from competition.

The franchise to hold a market could be 'owned' as a royal privilege requiring produce in the locality to be brought to that market and sometimes for tolls to be paid. The concept of a 'free market' at this time meant a privileged, monopolistic market controlled by a franchise owner, inverting the present connotation. Similar monopolist rights of this and earlier periods included jurisdictional rights for private courts such as the assize of bread and ale; ferry franchises; and the grim franchise granting jurisdiction to hang

[90] ii, 36; cf. *Co.Litt*. 56a. [91] ii, 37.

locally-convicted felons.[92] These franchises were formally rights of grant, but were often procured by long user implying grant by prescription. The Crown's use of writs of *Quo warranto* to rescind franchises of doubtful origin was continuously opposed by the propertied classes, protecting their local monopoly rights and jurisdictions from the larger monopoly of centralizing royal government.[93]

Blackstone discussed market franchises as follows:

> [I]f I am entitled to hold a fair or market, and another person sets up a fair or market so near mine that he does me a prejudice, it is a nusance to the freehold which I have in my market or fair.[94] But in order to make this out to be a nusance, it is necessary, 1. That my market or fair be the elder, otherwise the nusance lies at my own door. 2. That the market be erected within the third part of twenty miles from mine.... So that if the new market be not within seven miles of the old one, it is no nusance.[95]

The protection of franchised markets was not based on antiquity, custom, or origins of the market in prescription by long use. The right was based rather on a straightforward prior appropriation doctrine—whoever first has a market wins a monopoly right allowing suppression of competition from rival markets, no matter how recent the establishment of that first market. The rule concerning permissible distances between markets is from Bracton and the civil law, as interpreted by Hale; it was to ensure that each franchised market cover a region within one day's return journey, allowing any person bound by the franchise to attend that market a sufficient time 'in transacting his necessary business there'. The test for unfair competition was one of fact:

> If such market or fair be on the same day with mine, it is *prima facie* a nusance to mine, and there needs no proof of it, but the law will intend it to be so; but if it be on any other day, it *may* be a nusance; though whether it *is* or not, cannot be intended or presumed, but I must make proof of it to the jury.[96]

The doctrine might be interpreted as a rational rule to divide consumer markets between producers and ensure each an adequate market share—a common-law form of cartelization. There was, however, a crucial difference between monopoly in a fair or market and monopoly in some other good. A monopoly in a capital good or resource allows taking of monopoly profits or

[92] *Bracton*, f. 235–235b, iii, 198–9; F. Pollock and F. W. Maitland, *The History of English Law Before the Time of Edward I* (2nd edn., Cambridge, 1898, reprinted 1968) i, 571–84, 642–5; C. H. S. Fifoot, *History and Sources of the Common Law: Tort and Contract* (London, 1949) 96–7 (corn mill and franchise cases).

[93] iii, 262–4, 306–7. See further D. W. Sutherland, *Quo Warranto Proceedings during the Reign of Edward I* (Oxford, 1963); P. Brand, ' "Quo Warranto" Law in the Reign of Edward I: A Hitherto Undiscovered Opinion of Chief Justice Hengham', in P. Brand, *The Making of the Common Law* (London, 1993) 393, esp. at 427–34 (requirements of long-term seisin for proof of franchise grant). Mill-suit, requiring corn to be brought to the lord's mill, and the other typical production monopolies such as baking, brewing, and free bull, were seigneurial rights rather than governmental franchises emanating directly from the Crown.

[94] F.N.B. 140; 2 *Roll. Abdgt.* 140. [95] iii, 218–19. [96] iii, 219.

rents above the rate that could be procured under free competition. By contrast, a unified fair minimizes information and transaction costs for participating traders, and thereby promotes more efficient exchange than a series of isolated free markets. An example of a seemingly monopolist market promoting a more efficient free trade were the 'piece yards' of the early textile revolution in the West Riding of Yorkshire, where fully informed competitive trade was promoted by the enforcement of a compulsory textile exchange, which confined all sales of cloth in the region to the one place between certain hours only (generally Saturday mornings). This arrangement gathered together all information about prices, supply, and quality, and thus helped maintain bargaining rationality and equality.[97] The possibilities of franchised markets in improving exchange may explain why the common law long tolerated such rights; or at least explains why common lawyers of liberal mind such as Hale, Coke, and Blackstone found such franchises (together with the manorial monopolies) to be acceptable into modern times.

A further reason proposed by Blackstone for permitting monopolist rights by prior appropriation was to guarantee a return on sunk investment costs and so ensure the provision of public goods. His argument centres on prescriptive ferries, but can be applied also to tolled bridges, roads, and other fixed capital:

If a ferry is erected on a river, so near another antient ferry as to draw away it's custom, it is a nusance to the owner of the old one. For where there is a ferry by prescription, the owner is bound to keep it always in repair and readiness, for the ease of all the king's subjects; otherwise he may be grievously amerced:[98] it would be therefore extremely hard, if a new ferry were suffered to share its profits, which does not also share his burthen.

Blackstone stresses that only if there were sunk costs and public goods to be protected was this rule applicable:

But where the reason ceases, the law also ceases with it: therefore it is no nusance to erect a mill so near mine, as to draw away the custom, unless the miller also intercepts the water. Neither is it a nusance to set up any trade, or a school, in a neighbourhood or rivalship with another: for by such emulation the public are like to be gainers; and if the new mill or school occasions a damage to the old one, it is *damnum absque injuria.*[99]

Thus competition was valuable even where it destroyed the profits and viability of a prior business; but only price competition for trade was permitted, not physical competition for appropriated goods or capital such as water

[97] A magnificent piece yard (with museum) may be seen at Halifax. It is well worth a special visit; nearby are follies built to industrial scale by self-advertising local manufacturers.

[98] 2 *Roll. Abdgt.* 140.

[99] iii, 218–19, referring to Hale on F.N.B. 184; cf. cases cited in J. H. Baker and S. F. C. Milsom, *Sources of English Legal History. Private Law to 1750* (London, 1986) 592–610.

rights. This was an old principle for the regulation of competition extant in the medieval common law.[100]

'TRANSIENT' PROPERTY AND TITLE BY PRIOR APPROPRIATION—THE CASE OF WATER

The objects of dominion or property were things real, 'such as are permanent, fixed, and immoveable, which cannot be carried out of their place'; and things personal, 'goods, money, and all other moveables; which may attend the owner's person wherever he thinks proper to go'. Real property could be (1) land or 'all things of a permanent, substantial nature'; or (2) tenements which included corporeal and incorporeal rights over land; or (3) hereditaments, the largest classification which included all inheritable rights, corporeal or incorporeal; personal, real, or mixed. Blackstone also suggested a category of (4) transient property (with similar qualities to the Roman *res communes* and *res nullius*) which lay on the margins of the other main categories.

Blackstone regarded water as 'transient' property; and simultaneously as real property, being part of land. Water rights were not a form of personal property, even though water itself was transient and severable.[101] It was a corporeal object of property, a hereditament 'such as affect the senses; such as may be seen and handled by the body', rather than incorporeal property, or things which are 'not the object of sensation, can neither be seen nor handled, are creatures of the mind, and exist only in contemplation'.[102] Rights of water use were definitionally excluded from Blackstone's understanding of incorporeal rights in two ways. First, water use can be a natural amenity inherent in the possession of riparian or watered lands, and is therefore not always an 'accidental' or additional right of grant. Secondly, in some sense water may physically be appropriated by use or 'quasi-possessed', unlike purely abstract legal rights over land such as tithes.

Conspicuous by their absence in Blackstone's discussion were any incorporeal water rights akin to the Roman categories of *aquae ductus*, *aquae haustus*, and daily water. Allocation of natural waters by erecting praedial

[100] See *Resolution of the Judges* (1624) Hutt. 100; 123 E.R. 1128, citing 11 H.4. 27; and see *Viner's Abdgt.*, xv, 399–400. The case of water mills was complicated by the monopolist property rights of mill-suit, the customary and prescriptive rights attached to ancient mills, binding tenants of a manor or locality to grind only at that mill. See J. Blum, *The End of the Old Order in Rural Europe* (Princeton, NJ, 1990) 80–94; M. Bloch, 'The Advent and Triumph of the Watermill', in M. Bloch, *Land and Work in Mediaeval Europe: Selected Papers by Marc Bloch*, (trans. J. E. Anderson, London, 1967) 136; see Ch. 1, the text accompanying nn. 43–52 above.

[101] Cf. *Ferens* v. *O'Brien* (1883) L.R. 11 Q.B.D. 21 (Q.B.), holding that water as a severable form of property can be the subject of larceny.

[102] ii, 17–18.

rights connected to estates, and then protecting those rights by injunctions and real actions on the Roman plan, seems to have been an alien technique for Blackstone. Water rights as incorporeal property are expressly listed in the *Commentaries* only in the form of fishing rights: as common of piscary, and as the royal franchise of '*free fishery*, or exclusive right of fishing in a public river'.[103] Any type of analogy with classical Roman categories is contained only in Blackstone's discussion of common-law nuisance.[104] Nor is there resort to the later civilian ideas of praedial servitudes as *iura*, real rights, or *iura in re aliena*. This lacuna means that Blackstone's elaborate doctrines of custom and prescription for incorporeal rights have little or no application to water entitlements.[105]

Blackstone writes of rights over natural elements more as public goods than private interests:

> But, after all, there are some few things, which, notwithstanding the general introduction and continuance of property must still unavoidably remain in common; being such wherein nothing but an usufructuary property is capable of being had: and therefore they still belong to the first occupant, during the time he holds possession of them, and no longer. Such (among others) are the elements of light, air and water; which a man may occupy by means of his windows, his gardens, his mills, and other conveniences: such also are the generality of those animals which are said to be *ferae naturae*, or of wild and untameable disposition: which any man may seise upon and keep for his own use or pleasure. All these things, so long as they remain in possession, every man has a right to enjoy without disturbance; but if once they escape from his custody, or he voluntarily abandons the use of them, they return to the common stock, and any man else has an equal right to seise and enjoy them afterwards.[106]

The resonance with the Roman classifications of public goods as *res communes* or *res nullius* is striking, and is continued in a later passage:

> Corporeal hereditaments consist wholly of substantial and permanent objects; all of which may be comprehended under the general denomination of land only. For *land*, says sir Edward Coke,[107] comprehendeth in it's legal signification any ground, soil, or earth whatsoever; as arable, meadows, pastures, woods, moors, waters, marshes, furzes, and heath.... It is observable that *water* is here mentioned as a species of land, which may seem a sort of solecism; but such is the language of the law: and therefore I cannot bring an action to recover possession of a pool or other piece of water by the name of *water* only; either by calculating it's capacity, as, for so many cubical yards; or, by superficial measure, for twenty acres of *land covered with water*.[108] *For water is a moveable wandering thing, and must of necessity continue*

[103] ii, 39. [104] See the text accompanying nn. 190–202 below.

[105] For Blackstone's discussion of titles by prescription, custom, and limitation see ii, 29–32, 263–6, 365–71; iii, 188–9, 195–6, 306–8, 422–9.

[106] ii, 14.

[107] *Co.Litt.* 4.

[108] *Challenor* v. *Thomas* (1608) 1 Brownl. 142; 123 E.R. 718 (K.B.), see Ch. 3, the text accompanying n. 45.

common by the law of nature; so that I can only have a temporary, transient, usufructary, property therein wherefore, if a body of water runs out of my pond into another man's, I have no right to reclaim it.[109]

The transience of flowing water and its incapability of exclusive appropriation thus dictated that it be subject to use-rights only. Even incorporeal rights over free water, such as fishing franchises, were a suspect appropriation of common public goods:

A *free fishery*, or exclusive right of fishing in a public river, is . . . a royal franchise; and is considered as such in all countries where the feodal polity has prevailed; though the making such grants, and by that means appropriating what seems to be unnatural to restrain, the use of running water, was prohibited for the future by king John's great charter; and the rivers that were fenced in his time were directed to be laid open.[110]

However, in certain cases there could be property in still water, as forming part of land, a doctrine Blackstone adopted almost literally from Coke:[111]

But the land, which that water covers, is permanent, fixed, and immoveable: and therefore in this I may have a certain substantial property: of which the law will take notice, and not of the other.

Land hath also, in it's legal signification, an indefinite extent, upwards as well as downwards. *Cujus est solum, ejus est usque ad coelum* [who has the soil has also to the sky] is the maxim of the law. . . . So that the word 'land' includes not only the face of the earth, but everything under it, or over it. And therefore, if a man grants all his lands, he grants thereby all his mines of metal and other fossils, his woods, his waters, and his houses, as well as his fields and meadows. Not but the particular names of the things are equally sufficient to pass them, except in the instance of water; by a grant of which, nothing passes but a right of fishing: . . . but by the name of land, which is *nomen generalissimum*, every thing terrestial will pass.[112]

Water as Personal Property with Real Qualities

Property in water was also discussed at length under the heading of '*title* to things personal, or the various means of *acquiring*, and of *losing*, such property'. Personal property included things in action, chattels real, and chattels personal or moveables. Water fitted none of these categories, but had a 'mongrel amphibious nature' partaking of the qualities of each; it was

[109] ii, 17–18 (emphasis added). No direct authority was adduced for this key claim.

[110] ii, 39.

[111] ii, 17–18, following *Co.Litt.* 4a–b.

[112] Ibid. 4, 5, 6. M. Taggart, *Private Property and Abuse of Rights in Victorian England: The Story of Edward Pickles and the Bradford Water Supply* (Oxford, 2002) 120–1, notes that Blackstone seems to have innovated by extending the maxim *cujus est solum* to include downwards-facing ownership.

placed within the category of property in transient elements and public goods such as wild animals, in which 'a man can have no absolute property' but was permitted only a 'qualified property'.[113]

On acquisition of personal titles, Blackstone states:

> [A] property in goods and chattels may be acquired by *occupancy*: which we have more than once[114] remarked, was the original and only primitive method of acquiring any property at all; but which has since been restrained and abridged, by the positive laws of society, in order to maintain peace and harmony among mankind. For this purpose, by the laws of England, gifts, and contracts, testaments, legacies, and administrations have been introduced and countenanced, in order to transfer and continue that property and possession in things personal, which has once been acquired by the owner. And where such things are found without any other owner, they for the most part belong to the king by virtue of his prerogative; except in some few instances, wherein the original and natural right of occupancy is still permitted to subsist.
>
> . . .
>
> Thus . . . whatever moveables are found upon the surface of the earth, or in the sea, and are unclaimed by any owner, are supposed to be abandoned by the last proprietor; and, as such, are returned into the common stock and mass of things: and therefore they belong, as in a state of nature, to the first occupant. . . .[115]

Blackstone reiterates that water (that is, flowing water) was a transient thing that could not physically be occupied in the manner of land: but it could be occupied or appropriated by a first use or 'detention':

> Thus too the benefit of the elements, the light, the air, and the water, can only be appropriated by occupancy. If I have an antient window overlooking my neighbour's ground he may not erect any blind to obstruct the light: but if I build my house close to his wall, which darkens it, I cannot compel him to demolish his wall; for there the first occupancy is rather in him, than in me. If my neighbour makes a tan-yard, so as to annoy and render less salubrious the air of my house or gardens, the law will furnish me with a remedy; but if he is first in possession of the air, and I fix my habitation near him, the nuisance is of my own seeking, and may continue. *If a stream be unoccupied, I may erect a mill thereon, and detain the water; yet not so as to injure my neighbour's prior mill, or his meadow: for he hath by the first occupancy acquired a property in the current.*[116]

This 'prior appropriation' theory of title to water (or other appurtenances of land) impacts greatly on later common-law developments.

Water as 'Qualified Property'

Rights to personalty could be 'in *possession absolute*, which is where a man hath, solely and exclusively, the right, and also the occupation, of any

[113] ii, 390. [114] ii, 3, 8, 258. [115] ii, 401–3. [116] ii, 402–3 (emphasis added).

moveable chattels', and fully controlled their transfer and disposition;[117] or else a '*qualified*, *limited*, or *special* property; which is such as is not in it's nature permanent, but many sometimes subsist, and at other times not subsist'.[118] At the core of this category of qualified property were wild animals, characterized by their propensity to escape from appropriation. A title to these animals arose 'by a man's *reclaiming* and making them tame by art, industry, and education; or by so confining them within his own immediate power, that they cannot escape and use their natural liberty';[119] 'the property is not absolute, but defeasible: a property, that may be destroyed if they resume their ancient wildness, and are found at large'.[120] After giving a lengthy Romanist treatment of this subject, Blackstone continued:

> The qualified property which we have hitherto considered extends only to animals *ferae naturae*, when either reclaimed, impotent, or privileged. Many other things may also be the objects of qualified property. It may subsist in the very elements, of fire or light, of air, and of water. A man can have no absolute permanent property in these, as he may in the earth and land; since these are of a vague and fugitive nature, and therefore can admit only of a precarious and qualified ownership, which lasts so long as they are in actual use and occupation, but no longer. If a man disturbs another, and deprives him of the lawful enjoyment of these; if one obstructs another's antient windows, corrupts the air of his house or gardens, fouls his water[121] or unpens and lets it out, or if he diverts an antient watercourse that used to run to the other's mill or meadow;[122] the law will animadvert hereon as an injury, and protect the party injured in his possession. But the property in them ceases the instant they are out of possession: for, when no man is engaged in their actual occupation, they become again common, and every man has an equal right to appropriate them to his own use.[123]

Blackstone does not explain why a title to protect enjoyment of light and flowing water from interference can require 'antient windows' and 'antient watercourses'. The question therefore rises why a user of light or water must be ancient in order to attract protection, rather than simply take effect as an established first occupation or prior appropriation. Blackstone does not offer an explanation; and we may suspect that in fitting the law of appurtenances and natural rights into a framework of title by occupation, many of the complexities of preceding legal materials were simply glossed over. This is another example of Blackstone's 'superficiality in his interpretation of history',[124] which was, of course, part and parcel of his drive to present a rational and contained picture of the common law.

117 ii, 389. 118 ii, 391. 119 Ibid. 120 ii, 393.

121 *Aldred's Case* (1610) 9 Co. Rep. 57b; 77 E.R. 816 (K.B.); see Ch. 3, the text accompanying nn. 18–27.

122 *Russell* v. *Handford* (1583) 1 Leon. 273; 74 E.R. 248 (K.B.); *Prickman* v. *Tripp* (1693) Skin. 389; 90 E.R. 173 (K.B.); see Ch. 3, the text accompanying nn. 2, 94–95, 112–113.

123 ii, 395. 124 Baker, *Introduction to English Legal History*, 191.

The rule disallowing an exclusive and continuing title in non-occupied transient property may be compared to the policy excluding future property in personalty. This was a policy based on utility rather than the inherent nature of the thing as incapable of future property:

[P]ersonal goods ... being things transitory, and by many accidents subject to be lost, destroyed, or otherwise impaired, and the exigencies of trade requiring also a frequent circulation thereof, it would occasion perpetual suits and quarrels, and put a stop to the freedom of commerce, if such limitations in remainder were *generally* tolerated and allowed.[125]

In the context of titles by grant and contract, Blackstone analyses rights to future possession and enjoyment of goods in terms of contract more than property:

A true and proper gift or grant is always accompanied with delivery of possession, and takes effect immediately.... But if the gift does not take effect, by delivery of immediate possession, it is then not properly a gift, but a contract.[126]

The common law in the eighteenth and nineteenth centuries continued to grapple with the problem of whether a purported occupation of transient property such as water was in effect a claim to future property. The question was whether occupation rights could take effect as a proprietary claim or title ensuring potential enjoyment, even in the absence of present user—an ownership of the 'substance' as well as the 'use', to follow Blackstone's terminology.

To sum up Blackstone's analysis of water rights so far: first occupation is stressed as the basis of title to water. Water rights are not characterized as incorporeal rights or appurtenances, but as transient corporeal property acquired by appropriation. Water is subject to real rights, but its transient qualities give it some of the character of personal property, most significantly that occupation bestows title. Doctrines of long use or prescription are not employed as a source of title to water, barring one isolated reference to the idea that an ancient watercourse was a requirement to establish a claim to this qualified property.

HALE'S *DE JURE MARIS*

Sir Matthew Hale's *De Jure Maris* was a short manuscript treatise collecting together three shorter works dating from around 1670, and published in 1787, two decades after Blackstone's *Commentaries*, and like that work winning a wide readership—though it is far from clear that Blackstone

[125] ii, 397. [126] ii, 441.

had any knowledge of the manuscript.[127] Hale wrote these works for private study and pleasure, and they were not intended as descriptions of contemporary law. For our purposes Hale's work is significant chiefly for blending Romanist concepts of water as public goods with the English doctrines of royal prerogative and public nuisance.[128] Blackstone, by contrast, melded Roman ideas regarding water as *res communes* and *publici juris* within the categories of English private law, rather than public law. Hale's treatise thus serves as a counterweight to Blackstone's conceptual scheme.

'Concerning the Interest of Fresh Rivers'—Ownership of Soil of Streams

Hale begins with the conventional Roman view that riparian owners owned at least the soil underneath streams to the mid-way point of the channel.

> Fresh rivers of what kind soever, do of common right belong to the owners of the soil adjacent; so that the owners of the one side have, of common right, the propriety of the soil, and consequently the right of fishing, *usque filum aquae* [to the middle of the stream]; and the owners of the other side the right of soil or ownership and fishing unto the *filum aquae* on their side. And if a man be owner of the land of both sides, in common presumption he is owner of the whole river, and hath the right of fishing according to the extent of his land in length. With this agrees the common experience.... [129] But special usage may alter that common presumption;[130] for one man may have the river, and others the soil adjacent; or one man may have the river and soil thereof, and another the free or several fishing in that river.[131]

The Roman rules for alluvion, or change of riparian ownership where the bed of a stream shifts, are then reproduced.[132] Hale seems to count 'ownership' of a river in this instance as control of the subsoil, banks, and fishing rights, without discussing allocation of rights of user of the stream itself. He

[127] Sir Matthew Hale, *De Jure Maris* (*c.*1670), in Moore, *Foreshore*, 370–413. Hale's place in the treatise tradition is discussed in Simpson, 'Legal Treatise', 278–82. A bibliographical discussion of Hale's tracts is given in H. N. Scheiber, 'The Road to *Munn*: Eminent Domain and the Concept of Public Purpose in the State Courts', in D. Fleming and B. Bailyn (eds.), *Law in American History* (*Perspectives in American History*, v) (Boston, Mass., 1971) 329–402, at 334–5; and see C. Fairman, 'The So-called Granger Cases, Lord Hale, and Justice Bradley' (1953) 5 Stanford Law Review 587.

[128] Similar contemporary English adaptions of Roman public goods doctrine can be found in: R. Callis, *Reading Upon the Statute of Sewers, 23 Hen. VIII, c. 5* (London, 1622) 73–9; (4th edn. by W. J. Broderip, London, 1824) 90–8; J. Cowell, *The Institutes of the Lawes of England* (London, 1651) 54–5; J. Selden, *Mare Clausum Seu De Dominio Maris Libri Duo* (London, 1635), and *Of the Dominion or Ownership of the Sea* (translated by Marchamont Nedham, 1652).

[129] Citing: Y.B. Mich. 18–19 Edw. 1, B. R. Rot. Nott.; Trin. 2 Jac. B. R. *Owen et Dunch*, Vide 8 H. 7, 5, 22 Ass. 93.

[130] On special custom as varying general rules see Hale, *De Jure Maris*, 381.

[131] Ibid., ch. xv, 370–7; cf. Inst.2.1.2., 4.

[132] Inst.2.1.20.–24.

concludes the chapter by introducing the idea of public use-rights as a species of 'servitude':

Though fresh rivers are in point of propriety as before *prima facie* of a private interest; yet as well fresh rivers as salt, or such as flow and reflow; may be under these two servitudes, or affected with them; viz. one or prerogative belonging to the king, and another of publick interest, or belonging to the people generally.[133]

These 'servitudes' or burdens on private ownership consist of prerogative and public right, which are conceptually distinct.

'Of the Right of Prerogative in Private of Fresh Rivers'—Royal Franchises and Supervision

In the second chapter Hale states: 'The king by an ancient right of prerogative hath a certain interest in many fresh rivers, even where the sea doth not flow or reflow.' Three prerogative rights were specified: of ferry franchises where private persons were vested with the exercise of the prerogative in order to provide a monopolistic service; of the king's pleasure and recreation; and of the king's supervisory jurisdiction to maintain rivers as public highways.[134] The latter classification was rivalled by the next.

'Concerning Publick Streams'—Public Law Rights in Rivers as Highways

In the third chapter Hale describes rights to flowing water as a public good, blending Roman with feudal ideas:

There be some streams or rivers, that are private not only in propriety or ownership, but also in use, as little streams and rivers that are not a common passage for the king's people. Again, there, be other rivers, as well fresh as salt, whether they flow and reflow or not, are *prima facie publici juris*, common highways for man or goods or both from one inland town to another. Thus the rivers of Wey, of Severn, of Thames, and divers others, as well above the bridges and ports as below, as well above the flowings of the sea as below, and as well where they are become to be of private propriety as in what parts they are of king's propriety, are publick rivers *juris publici*.[135]

A test of navigability thus determined when a river or stream was *publici juris* or a public good, on the analogy of common highways. Hale seems to classify these rights as a public-law alternative to the established Crown prerogative jurisdiction over waterways. These ancient public rights were protected by ordinary local criminal jurisdictions, rather than by discretionary exercise of prerogative.[136]

[133] Hale, *De Jure Maris*, 372. [134] Ibid., 372–4. [135] Ibid., 374.

[136] Ibid., 374–5; citing *Glanvill* lib. 9. cap. 11; *Britton* f. 28, 29; *Co.Litt.* 277b, who describes the action thus:

The Doctrine of Dedication of Private Goods to Public Use

Just as a private ferry could be made subject to public regulation if it were offered as a public amenity, so private waters could be 'dedicated' as *publici juris* if they were seen to fall within a public sphere of navigation:

[I]f any person at his own charge makes his own private stream to be passable for boats or barges, either by making of locks or cutts, or drawing together other streams; and hereby that river, which was his own in point of propriety become now capable of carriage of vessels; yet this seems not to make it *juris publici*, and he may pull it down again, or apply it to his own private use. For it is not hereby made to be *publici juris*, unless it were done at a common charge, or by a publick authority, or that by long continuance of time it hath been freely devoted to a publick use. And so it seems also to be, if he that makes such a new river or passage doth it by way of recompence or compensation for some other publick stream that he hath stopped for his own conveniency; . . . So likewise if he purchaseth the king's charter to take a reasonable toll for the passage of the king's subjects, and puts it in use, these seem to be devoting and as it were consecrating it of the common use. . . . For no man can take a settled or constant toll even in his own private land for a common passage without the king's licence.[137]

The doctrine of dedication of private waters to public use was strongly to influence United States eminent domain doctrine.[138] Similar ideas of water as *publici juris* passed into the vocabulary of the nineteenth-century English common law, but without the stress on public navigation and tolls as the source of rights.

BLACKSTONE'S ANALYSIS OF REMEDIAL LAW

We return now to Blackstone's map of the law. He discusses the procedures and forms of possessory and proprietary actions in Book III of the *Commentaries*; and in the course of that discussion he has a great deal to say about the substantive principles of water law.

Purprestura est, &c., generaliter quoties aliquid fit ad nocumentum regii tenementi, vel regiae viae (vel aliquarum publicarum) vel civitatis, &c. [A purpresture] is properly when there is . . . an inclosure made of any part of the king's demesnes, or of an highway, or a common street, or public water, or such like public things, it is derived of the French word *pourpris*, which signifieth an inclosure, but specially applied, as is aforesaid, by the common law.

The common law later narrowed the extent of these rights: see *Ball* v. *Herbert* (1789) 3 T.R. 253; 100 E.R. 560 (K.B.); *Weld* v. *Hornby* (1806) 7 East. 196; 103 E.R. 75 (K.B.); and for public access to the sea-shore see *Blundell* v. *Catterall* (1821) 5 B. & Ald. 282; 106 E.R. 1190 (K.B.).

137 Hale, *De Jure Maris*, 375–6.

138 See D. R. Coquillette, 'Mosses from an Old Manse: Another Look At Some Historic Property Cases About the Environment' (1979) 64 Cornell Law Review 761, 799–820; Fairman, *Granger Cases*; H. N. Scheiber, 'Law and the Imperatives of Progress: Private Rights and Public Values in American Legal History', in J. R. Pennock and J. W. Chapman (eds.), *Ethics, Economics, and the Law*, Nomos XXIV (New York, 1982) 304–20 and 'Road to *Munn*'.

Tort Remedies for Possession and Property

Blackstone states repeatedly that the common law protects legal rights by providing remedies for wrongs, notably through the writs of disseisin and trespass. He elevates the procedural pragmatism of the tort remedies for real injuries into a general principle of remedial law.[139]

The idea that rights are enforced through remedies for wrongs was sometimes stated merely as an adjectival device, with analytic priority given to the substantive rights of persons and property recognized by municipal law. Thus wrongs 'for the most part convey to us an idea merely negative, as being nothing else but a privation of right'. Rights had to be defined before wrongs: 'the contemplation of what is *jus* being necessarily prior to what may be termed *injuria*, and the definition of *fas* precedent to that of *nefas*'.[140] Elsewhere in the *Commentaries*, wrongs are given priority, with the idea that the common law provides a writ or finds a remedy for every injury which ought to be redressed.[141] A larger idea expressed here is that justice is defined by the sense of injustice, of wrongful disturbance; we discover distributive justice by pursuing our intuitions about corrective justice. More practically, we must specify a wrong in order to understand our rightful legal entitlements. Blackstone stressed either substantive rights or remedies for wrongs, the two sides of the equation, as best suited his pragmatic and argumentative purposes.

The Complexity of Remedy-based Common Law

Blackstone defended the strictest adherence to the old forms of action, on the ground that the history of civil actions showed 'the establishment of some standard was undoubtedly necessary, to fix the true state of a question of right; left in a long and arbitrary process it might be shifted continually, and be at length no longer discernible'.[142] The forms of action could properly be adapted by statute, by issue of analogous writs, and above all by beneficial fictions.[143] Blackstone clearly felt the pressure of common-law tradition as a brake on rational re-ordering of the law.[144]

[139] i, 53–6, 121–5; iii, chs. 1–2, 8–10. See further D. Lieberman, 'Property, Commerce and the Common Law: Attitudes to Legal Change in the Eighteenth Century', in J. Brewer and S. Staves, *Early Modern Conceptions of Property* (London, 1995) 144–58.

[140] iii, 1–3; and see esp. iii, 116.

[141] iii, 108–9, 118–19, 183–4, 265–6, 421–4.

[142] iii, 116.

[143] iii, 42–3, 107–8, adumbrating Maine's formula of legal reform by legislation, equity, and fiction. Blackstone's conservatism in acceding to the cumbersome use of writs for wrongs to defend rights is stressed by Kennedy, 'Blackstone'; cf. Cairns, 'Blackstone', 350–2.

[144] See further iii, 222, 266–8, 325 ff., 421–4.

Romanizing the Forms of Action

Blackstone used a Roman institutional framework to order the forms of action. He drew a distinction between public and private wrongs, noting how the Crown's concern with keeping the peace led the royal courts to remedy not only public crimes and nuisances but also private disseisins and trespasses, thus opening up a wide jurisdiction to deal with all private wrongs and enforce all rights, both personal and proprietary. In the sphere of private rights there were personal, real, and mixed actions,[145] affording the respective remedies of damages, of recovery of title and possession, or both. Another distinction was between actions for wrongs with force or violence, or without, i.e. trespass *vi et armis* or case.[146] On a slim base of authority, Blackstone also erected a distinction between direct and indirect (or consequential) wrongs, again corresponding to the general trespass and case categories.[147] Finally, a distinction was drawn between injury to the enjoyment of property and injury to the rights of property:

With regard to the third absolute right of individuals, or that of private property, though the enjoyment of it, when acquired, is strictly a personal right; yet as it's nature and original, and the means of it's acquisition or loss, fell more directly under our second general division, of the *rights of things*; and as, of course, the wrongs that affect these rights must be referred to the corresponding division . . . of our commentaries; I conceive it will be more commodious and easy to consider together, rather than in a separate view, the injuries that may be offered to the *enjoyment*, as well as to the *rights*, of property.[148]

Injuries to real rights (corporeal and incorporeal) involved dispossession; injuries to enjoyment of property were interferences not involving dispossession, pre-eminently nuisance.

Injuries to Real Rights: Disseisin

Blackstone's discussion of real injuries demonstrates his drive to specify property rights as 'absolute', though defended through relative title by the ancient 'feodal' forms of action. He acknowledged that these actions were out of use by the eighteenth century: 'the title of lands is now usually tried in actions of *ejectment* or *trespass*'.

Such is the modern way, of obliquely bringing in question the title to lands and tenements, in order to try it in this collateral manner; a method which is now universally adopted in almost every case. It is founded on the same principle as the

145 iii, 1–3, 116–19.
146 iii, 118–19.
147 iii, 208–9; see discussion of *Reynolds* v. *Clerke* (1725) 1 Strange 634; 93 E.R. 747 (K.B.); see Ch. 3, the text accompanying nn. 133–138.
148 iii, 138.

antient writs of assise, being calculated to try the mere *possessory* title to an estate; and hath succeeded to those real actions, as being infinitely more convenient for attaining the end of justice;. . . . But a writ of ejectment is not an adequate means to try the title of all estates; for on those things, whereon an entry cannot in fact be made, no entry shall be supposed by any fiction of the parties. Therefore an ejectment will not lie of an advowson, a rent, a common, or other incorporeal hereditament.[149]

This view is consistent with seventeenth-century case law holding against ejectment for running water as incapable of physical, exclusive possession.[150]

The remedies for disseisin or dispossession were confined to cases of ouster from a freehold interest. There was limited scope for defence of water rights by these means, for exclusion from the use and enjoyment of water as 'qualified' property would not be the privation of a freehold; only an invasion of the territory of a freehold including the water would qualify. There was room for expansion of the real remedies for appurtenances to land such as water if the appurtenances could be reclassified as incorporeal rights, for '[d]isseisin may be effected in either corporeal inheritances, or incorporeal'. This varies from Coke, who states that 'disseisin . . . is understood only of such lands and tenements whereunto an entry may be made, and not of rents, commons, &c'.[151] However, Blackstone seemed to regard the notion of disseisin of an incorporeal thing as a procedural fiction only, allowed to a plaintiff where writs of right or entry would be inconvenient and where damages as well as restitution of the right were sought: the example given was disseisin of a rent.[152] Blackstone's statement of the form of the actions for disseisin also suggests how an interference with substantive enjoyment of natural property rights, such as water use, might be remedied as a real injury of disseisin:

Disseisin of things corporeal, as of houses, lands, *&c.* must be by entry and actual dispossession of the freehold.[153] . . . Disseisin of incorporeal hereditaments cannot be an actual dispossession; for the subject itself is neither capable of actual bodily possession, nor dispossession: but it depends on their respective natures, and various kinds; being in general nothing more than a disturbance of the owner in the means of coming at, or enjoying them.[154]

Injuries to Property Enjoyment: Trespass

Trespass actions could be used to recover possession and try title indirectly by sanctioning a wrongful possessor with damages penalties. However, the

[149] iii, 205–6.

[150] *Challenor* v. *Thomas* (1608) 1 Brownl. & Golds. 142; 123 E.R. 718 (K.B.); see Ch. 3, the text accompanying n. 45.

[151] *Co.Litt.* 181a. See also J. Lilly, 'Preface' to J. Lilly (ed.), *Reports and Pleadings of Cases in Assise [etc.]* (London, 1719) 1–17; 170 E.R. 1–13.

[152] iii, 169–70, 174.

[153] Referring to *Co.Litt.* 181, a text which Blackstone goes on to contradict.

[154] iii, 169–70; and see iii, 241–2.

main role of trespass was to compensate for loss caused by injury to rights. Blackstone continued:

[W]henever the act itself is directly and immediately injurious to the person or property of another, and therefore necessarily accompanied with some force, an action of trespass *vi et armis* will lie; but, if the injury is only consequential, a special action of trespass *on the case* may be brought.[155]

Trespass *vi et armis* for property-use rights was limited to cases where there was an intrusion onto the freehold property of the plaintiff, or trespass *quare clausum fregit*. The elements of the action flowed from the idea of physical interference with possession of a freehold estate falling short of dispossession. The freeholder had to have been in actual possession at the time of intrusion. Damage would be imputed for any invasion:

Every unwarrantable entry on another's soil the law entitles a trespass by *breaking his close*;... And every such entry or breach of a man's close carries necessarily along with it some damage or other: for, if no other special loss can be assigned, yet still the words of the writ itself specify one general damage, *viz.* the treading down and bruising of his herbage.[156]

Thus the trespass action could establish title by asserting a freehold right in possession, even in the absence of interference with actual enjoyment. Any special damage could be sued for additionally; and continuing or repetitive trespass injuries could be recovered by inclusion of a *continuando* clause.[157]

By the trespass action, physical intrusions interfering with enjoyment of elements of land possession (such as light, air, and water) were remedied with personal damages, which in effect asserted and maintained a continuing title to the right of enjoyment. The *continuando* pleading linked together individual injuries to rights as an invasion of a continuing property right, an intrusion on title.

Injuries to Property Enjoyment: Nuisance

Blackstone next listed '[a] third species of real injuries to a man's lands and tenements,... by *nusance*', which was the most important action for defence of water rights.

Nusance, *nocumentum*, or annoyance, signifies any thing that worketh hurt, inconvenience, or damage. And nusances are of two kinds: *public* or *common* nusances, which affect the public, and are annoyance to *all* the king's subjects; for which reason we must refer them to the class of public wrongs, or crimes and misdemeanours; and

155 iii, 208–9. 156 iii, 209–10, citing F.N.B. 87, 88. 157 iii, 212.

private nusances, which . . . may be defined, any thing done to the hurt or annoyance of the lands, tenements, or hereditaments of another.[158]

Nuisances were injuries to real property where the trespassory element of forceful intrusion onto the freehold was absent. A nuisance could affect or damage a man's corporeal or incorporeal hereditaments.

Nuisance to Corporeal Hereditaments

Blackstone divided this class of action between nuisances damaging dwellings and lands:

[T]he nusances which affect a man's *dwelling* may be reduced to these three: 1. Overhanging it: which is also a species of trespass, for *cujus est solum ejus est usque ad coelum*: 2. Stopping antient lights: and, 3. Corrupting the air with noisome smells: for light and air are two indispensable requisites to every dwelling. But depriving one of a mere matter of pleasure, as of a fine prospect, by building a wall, or the like; this, as it abridges nothing really convenient or necessary, is no injury to the sufferer, and is therefore not an actionable nusance.[159]

The theory uniting these categories of nuisance is not clear. The right protected from nuisance must be 'convenient or necessary' to enjoyment of the property, not a 'mere matter of pleasure'.[160] The rights to air and light are held to be necessary or essential natural rights concomitant to the possession of a freehold estate; but the right to light is also said to depend on the antiquity of the user as well as the necessity of light to a dwelling. The right against overhanging drains is justified not only by convenience, but by analogy to trespass *quare clausum fregit*.

Blackstone explains these seemingly disparate rights by reference to two other principles: the maxim *sic utere tuo* and the doctrine that priority be given to the first mode of user of lands. Both principles appear in the following passage:

If a man builds a house so close to mine that his roof overhangs my roof, and throws the water off his roof upon mine, this is a nusance, for which an action will lie.[161] Likewise to erect a house or other building so near to mine, that it obstructs my antient lights and windows, is a nusance of a similar nature.[162] But in this latter case it is necessary that the windows be *antient*, that is, subsisted there a long time without interruption; otherwise there is no injury done.[163] For he hath as much right to build a

[158] Sir Henry Finch, *Law, or, a Discourse Thereof (Nomotechnia)* (London, 1613, English edn; D. Pickering (ed.), London, 1729) 188.

[159] iii, 216–17, referring to *Aldred's Case* (1610) 9 Co. Rep. 57b; 77 E.R. 816 (K.B.); see Ch. 3, the text accompanying nn. 18–28.

[160] iii, 216. [161] F.N.B. 184. [162] 9 Rep. 58, *Aldred's Case* (1610).

[163] By 1805, the notion of ancient right to lights had shrunk to twenty years' enjoyment, as is noted in the 15th edn., 216, note (1): 'The judges now hold, that lights are sufficiently antient to support this action, of which there has been an uninterrupted enjoyment above twenty years.'

new edifice upon his ground as I have upon mine; since every man may erect what he pleases upon the upright or perpendicular of his own soil, so as not to prejudice what has long been enjoyed by another; and it was my folly to build so near another's ground.[164] ... Also, if a person keeps his hogs, or other noisome animals, so near the house of another, that the stench of them incommodes him and makes the air unwholesome, this is an injurious nusance, as it tends to deprive him of the use and benefit of the house.[165] A like injury is, if one's neighbour sets up and exercises any offensive trade; as a tanner's, a tallow-chandler's, or the like; for though these are lawful and necessary trades, yet they should be exercised in remote places; for the rule is, '*sic utere tuo, ut alienum non laedas*:' this therefore is an actionable nusance.[166]

...

As to nusance to one's *lands*: if one erects a smelting house for lead so near the land of another, that the vapour and smoke kills his corn and grass, and damages his cattle therein, this held to be a nusance.[167] And by consequence it follows, that if one does any other act, in itself lawful, which yet being done in that place necessarily tends to the damage of another's property, it is a nusance: for it is incumbent on him to find some other place to do that act, where it will be less offensive.

The legal ideas interwoven in this passage may be structured as follows:

(1) A nuisance is committed if the natural or necessary rights of land use are interfered with.

(2) This principle extends so far that nuisance rules can impose affirmative duties where this is required to protect a natural right: 'so also, if my neighbour ought to scour a ditch, and does not, whereby my land is overflowed, this is an actionable nusance'.[168]

(3) An owner is guilty of nuisance if he uses his property in such a way that a neighbour's convenience of property use is injured: the *sic utere tuo* principle.

(4) The *sic utere tuo* rights and the natural rights overlap and may be identical; together they are the rights 'convenient or necessary' to land enjoyment.

(5) Once a natural right is established by the *sic utere tuo* principle, that right cannot be interfered with merely because the act of interference produces social benefits; utilities of rival land uses are to be balanced by requiring activities damaging to natural rights, such as industry, to locate elsewhere. This principle was established in the early seventeenth-century cases, and in Blackstone's hands shades into a defence of delineated natural rights of property.[169]

[164] Citing *Bury* v. *Pope* (1588) Cro. Eliz. 118; 78 E.R. 375; 1 Leon. 168; 74 E.R. 155 (Ex. Ch.); *Rosewell* v. *Prior* (1701) 1 Ld. Raym. 1089, 1094; 91 E.R. 1375, 1570; S.C. 12 Mod.; 2 Salk. 460; Jac. 555 (K.B.); see Ch. 3, the text accompanying nn. 9, 96, 108.

[165] 9 Co. Rep. 58, *Aldred's Case* (1610).

[166] iii, 216–17, quoting *Morley* v. *Pragnel* (1638) Cro. Car. 510; 79 E.R. 1039 (K.B.); Ch. 3, n. 33 above.

[167] 1 *Roll. Abdgt.* 58.

[168] Hale on F.N.B. 427.

[169] Compare *Tonson* v. *Collins* (1761) 1 Blackstone W. 321; 96 E.R. 180, where Blackstone in argument uses *sic utere tuo* to propound natural rights to property in intangibles such as copyright.

(6) Damage to a neighbour's property is not a nuisance, even if in breach of natural rights, if the property use causing the damage is established first, that is, before the neighbour arrives, or before the neighbour builds or attempts some other activity harmed by the preceding land use. Thus a prior use of land can never be a nuisance: the damaged plaintiff who attempts a natural use of land after the defendant has commenced his incompatible use has 'come to the nuisance', and the damage is self-inflicted. An analogy can here be drawn with Blackstone's general ideas of possession and title by first appropriation: an owner can set the character of land use between tenements, in competition with his neighbours, by starting his own use first. This idea was also explored in Blackstone's discussion of monopolist franchises.[170]

(7) The requirement that a use of window light be ancient, as well as prior to any interference by a neighbour, is purely historical, and is not explained by the theory of nuisance. It belongs within a separate compartment of prescription law.[171]

Blackstone's discussion of water rights adds further complexities to his nuisance doctrine. Water rights at one point are characterized as simple corporeal property:[172]

> With regard to *other* corporeal hereditaments: it is a nusance to stop or divert water that uses to run to another's meadow or mill;[173] to corrupt or poison a water-course, by erecting a dye-house or a lime-pit for the use of trade, in the upper part of the stream;[174] or in short do any act therein, that in its consequences must necessarily tend to the prejudice of one's neighbour. So closely does the law of England enforce that excellent rule of gospel morality, of 'doing to others, as we would they shall do unto themselves.'[175]

It is not clear whether the water is to flow without interference because it has always flowed, and so is a natural right of the watered land or a customary right of the locale; or whether a prior use of the water (by meadow, mill, or other trade) is the significant factor setting up the right; or else whether any injury to the convenient use of watered land is actionable. Any of these principles may be derived from Blackstone's language. He is groping for a principle that riparian owners making a claim to a secure right to water must have some sort of rationing of access to the common pool so that they do not interfere with each other and destroy each other's common share. But he cannot explain how several individual titles founded on occupation can yield such a principle. This vagueness may also be traced to an intransigent policy dilemma affecting all forms of property, namely the

[170] See the text accompanying nn. 93–100 above.

[171] A. J. Kedar, 'History of Anglo-American Law of Light' (Harvard LL.M thesis, 1990).

[172] Cf. the classification of water as a corporeal part of land in the text accompanying nn. 101–126 above.

[173] F.N.B. 184.

[174] *Aldred*; 2 *Roll. Abdgt.* 141.

[175] iii, 218.

extent to which income rights from property should be stabilized by protection from competition.[176]

Protection of Incorporeal Rights of Grant from Nuisance

To summarize the ground covered: for Blackstone two sorts of rights were protected by the nuisance actions. First, there were the natural rights and *sic utere tuo* rights just examined—those rights 'convenient or necessary' to corporeal property, which were elements of freehold possession, independent of grant. Secondly, there were incorporeal hereditaments attached to landownership by grant:

As to *incorporeal* hereditaments, the law carries itself with the same equity. If I have a way, annexed to my estate, across another's land, and he obstructs me in the use of it, either by totally stopping it, or putting logs across it, or ploughing over it, it is a nusance: for in the first case I cannot enjoy my right at all, and in the latter I cannot enjoy it so commodiously as I ought.[177]

Blackstone does not sharply distinguish between incorporeal rights of land use originating in grant and the 'natural' rights of land use created or implied by law, lumping both classes of right under the heading of nuisances to land use—a similar merging to that of Bracton and the medieval law.[178] In Blackstone's work this merger is largely worked by his clumsy exposition of trespass on the case and actions for nuisance in the sphere of incorporeal rights. Blackstone gathers into a separate chapter the various nuisance remedies for particular incorporeal rights of grant such as franchises, ways, and commons, and describes this mixed bag of real actions, petty assizes, trespasses, and actions on the case, as a unified category of 'real injuries' separate to nuisances, which he labels with the neologism 'disturbances'.[179] But he is not able to go further and state (1) that 'nuisance' (in Blackstone's broad sense) is the appropriate action for natural rights appurtenant to land, and (2) 'disturbance' (generally varieties of action on the case) is apt for incorporeal rights of grant, because the historical structure of the forms of action at common law is against this radical re-ordering and simplification.

There may be a more substantial source of Blackstone's confusion of granted and natural rights, in addition to his difficulties in finding a new formal classification for nuisance and actions on the case. In Blackstone's overall philosophical framework of property and law, the appendant rights of land use based on necessity and *sic utere tuo* can easily be characterized as

[176] Cf. M. J. Horwitz, *The Transformation of American Law 1870–1960: The Crisis of Legal Orthodoxy* (New York, 1992) 148–56; O. W. Holmes, Jr., *The Common Law* (Boston, Mass., 1881; ed. with an introduction by M. De Howe, Boston, Mass., 1963) 80 and 'Privilege, Malice, and Intent' (1894) 8 Harvard Law Review 1. See further, Ch. 6, the text accompanying nn. 25–33 below (on modern *sic utere tuo* doctrine).

[177] iii, 218–19, quoting F.N.B. 183, 2 *Roll. Abdgt.* 140.

[178] See Ch. 2, text accompanying nn. 116–160 above.

[179] Ch. 16, iii, 236–52.

rights of implied grant—those rights which reasonable men should allow to each other in order to live together in a community. As has been seen, Blackstone ultimately justified all civil obligations as the accepted contractual duties of citizens, implied from their acceptance of the protection of society;[180] and in the sphere of mutual (and competing) uses of land, the idea of tacit, implied contractual rights and duties had an ample practical scope. Implied contract could operate freely here as a metaphor for the reasonable rights and obligations of man in society, contrasting with the principles of prescription where the presumptions and fictions of implied grant were taken rather more literally. In nineteenth-century land- and water-use law contractual ideas came increasingly to the fore.

The Forms of Action for Nuisance

Nuisance law was divided between the public and private forms; and within private nuisance Blackstone further identified the action on the case, the assize of nuisance, and the real remedies of *quod permittat.*

Blackstone explained public nuisance as follows:

> the law gives no *private* remedy for any thing but a *private* wrong. Therefore no *action* lies for a public or common nusance, but an *indictment* only: because the damage being common to *all* the king's subjects, no *one* can assign his particular proportion of it; or if he could, it would be extremely hard, if every subject in the kingdom were allowed to harass the offender with separate actions. For this reason, no person, natural or corporate, can have an action for a public nusance, or punish it; but only the king in his public capacity of supreme governor, and *pater-familias* of the kingdom.[181] Yet this rule admits of one exception; where a private person suffers some extraordinary damage, beyond the rest of the king's subjects, by a public nusance; in which case he shall have a private satisfaction by action.[182]

The public nuisance action was described as an indictment akin to a criminal prosecution; the private tort action or suit was appended to the public cause of prosecution. Blackstone gave the example where a person fell into a ditch dug across a public way: in this case the public or common nuisance has caused him a particular damage[183] so an individual nuisance action is allowed him.[184]

It has been shown how an interference with a public waterway or water-source causing particular damage could give rise to a private action separate

[180] See the text accompanying nn. 9–14 above.

[181] *Thomas* v. *Sorrel* (1674) Vaugh. 330, 341, 342; 124 E.R. 1098, 1104 (K.B.).

[182] iii, 219–20.

[183] The Editor adds Note (3): 'the damage sued must be direct, not consequential: *Bull N.P.* 26.' This aligns the private action for public nuisance with general trespass, under the new framework of tort developed in *Reynolds* v. *Clerke* (1725) 1 Strange 634; 93 E.R. 747 (K.B.); Ch. 3, the text accompanying nn. 133–138 above; it may be that this new classification was aimed to curb access to the remedy.

[184] *Co.Litt.* 56; *William's Case* (1592) 5 Co. Rep. 73; 77 E.R. 163 (K.B.).

from the indictment for public nuisance.[185] But private enforcement of common rights, pursued with some frequency in the seventeenth century and earlier,[186] falls off thereafter, perhaps reflecting the spirit of the times as common law and statute undermined common rights.[187]

Within the sphere of private nuisances, the chief legal remedy by Blackstone's time was:

[b]y action *on the case* for damages; in which the party injured shall recover a satisfaction for the injury sustained; but cannot thereby remove the nusance. Indeed every continuance of the nusance is held to be a fresh one;[188] and therefore a fresh action will lie, and very exemplary damages will probably be given, if, after one verdict against him, the defendant has the hardiness to continue it.[189]

This trespassory action with a *continuando* operated to establish title to the property use by the 'oblique' means of personal damages sanctioning the wrong-doer. If property rights were the basis of the nuisance tort, so also tort enforced title to the property.

Blackstone wished also to include the earlier real actions for nuisance in his scheme of remedies, and he suggested that these superseded remedies (assize of nuisance and *quod permittat* writs) were part of a plan of redress for those instances where personal actions on the case were too discretionary or impermanent to establish a stable and certain 'title' to user, in that case abatement by antique real remedies could be enforced.[190]

In his discussion of the proprietary nuisance actions, Blackstone brought out clearly the overlap between tort actions remedying a past wrong and proprietary actions maintaining a title projected into the future. Of the two real nuisance actions he wrote:

An *assise of nusance* is a writ: wherein it is stated that the party injured complains of some particular act done, *ad nocumentum liberi tenementi sui* [to the nuisance of the free tenement], and therefore commanding the sheriff to summon an assise, that is a jury, and view the premises, and have them at the next commission of assises, that justice may be done therein:[191] and, if the assise is found for the plaintiff, he shall have judgment of two things; 1. To have the nusance abated; and 2. To recover damages.[192]

[185] See Ch. 2, the text accompanying nn. 297–315 above.

[186] For examples see *Fowler* v. *Sanders* (1617) Cro. Jac. 446; 79 E.R. 382 (K.B.); *Robert Mary's Case* (1613) 9 Co. Rep. 111b, 113a; 77 E.R. 895, 898–9 (K.B.). Giles Jacob, *A New Law Dictionary* (London, 1729; 3rd edn., London, 1736) specifically describes as an actionable private nuisance the stopping of a communal watering place for cattle.

[187] Coquillette, 'Old Manse', 807 suggests that legal theory played a role in diminishing private rights to enforce access to *res communes*, quoting Hugo Grotius, *De Jure Belli Ac Pacis (On the Law of War and Peace)* (Paris, 1625, revised edn., Amsterdam, 1646; 2 vols., F. W. Kelsey (ed. and trans.), Oxford, 1925) bk. 2, ch. 3; Pufendorf, *De Jure Nature et Gentium* bk. 8.

[188] *Beswick* v. *Cunden* (1592) Cro. Eliz. 402; 78 E.R. 646 (K.B.), Ch. 3, the text accompanying n. 8 above.

[189] iii, 220.

[190] iii, 220–2, citing Finch, *Law*, 289.

[191] F.N.B. 183.

[192] 9 Rep. 55, *Aldred's Case* (1610).

The assize of nuisance here operated to entwine tort and property: by correcting particular wrongs committed by persons, it moved towards the stronger proprietary function of defending titles against all the world.

Formerly an assise of nusance only lay against the very wrong-doer himself who levied, or did the nusance; and did not lie against any person to whom he had aliened the tenements, whereon the nusance was situated. This was the immediate reason for making that equitable provision in statute Westmin. 2. 13 Edw.I, c. 24, for granting a similar writ, *in casu consimili*, where no former precedent was to be found.... For every continuation, as was before said, is a fresh nusance; and therefore the complaint is, as well grounded against the alienee who continues it, as against the alienor who first levies it.[193]

This action by petty assize replaced the full writ of right of *quod permittat*:

Before this statute, the party injured, upon any alienation of the land wherein the nusance was set up, was driven to his *quod permittat prosternere*; which is in the nature of a writ of right, and therefore subject to greater delays.[194] This is a writ commanding the defendant to permit the plaintiff to abate, *quod permittat prosternere*, the nusance complained of; and, unless he so permits, to summon him to appear in court, and shew cause why he will not.[195] And this writ lies as well for the alienee of the party first injured, as *against* the alienee of the party first injuring; as hath been determined by all the judges.[196] And the plaintiff shall have judgment herein to abate the nusance, and to recover damages against the defendant.[197]

The real nuisance remedies were not available where the injured property was possessed without a freehold interest,[198] or the interest protected is an incorporeal right in gross, not attached to any tenement.[199] The rise of action on the case for nuisance can be explained not only as a search for speedier, less cumbersome personal actions to replace real nuisance actions, but also as a means of effectively protecting the possession of the leaseholder or termor, as commercial and industrial land uses multiplied tenures less than freehold in modernizing England.

Self-help to Abate the Nuisance

Lastly Blackstone discusses the ancient right to self-help, allowing an individual who had suffered special injury to abate a private or public nuisance, without bringing action in court:[200]

[W]hatsoever unlawfully annoys or doth damage to another is a nusance; and such a nusance may be taken away or removed, by the party aggrieved thereby, so as he commits no riot in doing it....

And the reason why the law allows this private and summary method of doing one's self justice, is because injuries of this kind, which obstruct or annoy such things as are

[193] iii, 221. [194] *Co.Litt.* 405. [195] F.N.B. 124.
[196] *Penruddock's Case* (1597) 5 Rep. 100b, 101; 77 E.R. 210 (C.P.). [197] iii, 222.
[198] iii, 221. [199] e.g., a way in gross: iii, 241–2. [200] iii, 1–3.

of daily convenience and use, require an immediate remedy; and cannot wait for the slow progress of the ordinary forms of justice.[201]

Resort to self-help to redress private or public nuisance was an election excluding recourse to a court remedy.[202] Individual water users could thus remove nuisances preventing enjoyment of public waters, without such recourse appearing on the legal record.

In eighteenth-century practice, self-help and local litigation may have been a more important or frequent remedy than common-law court actions. By contrast, after Blackstone's time a steady flow of water rights cases appears in the central courts, and the judges relied heavily on Blackstone's new exposition of property torts and land-use doctrine in making their decisions. After a century of near inactivity, the common-law courts embarked on a remaking of servitude and nuisance doctrine.

[201] iii, 5–6; and see iii, 22–3, 167, 413.

[202] iii, 219–20.

5. *Appropriation Theory in the Courts*

NATURAL RIGHT AND PRESCRIPTION IDEAS IN THE COURTS AT THE TIME OF BLACKSTONE

The mid-eighteenth century case law presents a plurality of juristic bases for water rights. Four ideal types of right may be identified, though they were not clearly separated in application.

(1) There is a Blackstonian theory of prior appropriation, whereby flowing water is regarded as a *res nullius*, appropriated as the property of a riparian owner upon first use of the flow, so that the level of usage enjoyed by the owner is protected. It was not clear whether the usage had to be sustained following the first appropriation, in order to attract protection at the level of that commencing appropriation.

(2) There is a Romanist theory of natural rights, whereby all riparian owners have access to flowing water as a common right of possession. Sometimes the language of *res communes* is used, but the right is properly appurtenant to riparian ownership, not a right of the public at large. All riparian owners may use the water, but none has a private right exclusive of others. The limits of their 'natural' entitlements to water must then be set by law.

(3) There is a prescriptive theory, whereby only immemorial existence and user of a flow can establish a protected right to water use for a riparian owner. A long-standing natural flow of water to a tenement might then be interpreted as an ancient flow, prescriptively guaranteed to the riparian proprietor by a legally-presumed grant from neighbours. The grant is a legal fiction.

(4) There is a different prescriptive theory, whereby user of water in excess of common right, that is extraordinary use of natural flow, must be justified as a specialty, made by some form of factually-presumed grant. Complex legal and evidential rules of presumption of grant then operate, in order to decide whether a riparian owner's claim for a heightened usage against neighbours will be upheld. This type of prescriptive right can be combined with the Blackstonian appropriation theory by readily presuming an implied-in-fact grant from neighbours acceding to fresh occupations of a stream.

The waters are further muddied by the vagaries of procedure for asserting rights. Apart from the usual difficulties of formulating adequate and precise pleadings in this formalistic age, there were conceptual choices to be made in framing a claim.[1] The action on the case for nuisance to land enjoyment is a

[1] See e.g. *Fitzsimmons* v. *Inglis* (1814) 5 Taunt. 534; 128 E.R. 798 (C.P.); *Griffiths* v. *Marson* (1818) 6 Price 1; 146 E.R. 723 (Ex.); *Dukes* v. *Gostling* (1835) 1 Bing (N.C.) 588; 115 E.R. 341 (C.P.); *Ward* v. *Robins* (1846) 15 M. & W. 237; 153 E.R. 837 (Ex.).

damage-centred action; and it must be decided whether harm to a present usage of riparian flow must be shown before the case remedy is made available. If temporal damage is a requisite of the action on the case, then a plaintiff who is not using water flow will be unable to prevent a defendant starting a new use in excess of natural or common right, even if P had made past appropriations establishing title. If a more proprietary conception of entitlement and remedy is employed, it may be that injury to a right or title to water, even in the absence of harm to a present usage, will be actionable. Likewise the concept of *injuria sine damno* trailed in *Ashby* v. *White* will more readily protect a customary or natural title to water unsupported by present usage.

A vast amount of case law gathered around these doctrinal issues. But before turning to the decisions, it is necessary to identify some of the main developments of prescription doctrine for incorporeal rights after Bracton, in order to grasp the vocabulary of prescriptive and appropriative rights employed by eighteenth- and nineteenth-century judges.

THE MODERN DOCTRINE OF PRESCRIPTION AND PRESUMED GRANT

Prescription for Incorporeal Property and 1189

It has been seen that there was no true positive or negative prescription for corporeal property, only barring of actions; and that English law recognized acquisitive prescription for incorporeal rights only.[2] This rule applied in Roman law because the possession of incorporeal rights (the '*quasi*-possession') was not apparent, and hence could not readily raise a presumption of grant by acquiescence. English law followed a different rationale: there was no acquisitive prescription of servitudes, because of the medieval idea of prescriptions as miniature customs, binding individuals as specialties outside common law, or 'against common right'. Blackstone, for example, describes the patent inability to possess or have seisin in incorporeal things as the reason why prescriptions, providing a grant or legal origin of servitudes in lieu of possession, are generally necessary, thus inverting the Roman arguments derived from the policy of the *lex Scribonia*.[3] Corporeal property

[2] There is little secondary literature to turn to in this difficult area, especially for the modern law. J. Williams, *Rights of Common and Other Prescriptive Rights* (London, 1880), and T. A. Herbert, *The History of the Law of Prescription in England* (London, 1891), present a fascinating mass of evidence together with severely limited analysis.

[3] *Bl.Comm.*, ii, 264, following Christopher St. German, *Doctor and Student* (London, 1523–30) (T. F. T. Plucknett and J. L. Barton (eds.), Selden Society xci, London, 1974) dial. 1, c.8; Sir Henry Finch, *Law, or, a Discourse Thereof* (*Nomotechnia*) (London, 1613, English edn., D. Pickering (ed.), London, 1729) 132.

rights to land, by contrast with most servitudes, were common-law titles held by the general custom of the land, and readily proved by establishing the full seisin of an ancestor, according to the elaborate canons of the real and possessory actions.[4] Hence when the period of limitation for the writ of right was reduced to sixty years from the time of Henry VIII's limitation statute of 1540,[5] the courts saw fit to preserve 1189, being the entrenched statutory-cum-customary measure of time immemorial for the positive proof of custom and prescription, as the measure of time for prescriptive acquisition of those incorporeal rights which were specialities against common right—but not for incorporeal rights of common right, such as rents and pasture appendant to land.[6]

Reasonableness and Necessity in Presumptions of Grant

With the waning of the concepts of specialty rights and customs outside the common law, difficulties sprang forth as lawyers tried to make sense of precedents for which the medieval rationale had vanished. Coke tried to explain necessary, appendant incorporeal rights, such as pasture and estovers, as prescribed for by a necessarily implied grant, rather than as common rights attaching to land as a quality of seisin, independent of long user or special right.[7] A more significant problem for modern lawyers was the well-established requirement that prescriptions, like customs, should be reasonable if they were to attract legal recognition as immemorial and binding practice. Reasonableness here had a double meaning: that the right itself be reasonable, a substantive measure; or else that the right had a reasonable origin, a procedural test. For an example of the latter requirement, some putative bargain establishing the custom or prescription might be looked for, since persons would be unlikely to have agreed to special law without good consideration and reason. An example of such reasoning is given in a 1495 case where a fugitive tried to plead that a right of sanctuary had been attached to an old Templar's house. Hussey CJ in the King's Bench held that it was a long-held custom to accord a privilege based on custom or long use; but that: 'a sanctuary cannot lie in prescription, for the king may not grant to

[4] *Bl.Comm.*, ii, 264; J. W. Salmond, 'The History of the Law of Prescription', in J. W. Salmond, *Essays in Jurisprudence and Legal History* (London, 1891) 73, 99–102.

[5] 32 Hen. 8, c. 2. The 1623 statute of limitations, 21 Jac. 1, c. 16, reduced the limitation for ejectment to twenty years, setting a still shorter period for practical recovery of real property.

[6] *Co.Litt.* 110, 113a–114b, 122a; *Bl.Comm.*, ii, 30–1 and n.; *Angus* v. *Dalton* (1877) 3 Q.B.D. 85, 105 (Q.B.) per Cockburn CJ; *Dalton* v. *Angus* (1881) 6 App. Cas. 740, 810–12 (H.L.) per Lord Blackburn; Salmond, 'Law of Prescription', 98–103.

[7] *Co.Litt.* 122a–b; cf. A. W. B. Simpson, *A History of the Land Law* (2nd edn., Oxford, 1986) 111–12.

a man that he shall have a sanctuary; for in a sanctuary a party cannot have his remedy, and the king may not take away a party's action by his grant', that is such grants interfering with normal procedural rights would be unreasonable, 'yet they may be granted by parliament'.[8]

The tests of reasonableness survived strongly into the eighteenth century for customs;[9] but as prescriptions lost their legal quality as specialties, the judges began to elevate the procedural presumption of grant above substantive requirements of reasonableness. The emergent idea was that if long user indicated a voluntary grant of right some time in the past, then freedom of contract dictated that the rights had a good origin and had been supported by reason—even if they appeared now to be substantively unreasonable. By thus stressing the presumed grant, rather than the precedent fact of acquiescence in long user, as the immediate cause of right, the reasonableness doctrine for prescriptions was emptied of practical effect.[10]

Reasonableness and the Status of the Presumed Grant

The result of the changed test for good prescriptions was that by the time of Blackstone a new orthodoxy had hardened, namely:

> A prescription cannot be for a thing which cannot be raised by a grant. For the law allows prescription only in supply of the loss of a grant, and, therefore, every prescription presupposes a grant to have existed.[11]

According to Salmond, '[t]he rule that a prescription must be reasonable was thus wholly lost sight of, being supplanted by a new rule, which originated either as a somewhat illogical inference from the earlier or as a deliberate evasion of it'; and he continued:

> By the old theory, prescription was direct; by the new, it is indirect. By the old, immemorial user was beyond question itself a title; by the new, it is merely evidence of

[8] *Rollesley* v. *Toft* (1495) K.B. 27/936, m. 60, in *The Notebook of Sir John Port* (J. H. Baker (ed.), Selden Society, cii, 1986) Case 35, 31–6 at 31.

[9] *Littleton*, s. 212; *Co.Litt.* 140a; *Bl.Comm.*, i, 74–9. A powerful example of legal extinguishment of 'unreasonable' customary common rights was afforded by the case of *Steel* v. *Houghton et Uxor* (1788) 1 H.Bl. 51; 126 E.R. 32 (C.P.) which ended the right of gleaning after harvest: see P. King, 'Gleaners, Farmers and the Failure of Legal Sanctions in England 1750–1850' (1989) 125 Past and Present 116; P. King, 'The Origins of the Gleaning Judgement of 1788, A Case Study of Legal Change, Customary Right and Social Conflict in Late Eighteenth Century England' (1992) 10 Law and History Review 1; P. King, *Crime, Justice, and Discretion in England, 1740–1820* (Oxford, 2000) 361ff.; A. C. Loux, 'The Persistence of the Ancient Regime: Custom, Utility, and the Common Law in the Nineteenth Century' (1993) 79 Cornell Law Review 183.

[10] Salmond, 'Law of Prescription', 110–19; *Jenkins* v. *Harvey* (1835) 2 C. M. & R. 393; 150 E.R. 169 (Ex.); *Attorney-General* v. *Mathias* (1858) 4 Kay and Johnson 579, 70 E.R. 241; but cf. *Goodman* v. *Saltash Corporation* (1882) 48 L.T. 239 (H.L.).

[11] *Bl.Comm.*, ii, 265.

title. The difference is fundamental, and marks a distinct breach of logical continuity in the development of this branch of the law.[12]

The Fiction of the Lost Modern Grant

In the last phase of common-law development of prescription, the move from direct to indirect prescription led to invention of the fiction of the lost modern grant in the mid-eighteenth century.[13] The fixing of so distant a date as 1189 as the period of time immemorial for incorporeal prescription became palpably inconvenient and unworkable; but the judges were reluctant to apply the shorter statutory periods later set for the writ of right, preferring to create convoluted rules for advising juries when they could presume facts and rights from long user.[14] However, there was never any logical objection to having an archaically long period of proof, when user from time immemorial itself provided a direct title:

> But, when such user came to be regarded as not in itself a title, but merely evidence of a title, it became obvious that a very much shorter period of user might be equally effective. And, accordingly, [in the later eighteenth century], the period of twenty years came to be fixed upon as sufficient to raise a presumption of title.[15] The period was selected in analogy to the statutory limitation of the action of ejectment. Possession for twenty years constituted (in practice) a good title to a house, and it was only reasonable that it should be equally effective in the case of an easement belonging to the house. In the earlier cases we may trace a tendency to make twenty years' user not merely evidence of user, but a title itself. But this was too bold an innovation, and it soon became settled that the new form of prescription was not direct but indirect. The chance was lost of establishing by judicial decisions a satisfactory substitute for the old rule of immemorial prescription. The fiction of the modern lost grant was invented.[16]

To understand this notorious fiction, it is necessary to investigate the meaning of 'time immemorial' and the nature of the evidential presumptions made from long user. The setting of time of memory at 1189, being the old limitation for the writ of right, was reduced by limitation act in 1540 to sixty years for land by writ of right, and reduced again to twenty years for ejectment in 1623.[17] This reduced the inconvenience of distant, fixed dates of limitation which exposed titles to contrary evidence of absence of right or superior claim. The old common-law hearsay concept of time immemorial, as

[12] Salmond, 'Law of Prescription', 119; and see Simpson, *History of Land Law*, 110.

[13] Ibid., 266–9.

[14] Ibid.; and see *Co.Litt.* 110a, 114b, 115a–b; *Bl.Comm.*, ii, 30–1, 36, 265; *Dalton* v. *Angus* (1881) 6 App. Cas. 740, 810–15 (H.L.) per Lord Blackburn.

[15] See *Yard* v. *Ford* (1671) 2 Wms. Saund. 172; 85 E.R. 922, notes by Sjt. Williams and the cases there cited.

[16] Salmond, 'Law of Prescription', 120.

[17] N. 5 above.

the approximate limitation on evidence set by the last generation's direct witness, was often applied concurrently with the fixed statutory cut-off dates of legal memory. Coke quotes Littleton as stating that he did not know which measure of limitation of 'time immemorial' was correct at law, though Littleton inclined to the latter. Coke could shed no light on the matter.[18] An analysis from 1515–16 of acquisition of liberties and franchises demonstrates the persistence of hearsay concepts of time immemorial:

Franchises . . . may be forfeited for non-user or misuse. . . . One may use franchises by a general grant before time of memory, and special prescription, and allowance in eyre since time of memory. . . . *Time of memory means the memory of man and not the limitation in a writ of right.*[19]

Sir John Spelman in 1519 investigated the measurement of time immemorial pertaining to real actions, and seems thoroughly to contradict himself in cases A and B as given below:

First, prescription is something which has continued from time whereof memory runneth not. And that constitutes a good title even if the beginning was wrongful, inasmuch as the long continuance of the possession has purged the wrong. Therefore in every prescription it is said, 'whereof the memory of man is not to the contrary' (*cujus contrarii memoria hominum non existit*). And even if no man has memory to the contrary, nevertheless [A] *if it can appear that the claimant's possession began after King Richard [I] . . . the prescription fails.* For the limitation in the writ of right is from the time of King Richard. . . . But prescribing since the time of Richard is good; and if the prescription is traversed, the inquest shall only enquire concerning the time of men's memory. Suppose someone is seised in the time of Richard and continues all the time down to King Edward III and no longer, that does not make a prescription; but [B] if the seisin began in the time of King Edward III and continues through all the time since down to the present, that is a good prescription, for the memory of man is not to the contrary.[20]

Spelman's seemingly contradictory exposition captures the tendency of the courts to hold that if there was no hearsay evidence against the claim, thus fulfilling the common-law or customary limitation period, then this raised a further presumption that there was no evidence contrary to the grant within the statutory limitation period either. Case A involves proof of time immemorial in fact; Case B involves presumption in law. Establishing the ingredients of the short common-law prescriptive period thus went some way to establishing the longer statutory presumption in turn. However, the common-law evidential presumption was a rebuttable presumption of fact,

[18] *Littleton*, s. 170; E. Wambaugh, *Littleton's Tenures in English* (Washington, DC, 1903) 81–3, *Co.Litt.* 113a–115a; see Ch. 2, the text accompanying n. 252.

[19] Anon., 'A Reading on Magna Carta', *c*.9, Gray's Inn, *c*.1515/16, in *John Spelman's Reading on Quo Warranto delivered in Gray's Inn (Lent 1519)* (J. H. Baker (ed.), Selden Society, cxiii, 1997) 12–13.

[20] Lecture III on Prescription, ibid., 84–5; cf text B, 122–4.

whilst the statutory presumption established the legal facts conclusively, that is, it raised an irrebuttable legal fiction that the right was 'immemorial' in the sense of beginning before the medieval limitation points for real titles.

With the modern shortening of the limitation for property actions, the presumption of grant might have become a true conclusive presumption, whereby disproof of the possibility of an actual grant, or proof of a recent origin of enjoyment, would not prevail against the legal fact of twenty years' user or more. But the courts fumbled the nature of the presumption of grant, and sometimes spoke of factual presumptions operating after twenty years' lapse, but still being capable of disproof by evidence from any time after common-law memory. Sometimes, however, the twenty-year period of user was held to raise a conclusive legal presumption of lawful origin immune to rebuttal—the fiction of the lost modern grant, a means of turning rebuttable factual presumptions into conclusive legal ones. In Blackstone's doctrine, for example, current limitation periods are sometimes used to make conclusive legal presumptions of prescription, as a substantive rule defining what counts as time immemorial. Sometimes the period of prescription or limitation raises an evidential presumption of immemoriality, as a rebuttable inference of fact from partial evidence. Sometimes a factual presumption is made which further supports a conclusive legal presumption.[21] Lord Blackburn confessed in 1881 that he could not make sense of the intricate prescriptive presumptions of the preceding century.[22] Loux has identified some telling instances of judicial creativity in explaining the presumptions of immemoriality of custom.[23] For example, in *R* v. *Joliffe* the Court of King's Bench upheld a jury instruction that 'slight evidence [of custom enjoyed for more than twenty years], if uncontradicted, becomes cogent proof' of immemorial usage. Abbott CJ explained this as follows:

> A regular usage for 20 years, not explained or contradicted, is that upon which many private and public rights are held, there being nothing in the usage to contravene the public policy ... or any known rule or principle of law.[24]

This meant that if a practice could be proved for the past twenty years and was not obnoxious to law or public welfare, it could be ratified as 'immemorial custom' without more. In *Bryant* v. *Foot*[25] the court was blunt in its pragmatic approach to the doctrine:

> If we assume [that] ... neither judges nor juries have in reality believed ... that customs found to be immemorial had actually existed in the time of Richard I., still, if this state

[21] See Simpson, *History of Land Law*, 266–9; Loux, 'Persistence of the Ancient Regime', 210–12.

[22] See *Dalton* v. *Angus* (1881) 6 App. Cas. 740, 812–13 (H.L.).

[23] Loux, 'Persistence of the Ancient Regime', 210–12.

[24] (1823) 2 B. & C. 54, 59–60; 107 E.R. 303, 305 (K.B.) per Abbott CJ.

[25] (1868) L.R. 3 Q.B. 497 (Q.B.).

of the law, created by the judges to quiet titles, to protect rights derived from long user or enjoyment, and so, to supply the want of a just and enlightened legislation, be established by these decisions, we must accept it as we find it.... [26]

The court went on to hold that the fiction of grant was 'rendered absolutely necessary by the previous "judicial legislation", which established the reign of Richard I as the extent of legal memory'.[27]

The Prescription Act of 1832 sought to remove the possibility of disproof by evidence after the short modern time of common-law memory had elapsed. In the 1834 case of *Bright* v. *Walker*, Parke B stated that the purpose of the Act was to shorten the period of prescription and to allow possession as a bar to preceding title, or title of itself, as a matter of law without the intervention of a fact-finding jury.

For a series of years, prior to the... act, Judges had been in the habit, for the furtherance of justice and the sake of peace, to leave it to juries to presume a grant from a long exercise of an incorporeal right, adopting the period of twenty years by analogy to the Statute of Limitations. Such presumptions did not always proceed on a belief that the thing presumed had actually taken place.... 'A technical efficacy was given to the evidence of possession beyond its simple and natural force and operation;' and though in theory it was presumptive evidence, in practice and in effect it was a bar.... [S]o heavy a tax on the consciences and good sense of juries, which they were called on to incur for the sake of administering substantial justice, ought to [have been] removed by the legislature. The act in question is intended to accomplish this object, by shortening in effect the period of prescription, and making that possession a bar or title of itself, which was so before only by the intervention of a jury.[28]

The courts, however, did not allow this attempt at statutory simplification to resolve the tangles of legal history. Litigants were allowed an election between the statutory and common-law schemes of prescription, and the chance to create an integrated doctrine of prescription for corporeal and incorporeal property was missed.[29] The common-law doctrine of prescription declined further into a muddle of presumptions of mixed fact and law, requiring baroque instructions to be given to juries about the level of fictitious inference of fact they were permitted to make from the evidence of long user. Finally, the process or presumption hardened, from a search for reasonable evidence of likely grant to an assumption that so many years' user implied a grant that was presumptively reasonable in its origin, terms, and

[26] Ibid., 508.

[27] Ibid., 516. See also *Hammerton* v. *Honey* (1876) 24 W.N. 603, 604 (Ch.).

[28] (1834) 1 C.M. & R. 211, 217–18; 149 E.R. 1057, 1060 (Ex.) per Parke B; and see also *Manning* v. *Wasdale* (1836) 5 Ad. & E. 758; 111 E.R. 1353 (C.P.); *Drewitt* v. *Sheard* (1836) 7 C. & P. 465; 173 E.R. 206 (N.P.).

[29] *Dewhirst* v. *Wrigley* (1834) C.P. Cooper 319, 329; 47 E.R. 525, 529 (Ch., K.B.); *Eaton* v. *Swansea Waterworks Co.* (1851) 17 Q.B. 267; 117 E.R. 1282 (Q.B.); *Warrick* v. *Queen's College* (1871) L.R. 6 Ch. 278; *Ladyman* v. *Grave* (1871) L.R. 6 Ch. 763; *Aynsley* v. *Glover* (1875) L.R. 10 Ch. 283.

consideration, and more or less a final bar.[30] The judges thereby took prescription a long way towards Parke B's vision of a fictitious, conclusive presumption of right arising from long user; but impure elements were retained of a search for rebuttable evidence implied by long user, which could raise a factual presumption of grant reasonable in its origin and terms.[31]

The Policy of Prescription Doctrine

The convoluted development of common-law prescription for servitudes was given a more coherent structure by Lord Blackburn in the 1881 appeal of *Dalton* v. *Angus*.[32] He identified a number of policies for prescription: punishing laches; quieting titles long enjoyed from disturbance; allowing acquiescence as a mode of transferring titles by factual grant; and removing uncertainty of ownership. He offered a highly selective description of the history of prescription in England which largely omitted the role of custom and specialty rights. He used a Romanist *usucapio* idea to sum up the purpose and nature of the doctrine as one of quieting titles and establishing secure and certain ownerships. The elaborate rules for evidential presumptions and implied grants were dismissed as instruments and fictions directed to a utilitarian goal of stable ownership, a goal which Lord Blackburn found clearly adumbrated in the *usucapio* of Roman law. Thus he 'wiped the slate clean', superimposing a utilitarian and Romanist pattern on the unruly English materials.[33]

Notwithstanding Lord Blackburn's heroic work of redaction, complex historical ideas of the nature of prescription lived on into the nineteenth century. Next we return to the details of water law in the courts for examples of how these ideas played out in practice.

BROWN v. *BEST*

A good example of doctrinal pluralism (or confusion) is found in the 1747 King's Bench case of *Brown* v. *Best*,[34] decided immediately before Blackstone

[30] Simpson, *History of Land Law*, 266–8.

[31] See e.g. *Carlyon* v. *Lovering* (1857) 1 H. & N. 784; 156 E.R. 1417 (Ex.); *Rochdale Canal Co.* v. *Radcliffe* (1852) 18 Q.B. 287; 118 E.R. 108 (Q.B.); *Ivimey* v. *Stocker* (1865) L.R. 1 Ch. App. 396. (L.C.); and see generally H. J. W. Coulson and U. A. Forbes, *The Law Relating to Waters, Sea, Tidal and Inland and Land Drainage* (6th edn. by S. R. Hobday, London, 1952) 269–307; C. J. Gale, *A Treatise on the Law of Easements* (3rd edn., by W. H. Willes, London, 1862) 132–88; *Gale on Easements* (16th edn. by J. Gaunt and P. Morgan, 1997) 169–234.

[32] (1881) 6 App. Cas. 740, 810–29.

[33] S. Anderson, 'Easement and Prescription—Changing Perspectives in Classification' (1975) 38 Modern Law Review 641, 655–9; for later nineteenth- and twentieth-century developments, see W. S. Holdsworth, *A History of English Law* 13 vols. (London, 1922–52) vii, 343–52 and *An Historical Introduction to the Land Law* (Oxford, 1927) 276–88.

[34] (1747) 1 Wils. K.B. 174, 174–5; 95 E.R. 557, 559–60 (K.B.).

published his *Commentaries*. P brought a special action on the case for the diversion of a watercourse, 'declar[ing] upon his own possession of the place through which the water used to run', and stating that D had built dams, banks, pits, and ponds 'by which the water has been diverted in its antient course, and a great part of it sunk into these pits and ponds, so that little or no water has come to [P's] grounds, whereby [P] is damaged'. Significantly the pleadings make claim that possession of land containing an ancient watercourse gave right to the water, even if no special use of the water was declared. D demurred to the legal point; and also pleaded in defence that 'all the water springs in his ground, and that the two pits have been used since time immemorial'. D claimed he had only re-opened the pits that 'were choaked up with mud ... which he insists it is lawful for him to do, and denies that any other water has been obstructed'. The court supported P's declaration and rejected the defence. Lee CJ stated:

> I am of opinion that the declaration is very good, and that in the case of a watercourse which is jure naturae, this is the best way of declaring, for [P] being possessed of the place, declares that the water currere solebat [used to flow] through that place time out of mind, and that [D] has obstructed it.... [A]lthough there have been pits in [D's] ground time out of mind, yet he cannot enlarge them, but they must remain as they always have been, and so is the rule in the common and civil law.[35] [D] indeed might have cleansed the pits, keeping them as they were before, but cannot enlarge them; if I have a right from usage currere solebat, I have the right in such a manner as the usage has been; as to inconvenience to [D], it is nothing, and might be alledged in every case as this; and the maxim in Hetley 34,[36] is exactly applicable to the present case, sic utere tuo ut ne laedas alieno.[37]

Lee CJ's application of the *sic utere tuo* idea and rejection of convenience as a test of right served to emphasize that natural use-rights are protected absolutely from invasion and are not subject to a balancing of utilities. His analysis variously characterized the right to enjoy a watercourse as *jure naturae* or natural right; as based on a flow 'time out of mind'; and as derived from the *sic utere tuo* principle. These formulations are different expressions of one larger idea: that there may not be obstruction of a natural current which has always flowed through land, or which has flowed for so long as to become part of the land. The language of ancient flow 'time out of mind' and natural flow shades into one; there is no resort to further ideas of prescriptive long use or immemorial grant. However, Lee CJ also speaks of 'a right from *usage* as currere solebat ... [a] right *in such manner as the usage has been*',[38]

[35] Citing *Duncombe* v. *Sir Edward Randall* (1627–31) Hetley 32/3; 124 E.R. 320 (C.P.) (see Ch. 3, the text accompanying n. 40 above); and Dig. lib.3, sec.15.

[36] *Duncombe* v. *Randall*, n. 35 above.

[37] *Brown* v. *Best* (1747) 1 Wils. K.B. 174, 174–5; 95 E.R. 557, 558–9.

[38] Ibid. (emphasis supplied).

implying that the degree of customary use of water flow establishes the extent of the natural right, and perhaps suggesting that interference with the customary usage is an element of the action as based on special damage. His language recalls the Roman interdictal actions for daily water, whereby a water right was established by one season's sustained usage. Lee CJ's doctrine is so far removed from the common-law language of immemorial prescriptive use that some direct influence from Roman law may be inferred.

Dennison J stated that 'whatever the precedents may be in regard to watercourses to mills, yet as to natural watercourses this is the most proper way of declaring'—a hint that where denial of water specific to a mill (rather than denial to undeveloped riparian land) was at issue, then prescriptive water use by the mill may be required, in addition to pleading of a natural right based on possession. The search for a prescriptive basis of right emerges throughout Dennison J's judgment: 'as to [D's] plea . . . though I cannot properly call it a prescription, yet it has the same effect, for these pits &c. are said to be time out of mind'. D's declaration was then scrutinized for the indicia establishing a prescriptive claim:

> [D] says, that although there was a watercourse through your land, yet in my land there have been two large pits for watering cattle, &c. and for other purposes for the occupation of my land; [D] ought to have said for what purposes. . . .

This implies that a fairly precise use must be laid if a prescriptive right to water is to be shown. Further to this point,

> there is a direct allegation [by D] that these pits have been time out of mind, and that all the water except what was stopped for his purposes, was not hindered, so that really he has in effect alledged a right to keep all the water if he pleases, and this plea can only amount to the general issue.[39]

Because the issue was between two conflicting usages of water, it was not proper simply to claim an unspecified right to water use for one's purposes, in opposition to the neighbour's interests; the right must be specified: 'if [D] has any prescription, he ought to have traversed P's prescription, according to the case of *Murgatroyd* v. *Law*'.[40] According to the theory of prescription there could not be a number of conflicting rights all validly based on immemorial usage; one of the rights had to be spurious.[41] A view of water rights as prescriptive (based on user, being servitude rights of grant) rather than natural (based on seisin, being rights of possession) led Dennison J to conclude his judgment with a key phrase from *Sury* v. *Pigot*: 'And a watercourse is a quite distinct thing from the land'.

[39] 1 Wils. K.B. 174, 175; 95 E.R. 557, 559.
[40] *Murgatroyd* v. *Law* (1690) Carth. 116; 90 E.R. 672 (K.B.).
[41] See Ch. 3, the text accompanying nn. 72–74 above.

BLACKSTONIAN PRIOR APPROPRIATION THEORY IN THE COURTS

Blackstone's *Commentaries* (1765–9) were perceived by the courts to advocate a simple prior appropriation theory of water rights: namely, that first usage was an occupation creating a title to the water flow. This theory crowded out the natural and prescriptive right ideas found in *Brown* v. *Best*, for example. Blackstone's views were, as we have seen, far more complex and diverse, but were commonly reduced to a narrow collection of points wrenched away from his fuller arguments. In the result, Blackstone was cited as authority for the three propositions: (1) that 'water is a moveable, wandering thing, and must of necessity continue common by the law of nature; so that I can only have a temporary, transient, usufructary property therein';[42] (2) that water was among those things that 'belong to the first occupant, during the time he holds possession of them; and no longer';[43] and (3) that flowing water could be occupied by means of a mill: '[i]f a stream be unoccupied, I may erect a mill thereon, and detain the water; yet not so as to injure my neighbour's prior mill, or his meadow; for he hath by the first occupancy acquired a property in the current'.[44] Next will be discussed the reactions of the courts to these new doctrines.

Kames' Riposte—Romanist Natural Rights

The first response to the Blackstonian theory was outright rejection. In 1768 Lord Kames,[45] sitting in the Scottish Court of Session, strenuously maintained old Romanist and natural right principles against the new appropriation theory. His judgment in *Magistrates of Linlithgow* v. *Elphinstone*[46] was cited, if not followed, in most of the leading English cases of the nineteenth century. The facts of the case exemplify a typical conflict over water rights fought between different sectors of the economy in industrializing Britain. A number of mills were sited on a river supplied by an upstream lake. P and D were proprietors of riparian land and mill owners, with D having a tenement on the lake-shore. At P's downstream tenement, the water flow was 'far from sufficient to keep the mill in constant operation'. D decided to sell rights to water from his lake to a canal company; action was then brought by P against D on behalf of all the mill owners on the downstream river, who feared loss of their accustomed water flow through the takings for the canal. The action was commenced by declarator, in the nature of a common nuisance indictment.

[42] *Bl.Comm.*, ii, 18. [43] Ibid. [44] Ibid., ii, 403.

[45] For a brief intellectual biography of Kames, see P. G. Stein, *Legal Evolution* (Cambridge, 1980) 25–9.

[46] (1768) 3 Kames' Decisions 331 (S.C.S.).

Lord Kames discussed the abstract nature of riparian rights, drawing from Roman jurisprudence in order to counter the new prior appropriation theory:

At advising this cause, much darkness was occasioned by a notion which some of the Judges unwarily adopted, as if a river could be appropriated like a field or a horse. A river, which is in perpetual motion, is not naturally susceptible of appropriation; and were it susceptible, it would be greatly against the public interest that it should be suffered to be brought under private property. In general, by the laws of all polished nations, appropriation is authorized with respect to every subject that is best enjoyed separately; but barred with respect to every subject that is best enjoyed in common. Water is scattered over the face of the earth in rivers, lakes, *&c.* for the use of animals and vegetables. Water drawn from a river into vessels or into ponds, becomes private property; but to admit of such property with respect to the river itself, considered as a complex body, would be inconsistent with the public interest, by putting it in the power of one man to lay waste a whole country.[47]

Kames viewed running water as ineluctably a public good, and he not only resisted allowing persons private water rights in the form of exclusive property, but also rejected allowing lesser interests such as praedial servitudes to be held in water:

The same reasoning concludes equally against the subjecting a river to a servitude: they are both of them inconsistent with the public good; and the latter is rather less consistent with law than the former. There may be supposed a dominant tenement, a mill for example, that by long use has acquired right to an aqueduct from a neighbouring river; but can that river in any sense be considered as a servient tenement? Certainly not. Nor need we have recourse to the absurd notion of a servitude in cases of this nature, which can be explained clearly and simply as follows. A man who builds a mill is entitled to make an aqueduct, provided, after using the water for his mill, he restore it to the river from whence it was taken. This right he has from the law of nature without aid of prescription. But to carry the water another way without restoring it, will require 40 years possession to defend him by negative prescription against a challenge by inferior heritors [downstream owners].[48]

Kames identified a natural right to use and enjoy flowing water independent of any right of servitude, provided the water flow was restored after use—a right recalling the Roman regime of daily water protected by interdicts. To abstract water without restoration of flow required extinction by negative prescription of the concomitant natural right to water of riparian neighbours; the neighbouring tenements had to be made servient to the water-user's land. An English lawyer might have used the language of positive acquisition of incorporeal right by presumed grant from neighbours in place of Kames' ideas of extinctive prescription; but the result is the same.

[47] Ibid., 331–2. [48] Ibid., 332.

Kames finally preferred to summarize the principles of water law '[l]aying . . . aside arguments from property or servitude', partly because private-law doctrines ordering rival uses of property were inappropriate when delimiting use-rights in public goods. He stated the governing principles of water law as follows:

A river may be considered as the common property of the whole nation, but the law declares against separate property of the whole or part. 'Et quidem naturali jure communia sunt haec: aer, aqua profluens, et mare.'[49] A river is one subject composed of a trunk and branches. No individual can appropriate a river or any branch of it; but every individual of the nation, those especially who have land adjoining, are entitled to use the water for their private purposes. Hence it follows, that no man is entitled to divert the course of a river or of any of its branches; which would be depriving others of their right, *viz*. the use of the water.

But this restraint has its limits. There is not a moss nor a marsh but emits some moisture to a river: Nay, rivers are greatly fed by water running underground; and if such circumstances were comprehended under the general rule, we would be barred altogether from taking any liberty with water beyond the simple use; which would be as hurtful on the one hand as private property would be on the other. At that rate we would be prohibited to drain a marsh or a moss, or to intercept a spring by digging a pit within our own ground; for who knows whether these operations may not deprive a river of some of its secret feeders.

But what is the middle course that we are at liberty to take? An excellent practical rule is laid down in the Roman law, which is, that we cannot divert from a river any rill or runner that has a perennial course, but that we may use freedom with all other water within our bounds. And the distinction is sensible; for nothing properly can be considered as a part or branch of a river, but what, like itself, has a constant flow.[50]

[49] Inst.2.1.1.

[50] *Magistrates of Linlithgow*, ibid., 332–3. The Roman authority on which Kames purported to build his doctrine was a little more ambiguous than he suggests: see Ch. 2 above, passim. Lord Kames' riparian doctrine was adumbrated in his *Principles of Equity* (2nd edn., Edinburgh, 1767) 57–60, where he re-stated the principle of *sic utere tuo* as essential to reasonable intercourse of mankind, and then detailed some applications involving draining and flooding of neighbours' grounds. On water diversion for consumption he stated: 'Where a river is interjected between my property and that of my neighbour, it is not lawful for me to alter its natural course, whether by throwing it upon my neighbour's ground, or by depriving him of it', though equity and utility will permit some reasonable encroachment (at 58–9). He added that a pit may be dug to take water for use at a neighbour's expense, but only for use and not for spite (at 60). In a later edition (3rd edn., 1778; new edn. in one volume, Edinburgh, 1825, at 33–4), he elaborated:

> A river or any running stream directs its course through the land of many proprietors; who are thereby connected by a common interest, being equally entitled to the water for useful purposes. Whence it follows, that the course of the river or running stream cannot be diverted by any one of the proprietors, so as to deprive others of it. Where there is plenty for all, there can be no interference; but many streams are so scanty, as to be exhausted by using it with discretion; though hitherto, no rule has been laid down. To supply the defect in some measure, I venture to suggest the following particulars, which practice may in time ripen to a precise rule. . . . [I]f there be not a sufficiency of water for every purpose, those purposes ought to be preferred that are essential to the well-being of the adjacent proprietors. The most essential use is drink for man and beast; because they cannot subsist without

In the present case it was found that the lakes did not constantly discharge water into the river, and hence could not be seen as branches of the river 'which no man had power to divert from its natural course'; it followed that '[D], proprietor of these lakes, lay under no restriction from using them as he pleased'.

English Appropriation Doctrine *c.*1800

Unlike the Scots, the English courts did move towards Blackstonian appropriation doctrine, and for a time abandoned the Romanist doctrine of water as *res communes* that Kames claimed was the law of 'polished nations'. Many of the late eighteenth-century authorities on water rights reproduce a mix of natural-right and prescriptive analyses, as in *Brown* v. *Best*. In *Robinson* v. *Lord Byron*[51] in 1785, for example, a motion for injunction was brought in Chancery, 'to restrain Lord *Byron* from preventing the water flowing to a mill which the plaintiffs used for a cotton manufacture, or letting a greater quantity of water than usual flow upon the mill'. Lord Byron took water from upstream to fill ornamental lakes in his park over a period of twenty years, and then greatly increased his level of appropriation. P alleged that D did this maliciously in order to disrupt his mill operation and to extort money. Thurlow LC stated: 'The Court will not restrain what has been enjoyed for 20 years past; but if what has been so enjoyed is used in a different way, so as to do mischief, the Court may interpose.'[52] Water rights here appear as prescriptive with twenty years' enjoyment as a conclusive period establishing title. In the result, an injunction was issued to restrain use of the water in excess of the prescriptive level. What is conceptually interesting is the eschewal of the language of water as *res communes*.

Bealey v. *Shaw* and the Adoption of Prior Appropriation Theory

English law turned away from the *res communes* theory and decisively adopted the Blackstonian prior appropriation theory in the early nineteenth

it. What is next essential, is water for washing; because cleanness contributes greatly to health. The third is water for a corn-mill; which saves labour and cheapens bread. The fourth is watering land, for enriching it. The fifth is water for a bleach-field. And the lowest I shall mention, is water for machinery, necessary for cheapening the production of several arts. There may be more divisions; but these are sufficient in a general view. From this arrangement it follows, that one may use the water of a rivulet for drink, and for brewing and baking, however little be left for the inferior heritors. But a proprietor cannot be deprived of that essential use by one above him, who wants to divert the water for a mill, for a bleachfield, or for watering his land, unless he leaves sufficient for a mill below. . . . I may dig a pit in my own field for gathering water to my cattle, though it happens to intercept a spring that run underground into my neighbour's field and furnished him with water.

51 (1785) 1 Bro. C.C. 588; 28 E.R. 1315 (Ch.). The defendant was not the poet.

52 1 Bro. C.C. 588, 588–9; 28 E.R. 1315.

century, displacing also the rival theories of prescriptive and natural rights. The first significant case heralding the new doctrine was *Bealey* v. *Shaw*, a King's Bench decision of 1805.[53] This was an action on the case involving competition for the use of water between two Lancastrian mill owners. P declared that he was possessed of land and mills containing water-powered machinery for his trade as a whitster; further, that 'a stream of water used to flow out of the river Irwell through a watercourse through his land, and was used to work his said mills and machinery'; and that:

> [D] injuriously widened, deepened, and enlarged certain fenders, sluices, and watercourses, leading out of a part of the river Irwell higher than the commencement of [P]'s stream, and thereby drew off and diverted from the said river a greater quantity of water than used to flow and ought to have flowed into [D]'s fenders and sluices . . . and thereby prevented the same from flowing to the premises, &c. of [P].[54]

These pleadings embrace the traditional elements of a water-diversion action as developed in the seventeenth century—namely, an action on the case brought for injury to possession, specifying that water which naturally or customarily flowed to a tenement has been diverted, to the damage of some established usage of the water.

Bealey v. *Shaw* was decided with the greatest deliberation. Detailed evidence from the assize trial was carefully reviewed; four eminent counsel appeared on each side; and the four judges of the court each prepared a substantial opinion seeking to produce an authoritative determination of the law. The significant facts were that D's predecessors in title had built mills by the river in 1724, and enlarged the mills around 1770 and then again in 1791, with each enlargement resulting in an increase in the amount of water appropriated from the river channel. P built a mill in 1781, downstream from D's mill but upstream from D's exit-sluice, so that any water used by that mill was thereby denied to P. The 1791 appropriations left P with insufficient water to keep his mill running continually, and complaints were made; but D's predecessor [C] insisted on a right to exclusive appropriation of the water flow, and kept his sluices locked. C appointed a manager to allow water to flow to P's tenement when C did not need it, and P apparently agreed to this arrangement, even contributing to the manager's pay. P commenced his action against D in 1799 when D succeeded to C's mill and attempted to increase use of the stream further to benefit D's mill operations, rejecting the existing arrangement whereby D could control water appropriations to P's detriment.

In support of P, counsel cited *Prescott* v. *Phillips*,[55] which ruled:

[53] (1805) 6 East. 208; 102 E.R. 1266 (K.B.).
[54] 6 East. 208; 102 E.R. 1266, 1266–7.
[55] (1798) per Sjt. Adair, CJ of Chester.

that nothing short of 20 years undisturbed possession of water diverted from the natural channel, or raised by a weir, could give a party an adverse right against those whose lands lay lower down the stream, and to whom it was injurious; and that a possession of above 19 years, which was shewn in that case, was not sufficient.

The twenty-year rule, counsel argued, meant that D's increased diversion of 1791 was not sufficient to maintain a right against P. By requiring the full twenty-year user, prescription was characterized more as a substantive rule of law providing for a conclusive presumption of right—not an evidential rule creating a factual presumption.

D made three arguments for his untrammelled right of appropriation. First, he and his predecessors from 1724 to 1787 had 'had the free and exclusive enjoyment of so much of the water as they thought proper to appropriate to themselves', and P could not abridge that right by building a weir and mill on the portion of river hitherto controlled by D: 'he must take the river subject to [D]'s use of it'—an argument analogous to Blackstone's idea of 'coming to a nuisance'. Secondly, it was argued that P could acquire a right to use water adverse to D's needs only by establishing a prescription through twenty years' enjoyment, and here P had enjoyed C's superfluous water only from 1787 until the detrimental increases of 1791. The strict twenty-year rule was thereby turned against P. Finally, P should have brought action against C in 1791, but had instead acquiesced in C's appropriations and acceded in C's control of the water supply.

At trial Graham B found for P, stating the following doctrine of water rights:

That persons possessing lands on the banks of rivers had a right to the flow of the water in its natural stream, unless there existed before a right in others to enjoy or divert any part of it to their own use. That every such exclusive right was to be measured by the extent of its enjoyment; and if [C] had in 1791 taken more water from the river than had ever been done before... after [P] had appropriated what was before left to himself, by means of which his works were injured, this was a damage to him.[56]

P's supposed acquiescence was discounted by the judge as the product of ignorance or misapprehension of rights. D appealed, arguing that the jury should have been allowed to decide on the evidence whether the history of appropriations since 1724 had established an exclusive right in D or his predecessors, which could be abridged only by twenty years' adverse prescription by P. Counsel for D also 'denied the authority of *Prescott* v. *Philipps* to the extent it appeared to go, as it was common experience that juries were directed to presume a grant within 20 years under circumstances'[57]—an affirmation of the older evidential concept of prescription.

[56] 6 East. 208, 211–12; 102 E.R. 1266, 1268.

[57] 6 East. 208, 214; 102 E.R. 1266, 1269.

The King's Bench supported the judge's directions and the jury verdict for P; but the most diverse reasons were given explaining why P's existing usage of the superfluous water after 1787 should be protected. Lord Ellenborough stated:

The general rule... is, that, independent of any particular enjoyment used to be had by another, every man has a right to have the advantage of a flow of water in his own land without diminution or alteration. But an adverse right may exist founded on the occupation of another.... [I]f the occupation of the party so taking or using [the stream] have existed for so long time as may raise the presumption of a grant, the other party whose land is below must take the stream, subject to such adverse right. I take it that twenty years exclusive enjoyment of the water in any particular manner affords a conclusive presumption of right in the party so enjoying it, derived from grant or Act of Parliament. But less than twenty years enjoyment may or may not afford such a presumption according as it is attended with circumstances to support or rebut the right.[58]

Lord Ellenborough's statement of doctrine falls into the following propositions: (1) riparian owners have a right to natural flow; (2) the right may be abridged by another's adverse use or enjoyment; not because prior use or appropriation gives a direct title, but because it may indirectly evidence a grant against common right; (3) twenty years' enjoyment of water flow creates a legal 'conclusive presumption of right' derived from grant or Act;[59] (4) a lesser period of enjoyment can yet create a factual presumption of implied grant through neighbours' acquiescence in an adverse appropriation. Thus it would seem that even a short prior occupation can create a right of grant against common or natural right, if a jury holds the occupation to be sufficient evidence of grant.[60] The status of the implied grant in Ellenborough's doctrine is cloudy: as a 'conclusive presumption' the grant is a legal fiction applied for convenience; it does not matter that there is likely to be no grant or Act in existence, for the purpose of the implication is to protect water uses of twenty years' standing, and not in any real sense to provide evidence of a lost grant. But the factual implication of grant from less than twenty years' user is a real implication, a proxy for direct evidence. The twenty-year test can be seen as providing an arbitrary line separating real, factual, or evidential implications of grant from the purely legal fiction of conclusive grant which is derived from the fact of long enjoyment as a rule of convenience. The dividing line is blurred, however, by a description of the conclusive presumption as a factual substitute for evidence, as well as an instrumental legal fiction.

[58] 6 East. 208, 214–15; 102 E.R. 1266, 1269.

[59] On the invention of the modern grant fiction of prescription, see Simpson, *History of Land Law*, 266–9; Holdsworth, *History of English Law*, vii, 345–50; and *Land Law*, 281–4.

[60] See also *Woodyer* v. *Hadden* (1813) 5 Taunt. 125, 137–9; 128 E.R. 634, 639–40 per Chambre J (C.P.).

Applying these presumptions to the facts, Lord Ellenborough held that when P set up his mill in 1787 and employed all the available superfluous water, it could not then be said that D's prior partial appropriation allowed D to control the whole flow at will; for if D did not ever use the superfluous water, he could lay no claim to it. P had accepted an abridgement of his natural right to the full water flow without conceding D an exclusive right, as evidenced by the history of complaints and compromises over contentious water distribution. Hence there was no evidence between 1787 and 1791 or thereafter that D enjoyed a right by appropriation or grant to control the whole of the natural flow.

According to Grose J:

[P] had a right to all the water flowing over his own estate, subject only to the easement which [D] might have in it in respect of the premises which they occupied higher up the river.[61] D had established before 1787 a right by user to appropriate part of the stream; P therefore did not have the full natural rights of a riparian owner when he set up his mill, but was entitled only to the unappropriated surplus. D's increase of appropriation at P's expense in 1787 'incroached on his right, and deprived him of a benefit which was attached to his estate. It was an extension of the right before exercised by [D], and a material injury to [P]'. P had not waived his residual rights by acquiescing in D's scheme to divide the water at D's convenience, but had only submitted for the time being in order to avoid litigation.

Grose J's analysis postulates a natural right to water, which may be abridged by an 'easement' acquired by occupation of the flow by a rival. This was a novel usage of the language of incorporeal hereditament to describe water rights at common law. The basis of the water easement by occupation was not well elucidated: Grose J did not specify whether this amounted to a title by occupation or appropriation, or else a title by prescription or implied grant. His language suggests that occupation is the self-sufficient ground of the right.

Lawrence J stated a principle that the right to appropriate flow must involve a present use of water; hence there could be no right to appropriate natural water flow at discretion, beyond one's current level of use.[62] In the present case:

if the occupiers of [D's] premises could before have appropriated to themselves any part of the water flowing through their own lands, by the same rule those through whose lands it afterwards flowed might appropriate so much as had not been appropriated by others.[63]

Thus any unappropriated surplus flow may next be appropriated by a later user; and the successive appropriations will each be protected by law from

[61] 6 East. 208, 216–17; 102 E.R. 1266, 1269–70.
[62] 6 East. 208, 217–19; 102 E.R. 1266, 1270.
[63] 6 East 208, 218; 102 E.R. 1266, 1270.

later invasion. The judge then went closely into the evidence of the levels of appropriation by the parties, and determined that P had not exceeded his rights. Le Blanc J applied the same principle, stating:

> [T]he true rule is, that after the erection of works and the appropriation by the owner of the land of a certain quantity of the water flowing over it, if a proprietor of other land afterwards take what remains of the water before unappropriated, the first mentioned owner, however he might before such second appropriation have taken to himself so much more, cannot do so afterwards.[64]

To summarize the *Bealey* doctrines: two out of the four King's Bench judges, Lawrence and Le Blanc JJ, adopted a Blackstonian prior appropriation theory without reserve; Lord Ellenborough offered a prescriptive grant theory, founded partly on a fiction of the obligor's presumed consent and partly on an evidential or factual implication of consent; and Grose J used the language of an easement founded by pure occupation, a non-natural right based directly on the obligee's act of user. Blackstone is not cited in these judgments, but his influence may be presumed as the language of appropriation and occupation of water flow had not before been used by the English courts.

Edward Christian, the Downing professor of law at Cambridge, incorporated Lord Ellenborough's decision into the fifteenth edition of Blackstone's *Commentaries* in 1809. He noted the practical importance of this branch of law in England's transforming economy:

> Since the immediate extension of the woollen and cotton manufactures by machinery, a stream of water in many situations is become of great value to the owners of the grounds through which it flows. But though actions respecting injuries to mills, and the right to dam or divert the water in a stream, are now extremely frequent in the country, yet the whole law upon the subject seems to be comprized in the sentence of the text [If a stream be unoccupied, I may erect a mill thereon, and detain the water; yet not so as to injure my neighbour's prior mill, or his meadow: for he hath by the first occupancy acquired a property in the current].
>
> It seems now to be settled that persons possessing lands on the banks of rivers have a right to the flow of the water in its natural stream, unless there exists before a right in others to enjoy or divert any part of it to their own use. And that an enjoyment or diversion of it for 20 years establishes a right, or, in the words of Lord Ellenborough, it affords a conclusive presumption of right in the party so enjoying it, derived from grant or act of parliament.[65]

The Blackstonian theory of water title by appropriation, combined a little uneasily with Lord Ellenborough's evidential doctrine of prescriptive grant, was thus presented to the nineteenth-century reader of the *Commentaries* as the settled law of England.

[64] 6 East 208, 219; 102 E.R. 1266, 1270.

[65] *Bl.Comm.*, ii, 403, n. (1).

Applications of the Blackstonian Doctrine

In the 1818 case of *Saunders* v. *Newman*,[66] the King's Bench investigated the unresolved issue of whether riparian water rights were proprietary or possessory in character: that is, whether there was a natural or prescriptive title to claim access to water flow, regardless of usage, as a future-projected property right over a resource; or, alternatively, whether present usage was an essential foundation of right, in that interference with water flow was a tort against enjoyment of present occupation or possession.

The facts were that P, a mill owner, had enjoyed more than forty years' continuous use of a stream powering his mill at a certain level of water flow. P's mill burnt down in 1801 and was rebuilt with similar machinery; P later reduced his appropriation of flow by installing a more efficient water wheel. D, a downsteam mill proprietor, then raised the dam on his mill pond to a much higher level, forcing back water and so reducing the water fall available to P. P declared for injury to the accustomed flow, with the damage quantified by the water needs of the first, now-destroyed mill.

Burrough J at trial non-suited P on the ground that he had pleaded an injury for wrongful interference with the level of water use by the older mill, which in effect was to claim for damage done to a vanished level of appropriation. He stated:

> [t]hat as this was an action founded on [P's] possession, and for an injury to that possession, and as he had not enjoyed his mill in the state in which it was when the injury was sustained for the space of twenty years, he was not entitled to recover: that if the mill had remained in the state in which it was rebuilt in 1801, he would have been entitled to maintain his action for an injury, but he thought fit to alter it, and to make a wheel so materially different from the former, that the evidence of his right was gone.... [H]e could only support it by a medium of proof, not that this was the same wheel, but that if the old wheel had remained, the acts of [D] would have injured him in that state.[67]

The judge thus insisted on proof of a customary or prescriptive usage as the ground of title—not merely present usage of the natural flow.

The trial judge's approach was elaborated by counsel for D before the King's Bench, who argued that P must plead a title to an ancient mill, a right of common, a mill-suit, or other prescriptive right, which was interfered with or damaged by D's actions. 'Reasoning therefore from analogy, it must be inferred that this action being for an infringement on a mode of enjoying a mill, which mill is not claimed by prescription, [it] cannot be supported'. P had claimed a prescriptive right to receive the usual flow of water to his mill,

[66] (1818) 1 B. & Ald. 258; 106 E.R. 95 (K.B.).

[67] (1818) 1 B. & Ald. 258, 259; 104 E.R. 95, 96. Cf. *Drewett and Towle* v. *Sheard and Price* (1836) 7 C. & P. 465, 173 E.R. 206 (N.P., Berks. Assize).

and according to authority damage to a long use of the flow must be shown. For example, in Rolle's *Abridgment* the action is described in terms of damage to long use:

> If I have a mill by prescription, and another erect a new mill, and force back the water on my mill so as to do me an injury, I may have an action on the case.[68]

Rejecting the defence arguments, the King's Bench reversed the trial ruling and held that P had declared his action correctly. Lord Ellenborough held that an action lay 'if by any alteration lower down the stream the water be prevented from escaping as it usually has done, and that be to the prejudice of the owner of the mill'.[69] A plea declaring possession of a mill, to which water used to flow in a particular manner, sufficed to bring an action for interference with that flow; though if injury to a specific mill of given construction was pleaded, then evidence might have to be adduced of the precise harm to that mill. Lord Ellenborough indicated that obstruction of water could prejudice a mill owner even if he had not used the flow immediately prior to the diversion, and had suffered no harm to present usages. The owner's natural or prescriptive right to the water was thus protected as a future-directed title controlling a resource.

Bayley and Abbott JJ similarly stressed that P's efficient reduction of appropriation did not diminish P's right to accustomed water flow.[70] According to Bayley J:

> If a person stops the current of a stream which has immemorially flowed in a given direction, and thereby prejudices another, he subjects himself to an action.

The right was founded on ancient water flow—not prescriptive mill use of the flow. The notion of 'prejudice' specified here does not, however, clarify the problem of whether tortious damage to a present usage might be required in addition to interference with the stream, in order to found an action for trespass on the case.

Abbott J indicated that the original title to water required a prescriptive basis in ancient use, accepting that part of D's argument. However, once P's title was founded, only some usage was necessary in order to sustain a plea of actionable damage:

> When a mill has been erected upon a stream for a long time, it gives the owner a right that the water shall continue to flow to and from the mill, in the manner in which it has been accustomed to flow during all that time. The owner is not bound to use the water in the same precise manner, or to apply it to the same mill; if he were, that would stop all improvements in machinery. If . . . the alterations . . . prejudice the right of the lower mill, the case would be different.[71]

68 1 *Roll. Abdgt.*, 107, pl. 16.

69 1 B. & Ald. 258, 260; 106 E.R. 95, 96–7.

70 1 B. & Ald. 258, 261–2; 106 E.R. 95, 97.

71 Ibid. Cf. *Hall* v. *Swift* (1838) 4 Bing (N.C.) 381; 132 E.R. 834 (C.P.).

Of the four judges, only Holroyd J (who had appeared as counsel for the plaintiff in *Bealey* v. *Shaw*) chose to apply the Blackstonian prior appropriation theory. He cited Le Blanc J's version of the doctrine from *Bealey*, and then held that P, upon building the original mill, had 'by that act... appropriated to himself the water flowing in that particular way'. The quantum of flow originally used could not now be obstructed by D, because this would 'deprive [P] of an advantage which he had already lawfully acquired'. He did not confront the issue of which level of use ought to be the focus of the action:

> The change of wheel can make no difference; because at the time it was done it was certainly lawful for [P] to make the alteration.

Title apparently rested upon the first act of appropriation, and was not tied to present, perhaps reduced, usages of the appropriated resource.

Both Holroyd and Bayley JJ seem prompted by a desire to encourage innovating uses of water flow by industrialists through protection of the natural or customary flow to mill-sites, ignoring levels of established use. In effect, the Blackstonian appropriation doctrine was applied to allow a guaranteed level of access to natural water flow, rather than dividing access by protecting competitive occupations by rival users. By relaxing the formal requirements for declaring riparian rights, the courts apparently were promoting economic development by allowing newcomers access to resources.

Too much consistency and rigour cannot be read into the water decisions of this period. A good example is found in the case of *Cooper* v. *Barber*,[72] decided by the Common Pleas on circuit in 1810. The facts of the case were narrated at enormous length at trial, and then twice before the Common Bench, which tried to dispose of the matter by referring it to arbitrators as a question of pure fact. The legal conflict had started when D resorted to heavy-handed self-help after years of bickering, invading P's land in force in order to throw down his dams and penstocks, and dumping the building materials into P's watercourse. D had become incensed by damage caused through P's damming back of the water of an ancient artificial watercourse running from the river Lavant in Horsham, Sussex. Release of waters from P's dam had caused severe flooding of D's dwelling house; and the unnatural collection of water had further caused the soil under his house to subside. Despite causing this damage, P had refused to restore the water to its natural and accustomed course and persisted in his unreasonable user; D had then forcibly abated the nuisance. P pleaded an immemorial right to divert the water to the benefit of his own estate, showing that he had built the dam thirty or forty years earlier and had enjoyed its use without interruption for

[72] (1810) 3 Taunt. 99, 108–9; 128 E.R. 40, 44 (C.P.).

at least thirty years. P further claimed that his user had been reasonable at all times; he sued D for damage to his dams and other structures, in breach of his prescriptive rights of enjoyment. The trial judge went into detailed evidence of the water levels of each dam and watercourse, and the flood damage occurring at different seasons. The evidence of witnesses and surveyors was contradictory; it appeared that P may have more than doubled the levels of damming during the period of the thirty years' claimed prescriptive enjoyment. On that issue Heath J directed the jury to decide the 'reasonableness' of P's behaviour by reference to the existence of any prescriptive right, as it was clear that P's dams had injured D's dwelling:

> If [P] had possessed an uninterrupted right to raise the penstock to a certain height, it would not derogate from that right that [D] had thought proper to build a house... but [P]'s enjoyment had not been very peaceable; for whenever the neighbouring inhabitants felt any inconvenience, they went and pulled down the penstock.... [T]here was conclusive evidence that the penstock had been enhanced of late years... and if the jury should be of that opinion [they should] find a verdict for [D]....[73]

D moved for a retrial, claiming that a prescriptive right did exist and could not be defeated by D's rights to enjoy a dwelling built only six or seven years earlier. Lawrence J rejected this plea on the basis that a prescriptive right must be adverse in order to indicate the implied grant of a right. Without a lengthy period of use actually harmful to the neighbour's estate, that neighbour cannot have acquiesced in the user in the eyes of the law. Long user by itself bestowed no right. Lawrence J blended this idea of prescription as adverse use with the doctrine of *sic utere tuo*:

> [P] may pen the water there [in his own lands] as he will, until he does a damage to a neighbour.... Is it not law that you must so use your own as not to prejudice your neighbour? And until you prejudice your neighbour by penning the water, you do that which you have a right to do; but where you begin to injure your neighbour, there the right terminates. If there had been an ancient house, into which you had... immemorially caused the water to flow, without being encountered by obstruction, it would have been evidence of grant; but here is no such evidence.[74]

Mansfield CJ and Chambre J seemed to agree with Lawrence J's argument, but the retrial never took place and the issues of fact were left unresolved. The case is significant because Lawrence J and the court made no mention of any prior occupancy doctrine, but assumed that rights to expanded, non-natural water use are based on adverse user as real evidence of grant, to be established by minute factual inquiry into the behaviour of the parties. Other cases at this time stressed that pleadings for interference with water flow

[73] *Cooper* v. *Barber* (1810) 3 Taunt. 99, 108–9; 128 E.R. 40, 44 (C.P.).
[74] 3 Taunt. 99, 110; 128 E.R. 40, 45.

should show that the regular supply to a riparian site and use of the water there had actually been interrupted.[75]

Equity Leads the Law

In 1823 Leach VC outlined a synthesis of riparian doctrine which was frequently to be cited and applied in later case law—an instance of equity doctrine fusing new ideas into common-law thought. *Wright* v. *Howard*[76] was a suit in Chancery for specific performance of a sale of riparian land, where the vendor (P, seeking execution of the conveyance) could not deliver good title to valuable water privileges appurtenant to the tenement, as had been promised to D in the contract. P held a long lease of the property and had not negotiated a right to divert water away from three riparian tenements neighbouring his land, as would have been required under the contract with D. When D refused to proceed, P won a new long demise from his lessor granting him unrestricted enjoyment of the stream during the lease; P then insisted on execution of the contract, arguing that he had successfully 'fed' water title to the land. D resisted completion of the conveyance on grounds that a finite leasehold right to the water was insufficient, that two of the riparian neighbours had not agreed to grant the right, and that the fourteen-year delay of the commercial agreement and resulting waste of the tenement had rendered the agreement nugatory.

The circumstances of the case elucidate the economics of water exploitation. Under the contract, the channel for the mill-stream was to be directed back to the river at a point along the river allowing 'a greater fall by three feet.... This additional fall was of great importance to the cotton manufactory.... [T]he privileges as to the use of the water...constituted the most valuable part of the subject of the contract'. The property was sold for £6,600, but was worth only £2,200 without the specified water rights; the cotton mill to be erected by the purchaser on the land would have cost an additional £15,000. Thus total projected capital outlay premissed on the quality of water power available on site neared the considerable sum of £20,000.

Counsel for P argued that the riparian neighbours could not have restrained the proposed water use, as '[a]ccording to the principles of the law on this subject, a proprietor of the land on the banks of a river has a right to divert the water, unless he does it so as to occasion an actual injury to a neighbour. Without an actual injury there can be no right of action'. By 'actual injury' he meant damage to a proprietor's own current use of the water; in other words, an actionable right to water depended on the owner

[75] *Griffiths* v. *Marson* (1818) 6 Price 1; 146 E.R. 723 (Ex.).
[76] (1823) 1 Sim. & St. 192; 57 E.R. 76 (V.C.).

having made a prior appropriation. A further argument was made from presumed grant: that P's long use of the water without protest by his neighbours indicated that they had made acquiescence and surrender of rights to the water, as well as suggesting they had not been harmed in their established uses.

Counsel for D argued that P had won no title to the water 'either by grant or prescription' binding his neighbours, and so was liable to equitable injunction to remove the weir diverting water for the mill-site. A theory of natural riparian right was opposed to P's appropriation theory:

> The mere erection of the weir and the diversion of the water so as to diminish the quantity which passed their land was injury enough. Taking away the water must, of itself, be injurious.[77]

Leach VC found against specific performance, on the ground that a title to the water could not be made out by P against the riparian neighbours, either by grant or prescription. Furthermore, too much time had lapsed to allow any new steps to perfect title for what was always a speculative commercial transaction requiring rapid completion.

The doctrines applied by the Vice Chancellor were as follows:

(1) '*Prima facie*, the proprietor of each bank of a stream is the proprietor of half the land covered by the stream, but there is no property in the water'. This restated the position of Roman law.[78]

(2) The basic rule of water law is that riparian owners enjoy a common right to natural water flow:

> Every proprietor has an equal right to use the water which flows in the stream, and consequently no proprietor can have the right to use the water to the prejudice of any other riparian proprietor. Without the consent of the other proprietors, who may be affected by his operations, no proprietor can either diminish the quantity of water which would otherwise descend to the proprietors below, nor throw the water back upon the proprietors above.

(3) To maintain a claim to divert water beyond this common right, a proprietor must either (i) 'prove an actual grant or licence from the proprietors affected by his operations'; or (ii) 'prove an uninterrupted enjoyment of twenty years . . . which term . . . is now adopted upon a principle of general convenience, as affording conclusive presumption of a grant'. The language of conclusive presumption indicates that prescription has now become a direct mode of acquiring rights, departing from its origins as a

[77] 1 Sim. & St. 192, 198; 57 E.R. 76, 79.

[78] English judges sometimes flirted with the idea that a riparian proprietor owned the body of water as it flowed over his land, though the heresy was seldom enunciated: see *R.* v. *Wharton* (1701) 12 Mod. 510; 88 E.R. 1483 (K.B.); *Lyon* v. *Fishmongers' Company* (1876) 1 App. Cas. 673, 683 (H.L.) per Lord Selborne LC.; and authorities discussed in Coulson and Forbes, *Law Relating to Waters*, 93–100.

principle of real evidence, and reducing the implication of grant to an irrebutable legal presumption, an instrumental fiction.

(4) '[N]o action will lie for water diversion except by a person who sustains an actual injury'. This seems to be a separate requirement of substantial right-infringement sufficient to warrant injunctive relief in equity, and is distinct from those principles establishing the right. However, 'actual injury' in the context of action on the case might embrace *injuria sine damno*, or damage implied from right-infringement, as explained by Holt CJ in *Ashby* v. *White*.

(5) It appears that in the absence of a use of the stream, a riparian owner cannot sue to defend his natural rights against invasion. This may mean that an owner who attempts to use a natural stream for the first time but is defeated by another's diversion of the stream has thereby suffered 'actual injury'; but there can be no action for prospective denial of water flow.

(6) An action against a diverter-defendant 'must lie at any time within twenty years when the [actual] injury happens to arise, in consequence of a new purpose of the party [the plaintiff] to avail himself of his common right'. That is, if a riparian proprietor newly attempts to exercise his natural or common right to water, but is pre-empted by another's expanded non-natural user of the stream, then the denial of the use amounts to an 'actual injury' founding an action. This suggests that a diverter must show at least twenty years' enjoyment injurious to another's purposes of use in order to found a prescriptive right.

The doctrines stated by Leach VC combine natural flow and direct prescription theories of title, without broaching Blackstonian prior appropriation theory. Unlike in preceding nineteenth-century decisions, there seems to be no factual implication of grant derived from acquiescence in less than twenty years' use;[79] nor is there recognition of any title by appropriation, formed immediately by an occupation of water against common right. The rule that a natural right could be neither defended nor abridged by prescription, without showing harm to an actual or attempted use by the riparian proprietor, may be seen as merely an accession to the form of the action on the case. The requirement of damage to use might then be circumvented by Holt's doctrine importing damage into any type of right infringement. But if proof of actual use was indeed a necessary element of action, then Leach VC was proposing a doctrine that physical appropriation was still necessary in order to establish or maintain riparian rights. It might have been that equity courts looked more to substance before granting the powerful remedies of specific performance or injunction; but the line between deciding on equitable remedy and adjudicating on legal rights could be fine. The praised clarity

[79] Though Leach VC hints that if P had acted to divert water for ten to fourteen years with acquiescence from neighbours, a grant may have been presumed: 1 Sim. & St. 192, 205; 57 E.R. 76, 82.

of Leach's judgment thus dissolves upon closer scrutiny, with crucial doctrinal choices remaining unresolved, to trouble later case law.[80]

Blackstonian Appropriation Theory Revived in the Court of King's Bench

A prior appropriation theory was strongly upheld by the King's Bench in the 1824 decision of *Williams* v. *Morland*,[81] without referring to the detailed doctrines outlined in *Wright* v. *Howard* only the year before.

The case turned on the validity of the pleadings. P, a downstream proprietor, declared that he was possessed of riparian land and therefore had and ought to have the benefit and advantage of the stream. The claim was based solely on riparian possession, without prescription. P further counted that D had erected a dam upstream which had 'wrongfully prevented the water of the stream from running in its usual and regular course, and in its usual calm, moderate and smooth manner'; and that this interference with the natural flow had caused damage to the banks and premises of P's land.

At the Kent Assize, the jury found that the damming of the water had not caused the claimed damage, but they appended to their verdict a holding that D 'should not stop the water in the summer-time'. Graham B at trial ruled that P had complained of the alteration of natural flow damaging his banks, not that he had been deprived of water. The jury verdict could not be supported, because notwithstanding obstruction of the stream, P's pleadings had revealed no injury or deprivation of usage. The issue before the King's Bench was whether P's declaration sufficed to bring action on the case for diversion of the water, without otherwise specifying damage.

Chitty in support of P's verdict argued:

> The stoppage of that water of itself is an injury, although no actual pecuniary damage ensue. In trespass to land it is not necessary to prove any actual damage; and if special damage be alleged, it need not be proved.... [W]rongfully prevent[ing] the water from coming to [P's] premises... of itself constitutes an injury, and then it was unnecessary to prove the special damage alleged.[82]

The court rejected Chitty's analogy with trespass *quare clausum fregit*; interference with water was not comparable to physical invasion of land, and in order to bring an action on the case, actual injury to some existing use or appropriation of the water flow had to be pleaded. Water titles thus were conceived as maintaining established appropriations, not as property rights guaranteeing future access to resources.

[80] Cf. *Dewhirst* v. *Wrigley* (1837) C P Cooper 319, 47 E.R. 525 (L.C.); *Elmhirst* v. *Spencer* (1849) 2 Macnaghten and Gordon 45, 42 E.R. 18 (L.C.); *Ennor* v. *Barwell* (1860) 2 Giffard 410, 66 E.R. 171 (V.C.); *Elwell* v. *Crowther* (1862) 31 Beavan 163; 54 E.R. 1100 (Ch., M.R.).

[81] (1824) 2 B. & C. 910; 107 E.R. 620 (K.B.).

[82] 2 B. & C. 910, 913; 107 E.R. 620, 621.

Bayley J grounded this result by faithfully adopting the Blackstonian appropriation doctrine:

My judgment in this case is founded on the nature of flowing water, and the manner in which an exclusive right to it is obtained. Flowing water is originally publici juris. So soon as it is appropriated by an individual, his right is coextensive with the beneficial use to which he appropriates it. Subject to that right all the rest of the water remains publici juris. The party who obtains a right to the exclusive enjoyment of the water does so in derogation of the primitive right of the public.[83]

According to Bayley J, there was no right in water until used or 'beneficially' appropriated. Unappropriated or surplus flow remained *publici juris*, but would in turn be subjected to private property when appropriated. It followed that 'a party complaining of the breach of such a right ought to shew that he is prevented from having water which he has acquired a right to use for some beneficial purpose'.[84]

Holroyd J struggled with the Blackstonian doctrine that '[r]unning water is not in its nature private property', and sought for a language of property rights with which to explain the character of water titles:

At least [running water] is private property no longer than it remains on the soil of the person claiming it. Before it came there it clearly was not his property. It may, perhaps, become, quasi, the property of another before it comes upon his premises, by reason of his having appropriated to himself the use of the water accustomed to flow through his lands before any other person had acquired a prior right to it [*Bealey* v. *Shaw*]. . . . If [P] . . . had shewn . . . a right to the unappropriated water of the stream, and had alledged as the ground of his complaint that he had been deprived of the use of that surplus water, he might then have been entitled to a verdict. . . . The mere obstruction of the water which had been used to flow through his lands does not of itself give any right of action. In order to entitle himself to recover, he should shew the loss of some benefit, or the deterioration of the value of the premises.[85]

Holroyd J ended up dismissing P's case, but his reasons were opaque. His judgment stated the following doctrines: (1) a riparian proprietor has 'property' in water whilst it flows over his land; (2) an established use of the flow gives the owner a 'quasi-property' in unobstructed upstream waters; (3) loss of benefit of appropriated water is the gist of an action; but also that (4) diversion of unappropriated water may be an actionable injury to riparian ownership, as a 'depriv[ation] . . . of surplus water' or a 'deterioration of the value of the premises'—suggesting that water titles can be protections of future as well as present usages.[86]

Littledale J held that P must show actual damage accruing from D's diversion. He conceded that in actions for trespass by wrongful invasion

[83] 2 B. & C. 910, 914; 107 E.R. 620, 621.
[84] Ibid.
[85] 2 B. & C. 910, 915–16; 107 E.R. 620, 622.
[86] 2 B. & C. 910, 914; 107 E.R. 620, 621–2.

and by obstruction of rights of common and way, 'damage is presumed to have been sustained, though no pecuniary damage be actually proved'. Nonetheless, in water actions real damage was necessary:

> The doing of any act calculated to injure that right is a sufficient ground of action, but, generally speaking, there must be a temporal loss or damage accruing from the wrongful act of another, in order to entitle a party to maintain an action on the case.
>
> . . .
>
> Water is of that peculiar nature, that it is not sufficient to allege in a declaration, that [D] prevented the water from flowing to [P's] premises. The mere right to use the water does not give a party such a property in the new water constantly coming, as to make the diversion or obstruction of the water, per se, give him any right of action. All the King's subjects have a right to the use of flowing water, provided that, in using it, they do no injury to the rights already vested in another by the appropriation of the water.[87]

THE GENERALIZATION OF APPROPRIATION THEORY

Building on *Williams* v. *Morland*, the courts soon developed an elaborate appropriation theory of proprietary incidents applying to rights of light and air as well as water.[88] All rights of natural amenity were now said to be constituted as actionable rights by appropriation with possessive intent, and lost upon non-user. By contrast, non-natural amenities or appurtenances, such as rights of common or way, were acquired (or lost) only by grant or prescription, not simply by intentional possession or abandonment.[89]

Moore v. *Rawson*,[90] decided by the King's Bench in 1824 shortly after *Williams* v. *Morland*, helped to crystallize these developments. The case involved loss of a right to ancient lights by a plaintiff who had blocked an ancient window with a blank wall for some seventeen years. This was held sufficient to terminate the right through abandonment. The Court rejected P's argument that since the right was won by prescriptive enjoyment of twenty years or more, it could be terminated only by twenty years' non-enjoyment, that is through a negative prescription for a counter-servitude in D's favour. The doctrine finally adopted by the court was that argued for D by Denman, who some time later redefined riparian doctrine as Chief Justice of the King's Bench. Denman argued:

[87] 2 B. & C. 910, 916–17; 107 E.R. 620, 622.

[88] See *Moore* v. *Rawson* (1824) 3 B. & C. 332; 107 E.R. 756 (K.B.); *Canham* v. *Fisk* (1831) 2 Tyrwh. 155; 2 Cro. & J. 125; 149 E.R. 53 (Ex.) per Bayley J.

[89] *Moore* v. *Rawson*, (1824) 3 B. & C. 332, 339–41; 107 E.R. 756, 759–60, per Littledale J. Cf. *Bliss* v. *Hall* (1838) 4 Bing. (N.C.) 183; 132 E.R. 758 (C.P.), using prior appropriation ideas as a defence to nuisance.

[90] (1824) 3 B. & C. 332; 107 E.R. 756 (K.B.).

Light, air, and water are prima facie publici juris, but individuals may acquire a right to them by occupancy or enjoyment, and if the right is acquired by enjoyment, it may also be lost by a discontinuance of it. The period of enjoyment necessary to give an individual an exclusive right to enjoy light, air, and water, is fixed by the municipal law of this country, and, by the law of England, that period is twenty years, but as the right is acquired by enjoyment, it may be lost by non-user, unless the party who has appropriated to himself the light, air, or water, at the time when he discontinues the use, does some act to indicate to others his intention to resume it within a reasonable time.[91]

Bayley J (Holroyd J concurring) followed Denman's doctrine without variation, stating:

The right to light, air, or water, is acquired by enjoyment, and will... continue so long as the party either continues that enjoyment or shews an intention to continue it.[92]

Littledale J decided the case upon a distinction between use and occupation. The acquisition of rights of common or way by twenty years' user or enjoyment involved a prescriptive presumption of grant, such that an equivalent period of twenty years' non-enjoyment might be required in order to ground a presumption of release. He then added:

But there is a material difference between the mode of acquiring such rights and a right to light and air. The latter is acquired by mere occupancy; the former can only be acquired by user, accompanied with the consent of the owner of the land.

Expanding this insight, Littledale J suggested that exercise of a common or way over land without grant was intrinsically a wrong, a trespass; the continuance of the wrong for twenty years gave rise to a fictitious presumption that the owner had consented and granted the right at a time before the exercise began; this antedated consent was necessary to make lawful the initial acts of user. By contrast the first use or appropriation of light and air was intrinsically lawful or privileged and no trespass, though such enjoyment was not protected against interference by neighbours until such occupation had extended for twenty years. This lapse of time creates a presumption of covenant between neighbours, granting a negative right that free use of the light and air not be obstructed or interfered with in the future; by this presumption the privilege is converted into a right. There is no need for a retroactive grant of positive right, for there is no wrongful act to be legitimized. Because there is no grant of right, but only a forbearance to interfere with a lawful occupation, it followed that if the occupation was ended for a time sufficient to show intention to abandon, then the foundation of the right was removed. Littledale J here provided a reasoned reformulation of the juristic relationship between appropriation and prescriptive grant doctrine. He did not, however, expressly extend his general analysis of incidental property rights to the case of water.

[91] (1824) 3 B. & C. 332, 334; 107 E.R. 756, 758.
[92] (1824) 3 B. & C. 332, 336; 107 E.R. 756, 758.

Two 1831 cases further supported the emergent general theory of appropriation. In *Canham* v. *Fisk*[93] land with running water was divided and the downstream part sold to P, with D retaining the upstream tenement. P enjoyed the flow of water to his land for less than twenty years when D diverted the flow by dams and sluices. In an action on the case brought before the Exchequer of Pleas, P argued that there was 'a title by appropriation and enjoyment, quite sufficient to sustain the action, without any prescriptive right'.[94] D argued that there was no title to receive the water, as the closes had been in a unity of ownership extinguishing any possible easement; there was no actual grant, nor was there a sufficient period of enjoyment to prescribe by presuming a grant; and these were the only three possible modes for acquiring a title. Bayley B responded:

> There is a fourth mode of acquiring such a right, viz. by appropriation. If a man find water running through his land, he may appropriate it, and thus acquire a title to the water.[95]

The court also held that if a conveyance of land is to exclude rights to appurtenant water or light, the instrument must state so expressly: 'This land is purchased with the water running upon it, and the conveyance passes the land with the easements existing at the time'. 'Easement' was here used in an imprecise manner similar to Bracton, connoting both natural and granted appurtenances attached to possession.

The most fully developed analysis of appropriation as a source of title was offered in the Common Pleas decision of *Liggins* v. *Inge*, also from 1831.[96] The idea that continuing appropriation depended on possessive intention, as stated by Littledale J in *Moore* v. *Rawson*, was here expressly extended to water rights. This was an action on the case brought by P, the owner of an ancient corn mill, against D, the owner of another ancient mill upstream on the same river, for diversion of water to the damage of P's business. The pleadings were entirely standard, declaring a customary flow, used for a long period to beneficial purpose, and then interfered with by D with knowledge of the ensuing injury and special damage to P. At first trial the large sum of £500 was awarded for loss of profits. It then emerged at a later arbitration that P's father had given D an oral permission to dam and divert the water. The arbitrator determined that this licence had been revoked by P's later claim; that nominal damages were now to be paid in order to establish P's title to the unimpeded water since revocation; and that D was to remove the dam.

The main issue before the court was whether the parol licence had irrevocably transferred a property right to D, or whether the licence could not be

93 (1831) 2 Tyrwh. 155; 2 Cro. & J. 126; 149 E.R. 53 (Ex.).
94 Citing *Williams* v. *Morland*, in the text accompanying nn. 81–87 above.
95 Citing *Bealey* v. *Shaw*, in the text accompanying nn. 53–65 above.
96 (1831) 7 Bing. 682; 131 E.R. 263 (C.P.).

countermanded because D had acted and relied upon the permission by building the dam. Tindal CJ found that the licence could not be retracted, as D had been authorized to change his position and expand his milling operation, at great expense, on the strength of the licence to appropriate water:

[T]his is not a licence to do acts which consist in repetition, as to walk in a park . . . to fish in the waters of another, or the like: which licence, if countermanded, the party is but in the same situation as he was before it was granted; but this is a licence to construct a work, which is attended with expense to the party using the licence; so that, after the same is countermanded, the party to whom it was granted may sustain a heavy loss. It is a licence to do something that, in its own nature, seems intended to be permanent and continuing.[97]

This decision was a foundation of later licence and estoppel doctrine, including the leading case of *Plimmer* v. *Mayor and Corporation of Wellington*.[98]

In addition to the express irrevocable licence, Tindal CJ found that P had a title to the water by appropriation after it had been relinquished from D's upstream tenement. The licence did not transfer any title, but was an acknowledgment 'that he [P's predecessor] wanted such water no longer for the purposes of his mill; and that he gave back again and yielded up' the water that D then appropriated by erection of the dam. The general doctrine grounding the decisison was stated as follows:

[97] 7 Bing. 682, 693–4; 131 E.R. 263, 268.

[98] (1884) 9 App. Cas. 714 (P.C.). For use of licence and estoppel doctrine to order land-use and water rights, especially in the case of leaseholds, see *Fentiman* v. *Smith* (1803) 4 East. 107; 102 E.R. 770 (K.B.); *Winter* v. *Brockwell* (1807) 8 East. 308; 103 E.R. 359 (K.B.); *Alder* v. *Savil* (1814) 5 Taunt. 454; 128 E.R. 766 (C.P.); *Taylor* v. *Waters* (1816) 7 Taunt. 374; 129 E.R. 150 (C.P.); *Hewlins* v. *Shipham* (1826) 5 B. & C. 221; 108 E.R. 82 (K.B.); *Bryan* v. *Whistler* (1828) 8 B. & C. 288; 113 E.R. 1050 (K.B.); *Liggins* v. *Inge* (1831) 7 Bing. 682; 131 E.R. 263 (C.P.); *Mason* v. *Hill* (1833) 5 B. & Ad. 1, 14–16; 110 E.R. 692, 697–8 (K.B.) per Denman CJ and the court; *Cocker* v. *Cowper* (1834) 1 C. M. & R. 418; 5 Tyrw. 103; 149 E.R. 1143 (Ex.); *Blatchford* v. *Mayor of Plymouth* (1837) 3 Bing. N.C. 691; 132 E.R. 577 (C.P.); *Rochdale Canal* v. *King* (1851) 2 Sim. (N.S.) 28; 61 E.R. 270 (V.C.); *Duke of Devonshire* v. *Eglin* (1851) 14 Beav. 530; 51 E.R. 389 (Rolls.); *Attorney-General* v. *Sheffield Gas Consumers Company* (1853) 3 De. G.M. & G. 304; 43 E.R. 119 (Ch.); *Northam* v. *Hurley* (1853) 1 El. & Bl. 665; 118 E.R. 586 (Q.B.); *Rawstron* v. *Taylor* (1855) 11 Exch. 369; 156 E.R. 873. (Ex.); *Cawkwell* v. *Russell* (1856) 26 L.J. Ex. 34 (Ex.); *Somerset Coal Canal Co.* v. *Harcourt* (1857) 24 Beav. 571; 53 E.R. 478 (Rolls.); *Moore* v. *Webb* (1857) 1 C.B.N.S. 673; 140 E.R. 277 (C.P.); *Lee* v. *Stevenson* (1858) 27 L.J.Q.B. 263 (Q.B.); *Whitehead* v. *Parks* (1858) 2 H. & N. 870; 157 E.R. 358 (Ex.); *Wardle* v. *Brocklehurst* (1859) 1 El. & El. 1058; 120 E.R. 1207 (Q.B.); *Hodgkinson* v. *Ennor* (1863) 4 B. & S. 229; 122 E.R. 446 (Q.B.); *Hall* v. *Lund* (1863) 1 H. & C. 676; 158 E.R. 1055 (Ex.); *Chadwick* v. *Marsden* (1867) L.R. 2 Ex. 285; *Watts* v. *Kelson* (1870) L.R. 6 Ch. 166; *Bankart* v. *Tennant* (1876) L.R. 10 Eq. 141; *Cooke* v. *Chilcote* (1876) 3 Ch. D. 694; *Taylor* v. *St. Helens* (1877) 6 Ch. D. 264 (C.A.); *Brain* v. *Marfell* (1879) 41 L.T. (N.S.) 457; *Countess of Rothes* v. *Kirkcaldy Waterworks* (1882) 7 App. Cas. 694; C. J. Gale, *Treatise on the Law of Easements* (3rd edn., London, 1862) 39–45, 187–8; Coulson and Forbes, *Law Relating to Waters*, 243–69.

Water flowing in a stream, it is well settled, by the law of England, is publici juris. By the Roman law, running water, light, and air, were considered as some of those things which had the name of res communes, and which were defined 'the property of which belong to no person, but the use of all.' And, by the law of England, the person who first appropriates any part of the water flowing through his land to his own use, has the right to the use of so much as he thus appropriates, against any other. *Bealey* v. *Shaw*. . . .

And it seems consistent with that same principle, that the water, after it has been so made subservient to private uses by appropriation, should again become publici juris by the mere act of relinquishment. There is nothing unreasonable in holding that a right which is gained by occupancy should be lost by abandonment.[99]

The test of occupancy was a factual test of intention—whether an occupant by acts or words has decided to surrender, as opposed to disuse temporarily, the water flow (or other amenity).[100]

REFORM OF THE PRIOR APPROPRIATION THEORY—*MASON* v. *HILL*

The new general theory of prior appropriation was not to last long. In the landmark 1833 decision of *Mason* v. *Hill*[101] the King's Bench constructed a new riparian theory re-emphasizing natural rights.

The facts of the case were that P's predecessor in title to riparian land had sporadically appropriated water flow from a stream for irrigation for twenty years before 1818. By parol agreement P then licensed D, an upstream proprietor, to dam back the bulk of the water at a particular point, the water to be returned to its course after use. P built a mill in 1823 using the surplus water flow from D's dam; in 1828 P installed steam power in this mill and extended his use of the water to appropriate all the surplus. The next year P revoked the licence, demolished D's dam, and demanded that the whole natural flow of the stream descend to his lower tenement without obstruction. D responded by erecting a new dam lower down the stream, appropriating still more of the flow and heating the water before returning it to its natural course. P brought action on the case against D for interference with the natural stream, declaring on the following grounds: possession of land with mill; water that used to and ought to flow to the land; beneficial use of the water by the mill; and wrongful interference with the water, 'whereby [P] was prevented from using his mill . . . in so extensive and beneficial a manner as he otherwise would have done'. The pleadings did not allege a prescriptive use of the water by the mill; nor was special damage to the mill's operation

[99] *Liggins* v. *Inge* (1831) 7 Bing. 682, 692–3; 131 E.R. 263, 268.
[100] 7 Bing. 682, 693–4; 131 E.R. 263, 268.
[101] (1832) 3 B. & Ad. 304; 110 E.R. 112; (1833) 5 B. & Ad. 1; 110 E.R. 692 (K.B.).

itemized; the action was brought on the possession of riparian land alone, the injury being interference with natural flow preventing a new beneficial appropriation.

The verdict gave a detailed statement of evidence, listing past appropriations of water from various springs and streams by both parties, and summarizing their negotiations and transactions. The jury described the main stream as 'an ancient and natural course', characterizing as ancient the flow of water, rather than the use to which the water was put. The jury found for P and awarded one shilling for each of the four interferences alleged, indicating that this was a determination of title by oblique means of a tort action, to be enforced by damages, costs, and injunction rather than by declaration of real rights.

At the first King's Bench hearing of 1832,[102] after lengthy review of the authorities the court preferred the natural-right theory to the appropriation doctrine of water rights. Lord Tenterden CJ described the issues of the case with great clarity:

> [F]or the defendants it was insisted that, they having first appropriated the water beneficially to their use at a time when the appropriation was not injurious to [P], had a right to the water and the use of it, notwithstanding the diversion had by subsequent acts of [P] become injurious to him. [P], on the other hand, insisted that [D] did not, nor could by law, acquire a right to the water by a diversion and enjoyment for a period less than twenty years.[103]

The court held that P could not expand his right to the natural flow of water by past appropriations, but few reasons were given for the decision beyond approval of the *ratio* of *Wright* v. *Howard.*

According to P's counsel in the appellate hearing, Lord Tenterden's decision determined that a riparian proprietor, as soon as he was injured by the diversion of water from its natural course, might maintain an action against the diverter; and that prior use of the stream by the diverter was no answer unless the stream had been enjoyed without disturbance for twenty years, giving prescriptive title for the non-natural use. In the present case P's predecessor had sufficiently established an actionable title by appropriating and using the water for irrigation and husbandry. The licence was revocable because in the circumstances it amounted to an easement to abstract water from a particular spot, and hence was a real interest that could pass by deed only.

Counsel for D responded by demonstrating that the weight of recent authorities (including Blackstone) 'shew that the right to flowing water is acquired by appropriation and occupancy'; and it was D who had first

[102] (1832) 3 B. & Ad. 304; 110 E.R. 114.

[103] (1832) 3 B. & Ad. 304, 311–12; 110 E.R. 112, 116–17.

appropriated the water by damming the stream for his mill under licence. The first King's Bench hearing was flawed because it had relied solely on the doctrine of *Wright* v. *Howard*, an equity decision which did not cite the relevant common-law authorities. Moreover, a deed to pass an easement for water was necessary only for an aqueduct or passage across another's land,[104] not for the more abstract right to water use, for which there was recent authority stating that a parol licence acted upon by the licensee was irrevocable.[105]

Denman CJ (Littledale and Parke JJ concurring) held that P had an undoubted right to the surplus water left after D built the 1818 dam, where P had applied that water to his own mill:

> In any view of the law on this subject—whether the right to the use of flowing water be in the first occupant . . . or in the possessor of land through which it flows in its natural course . . . [P] was entitled to the surplus, for he filled both characters; he was the first occupant of it, and the owner and occupier of the land through which it flowed.

This left the question whether P could claim the full natural flow to his land, reversing D's appropriations under the 1818 licence, and also claim the water appropriated by D outside the licence. The water appropriated outside the licence was only later required for P's expanded milling operations.

The licence was held by the court to be revocable because it authorized appropriations only at a particular site, and D was claiming a right to abstract licensed water from any place on the river. Denman CJ's reasoning was scant on this issue, and did not explain why D's expenses in erecting a dam at the authorized place did not attract protection of his rights, following the principle of *Liggins* v. *Inge*.[106] D's plea of prior appropriation of all waters dammed up to 1829 was rejected on the unlikely ground that P's predecessor had already laid indefeasible title to the whole of the water flow by first use, notwithstanding that this usage, being agricultural, was partial and intermittent, had lapsed for ten years, and was not adverse, that is, D's appropriation had not interfered with P's needs during those ten years and no actual damage had been sustained in that time. Denman CJ recognized that his factual conclusions did not address any problems of doctrine, and so added a long disquisition on the general law of riparian titles, 'to settle the principle upon which rights of this nature depend'.

First, Denman CJ carefully set out the rival theories of water title so that a considered choice could be made between them. The natural-right theory was stated as follows:

[104] As in *Hewlins* v. *Shipham* (1826) 5 B. & C. 221; 108 E.R. 82 (K.B.); *Cocker* v. *Cowper* (1834) 1 C. M. & R. 418; 5 Tyrw. 103; 149 E.R. 1143 (Ex.).

[105] *Liggins* v. *Inge* (1831) 7 Bing. 682; 5 M. & D. 712; 131 E.R. 263 (Ex.); *Taylor* v. *Waters* (1816) 7 Taunton 374; 129 E.R. 150 (C.P.).

[106] (1831) 7 Bing. 682; 131 E.R. 263 (C.P.).

[T]he possessor of land, through which a natural stream runs, has a right to the advantage of that stream, flowing in its natural course, and to use it when he pleases, for any purposes of his own, not inconsistent with a similar right in the proprietors of the land above and below—that neither can any proprietor above diminish the quantity, or injure the quality of water, which would otherwise descend, nor can any proprietor below throw back the water without his licence or grant:—and that, whether the loss by diversion, of the general benefit of such a stream be or be not, such an injury in point of law, as to sustain an action without some special damage, yet, as soon as the proprietor of the land has applied it to some purpose of utility, or is prevented from so doing by the diversion, he has a right of action against the person diverting.[107]

Next, the prior appropriation theory was set out for comparison:

[T]he right to flowing water is publici juris, and . . . the first person who can get possession of the stream, and apply it to a useful purpose, has a good title to it against all the world, including the proprietor of the land below, who has no right of action against him, unless such proprietor has already applied the stream to some useful purpose also, with which the diversion interferes; and in default of his having done so, may altogether deprive him of the benefit of the water.[108]

Denman CJ adopted the natural-right theory more or less wholesale, justifying this both by legal precedent and by policy requirements. But first the extant prior appropriation theory had to be neutralized or assimilated:

The position that the first occupant of running water for a beneficial purpose has a good title to it, is perfectly true in this sense, that neither the owner of the land below can pen back the water, nor the owner of the land above divert it to his prejudice. In this, as in other cases of injury to real property, possession is a good title against a wrongdoer: and the owner of the land who applies the stream that runs through it, to the use of a mill newly erected, or other purposes, if the stream is diverted or obstructed, may recover for the consequential injury to the mill: *The Earl of Rutland* v. *Bowler*.

The principle that possession and use founded an action for damages wherever current use was denied did not exclude a natural right to water flow, a right existing independently of usage:

[I]t is a very different question whether [one] can take away from the owner of the land below, one of its natural advantages, which is capable of being applied to profitable purposes, and generally increases the fertility of the soil, even when unapplied; and deprive him of it altogether by anticipating him in its application to a useful purpose. If this be so, a considerable part of the value of an estate, which, in manufacturing districts particularly, is much enhanced by the existence of an unappropriated stream of water with a fall, within its limits, might at any time be taken away; and by parity of reasoning, a valuable mineral or brine spring might be abstracted from the proprietor in whose land it arises, and converted to the profit of another.[109]

[107] *Mason* v. *Hill* (1833) 5 B. & Ad. 1, 17; 110 E.R. 692, 698.
[108] Ibid. [109] 5 B. & Ad. 1, 18; 110 E.R. 692, 698–9.

Denman CJ then boldly asserted that none of the leading authorities for the prior appropriation theory permitted a first user of water to deprive other riparian owners of their continuing title to natural flow. Prior appropriation could create a more substantial title only in the sense that diversion or obstruction of natural flow by another would then be actionable as a wrong to present use, as well as an interference with prospective enjoyment of the natural property right. He held that from *Cox* v. *Matthews* onwards, the true principle was that natural user could be exceeded only by grant from neighbours, or else by prescription or user for a time sufficient to imply a grant. Lord Hale's judgment in *Cox* was interpreted as stating that a prescriptive use contrary to natural right was required as a defence to diversion of the stream from its customary course. Lord Ellenborough's decision in *Bealey* and Sir John Leach VC's 'luminous judgment' in *Wright* v. *Howard* were interpreted in similar vein.

How did Denman CJ face down the authorities directly supporting a theory of prior appropriation, whereby water titles arose through occupation of *res communes*? He stated that the doctrines presented in *Bealey* v. *Shaw*, *Saunders* v. *Newman*, *Williams* v. *Morland* (and in Blackstone's *Commentaries*) were open to varying interpretations in different situations of fact, and hence all were distinguishable as precedents:

None of these dicta, when properly understood with reference to the cases in which they were cited, and the original authorities in the Roman law, from which the position that water is *publici juris* is deduced, ought to be considered as authorities, that the first occupier or first person who chooses to appropriate a natural stream to a useful purpose has a title against the owner of the land below, and may deprive him of the benefit of the natural flow of the water.[110]

The Roman roots of the Blackstonian doctrine were then explored in order to discover its true meaning: common-law muddle was to be clarified and corrected with civilian learning. Beginning with Justinian's statement that 'the things which are naturally everybody's are air, flowing water, the sea, and the sea-shore', it was noted that Fleta omitted *aqua profluens* from his enumeration of the *res communes*, and that Vinnius in commenting on the Institutes distinguished between a river and its water, 'the former being . . . a perpetual body, and under the dominion of those in whose territories it is contained; the latter being continually changing, and incapable, whilst it is there, of becoming the subject of property, like the air and sea'.[111] Further, according to the Digest:

[110] 5 B. & Ad. 1, 23; 110 E.R. 692, 700.

[111] Arnold Vinnius (1588–1657), a Dutch civilian, published his commentary on the Institutes of Justinian (*Institutionum imperialium commentarius*) in Amsterdam in 1642; it became the established teaching text for Roman law in Europe: see P. G. Stein, 'The Fate of the Institutional System', in P. G. Stein, *The Character and Influence of the Roman Civil Law. Historical Essays*

[I]n public rivers, whether navigable or not, it appears that every one was forbidden to lower the water or narrow the course of the stream, or in any way alter it, to the prejudice of those who dwelt there.[112] [D.43.12. (Ulpian)] distinguishes between public and private rivers; and in [D.43.12.4. (Ulpian)] it is said, that private rivers in no way differ from any other private place. From these authorities, it seems that the Roman law considered running water, not as bonum vacans, in which any one might acquire a property; but as public or common, in this sense only, that all may drink it, or apply it, to the necessary purposes of supporting life; and that no one had any property in the water itself, except in that particular portion, which he might have abstracted from the stream, and of which he had the possession; and during the time of such possession only.

We think that no other interpretation ought to be put upon the passage in Blackstone, and that the dicta of the learned judges . . . in which water is said to be publici juris, are not to be understood in any other than this sense; and it appears to us there is no authority in our law, nor as far as we know, in the Roman law (which, however, is no authority in ours), that the first occupant (though he may be the proprietor of the land above) has any right, by diverting the stream, to deprive the owner of the land below, of the special benefit and advantage of the natural flow of water therein.[113]

On the crucial question whether injury to right *sine damno* could found an action, Denman CJ hesitated. 'Whether [P] could have maintained an action before he had constructed his mill, or applied the water of the stream to some profitable purpose, we need not decide'. Holt CJ's statement in *Palmer* v. *Keblethwaite*[114] that some use must be laid to bring action on the case for diversion of water was quoted; but this was contrasted with Pollexfen's argument in the same case that an action lay for diverting a stream, though no mill was erected.[115] The court in *Palmer* apparently accepted this argument, but '[t]he final result of that case does not appear in the books, and the roll has been searched in vain'. *Glynne* v. *Nichols* was seen to incline to a position that actionable diversion did not require interference with a present use. Denman CJ was therefore prepared to hold (*obiter*) that:

It must not . . . be considered as clear that an occupier of land may not recover for the loss of the general benefit of the water, without a special use or special damage shown.[116]

He then concluded for the court: 'Be that as it may, the plaintiff in this case, who has sustained actual damage, is entitled to . . . judgment.' Thus

(London, 1988) 73, 81. Lord Mansfield recommended Vinnius's work for beginners in civil law (C. H. S. Fifoot, *Lord Mansfield* (London, 1936) 29), and it is quoted *in extenso* in Denman CJ's judgment.

112 D.43.13. (Ulpian).

113 *Mason* v. *Hill* (1833) 5 B. & Ad. 1, 24–5; 110 E.R. 692, 701.

114 1 Show. K.B 64, 89 E.R. 451, see Ch. 3, the text accompanying nn. 90–92 above.

115 See Ch. 3, the text accompanying nn. 82–88 above.

116 *Mason* v. *Hill* (1833) 5 B. & Ad. 1, 27; 110 E.R. 692, 701 (K.B.).

for all Denman CJ's ambition to map out the law of riparian rights, he deliberately left unclear the role of damage in water actions—though some favour was given to the notion that injury to a right without interference with use was actionable, in order to maintain the stability of title to land and its appurtenances.

RIGHTS IN ARTIFICIAL WATERCOURSES

Investment in industrializing England in mines, water-powered industry, and waterways led to the construction of hundreds of miles of drains, mill-leats, canals, and other artificial watercourses. In these cases, natural-flow ideas were not readily available to describe the status of rights to water in the channel.[117] Sometimes the flow was a drain discharging water onto another's land; and the discharger might then wish to establish a right to continue that flow. Sometimes the flow of water was to the benefit of owners receiving the flow, as where the water ran pure from a spring or river; in that case the dischargee might wish to acquire a right to receive. The courts used doctrines of grant and prescription extensively to order rights in these various situations. For large-scale water works for canal transport and municipal supply, private-law mechanisms would be replaced by the private bill mechanism; but mill owners and other single riparian users did not avail themselves of such methods, but were more or less dependent on common-law entitlements and treaties with neighbours.

Arkwright v. *Gell*

This 1839 case[118] concerned artificial channels, but in making its decision the Court of Exchequer reinforced a more general division of water titles between absolute natural rights inherent in possession and constituted rights of grant. The court also stressed the evidential basis of prescriptive rights in factually-presumed grants or implied contractual consent, rather than rights derived directly from long enjoyment.

Arkwright v. *Gell* was stated as a special case where the bench sat as jury as well as court of law; the facts were therefore narrated at enormous length for the court record. According to the report, Sir Richard Arkwright, the pioneering industrialist, erected textile factories at Cromford in Derbyshire in 1772, locating these on the site of an ancient cornmill. The factories were powered by water from a small stream called Bonsall Brook, which was

[117] Cf. Roman and Bractonian doctrine of natural source, see Ch. 2, the text accompanying nn. 152–153 above.

[118] *Arkwright* v. *Gell* (1839) 5 M. & W. 203; 151 E.R. 87 (Ex).

partly fed with water from the Cromford Sough, an artificial drain leading water from a mineral field a small distance from the mills. The mill-site was held on long lease, and the terms of the lease took account of the artificial and precarious nature of the water supply, providing for re-location of the mills if the water supply was diminished. In 1789, Arkwright bought the freehold of the land on which his mills stood, and also the land through which the mine sough was laid, in order better to secure his water supply.[119] The owners of the mineral field had meanwhile opened a new drain for their mines, which diverted water from the Cromford Sough. By 1836 this drain was denying sufficient flow of water to the Bonsall Brook to disrupt Arkwright's manufacturing operations which depended on that water. Following negotiation, informal arrangements allocating the scarce water between the parties were tried, but failed. Arkwright's son, P, sued to maintain the customary water flow through the Cromford Sough, arguing that an enforceable title to the water arose first from his possession of the watercourse, and secondly from a presumption of grant derived from lengthy enjoyment of the Sough. In effect, this was a claim to a perpetual water supply from an artificial channel draining another's mine.

The statement of evidence also described the legal results of the Cromford Canal Acts of 1789–90.[120] At the time of the Act there was intense competition for water resources in the valley of the Derwent River. A canal company was seeking to abstract the waters of the Derwent under Parliamentary licence, using the water to feed navigations for the transport of coal and heavy goods. These developments were fiercely opposed by local mill owners and mine owners whose operations depended on the water. Joseph Strutt, Arkwright's first collaborator and a major textile industrialist himself at nearby Belper, wrote to his brother William on 28 July 1789:

> I thought it necessary to go to my father to talk with him about Belper Weir.[121] He thinks that if the [Cromford] Bill is likely to pass, such a clause should be introduced as will impower all the owners of weirs to raise them at particular seasons, making compensation for the injury that may be done and that this compensation the proprietors of the canal should defray.[122]

[119] See Ch. 1, the text accompanying nn. 90–100 above.

[120] 29 Geo. 3, c. 74, 30 Geo. 3, c. 56.

[121] This was the Strutts' vast reservoir powering their factory complex.

[122] *A Memoir of William Strutt*, quoted in R. S. Fitton and A. P. Wandsworth, *The Strutts and the Arkwrights, 1758–1830* (Manchester, 1958) 222–3. The indispensable guides to the private bills are: G. Bramwell, *An Analytical Table of the Private Statutes, 1727–1812* (London, 1813); T. Vardon, *Index to the Local and Personal and Private Acts 1798–1839* (London, 1840) and *An Index to the Statutes, Part II: The Local and Personal Acts, Local and Private Acts and Private Acts* (Select Committee of the Library of the House of Lords, London, 1867). See further Conclusion, the text accompanying nn. 64–66, below. Local and Personal Acts governing water resources are thick in the statute book throughout this era; for some late examples see 2 Geo. 4, c. 50 (a telling canal case granting a company legal powers to confiscate waters from riparian owners); and see also 2 Geo. 4, c. 51, 53, 55, 57.

Mill and land owners of the Derwent valley, fearing harm to their interests, issued petitions protesting against the Cromford Canal Bill's provisions legalizing takings of water from the Derwent river. One petition declared the mill owners' 'Dissent ... and their disapprobation of the said Project'; whilst another stated: 'That your Petitioners are well satisfied and convinced that their several Mills and other Works on the said River Derwent will be materially injured and affected if the said Bill passes into a Law in the present form ... '. The Lords are then asked 'to protect the said Property of your Petitioners from essential Injury'.[123] The issues were aired in the lengthy contested hearings before House of Lords committees. However, it was finally decided by Parliament that the benefits of cheaper transport and coal-based industry outweighed the losses inflicted on existing water users, and that legislation should be passed curtailing the riparian rights of property owners in favour of the Canal Company. The Acts set out a compromise granting water to the Company, whilst protecting the local mills and mines from water abstractions interfering with their operation. The Company was authorized to abstract a certain amount of Derwent water from its canal, and to make compulsory acquisitions of certain lands of the Arkwrights' that were necessary for construction of the navigation. The rights of local mine owners to water and drain their diggings were also guaranteed by the legislation. The Acts thereby attempted to strike a balance between the utilities of contending interests. Water rights were allocated in order to maximize the public interest, following a cost-benefit analysis of the relative worth of water resources to millers, miners, and canal companies, without restraint by requirements of due judicial process and compensation for existing private property rights.

Returning now to the case of *Arkwright* v. *Gell*, counsel justified Arkwright's entitlement to the drained mine waters by the following principle:

> [T]he general proposition of law is, that if a stream run through my land, the owner of adjoining land cannot use it for any purposes—whether for mining or quarrying, or otherwise,—so as to stop my enjoyment of it after twenty years' user. If by lapse of time I have acquired a right to water upon my land—whether it be a well or an open watercourse—no proprietor of adjoining land can use it to my detriment.

The case of *Balston* v. *Bensted* was cited to support the doctrine. In this action at Nisi Prius of 1808, a paper manufacturer sued to prevent diversion of water from a spring by a quarry owner, whose workmen had drained underground water and choked off the supply to the spring. For the quarry owner it was argued that:

[123] *House of Lords Petitions* (1789), LP 281/29 and 41 (H.L.R.O.). There were twelve subscribers to the first petition, only ten of whom could sign their names. See also Ch. 1, the text accompanying nn. 140–141 above.

the principle on which 20 years' enjoyment of running water confers a right to it, appeared from the cases to be, that after an adverse possession for so long a time, a grant was to be presumed from the owners of the land farther up the stream; and such a grant could not be presumed here, as, previously to the drain being made, probably no individual knew that [P's] spring was fed by water percolating through the strata in the close now occupied by [D].

Lord Ellenborough in that case replied:

that the only question was, whether the diminution of the supply of water [to the spring] had been caused by the drain dug by [D], and that there could be no doubt but that 20 years' exclusive enjoyment of water in any particular manner affords a conclusive presumption of right in the party so enjoying it.[124]

Arkwright's counsel argued that this statement should be taken as sound common-law principle; that recent decisions such as *Bealey* v. *Shaw* supported Lord Ellenborough's approach; and that the great point settled in *Mason* v. *Hill* was that 'a party through whose lands a stream had run for twenty years, although he had never appropriated it to any particular purpose, had a right of action against the owner of adjoining land who diverted it'. Parke B interjected at this point:

I think the case was not actually decided on that ground: the object of the judgment was to set right the mistaken notion which had got abroad in consequence of certain dicta in *Williams* v. *Morland* that flowing water is publici juris, and that the first occupant of it for a beneficial purpose may appropriate it.

Counsel responded that the *Mason* court had offered strong support to an absolute rule protecting rights to flow in any watercourse of twenty years' standing. The final case cited was *Birmingham Canal Company* v. *Lloyd*[125] where the Lord Chancellor had indicated that injunction might be made available where the draining of a mine prejudiced the use of a canal.

Apart from common-law rights, P pleaded a statutory right under Lord Tentedern's Act of 1832 (the Prescription Act 2 & 3 Will. 4 c.71). Section 2 of the Act states:

That no claim which may be lawfully made by any custom, prescription, or grant, to any watercourse, or the use of any water which shall have been actually enjoyed by any person claiming right thereto without interruption for the full period of twenty years, shall be defeated or destroyed by shewing only that such way was first enjoyed at any time prior to such period of twenty years, but nevertheless such claim may be defeated in any other way by which the same is now liable to be defeated; and when

[124] *Balston* v. *Bensted* (1808) 1 Camp N.P. 463, 465; 170 E.R. 1022, 1023 (N.P.).

[125] *Birmingham Canal Company* v. *Lloyd* (1812) 18 Ves. 515; 34 E.R. 413, 1220 (Ch.). Also relevant was *Bower* v. *Hill* (1835) 1 Bing. (N.C.) 549; 131 E.R. 1229 (C.P.) where Tindal CJ held that a canal owner could sue for interference with an artifical watercourse for navigation without a showing of damage, in order to prevent prescription; and to like effect was *Lord Falmouth* v. *Innys* (1729) Mosely 87, 25 E.R. 287 (Ch. L.C.).

such way shall have been so enjoyed for a full period of forty years, the right thereto shall be deemed absolute and indefeasible.

Counsel argued that this section vested title in watercourses directly, without resort to presumptions of grant, following an actual unbroken enjoyment for twenty years. It vested a possessory title which became real and indefeasible after forty years, notwithstanding proof of a recent actual commencement of the enjoyment or proof of absence of grant. The statutory form of prescription was said to replace the common-law presumption of modern grant; the statutory fiction buttressed P's claim in the instant case, as it was improbable that any mine owner would ever in fact have granted a right to another to the perpetual continuance of a flow of drain water. A final claim made for P was that the Acts of 1789–90 evidenced an agreement or consent that the Arkwrights' water supply would not be diverted by neighbours.

Counsel for D (Erle, later Chief Justice of the Common Pleas) gave two arguments against P's title to the artificial waters. First, a right to the flow of water to one's land did not mean a right to waters artificially discharged by the positive act of a neighbour:

The parties who had the easement to drain the mines, had for seventy or eighty years poured it out over his land; [P] had acquiesced in their doing so; but he had gained no right thereby. If poured over his land for twenty years, they would acquire thereby the right of continuing so to pour it, but [P] would acquire no right whatever.

Further, the principle that water titles arose from natural right with augmentation by grant or prescription, excluded title to artificial watercourses:

The old notion was, that running water was publici juris;... [this] was corrected in *Mason* v. *Hill*, in which all the authorities were examined: and the law is now established, that the flow of a natural stream belongs to him through whose land it goes by nature. The recent statute [2 & 3 Will.4 c.71] makes no difference: the title must still be derived out of such a user as, before the statute, would have led to the presumption of a grant. Such is the law as to the right to a natural stream, as contradistinguished from an artificial one. All the cases proceed upon the ground, that the first title to the water is 'donum naturae', and speak of a 'natural stream'—of the 'natural channel' of the water.... The title to water is therefore to be tried by ascertaining in the first place, where, by the laws of nature, it would flow; and, if a secondary title to it be claimed, whether there has been such a user of it, from which, before the stat[ute], a grant would have been presumed.

The user must have been as of right, 'not by stealth or permission, or in any way which which would negative a grant'.[126] To receive an artificial discharge

[126] *Partridge* v. *Scott* (1838) 3 M. & W. 220; 150 E.R. 1124 (Ex.); *Bright* v. *Walker* (1834) 1 C. M. & R. 211; 149 E.R. 1057 (Ex.); *Tickle* v. *Brown* (1836) 4 Ad. & E. 369; 111 E.R. 826 (K.B.); *Beasley* v. *Clarke* (1836) 2 Bing. N.C. 705; 132 E.R. 271 (C.P.); *Monmouthshire Canal Company* v. *Harford* (1834) 1 C. M. & R. 614; 149 E.R. 614 (Ex.).

of water from a neighbour is not to use that discharge as of right, nor to imply a grant.

Erle argued further that '[s]ubterraneous water, inaccessible to man, is not appropriated', in that no-one can control the use of such water without throwing an intolerable onus on neighbours to leave their land in its natural state. All previous cases concerned a natural surface flow; this case raised a new point uncontrolled by precedent, which should be decided on policy grounds.

This is a case where water percolates in various directions through many points into this sough. If the principle contended on the other side be tenable, the tapping of such water at any distance would be actionable; therefore the first person who were to sink a well, would acquire a right to all the water, to the exclusion of all the landowners whose waters drained towards his well, and who would be under the burthen of keeping their lands inundated to that height; and that, although they might have known nothing of the water percolating to the well, and if they had, could not stop the party from exercising his lawful right of digging in his own soil.... A party cannot, by an act of ownership in his land, deprive his neighbour of rights in his land, unless the facts raise the presumption of a grant. Here, no assent could exist on which a grant could be presumed. This is in truth a claim to stop all the mineral operations of the district, in order to keep up the plaintiff's mill.[127]

Abinger CB and the court found for D, more or less adopting Erle's novel arguments. The following principles were set out:

(1) The possessor of land adjoining a natural water course has a right to the advantage of its natural flow; but there is no such right of user in an artificial watercourse. In the present case:

This was an artificial watercourse, and the sole object for which it was made, was to get rid of a nuisance to the mines, and to enable their proprietors to get the ores which lay within the mineral field drained by it: and the flow of water through that channel was, from the very nature of the case, of a temporary character, having its continuance only whilst the convenience of the mine-owners required it, and... would, most probably, cease when the mineral ore above its level should have been exhausted.

(2) A user for twenty years or more operated at common law to raise a presumption of grant. To make the presumption, an actual grant had to be factually possible in the circumstances. It was impossible, however, to expect that any owner would burden his land with a servitude to maintain an artificial stream of water onto a neighbour's land. For a mine owner so to bind himself would be to destroy his ability to exploit his mine effectively. Acquiescence in another's user of an artificial watercourse could not betoken consent to a grant of perpetual right to the water, for there was no convenient way to prevent or protest that user.

[127] *Arkwright* v. *Gell* (1839) 5 M. & W. 203, 222–6; 151 E.R. 87, 94–6.

(3) The 1832 Prescription Act required enjoyment of a watercourse for a specific period 'without interruption', where the right was of a type which could have been acquired by long user at common law before the Act. This meant that the user had to be 'of right', exercised against some one 'capable of resisting the claim'. For the reasons set out above, a right to artificial water could not be exercised as of right: dissent by the owner of the servient tenement could not readily be shown, and so acquiescence was inadequate as a token of consent.[128]

In the present case, D's draining of mine water was held to be temporary only, being wholly a convenience of day-to-day mining operations. P was well aware, from the terms of the lease and the private legislation, that his enjoyment of the water was precarious. P's user therefore could not be said to be an exercise of right against an acquiescing owner, and hence no right by grant or prescription could arise either at common law or statute.

The doctrine developed in *Arkwright* strongly departed from any concept of occupancy or appropriation as a sufficient ground of title. Rights arising from user through prescription were now tied to factual presumption of grantor's intention, rather than the possessive intentions of the appropriator.

Magor v. *Chadwick*

In 1840 the Court of Queen's Bench reviewed again the nature of the presumed intention to grant rights in an artificial channel in the case of *Magor* v. *Chadwick*.[129] The facts were that an adit was built to drain a copper-mine in Cornwall. Eventually the mine was closed and the adit began to run with pure water. P then built a brewery nearby at a considerable investment, taking advantage of this pure water source. After more than twenty years' enjoyment of the water by P, D opened some mines nearby and used the old adit for disposing of ore-waste, thereby fouling the water and rendering it unfit for P's use. P brought an action on the case, declaring on his possession of land adjoining the adit and also on his enjoyment of the water for the period of prescription.

It was contended for P that there was no relevant distinction between an artificial and natural watercourse; *Arkwright* turned on its particular facts and did not declare a principle governing the present case. Against this, D argued that *Arkwright* did negate the possibility of title to waters in an artificial channel; and D further pleaded an old Cornish custom that adits should always keep their character as drains for mining operations.

[128] See also *Rolle* v. *Whyte* (1868) L.R. 3 Q.B. 286 (Q.B.); *Bradford Corporation* v. *Ferrand* (*No. 2*) [1902] 2 Ch. 655 (Ch.).

[129] (1840) 11 Ad. & E. 572; 113 E.R. 532 (Q.B.).

Counsel for P distinguished away *Arkwright* as a finding that the maker of an artificial watercourse is unlikely to intend to guarantee a source of water to his neighbours; hence no presumption of grant can generally be made arising from long use of such a channel. That left two unresolved issues. First, was the *Arkwright* court laying down a general rule of law distinguishing natural from artificial channels? Or was the court merely making a finding of fact, or perhaps erecting a presumption of evidence, that an artificial sough is usually created subject to closing or diversion? The second related issue was whether modern prescription operated through some evidential presumption of grant requiring a factual possibility of consent; or whether twenty years' user now supplied a conclusive (fictitious) presumption of right, wholly independent of implied (actual) consent.

On the first point, counsel for P argued:

> The distinction between natural and artificial water-courses ... has no foundation. The stream, when discharged from the adit's mouth, pursues its natural course. The flow of all waters, when made through channels made by art, is itself natural.... The 'sole object' of [a] gutter and ditch is to 'get rid of the nuisance;' yet the right to the water, when appropriated for a sufficient time by the owner of the meadow or mill [receiving the flow], is undeniable. A leat, cut artificially to supply a mill by waters which afterwards turn another mill or water a close below, cannot be so altered, after long user, as to injure them. A window, though wholly artificial, may nevertheless gain for the owner of the house a right to the uninterrupted flow of light and air.[130]

As to the second point regarding the nature of presumptions, it was argued that under the modern common law of prescription, proof of the impossibility of grant at some time before the prescriptive period was no longer a bar: 'Where ... prescriptive existence [of a right of this kind] could be disproved, and no grant could be shewn, a series of decisions established the rule that an unexplained user for twenty years was conclusive evidence of a grant.' It was conceded that when the adit was built fifty years ago, the water then discharged was unfit for brewing, and that no grant of use could plausibly be claimed at that time or later. However, modern prescription was based on conclusive presumptions, and did not involve a search for rebuttable evidence of grants. Thus the *Arkwright* court was pursuing the wrong path when it stated that the mine owners 'could not have meant to burthen themselves with such a servitude, so destructive to their interests':

> But the Court cannot speculate on the probability of the case, or the actual intention of parties who permit the enjoyment. In *Eldridge* v. *Knott*[131] Lord Mansfield says that grants are presumed 'not that the Court really thinks a grant has been made,' which may be very improbable, but 'from a principle of quieting the possession.'[132]

[130] 11 Ad. & E. 572, 575–6; 113 E.R. 532, 534.
[131] *Eldridge* v. *Knott* (1774) 1 Cowp. 214; 98 E.R. 1050 (K.B.).
[132] *Magor* v. *Chadwick* (1840) 11 Ad. & E. 572, 576; 113 E.R. 532, 534.

The irrelevance of actual intentions undercut the argument that no prescription can arise where a party sends an artificial stream onto another's land, because the first party cannot reasonably or conveniently signal an intention that the recipient not commence a long and continuous user. For example, 'a right to unobstructed light is often only to be prevented by expensive erections', yet long enjoyment of window light does grow into a right:

> Whether the expense and trouble of interrupting a growing right be great or small, cannot be taken into consideration. It would destroy the simplicity of the legal rule, and be at variance with first principles.[133]

Finally the effect of the Prescription Act 1832 was discussed. The *Arkwright* court's interpretation was 'that the Act applies only to cases where a grant would before have been presumed'. Counsel continued:

> The preamble [to that Act] shows, however, that the object was to shorten the period of legal prescription, and to make it unnecessary to go back to the reign of Richard I. Twenty years' user was before only evidence: *Rex* v. *Joliffe*,[134] *Jenkins* v. *Harvey*.[135] It is now a title in itself, and after forty years an indefeasible one, unless a written origin be shewn for it. The necessity for resorting to the fiction of grant is at an end; and all enquiry about the probability of one is superfluous and irrelevant. It has been suggested that the use of water cannot be 'of right' if it be not the subject of an action, nor capable of interruption 'by any reasonable mode'.[136] But rights may be gained by acts which are perfectly legal, as by opening a window; and it is difficult to conceive a right incapable of interruption. The reasonableness of the means of interruption cannot be taken into consideration. The words 'of right' mean proprio vigore, without leave or licence, or any payment or acknowledgment of an adverse title.... The statute operates where no valid grant could before have been presumed.... It is fallacious to assume that the Legislature has interposed its protection in aid only of titles presumably good in their origin. It rather supplies a title which would clearly be wanting without it. This is the object of all Statutes of Limitations, which would be defeated if the doctrine of presumed intention were to be admitted.[137]

Counsel for D opposed these arguments with a prior appropriation theory meaning that D's first user of the adit was protected. Next, the unreasonableness of requiring an owner to continue draining water through an artificial channel was stressed: '[c]an one, who has been obliged to drain his land for twenty years, be compelled to continue draining it forever?' Such a ruling would render land unprofitable by freezing its mode of user. The patent unreasonableness of enforcing a pure discharge from the adit showed that

[133] 11 Ad. & E. 572, 577; 113 E.R. 532, 535.
[134] (1823) 2 B. & C. 54; 107 E.R. 303 (K.B.); and see the text accompanying n. 24 above.
[135] (1835) 2 C. M. & R. 393; 150 E.R. 169 (Ex.).
[136] Referring to D.8.1.15. (Pomponius).
[137] *Magor* v. *Chadwick* (1840) 11 Ad. & E. 572, 578–9; 113 E.R. 532, 535–6.

there was never any intention that the adit be continued as permanent by the owner of the mine. Moreover, such an extraordinary purpose would have been known to P, negativing both any possible intention to grant such a right to D or to acquiescence in D's enjoyment as of right. This negativing of intention excluded prescription, both at common law and statute, for '[t]hough a presumed grant is dispensed with by the statute, the right must be one capable of originating in a grant: mere user of that which is no longer under my control will establish no easement against me'. *Arkwright* was directly in point, both in fact and law. Further, section 2 of the Prescription Act 1832 stated that the circumstances of a user and enjoyment can be shown to negative user as of right; the present case fell within such a category. Rights to light and air from an artificial opening were not comparable, as the servient owner in such cases need perform no positive act in order to create or continue the right.

In the result, Denman CJ and the court upheld P's right to the water, finding that D had failed sufficiently to declare the existence of a local custom in Cornwall, nor had he proved the custom as a question of fact. Therefore custom could not be employed to establish that enjoyment of the water by P had not been as of right. On these confined pleading points the decision was rested. The court declined to address the broader questions of law raised so ably in argument, stating only the following limited conclusions:

> We are by no means prepared to say that the circumstances under which a water-course has been enjoyed may not prove it to have been without right; or that a universal practice in the neighbourhood might not lead to fix the party with knowledge that those who cleared a mine by an adit notoriously reserved to themselves the right of working the mine at any time....
>
> The imputed misdirection is, that the law of water-courses is the same, whether natural or artificial.... [T]his was no misdirection, but clearly right. The contrary proposition, that a water-course, of whatever antiquity, and in whatever degree enjoyed by numerous persons, cannot be so enjoyed as to confer a right to the use of the water, if proved to have been originally artificial, seems to us quite indefensible.... [*Arkwright*] leads to no such conclusion.[138]

Wood v. *Waud*

In the 1849 case of *Wood* v. *Waud* the Court of Exchequer propounded a new doctrine of artificial watercourses, whereby the intentions of the maker of a channel determined whether others could acquire use-rights by occupancy or long enjoyment of the water. In *Wood* v. *Waud*,[139] as in *Arkwright* v. *Gell*, P enjoyed a long use of water through an artificial watercourse draining a

[138] 11 Ad. & E. 572, 585–6; 113 E.R. 532, 538.
[139] (1849) 3 Exch. 748; 154 E.R. 1047 (Ex.).

colliery. The flow was then diverted, not by the colliery owner who built the drain, but by an upstream mill owner. It was agreed that no right by grant or prescription arose against the colliery owner; the question was whether a proprietary right in the water could be asserted against other neighbours. The court decided not to allow such a right:

> [N]o action lay for an injury by the diversion of an artificial watercourse, where, from the nature of the case, it was obvious that the enjoyment of it depended upon temporary circumstances, and was not of a permanent character; and where the interruption was by the party who stood in the situation of the grantor.

Magor v. *Chadwick* was distinguished as dealing not with the diversion but the fouling of a watercourse, an anti-social act with qualities of public nuisance, which was presumptively prohibited in every case of watercourse or reservoir.[140] But diversion of artificially conducted water was governed by a different rule:

> The right to artificial watercourses, as against the party creating them, surely must depend upon the character of the watercourse, whether it be of a permanent or temporary nature, and upon the circumstances under which it was created. The enjoyment for twenty years of a stream diverted or penned up by permanent embankments clearly stands upon a different footing from the enjoyment of a flow of water originating in the mode of occupation or alteration of a person's property, and presumably of a temporary character and liable to variation.[141]

The presumed state of mind of the owner creating the watercourse was paramount: did he intend to create a channel forming a permanent part of the land? Only then could his tenement be burdened with an obligation to supply water to other tenements as if the channel were a natural watercourse. This doctrine of presumptive intention was illustrated as follows:

> The flow of water for twenty years from the eaves of a house could not give a right to the neighbour to insist that the house should not be pulled down or altered, so as to diminish the quantity of water flowing from the roof. The flow of water from a drain for the purposes of agricultural improvements for twenty years could not give a right to the neighbour so as to preclude the proprietor from altering the level of his drains for the greater improvement of the land.[142] The state of circumstances in such cases shows that one party never intended to give, nor the other to enjoy, the use of the stream as a matter of right.[143]

[140] See *Carlyon* v. *Lovering* (1857) 1 H. & N. 784; 156 E.R. 1417 (Ex.), the text accompanying nn. 150–158 below.

[141] *Wood* v. *Waud* (1849) 3 Exch. 748, 777–8; 154 E.R. 1047, 1059.

[142] For this very example see *Greatrex* v. *Howard* (1853) 8 Ex. 291; 155 E.R. 1357 (Ex.); see also *Murgatroyd* v. *Robinson* (1857) 26 L.J. Q.B. 233 (Q.B.).

[143] *Wood* v. *Waud* (1849) 3 Ex. 748, 778; 154 E.R. 1047, 1059. Cf. *Baily & Co.* v. *Clark Son & Morland* [1902] 1 Ch. 649 (Ch.); *West Riding of Yorkshire Rivers Board* v. *Reuben Grant and Sons Ltd* (1903) 67 J.P. 183.

A distinction was drawn between interferences by acts affecting the stream while it flowed over one's land; and interferences with the sources of the stream from outside one's land. The court elaborated:

It appears to us to be clear, that, as [the plaintiffs] have a right to the... natural stream... as incident to their property on the banks and bed of it, they would have the right to all the water which actually formed part of the stream, as soon as it had become part, whether such water came by natural means, as from springs, or from the surface of the hills above, or from rain or melted snow, or was added by artificial means, as from the drainage of lands or of colliery works; and if the proprietors of the drained lands or of the colliery augmented the stream by pouring water into it, and so gave it to the stream, it would become part of the current; no distinction could then be made between the original natural stream and such accessions to it.[144]

This rule can be seen as a protection of land from trespass by direct interference with the appurtenances of possession. But interferences with non-natural water sources by acts outside a person's lands need not attract protection, because the analogy with direct trespass was absent:

[W]ith respect to an artificial stream not yet united to the natural one... [t]he proprietor of the land through which [such a natural stream] flows has no right to insist on the colliery owners causing all the waters from their works to flow through their land. The owners merely get rid of a nuisance to their works by discharging the waters into the [artificial] sough, and cannot be considered as giving it to one more than another of the proprietors of the land through which that sough is constructed; each may take and use what passes through his land, and the proprietor of land below has no right to any part of that water until it has reached his own land: he has no right to compel the owners above to permit the water to flow through their lands for his benefit; and, consequently, he has no right of action if they refuse to do so. If they pollute the water, so as to be injurious to the tenant below, the case would be different.[145]

Artificial Conduits and Artificially Obtained Water

In the 1856 Queen's Bench case of *Beeston* v. *Weate*[146] a distinction was drawn between rights to artificially obtained water (such as water drained from a mine), and water from a natural stream obtained by diversion through a man-made conduit, in which latter case user-rights could more readily be ascribed.

The facts were that for more than forty years, and as far back as living memory extended, P had regularly entered D's neighbouring land, in order to divert water into an old artificial channel by damming and diverting a natural stream or brook running through D's land. The water was used to supply P's cattle with water whenever required, excepting those times when D

[144] 3 Exch. 748, 779; 154 E.R. 1047, 1060.
[145] 3 Exch. 748, 779; 154 E.R. 1047, 1060.
[146] (1856) 25 L.J.Q.B. 115; 5 E. & B. 986; 119 E.R. 748 (Q.B.).

needed the water for irrigation and the level fell too low for P to divert it. P conveyed the water after use back to the natural brook. D eventually pulled down P's dam and refused him access to the stream. P asserted a prescriptive right to take the water, arguing that according to the criteria laid down by recent case law, a right could be acquired in an artificial stream where the circumstances of long user and acquiescence implied a grant.

The court found for P on grounds that the law now permitted prescriptive rights to arise in artificial watercourses. Prior cases had excluded such rights only as a determination of particular fact; to exclude rights in all artificial watercourses as a general doctrine 'would destroy the right to the great majority of mill leats all over the kingdom':

> for the water invariably runs through them in an artificial cut from the weir across the natural current of the river where they begin, till the water is restored to the natural current of the river: and it very frequently happens that in part the soil belongs, not to the owner of the mill, but to a stranger. Nevertheless, if the water has flowed immemorially, or for a considerable period of time, from the river through the leat, to turn the mill, and the owner of the mill has been in the habit of going on the soil of another to clean out the leat and to repair its banks, we conceive that the right to do so might be established, and that an obstruction to the flow of water through the mill leat would be actionable. In the [earlier] cases... regard was had to the water being obtained artificially by the owner of the servient tenement, rather than to the water running through an artificial cut. Here the water in question is part of the water of a stream which has flowed on the surface of the country from the time that our globe took its present configuration. But the strength of [P's] case (distinguishing it from [prior] cases)... is that here the occupier of the dominant tenement, for the purposes of letting in the water from the natural current of the river into the artificial cut, and from the artificial cut into his pond [for watering his cattle], was constantly going upon the servient tenement, with notice to the occupier of the servient tenement, and doing acts which, without the easement, would be trespasses. Such has been the practice as far back as living memory goes, and may have been the practice from time immemorial....
>
> Great stress was laid by [D] on the often repeated assertion that the artificial cut was made for a temporary purpose. The water flowing through the cut has, as far back as living memory goes, and probably much longer, been constantly applied to two purposes... irrigation... and the watering of the cattle pasturing on [P's] meadow.... These purposes cannot be considered temporary in their nature, although there is no certainty that the meadows may not at some remote time become the sites of streets or squares in a town. [D] argued strongly against the probability of such a grant, whereby the owner of the servient tenement would have deprived himself of the power of converting it to any purpose inconsistent with the easement granted. But it is part of the generally fictitious supposition of a grant, that it proceeds upon an adequate consideration.[147]

[147] 5 E. & B. 986, 996–8; 119 E.R. 748, 753–4. See also *Ennor* v. *Barwell* (1860) 2 Giff. 410; 66 E.R. 171 (V.C.).

This argument inverted the doctrine that an easement carries with it appurtenant rights of access and repair in order to give effect to the easement. Here P was presumed to have a right of aqueduct because of D's long acquiescence in P's exercise of the subsidiary rights of way and repair, for these apparent easements evidenced the larger water right. Long user with acquiescence was now clearly emerging in the law as a direct source of prescriptive right, with presumed grant characterized as a wholly instrumental fiction. The common law was thus moving towards a similar position to that of the Prescription Act 1832.[148] Finally, it may be noted that there is no advertence to the Roman and Bractonian idea that servitudes can only inhere in permanent natural sources of water.[149]

Local Custom and Rights in Artificial Channels

Two Exchequer cases of 1857 elaborated the common-law doctrine dealing with the right to pure water, and the interaction between mining rights, local custom, and prescriptive rights in watercourses.

In *Carlyon* v. *Lovering*[150] D was possessed of a tin-mine upstream from P's land, and claimed a right to wash ore and discharge refuse from the mine by means of the stream. This mode of using the stream was claimed to have existed either for twenty or forty years, invoking the statutory form of prescription under Lord Tenterden's Act. Suing against D's pollution of the stream, P 'contended that such a privilege could not be the subject matter of grant, inasmuch excessive user might injure [P's] property to such an extent as to exclude [P] from the entire enjoyment of his land'. According to the court, 'the question is, whether such privilege . . . could be the subject matter of a grant, for if it could not, the pleas would not be supported'.[151] The issue was whether a practice of fouling water was so destructive of a neighbour's interest in land as to amount to a surrender of possessory rights, a practice so unreasonable that it could not have been the subject of voluntary grant. If the Prescription Act 1832 operated with a conclusive and fictitious presumption of grant as the basis of prescriptive rights, then the reasonableness test for prescriptions might fall away, such that impossibility or improbability of actual grant would no longer be a bar to finding prescriptive rights.[152]

[148] See also *Rameshur Pershad Narain Singh* v. *Koonj Behari Pattuk* (1878) 4 App. Cas. 121, 126 (P.C.) per Sir Montague Smith.

[149] See Ch. 2, the text accompanying n. 153 above.

[150] (1857) 1 H. & N. 784; 156 E.R. 1417 (Ex.).

[151] 1 H. & N. 784, 797–8; 156 E.R. 1417, 1423–4, citing *Rochdale Canal Co.* v. *Radcliffe* (1852) 18 Q.B. 287; 118 E.R. 108 (Q.B.); *Mill* v. *Commissioners of New Forest* (1856) 18 C.B. 69; 139 E.R. 1286 (C.P.).

[152] See also *Wright* v. *Williams* (1836) 1 M. & W. 77; 150 E.R. 353 (Exch.), where forty years' acquiescence in discharge of a watercourse polluted with heavy metals could amount to tacit consent to the discharge as an easement.

Watson B for the court proposed the following doctrine:

The plaintiff, as a riparian proprietor, has a right to have the water of this natural stream run through his land in its accustomed purity, without being polluted by any riparian proprietors or others higher up the stream, but that right he may abandon by allowing an user to have continued for twenty or forty years; or he may grant the privileges to an owner higher up the stream, for his advantage, of invading that right to the detriment of the water flowing through the plaintiff's lands. We can see no reason why such a privilege, although injurious to [P] to a great extent, might not be granted.[153]

The test for unreasonableness of prescriptions was the same as that for custom, namely 'these pleas are good if the claim could be the subject matter of a valid grant, without reference to prescription or custom'. The doctrine that grants cannot be presumed which entirely destroy the grantor's interest was accepted, according to the dictum that:

a claim destructive of the subject matter of the grant cannot be set up by any. Even if the grant could be produced in specie, reserving a right in the lord to deprive his grantee of the enjoyment of the thing granted, such a clause must be rejected as repugnant and absurd.[154]

However, polluting a stream of water was no destruction of P's property interest, even if it detracted from enjoyment of his land; a right to pollute was not comparable, for example, to a claim of right to strip land for minerals which could not reasonably be the subject of presumed grant.[155] Reasonableness standards inherent in the implication of grants therefore survived the reformation of prescription by the Act. In the instant case D's interferences with water enjoyment were found to be unreasonable, and hence not capable of prescription.

D pleaded additionally a right to foul the water based on local mining custom. The court stated:

It is settled that a custom to be valid in law must be reasonable, certain and defined. It was objected that the custom as pleaded in the present case was unreasonable and indefinite, as the exercise of the custom might go to the destruction of [P's] land adjoining the stream; that there was no limit to the user as to times of user or extent of user.[156]

The court held that the custom was not unreasonable; it was beneficial and necessary for mining in the area; and the damage to P was tolerable in light of

[153] 1 H. & N. 784, 798; 156 E.R. 1417, 1423, following *Wright* v. *Williams* (1836) 1 M. & W. 77; 150 E.R. 353 (Exch.).

[154] *Hilton* v. *Lord Greville* (1845) 5 Q.B. 701; 114 E.R. 1414 (Q.B.); and see also *Clayton* v. *Corby* (1843) 5 Q.B. 415; 114 E.R. 1306 (Q.B.).

[155] See also *Cator* v. *Board of Works of Lewisham* (1864) 5 B. & S. 115; 122 E.R. 775 (Q.B.); *Goldsmid* v. *Tunbridge Wells Commissioners* (1865) L.R. 1 Ch. 161 (M.R.); (1866) 1 Ch. Ap. 349 (Ch. Ap.); *Attorney-General* v. *Halifax* (1969) 39 L.J. Ch. 129.

[156] *Carlyon* v. *Lovering* (1857) 1 H. & N. 784, 800; 156 E.R. 1417, 1423.

the benefits to all. This finding involved an openly utilitarian balancing of the parties' rights and interests:

> The exercise of the privilege as claimed, was in respect of working a mine and winning the ore where the stream passed through the defendant's land. Thus the user is limited to the necessary working of the mine[157] ... [This custom] is not to take the land or any part of it, but merely to pollute the water of this stream in the course of working the mine. We do not see that this has a tendency to destroy [P's] land or exclude [P] from the user of his land, except to a partial extent. We think that the custom alleged is sufficiently definite and is not unreasonable.[158]

By this approach, the old common-law reasonableness test for customs and prescriptions was read down to vanishing point, as only a complete expropriation of user-rights of others could amount to an unreasonable claim.

In *Whaley* v. *Laing*,[159] the other 1857 Exchequer case, a coal-mine owner at Wigan suffered damage when a chemical works opened upstream, polluting the water with which he worked his mine engines. P declared that he was possessed of a coal mine with machinery; that he used and enjoyed the benefit of clear canal water to work the machinery; and that this water 'had been used, and then ought, to have run and flowed, and been without disturbance, fouling and pollution'. No right to receive the flow of water as riparian owner was claimed, only a right to have the waters come without fouling. Parke B summarized the material facts as follows:

> [P], by permission of a canal company, made a communication from the canal to his own premises, by which water got to those premises, and with which water he fed his boilers.... [D] fouled the water in the canal, whereby the water as it came into [P's] premises was fouled, and by the use of it [P's] boilers were injured; [D] having no right or permission to do this from the canal owners.[160]

D's defence was that P's injury was self-inflicted, as he had poured the fouled water into engines by his own act; and also that P had only a permissive licence to take water from the canal as an artificial watercourse, giving him no right to the water, pure or impure, which could bind either the canal company or any third person.[161] The defence claims were illustrated by analogy with rights in a bailed chattel:

[157] *Wilkes* v. *Broadbent* (1744) 1 Wils. K.B. 63; 95 E.R. 494 (K.B.).

[158] *Carlyon* v. *Lovering* 1 H. & N. 784, 800; 156 E.R. 1417, 1423–4. See also *Wood* v. *Sutcliffe* (1852) 2 Sim. (N.S.) 163; 61 E.R. 303 (V.C.); *Moore* v. *Webb* (1857) 1 C.B.N.S. 673; 140 E.R. 277 (C.P.); *Murgatroyd* v. *Robinson* (1857) 26 L.J. Q.B. 233; 7 El. & Bl. 391; 119 E.R. 1292 (Q.B.); *Crossley* v. *Lightowler* (1866) L.R. 3 Eq. 279 (Ch.); (1867) L.R. 2 Ch. App. 478 (V.C.); *Baxendale* v. *McMurray* (1867) L.R. 2 Ch. 790.

[159] (1857) 2 H. & N. 476; 157 E.R. 196 (Ex.); (1858) 3 H. & N. 675, 901; 157 E.R. 639, 733 (Ex. Ch.); (1860) 5 H. & N. 480; 157 E.R. 1269 (costs only).

[160] 2 H. & N. 476, 485; 157 E.R. 196, 200.

[161] *Arkwright* v. *Gell* (1839) 5 M. & W. 203; 151 E.R. 87 (Ex.), the text accompanying nn. 118–128 above, was cited as authority.

Mere possession of a chattel is sufficient to enable a bailee to maintain an action against a wrongdoer, for whilst he has possession of the chattel, his title is as complete as that of the real owner. But in order to bring the case of water within that principle, it ought to appear that the water, which is the subject-matter of complaint, is the identical water which the owner allowed the party complaining to take. The right of a riparian owner is not a possessory right until he has appropriated the water.... The fouling of the water was not wrong as against [P]; for they had no title to the water at the time it was fouled; and the allowing foul water to flow into their pit was their own act.... A person seeking to recover damages must shew that he has a legal right; but here [P] had no right to the water until they took it, and before they did so the water was fouled. It is the same as if [P] had fetched the foul water from the canal in a bucket and put it in their cistern.[162]

The court rejected these arguments and held for P. Bramwell B held that D's responsibility for acts of pollution causing the damage was not overtaken by the minor intervening cause of P drawing water into his cistern for use by his machinery. Further, D had not denied fouling the water, nor questioned the amount of damage, but had simply traversed P's declaration, 'viz. that the water "ought to flow without being fouled in the canal"'. This pleading was taken to mean, 'not an assertion of title in the plaintiff, but that the defendant had no right to foul the water there'. No opinion was given as to whether P had a possessory title to water in the canal, or whether D could stop its flow to P, or whether P would have had an action if the fouled water had been abstracted by a bucket or engine rather than by allowing it to flow into a cistern:

Our opinion proceeds... on the ground that [D] caused foul water to flow on to [P's] premises without right to do so. And this opinion is warranted by the cases cited, which shew that though there may be no right to water, there may be a right, if it comes or is sent, to have it come or sent without pollution.[163]

The gist of the doctrine was given by Martin B in argument: 'If a person allows his neighbour to water his cattle in his pond, and a third person poisons the water whereby the cattle die, would he not be responsible?'[164]

The decision was taken on error to the Exchequer Chamber, where the judges decided by four to two to arrest the judgment of the Court of Exchequer. Three judges found for P on the substantive issue of law and three against; only two of the six judges held that P's declaration of fact sufficiently disclosed a cause of action. Crowder J held that P's declaration of a rightful or permitted enjoyment (rather than possession) of the water founded a right to pure water:

[162] *Whaley* v. *Laing* (1857) 2 H. & N. 476, 483–4; 157 E.R. 196, 200.
[163] 2 H. & N. 476, 486; 157 E.R. 196, 200–1.
[164] 2 H. & N. 476, 483–4; 157 E.R. 196, 200.

[I]t sufficiently appears that [P] were in lawful enjoyment of a beneficial flow of clear water from the branch canal, and that [D] wrongfully polluted the stream, and thereby damaged [P], which appears to me a sufficient statement of a good cause of action.[165]

Willes J concurred in Bramwell B's judgment, adding that P was 'in possession of the water and [D] was a wrongdoer'. This went a little further than the lower court, being a finding that P had an actionable possessory right to the water, in addition to his right not to suffer a nuisance by pollution.

Williams J agreed that as a question of law the correct form of action was an 'allegation that the waters ought to have been free from pollution, viz., that it means not an assertion of title in [P], but that [D] had no right to foul the waters'. But P's declaration had not alleged how he was 'rightfully in enjoyment of the benefit of the waters'; there was nothing to show that P was not a wrongdoer in taking the water for working his engines, and rightful enjoyment could not be presumed, in contrast to the assumption of rightful possession in ordinary trespass and actions on the case. P had thus failed to plead all necessary elements of his action, even if a substantial right may otherwise have existed to take water free of pollution.

Crompton J, with Erle J's concurrence, held that there could be no action defending the pure quality of a water flow without declaring a substantial possessory right to the water; and rightful enjoyment alone was inadequate to establish such right:

[T]his declaration . . . can only be supported on the ground of its claiming a right to the water for the supply of, or by reason of the possession of, the works in question. It states the possession of the mines and works and the use of the water for the supply of the works; and then avers that the water ought to flow unpolluted, and that [D] polluted it near to the place from which the supply was drawn, The word ought seems to me to import an allegation of right; and I think that the allegation that the water ought to flow unpolluted, in order to support the declaration after verdict, must be taken as meaning that the water ought to flow to the place in question, and ought to flow there unpolluted.

The added requirement that P prove 'the existence of the right to the flow of the unpolluted water' excluded P's action. Crompton J went on to analyse the right to freedom from pollution, not in terms of property rights to purity of resources, involving strict liability for damage, but rather as a case of fault liability in tort. He took Martin B's example of the watering of cattle as his text:[166]

Where a man has the permission of the owner of a pond to get water from it for his cattle, and a defendant, knowing of such permission and knowing the probable and

[165] (1858) 3 H. & N. 675, 680; 157 E.R. 639, 641 (Ex. Ch.).
[166] (1858) 3 H. & N. 675, 681; 157 E.R. 639, 642 (Ex. Ch.).

natural effect and consequence of his act, poisons the water of such pond so as that the cattle are injured, probably an action would lie. Such an action is founded, not on the title or right to the water, but on the injury to the property of the plaintiff.

In the present case P had made only:

an informal declaration of the usual kind of declarations for an injury to a right of water connected with a mill or other works.... [A]nd in such a case a right must... be proved, according to the rule laid down in the note (*c*) to *Coryton* v. *Lithebye*[167] and the case of *Fentiman* v. *Smith*.[168]

That rule required that the right to water or way be declared as appurtenant or appendant to a possession; and P had not shown any deed, licence, or other evidence of possessory right in the canal or cistern sufficient to establish rights to the flow of water. Hence there could be no actionable injury to P's property or possession by fouling of the water:

It was said that [D] had rights as riparian proprietors on an artificial watercourse; but they were not the owners or occupiers of the soil on the banks, nor was the canal from its nature a watercourse in which persons having adjoining land would generally have riparian rights; and there was nothing to shew the existence of such rights in this particular case.[169]

Wightman J argued that in the absence of natural or possessory riparian rights, it was as easily said that D had a right to pollute as that P had a right to no pollution—an adumbration of twentieth-century economic analysis of pollution rights.[170] He stated:

The plaintiffs allege no right whatever to take the water of the canal; they merely say that they had used and enjoyed the benefit of the water. They do not state how long they have used it, nor how long they have had the coal mines, nor that they had or used the benefit of the water of the canal by reason of their possession of the coal mines; and though they say that the water used and ought to run and flow without being polluted, they do not allege any reason why it ought to run and flow without being polluted, or that the defendant as against them had not as much right to pollute it for his purposes, as they had to take it for theirs. The allegation traversed, that the water ought to flow without being fouled or polluted, does not amount... to any assertion of right in [P]; but if it did, [then] upon the facts stated in the case, there was no proof of any right in [P].... I can find nothing in the declaration to shew that [D], by fouling the water, injured any right of [P], nor that, as against [P], he can be considered a wrong doer.[171]

167 (1671) 2 Wms. Saund. 112; 85 E.R. 814 (K.B.).
168 (1803) 4 East 107; 102 E.R. 770 (K.B.).
169 *Whaley* v. *Laing* (1857) 3 H. & N. 675, 682; 157 E.R. 639, 642.
170 Cf. R. H. Coase, 'The Problem of Social Cost' (1960) 3 Journal of Law and Economics 1; J. Getzler, 'Theories of Property and Economic Development' (1996) 26 Journal of Interdisciplinary History 639, 658–64.
171 *Whaley* v. *Laing* (1858) 3 H. & N. 675, 684–5; 157 E.R. 639, 643 (Ex. Ch.).

This approach was not followed by later judges. In 1885 Brett MR could state that 'No one is justified in injuring the right of appropriation which everybody else has',[172] by which he encompassed non-proprietary privileges to take water free of trespassory interferences. Shortly afterwards an Irish court stated: 'Mere possession of rights corporeal and incorporeal is sufficient to maintain an action against a wrongdoer'.[173] Sometimes the principle was grounded on the simple idea that a factual grant of 'reasonable' amenities should be implied whenever property was divided into adjoining tenements, as an easement of necessity;[174] where there was no property division, the 'easement' might be implied by law, independently of grant. The courts seemed particularly concerned to give remedies against water pollution, even in the absence of possessory interests or sensible damage to property.[175] For one example, in *Hodgkinson* v. *Ennor*,[176] Blackburn J held that there was a right to receive waters percolating through the soil without pollution, even if there was no right to the undiminished natural flow of the water itself:

I take the law to be as stated in *Tenant* v. *Gouldwin*, that you must not injure the property of your neighbour, and that, consequently, if filth is created on any man's land, then, in the quaint language of the *Report in Salk*. 361, 'he whose dirt it is, must keep it that it may not trespass.' Now here... the foul water was not kept by [D] so that it shall not trespass, in consequence of which the water which [P] had a right to have pure and unpolluted... was corrupted. That is both damnum and injuria.[177]

[172] *Ballard* v. *Tomlinson* (1885) 29 Ch. D. 115, 122 (Ch.).

[173] *Pullan* v. *Roughfort Bleaching Co.* (1888) 21 L.R. Ir. 73. See further *Womersley* v. *Church* (1867) 17 L.T. 190 (Ch., M.R.); *Foster* v. *Warblington Urban Council* [1906] 1 K.B. 648 (K.B.); *Owen* v. *Faversham Corporation* (1909) 73 J.P. 33 (C.A.).

[174] *Ewart* v. *Cochrane* (1861) 4 McQ. Scotch App. 117 (H.L.(Sc.)); *Pyer* v. *Carter* (1833) 1 H. & N. 916; 156 E.R. 1472 (Ex.). This approach echoes the servitude doctrines of Bracton and the seventeenth-century line of authority stretching from *Luttrell's Case* (1601) 4 Co. Rep. 84b. 86a; 76 E.R. 1063, 1065 (K.B.); *Nicholas* v. *Chamberlain* (1606) Cro. Jac. 121; 79 E.R. 105 (K.B.); and *Sury* v. *Pigot* (1625) Poph. 166; 79 E.R. 1263; 3 Bulst. 339; 81 E.R. 280 (K.B.), Ch. 3, the text accompanying nn. 12–17 and 41–63 above. The nineteenth-century courts made a meal of the doctrine implying easements upon severance and grant of adjoining tenements: for the contradictory authorities see Coulson and Forbes, *Law Relating to Waters*, 255–69; *Gale on Easements* (16th edn.) 109–54.

[175] *Attorney-General* v. *Birmingham Borough Council* (1858) 4 Kay & J. 528; 70 E.R. 220 (V.C.); *Goldsmid* v. *Tunbridge Wells Commissioners* (1865) L.R. 1 Ch. 161 (M.R.); (1866) 1 Ch. Ap. 349 (Ch. Ap.); *Crossley* v. *Lightowler* (1866) L.R. 3 Eq. 279 (Ch.); (1867) L.R. 2 Ch. App. 478 (V.C.); *Pennington* v. *Brinsop Hall Company* (1875) 5 Ch.D. 769 (Ch.); *Clarke* v. *Somerset Drainage Commissioners* (1888) 57 L.J.M.C. 96; *Blackburn* v. *Somers* (1879) 5 L.R. Ir. 1; *McIntyre* v. *McGavin* [1893] A.C. 268 (H.L.(Sc.)); and see further Coulson and Forbes, *Law Relating to Waters*, 191–220, 284–8.

[176] (1863) 4 B. & S. 229; 122 E.R. 446 (Q.B.).

[177] 4 B. & S. 229, 241–2; 122 E.R. 446, 450, per Blackburn J; and see *Womersley* v. *Church* (1867) 17 L.T. (N.S.) 190 per Lord Romilly MR; *Ballard* v. *Tomlinson* (1885) 29 Ch. D. 115 (C.A.).

Non-riparian Statutory Rights to Water: The Canal and Utility Cases

An important public dimension to the law of water rights was added by legislation which granted powers to canal and water companies and to local authorities permitting diversion of natural waters into artificial reservoirs and channels. This aspect will not be treated in detail in the present work. Legislation and judicial interpretation were characterized in the sphere of water law by pragmatic and *ad hoc* reasoning, and this law had little or no impact on the development of general common-law riparian doctrine.[178] The

[178] For further examples see: *Carlisle, Mayor of* v. *Blamire* (1807) 8 East. 487; 103 E.R. 430 (K.B.); *R.* v. *Directors of the Bristol Dock Company* (1810) 12 East. 429; 104 E.R. 167 (K.B.); *Agar* v. *Regent's Canal Company* (1815) G. Coop. 77, 212, 221; 35 E.R. 221, 483, 534 (Ch.); *Finch* v. *Birmingham Canal Co.* (1826) 5 B. & C. 820; 108 E.R. 305 (K.B.); *Dudley Canal Navigation Co.* v. *Grazebrook* (1830) 1 B. & A. 59; 109 E.R. 709 (K.B.); *Blakemore* v. *Glamorganshire Canal Company* (1832) 1 My. & K. 154; 39 E.R. 639 (Ch.); *R.* v. *Brecknock & Avergavenny Canal Company* (1835) 3 Ad. & E. 217; 111 E.R. 395 (K.B.); *Thicknesse* v. *Lancaster Canal Company* (1838) 4 M. & W. 472; 150 E.R. 1515 (Ex.); *Arkwright* v. *Gell* (1839) 5 M. & W. 203; 151 E.R. 87 (Ex.); *South Shields* v. *Cookson* (1845) 15 L.J. Ex. 315; *Cromford Canal Co.* v. *Cutts* (1848) 5 Oliver & Beavan's Rail. Cas. 442 (V.C., L.C.); *Rochdale Canal Company* v. *King* (1849) 14 Q.B. 120; 117 E.R. 49 (Q.B.); *East and West India Docks Company* v. *Gattke* (1851) 3 Mac. & G. 168; 42 E.R. 220 (Ch.); *Dickinson* v. *The Grand Junction Canal Company* (1852) 7 Exch. 282; 155 E.R. 953 (Ex.); *Rochdale Canal Co.* v. *Radcliffe* (1852) 18 Q.B. 287; 118 E.R. 108 (Q.B.); *Attorney-General of the Prince of Wales* v. *Bristol Waterworks Company* (1855) 10 Ex. 884; 156 E.R. 699 (Ex.); *Blyth* v. *Birmingham Waterworks Company* (1856) 11 Ex. 780; 156 E.R. 1047 (Ex.); *Llewellyn* v. *Swansea Canal Navigation, Proprietors* (1856) 1 H. & N. 343; 156 E.R. 1235 (Ex.); *Caledonian Railway Company* v. *Ogilvy* (1856) 2 Macq. H.L. 257 (H.L.); *Busby* v. *Chesterfield Waterworks and Gas Light Co.* (1858) El. Bl. & Bl. 176; 120 E.R. 474 (Q.B.); *Lord* v. *Commissioners for the City of Sydney* (1859) 12 Moore P.C. 473; 15 E.R. 472 (P.C.); *National Manure Co.* v. *Donald* (1859) 28 L.J. Ex. 185 (Ex.); *New River Company* v. *Johnson* (1860) 2 El. & El. 435; 121 E.R. 164 (Q.B.); *Stourbridge Canal* v. *Dudley* (1860) 30 L.J.Q.B. 108; *Medway Navigation Co.* v. *Romney* (1861) 9 C.B.N.S. 586; 142 E.R. 226 (C.P.); *Birmingham Canal Navigation Co.* v. *Earl of Dudley* (1862) 7 H. & N. 968; 158 E.R. 764 (Ex.); *Hill* v. *Tupper* (1863) 2 H. & C. 121; 159 E.R. 51 (Ex.); *R.* v. *Metropolitan Board of Works* (1863) 3 B. & S. 710; 122 E.R. 266 (Q.B.); *Cator* v. *Board of Works of Lewisham* (1864) 5 B. & S. 115; 122 E.R. 775 (Q.B.); *R.* v. *Bradford Navigation Co.* (1865) 6 B. & S. 631; 122 E.R. 1328 (Q.B.); *Goldsmid* v. *Tunbridge Wells Commissioners* (1865) L.R. 1 Eq. 161 (M.R.); (1866) 1 Ch. Ap. 349 (Ch. Ap.); *Midland Railway* v. *Checkley* (1867) L.R.4 Eq. 19; *R.* v. *Metropolitan Board of Works* (1869) L.R. 4 Q.B. 265 (Q.B.); *Grand Junction Canal Company* v. *Shugar* (1871) L.R. 6 Ch. Ap. 483 (L.C.); *Mason* v. *Shrewsbury & Hereford Railway Co.* (1871) L.R. 6 Q.B. 578 (Q.B.); *Dunn* v. *Birmingham Canal* (1872) L.R. 8 Q.B. 42; *M'Carthy* v. *Metropolitan Board of Works* (1873–4) L.R. 8 C.P. 196 (C.P.); *Swindon Waterworks Company* v. *Wilts and Berks Canal Navigation Company* (1874) L.R. 9 Ch. 453 (Ch.); (1875) L.R. 7 H.L. 697 (H.L.); (1876) 45 L.J. Ch. 638 (Ch.); *Rhodes* v. *Airedale Drainage Commissioners* (1876) 1 C.P.D. 398, 402 (C.P.); *Geddis* v. *Proprietors of the Bann Reservoir* (1878) L.R. 3 H.L.(I.) 430; *Bradford Corporation* v. *Pickles* [1894] 3 Ch. 53; [1895] A.C. 587 (H.L.); *Roberts* v. *Gwyrfai District Council* [1899] 2 Ch. 608 (C.A.); *Attorney-General* v. *Great Northern Railway* [1909] 1 Ch. 775 (Ch.). Cf. A. W. B. Simpson, 'Legal Liability for Bursting Reservoirs: The Historical Context of *Rylands v. Fletcher*' (1984) 13 Journal of Legal Studies 209, revised and reprinted as 'Bursting Reservoirs and Victorian Tort Law: *Rylands and Horrocks* v. *Fletcher* (1868)' in A. W. B. Simpson, *Leading Cases in the Common Law* (Oxford, 1995) 195–226. The impact of statute-authorized interferences with water rights for the purposes of navigation, ferries, bridge-making, and highways is treated exhaustively in Coulson and Forbes, *Law Relating to Waters*, 492–631; the law of water supply, ibid., 369–404; the law for sewerage and land drainage, ibid., at 759–837; the law of canals, ibid., 308–58; and for an exhaustive treatment,

courts affirmed again and again that the question of allowing canal companies a special property in riparian waters was a question of construction of the particular statute before them; and little discernible pattern therefore emerged from the judicial decisions. Sometimes the canal companies' rights were tightly circumscribed; sometimes they were given virtually absolute control of riparian waters such that proprietors could use the waters only by licence. Willes J delivered a representative judgment dealing with these issues in the case of *Medway Navigation Company* v. *Romney*.[179] In that case a canal company, P, was given statutory powers compulsorily to acquire land and waters for the purpose of navigation; under the legislation,[180] 'the said river and streams so as to be made navigable, and all lands, etc., to be used for the benefit of the navigation were vested in the company for ever'. The defendant, D, then took riparian waters for the purpose of supplying a county gaol and asylum not adjacent to the waterfront. Willes J and the court held that this infringed P's statutory rights in the water, even though the navigation had not been harmed.

Looking to the objects which were contemplated by the Acts of Parliament, to which our attention has been directed, we cannot construe the statute... as giving the plaintiffs any such limited right in the river as a private grant of the 'said river and stream' might have conveyed, but as creating a new species of statutory property and interest in the water, which, in our opinion, was interfered with by the abstraction of it... by [D]... [for] purposes [that] were more extensive than those for which a riparian proprietor, as such, could insist upon appropriating the stream as it passed by his land. In our view of the correct construction of the Act of Parliament, it is not necessary that there should be an actual damage to the navigation; because we think that the legislature intended to give the company such an interest in all the water of the river for the purposes of the navigation as is interfered with by the abstraction of any part thereof. Whether or not riparian proprietors can exercise, for the benefit of their land adjoining the river, the rights which ordinarily belong to such proprietors, it is unnecessary to express an opinion.[181]

In other cases, canal companies were held to have a statutory title to water inadequate to allow them to make a grant of water to other riparian users; hence those users were unable to set up prescriptive users against the companies in lieu of actual grant.[182]

R. G. Webster, *The Law Relating to Canals, Comprising a Treatise on Navigable Rivers and Canals* (London, 1885). The use of English authority in America is explored in D. J. Hulsebosch, 'Writs to Rights: "Navigability" and the Transformation of the Common Law in the Nineteenth Century' (2002) 23 Cardozo Law Review 1049.

[179] (1861) 9 C.B.N.S. 586; 142 E.R. 226 (C.P.).

[180] 13 Geo. 2, c. 26, s. 2.

[181] (1861) 9 C.B.N.S. 586, 591–2; 142 E.R. 226, 232–3 (C.P.).

[182] *Ellwell* v. *Birmingham Canal* (1852) 3 H.L.C. 812; 10 E.R. 323 (H.L.); *Rochdale Canal Company* v. *Radcliffe* (1852) 18 Q.B. 287; *National Manure Co.* v. *Donald* (1859) 28 L.J. Ex. 185 (Ex.); *Staffordshire Canal* v. *Birmingham Canal* (1866) L.R. 1 H.L. 254.

In the 1865 case of *Gaved* v. *Martyn*[183] the Court of Common Pleas reviewed the accumulating doctrine of artificial watercourses. The case was elaborately presented in court, with maps and diagrams supplementing a description of respective water uses by miners, farmers, and manufacturers in Cornwall from 1830. In that year, the proprietor of a clay-works was given permission by a neighbour to cut a leat from the neighbour's stream to his clay-works. The artificial watercourse was enjoyed to 1835 when P succeeded to the clay-works, continuing the enjoyment until 1855. D, the new owner of the natural stream, then purported to rescind the original licence and cut off the supply of water to the leat. According to Erle CJ, 'the question is whether the enjoyment in fact for more than twenty years established an indefeasible right in [P], or left it as a question for the jury whether [P] was not limited to the same right as [his predecessor in title] had', viz. by virtue of the 1830 licence.

P suggested that the Prescription Act 1832 supplied a simple rule that twenty years' enjoyment gave a prescriptive right, notwithstanding the precarious origin of the enjoyment. Erle CJ firmly rejected this interpretation:

> Before the statute, such a right could only be claimed by prescription, and might have been defeated by shewing the origin of the enjoyment: and the 2nd section provides that the claim shall not be defeated or destroyed by shewing only that the right was first enjoyed at any time prior to such period of twenty years (that is, by shewing its origin); provided the person claiming has enjoyed claiming a right thereto.... The leat was made by [P's predecessor] through the farm in his occupation; and, on the face of it, it was an artificial course, and the owner of the soil from which it was brought at the end of twenty years claimed a right to stop it.... [T]here was evidence from which the jury was warranted in finding that there had not been an enjoyment for twenty years...as of right; but that the enjoyment was precarious, and procured by the permission of the owner of the soil.[184]

According to Willes J:

> A plaintiff who is seeking to establish an enjoyment for the statutable period of twenty years, must,—with this exception, that he need not satisfy the jury of the fact of there having been a lost grant, or that the enjoyment commenced from before the time of living memory,—make out that his enjoyment has been under a claim of right.[185]

If it could be proved that 'the enjoyment originated under an agreement with the tenant or owner of the servient tenement, and therefore was precarious and not as of right', then no prescriptive claim could be brought.[186]

The court's test for an adverse possession capable of founding a right thus seemed to depend on the intentions of the maker who allowed another to use

183 (1865) 19 C.B.N.S. 732; 144 E.R. 974 (C.P.).
184 19 C.B.N.S. 732, 744; 144 E.R. 974, 980.
185 19 C.B.N.S. 732, 745–6; 144 E.R. 974, 980.
186 19 C.B.N.S. 732, 746; 144 E.R. 974, 980.

his watercourse; but this only begged further questions. Did the maker intend a temporary channel that was subject to closure? Or was the channel intended to become a permanent part of the land—a creation or extension of a natural or ancient watercourse by man-made means? Ultimately it was a factual, not a doctrinal question, whether an original licence was intended by the grantor to be permanent or precarious; or whether a licensee's successor started up a new, adverse possession as of right, or only continued the permissive use of his predecessor.

These issues were raised in two later hearings of the case, concerning the fouling of two other artificial soughs conveying water to P's clay-works. Both soughs were dug by P himself and intended to be permanent; one collected water on D's land and transmitted it to P's works, the other received water from D's mine at the boundary of the tenements. The pollution to the water was caused by tin-streaming or washing of ore in the lands from which the water was collected. One of the soughs had been abandoned during the perod of P's use, the other being still in use.

D claimed in defence that the mining customs of Cornwall (the stannary laws) preserved the right of miners to channel water, drain mines, and wash ore as was required for their operations, notwithstanding any inconsistent rights of private property. Local custom therefore excluded the operation of any prescriptive title to clear, uninterrupted water, because even if an owner had twenty years' untroubled enjoyment, this was always subject to the contingent customary rights of the tin-bounders, and hence was a precarious enjoyment excluding presumed grant.

Erle CJ rejected out of hand D's customary defence in relation to the abandoned sough:

> If the rights of the tin-bounders are in operation, the custom of Cornwall, which may be called the common law of Cornwall, may operate in the way suggested, But, if they are not in operation, the general law of the land applies to Cornwall as to any other county. The man who has dug a channel, and has conducted water along it for twenty years without interruption, acquires a right to it, though its source may be in lands which are subject to tin-bounders' rights.

Willes J added that the leats had been intended by their maker to be permanent, and hence under the doctrine of *Wood* v. *Waud* could be made subject to prescriptive rights. As to the defence argument that stannary custom prevented the application of the Prescription Act 1832, he stated:

> [t]he right of the tin-bounders by custom is one apart from the ownership of the soil, or the enjoyment of any right connected with the soil, with the exception of the single right to search for tin and to take all reasonable means for producing it, subject to the payment of a toll to the owner of the land. I apprehend that the rights of the owner of the land, and any incorporeal rights or hereditaments arising out of it, may be determined by the ordinary law under the Prescription Act, irrespective of the rights

of the tin-bounder, which may not inaptly be described as rights paramount under the custom. I do not see why the inhabitants of Cornwall should be in a worse position with reference to the acquisition of prescriptive rights to water than the inhabitants of other parts of the kingdom.[187]

Prescription was thus characterized not as a grant against common right, but as a right created by general custom or common law (and statute), which was not subject to derogation by local custom. This was a transformation of the orthodoxies of earlier common-law theory.[188]

In the case of the second sough, the water was brought to the surface and conveyed to P's artificial watercourse by the operations of tin-miners. The miners claimed that their drainage operations and their use of the stream were done in pursuance of customary rights that had never been abandoned; therefore the rule that an unexercised customary right does not bar a prescription did not apply.

The court denied P's claim, not because of the paramountcy of custom, but due to the stream being non-natural:

[P] acquired no right to this stream by user thereof for twenty years, because the stream was an artificial stream made to flow over [D]'s land by the operations of miners, and the miners had not permanently abandoned their right of control over the water in the stream when P diverted it by the [sough] to his works.[189]

A considered statement of doctrine was then made, which must be pondered in its full length:

Rights and liabilities in respect of artificial streams when first flowing on the surface are entirely distinct from rights and liabilities in respect of natural streams so flowing. The water in an artificial stream flowing in the land of the party by whom it is caused to flow, is the property of that party, and is not subject to any rights or liabilities in respect of other persons. If the stream so brought to the surface is made to flow upon the land of a neighbour without his consent, it is a wrong for which the party causing it so to flow is liable. If there is a grant by the neighbour, the terms of the grant regulate the rights and liabilities of the parties thereto. If there is uninterrupted user of the land of the neighbour for receiving the flow as of right for twenty years, such user is evidence that the land from which the water is sent into the neighbour's land has become the dominant tenement, having a right to the easement of so sending the water, and that the neighbour's land has become subject to the easement of receiving that water. But such user of the easement of sending on the water of an artificial stream is of itself no evidence that the party enjoying it has become subject to the servitude of being bound to exercise the easement for the benefit of the neighbour. A right of way is no evidence that the party entitled thereto is under a duty to walk; nor a right to eaves-dropping on the neighbour's land, that the party is bound to send on his rain water to that land. In like manner, we consider that a party by the mere exercise

187 19 C.B.N.S. 732, 754; 144 E.R. 974, 983.
188 See Salmond's analysis of prescription, Ch. 2, the text accompanying nn. 238–252 above.
189 19 C.B.N.S. 732, 757; 144 E.R. 974, 984–5.

of a right to make an artificial drain into his neighbour's land either from mine or surface, does not raise any presumption that he is subject to any duty to continue his artificial drain, by twenty years' user, although there may be additional circumstances by which that presumption would be raised or the right proved. Also, if it be proved that the stream was originally intended to have a permanent flow, or if the party by whom or on whose behalf the artificial stream was caused to flow is shewn to have abandoned permanently without intention to resume the works by which the flow was caused, and given up all right to and control over the stream, such stream may become subject to the laws relating to natural streams.

...

The law relating to natural streams is entirely different. The flow of a natural stream creates natural rights and liabilities between all the riparian proprietors along the whole of its course. Subject to reasonable use by himself, each proprietor is bound to allow the water to flow on without altering the quantity or quality. These natural rights and liabilities may be altered by grant or by user of an easement to alter the stream, as by diverting, or fouling, or penning back, or the like. If the stream flows at its source by the operation of nature, that is, if it is a natural stream, the rights and liabilities of the party owning the land at its source are the same as those of the proprietors in the course below.

If a stream flows at its source by the operation of man, that is, if it is an artificial stream, the owner of the land at its source of the commencement of the flow, is not subject to any rights or liabilities towards any other person in respect of the water of that stream. The owner of such land may make himself liable to duties in respect of such water, by grant or contract: but the party claiming a right to compel performance of those duties must give evidence of such rights, beyond the mere suffering by him of the servitude of receiving such water.[190]

In the present case, there could be no servitude requiring D to continue sending the water to P's land without interference, for there had been no use of the water flow as of right on P's part, nor was there *patientia* or acquiescence by D in any use as of right: 'and so there was no presumption of a grant by [D], no evidence of a right in [P]'. The court reviewed previous authorities at length, summarizing *Arkwright* as follows:

The important and extensive rights and interests connected with mining are protected in due relation to the rights of surface owners. In this case [*Arkwright*], the question arose between the surface owner and the mining owner: and it was held that the mining owner who had brought the water to the surface on [P]'s land for draining a mine, might divert it where deeper draining was required; and all the mines of the district that might be unwatered by the drain were properly treated as one interest.[191]

This decision provided a doctrinal resting point in the field.[192]

[190] 19 C.B.N.S. 732, 757–9; 144 E.R. 974, 985.

[191] 19 C.B.N.S. 732, 760–1; 144 E.R. 974, 986.

[192] See further *Holker* v. *Porrit* (1875) L.R. 10 Ex. 62 (Ex.); *Roberts* v. *Richards* (1881) 50 L.J. Ch. 297 (Ch.); *Burrows* v. *Lang* [1901] 2 Ch. 502 (Ch.); per Farwell J, who cites Coke and Bracton's definitions of precarious enjoyment of rights to supplement the *Gaved* tests. See also

Refining the Factual Presumption of Prescriptive Title

In the Chancery appeal case of *Ivimey* v. *Stocker* in 1866,[193] Lord Cranworth LC held that prescriptive rights could be acquired in artificial watercourses where practice and custom showed that they had been intended to be permanent.[194] The case is significant as it gives a new description of the nature of the presumptions of fact founding prescriptive titles.

In this case P, the owner of a Cornish tin-mine, sought to succeed to a prescriptive title in a watercourse, which title had been acquired by personal licensees in factual possession who lacked any estate at common law. From time before memory P's tin-mine had been worked by tin-bounders under a custom of Cornwall, which accorded a licence to occupiers of unused land to exploit the land for minerals without the consent of the owner, upon payment of a portion of the profits for ore recovered. Also since time immemorial, the bounders had used an artificial stream emanating from D's land for their mining operation. Lord Cranworth defined time immemorial in this context as 'a period... beyond living memory, and as to which there is nothing to shew when the [user] commenced'. This was the older common-law conception of prescriptive time as a human limit on evidence. The bounders abandoned their works in 1856, and the mine was then taken into factual possession by P, who continued to work it by contracting out to licensees. D later diverted the stream from P's land for the benefit of his own newly-erected clay works; P then sued under a prescriptive title to the water based on the bounders' user, as he and his predecessors had not personally used the stream as owners before 1856. It was decided by the court that through immemorial use of the water, the bounders had prescribed in a que estate and not in their capacity as bounders holding mere personal licences not derived from the owner's estate. Hence the bounders' prescription annexed an easement to the owner's land, which could be enforced by equitable injunction against D.[195]

Lord Cranworth analysed the nature of common-law titles by prescription in terms of a search for sensible factual presumptions where express proof was lacking. The parties' rights would have been clear if the stream had been a natural flow, in which case the running water 'forms part of the land bounded'. But it was the intentions of the makers and recipients of an artificial stream which determined the existence of rights in that stream. In

H. J. W. Coulson and U. A. Forbes, *The Law Relating to Waters, Sea, Tidal and Inland* (1st edn., London, 1880) 221 ff., and D. A. Stroud, *The Law of Easements, Founded on Select Cases* (London, 1934) 182–206, which gives exhaustive treatment of the law after 1870.

[193] (1865) L.R. 1 Ch. App. 396 (L.C.).

[194] See also *Bastard* v. *Smith* (1836) 5 Ad. & E. 827; 111 E.R. 1380 (Ex.); *Harrop* v. *Hirst* (1868) L.R. 4 Ex. 43.

[195] Reversing the decision of Kindersley V.C.

the present case, tin-mining would not have been commenced without a water supply for the bounds; the bounders would probably not have begun operations and then received a grant of water rights. It was also highly unlikely that the bounders could have secured a water supply to commence mining without arrangement with the owner, whose land was thereby physically altered. There was no extant custom allowing bounders to water any mining land they chose without the owner's consent. At the same time, the watering of a tin mine could be a benefit to the owner by securing him increased production royalties, and this advantage he would probably wish to continue once it commenced, and not leave the availability of the benefit to the personal discretion of the bounders.[196] Lord Cranworth concluded:

> If therefore it is important that a stream of water should be brought from adjoining lands for the use of the works, which cannot be done without the consent of the owner, the great probability is that any arrangement made for that object in which the owner has an immediate and a possible quasi-reversionary interest should be made with him, and not merely with those who have the comparatively uncertain rights of tin-bounders.[197]

In establishing a common-law prescriptive title, Lord Cranworth used the technique of presuming grant from the evidence of user, as a matter of reasonable factual inference and implication. The technique of the Prescription Act 1832, which moved the presumption of grant away from fact towards the fiction of legally conclusive presumptions upon lapse of limitation, was mentioned in his judgment, but not applied. Lord Cranworth's approach may have been dictated by the special nature of customary possession intersecting with common-law title; but it may also indicate that courts of equity pursued a more fact-specific, evidential approach to prescription than courts of law, and were prepared to apply common-law doctrine in a distinctively equitable style of presuming relevant fact from available evidence.[198]

LIABILITY FOR ESCAPES AND *SIC UTERE TUO* BEFORE THE RULE OF *RYLANDS* v. *FLETCHER*

Two parallel issues arising from the draining of mines were the right to prevent a mine owner diverting water from one's lands; and the right to prevent a mine owner (or other proprietor) from discharging unwanted water onto one's lands. The first issue is properly a problem of water law, and will be discussed in some detail shortly. The latter issue belongs properly

[196] *Ivimey* v. *Stocker* (1866) 1 Ch. App. 396, 404–6.
[197] Ibid., 406. See also *Ewart* v. *Cochrane* (1861) 4 Macq. 116 (H.L.(Sc.)).
[198] Cf. M. R. T. Macnair, *The Law of Proof in Early Modern Equity* (Berlin, 1999) 267–75.

to the law of nuisance for escapes rather than the law of water rights, and was eventually addressed in the great case of *Rylands* v. *Fletcher*.[199] Before the formulation of the well-known *Rylands* rule of strict liability for discharges, a clear rule was established that in the ordinary use of land inconvenient water could be expelled onto another's land to his or her damage without infringement of right—a case of *damnum sine injuria* falling outside the *sic utere tuo* rule.

Fault Liability for Flooding

The leading case of *Smith* v. *Kenrick*[200] was decided in the Common Pleas in 1849, and involved a claim for the flooding of a coal mine by the operation of an adjoining mine. Cresswell J found no clear rules for such flooding in the numerous authorities cited to the court, and stated his own original doctrine:

> Treating the question as a new one, not governed by the authority of any decided case . . . it would seem to be the natural right of each of the owners of two adjoining coal mines,—neither being subject to any servitude to the other,—to work his own in the manner most convenient and beneficial to himself, although the natural consequence may be, that some prejudice will accrue to the owner of the mine, so long as that does not arise from the negligent or malicious conduct of the party.[201]
>
> . . .
>
> There are many cases where the principle has been recognised, that one land owner cannot, by altering the condition of his land, deprive the owner of the adjoining land of the privilege of using his own as he might have done before. Thus, he cannot, by building a house near the margin of his land, prevent his neighbour from excavating his own land, although it may endanger the house; nor from building on his own land, although it may obstruct windows, unless, indeed, by lapse of time, the adjoining land has become subject to a right analagous to what in the Roman law was called a servitude. So, also, in *Acton* v. *Blundell*,[202]—where the subject was very much dis-

[199] (1865–68) 3 H. & C. 774; 159 E.R. 737 (Ex.); L.R. 1 Ex. 265 (Ex. Ch.); L.R. 3 H.L. 330 (H.L.). For discussion of the 'rule in *Rylands* v. *Fletcher*', see C. Dalton, *Losing History: Tort Liability in the Nineteenth Century and the Case of Rylands v Fletcher* (MS., 1987); F. Bohlen, 'The Rule in Rylands v Fletcher' (Parts 1–3) (1911) 59 University of Pennsylvania Law Review 298, 373, 423, reprinted in F. Bohlen, *Studies in the Law of Torts* (Indianapolis, Ind., 1926) 344–440; cf. R. T. Molloy, '*Fletcher* v. *Rylands*' (1941–2) 9 University of Chicago Law Review 266; Simpson, 'Legal Liability for Bursting Reservoirs'. For modern appraisals of the rule, absorbing it into a general negligence standard, see: S. J. Stoljar, 'Concerning Strict Liability' in P. D. Finn (ed.), *Essays on Tort* (Sydney, 1989) 267–93; *Burnie Port Authority* v. *General Jones Pty Ltd* (1994) 179 C.L.R. 520, 526–60 per Mason CJ, Deane, Dawson, Toohey and Gaudron JJ; 560–81 per Brennan J (dissenting); 581–95 per McHugh J (dissenting); also in (1994) 120 A.L.R. 42 (High Court of Australia); *Cambridge Water Co.* v. *Eastern Counties Leather Plc* [1994] 2 A.C. 264, 290–309 per Lord Goff (H.L.); cf. *Transco plc* v. *Stockport M.B.C.* [2003] 3 W.L.R. 1467 (H.L.).

[200] (1849) 7 C.B. 515; 137 E.R. 205 (C.P.).

[201] Cf. *Chasemore* v. *Richards* (1859) 7 H.L.C. 349; 11 E.R. 140 (H.L.), and *Bradford Corporation* v. *Pickles* [1894] 3 Ch. 53 (Ch.); [1895] A.C. 587 (H.L.), both in Ch. 6, the text accompanying nn. 111–159 below.

[202] (1843) 12 M & W. 324; 152 E.R. 1223 (Ex. Ch.), the text accompanying nn. 207–224 below.

cussed—the court held that one landowner, having dug a well on his own land, could not maintain an action against a party who afterwards sunk a coal-pit in the neighbourhood, which had the effect of drawing the water away from his well; the act not being done by the defendant negligently or maliciously, but in a proper manner, for the purpose of winning his own coal.

We think the same principle is applicable to the present case. The water is a sort of common enemy,—as was said by Lord Tenterden, in *Rex* v. *The Commissioners of Sewers for Pagham Level*,[203]—against which each man must defend himself. And this is in accordance with the civil law, by which it was considered that land on a lower level, owed a natural servitude to that on a higher, in respect of receiving, without claim to compensation, the water naturally flowing down to it (Dig. lib. 39, tit. 3).[204]

This decision suggests that mid-nineteenth-century law tended to favour the exercise of quite untrammelled rights to exploit land, even at the expense of neighbours' amenities. If the rider that damage must not be negligently or maliciously caused was super-added in, its effect was not specified, and indeed the rider was later abandoned.[205] The doctrine is important in the context of riparian law as it demonstrates that the *sic utere tuo* maxim was not being used at this time to generate new notions of reasonable limit or restraint on property use.[206] The fullest discussion of these issues is found in the earlier decision of *Acton* v. *Blundell*.

Subterranean Watercourses and the Plenitude of Ownership

In the leading decision of *Acton* v. *Blundell* in 1843[207] the Exchequer Chamber carefully investigated the doctrinal foundation of water rights. This case may

[203] (1828) 8 B. & C. 355; 108 E.R. 1075 (K.B.); and see *Fay* v. *Prentice* (1845) 1 C.B. 828; 135 E.R. 769 (C.P.); *Bagnall* v. *London and North Western Railway Company* (1861) 7 H. & N. 423, 158 E.R. 538 (Ex.).

[204] *Smith* v. *Kenrick* (1849) 7 C.B. 515, 565–6; 137 E.R. 205, 225. This doctrine was approved in *Baird* v. *Williamson* (1863) 15 C.B.N.S. 392; 143 E.R. 831 (C.P.); *Rylands* v. *Fletcher* (1865–68) 3 H. & C. 774; 159 E.R. 737 (Ex.); L.R. 1 Ex. 265 (Ex. Ch.); L.R. 3 H.L. 330 (H.L.); and *Mason* v. *Shrewsbury & Hereford Railway Co.* (1871) L.R. 6 Q.B. 578 (Q.B.); but the doctrine was distinguished or evaded as often as it was applied in the later nineteenth century. The strict liability rule of *Rylands* v. *Fletcher* by contrast dealt with escapes of collected water in artificial reservoirs and the like: the case addresses the problem of damage caused by man-made, not natural, hazards: see further Simpson, 'Legal Liability for Bursting Reservoirs'; Dalton, *Losing History*; H. J. W. Coulson and U. A. Forbes, *The Law Relating to Waters* (6th edn. by S. R. Hobday, London, 1952) 161–91.

[205] *Chasemore* v. *Richards* (1859) 7 H.L.C. 349; 11 E.R. 140 (H.L.); *Bradford Corporation* v. *Pickles* [1894] 3 Ch. 53 (Ch.); [1895] A.C. 587 (H.L.); Ch. 6, the text accompanying nn. 111–159 below.

[206] See also *Alston* v. *Grant* (1854) 3 El. & Bl. 128; 118 E.R. 1089 (Q.B.); *New River* v. *Johnson* (1860) 2 El. & El. 435; 121 E.R. 164 (Q.B.); *Black* v. *Ballymena Commissioners* (1886) 17 L.R.Ir. 459 (Ch.(I.)); *Dickinson* v. *The Grand Junction Canal Company* (1852) 7 Exch. 282; 155 E.R. 953 (Ex.); *Broadbent* v. *Ramsbotham* (1856) 11 Exch. 602; 156 E.R. 971 (Ex.); *Rawstron* v. *Taylor* (1855) 11 Exch. 369; 156 E.R. 873. (Ex.); *Chamber Colliery Company* v. *Hopwood* (1886) 32 Ch. D. 549.

[207] (1843) 12 M.& W. 324; 152 E.R. 1223 (Ex. Ch.).

be seen as a transitional opinion, experimenting with Roman doctrine and English precedent in order to give substantive content to the idea of *sic utere tuo* as a balancing and restraint of rival property uses. Ultimately that balance rested not on clear-cut doctrinal tests, but upon utilitarian intuitions.

The issue before the court in *Acton* v. *Blundell* was whether natural rights inhered in the flow of a subterranean watercourse. The facts were that P owned cotton mills and used underground water to drive his machinery; D then sunk mining pits and drains which cut off the stream. P's use of the water had been for less than twenty years, and he did not raise a claim that right or immunity had been gained through lapse of time.

Counsel for P claimed that there were natural rights in all flows of water supplying land, including subterranean sources, so that an owner in P's position could restrain interceptions of the water interfering with his mills. *Sic utere tuo* was stressed as the paramount principle:

> [G]enerally . . . a party may sink pits and work the coal in his own land, and there is no provision against it; but that is an imperfect view of the case. The law does not say that a party may so work whatever the consequences may be, or how far soever beyond the property of the party the effects may extend; it does not give the party an absolute unqualified right independent of all circumstances; but that right must be subject to another and paramount rule—sic utere tuo ut alienum non laedas: and the question comes to this, whether there was any peculiar privilege on account of the act being done by the defendants in carrying on mining operations, but assuming that the doing of the act was, abstractedly speaking, lawful, it is submitted that, if water passes in its natural course through a person's land, he has a right to the use of it as it passes, and to be protected against another obstructing it, or altering the stream so as to prevent such user, unless the other has gained some right or servitude . . . by grant or otherwise; and here the defendants do not allege they have gained any such right. The right contended for by [P] is incident to, and follows from, the possession and occupation of the land, and requires no length of time to acquire it. Such right is almost self-evident. The water is the party's as long as it is on his land, as every thing is his that is above or below it. This is not disputed as to water flowing on the surface of the land, but the question is whether it makes any difference that it flows below it. It cannot; for the right arises from the occupation of the land, and must equally apply to water running under the surface. Indeed, from the nature of watercourses, there can be no difference between them on this point, whether superficial or not; for all water is originally underground, and this stream may at some distance be on the level with and flow along the surface. If there were any difference, a party might go, even in the case of surface water, to some place before it reached the surface, and cut off the stream . . . with impunity.[208]

Counsel for D replied that *sic utere tuo* was not an injunction to avoid all interferences with others' interests, independently of any prior recognized right. The principle was more modest, entailing mutual respect for the existing legal rights of neighbours.

[208] 12 M. & W. 324, 331–2; 152 E.R. 1223, 1226.

[T]he direct consequence [of P's approach] is this, that if any person, a mere cottager for instance, sink a well in his ground, the mines of the surrounding neighbourhood, however extensive and valuable, can afterwards never be worked . . . if the doing so would have the effect of materially diminishing the water in the well. . . . Where the consequences to other proprietors are so strikingly disproportionate, some very clear authorities ought to be produced in support of such a right; but none such have been adduced. The maxim sic utere tuo ut alienum non laedas, does not go to forbid damna generally, but damna injuriosa. To constitute a violation of that maxim, there must be injuria as well as damnum. There are many cases in which a man may lawfully use his own property so as to cause damage to his neighbour, so as it be not injuriosum. He may build a wall on his own ground so as to obstruct the lights of his neighbour, who may not have acquired a right to them by grant or adverse user. He may build a mill near the mill of his neighbour to the grievous damage of the latter by loss of custom, and so in other cases. . . . To derive, therefore, any aid from the maxim, sic utere, &c., the plaintiff must shew that he has sustained injuriam, which is the whole question.[209]

Bracton was then quoted to illustrate the distinction between *damnum* and *injuria* in nuisance.[210] Counsel on both sides displayed extensive learning, citing authorities from Justinian through to Bracton and the Year Books in order to support their arguments.

Tindal CJ, giving the judgment of the court, began by confirming the natural-flow riparian doctrine of *Mason* v. *Hill*,[211] stating:

[I]f the right to the enjoyment of underground springs, or to a well supplied thereby, is to be governed by the same law, then undoubtedly [D] could not justify the sinking of the coal pits.

Tindal C.J. then confined the application of the riparian doctrine to surface streams. He characterized all water rights, both natural and granted, as based on the knowledge and intentions of riparian proprietors. It followed that hidden underground streams could not be subject to natural rights of ownership, for their flow was usually unknown:

[W]e think, on considering . . . the law which is held to govern running streams, the consequences which would result if the same law is made applicable to springs beneath the surface, and, lastly, the authorities to be found in the books . . . that there is a marked and substantial difference between the two cases, and that they are not to be governed by the same rule of law.

The ground and origin of the law which governs streams running in their natural course . . . [is] that the right enjoyed by the several proprietors of the lands over which

[209] Per Addison, 12 M. & W. 324; 152 E.R. 1223, 1230; for similar arguments minimizing the effect of *sic utere tuo* by interpreting it in terms of rights, not interests, see Ch. 6, the text accompanying nn. 24–33 below.

[210] Henry de Bracton, *De Legibus et Consuetudinibus Angliae* 4 vols. (ed. by G. E. Woodbine, trans. S. E. Thorne, Cambridge, Mass., 1977) f. 221, iii, 163–4; see Ch. 2, the text accompanying nn. 68–72 above.

[211] *Mason* v. *Hill* (1832) 3 B. & Ad. 304; 110 E.R. 112; (1833) 5 B. & Ad. 1; 110 E.R. 692 (K.B.), the text accompanying nn. 101 and ff above. Tindal CJ in *Acton* v. *Blundell* (12 M. & W. 324, 348–9; 152 E.R. 1223, 1233) interpreted *Mason* v. *Hill* and *Wright* v. *Howard* (1823) 1 Sim. & St. 192; 57 E.R. 76 (V.C.) (the text accompanying nn. 76–80 above) as propounding the same doctrine.

they flow is, and always has been, public and notorious: that the enjoyment has been long continued—in ordinary cases, indeed, time out of mind—and uninterrupted; each man knowing what he receives and what has always been received from the higher lands, and what he transmits and what has always been transmitted to the lower. The rule, therefore, either assumes for its foundation the implied assent and agreement of the proprietors of the different lands from all ages, or perhaps it may be considered as a rule of positive law, (which would seem to be the opinion of Fleta and Blackstone), the origin of which is lost in the progress of time, or it may not be unfitly treated, as laid down by Mr. Justice Story, in his judgment in the case of *Tyler* v. *Wilkinson*, in the courts of the United States[212] . . . as 'an incident to the land; and that whoever seeks to found an exclusive use must establish a rightful appropriation in some manner known and admitted by the law'.[213]

But in the case of a well sunk by a proprietor in his own land, the water which feeds it from a neighbouring soil does not flow openly in the sight of the neighbouring proprietor, but through the hidden veins of the earth beneath its surface; no man can tell what changes these underground sources have undergone in the process of time: . . . again, no proprietor knows what portion of water is taken from beneath his own soil: how much he gives originally, or how much he transmits only, or how much he receives: on the contrary, until the well is sunk, and the water collected by draining into it, there cannot properly be said, with reference to the well, to be any flow of water at all. In the case, therefore of the well, there can be no ground for implying any natural consent or agreement, for ages past, between the owners of the several lands beneath which the underground springs may exist . . . ; nor, for the same reason, can any trace of a positive law be inferred from long-continued acquiescence and submission, whilst the very existence of the underground springs or of the well may be unknown to the proprietors of the soil.

Apart from these doctrinal objections, the practical consequences of allowing rights to underground water flow were unattractive. Such rights would sterilize the use of much land, for ability to exploit the soil depended greatly on power to drain or otherwise interfere with water in the subsoil, often at the expense of neighbours.

In the case of the running stream, the owner of the soil merely transmits the water over its surface: he receives as much from his neighbour as he sends down to his neighbour below: he is neither better nor worse off: the level of the water remains the same. But if the man who sinks the well in his own land can acquire by that act an absolute and indefeasible right to the water that collects in it, he has the power of preventing his neighbour from making any use of the spring in his own soil which shall interfere with the enjoyment of the well. He has the power, still further, of debarring the owner of the land in which the spring is first found, or through which it is transmitted, from

212 (1827) 4 Mason's (U.S.) Rep. 401; 24 Fed. Cas. 472 (Case No. 14,312), discussed in Ch. 6, the text accompanying nn. 22–33 below.

213 *Acton* v. *Blundell* (1843) 12 M. & W. 324, 349–50; 152 E.R. 1223, 1233 per Tindal CJ, citing *Tyler* v. *Wilkinson* per Story J, 24 Fed. Cas. 472, 474, discussed in Ch. 6, the text accompanying nn. 22–32 below.

draining his land for the proper cultivation of the soil: and thus, by an act which is voluntary on his part, and which may be entirely unsuspected by his neighbour, he may impose on such neighbour the necessity of bearing a heavy expense, if the latter has erected machinery for the purposes of mining, and discovers, when too late, that the appropriation of the water has already been made. Further, the advantage on one side and the detriment to the other may bear no proportion. The well may be sunk to supply a cottage or a drinking place for cattle: while the owner of the adjoining land may be prevented from winning metals and minerals of inestimable value. And, lastly, there is no limit of space within which the claim of right to an underground spring can be confined: in the present case, the nearest coal-pit is at the distance of half a mile from the well: it is obvious the law must equally apply if there is an interval of many miles.[214]

The lengthy submissions and citations of authority by counsel were held to be mostly beside the point:

No case has been cited on either side bearing directly on the subject in dispute. The case of *Cooper* v. *Barber*,[215] which approaches nearest to it, seems to make against [P's arguments]. . . . In that case the defendant had, for many years penned back a stream for the purpose of irrigation, in consequence of which the water had percolated through a porous and gravelly soil into the plaintiff's land: but as this percolation had been insensible, and unknown by the plaintiff until the land was applied for building purposes, the Court held, that the defendant had gained no right thereby, so as to justify its continuance.[216]

The arguments of counsel culled from Roman texts[217] were also held to be inconclusive. After accepting the persuasive status of Roman doctrine in English law,[218] Tindal CJ observed:

The authority of one at least of the learned Roman lawyers appears decisive upon the point in favour of the defendants; of some others the opinion is expressed with more obscurity. In the Digest [39.3.1.12. (Marcellus)]: '[no action, not even the action for fraud, can be brought against a person who, while digging on his own land, diverts his neighbour's water supply. And of course the latter ought not to have even the action

[214] *Acton* v. *Blundell* (1843) 12 M. & W. 324, 349–54; 152 E.R. 1223, 1233–55 per Tindal CJ.

[215] (1810) 3 Taunt. 99; 128 E.R. 405 (C.P.), discussed in the text accompanying nn. 72–75 above.

[216] *Acton* v. *Blundell* (1843) 12 M. & W. 324, 352; 152 E.R. 1223, 1234.

[217] Citing, *inter alia*, Inst.2.1.1.; D.39.3.1.12. (Marcellus); D.39.3.1.21. (Ulpian, Labeo); C.3.34.10., 12.; and also Bracton, f. 221–2, 232. See generally D.39.3.1.pr.–23. (Ulpian); D.39.3.2.6., 9. (Labeo); D.39.3.2.pr., 3.; D.39.3.14. (Paul); D.39.3.6.4.–8.; D.39.3.16. (Ulpian); D.39.2.19.–20. (Pomponius); D.39.3.24.pr. (Alfeus), allowing interference with natural flow for purposes of cultivation, or by custom or consent.

[218] Cf. *Bradford Corporation* v. *Pickles* [1894] 3 Ch. 53 (Ch.); [1895] A.C. 587 (H.L.); Ch. 6, the text accompanying nn. 158–161 below; M. Taggart, *Private Property and Abuse of Rights in Victorian England: The Story of Edward Pickles and the Bradford Water Supply* (Oxford, 2002) 49–74 and passim.

for fraud, assuming the other person acted not with the intention of harming his neighbour, but with that of improving his own field.]'[219]

Cowling, P's counsel, argued that Marcellus's doctrine, allowing abstraction of underground water in the absence of malice, ought not be applied in modern times. His celebrated exchange with Maule J on this point reveals the policy choices presented to the court, in the guise of interpretative debates:

[Maule J:] It appears to me that what Marcellus [D.39.3.12.] says is against you....
[Cowling:] His language is to be construed according to the state of things at the period he used it. Mining was then altogether unknown, at least on the scale and with the means now applied to it. He meant therefore, probably, digging a well in order to obtain access to the stream, that he might use it for occupation purposes: and it may be admitted... that the occupiers of the land have a right to the use of the water flowing through it for occupation purposes, though such use may possibly, and in rare instances, prejudice their neighbours. Such use, however, is very different from that in the present case, where, by means of steam-engines, &c., the defendants continually abstract all the water from the plaintiff's land. That the Romans knew little about cutting off or using under-ground currents of water appears from their use of aqueducts.
[Maule J:] That is not conclusive; it is certain that they, in some instances, used water-pipes for their dwelling-houses. What do you understand by user for occupation purposes?
[Cowling:] Such purposes as Vinnius refers to [in his commentaries on the Institutes], ad lavandum et potandum, for the use of the family or cattle. It may be difficult to define the exact boundary of those purposes; the same difficulty would have applied to the doctrine in *Mason* v. *Hill*, and yet was not noticed.... A right like the present seems acknowledged from the remotest times; for wells have always been considered as of the highest value: habitations and towns have grown up about them, and yet, if the defendants are right, all this is held at the caprice of the owner of neighbouring mines, who may lay those wells dry at any moment they please; for it is very difficult to say, that, if the mine-owner may do so within twenty years, he can be barred by any lapse of time.[220]

Notwithstanding extensive arguments offered to the court by counsel, Tindal CJ finally excluded from consideration all theories of *sic utere tuo*, natural right, implied contractual forebearance, and presumed grant. The various Roman law texts were held by Tindal CJ to be of persuasive authority only, though Marcellus's opinion in this instance was found to be 'decisive in favour of [D]'.[221] Cowling made a belated attempt to withdraw the Digest text from the discussion: 'The extracts from the civil law are, at most, conflicting... when the Roman lawyers speak of cutting off veins of water, they are alluding solely to the doing so for occupation purposes [i.e. not for

[219] (1843) 12 M. & W. 324, 353; 152 E.R. 1223, 1234–5 (translation supplied).
[220] 12 M. & W. 324, 336; 152 E.R. 1223, 1228.
[221] 12 M. & W. 324, 353; 152 E.R. 1223, 1235.

draining]'.[222] It is not clear whether Cowling's rather inept display of Roman learning assisted P's case all that much in the end; it probably harmed it.[223] Tindal CJ's judgment finally rested on a simple absolutist concept of land-ownership *usque ad coelum et ad infernos*, a philosophical rather than a historicist approach, calculated to promote an individualistic or libertarian plenitude of power for the land owner:

> [W]e intimate no opinion whatever as to what might be the rule of law, if there had been an uninterrupted user of the right for more than the last twenty years; but, confining ourselves strictly to the facts stated in the bill of exceptions, we think the present case, for the reasons above given, is not to be governed by the law which applies to rivers and flowing streams, but that it rather falls within that principle, which gives to the owner of the soil all that lies beneath his surface; that the land immediately below is his property, whether it is solid rock, or porous ground, or venous earth, or part soil, part water; that the person who owns the surface may dig therein, and apply all that is there found to his own purposes as his free will and pleasure; and that if, in the exercise of such right, he intercepts or drains off the water collected from underground springs in his neighbour's well, this inconvenience to his neighbour falls within the description of damnum absque injuria, which cannot become the ground of an action.[224]

This considered statement was not the last word on the subject. The English common law of property use was soon to be rewritten yet again, under the impact of fresh influences. There was a new specialist treatise literature; a more serious engagement with civilian doctrine and technique; and, most importantly, exposure to the confident and articulate judgments of the American common-law courts.

222 12 M. & W. 324, 347; 152 E.R. 1223, 1232.

223 Cf. A. D. E. Lewis, '"What Marcellus says is against you": Roman Law and Common Law', in A. D. E. Lewis and D. J. Ibbetson (eds.), *The Roman Law Tradition* (Cambridge, 1994) 199–208.

224 *Acton* v. *Blundell* (1843) 12 M. & W. 324, 353–4; 152 E.R. 1223, 1235 (Ex. Ch.).

6. *The Establishment of Modern Riparian Doctrine*

THE INFLUENCE OF CIVILIAN AND AMERICAN RIPARIAN DOCTRINE IN THE NINETEENTH CENTURY

Roman Doctrine and the Rise of Treatise Literature

Roman law has always been a presence in English legal thought, and its influence strengthened in the early nineteenth century. Roman doctrine was received into common-law reasoning by a number of paths. Legal intellectuals employed Roman concepts in generalizing or describing the common law, as had Blackstone and Hale a century earlier;[1] civil law was taught in the new reformed and university-based legal education; and above all there was much study and adoption of the details of Roman doctrine by practising lawyers seeking solutions to the new problems of the industrial age. The rise of a new treatise literature restating and shaping the law in specific subject-areas involved heavy reliance on Roman principles, sometimes taken directly from the Justinianic sources, often derived from the French civilian law. The resort to Pothier's *Treatise on the Law of Obligations*[2] by the creators of modern contract law is a well-known instance.[3] In the sphere of property law, the *Code Civil*, Domat, Vinnius, and other civilian sources provided direct models for Charles Gale as he gathered together the English doctrines dealing with easements and rights of property use incidental to ownership.[4] In the preface to the first edition of his treatise in 1839 Gale wrote:

[1] Sir Henry Maine and John Austin being two prominent examples: see P. G. Stein, *Legal Evolution* (Cambridge, 1980) 71–2, 86–98; J. Morison, *John Austin* (London, 1982). The literature here is vast: for an overview see P. G. Stein, 'Continental Influences in English Legal Thought, 1600–1900', in P. G. Stein, *The Character and Influence of the Roman Civil Law. Historical Essays* (London, 1988) 209–29; M. H. Hoeflich, *Roman and Civil Law and the Development of Anglo-American Jurisprudence in the Nineteenth Century* (Athens, Ga., 1997).

[2] R. Pothier, *Traité des obligations* (*Treatise on the Law of Obligations*) (Paris, 1761–4; W. D. Evans (trans.), London, 1806).

[3] See A. W. B. Simpson, 'Innovation in Nineteenth Century Contract Law', in A. W. B. Simpson, *Legal Theory and Legal History. Essays on the Common Law* (London, 1987) 171, 178 ff.; P. S. Atiyah, *The Rise and Fall of Freedom of Contract* (Oxford, 1979) 399–408; A. D. E. Lewis, '"What Marcellus says is against you": Roman law and Common law', in A. D. E. Lewis and D. J. Ibbetson (eds.), *The Roman Law Tradition* (Cambridge, 1994) 199–208. It is not entirely clear how far treatise writers influenced the courts, in part because of the convention of not citing academic authors (especially live ones), a theme investigated in N. Duxbury, *Jurists and Judges: An Essay on Influence* (Oxford, 2001).

[4] C. J. Gale, *A Treatise on the Law of Easements* (1st edn., with T. D. Whatley, London, 1839). Gale's original co-author remains entirely obscure to this day. The success of the work may be

The difficulties which arise from the abstruseness and refinements incident to the subject [of Easements], have been increased by the comparatively small number of decided Cases affording matter for defining and systematizing this branch of the law. Upon some points, indeed, there is no authority at all in the English Law;–of the decisions, some depend on the circumstances of the particular case, and some are irreconcilable with each other.... Water-courses are the only class of Easements with regard to which the law has been settled with any degree of precision.

...

As in many other branches of the law of England, the earlier authorities upon the law of easements appear to be based upon the Civil Law, modified, in some degree, probably, by a recognition of customs which existed among our Norman ancestors. The most remarkable instance of an adoption by the English law of this source is the doctrine known in the French law by the title of 'Destination du père de famille.'[5]

In the majority of the cases, both ancient and modern, probably from a consideration of this being the origin of the law, recourse has been had for assistance to the Civil Law. It has, therefore, been considered that the utility of the work would be increased by the introduction of many of the provisions of that refined an elaborate system with respect to Praedial Servitudes, and the doctrine of Prescription; as well as some of the observations of Pardessus—an eminent French writer on Servitudes.[6]

In Gale's second edition of 1849 the preface stated:

The introduction of the Civil Law, 'The collected wisdom of the ages', into this Treatise, has, it is believed, been found extremely useful; and, indeed, on this branch of our law the opinions of the civilians seem to be now almost adopted as authority.[7]

measured from its multiple editions: 2nd edn., 1849; 3rd edn. by W. H. Willes, 1862; 4th edn. by D. Gibbons, 1868; 5th edn., 1876; 6th edn. by G. Cave, 1888; 7th edn., 1899. The work lives on as a modern text, in the 16th edn. by J. Gaunt and P. Morgan, London, 1997. Comparable specialists texts included J. L. Goddard, *A Treatise on the Law of Easements* (1st edn., 1871, 2nd edn., London, 1877); and particularly in relation to water rights, W. Bainbridge, *A Treatise on the Law of Mines and Minerals* (1st edn., 1841; 2nd edn., London, 1856); D. Gibbons, *A Treatise on the Law of Dilapidations and Nuisances* (London, 1849) ch. X, 366–9; J. B. Phear, *A Treatise on Rights of Water, including Public and Private Rights to the Sea and Sea-Shore* (London, 1859); O. S. Round, *Riparian Rights, Being a Concise Review of the Law Relating to Running Streams, Angling, and the Sea Shore* (London, 1859); H. W. Woolrych, *A Treatise on the Law of Waters* (2nd. edn., London, 1851); G. V. Yool, *An Essay on Waste, Nuisance, and Trespass, Chiefly with Reference to Remedies in Equity* (London, 1863) 123–48; H. J. W. Coulson and U. A. Forbes, *The Law Relating to Waters, Sea, Tidal and Inland* (1st edn., London, 1880); S. M. Leake, *A Digest of the Law of Uses and Profits of Land* (London, 1888); J. M. Gould, *A Treatise on the Law of Waters, including Riparian Rights* (Chicago, Ill., 1883).

[5] See further the text accompanying nn. 65–70 below; A. W. B. Simpson, 'The Rule in Wheeldon v. Burrows and the Civil Code', in Simpson, *Legal Theory and Legal History*, 163–70.

[6] Gale, *Easements*, pp. vii–ix. The reference to (presumably) Jean Marie Pardessus (1772–1853) is slightly obscure; Pardessus wrote on French legal history, commercial law, and maritime law and law of the sea, publishing much of his work in the 1840s.

[7] Gale, *Easements* (2nd edn., London, 1849) p. v.

Romanism in the Modern Courts

It was not only the treatise writers such as Gale who followed the path to Roman law in the nineteenth century. English judges of this classical period of the common law also accorded great respect to Roman and civilian doctrine, both as an intellectual achievement and as a source of working precedents to help them in their labours; and this tendency was especially strong in property law. The concepts of easement, prescription, customs, commons, and natural right which structured the English law of land use had undergone centuries of separate common-law development since the time of Bracton; and these doctrines were now further developed and recast by self-conscious infusions of Romanism. For example, in *Acton* v. *Blundell*, Tindal CJ quoted extensively from Justinian's *Institutes* and Digest to support his judgment, and further stated:

The Roman law forms no rule, binding in itself, upon the subjects of these realms; but, in deciding a case upon principle, where no direct authority can be cited from our books, it affords no small evidence of the soundness of the conclusion at which we have arrived, if it proves to be supported by that law, the fruit of the researches of the most learned men, the collected wisdom of ages and the groundwork of the municipal law of most of the countries in Europe.[8]

In an 1829 Privy Council case defining the nature of prescriptive rights controlling land use, the judges stated:

The Roman law relative to prescription has been adopted into the law of Normandy, which prevails in Jersey. We profess to act on the same principles. We say, on the authority of the commentators of the civil law, that the right which is to be supported by prescription must have existed beyond the memory of man. (Domat. Lois Civiles, lib. 3, tit. 7, sec. 4.) They have fixed on the term of 30 years as exceeding that period. Our law has carried the time of legal memory back to the return of Richard I. from the Holy Land. The sort of possession that is required to establish a prescription, is the same in the civil law, the law of Jersey, and of our common law. Whoever, indeed, will take the trouble to read Bracton, and our other early writers on the common law, will be surprised to find the number of doctrines they have adopted, and even whole passages they have transcribed from the civil law.[9]

And in the prescription case of *Dalton* v. *Angus* in 1881, Lord Blackburn displayed a close familiarity with Roman law and acknowledged its place in shaping the common law. More generally he stated:

No one who has ever looked at the Digest will complain of [the] Praetorian law as brief; nor will any one who has read any portion of it fail to admire the skill with

[8] *Acton* v. *Blundell* (1843) 12 M. & W. 324, 353; 152 E.R. 1223, 1234 (Ex.) per Tindal CJ.

[9] *Benest* v. *Pipon* (1829) 1 Knapp. 60, 69–70; 12 E.R. 243 (P.C., Jersey). The judgment also discusses Bracton, Domat, and the *Code Civil*. Brougham and Denman, leading judges of the next generation of common lawyers, were counsel citing civilian authorities in this case.

which legal principles are worked out. Some of the edicts of the Praetors are so obviously just and expedient, and are so tersely expressed, that they have been generally adopted, and are quoted as legal maxims by those who often do not know whence they came.... [T]he English law as to prescription was, beyond controversy, greatly derived from the Roman law, the very words of which are often quoted in the earliest English authorities.... [10]

American Civilianism and Riparian Law

Further cosmopolitan influence came from English adoption of much American common-law doctrine, especially that created by James Kent and Joseph Story. These two great scholar-judges were steeped in Roman and civilian law, and resorted to it with alacrity as a 'republican' source of principles from which to construct an American common law distinct from its pre-revolutionary English beginnings.[11] Wiel has demonstrated how Kent and Story's water law in particular was directly influenced by the French *Code Civil*, which codified many of the Roman principles.[12] This American doctrine in turn helped shape the emergent common law of easements back in England, a reciprocal influence which was another contribution of Charles Gale to the subject. He wrote in the first edition of his *Law of Easements*:

With the same view [of using civilian law] the authority of decisions in the American Courts has been called in aid upon the question of water-courses—questions which the value of water as a moving power, and the frequent absence of ancient appropriation, have often given rise to in the United States. In those judgments the law is considered with much care and research, and the rights of the parties settled with

[10] *Dalton* v. *Angus* (1881) 6 App. Cas. 740, 819, 822 (H.L.).

[11] P. G. Stein, 'The Attraction of the Civil Law in Post-Revolutionary America', in Stein, *Historical Essays*, 411–42; G. E. White, *The American Judicial Tradition. Profiles of Leading American Judges* (2nd edn., New York, 1988) ch. 2, 35–63; J. H. Langbein, 'Chancellor Kent and the History of Legal Literature' (1993) 93 Columbia Law Review 547; R. H. Helmholz, 'Use of the Civil Law in Post-Revolutionary American Jurisprudence' (1992) 66 Tulane Law Review 1649; Hoeflich, *Roman and Civil Law and the Development of Anglo-American Jurisprudence*; cf. A. Watson, 'Chancellor Kent's Use of Foreign Law', in M. Reimann (ed.), *The Reception of Continental Ideas in the Common Law World 1820–1920* (Berlin, 1993), 45 (arguing that Kent's use of civilian sources was rhetorical rather than authoritative).

[12] S. C. Wiel, 'Origin and Comparative Development of the Law of Watercourses in the Common Law and in the Civil Law' (1917–18) 6 California Law Review 245, 342 and 'Waters: American Law and French Authority' (1919) 33 Harvard Law Review 133. The French versions of Roman doctrine are contained in the *Code Civil* liv. II, tit. IV (Servitudes or Land Services) arts. 637–639, and ch. I (Servitudes which Derive from the Situation of the Premises) Arts. 640–645; see J. B. J. Pailliet, *Manuel de Droit Français* 2 vols. (Paris, 1837) i, 216–21; *The French Civil Code* (trans. J. H. Crabb, South Hackensack, NJ, 1977) 145–6; see further the text accompanying nn. 65–70 below. By contrast there seems to have been little influence from the fertile contemporary German sources: see H. W. Baade, 'Springs, Creeks, and Groundwater in Nineteenth-Century German Roman-Law Jurisprudence with a Twentieth Century Postscript', in D. S. Clark (ed.), *Comparative and Private International Law. Essays in Honour of John Henry Merryman on his Seventieth Birthday* (Berlin, 1990) 61.

precision. The result of the authorities is stated by Chancellor Kent, in his well-known Commentaries, with his usual ability.[13]

So when the English courts of King's Bench and Exchequer relied on the authority of Story and Kent (together with Pothier and the *Code Civil*) in deciding some of the pivotal water rights cases of the nineteenth century, the influence of Roman law was again at work within the common law.

American riparian doctrines date from the early nineteenth century, when industrialization in New England and the north-eastern states led to intense competition for water power for textile mills and other manufactures.[14] The American courts addressed many of the unresolved issues of English water law in a series of elaborate, open-textured decisions. American doctrine was based on English common law; but there was much variance from jurisdiction to jurisdiction, producing ambiguous rules affording judges considerable discretion in specific cases.[15] Here will be summarized the main doctrines that influenced English judges and jurists.

Around 1800 a natural-right theory was commonly propounded in the American courts. This allowed riparian proprietors the use of a stream at will, provided they did not interfere with natural flow beyond the level of insignificant abstractions for domestic use, agriculture, and husbandry. Some jurisdictions allowed diversion of the natural flow of water to any degree, provided necessary uses of neighbours were not disrupted; or even beyond that level if a prescriptive right to divert water was established by long enjoyment. *Shorey* v. *Gorrell*[16] used the prescriptive idea to stand natural-

[13] Gale, *Easements* (1st edn., 1839) p. vii. In the second edition of 1849, at p. vi, Gale noted that '[i]n *Acton v. Blundell* the Court of Exchequer Chamber cited American authority as, at least proper to be weighed and examined in deciding a case upon principle'.

[14] Full acounts are given in T. Steinberg, *Nature Incorporated: Industrialization and the Waters of New England* (New York, 1991); L. C. Hunter, *Waterpower in the Century of the Steam Engine*, Vol. 1 of L. C. Hunter, *A History of Industrial Power in the United States, 1780–1930* (Charlottesville, Va., 1979).

[15] For the history of American riparian law see M. J. Horwitz, *The Transformation of American Law 1780–1860* (henceforth *Transformation*) (Cambridge, Mass., 1977) 31–53; Steinberg, *Nature Incorporated*; W. W. Fisher III, *The Law of the Land: An Intellectual History of American Property Doctrine, 1776–1940* (MS., Harvard Law School, 1990) 149–206; C. M. Rose, 'Energy and Efficiency in the Realignment of Common Law Water Rights' (1990) 19 Journal of Legal Studies 261, 277–88. For the divergence of water law in the eastern and western states see D. J. Pisani, 'Enterprise and Equity: A Critique of Western Water Law in the Nineteenth Century' (1987) Western Historical Quarterly 18, *Water, Land, and Law in the West: The Limits of Public Policy, 1850–1920* (Lawrence, Kan., 1996), *To Reclaim a Divided West: Water, Law, and Public Policy, 1848–1902* (Albuquerque, N. Mex., 1992), and *From the Family Farm to Agribusiness: The Irrigation Crusade in California and the West 1850–1931* (Berkeley, Calif., 1984); D. Worster, *Rivers of Empire: Water, Aridity, and the Growth of the American West* (New York, 1985). The law is stated concisely in C. Donahue Jr., T. E. Keeper, and P. W. Martin, *Property: An Introduction to the Concept and the Institution. Cases and Materials* (3rd edn., St. Paul, Minn., 1993) 244–60; S. F. Kurtz and H. Hovenkamp, *Cases and Materials on American Property Law* (2nd edn., St Paul, Minn., 1993) 1–41.

[16] (1783) Mass. S.C., ref. in Horwitz, *Transformation*, 274, n. 10.

right theory on its head, stating that there was a right to obstruct water flowing to a neighbour unless the neighbour had secured a right to the natural flow by prescriptive use. Other Massachusetts cases indicated that a right-creating user could mean only possession of land to which water had always flowed, and did not necessitate an actual water appropriation in order to maintain a title. There were also a number of decisions upholding a more severely competitive regime, allowing the first appropriator for a beneficial purpose to deny other users access to water, even in the absence of prescriptive title augmenting his common right—a rule favouring upstream at the expense of downstream proprietors, and large dam-builders and water users at the expense of smaller users.

The 1805 New York case of *Palmer* v. *Mulligan*[17] put forward a novel doctrine, allowing each riparian owner a right to the natural flow, subject to reasonable interferences in their own usage in order to allow beneficial usage by rival owners. The new rule was necessary to prevent the natural rights restraining application of water flow to productive milling operations: the common-law right to water 'must be restrained within reasonable bounds so as not to deprive a man of the enjoyment of his property'. Sometimes this rule of reasonable forbearance was subsumed within the idea of *sic utere tuo*: for example in the 1818 case of *Platt* v. *Johnson*, a mill use occasionally denying water to downstream users was justified by the *sic utere tuo* maxim, which 'must be taken and construed with an eye to the natural rights of all'. This approach was a radical recasting of the seventeenth-century English use of *sic utere tuo* expressed in *Aldred's Case*, which enforced strict natural rights emphatically without engaging in the utilitarian balancing of interests. By contrast, according to New York law:

> Although some conflict may be produced in the use and enjoyment of such [natural water] rights, it cannot be considered, in judgment of law, an infringement of right. If it becomes useful to one, in consequence of the enjoyment by another, it is by accident, and because it is dependent on the exercise of the equal rights of others.

Joseph Angell's exhaustive 1824 treatise on the Anglo-American law of watercourses attacked the tendency of the eastern states' courts to permit 'reasonable' interferences with natural flow in the name of utility and *sic utere tuo*.[18] Angell argued that trivial or immaterial interferences should be allowed, but criticized any rule allowing substantial expropriation of natural flow merely because the court thought this justified by utility; such a principle was against all common-law precedent and policy. As late as 1840, Angell insisted that water rights could not be appropriative:

[17] (1805) 3 Cai. R. 307 (N.Y. Sup. Ct.).

[18] J. K. Angell, *A Treatise on the Law of Watercourses* (1st edn., Boston, Mass., 1824) 37–41; see also his *An Inquiry into the Rule of Law Which Creates a Right to an Incorporeal Hereditament by an Adverse Enjoyment of Twenty Years with Remarks on the Application of the Rule to Light, and in Certain Cases to a Water Privilege* (Boston, Mass., 1827).

[A] watercourse begins *ex jure naturae*, and having taken a certain course naturally, cannot be diverted ... water flows in its natural course, and should be permitted thus to flow, so that all through whose land it naturally flows, may enjoy the privilege of using it. The property in the water therefore, by virtue of the riparian ownership, is in its nature usu-fructuary, and consists not so much of the fluid itself, as the advantage of its impetus.[19]

Angell's argument could, however, be accommodated within the new utilitarian theory by subsuming his idea of permissible 'insignificant deprivation' of natural flow within the test of 'reasonable' usage.[20] A stable synthesis of the reasonable and natural usage tests was soon developed by the eminent Justice Story in a series of cases beginning with *Tyler* v. *Wilkinson* in 1827.[21]

Tyler v. *Wilkinson* and the Story Doctrine

Story J stated in *Tyler* that he had studied the entire corpus of English and American water law to prepare his judgment, and his lengthy opinion touched upon many or most of the ideas of riparian law that went before, though Story quoted no case law directly and cited English authority only at the vaguest level of generality. The significant portion of his opinion was printed at length in Gale's *Law of Easements*, providing an important path for American ideas to enter the English law. Gale stated that 'the Courts of the United States ... recognize and profess to be guided by the principles of the English law'; and further argued that Story J had merely affirmed Bractonian doctrine, viz. that riparian owners have a natural water right, subject to variation by prescription and grant. For Gale, the essence of *Tyler* was that:

[T]he right to have a stream flow in its accustomed course is ... a right universally incident to the property in the adjoining land, a right which can only be interfered with by the acquisition of an easement; and the ordinary rights of the owners of the adjacent land to the natural flow of the stream are distinguished ... from the acquisitions in derogation of the common rights made by an exclusive appropriation of the water.[22]

This was a standard and rather uninformative analysis of the problems. More significant was Story J's theory of the extent of the common right arising naturally from riparian possession, and how this related to prior appropriations.

[19] J. K. Angell, *A Treatise on the Law of Watercourses* (3rd edn., Boston, Mass., 1840) 11.
[20] Horwitz, *Transformation*, 38–9.
[21] (1827) 4 Mason (U.S.) 397; 24 Fed. Cas. 472 (Case No. 14,312).
[22] Gale, *Easements* (1st edn., 1839) 130–1; (3rd edn., 1862, by W. H. Willes) 190–1.

Nine relevant propositions may be extracted from Story's *Tyler* judgment:[23]

(1) 'Prima facie every proprietor upon each bank of a river is entitled to the land, covered with water, in front of his bank, to the middle thread of the stream, or ... usque ad filum aquae.' This was a straightforward restatement of Roman principle.

(2) 'In virtue of this ownership he has a right to the water flowing over it in its natural current, without diminution or obstruction. But ... he has no property in the water itself; but a simple use of it, while it passes along.'

(3) '[N]o proprietor has a right to use the water to the prejudice of another.... [T]he right being common to all the proprietors on the river, no one has a right to diminish the quantity which will, according to the natural current, flow to a proprietor below, or to throw it back upon a proprietor above'. At face value this is an uncompromising statement of natural right theory, prohibiting any interference with the natural current. Story J emphasized the absolutism of the common natural right in characteristically grand language: 'The natural stream, existing by the bounty of Providence for the benefit of the land through which it flows, is an incident annexed, by operation of law, to the land itself'; it was a 'perfect equality of right among all the proprietors ... common to all'.

(4) The apparent absolutism of the common natural right to water was then moulded by Story J into something quite different: a theory of reasonable rights to the natural stream. The key passage is as follows:

> When I speak of this common right, I do not mean to be understood, as holding the doctrine, that there can be no diminution whatsoever, and no obstruction whatsoever, by a riparian proprietor, in the use of the water as it flows; for that would be to deny any valuable use of it. There ... must be allowed of that, which is common to all, a reasonable use. The true test of the principle and extent of the use is, whether it is to the injury of the other proprietors or not. There may be a diminution in quantity, or a retardation or acceleration of the natural current indispensable for the general and valuable use of the water, perfectly consistent with the existence of the common right. The diminution, retardation, or acceleration, not positively and sensibly injurious by diminishing the value of the common right, is an implied element in the right of using the stream at all. The law here ... acts with a reasonable reference to public convenience and general good, and it is not betrayed into a narrow strictness, subversive of common sense, nor into an extravagant looseness, which would destroy private rights. The maxim is applied, 'Sic utere tuo, ut non alienum laedas.'

Story J here transforms strict natural rights into reasonable rights by playing on the ambiguity of the notion of 'injury', both at law and in common speech. Injury can mean either invasion of right or damage and loss; hence Story J could say that there is a right to the full natural flow, but

[23] (1827) 24 Fed. Cas. 472, 474–5; also reprinted in Gale, *Easements*, (3rd edn.) 191–4.

at the same time assert that this was a right only to a reasonable access to the natural flow, for by his definitions there was no injury to rights if proprietors were allowed to vary natural flow for productive purposes, and thereby cause a permissible loss to other proprietors' interests by curbing or displacing their access to water. The level of 'reasonable' or permitted abstraction under the new test was defined as user causing no 'sensible injury' to other riparian proprietors, so that appropriation did not diminish the value of the common right. Common rights in a shared resource, such as water, were not valuable unless some encroachment on others was permitted, some form of reciprocal compromise. However, this principle of forbearance of itself could provide no bright line between acceptable encroachment and wrongful invasion of others' rights. Ultimately the test rested on the criteria of 'reasonableness' or common sense—in other words, the text bestowed a strong judicial discretion allowing courts to balance the interests and utilities of competitors. This was a neat inversion of the seventeenth-century application of *sic utere tuo*.

The final elements of Story J's doctrine in *Tyler* may be dealt with swiftly:

(5) '[O]f a thing, common by nature, there may be an appropriation by general consent or grant. Mere priority of appropriation of running water, without such consent or grant, confers no exclusive right. It is not like the case of mere occupancy, where the first occupier takes by force of his priority of occupancy'.
(6) '[W]hoever seeks to found an exclusive use, must establish a rightful appropriation, either by a grant from all the proprietors, whose interest is affected by the particular appropriation, or by a long exclusive enjoyment, without interruption, which affords a just presumption of right'.
(7) '[U]pon principles of public convenience, the term of twenty years of exclusive uninterrupted enjoyment has been held a conclusive presumption of a grant or right'. As a conclusive presumption, the 'grant' was effectively a fiction providing for direct prescription of right from enjoyment; hence it did not matter if it was proved that a real grant could not actually have been made in the circumstances.
(8) A mill owner, or other user, therefore had two types of water title: his general common right to the reasonable use of natural flow and additional rights won by prescriptive appropriation, or by express grant in excess of common right.
(9) It followed that no title to water could be derived from a mill use falling short of the prescriptive period; and further that surplus water not legally appropriated by grant or prescription was open to general competitive appropriation by other proprietors.

A Closer Look at *Sic Utere Tuo*

The reshaped doctrine of *sic utere tuo* was the keystone of Story J's argument. The doctrine was sometimes described as the Golden Rule in common-law guise—'do to others what you would have them to you'.[24] Burrough J outlined just such a concept of *sic utere tuo* in *Deane* v. *Clayton*,[25] an 1817 case in the Court of Common Pleas concerning rights to destroy neighbours' animals trespassing on one's property:

> This principle is, in all its parts, restrictive of the use a man may make of his own property. It shews he is not to make any use he pleases of it, as not thereby to injure another: he must look forward to the situation of others. Another may be injured in his person or his property: he is not to injure another in the enjoyment of his rights or property.... The noxious trade... considered abstractedly from the rights of others, is perfectly innocent; but if another has an existing right, and is in consequence injured by it, or prevented from the reasonable enjoyment of such right, he sustains an injury, for which an action may be maintained.[26]

But as later commentators and judges were to note, there could be divergent views on which conduct one might reasonably expect from one's neighbours, and hence how one would define one's own good conduct.[27] A follower of Hobbes, or of Kant, or of the Gospels might hold different interpretations of the standard of conduct to be expected under an abstract, normatively contentless Golden Rule. The structure of expectations between persons involves assessment of the conduct one is likely to receive from others; it is dependent on rules laid down by institutions and by culture, and cannot straightforwardly be discovered in natural law or reason.[28] In *Deane* v. *Clayton*, Dallas J made this point very clearly, seeking to curtail the *sic utere tuo* doctrine raised by Burrough J and assimilate it to absolute property ideas.

[24] *Bl.Comm.* iii, 218, Ch. 4, the text accompanying nn. 161–175 above. See further *Morley* v. *Pragnel* (1638) Cro. Car. 510; 79 E.R. 1039 (K.B.); *Turberville* v. *Stamp* (1697) 12 Mod. 152; 88 E.R. 1228; Comyn. Rep. 32, 33; 92 E.R. 944, 945 (K.B.); *Tenant* v. *Goldwin* (1704) 2 Ld. Raym.' 1089; 92 E.R. 222; 3 Ld. Raym. 324; 92 E.R. 712; 6 Mod. 311; 87 E.R. 1051 (K.B.); cases cited in J. H. Baker and S. F. C. Milsom, *Sources of English Legal History. Private Law to 1750* (London, 1986) 592–610. For later formulations of the doctrine see *Backhouse* v. *Bonomi* (1857–8) El. Bl. & El. 622, 643; 120 E.R. 643, 651 (Q.B.); (1859) El. Bl. & El. 646; 120 E.R. 652 (Ex. Ch.); (1861) 9 H.L.C. 503; 11 E.R. 825 (H.L.); *Rowbotham* v. *Wilson* (1856) 6 B. & El. 593; 119 E.R. 985 (Q.B.); (1857) 8 B. & El. 123; 125 E.R. 45 (Ex. Ch.); (1860) 8 H.L.C. 347; 11 E.R. 463 (H.L.).

[25] (1817) 7 Taunt. 489; 129 E.R. 196 (C.P.).

[26] 7 Taunt. 489, 499–500; 129 E.R. 196, 200–1. See further J. Getzler, 'Judges and Hunters: Law and Economic Conflict in the English Countryside, 1800–60' in C. Brooks and M. Lobban (eds.), *Communities and Courts in Britain 1150–1900* (London, 1997) 199, 227–8.

[27] See C. Dalton, *Losing History: Tort Liability in the Nineteenth Century and the Case of Rylands v Fletcher* (MS., 1987) 132–76, esp. 151–72.

[28] This is a fundamental insight given by game theory, or the study of strategic behaviour where interacting parties' conduct is predicated on mutual predictions of conduct: J. F. Nash, 'The Bargaining Problem' (1950) 18 Econometrica 155; D. M. Kreps, 'Nash Equilibrium', in J. Eatwell, M. Milgate, and P. Newman, *The New Palgrave: A Dictionary of Economics* 4 vols. (London, 1987) iii, 584–8; D. M. Kreps, 'Nash Equilibrium' in *The New Palgrave: A Dictionary of Economics* 4 vols. (J. Eatwell, M. Milgate, and P. Newman (eds.), London, 1987) iii, 584–8.

[I]t is further said, you shall make such use of your own property as not to injure that of another; and to this also I agree, in the true sense of the maxim, which is, the right of another, for, if, in breach of this rule, my right be invaded by another, what is done by me, if only adequate to repel such invasion, is not an infringement of his right, but a defence of my own, and must turn on the consideration of what, to defend such rights, I am permitted by law to do.

On this foundation stands the whole law of actions on the case for consequential damages, and the doctrine of nuisance, as it may affect individuals or the public, in all its variation of form. The difference is, between absolute and relative rights, between that which is mine, exclusive of any right in others, present or future, and that which is of a spreading, shifting possession, as air, water, &c., in which I have but a qualified possession, a possession subservient to the future use by others.[29]

Erle CJ took a similar line in cases of 1858 and 1867:

As a general principle it is difficult to conceive a cause of action from damage when no right has been violated and no wrong has been done. The maxim sic utere tuo ut non alienum laedas is mere verbiage. A party may damage the property of another where the law permits, and he may not where the law prohibits: so that the maxim can never be applied til the law is ascertained, and, when it is the maxim is superfluous.[30]

The maxim 'sic utere tuo ut non alienum laedas' is no help to decision, as it cannot be applied till the decision is made; and the use of the word nuisance prolongs the dispute, because it means both annoyance that is actionable, and also that which is not actionable . . . [it] introduces an equivocation which is fatal to any hope of a clear settlement.[31]

And in 1894, Justice Holmes lumped *sic utere tuo* together with *damnum sine injuria* as simple-minded evasions of policy questions:

[Policy] decisions for or against the privilege [to inflict damage], . . . often are presented as hollow deductions from empty general propositions like *sic utere tuo ut alienum non laedas*, which teaches nothing but a benevolent yearning, or else are put as if they themselves embodied a postulate of the law and admitted of no further deduction, as when it is said that, although there is temporal damage, there is no wrong; whereas, the very thing to be found out is whether there is a wrong or not, and if not, why not.[32]

[29] *Deane* v. *Clayton* (1817) 7 Taunt. 489, 522; 129 E.R. 196, 209 per Dallas J.

[30] *Backhouse* v. *Bonomi* (1858) El. Bl. & El. 622, 643; 120 E.R. 643, 651 (Q.B.).

[31] *Brand* v. *Hammersmith and City Railway* (1867) L.R. 2 Q.B. 223, 247 (Ex. Ch.).

[32] O. W. Holmes Jr., 'Privilege, Malice and Intent' (1894) 8 Harvard Law Review 1, 3. A similar insight was offered later by Hohfeld with his distinction between 'rights' absolutely protected by law, and 'privileges', where permitted actions may legally be interfered with: see W. N. Hohfeld, *Fundamental Legal Conceptions as Applied in Judicial Reasoning* (New Haven, Conn., 1919); F. Bohlen, 'Incomplete Privilege to Inflict Intentional Invasions of Interests of Property and Personality' (1926) 39 Harvard Law Review 307, reprinted in F. Bohlen, *Studies in the Law of Torts* (Indianapolis, Ind., 1926) 614–35; R. A. Posner, *Tort Law: Cases and Economic Analysis* (Boston, Mass., 1982) 737–56; J. Singer, 'The Legal Rights Debate in Analytical Jurisprudence from Bentham to Hohfeld' [1982] Wisconsin Law Review 975; M. J. Horwitz,

An inverse justificatory principle which tends to shield actors and owners from liability for nuisance rather than establish liability was the 'live and let live' rule permitting 'reciprocal nuisances' in the course of everyday life, enunciated by Bramwell B in *Bamford* v. *Turnley*; this test was likewise entirely dependent on fact discretion and had no predictive quality.[33]

Returning to the sphere of water rights, Story J in *Tyler* used the inherent ambiguity of *sic utere tuo* as a pliable version of social contract theory, enabling the court to mould parties' behaviour according to free evaluative discretion, whilst purporting to follow a strictly ministerial or self-executing rule of law. The indeterminacy of the *sic utere tuo* rule was used to reduce barriers to water exploitation, and to introduce a controlling judicial discretion regulating the ensuing conflict and competition for resources.

After *Tyler* v. *Wilkinson*

In later cases, Story J indicated that he did not wish to see wide judicial discretion used to permit appropriations interfering with natural flow beyond a narrow threshold. Sizeable interference with natural flow was to be characterized as an invasion of right even if the injury occasioned no temporal damage.[34] This stance was consistent with his original *Tyler* doctrine; other judges however, were wont to allow far greater interferences with natural flow as legally and socially justified 'reasonable use'. It is incorrect to describe Story J's post-*Tyler* decisions as a return to an absolute natural-right theory contrary to his proportionality test in *Tyler*; his later decisions simply apply the *Tyler* test, but conservatively, to allow like interference with natural water flows.

In the 1838 case of *Webb* v. *Portland Manufacturing Co.*[35] Story J explained the conservative riparian test in terms of the idea of *injuria sine damno*. To this end he analysed the role of tort actions in defending property titles, reviewing the corpus of English doctrine including Lord Holt's judgment in *Ashby* v. *White*. *Webb* concerned a diversion of water by an upstream riparian owner, which did not interfere with the downstream mill owner's water use, but which sizeably reduced the water flow potentially available to him. Nominal damages and equitable injunction were made available in order to establish the title of the downstream owner against

The Transformation of American Law 1870–1960: The Crisis of Legal Orthodoxy (henceforth *Crisis*) (New York, 1992) 148–56; A. W. B. Simpson, 'The Timeless Principles of the Common Law: *Keeble* v. *Hickeringill* (1707)', in A. W. B. Simpson, *Leading Cases in the Common Law* (Oxford, 1995) 45–75, at 72–5.

33 (1862) 3 B. & S. 66, 83–4; 122 E.R. 27, 32–3, analysed in R. A. Epstein, 'Nuisance Law: Corrective Justice and its Utilitarian Constraints' (1979) 8 Journal of Legal Studies 49, 82–7; R. A. Epstein *Torts* (London, 1999) 372–5.

34 *Whipple* v. *Cumberland Manufacturing Co.* (1843) 29 Fed. Cas. 934 (No. 17, 516) (C.C.D. Me.), cited in Horwitz, *Transformation*, 275–6.

35 (1838) 3 Sumn. 189; 3 Law Rep. 374; 29 Fed. Cas. 506 (No. 17,322).

such encroachment, and to restrain further interferences. Story J held that in such cases *injuria sine damno* was the guiding concept:

I can very well understand that no action lies in a case where there is damnum absque injuria, that is, where there is damage done without any wrong or violation of any right of the plaintiff. But I am not able to understand, how it can correctly be said, in a legal sense, that an action will not lie, even in a case of a wrong or violation of a right, unless it is followed by some perceptible damage, which can be established, as a matter of fact; in other words, that injuria sine damno is not actionable. On the contrary, from my earliest reading, I have considered it laid up among the very elements of the common law, that, wherever there is a wrong, there is a remedy to redress it; and that every injury imports damage in the nature of it; and, if no other damage is established, the party injured is entitled to a verdict for nominal damages. A fortiori, this doctrine applies where there is not only a violation of a right of the plaintiff, but the act of the defendant, if continued, may become the foundation, by lapse of time, of an adverse right in the defendant; for then it assumes the character, not merely of a violation of a right, tending to diminish its value, but it goes to the absolute destruction and extinguishment of it.[36]

Story J then reasserted his test of reasonable usage of natural riparian flow, claiming that though 'there were formerly many vexed questions, and much contrariety of opinion', the principles were now well settled.[37] *Wright* v. *Howard* and *Mason* v. *Hill* were invoked as supporting the same reasonableness doctrine; even *Sury* v. *Pigot*, *Bealey* v. *Shaw*, and *Saunders* v. *Newman* were pressed into service to clothe the newly-formulated test with the semblance of settled common-law authority. American applications of the *Tyler* doctrine, which did require sizeable damage to a present use in order to ground an action, were deplored by Story J for confusing temporal loss with interference with rights. He added a final argument that interference with future rights could be characterized as present injury:

Now, the value of the mill privileges must essentially depend, not merely upon the velocity of the stream, but upon the head of water, which is permanently maintained. The necessary result of lowering the head of water permanently, would seem, therefore, to be a direct diminution of the value of the privileges. And if so, to that extent it must be an actual damage.[38]

[36] 29 Fed. Cas. 506, 507–8. For a wealth of English authority supporting the principle that injuries without damage are actionable to maintain rights and prevent adverse rights by acquiescence, see the arguments of counsel in *Embrey* v. *Owen* (1851) 6 Ex. 353, 363–6; 155 E.R. 579, 583–5 (Ex.).

[37] See also *Blanchard* v. *Baker* (1832) 8 Greenleaf 253 (S. C. Maine), and the text accompanying n. 39 below. Ultimately the reasonable usage test prevailed in the eastern states, but prior appropriation doctrine could be re-asserted on occasion: see e.g. *Cary* v. *Daniels* (1844) 49 Mass. (8 Met.) 466 (Mass. S.C.). In the drier western states, by contrast, a prior appropriation doctrine took root: see Donahue, Keeper, and Martin, *Property*, 244–60.

[38] 29 Fed. Cas., 510.

Story J approved the Maine case of *Blanchard* v. *Baker*, where similar ideas were propounded in the following terms:

A mill privilege not yet occupied is valuable for the purposes to which it may be applied. It is a property which no one can have a legal right to impair or destroy, by diverting from it the natural flow of the stream, upon which its value depends, although it may be impaired by the exercise of certain lawful rights, originating in prior occupancy. If an unlawful diversion is suffered for twenty years, it ripens into a right which cannot be controverted. If the party injured cannot be allowed, in the meantime, to vindicate his right by action, it would depend on the will of others, whether he should be permitted or not to enjoy that species of property.[39]

In conclusion, Story J's contribution to riparian doctrine may be summarized in terms of two key doctrines. First, the right to water is measured by the court's discretionary determination of the reasonable usage each proprietor should receive, in the circumstances of the particular case. Secondly, if the level of diversion or obstruction of water is an injury to that reasonable right, then it is an actionable wrong to title, even in the absence of any temporal damage to a present use. Thus the title to a reasonable flow of water is maintainable in the absence of an interference with present appropriations; the *Ashby* v. *White injuria sine damno* principle thereby pulls the law towards a natural-right theory of water entitlement.

A reproduction of Story J's *Tyler* doctrine was offered by James Kent in the third edition of his *Commentaries*,[40] and this source disseminated the doctrine widely on both sides of the Atlantic. It was cited with approval by Story J in *Webb*, and also quoted *in extenso* and adopted by Parke B in *Embrey* v. *Owen*, the classical English judgment on water rights.[41] Chancellor Kent concluded his discussion with a statement capturing the gist of Story's doctrine:

[T]his rule [of right to natural flow] must not be construed literally, for that would be to deny all valuable use of the water to the riparian proprietors. It must be subjected to the qualifications which have been mentioned [that proprietors should use the water in a reasonable manner, etc.], otherwise rivers and streams of water would become utterly useless, either for manufacturing or agricultural purposes. The just and equitable principle is given in the Roman law:—'*Sic enim debere quem meliorem agrum suum facere, ne vicini deteriorem faciat*'.[42]

[39] (1832) 8 Greenleaf 253, 268 (S. C. Maine).

[40] J. Kent, *Commentaries on American Law* 4 vols. (1st edn., Boston, Mass., 1826; 3rd edn., Boston, Mass., 1840) iii, lect. 52, 439–45.

[41] (1851) 6 Ex. 353, 369–71; 155 E.R. 579 (Ex.).

[42] D.39.3.1.4. (Ulpian): 'one must only improve one's field in such a way as not to reduce the quality of one's neighbour's field' (from A. Watson (ed.), *The Digest of Justinian* (trans. Watson *et al.*, Philadelphia, Pa., 1985, rev. edn., 1998).

The Role of Gale's *Law of Easements*

It has often been suggested that Gale played a leading role in new conceptualizations of water rights and other incidents of land use in the mid-nineteenth century.[43] However, the text does not make any significant contribution to leading English decisions, save as a convenient digest of extant Roman, French, and especially American doctrine. Gale did not take positions on key problems of water law, but simply reported the state of current law as he found it in each of his successive editions from 1839. His approach contrasts with that of writers such as Angell and Kent in America, who asserted their interpretations of how the law ought to be.

Gale's approach was not to write a reasoned exposition or synthesis of legal principle, but rather to illustrate the law by extracting lengthy portions of doctrine from judgments and treatises. His contribution was to arm counsel and judges with a range of doctrine to deploy as they struggled with the problems of new litigation. *Gale on Easements* and other leading texts on land and easement law such as *Goddard*[44] are best viewed as source-books of law—not as a site of law-making itself. This position reflects the weak role of nineteenth-century English academics and text-writers in clarifying and formulating doctrine for use in the courts. There was little tradition of jurists outside the courts taking a lead in doctrinal developments. The emergence of authoritative, intellectually rigorous texts dealing with legal subjects in an analytical fashion begins (albeit weakly) after the Judicature Act reforms and the establishment of modern university education in English law around 1870, an academic movement led by scholars such as Anson, Maitland, Pollock, Salmond, and later Holdsworth and Cheshire.[45] Before their day, the law was shaped almost exclusively in court-room arguments and judgments, and not through textbook formulations.

A DOCTRINAL TERMINUS

From about 1850, English courts followed the American lead and began to stress a natural right to 'reasonable' water use. At the same time the judges

[43] B. Nicholas, *An Introduction to Roman Law* (3rd edn., Oxford, 1962) 148; A. W. B. Simpson, *A History of the Land Law* (2nd edn., Oxford, 1986) 262; W. S. Holdsworth, *A History of English Law*, 13 vols. (London, (1922–52) vii, 323–4; C. H. S. Fifoot, *History and Sources of the Common Law: Tort and Contract* (London, 1949) 95, n. 16.

[44] J. L. Goddard, *A Treatise on the Law of Easements* (1st edn., London, 1871, 2nd edn., London, 1877), and see references in n. 4 above.

[45] A. W. B. Simpson, 'The Rise and Fall of the Legal Treatise: Legal Principles and the Forms of Legal Literature', in A. W. B. Simpson, *Legal Theory and Legal History: Essays on the Common Law* (London, 1987) 273–320; D. Sugarman, 'Legal Theory, the Common Law Mind and the Making of the Textbook Tradition', in W. Twining (ed.), *Legal Theory and Common Law* (Oxford, 1986) 26–61; J. S. Anderson, 'Land Law Texts and the Explanation of 1925' (1984) 37 Current Legal Problems 63.

sought to minimize the role of appropriations, prescriptions, and presumed grants as means of allocating water titles. Social contractarian ideas were sometimes used so as to justifiy binding riparian owners to an implicit agreement whereby each party's water use was limited to reasonable levels. For example, in *Wood* v. *Waud*, the court observed:

It is said that the true rule... is laid down by Chancellor Kent (3 Com. 439, 440), that streams are meant for the use of men, and that it would be unreasonable, and contrary to the universal consent of mankind, to debar each riparian proprietor from [water use]... provided the use... work[s] no material injury to his neighbour.[46]

But the new decisions generally rejected intention-based concepts of right extant around 1840.[47] In the leading 1851 Exchequer case of *Embrey* v. *Owen*,[48] for example, no consensual theories of riparian right were propounded.

Embrey v. *Owen*: The Arguments

The issue to be decided in *Embrey* was whether abstraction of water by D for irrigation of his fields gave P, a downstream neighbour, an action for breach of natural right, where the abstraction caused no appreciable loss or damage to P's corn-milling operation. P declared that D had wrongfully diverted the stream; that P was lawfully possessed of the mills at the time of the diversions; that he had a right to enjoy the benefit and advantage of the water 'which had been used to run and flow... and still of right ought to run and flow unto the said mills, for the supplying the same with water for the working thereof'; that other proprietors had a right to use the stream only as was reasonable and necessary for irrigation and watering of their closes, and that D had taken more than was reasonable and for purposes other than irrigation; and as a result, that P 'for want of sufficient water, could not during that time use the said mills, or follow, use, or exercise their trade or business therein, in so large, extensive, and beneficial manner as they might and otherwise would have done'.

D claimed in defence that the diversions were reasonable for his irrigation needs; that most of the water was returned to the stream after use; that the diversions were intermittently made in the wet season so that P's mill suffered no significant or appreciable shortfall and no damage. D also claimed an independent right to water use, arising from possession of riparian land 'up to the middle of the said stream or watercourse, [which] hath, from the time whereof the memory of man runneth not to the contrary,

[46] (1849) 3 Exch. 748, 780; 154 E.R. 1047, 1060 (Ex.) per Pollock CB.

[47] See *Wood* v. *Waud* (1849) 3 Exch. 748, 775–6, 780–1; 154 E.R. 1047, 1058, 1060–1 (Ex.) per Pollock CB; *Dickinson* v. *Grand Junction Canal Company* (1852) 7 Exch. 282, 299–301; 155 E.R. 953, 960–1 (Ex.) per Pollock CB.

[48] (1851) 6 Exch 353; 155 E.R. 579 (Ex).

been . . . covered with the water of the said stream or watercourse; which . . . hath been used and accustomed to run and flow in its usual flow, stream and current . . . by the said . . . closes, for the watering, fertilization, and general benefit and advantage thereof'. A further justification for D's water use was that his irrigations improved and cultivated the land, 'rendering the same fertile and productive and conducive to the public and general weal and advantage'.

The trial judge instructed the jury to acquit if the diminution of flow was 'inappreciable', that is, 'so inconsiderable as to be incapable of price or value'. An alternative test was whether there had been 'any sensible diminution of the natural flow of the water by means of the diversion', a stricter test relying on observable interference rather than material damage as the measure of injury. Expert witnesses adduced that only 5 per cent of the water flow at most had been abstracted at any time by D; the jury therefore returned negative answers to both tests. Leave was then given for P to seek nominal damages and an authoritative appellate ruling of law.

Bramwell appeared as counsel for D in the action before the Court of Exchequer.[49] He warned that P's claim of a right to all the water would realize the anarchist dogma of Proudhon: '*La proprieté, c'est le vol*'.[50] Bramwell then argued that a rule forbidding abstraction by upstream proprietors in favour of the lower owner's absolute right to the natural flow would undermine the natural rights of all land owners:

> Rivers flow for the benefit of all persons through whose lands they pass, and not for the benefit of those persons only whose lands lie at the mouth of the stream. . . . Every riparian proprietor is entitled to use the stream for all natural and normal purposes, domestic and agricultural, provided he does not interfere with the rights of other riparian proprietors. For instance, he may, either by himself, his family, or his cattle, drink the water; he may bathe in it, use it in his habitation, and for watering his garden.[51]

Bramwell's basic needs test was derived from a range of civilian, English, Scottish, and American authorities. He also cited treatise literature such as Hutcheson, Gale, and *Starkie on Evidence*, which stated:

> The water of a running stream is publici juris, which each successive proprietor has a right to use in passing, but which is the property of no one; but if one of such owners appropriates the water by applying it to a particular purpose, he has a right to do so, provided he does not thereby prejudice any other owner in his previous use and appropriation of the water to other purposes.[52]

[49] Which court he was to join five years later in 1856, taking Parke B's place.

[50] (1851) 6 Exch. 353, 359–62; 155 E.R. 579, 582–3.

[51] 6 Exch. 353, 359; 155 E.R. 579, 582.

[52] T. Starkie, *A Practical Treatise of the Law of Evidence* 3 vols. (3rd edn., London, 1842) iii, Tit. 'Watercourse', 1249.

This formulation seems to require damage to present use as a sine qua non of action. In argument Parke B doubted, however, whether English authority supported a right to abstract water in the absence of harm to present uses of neighbours:

It has not yet been decided in this country that a riparian proprietor has an equal right to use the water for the purpose of irrigating his land. In America, a far more liberal use of water is allowed: Angell on Watercourses (page 23). Assuming, therefore, that every proprietor has a right to to use the stream for certain purposes, domestic and agricultural, is irrigation one of them?[53]

Comyn's *Digest*[54] was found to be reticent on this point, stating that no action will lie 'if a man use water in his own land out of a watercourse running through his land to the pond of B, whereby B's pond is not so full, if he do not divert the watercourse'.[55] *Wood* v. *Waud* was also held to be inconclusive on this key issue. Alderson B then adduced authority suggesting that any interference with natural flow was actionable, whether or not any damage was caused to present uses:

There was a case of *Dakin* v. *Cornish* (not reported) tried before me, at Leeds, in 1845, where water was taken from the river Ayr to work a steam-engine: there was an artificial channel from the river to a reservoir in the yard of a mill; the water was there mixed with other water obtained from the earth; the whole was then used for the steam engine, and what remained was transferred into another tube and carried back to the river. The question was, whether that was an injury to some other mills lower down on the stream. I left it to the jury to say, whether the same quantity of water continued to run in the river, as if none of its water had entered the premises of the defendant; telling them, that if they were of that opinion, they should find a verdict for the defendant.[56]

As Alderson B indicated, a strict rule forbidding diminution of natural flow had to be interpreted and applied by a jury; and jurors exercising their unfettered discretion to determine relevant fact might reasonably hold that a minimal abstraction or diversion of a stream was no significant injury to rights. Bramwell suggested this approach should govern the present case:

It is found as a fact, that the quantity of water diverted was 'inappreciable'; and therefore [D] is entitled to retain the verdict on the general issue. 'Not guilty' puts in issue the taking of an injurious quantity of water. The maxim 'de minimis non curat lex' applies. A person who keeps a large fire burning a mile distant from the house of another, in some degree destroys the oxygen; but that is clearly not an injury for which an action would lie.

53 *Embrey* v. *Owen* 6 Exch. 353, 359–60; 155 E.R. 579, 582.

54 J. Comyns, *Digest of the Laws of England* (1st edn., London, 1767; 4th edn., London, 1793) Title: 'Action Upon the Case for a Nuisance'.

55 Per St. John, at Suffolk Ass., 1657, between Smart and Stisted.

56 6 Exch. 353, 360; 155 E.R. 579, 582.

Only one case appeared to contradict this view, as reported by Starkie:

[In a case] before Wood B., at Carlisle, where the water, having been used for the purpose of irrigation, was afterwards returned into the ordinary channel; the learned Judge nonsuited the plaintiff; but as it appeared that by so doing a portion was lost in consequence of absorption and irrigation, the Court of King's Bench ... afterwards set aside the nonsuit.[57]

Against Bramwell, counsel for P argued that common-law doctrine, culminating in *Mason* v. *Hill*, guaranteed the full natural flow of streams through riparian land:

The right to flowing water, like the right to light or air, is publici juris, so that every riparian proprietor has a right to have the stream flow on in its full, natural, and unimpeded current, subject only to those small and uninjurious exceptions which the common law has introduced, viz.—that every person, whether riparian proprietor or not, may take from it, as it flows, water for domestic purposes, or by the mouths of his cattle,—purposes which in no degree disturb or change the natural course of the stream, or prejudicially alter its character. No other exception is engrafted by the law of England on the general right, and it is not easy to apply to that law any modification of the right, which America, with its large rivers, may have conveniently adopted. It follows, that every disturbance of this right, by any other than the excepted means,—that is, every act, by which the water is diverted out of its natural course, or by which, while flowing in its natural course, it is fouled or heated, or its quality is otherwise deteriorated,—even though by such act no pecuniary damage is sustained,—is the subject of an action, on the ground that a continued disturbance of the right by such means would establish an easement, and so create an adverse right.[58] And if, by diversion of the water for the purpose of irrigation or otherwise, some may be abstracted, or ... its character is prejudiced, although the quantity abstracted be ever so small, or the prejudice to its character be ever so minute, the right of action still subsists, because there is an injury to the right; and it is no element in the case whether the amount abstracted be sensible and appreciable, or not.[59]

Many authorities supported the doctrine of *injuria sine damno*, a prophylactic principle of right-maintenance against all insignificant interferences, however insignificant. A telling illustration of the principle was given:

If [D] were allowed to take an inappreciable quantity of water for the purpose of irrigation, fifty other persons might do the same, and thus an appreciable, nay, a considerable quantity would be taken, by which actual pecuniary damage might be done, and yet for which no one would be liable; and in time an adverse right would

[57] 6 Exch. 353, 362; 155 E.R. 579, 583, quoting Starkie, *Law of Evidence*, 1250.

[58] Citing *Ashby* v. *White* (1703) 2 Ld. Raym. 938; 92 E.R. 126 (K.B.); *Williams* v. *Mostyn* (1838) 4 M. & W. 145; 150 E.R. 1379 (Ex.).

[59] Citing *Bower* v. *Hill* (1835) 1 Bing. N.C. 549; 131 E.R. 229 (C.P.); *Moore* v. *Browne* (1572) Dyer 319b; 73 E.R. 723 (K.B.); *Weller* v. *Baker* (1769) 2 Wils. 414; 95 E.R. 892 (K.B.); *Marzetti* v. *Williams* (1830) 1 B. & Ad. 415; 109 E.R. 842 (K.B.).

be established by all those parties.[60] ... But the authorities clearly establish this principle, that wherever there is an injury to a right, which if acquiesced in, would in the course of time create an adverse right in the wrongdoer, there an action is maintainable without proof of any specific injury.[61]

Embrey v. *Owen*: The Decision

Bramwell's defence was successful. The court found for D on the basis of the jury finding that 'no sensible diminution of the natural flow of the stream to [P's] mill was caused by the abstraction of the water... the working of the mill was not in the least impeded'. Parke B, already regarded as the leading common lawyer of his time, delivered the court's judgment. He began with a careful analysis of the nature of water rights and the place of damage to user in establishing an action. He summed up P's arguments as follows:

[Proprietors have] a right to the full flow of the water in its natural course and abundance, as an incident to their property in the land through which it flowed; and... any abstraction of the water, however inconsiderable, by another riparian proprietor, and though productive of no actual damage, would be actionable, because it was an injury to a right, and, if continued, would be the foundation of a claim of adverse right in that proprietor.

Parke B agreed that there was a principle allowing action for injury without damage, which held for 'every description of right':

Actual perceptible damage is not indispensable as the foundation of an action; it is sufficient to shew the violation of a right, in which case the law will presume damage; injuria sine damno is actionable, as was laid down in the case of *Ashby* v. *White* by Lord Holt, and in many subsequent cases, which are all referred to, and the truth of the proposition powerfully enforced in a very able judgment of the late Mr. Justice Story in *Webb* v. *The Portland Manufacturing Company.*

However, the *injuria sine damno* rule was to be distinguished and narrowed in the special instance of amenities of land enjoyment, where the utilities of rival owners had to be balanced and the full extent of natural rights compromised:

But in applying this admitted rule to the case of rights to running water, and the analogous cases of rights to air and light, it must be considered what the nature of those rights is, and what is a violation of them.

[60] Citing, inter alia, *Bracton*, f. 221; Gale, *Easements*, 137; *Wood* v. *Waud* (1849) 3 Exch. 748; 154 E.R. 1047 (Ex.); *Tyler* v. *Wilkinson* (1827) 4 Mason's (U.S.) Rep. 401; 24 Fed. Cas. 472; *Blanchard* v. *Baker* (1832) 8 Greenleaf 253 (S. C. Maine); *Mason* v. *Hill* (1833) 5 B. & Ad. 1; 110 E.R. 692; *Palmer* v. *Keblethwaite* (1682) Skin. 65; 90 E.R. 31; S.C. 2 Show. K.B. 243, 249; 89 E.R. 916, 921; *Glynne* v. *Nichols* (1687) 2 Show. K.B. 507; 89 E.R. 1069; Comb. 43; 90 E.R. 333.

[61] *Hobson* v. *Todd* (1790) 4 T.R. 71; 100 E.R. 900 (K.B.); *Pindar* v. *Wadsworth* (1802) 2 East. 154; 102 E.R. 328 (K.B.).

The law as to flowing water is now put on its right footing by a series of cases[62] ... and is fully settled in the American courts.[63]

The right to have the stream to flow in its natural state without diminution or alteration is an incident to the property in land through which it passes; but flowing water is publici juris, not in the sense that it is bonum vacans [a vacant good], to which the first occupant may acquire an exclusive right, but that it is public and common in this sense only, that all may reasonably use it who have a right of access to it, that none can have any property in the water itself, except in the particular portion which he may choose to abstract from the stream and take into his possession, and that during the time of his possesssion only. But each proprietor of the adjacent land has the right to the usufruct of the stream which flows through it.[64]

This right to the benefit and advantage of the water flowing past his land, is not an absolute and exclusive right to the flow of all the water in its natural state; if it were, the argument... that every abstraction of it would give a cause of action, would be irrefragable; but it is a right only to the flow of the water, and the enjoyment of it, subject to the similar rights of all the proprietors of the banks on each side to the reasonable enjoyment of the same gift of Providence.

It is only therefore for an unreasonable and unauthorised use of this common benefit that an action will lie; for such an use it will; even, as [*Webb* per Story J] shews, though there may be no actual damage to the plaintiff.

Parke B then unreservedly adopted the American reasonable doctrine developed by Story and Kent. After quoting extensively from Kent's *Commentaries* he commented:

In America... a very liberal use of the stream for the purposes of irrigation and for carrying on manufactures is permitted. So in France, where every one may use it 'en bon père de famille, et pour son plus grand avantage:'.[65]

Parke B drew here from article 640 of the French *Code Civil*, which stated:

Lower lands are subjected to those which are higher to receive waters which flow naturally therefrom without the hand of man having contributed thereto.

The lower owner may not raise a dike which prevents such flow.

The higher owner may do nothing which aggravates the servitude on the lower lands.[66]

The *Code* condensed much of the Roman law of servitudes and interdicts concerning water rights to a few paragraphs.[67] Article 639 states that a

[62] *Wright* v. *Howard* (1823) Sim. & St. 192; 57 E.R. 76; *Mason* v. *Hill* (1833) 5 B. & Ad. 1; 110 E.R. 692; *Wood* v. *Waud* (1849) 3 Exch. 748; 154 E.R. 1047.

[63] Citing Kent, *Commentaries*, iii, lect. 52, 439–45.

[64] Citing Roman materials from Denman CJ's judgment in *Mason* v. *Hill* (1833) 5 B. & Ad. 1, 24; 110 E.R. 692, 700–1.

[65] J. B. J. Pailliet, *Manuel de Droit Français* 2 vols. (Paris, 1837) i, note a. to *Code Civil*, art. 640, 217–19.

[66] *Code Civil*, art. 640, Pailliet, *Droit Français*, 217–18; translated Crabb, *Code*, 145.

[67] See Wiel, 'Origin and Comparative Development' and 'Waters: American Law and French Authority'; cf. J. Gordley, 'Water Rights', in J. A. R. Nafziger and S. C. Symeonides (eds.), *Law and Justice in a Multistate World* (Ardsley, NY, 2002) 683, 698–703.

servitude between lands 'derives either from the natural situation of the premises or from obligations imposed by law, or from agreements between the owners'.[68] Articles 641–645 deal with rain, spring, and subterranean waters and rights to water by prescription.[69] Article 645 states a utilitarian rule for water allocations:

> If a dispute arises among owners to whom such [riparian] waters may be useful, the courts, in deciding, should reconcile the interest of agriculture with the respect due to ownership; and, in all cases, particular and local rules on waters and use of waters should be observed.[70]

After citing the French law, Parke B continued:

> He [the riparian owner] may make trenches to conduct the water to irrigate his land, if he returns it with no other loss than that which irrigation caused. In... *Wood* v. *Waud*, it was observed, that in England it is not clear that an user to that extent would in every case be deemed a lawful enjoyment of the water, if it was again returned into the river with no other diminution than that which was caused by the absorption and evaporation attendant on the irrigation of the lands of the adjoining proprietor. This must depend upon the circumstances of each case. On the one hand, it could not be permitted that the owner of a tract of many thousand acres of porous soil, abutting on one part of the stream, could be permitted to irrigate them continually by canals and drains, and so cause a serious diminution of the quantity of water, though there was no other loss to the natural stream than that arising from the necessary absorption and evaporation of the water employed for that purpose; on the other hand, one's common sense would be shocked by supposing that a riparian owner could not dip a watering-pot into the stream, in order to water his garden, or allow his family or his cattle to drink it. It is entirely a question of degree, and it is very difficult, indeed impossible, to define precisely the limits which separate the reasonable and permitted use of the stream from its wrongful application; but there is often no difficulty in deciding whether a particular case falls within the permitted limits or not; and in this we think, that as the irrigation took place, not continuously, but only at intermittent periods, when the river was full, and no damage was done thereby to the working of the mill, and the diminution of the water was not perceptible to the eye, it was such a reasonable use of the water as not to be prohibited by law. If so, it was no infringement of [P]'s right at all; it was only the exercise of an equal right which [D] had to the usufruct of the stream. We are therefore of the opinion that there has been no injury in fact or law in this case.[71]

A general theory of land use was then constructed from these principles:

[68] Pailliet, *Droit Français*, 216; Crabb, *Code*, 145.

[69] Pailliet, *Droit Français*, 217–21; Crabb, *Code*, 145–7.

[70] Pailliet, *Droit Français*, 221; Crabb, *Code*, 146. Civilian riparian law could also find its way into English courts through Privy Council appeals: see e.g. *St Louis* v. *St Louis* (1841) 3 Moore 398, 13 E.R. 161 (P.C., Quebec) per Dr Lushington; *Van Breda* v. *Silberbauer* [1869] 6 Moore N.S. 319, 16 E.R. 746 (P.C., Cape of Good Hope).

[71] *Embrey* v. *Owen* 6 Exch. 353, 371–2; 155 E.R. 579, 586–7.

The same law will be found to be applicable to the corresponding rights to air and light. These also are bestowed by Providence for the common benefit of man; and so long as the reasonable use by one man of this common property does not do actual and perceptible damage to the right of another to the similar use of it, no action will lie. A man cannot occupy a dwelling and consume fuel in it for domestic purposes, without its in some degree impairing the natural purity of the air; he cannot erect a building, or plant a tree, near the house of another, without in some degree diminishing the quantity of light he enjoys: but such small interruptions give no right of action; for they are necessary incidents to the common enjoyment by all.[72]

Parke B's judgment managed to incorporate most of the ideas produced by prior centuries of legal development, notably the doctrine of natural rights incident to property; and the notions of *injuria sine damno* and *damnum sine injuria* governing the doctrine of nuisance. In effect, he drew a simple dichotomy between 'reasonable use' of a stream, which reduces the natural flow yet is not actionable; and an unreasonable use diminishing the flow available to neighbours, which is an actionable interference with natural rights even if causing no actual damage to other users. The notion of 'reasonableness' imbued Parke B's whole doctrine, arming judges in the future with a strong discretion to decide conflicts by the interpretation of fact. All would depend on 'the circumstances of the case', allowing courts to balance conflicting calls on water resources as they saw fit.

Acceptance and Elaboration of the *Embrey* Doctrine

Embrey v. *Owen* proved to be the authority finally settling common-law riparian doctrine regarding natural surface streams. In *Dickinson* v. *The Grand Junction Canal Company*,[73] Pollock CB stated:

Questions of rights to flowing water have been much discussed in modern times in several cases, *Mason* v. *Hill*, *Wood* v. *Waud*, *Embrey* v. *Owen*, and placed on their proper foundation. We consider it as settled law, that the right to have a stream running in its natural course is, not by a presumed grant from long acquiescence on the part of the riparian proprietors above and below, but is ex jure naturae: *Shury* v. *Piggot*, *Tyler* v. *Wilkinson*; and an incident of property, as much as the right to have the soil itself in its natural state, unaltered by the acts of a neighbouring proprietor, who cannot dig so as to deprive it of the support of his land.[74]

[72] 6 Exch. 353, 372–3; 155 E.R. 579, 587; judgment followed in *Dickinson* v. *The Grand Junction Canal Company* (1852) 7 Exch. 282, 299–301; 155 E.R. 953, 960–1 (Ex.) per Pollock CB; *Sampson* v. *Hoddinott* (1857) 1 C.B.N.S. 590; 140 E.R. 242 (C.P.) per Cresswell J; see J. L. Goddard, *A Treatise on the Law of Easements* (2nd edn., London, 1877) 52–5, 202–3, 239–46 for collected authorities.

[73] (1852) 7 Ex. 282; 155 E.R. 953 (Ex.).

[74] 7 Ex. 282, 299–300; 155 E.R. 953, 961.

In the 1857 case of *Sampson* v. *Hoddinott*[75] Cresswell J of Common Pleas set out an authoritative version of the *Embrey* doctrine, incorporating within it the principles of prescription:

> [A]ll persons having lands on the margin of a flowing stream have, by nature, certain rights to use the water of that stream, whether they exercise those rights or not; and... they may begin to exercise them whenever they will. By usage, they may acquire a right to use the water in a manner not justified by their natural rights: but such acquired right has no operation against the natural rights of a landowner higher up the stream, unless the user by which it was acquired affects the use that he himself has made of the stream, or his power to use it, so as to raise a presumption of grant, and so render the tenement above a servient tenement. If the user of the stream by the plaintiff... was merely an exercise of his natural right, such user, however long continued, would not render the defendant's tenement a servient tenement, or in any way affect the natural rights of the defendant to use the water....
>
> But if the user by the defendant has been beyond his natural right, it matters not how much the plaintiff has used the water, or whether he has used it at all. In either case, his right has been equally invaded, and the action is maintainable.[76]

This affirms a pure principle of *injuria sine damno*, whereby interference with natural water rights is actionable regardless of usage.[77] However, Cresswell J also adopted Parke B's *Embrey* doctrine that 'every proprietor of lands on the banks of a natural stream has a right to use the water, provided he so uses it as not to work any *material injury* to the rights of other proprietors above or below on the stream'.[78] The concept of material injury (like its synonyms 'perceptible' or 'sensible' injury, 'serious diminution') imports a judicial discretion to hold some acts of invasion legally inconsequential (*damnum sine injuria*). In the present case it was held that an extensive use of water for irrigation sensibly interfering with a lower proprietor's use of the natural river fell within the *Embrey* doctrine as a breach of rights. Through their factual assessment of the interference, the judges could decide which principle to uphold—strict right-maintenance or reasonable usage—and thus shape doctrine to yield the preferred result. For an example of this discretionary power, in the 1875 Irish appeal of *Devery* v. *Grand Junction Canal Company*,[79] the Exchequer Chamber held that a

[75] (1857) I C.B.N.S. 590; 140 E.R. 242 (C.P.).

[76] 1 C.B.N.S. 590, 611; 140 E.R. 242, 251–2.

[77] This principle was affirmed, inter alia, in *Edleston* v. *Crossley & Sons* (1868) 18 L.T. 15; 7 Bar Rep. 15 (V.C.); *Holker* v. *Porrit* (1875) L.R. 10 Ex. 62 (Ex.); *Pennington* v. *Brinsop Hall Company* (1875) 5 Ch.D. 769 (Ch.); *Chasemore* v. *Richards* (1857) 2 H. & N. 168, 191; 157 E.R. 71, 80 (Ex.); (1859) 7 H.L.C. 349; 11 E.R. 140 (H.L.); *Attorney-General* v. *Birmingham Borough Council* (1858) 4 Kay & J. 528; 70 E.R. 220 (V.C.).

[78] 1 C.B.N.S. 590, 611; 140 E.R. 242, 251–2, per Cresswell J (emphasis added). See also *Northam* v. *Hurley* (1853) 1 El. & Bl. 665; 118 E.R. 586 (Q.B.) per Coleridge J.

[79] (1875) Ir. R. 9 C.L. 194 (Ex. Ch.).

right-infringement against a riparian owner's interests in 1866 was renewed as a fresh cause of action, when that same infringement finally caused material flooding damage in 1873; the Statute of Limitations was therefore allowed to run from the date of damage rather than injury.

Affirmation by the House of Lords: *Miner* v. *Gilmour*

The Privy Council case of *Miner* v. *Gilmour* in 1858,[80] being an appeal from Lower Canada, was the first opportunity for the law lords to comment upon and develop the *Embrey* doctrine. Counsel cited to the court French-Canadian doctrine derived from Roman law, Pothier, and the *Code Civil*,[81] together with the riparian doctrine of Story and Kent[82] and recent English case law. Lord Kingsdown stated that for the purposes of riparian doctrine there was no material distinction between the French and English law. The facts of the case were that D channelled water to his downstream grist mill, diverting the water from P's tannery upstream. P argued that this diversion was injurious to his rights, those rights deriving from three sources: a conveyance of the riparian land with dam and water privileges from the original owner of the river; ten years' continuous use by P; and, finally, by virtue of P 'being the proprietor of land on the bank of the river'. P declared damage including deprivation of water flow, permanent harm to P's sluices and dam, and impairment of potential water power available to his site. Sizeable money damages were sought in addition to a declaration of P's rights.

D's defence, in short, was that P had come to the nuisance. According to D, when the original owner had conveyed the downstream site to P, he had retained by that grant those water privileges necessary to run a grist mill to be built on the upstream site. The grist mill was built as planned and had drawn water continuously for more than twenty years. Hence P had bought and occupied his tannery site with full knowledge that a prior use of the stream had been reserved for the owner and his successors.

Detailed evidence was collected at trial concerning the terms of the conveyances and the history of the parties' respective appropriations of water. It was determined that D had not acquired a right to divert the water from P's site at a high level injurious to P's interests; no such right had been constituted either by conveyance or by later usage. On appeal, the reverse finding was made: that the sale of land to P had granted a water privilege 'subordinate to the vendor [and successors] using the water for a grist mill, which was to have the preference, that is to say, the use of the water retained by the

[80] (1858) 12 Moo. P.C. 131; 14 E.R. 861 (P.C.).

[81] D.43.13.1. (Ulpian); R. Pothier, *Oeuvres complètes*, 25 vols. (St. A. Berville (ed.), Paris, 1821–24), xvii, 520; Douet, *Principles of the Law of Lower Canada*, Art. 186, at 189, 265.

[82] Kent, *Commentaries*, iii, 544; *Tyler* v. *Wilkinson*, the text accompanying nn. 21–23 above.

[upper] dam in preference to that which [P] obtained permission to employ for his tannery'. Both upper and lower courts searched carefully for the contractual intentions underlying the grants of riparian land; the upper court determined that P had a right to unimpeded water, but it refused to award damages in the absence of proof of wrongful or malicious intention to divert the water from P's operation. A distinction was thus impliedly drawn between tort actions obliquely establishing title and those compensating wrongful damage.

On appeal before the Judicial Committee, the evidence and pleadings were pored over in minutest detail. Lord Kingsdown concluded:

> that [P] having purchased the right to use the water, subject only to a preference in favour of a mill thereafter to be built, and which preference is to be exercised in a particular mode, cannot be bound by its exercise in a different mode and in favour of a different mill.

Thus interpretation of the conveyance yielded no special right permitting D to divert. 'The question, therefore, must depend on the general rules of law as applied to the facts appearing in the case.' Lord Kingsdown observed that if D took sufficient water for his operations by sluice from the river, then P's tannery would be deprived of necessary water; but that if D curtailed his abstractions then D's grist mill would not be workable; therefore one of the parties was inevitably going to lose valuable rights in the conflict. Established usages could not supply a conventional priority of rights:

> With respect to the usage which has prevailed . . . this gate has always been kept open whenever the use of the grist mill required it, and that though no such usage has been proved as to constitute in itself a prescriptive right in favour of the mill, there is abundantly sufficient to show that there has not been any acquiescence, by the owner of the grist-mill, in any obstruction created by the upper dam, nor any compromise or abandonment of his right to the use of the water, whatever that right may originally have been.
>
> It being necessary, therefore, that the tannery should suffer if the gate be opened, and that the mill should suffer if the gate be closed, the question for determination is, whether [P] has established a right to have the gate kept closed, and has proved that [D] is a wrong-doer in opening it. The *onus* is upon him.

The following riparian doctrine was then derived from English and French authority:

> By the general law applicable to running streams, every riparian proprietor has a right to what may be called the ordinary use of the water flowing past his land; for instance, to the reasonable use of the water for his domestic purposes and for his cattle, and this without regard to the effect which such use may have, in case of a deficiency, upon proprietors lower down the stream. But, further, he has a right to the use of it for any purpose, or what may be deemed the extraordinary use of it, provided that he does not thereby interfere with the rights of other proprietors, either above or below him.

Subject to this condition, he may dam up the stream for the purpose of a mill, or divert the water for the purpose of irrigation. But, he has no right to interrupt the regular flow of the stream, if he thereby interferes with the lawful use of the water by other proprietors, and inflicts upon them a sensible injury.

This elaboration of the *Embrey* doctrine fell into three parts. First, a natural riparian right to water was upheld, that is a right independent of established usage, or prior appropriation, or real or presumed grant. There was, however, no outright protection of natural flow from all forms of interference. For example, an 'ordinary use' of water for domestic and livestock needs was permitted even if it interfered with neighbours' uses; this was *damnum sine injuria*. Secondly, the judgment preserved the category of *injuria sine damno*. In the absence of grant, an 'extraordinary use', or unreasonable abstraction or pollution of water, was permitted only if neighbours' rights were not materially affected. Finally, both these last criteria of judgment depended on a strong judicial discretion to decide what was 'reasonable' in the light of the facts, including interpretation of any conveyances or informal agreements and understandings between the parties. In the present case, D's water use was held to be reasonable even though it caused P damage:

[P] cannot say that the use of the water by [D] for his mill is not a lawful use; for such rights as he had, were acquired from the person under whom [D] claims, and with knowledge of the previous grant made to [D].

Lord Kingsdown's *Miner* judgment was regarded as a definitive reworking of Parke B's *Embrey* test for the rest of the nineteenth century and beyond.

The *Embrey* Test and Jury Directions

The highly discretionary 'sensible injury' test from *Embrey* and *Miner* was given some practical elaboration by Martin B in his directions to the jury at the Kent Assizes of 1862. In the case of *Lord Norbury* v. *Kitchin*,[83] P, an earl and large landowner, complained that a mill owner (D), by increasing by one-fortieth his abstraction of waters from a stream for his machinery, had denied water to the earl's ornamental lake in his country park. After citing the test for reasonable water use as set out in *Miner* v. *Gilmour*, Martin B instructed the jury that:

[t]he question as to whether the quantity of water taken was reasonable, must in a degree depend upon the entire quantity of water in the stream, and it was for the jury to consider whether [D] took an unreasonable quantity of the water.

[83] (1862) 3 F. & F. 292; 176 E.R. 132 (N.P.).

In exercising its discretion, the jury was to look at the manner of the taking and the surrounding circumstances. In the South where water power was not much used, a relaxed approach to large abstractions could be adopted; '[i]t was otherwise in the North, where by reason of the value of the water for manufacturing purposes, such questions were often litigated'. A temporary inconvenience to a water user was not enough; the plaintiff must have 'really suffered in his supply of water'. Moreover, the law did not aim to protect such uses as ornamental lakes: persons 'could only take the water away for the purposes of utility'.[84] These comments were not a formal opinion of law but jury instructions; they suggest that the developed nineteenth-century riparian doctrines of the superior courts were implemented with but little precision.[85] In the result, the assize jury gave a farthing in nominal damages stating that P's rights had been interfered with, but that no actual loss had been sustained. There was a supplementary action in Chancery: P went on to seek injunctions to preserve water supplies to his park. Wood VC granted the injunction on grounds that even in the absence of temporal damage, the interference with the water right suggested a possibility of future loss which entitled present equitable relief. This suggests that the courts of equity were readier than courts of law to prevent right-infringement in the absence of 'sensible injury'.[86] Equitable injunctions would usually have been unnecessary in the circumstances of riparian rights. Bullen and Leake wrote in this context:

> A riparian proprietor is entitled to an action for any injury to ... natural or acquired rights; as by diverting the stream, or by abstracting ... or by fouling the water. And he is entitled to nominal damages in order to prevent the injury, although no actual damage be sustained.[87]

[84] 3 F. & F. 292, 295–6; 176 E.R. 132, 133–4.

[85] See also *Kensit* v. *Great Eastern Railway* (1884) 27 Ch.D. 122 (C.A.).

[86] See *Wright* v. *Howard* (1823) 1 Sim. & St. 190; 57 E.R. 76 (V.C.); *Blakemore* v. *Glamorganshire Canal Company* (1832) 1 My. & K. 154; 39 E.R. 639 (Ch.); *Beaufort, Duke of* v. *Morris* (1847) 2 Ph. 683; 41 E.R. 1107 (Ch.); (1848) 6 Hare 340; 41 E.R. 1197 (V.C.); *Goldsmid* v. *Tunbridge Wells Improvement Commissioners* (1865) L.R. 1 Ch. 161 (M.R.); *Bickett* v. *Morris* (1866) L.R. 1 H.L. Sc. Ap. 47. (H.L.(Sc.)); *Swindon Waterworks Company* v. *Wilts and Berks Canal Navigation Company* (1874) L.R. 9 Ch. 453; (1875) L.R. 7 H.L. 697 (H.L.).

[87] E. Bullen and S. M. Leake, *Precedents of Pleading in the Superior Courts of Common Law* (3rd edn., London, 1868) 425. Authorities cited for this principle included *Wood* v. *Waud* (1849) 3 Exch. 748; 154 E.R. 1047 (Ex.), Ch. 5, the text accompanying nn. 139–145 above; *Embrey* v. *Owen* (1851) 6 Exch. 353; 155 E.R. 579 (Ex.), the text accompanying nn. 48–72 above; and *Crossley* v. *Lightowler* (1867) L.R. 2 Ch. App. 478 (V.C.). Examples of such actions were: *Northam* v. *Hurley* (1853) 1 El. & Bl. 665; 118 E.R. 586 (Q.B.); *Insole* v. *James* (1856) 1 H. & N. 243; 156 E.R. 1194 (Ex.); *Hall* v. *Swift* (1838) 4 Bing. N.C. 381; 132 E.R. 834 (C.P.); *Attorney-General of the Prince of Wales* v. *Bristol Waterworks Company* (1855) 10 Ex. 884; 156 E.R. 699 (Ex.). See also *Lord Egremont* v. *Pulman* (1829) Moo. & M. 404; 173 E.R. 1204 (N.P.); *Shadwell* v. *Hutchinson* (1829) Moo. & M. 350; 173 E.R. 1185 (N.P.) per Lord Tenterden CJ; *Baxter* v. *Taylor* (1832) 4 B. & Ad. 72; 110 E.R. 382 (K.B.); *Bell* v. *Twentyman* (1841) 1 Q.B. 766; 113 E.R. 1324 (Q.B.); *Battishill* v. *Reed* (1856) 18 C.B. 696; 139 E.R. 1544 (C.P.) (injury to rights of reversioner implies actionable damage).

In this view, an award of damages protected title rather than compensated for loss; and a recalcitrant injurer who paid nominal damages (and shouldered costs in the action) might then face further injunctive restraint as in *Norbury* v. *Kitchin*.

COMPLETING THE STRUCTURE OF WATER LAW: SUBTERRANEAN WATERS; INDEFINITE SURFACE WATERS; AND ASSIGNABILITY

A set of principles dealing with rights to artificial watercourses had been developed in *Magor* v. *Chadwick* and *Arkwright* v. *Gell*.[88] This left three major problems of water doctrine to be resolved after *Embrey* v. *Owen* in 1851, namely the nature of rights in underground waters (which had been inconclusively addressed in *Acton* v. *Blundell*); the nature of rights to indefinite surface waters forming no channel; and the extent to which water rights as a species of property incidental to land ownership could be assigned to persons with no riparian land or privity of estate. A good deal of theorizing on the nature of water- and land-use rights emerged from these questions.

Rights in Underground Watercourses—Theorizing in the Court of Exchequer

The 1852 case of *Dickinson* v. *The Grand Junction Canal Company*[89] launched a series of difficult cases on underground water heard in the Court of Exchequer. The facts of the case begin with private legislation passed in 1793, granting the defendant company powers to acquire land by compulsory sale and to divert river-water for the purposes of a canal navigation. The legislation specified that a reservoir be built by D, ensuring that supplies of water power to mill sites on the river were not adversely affected by the canal abstractions. The reservoir proved to be an expensive failure, requiring the pumping of water upstream by steam power. After a number of disputes between mill owners and the company, a new agreement was made varying the line of the canal and thereby removing the strain on river water-levels. A second private bill went to Parliament in 1818, passing this agreement into private legislation binding all parties whether privy to the agreement or not.

A paper manufacturer, P, owned two ancient mills on the river, and two modern mills of more than twenty years' operation. P sued for breach of his common-law and statutory rights when the company, D, reduced the flow of water to P's mills by sinking a well intercepting underground water that otherwise would have supplied the river by infiltration through the soil. P

[88] Ch. 5, the text accompanying nn. 118–138 above.
[89] (1852) 7 Exch. 282; 155 E.R. 953 (Ex.).

laid his claim variously as a natural right to the full flow of water to riparian property, a prescriptive right arising from long use, and a right of express grant arising from the agreement between D and the river users and the ensuing legislation of 1817–18.

The Court of Exchequer found for P on the third, statutory basis of claim; but it also addressed common-law entitlements, as requested in the reference of law from the Master of Rolls. Pollock CB developed the doctrinal position at some length:

> [I]n the much considered case of *Acton* v. *Blundell*... a distinction is made for the first time between under-ground waters and those which flow on the surface; and it was held, that the owner of a piece of land, who has made a well in it, and thereby enjoyed the benefit of underground water, but for less than twenty years, has no right of action against a neighbouring proprietor, who, in sinking for and getting coals from his soil in the usual and proper manner, causes the well to become dry. The decision goes no further. In such a case the existence and state of under-ground water is generally unknown before the well is made; and after it is made there is difficulty in knowing certainly how much, if any indeed, of the water of the well, when the ground was in its natural state, belonged to the owner in right of his property in the soil, and how much belonged to that of his neighbour, who, in digging a mine or another well, may possibly be taking back his own. These practical uncertainties make it very reasonable not to apply the rules which regulate the enjoyment of streams and waters above ground to subterranean waters, especially when the result would be to limit the full enjoyment of the rights of property in the neighbouring owner, and to prevent him from extracting valuable metals or minerals from his own soil, or making some other beneficial use of it. When water is on the surface, the right of the owner of the adjoining land to the usufruct of the water is not a doubtful matter of fact; it is public and notorious, and such a right ought as a matter of course to be respected by every one: and indeed, if the course of a subterranean stream were well known... the owner of the soil under which the stream flowed could... maintain an action for the diversion of it, if it took place under such circumstances as would have enabled him to recover if the stream had been wholly above ground. When, however, the springs come to the surface and form streams and rivers, the established rules apply that each riparian owner is entitled, not to the property in the flowing water, but the usufruct of its stream for all reasonable purposes, to drink, to water his cattle, or to turn his mills, according to the nature and situation of the stream.[90]

The facts of the present case distinguished it from *Acton* v. *Blundell* and gave P a right of action at common law: 'the water is proved to have been taken from the river after it formed part of its stream, not by the reasonable use of it by another riparian proprietor, but by the digging of a well, which is clearly a diversion'. Pollock CB suggested that where use of underground water impairs another's rights without knowledge (or means of knowledge) of the diversion, nor possibility of restitution, then the action for interference

[90] 7 Exch. 282, 300–1; 155 E.R. 953, 960–1.

with property rights to the water flow might not be maintainable; but this approach was suggested only tentatively. More surprising was the position regarding abstraction of underground waters before they joined the river. Pollock CB categorized such abstractions as a species of legal injury or *injuria sine damno*; but he went on to say:

As to the abstraction of the water which never did form part of the rivers, but has been prevented from doing so in its natural course, by the excavation of the well, whether the water was part of an under-ground watercourse or percolated through the strata, we are also of opinion that an action would lie. The mill-owners were entitled to the benefit of the stream in its natural course; and they are deprived of part of that benefit if the natural supply of the stream is taken away.[91]

This finding seems to contradict not only Pollock CB's prior statements, but also the express doctrine of *Acton* v. *Blundell*.

The Court of Exchequer examined rights to underground water again in 1855 in *Rawstron* v. *Taylor*.[92] This was an action for damages to P's mills, manufactures, cottages, and premises, caused by D diminishing the supply of water by draining operations. D had laid an elaborate system of ditches and pipes in his estate, an instance of the improvement of agricultural land which engrossed the energies and spare capital of the landholding classes in the mid- to late nineteenth century.[93] D's drainage system diverted the sources of water from a stream supplying P's mills, thereby injuring his manufacturing enterprise. The interferences were evidenced by lengthy submissions of evidence, including maps of the respective estates and the network of watercourses, reservoirs, and drains linking them. P declared that D had not only diverted underground water from P's land, but had diverted water from an artificial watercourse for D's own use, and failed to return the surplus of unused waters. Such restitution of surplus was required under a deed of 1845, conveying a piece of land from D to P with guaranteed supplies of water by means of the artificial watercourse. Special damages and a declaration of right were sought in remedy. D pleaded in defence that he had not denied to P any waters in excess of his rights to appropriate or divert at common law, or by the terms of the deed. At the Liverpool assizes verdict for P was entered, subject to a ruling of law by the Exchequer court on a special case.

Counsel for P proposed a natural right to the underground water feeding P's mills. *Greatrex* v. *Howard* and *Wood* v. *Waud*[94] could be distinguished on

[91] 7 Exch. 282, 302; 155 E.R. 953, 961.

[92] (1855) 11 Exch. 369; 156 E.R. 873 (Ex.).

[93] See F. M. L. Thompson, *English Landed Society in the Nineteenth Century* (London, 1963) 247–58; C. O'Grada, 'The Landlord and Agricultural Transformation, 1870–1900: A Comment on Richard Perren's Hypothesis' (1979) 27 Agricultural History Review 40, 40–2; S. Wade Martins, *A Great Estate at Work: The Holkham Estate and Its Inhabitants in the Nineteenth Century* (Cambridge, 1980); A. Offer, *The First World War: An Agrarian Interpretation* (Oxford, 1989) 108–10.

[94] Ch 5, the text accompanying nn 139–145 above.

the basis that absolute rights of drainage were predicated on a bona fide purpose of draining land, and did not license the profitable extraction and use of the water, as was alleged to be D's purpose in the present case. The court doubted, however, if motive could ever be a test for determining the legality of acts of abstraction and drainage.[95]

Counsel for P then argued that the doctrine of *Dickinson* v. *Grand Junction Canal* supported his case, as D in effect was diverting a known ancient spring of water supplying P's land. It followed that the rule allowing absolute diversion of underground springs was no justification or defence. This characterization of the nature of the intercepted waters was challenged by Parke B, who held that the source was not a spring but a gathering of surface water, and went on to state:

It must be shewn that [P] possesses some definite right, in order to deprive [D] of his general right to cultivate his land in the manner he may think most advantageous to him, with a view to make the most of it.... [T]his is not a stream which [P] is entitled ex jure naturae to enjoy without diminution. If [P's] argument were correct, [D] would not be entitled to drain his land for the purpose of building upon it.[96]

As regards the right to unobstructed water on the land conveyed in 1845, Parke B rejected P's argument that the diversion from the artificial watercourse was a breach of a prescriptive right from long enjoyment independent of grant: *Magor* v. *Chadwick* was interpreted as excluding all such rights arising in man-made channels. The question was whether D's claim to abstract the water derogated from his grant of land to P with extensive water privileges.[97] Parke B judged the case as follows:

This is the case of common surface water rising out of springy or boggy ground, and flowing in no definite channel, although contributing to the supply of [P's] mill. This water having no defined course, and its supply being merely casual, [D] is entitled to get rid of it in any way he pleases... for the purpose of cultivating his land in any way he pleases.[98]

As to the deed granting rights to water by artificial channel:

[T]his right to this water would not pass independently of the deed, as the plaintiff would have no right to water in alieno solo. Natural watercourses are like ways of necessity. The right to have a stream running in its natural direction does not depend on a supposed grant, but is jure naturae: *Shury* v. *Pigott*. But if the stream is artificial no such right exists. This is not a natural watercourse; but [P] is entitled to the flow of this water, under the conveyance which gives it to him, by the terms of the grant.[99]

[95] Cf. *Bradford Corporation* v. *Pickles* [1894] 3 Ch. 53 (Ch.); [1895] A.C. 587 (H.L.), the text accompanying nn. 158–162 below.

[96] *Rawstron* v. *Taylor* (1855) 11 Exch. 369, 380–1; 156 E.R. 873, 880 *in arguendo*.

[97] Following *Northam* v. *Hurley* (1853) 1 El. & Bl. 665; 118 E.R. 586 (Q.B.).

[98] *Rawstron* v. *Taylor* (1855) 11 Exch. 369, 382; 156 E.R. 873, 880.

[99] 11 Exch. 369, 382–3; 156 E.R. 873, 880.

The court agreed that P should have verdict for breach of the covenant of the deed, but had failed to establish a right at common law. Platt B stated: 'this was merely surface water, and [D] had a right to drain his land, and [P] could not insist upon [D] maintaining his fields as a mere water-table'.[100] Martin B agreed in libertarian terms of freedom of property, implicitly assailing the *sic utere tuo* doctrine:

[D] is at liberty to get rid of the surface water in any manner that may appear most convenient to him; and I think that no one has a right to interfere with him, and that the object he may have in so doing is quite immaterial.[101]

P's verdict could therefore rest only on the 1845 deed:

[D] grants all the waters, and cannot derogate from his own grant by cutting off the supply.... *Northam* v. *Hurley*[102] shews, that the correct rule of law is, that where a party is entitled to a grant of water under a deed, the grantor is liable in damages if he derogate from his grant by diverting the water, although the grantee be not deprived of the use of any of the water by such diversion.

Rights in Indefinite Surface Waters

In *Broadbent* v. *Ramsbotham*,[103] decided in the Court of Exchequer one year later in 1856, an action was brought by a mill owner seeking to prevent the diversion of water from a pond, a marsh, and two wells on D's land, the diversion denying water to P's downstream mill. The court extended the principle of *Rawstron*, allowing unobstructed drainage of underground water, into a rule that all indefinite flows of water, whether underground or on the surface, could be appropriated or diverted at discretion, even if this was at the expense of a neighbouring land owner; only definite natural channels of water were subject to the natural rights of neighbours. Alderson B stated this new doctrine as follows:

The right to the natural flow of the water... cannot extend further than a right to the flow in the brook itself, and to the water flowing in some defined natural channel, either subterranean or on the surface, communicating directly with the brook itself. No doubt, all the water falling from heaven and shed upon the surface of a hill, at the foot of which a brook runs, must, by the natural force of gravity, find its way to the bottom, and so into the brook; but this does not prevent the owner of the land on which this water falls from dealing with it as he may please and appropriating it.[104]

An alternative case report introduces an observation of Parke B *in arguendo*, stressing that the doctrine of natural rights applied to all definite streams whether above or below ground, and hence departing from the rule

[100] 11 Exch. 369, 383; 156 E.R. 873, 881.
[101] 11 Exch. 369, 384; 156 E.R. 873, 881.
[102] (1853) 1 El. & Bl. 665; 118 E.R. 586 (Q.B.).
[103] (1856) 11 Exch. 602; 156 E.R. 971 (Ex.).
[104] 11 Exch. 602, 615; 156 E.R. 971, 976.

in *Acton* excluding all subterranean waters from the protection of natural right doctrine. Parke B stated:

This Court, and I believe all other Courts, disapprove of that part of the judgment [of *Acton* v. *Blundell*] which denies the natural right to the water. In *Wood* v. *Waud*, it was held that there was no distinction with respect to water running under ground. For instance, there would be no right to divert [a river or stream] which is subterranean in a known course for a mile. *Dickinson* v. *The Grand Junction Canal Company*[105] shows the right to feeders, unless the owners' necessities require them.[106]

A similar line to that of Parke B was followed in the 1857 Exchequer case of *Dudden* v. *The Guardians of Clutton Union*.[107] The facts were that an owner of land on which a spring rose gave a licence to D to abstract the stream at source in order to supply a Poor Law workhouse with water. This diversion deprived P of spring water flowing through a natural course to his mill. The case was decided without adverting to the legality of the licence to abstract water. The court's approach, building on prior decisions, was summed up by Pollock CB in argument:

The real question is, whether there is a natural watercourse which, but for the acts done by [D], would have conveyed water to the stream, and from thence to the mill of [P]. If there is a natural spring, the water from which flows in a natural channel, it cannot lawfully be diverted by any one to the injury of the riparian proprietors. When the stream is above ground, a grant must be presumed, not only of the thing itself, but of all things necessary to the complete enjoyment of it. If the channel or course underground is known . . . it cannot be interfered with. It is otherwise when nothing is known as to the sources of supply; in that case, as no right can be acquired against the owner of the land under which the spring exists, he may do as he pleases with it, and if mining or draining his land he taps a spring, he cannot be made responsible.[108]

In his judgment Pollock CB decided that neither D nor the owner of the spring had any right to divert the spring water:

This was a natural spring, the waters of which had acquired a natural channel from its source to the river. It is absurd to say that a man might take the water of such a stream four feet from the surface.[109]

Watson B gave a similar opinion; and Martin B added:

The owners of lands adjoining a stream, from its source to the sea, have a natural right to thc usc of the water of it. A river begins at its source, when it comes to the surface,

105 (1852) 7 Exch. 282; 155 E.R. 953 (Ex.).

106 (1856) 25 Law Journal (N.S.) 115, 121 (Ex.), quoted by counsel in *Chasemore* v. *Richards* (1859) 7 H.L.C. 349, 360; 11 E.R. 140, 145. This statement was expressly affirmed in *Grand Junction Canal Company* v. *Shugar* (1871) L.R. 6 Ch. Ap. 483 (L.C.) per Lord Hatherley LC.

107 (1857) 1 H. & N. 627; 156 E.R. 1353 (Ex.).

108 1 H. & N. 627, 630; 156 E.R. 1353, 1354.

109 Ibid.

and the owner of the land on which it rises cannot monopolize all the water at the source so as to prevent its reaching the lands of other proprietors lower down.[110]

Chasemore v. *Richards*: Indefinite Waters and Assignability

The House of Lords finally reviewed the gathering body of doctrine governing riparian, underground, and surface water in *Chasemore* v. *Richards* in 1859.[111] The case involved abstraction of water by a local health board by means of a well on Croydon town land, for the purpose of supplying water to the town's large population, and not for uses connected to the land within which the well was sunk. A very large quantity of underground water and rain water was collected by the well, and thereby prevented from flowing to a river which had supplied P's mill for over sixty years. The agreed facts of the case stated:

> [i]t is impossible to know beforehand the precise or complete effect which the sinking of a new well, and pumping from it in any part of the district . . . may have upon springs or streams in the vicinity; the effect may be instantly sensible and considerable, or for a long time no sensible effect may appear; but the natural effect of abstracting a large quantity of water at any spot . . . is to diminish the quantity at every other spot throughout the district, though the amount of diminution at particular spots may be infinitesimally small; and the natural effect to be reasonably expected from sinking a new well . . . and from continually . . . pumping thence large quantities of water for a long time, must be the sensible diminution of the water supply of springs and streams in the vicinity.[112]

The facts indicated that the Board had acted without bad faith in abstracting the water; and had taken no water directly from the river itself; but that D also 'had reasonable means of knowing the probable and natural effects of their said acts and works'.

P's action against the diversion failed on the ground that principle precluded any possible right, either natural or by easement, in indefinite underground streams. The case raised the further problem of whether water resources were freely alienable property, wholly distinct or severable from land, or else were confined to uses associated with the soil of origin.

The case was heard at no fewer than four levels of superior court, before most of the leading appellate judges of the time. In the Court of Exchequer it was held that *Broadbent* v. *Ramsbotham* provided direct authority excluding

[110] 1 H. & N. 627, 630–1; 156 E.R. 1353, 1354. See also *Bowers* v. *Sandford* (1889) 5 Times L.R. 570 (Q.B.) per Denman J; *Bradford Corporation* v. *Pickles* [1894] 3 Ch. 53, 68–70 (Ch.) per North J; *Mostyn* v. *Atherton* (1899) 81 L.T. 356 (Ch.).

[111] (1859) 7 H.L.C. 349; 11 E.R. 140 (H.L.); followed in *Lord Norbury* v. *Kitchin* (1862) 3 F. & F. 292; 176 E.R. 132 (N.P.); *Gaved* v. *Martyn* (1865) 19 C.B. N.S. 732; 144 E.R. 974 (C.P.); *Dalton* v. *Angus* (1881) 6 A.C. 741, 805 per Lord Penzance.

[112] *Chasemore* v. *Richards* 7 H.L.C. 349, 351–2; 11 E.R. 140, 141.

P's action. The Exchequer Chamber affirmed, with Coleridge J dissenting; he argued that natural rights akin to riparian rights should not be denied to underground springs, simply on the basis of the lack of knowledge of proprietors of the flows of water beneath their soil. This ignorance could not be 'material, in respect of a right which does not grow out of the assent or acquiescence of the landowner, as in the case of a servitude, but out of the nature of the thing itself'. Coleridge J wished to base rights to underground water on long user as a self-sufficient ground, separating this source of right from the traditional prescriptive ground of presumed consent. He stressed notions of *sic utere tuo* and a policy of protecting quiet enjoyment of established property uses.

Following these determinations, Lord Chelmsford LC called for an opinion of the common-law judges to be delivered for the Lords' deliberation.[113] In argument before the conference of judges, counsel for P stated that '[t]he ordinary right to water is the same as the right to light and air, Blackstone (Comm. vol.ii p.14); and any additional right must be established by grant or prescription'. P had enjoyed long use of an ancient mill stream, and D's abstraction of water had interfered with that enjoyment and denied water to owners in a large vicinity. 'This is an excess for which [D] is answerable. Each owner may have the reasonable use of water coming to his land, but the use must be confined within reasonable limits. That is the law of England, and it applies even in the cases on the subject of irrigable meadows.' A large body of authority was marshalled to support this statement of doctrine. In *Balston* v. *Bensted* of 1808, Lord Ellenborough held that where a spring was diverted from a pond by the digging of a quarry and drain, so that a paper manufactory was deprived of its requisite supply of spring water,

> the only question was, whether the diminution of the supply of water to [P's] bath had been caused by the drain dug by [D]? and that there could be no doubt but that 20 years' exclusive enjoyment of water in any particular manner affords a conclusive presumption of right in the party so enjoying it.[114]

Ellenborough added no qualification that the spring water should flow in a known or ascertainable channel at the point of appropriation. *Race* v. *Ward*[115] decided that the right to use water issuing from a well was not a profit-à-prendre but an easement, indicating that the flow of the spring was protected as a property right, a more extensive protection than merely a personal right to take water from the well. Recent English[116] and

[113] The judges summoned were Wightman, Williams, and Crompton JJ and Martin, Bramwell, and Watson BB.

[114] (1808) 1 Camp. 463, 465; 170 E.R. 1022, 1023 (N.P.).

[115] (1855) 4 El. & Bl. 702; 119 E.R. 259 (Q.B.); and see A. C. Loux, 'The Persistence of the Ancient Regime: Custom, Utility, and the Common Law in the Nineteenth Century' (1993) 79 Cornell Law Review 183, 205–6.

[116] *Mason* v. *Hill* (1833); *Embrey* v. *Owen* (1851); *Wood* v. *Waud* (1849).

American[117] riparian authorities were held to extend rights to the reasonable use of natural flow to every type of waters: 'All these authorities apply as much to water flowing under ground as to that which flows on the surface, and whose course is visible to all'. This position was held to be supported in the civil law, though Cujacius only was cited and no original Roman authorities.[118] Cujacius doubted if the Digest texts directly supported a right to appropriate or intercept underground and spring water, even where some grant had been made, and then only if the grant was necessary or useful to the needs or use of the grantee as owner of the land. In the present case, however, there was no grant and no taking of the water for the use of the Local Board as landowner. P's counsel concluded:

> The rule to be deduced from these authorities seems to be that the owner or occupier of the land has a right to take the water flowing through it to a reasonable extent, and for purposes connected with the land through which it flows, but not otherwise.... If [D] may take the water from all the land immediately around his own merely because he is about to employ it for the benefit of the town of Croydon, he may take it in like manner, and carry it to London, for the purposes of the metropolis.[119]

An appurtenancy rule was thus applied to control the permissible extent of property use-rights. Further supporting authority was found in *Dickinson* v. *The Grand Junction Canal Company*, deciding that the right to use underground water was subject to the same reasonableness restraints as pertained to surface water. Lord Brougham interjected to doubt this claim:

> Suppose a man sank an artesian well for his use, and got an ample supply of water, he must obtain part at least of it from what would otherwise find its way into neighbouring streams. Suppose it was like the artesian well at Grenelle, which affects streams for forty or fifty miles around; would every proprietor and millowner within such a circle have a right of action?

Counsel in reply distinguished the cases of *Rawstron* and *Broadbent* as dealing only with the right of landowners to drain surface water from their land where it formed no distinct channel; this principle did not allow owners to abstract any amount of underground water. Parke B's statement in *Broadbent* was then cited, criticizing *Acton* v. *Blundell* for its exclusion of a natural right to underground water.[120]

Counsel for the defendant at this hearing was the Attorney-General, arguing the case for the Local Board as a public authority. He attacked P's application of the reasonable usage test to both underground and surface

[117] *Tyler* v. *Wilkinson* (1827) 4 Mason (U.S.) 397; Kent, *Commentaries*, 544.

[118] Citing J. Cujacius, *Opera Omnia* (Paris, 1658, Naples, 1758) vii, *Ad diversos titulos Pandectarun* Tit. I., De Servitutibus Col. 399; Tit. IV., Comm, Praed. Col. 443.

[119] *Chasemore* v. *Richards* (1859) 7 H.L.C. 349, 357–8; 11 E.R. 140, 144.

[120] See the text accompanying nn. 105–106 above.

water, as this was inadequate to resolve 'the conflict of rights of all the owners whose lands are on the same level'. Each owner might take reasonable amounts of water passing through his lands, for example by sinking a well for domestic and agricultural water needs; each of these wells might have an imperceptible or tolerable impact on the amounts of water left for neighbours; but if every neighbour sank a well and this resulted in a significant curtailment of the supply for all, there would be no means of determining who had caused the injury, or who had taken water unreasonably. The American doctrine of reasonable access to all forms of water, it was argued, courted exhaustion of water supplies by over-use of a common resource. It was noted that Chancellor Kent included manufacturing purposes in his rough list of reasonable or permissible uses; this raised the question whether English conditions permitted draining, irrigation, or the making of ornamental lakes as at Blenheim Park. Lord Wensleydale (formerly Parke B) interjected that English cases had not gone so far as American authorities in permitting common use of water for irrigation. *Embrey* v. *Owen* had concerned a taking for irrigation alleged to be unreasonable, but that action had been dismissed as no perceptible injury was occasioned. *Embrey* thus left undecided the propriety of sizeable irrigation uses depleting water supplies available to other owners.

The Attorney-General further argued that there was no distinction in propriety between the abstraction of water by many small wells and abstraction by one large well undertaken by public bodies on behalf of a community; takings by a public agency for the benefit of many persons therefore legitimately circumvented the appurtenancy rule. Next, Blackstone[121] had held that where water passed through land, the owner had rights to water as part of his land, just as he had rights to take rain water. Because there was no property in indefinite water until it passed into one's own land, P's setting up of a prescriptive right based on his long enjoyment of the percolating underground flow was the equivalent of a prescription in his own land, a right which by definition could not be supported.[122] As for recent authority, *Dickinson* could be distinguished as dealing with water emerging from an indefinite underground source, then forming a defined stream subject to the ordinary riparian rights and duties. The only apposite case was *Acton* v. *Blundell*, which 'establishes the doctrine of the absolute right of the owner of the land through whose land water percolates, to use that water'. *Acton* authoritatively reviewed the Roman and civilian sources, and counsel advocated that its doctrinal conclusions be accepted and applied to the present case. The juristic basis for the *Acton* doctrine was that:

[121] *Bl.Comm.*, ii, 14.

[122] Citing *Cooper* v. *Barber* (1810) 3 Taunt. 99; 128 E.R. 40 (C.P.); *Acton* v. *Blundell* (1843) 12 M. & W. 324; 152 E.R. 1223 (Ex.) per Tindal CJ.

while as to streams flowing on the surface everything about them is known, there is an absolute impossibility for anyone to know what are the underground currents, where they begin, what they produce, and in what direction they run, and consequently an absolute impossibility of knowing what are the rights in relation to them.[123]

Wightman J delivered the opinion of the judges' conference. First, the law governing rights to water flowing in definite, visible channels was held to be settled by the cases culminating in *Embrey*;

But the law, as laid down in those cases, is inapplicable to the case of subterranean water not flowing in any definite channel, nor indeed at all, in the ordinary sense, but percolating or oozing through the soil, more or less, according to the quantity of rain that may chance to fall.[124]

This position was said to be supported by all recent authorities.[125] The only contrary dictum was that of Lord Ellenborough in *Balston* v. *Bensted*, but that Nisi Prius case was not brought to final decision and was no strong authority. Moreover, the reasoning that prescriptive rights to underground waters could arise by long user was expressly excluded by later authorities, including *Dickinson* v. *Grand Junction Canal* upon which P chiefly relied. However, *Dickinson* itself was to be confined as an authority: first, its result could have rested on the private Act of Parliament setting out the water entitlements of the parties; and, secondly, the Court of Exchequer in that case fully accepted the reasoning of *Acton*, namely that a special regime of rules applied to underground and percolating water flows. The natural state of such waters was unknown to proprietors and unascertainable; it was therefore impossible to determine natural or reasonable levels of use, as could be done with surface waters. The *Dickinson* court unaccountably failed to apply this obvious principle to the facts before them, holding that as the right to underground waters was not based on presumed grant from long acquiescence, it must be *ex jure naturae* and subject to the same rules as surface streams. The natural-right reasoning of *Dickinson* was therefore to be rejected, even if the result could stand.

Turning to P's argument from long user, the judges held that prescriptive rights could not be divorced from factual presumptions of grant; the presumption was not to be a legal fiction impossible in fact.

[W]hat grant can be presumed in the case of percolating waters, depending upon the quantity of rain falling or the natural moisture of the soil, and in the absence of any visible means of knowing to what extent, if at all, the enjoyment of [P's] mill would be affected by any water percolating in and out of [D's] or any other land? The presump-

[123] *Chasemore* v. *Richards* (1859) 7 H.L.C. 349, 364; 11 E.R. 140, 146.

[124] 7 H.L.C. 349, 366–7; 11 E.R. 140, 147.

[125] E.g. *Rawstron* v. *Taylor* (1855) 11 Exch. 369; 156 E.R. 873 (Ex.) per Parke B; *Broadbent* v. *Ramsbotham* (1856) 11 Exch. 602; 156 E.R. 971 per Alderson B; *Acton* v. *Blundell* (1843) 12 M. & W. 324; 152 E.R. 1223 (Ex. Ch.).

tion of a grant only arises where the person against whom it is to be raised might have prevented the exercise of the subject of the presumed grant; but how could he prevent or stop the percolation of water.[126]

Enforcement of P's claimed right would also have disastrous policy implications:

It is impossible to reconcile such a right with the natural and ordinary rights of landowners, or to fix any reasonable limits to the exercise of such a right.... [It] would interfere with, if not prevent, the draining of land by the owner.

...

If the rain which has fallen may not be intercepted whilst it is merely percolating through the soil, no man could safely collect the rain water as it fell into a pond; nor would he have a right to intercept its fall, before it reached the ground, by extensive roofing, from which it may be conveyed to tanks, to the sensible diminution of water which had, before the erection of such impediments, reached the ground, and flowed to [P's] mill.[127]

According to this view, it was necessary to deny a general right to all types of natural flow of water, as this would irrevocably assign property rights in the water to certain owners at the expense of others, who might value those rights the higher. To expand on the example given, persons draining their houses of rain-water and collecting it as drinking water should not be restrained from so using their property by a neighbour who wished to see the natural flow of water trickle to his field; it made better sense to have that field owner procure a right to irrigation water if it was of significant value to him, rather than legally assign him the right, at considerable expense to the neighbours' freedom to use their land.[128]

Following the negative opinion of the judges' conference, the members of the House of Lords gave their own separate judgments, with Lord Chelmsford delivering the leading speech. He began by restating P's arguments: first, that landowners were permitted to appropriate invisible or indefinite underground waters, such use being restricted to reasonable appropriation for domestic purposes and agriculture, and perhaps also for manufacturing; secondly, that in mining operations an incidental interference with subterranean water was countenanced in order to promote exploitation of mineral wealth; but where abstraction of water for use or sale was the direct object of the diversion, such actions could be restrained; finally, that user of underground waters must be connected to the tenement, disallowing abstraction

[126] *Chasemore* v. *Richards* (1859) 7 H.L.C. 349, 370; 11 E.R. 140, 148–9.

[127] 7 H.L.C. 349, 371–2; 11 E.R. 140, 149.

[128] The judges thus anticipated some of the economic analysis of property rights pioneered in R. H. Coase, 'The Problem of Social Cost' (1960) 3 Journal of Law and Economics 1, and G. Calabresi and A. D. Melamed, 'Property Rules, Liability Rules, and Inalienability Rules: One View of the Cathedral' (1972) 85 Harvard Law Review 1089.

for use by others, or for public purposes such as municipal water and sanitation.

P's arguments were thus laid out only to be rejected. The reasonable-use doctrine as settled by recent authorities applied only to 'water flowing in a certain and defined course, whether in an open visible stream or in a known and subterranean channel':[129]

> [T]he principles which apply to flowing water in streams or rivers, the right to the flow of which in its natural state is incident to the property through which it passes, are wholly inapplicable to water percolating through underground strata, which has no certain course, no defined limits, but which oozes through the soil in every direction in which the rain penetrates.
>
> There is no difficulty in determining the rights of the different proprietors to the usufruct of the water in a running stream. Whether it has been increased by floods or diminished by drought, it flows on the same ascertained course, and the use which every owner may claim is only of the water which has entered into and become part of the stream. But the right to percolating underground water is necessarily of a very uncertain description.... If the owner of land through which the water filters cannot intercept it in its progress, can he prevent its descending to the earth at all, by catching it in tanks and cisterns? And how far will the right to this water supply extend?

It would curb exploitation of land too much if proprietors were required to avoid activities harming natural water flows the extent of which they could not discover. It followed that no limit could be placed on the use proprietors could make of indefinite water flows; use of underground waters was therefore to be unregulated.[130] This argument did not base rights (or no-rights) directly on the state of knowledge or ignorance of proprietors; following the new natural-right orthodoxy, knowledge could not be 'material in respect of a right which does not grow out of the assent or acquiescence of the landowner, as in the case of a servitude, but out of the nature of the thing itself'.[131]

Finally, Lord Chelmsford observed that the 'distinction between water flowing in a definite channel, and water whether above or underground not flowing in a stream at all, but either draining off the surface of the land, or oozing through the underground soil in varying quantities and in uncertain directions, depending upon the variations of the atmosphere, appears to be well settled by the cases cited in argument'. The previous authorities on the subject were reviewed extensively, and Wightman J's reading down of the contrary authorities was adopted.

[129] *Chasemore* v. *Richards* (1859) 7 H.L.C. 349, 374; 11 E.R. 140, 150, following *Dickinson* v. *The Grand Junction Canal Company* (1852) 7 Exch. 282, 300–1; 155 E.R. 953, 961 (Ex.) per Pollock CB.

[130] 7 H.L.C. 349, 374–9; 11 E.R. 140, 150–2.

[131] 7 H.L.C. 349, 375; 11 E.R. 140, 150 quoting Coleridge J (diss.) at first appeal (1857) 2 H. & N. 168, 191; 157 E.R. 71, 80 (Ex.).

The other lords concurred in Lord Chelmford's judgment.[132] Lord Cranworth added:

The right to running water has always been properly described as a natural right, just like the right to the air we breathe; they are the gifts of nature, and no one has a right to appropriate them. There is no difficulty in enforcing that right, because running water is something visible, and no one can interrupt it without knowing whether he does or does not do injury to those who are above or below him. But if the doctrine could be applied to water merely percolating... through the soil, and eventually reaching some stream, it... would require the evidence of scientific men, to state whether or not there had been interruption... or... injury. It is a process of nature not apparent, and therefore such percolating water has not received the protection which water running in a natural channel on the surface has always received. If the argument of P were adopted, the consequence would be that every well that ever was sunk would have given rise, or might give rise, to an action.[133]

As to the argument that the water was used for purposes not appurtenant to the land,

[T]hat argument does not affect my mind at all... it seems to me to be exactly the same thing whether the water is abstracted by one large well, which supplies the whole community, or by a thousand small wells, by which each individual of the community supplies himself.[134]

In the 1871 case of *Grand Junction Canal Company* v. *Shugar*,[135] Lord Hatherley LC restated the *Chasemore* majority doctrine of defined subterranean waters as follows:

[Y]ou have a right to all the water which you can draw from the different sources which may percolate underground; but... water which is in a defined channel... you are not to touch.... You are not by your operations... to diminish the water which runs in this defined channel, because that is not only for yourself, but for your neighbours also, who have a clear right to use it, and have it come to them unimpaired in quality and undiminished in quantity.[136]

[132] Lords Kingsdown, Cranworth, Wensleydale, and Brougham.

[133] 7 H.L.C. 349, 379; 11 E.R. 140, 152.

[134] 7 H.L.C. 349, 379–80; 11 E.R. 140, 152. See also *New River Company* v. *Johnson* (1860) 2 El. & El. 435; 121 E.R. 164 (Q.B.).

[135] (1871) L.R. 6 Ch. Ap. 483 (L.C.).

[136] Ibid., 488; and see further *Ewart* v. *Belfast Poor Law Guardians* (1881) 9 L.R. Ir. 172; *Black* v. *Ballymena Township Commissioners* (1886) 17 L.R. Ir. 459; *M'Nab* v. *Robertson* [1897] A.C. 129 (H.L.(Sc.)); *Jordeson* v. *Sutton, Southcoates, and Drypool Gas Co.* [1899] 2 Ch. 217; *Bradford Corporation* v. *Ferrand* [1902] 2 Ch. 655; *English* v. *Metropolitan Water Board* [1907] 1 K.B. 588. The law governing canal channels and aqueducts sometimes took a different direction: see *Dudley Canal* v. *Grazebrook* (1830) 1 B. & A. 59; 109 E.R. 709 (K.B.); *Cromford Canal Co.* v. *Cutts* (1848) 5 Oliver & Beavan's Rail. Cas. 442 (V.C., L.C.); *Stourbridge Canal* v. *Dudley* (1860) 30 L.J.Q.B. 108; *Birmingham Canal Navigation Co.* v. *Earl of Dudley* (1862) 7 H. & N. 968; 158 E.R. 764 (Ex.); *Midland Railway* v. *Checkley* (1867) L.R. 4 Eq. 19; *Dunn* v. *Birmingham Canal* (1872) L.R. 8 Q.B. 42; H. J. W. Coulson and U. A. Forbes, *The Law Relating to Waters, Sea, Tidal and Inland and Land Drainage* (6th edn. by S. R. Hobday, London, 1952) 320–36.

Lord Wensleydale joined the majority decision in *Chasemore* v. *Richards*, but effectively dissented on most matters of principle.[137] He stated that the doctrine of *Dickinson* had not been overruled by *Rawstron* and *Broadbent*: having participated in all three of those cases, he asserted that *Dickinson* had been carefully and correctly decided, and that the latter cases had not reversed any doctrine but had turned on differing facts, namely that the intercepted percolating water had not contributed to the flow of the stream used by the plaintiff.

Next, he agreed that recent authorities had firmly established a natural right theory for ordinary riparian water rights:

> It has now been settled that the right to the enjoyment of a natural stream of water on the surface, *ex jure naturae*, belongs to the proprietor of the adjoining lands, as a natural incident of the right to the soil itself, and that he is entitled to the benefit of it, as he is to all the other natural advantages belonging to the land of which he is the owner. He has the right to have it come to him in its natural state, in flow, quantity and quality, and to go from him without obstruction; upon the same principle that he is entitled to the support of his neighbour's soil for his own in its natural state.[138] His right in no way depends upon prescription, or the presumed grant of his neighbour.[139]

These principles were established by Denman CJ in *Mason* v. *Hill* and were moreover extant in earlier law[140] and affirmed by 'the best' American authorities,[141] including 'the very able treatise on watercourses by Mr. Angel [*sic*]'.[142] American authorities were invoked to help determine the controversial scope of *injuria sine damno*:

> And it has been held in America that the law implied damage from the violation of the right, *vide* Angel [*sic*] on water,[143] *Pastorius* v. *Fisher*;[144] a matter which has sometimes been doubted, though probably without sufficient reason.[145]

137 *Chasemore* v. *Richards* (1859) 7 H.L.C. 349, 380–9; 11 E.R. 140, 152–6. Wensleydale suggested that Bramwell B, sitting with the panel of judges, had prepared a reasoned dissent with which he agreed, which had not, however, been delivered to avoid differences. Lord Wensleydale was the ennobled Parke B, who had settled many of the principles of water law in *Embrey*. Parke's elevation to the House of Lords purely as a legal functionary provoked a major constitutional controversy concerning the hereditary principle of aristocracy. He was regarded as one of the greatest common lawyers of his day; his judgments commonly displayed both extreme legal formalism and a warm embrace of the principles of political economy: see P. S. Atiyah, *The Rise and Fall of Freedom of Contract* (Oxford, 1979) 368–9, 395, 498, 502, 522.

138 Cf. *Dalton* v. *Angus* (1881) 6 App. Cas. 825 (H.L.).

139 *Chasemore* v. *Richards* (1859) 7 H.L.C. 349, 382; 11 E.R. 140, 153.

140 Citing *Sury* v. *Pigot* (1625) Poph. 166; 79 E.R. 1263; 3 Bulst. 339; 81 E.R. 280 (K.B.); *Brown* v. *Best* (1747) 1 Wils. K.B. 174; 95 E.R. 557 (K.B.); *Wright* v. *Howard* (1823) 1 Sim. & St. 192; 57 E.R. 76 (V.C.); and *Dickinson* v. *The Grand Junction Canal Company* (1852) 7 Exch. 282; 155 E.R. 953 (Ex.).

141 *Tyler* v. *Wilkinson* (1827) 4 Mason's (U.S.) Rep. 401; 24 Fed. Cas, 472 (Case No. 14, 312) per Story J; Kent, *Commentaries*, iii, lect. 52, 439–55.

142 Angell, *Watercourses*, 1, 21, 22.

143 Ibid., 98.

144 (1828) 1 Rawle. Pennsylvania Reports 27, 28, per Gibson CJ ('the action may be brought to try the right').

145 *Chasemore* v. *Richards* (1859) 7 H.L.C. 349, 383–4; 11 E.R. 140, 154–5.

Various authorities supporting the implied consent and prior occupation theories were then assailed:

We may consider, therefore, that this proposition is indisputable, that the right of the proprietor to the enjoyment of a watercourse on the surface is a natural right, and not acquired by occupation of the stream itself, or presumed grant. And the expressions used by [Bayley J] in *Williams* v. *Morland*, and by [Tindal CJ] in *Liggins* v. *Inge*, that water flowing in a stream is *publici juris*, and the property of the first occupier, are founded on a mistake between the property in the water itself and the right to have its continual flow.

The observations, also, of [Tindal CJ] in the case of *Acton* v. *Blundell* and of [Maule J] in *Smith* v. *Kenrick*, as to the origin of the right to the continual flow of a superficial stream, being the presumed acquiescence of the proprietors above and below, and which is the foundation of the distinction made by [Tindal CJ] between those streams and subterranean watercourses, cannot be supported.

Further criticisms were made of the theory of prescription or presumed grant proposed by Coleridge J in the Exchequer hearing of *Chasemore*, and by Lord Ellenborough in the earlier case of *Balston* v. *Bensted*. According to Lord Wensleydale, notional consent derived from acquiescence in the long user of underground water could not reasonably be presumed at law, because an owner could not plausibly be expected to negate consent to another's user of percolating or underground waters by somehow cutting off the flow of water through his land:

I do not think that the principle on which prescription rests can be applied; it has not been with the permission of the proprietor of the land that the streams have flowed into the river for twenty years or upwards: *qui non prohibit quod prohibere potest, assentire videtur*.[146] But how here could he prevent it? He could not bring an action against the adjoining proprietor; he could not be bound to dig a deep trench in his own land to cut off the supplies of water, in order to indicate his dissent. It is going very far to say, that a man must be at the expense of putting up a screen to window lights, to prevent a title being granted by twenty years' enjoyment of light passing through a window. But this case would go very far beyond that. I think that the enjoyment of the right to these natural streams cannot be supported by any length of user if it does not belong of natural right to the Plaintiff.[147]

Lord Wensleydale saw prescriptive rights as founded on some type of real consent evidenced by acquiescence in user—not a wholly fictional consent that may be so unlikely as to be nigh-impossible, but which is implied by law in order to protect long enjoyment. Here he criticized the theory espoused by Coleridge J in the lower court. Further, in departing from the majority opinions, Lord Wensleydale went on to assert that a natural right inhered

[146] A man who has power to prevent and does not prevent is held to assent. Cf. D.50.17.109. (Paul).

[147] *Chasemore* v. *Richards* (1859) 7 H.L.C. 349, 385–6; 11 E.R. 140, 154. See further *Sturges* v. *Bridgeman* (1879) 11 Ch. D. 855 (C.A.); *Harris* v. *De Pinna* (1886) 33 Ch. D. 259 (Ch.).

both in defined and indefinite subterranean water flows, claiming that the two types of flow were closely analogous:

Now the right to a natural stream flowing in a definite channel is not confined to streams on the surface, but the right to an underground stream flowing in a known and definite channel is equally a right *ex natura*, and an incident to the land itself, as a beneficial adjunct to it, as was determined in the case of *Wood* v. *Waud*.[148]

If the [r]iver... in this case had been supplied by natural streams flowing into the river above ground, or in known definite channels below ground, the cutting off those streams to which the person entitled to the use of the river was entitled *ex natura* as feeders of the river, would be an injury to him, and give a right of action. And if this be true with regard to underground streams finding their way into the river, then comes the difficulty how to distinguish the smaller rivulets, and the drops of water which flow and percolate into and supply the river. They are all flowing water, the property in which is not vested in the owner of the soil, any more than the property in the water of a river which flows through it on the surface.

Support for this doctrine was drawn from Tindal CJ's statements in *Acton*; first, that underground water was part of a man's property in land under 'the principle which gives to the owner of the soil all that lies beneath his surface'; and, secondly, that 'the person who owns the surface may dig therein, and apply all that he finds to his own purposes, at his free will and pleasure'. Lord Wensleydale suggested that, at least in the case of water resources, this principle should be adapted to avoid the notion of absolute ownership and control of all physical matter beneath the soil:

If this applies to water underground in a natural course of transit (and it must do so to be applicable to all), and not to mere stagnant water, I agree with Mr. Justice Coleridge[149]... that the reason why it is, as such, more the subject of property than the water flowing above ground, is not explained. Surely the use of the flowing water in each case, and not the property in it, belongs to the proprietor of the surface.[150]

In sum, a natural right of user was to be applied to all forms of water flow. Wensleydale acknowledged that a significantly different regime should apply to water flows above and below ground, but unlike the majority he did not focus on the presumed lack of knowledge of underground waters in order to deny rights to the uninterrupted flow of such waters. His reasoning was grounded on utilitarian rather than contractarian grounds:

What, then, is the distinction between superficial streams and subterranean waters? With respect to underground waters percolating the strata, two considerations arise which make a material difference between them and the right to superficial streams. In the first place, these subterraneous waters cannot be actually enjoyed (and all things are given to be enjoyed) without artificial means. The water must be reduced into

148 *Chasemore* v. *Richards* (1859) 7 H.L.C. 349, 384; 11 E.R. 140, 154.
149 *Chasemore* v. *Richards* (1857) 2 H. & N. 168, 192; 157 E.R. 71, 80 (Ex.) per Coleridge J.
150 *Chasemore* v. *Richards* (1859) 7 H.L.C. 349, 385; 11 E.R. 140, 154.

possession before it can be used, and some mode of reducing into possession must be permitted by law. If there be no such right, underground water is comparatively useless. A man may dig therefore for his own supply, or make a well for his own use and that of his family, and, in so doing, he may deprive his neighbour's land of moisture, and even tap a copious spring, and prevent it from flowing into his neighbour's close. It can rarely happen that in excavating, in order to obtain the use of the water, some injury will not be caused in the subterraneous supplies of a neighbour, especially as the precise course and direction of the water can seldom be known accurately beforehand.

In the second place, as the great interests of society require that the cultivation of every man's land should be encouraged, and its natural advantages made fully available, the owner must be permitted to dig his own soil, and, in so doing, he can very rarely avoid interfering with the subterraneous waters flowing or percolating in his neighbour's land.[151]

The second argument was derived from Roman law, which provides 'many instances in which it is allowed to cut off subterraneous supplies, if it is done in the cultivation of the soil'. Digest texts were quoted showing the latitude of this principle:[152]

It would seem ... that if the sources of a fountain or spring in an adjoining piece of land were cut off by excavating, in order to get the minerals in any place, it would be deemed by the Roman law to fall within the principle of the improvement of the land, and not be actionable.[153]

Concluding this train of reasoning, it was held that all flows of water were protected by natural rights, though only surface water attracted a strong protection from obstruction. Productive use of land inevitably interfered with indefinite subsoil waters, so that only a lesser protection of those waters could be afforded; interferences of considerable scope were 'reasonable' and permitted. The result of *Acton* was explained as turning on this ground of utility, rather than any absolute proprietary right to exploit the subsoil: 'the injury to [P's] well was caused by the lawful exercise of [D's] right to get the minerals in his land; and unless he had that right, the public would have lost the benefit of a valuable gift of Providence'.

The natural right of user of underground water flow was not to be unregulated, but was to be exercised according to a reasonableness test less stringent than that for surface waters. Wensleydale summed up his doctrine as follows:

[E]very man has a right to the natural advantages of his soil—[P] to the benefit of the flow of the water in the river and its natural supplies, [D] to the enjoyment of his land, and to the underground waters on it, and he may, in order to obtain that water, sink a well. But according to the rule of reason and law, '*sic utere tuo ut alienum non laedas*,'

[151] 7 H.L.C. 349, 386–7; 11 E.R. 140, 155.

[152] D.39.3.1. (Ulpian). Wensleydale used the Pothier edition, and described the Digest titles very obscurely, save for the famous text D.39.3.1.12. (Marcellus).

[153] *Chasemore* v. *Richards* (1859) 7 H.L.C. 349, 337–8; 11 E.R. 140, 155.

it seems right to hold, that he ought to exercise his right in a reasonable manner, with as little injury to his neighbours' rights as may be.[154]

An example of unreasonable use of rights might be an act done with malicious intent to harm a neighbour—though it was acknowledged that this civilian and Scots principle had not found a place as a general doctrine of English law.[155]

Finally, it was suggested that a reasonable manner of exercise of rights to underground water extended only to uses by the proprietor on his own land—an application of the appurtenancy principle as a general limitation on the enjoyment of incidents of property:

Had he [D] made the well and used the steam-engines for the supply of water for the use of his own property, and those living on it, there could have been no question. If the number of houses upon it had increased to any extent, and the quantity of water for the families dwelling on the property had been proportionately augmented, there could have been no just grounds of complaint. But I doubt very greatly the legality of [D's] acts in abstracting water for the use of a large district in the neighbourhood, unconnected with his own estate, for the use of those who would have no right to take it directly themselves, and to the injury of those neighbouring proprietors who have an equal right with themselves. It does not follow that each person who was supplied with water by [D] could have dug a well himself on his own land, and taken the like quantity of water, so that [D] may have taken much more than would have been abstracted if each had exercised his own right.

The same objection would not apply to the abstraction of water for the use of the dwellers on [D's] land, even though they carried on trades requiring more water (breweries, for example) than would be used for mere domestic purposes; it would be still for their purposes only. But in this case there has been an abstraction of water for purposes wholly unconnected with the enjoyment of [D's] land.[156]

All the judgments of this elaborate litigation, both majority and minority, pointed to the extent to which the new reasonableness test for water use had discarded notions of equal natural rights and moved in the direction of absolute rights of competitive land exploitation.[157] The magnitude of the *Chasemore* decision as a restatement of the law was noted by many of the judges. Lord Wensleydale stated 'this case is of the greatest importance, and requires the most full and attentive consideration. No question that has occurred in my time has been so worthy of the most careful examination'. Lord Kingsdown expressed the House's thanks to 'those learned persons',

[154] 7 H.L.C. 349, 388; 11 E.R. 140, 155.

[155] An issue to erupt later in the great case of *Bradford Corporation* v. *Pickles* [1894] 3 Ch. 53 (Ch.); [1895] A.C. 587 (H.L.), the text accompanying nn. 158–162 below.

[156] *Chasemore* v. *Richards* (1859) 7 H.L.C. 349, 388–9; 11 E.R. 140, 155–6.

[157] For continuation of this policy see *Grand Junction Canal Company* v. *Shugar* (1871) L.R. 6 Ch. Ap. 483 (L.C.); *Lyon* v. *Fishmongers' Company* (1876) 1 App. Cas. 673 (H.L.); *Dalton* v. *Angus* (1881) 6 App. Cas. 825 (H.L.); *Bradford Corporation* v. *Pickles* [1894] 3 Ch. 53; [1895] A.C. 587 (H.L.); *Black* v. *Ballymena Commissioners* (1886) 17 L.R. Ir. 459 (Ch.(I.)).

the counsel and judges, 'for the admirable reasoning by which they appear to have removed all doubt upon one of the most important questions that ever came under the consideration of a court of justice'. This last claim was not quite accurate, for the problem of the assignability of water rights was left unresolved, to be litigated in another series of large-scale cases.

Bradford Corporation v. *Pickles*: Motive and the Exercise of Property Rights

Before we turn to this final issue of severability and assignment, the well-known decision of *Bradford Corporation* v. *Pickles*[158] can be cited as the apogee of doctrines of absolute rights of property exploitation in English law. An owner (D) sunk a well and intercepted percolating underground water with the tacit purpose of coercing a local authority (P) into buying out his land at a premium in order to secure the municipal water supply, and not in order to use the underground water for his own purposes. P argued that D's conduct breached the implicit principle that a nuisance motivated by malice is always wrongful. The House of Lords held that such a principle of abuse of rights, even if it had any place in English law, could not be applied to economically self-interested actions. Lord Macnaghten outlined a highly individualistic principle governing such cases:

> [P] say[s] that under the circumstances the operation which [D] threatens to carry out is something in excess of his rights as a landowner.... The position of [P] is one which it is not very easy to understand.... They say that [D]'s action in the matter is malicious, and that because his motive is a bad one, he is not at liberty to do a thing which every landowner in the country may do with impunity if his motives are good.... Well, he has something to sell, or, at any rate, he has something which he can prevent other people enjoying unless he is paid for it.... He prefers his own interest to the public good. He may be churlish, selfish, and grasping. His conduct may seem shocking to a moral philosopher. But where is the malice?... [I]n such a case motives are immaterial. It is the act, not the motive for the act, that must be regarded.[159]

It is not true that there were no doctrines of abuse of rights in English jurisprudence. Chancery jurisdiction, for example, has always been devoted to restraining unconscientious abuse of legal rights.[160] But *Bradford* v.

[158] [1895] 3 Ch. 53 (Ch.) per North J; [1895] A.C. 587 (H.L.). For close analysis see A. W. B. Simpson, 'Victorian Law and the Industrial Spirit' (Selden Society Lecture, 1995), and M. Taggart, *Private Property and Abuse of Rights in Victorian England: The Story of Edward Pickles and the Bradford Water Supply* (Oxford, 2002).

[159] [1895] A.C. 587, 603–5. For modern restatements of the doctrine see *Langbrook Properties Ltd* v. *Surrey County Council* [1970] 1 W.L.R. 161; *Stevens* v. *Anglian Water Authority* (1987) 137 N.L.J. 829. For some of the historical antecedents of the doctrine see Simpson, 'The Timeless Principles of the Common Law: *Keeble* v. *Hickeringill* (1707)'.

[160] L. D. Smith, 'The Motive Not the Deed', in J. Getzler (ed.), *Rationalizing Property, Equity and Trusts. Essays in Private Law in Honour of Edward Burn* (London, 2003) 53–81, arguing that fiduciary law remains essentially motive-based.

Pickles did exclude any application of the general abuse of rights theory found in civilian systems, especially French law, to property rights in land. Further the *Pickles* decision, by rejecting any doctrine of property tort based on malicious motive or intent or other moralistic test of behaviour, may have saved English common law from the general adoption of a malice test in contract and tort when the issue came before the Lords in the great 1898 case of *Allen* v. *Flood*.[161] In other words the unlovely *Pickles* doctrine headed off the greater danger of a motive test infecting the law of obligations, as with the American doctrine of prima facie torts.[162] But this theme takes us beyond the scope of this study.

ASSIGNABILITY OF WATER RIGHTS AND THE APPURTENANCY RULE

Lord Wensleydale clearly identified the problem of appurtenancy in *Chasemore*: could natural water rights be enjoyed only for purposes connected to the riparian tenement?[163] The issue arose squarely in the Court of Exchequer case of *Stockport Waterworks Company* v. *Potter* in 1864.[164] Riparian rights were acquired by M in 1809 upon purchasing a mill site on the river Mersey, including the right to channel water into a weir. In 1811 M began supplying the town of Stockport with water, and expanded his water use by constructing further channels taking water from the river to treatment works near the

[161] [1898] A.C. 1 (HL).

[162] For development of this argument see J. Getzler, 'The Fate of the Civil Jury in Late Victorian England: Malicious Prosecution as a Test Case', in G. R. Rubin and K. O'Donovan (eds.), *Human Rights and Legal History: Essays for Brian Simpson* (Oxford, 2000) 205–24, reprinted in J. W. Cairns and G. McLeod (eds.), *'The Dearest Birth Right of the People of England': The Jury in the History of the Common Law* (Oxford, 2002) 217–37; cf. Taggart, *Private Property and Abuse of Rights*, 167–93, who marshalls arguments in favour of the motive test in private law, but does not give weight to the problem of common-law suppression of labour action as exemplified in *Allen* v. *Flood*. See Tony Weir, *Economic Torts* (Oxford, 1997) passim; cf. R. Bagshaw, 'Inducing Breach of Contract', in J. Horder (ed.), *Oxford Essays in Jurisprudence, Fourth Series* (Oxford, 2000), 131. For the downside of good-faith tests in contract generally see H. K. Lücke, 'Good Faith and Contractual Performance', in P. D. Finn (ed.), *Essays on Contract* (Sydney, 1987) 155.

[163] Cf. *Hill* v. *Tupper* (1863) 2 H. & C. 121; 159 E.R. 51 (Ex.); *Keppel* v. *Bailey* (1834) 2 My. & K. 517; 39 E.R. 1042 (Ch.) (new property rights cannot be created by contract to run with land and bind third parties at the will of contracting parties; they must be recognized easements or profits); *Dempster* v. *Cleghorn* (1813) 2 Dow. 40; 3 E.R. 780 (H.L.); *Manning* v. *Wasdale* (1836) 5 Ad. & E. 758; 111 E.R. 1353 (C.P.); *Fentiman* v. *Smith* (1803) 4 East. 107; 102 E.R. 770 (K.B.); *Tyler* v. *Bennett* (1836) 5 Ad. & E. 377; 111 E.R. 1208 (C.P.); *Race* v. *Ward* (1855) 4 El. & Bl. 702; 119 E.R. 259 (Q.B.) (rights to water cattle or other rights to take water are praedial easements requiring dominant and servient tenements, not profits-à-prendre in gross); *Rangeley* v. *Midland Railway Co.* (1865) L.R. 3 Ch. App. 310, 311 (Ch. App.) (no easements in gross in English law).

[164] (1864) 3 H. & C. 300; 159 E.R. 545 (Ex.). See also *Laing* v. *Whaley* (1858) 3 H. & N. 675, 901; 157 E.R. 639, 733 (Ex.).

town. These actions provoked disputes with neighbours, leading to an Act of Parliament in 1825 formally approving M's right to divert water for his commercial purposes. By 1850, the bulk of Stockport's water was supplied from M's works, taking water directly from the Mersey as the town's artesian sources had dried up. A neighbouring riparian owner brought an action seeking to restrain the heightened takings of river water. An arbitrator determined that M had not established a prescriptive right to the present levels of water use, and ordered that reservoirs be built in order to prevent shortages being suffered by other users. In 1850 a utility company (P in the present action) took over the supply of water to Stockport; and in 1853 M granted P all rights in his water works, including rights to take water from the Mersey via the existing weirs and channels to the town water works some distance away. P was not, however, granted possession of the riparian land itself, nor the land within which the weirs and channels were built, those lands remaining in M's ownership.

In 1863 P sued an upstream proprietor, D, for polluting the stream by arsenic emissions from a calico factory nine miles upstream. P claimed a right to unpolluted water binding all persons, arising from the 1853 grant transferring M's vested water rights to P. P also claimed a separate prescriptive right to pure water flow, an easement created by the combined period of enjoyment of the high level of water use by P and his predecessor M from 1850 or earlier.

The Court of Exchequer majority[165] held that P's claim amounted to a novel right of action unsupported by authority, and P was therefore non-suited. Pollock CB expressly adopted the defence arguments, which divided into three. First, P could not claim the benefit of another riparian landowner's natural water privileges, for these were annexed to the land:

> [A]lthough the right to pure water is the right of a riparian proprietor, the plaintiffs are not riparian proprietors . . . nor assignees of a riparian proprietor. For . . . the law knows of no such right as the subject of assignment separate from the land in respect of which it arises. . . . And . . . there is no authority for the proposition that these rights in respect of water, which, in *Embrey* v. *Owen* and other modern cases have been for the first time defined and attributed to the ownership of land by the side of a river, can be dealt with in gross and assigned in any way except in conjunction with such land.[166]

Secondly, even if P could have a right in gross to the use of the river, the appurtenancy principle excluded any right to take water for the use of others:

[165] Pollock CB and Channell B, Wilde B concurring.

[166] *Stockport Waterworks Company* v. *Potter* (1864) 3 H. & C. 300, 324; 159 E.R. 545, 555 per Pollock CB. Pollock CB and the majority rejected any analysis of flowing water as itself a servient tenement subjected to the requirements of a neighbouring or distant dominant tenement: 3 H. & C. 300, 327–8; 159 E.R. 545, 556–7; see also *Ackroyd* v. *Smith* (1850) 10 C.B. 164, 187–8; 138 E.R. 68, 77–8 (C.P.); Holdsworth, *History of English Law*, vii, 331–3.

[T]he rights even of a riparian proprietor himself would not extend to the abstraction from the stream of water for the use of a populous town situated on land in no way connected with such stream, and the conveyance of it away from the river-side to a considerable distance for that purpose without returning it into the stream.[167]

Finally, the prior enjoyment of pure water for more than twenty years at the downstream site could found no prescription, because D's property and activities were not adversely affected by M and P's downstream abstractions:

No amount of water abstracted by [P] or those under whom they claim could possibly be felt by [D]. If the water was abstracted unlawfully or in excessive quantities, or not returned into the river the proprietors below might have cause to complain, but D could not, because they could not be affected by it. They had neither the will nor the power to interfere with P's use nor to take legal proceedings against them. No grant could therefore be presumed by [D] because no user ever existed adverse to their full enjoyment of the water.... [168]

It followed that failure to pollute could not be construed as reasonable acquiescence by D in P's right to pure water, and could not establish an easement for pure water. The cases of *Magor* v. *Chadwick* and *Whaley* v. *Laing*[169] concerning rights against fouling were not here cited; though earlier in argument the judges indicated that these authorities excluded any natural right to pure water accorded to non-riparian users.

Pollock CB summed up the majority opinion as follows:[170]

[A] riparian proprietor [cannot] keep the land abutting on the river the possession of which gives him his water rights, and at the same time transfer those rights or any of them, and thus create a right in gross by assigning a portion of his rights appurtenant.

[T]he rights which a riparian proprietor has with respect to the water are entirely derived from his possession of land abutting on the river. If he grants away any portion of his land so abutting, then the grantee becomes a riparian proprietor and has similar rights. But if he grants away a portion of his estate not abutting on the river, then clearly the grantee of the land would have no water rights by virtue merely of his occupation. [B]y express grant... he can have them against the grantor but not so as to sue other persons in his own name for an infringement of them.... *Hill* v. *Tupper*[171] ... is an authority for the proposition that a person cannot create by grant new rights of property so as to give the grantee a right of suing in his own name for an interruption of the right by a third party.

The abstraction of the water from the stream took place at a spot situated on land other than that now called the dominant tenement, and in no sort of way affected the enjoyment of the water at what is now called the servient tenement. If the waterworks could be considered a dominant tenement

167 *Stockport Waterworks Company* v. *Potter* (1864) 3 H. & C. 300, 324–5; 159 E.R. 545, 555.

168 3 H. & C. 300, 324–6; 159 E.R. 545, 555–6, citing *Sampson* v. *Hoddinott* (1857) 1 C.B.N.S. 590; 140 E.R. 242 (C.P.).

169 See Ch. 5, the text accompanying nn. 129–138 and nn. 159–177 above.

170 *Stockport Waterworks Company* v. *Potter* (1864) 3 H. & C. 300, 326–7; 159 E.R. 545, 556.

171 (1863) 2 H. & C. 121; 159 E.R. 51 (Ex.).

every house in Stockport to which the water flowed through pipes might equally be so.

And as in modern times water is often conveyed many miles under ground in pipes for the supply of large towns, the dominant and servient tenements might not only be many miles apart, but have no other connexion with each other than the artificial one created by miles of pipes.[172]

Bramwell B dissented, offering a radical utilitarian justification for according water rights of grant and in gross a proprietary protection against third parties. He ignored or interpreted away contrary authority, reasoning from the higher premise of freedom of contract:

[W]e must suppose that the grantor [the riparian proprietor] and grantee have found the arrangement to be to their mutual advantage, that the stream can be more beneficially used this way than otherwise. Consequently that such an arrangement is for the public good. Why, then, should it not be effectual against a person [i.e. a polluter], who as against the riparian proprietor is a wrongdoer?[173]

Bramwell's argument was that all persons were subject to a general obligation not to foul or obstruct rivers; hence there could be no objection to allowing an assignee of water rights a power to enforce that already-existing obligation, even though this might create a greater incidence of liability than under a privity of estate regime:

It imposes no additional burden on the riparians or others above. If they are wrongdoers by fouling now, so were they before. They could be restrained by injunction before if they can now. No doubt they might be made liable to larger damages than they would have been before, but their rights are not altered.

The power to make such a grant then is for the benefit of the grantor, and grantee, and the public; and the only prejudice by it to the riparian or wrongdoer above is the liability to greater damages and to an action and injunction at the suit of persons additional to the riparians below.[174]

Bramwell B further held that this obligation did not annex new property burdens to tenements of land (as proscribed in *Keppel* v. *Bailey*[175]), for if one viewed the obligation from the side of the obligee (rather than the obligor claiming the right) the duty not to divert or pollute water was not itself attached to any estate but was a rule of right-conduct binding all persons in tort.[176] Apart from the argument from tort duties, the recognition of the

[172] *Stockport Waterworks Company* v. *Potter* (1864) 3 H. & C. 300, 327–8; 159 E.R. 545, 556–7. See further *Holker* v. *Porrit* (1875) L.R. 10 Ex. 62 (Ex.); *Kensit* v. *Great Eastern Railway* (1884) 27 Ch.D. 122 (Ch.); *Ormerod* v. *Todmorton Mill Co.* (1883) 11 Q.B.D. 155 (Q.B.); *McCartney* v. *Londonderry &c., Railway* [1904] A.C. 315 (H.L.); *Elmhirst* v. *Spencer* (1849) 2 Mac. & G. 45; 42 E.R. 18 (Ch.).

[173] *Stockport Waterworks Company* v. *Potter* (1864) 3 H. & C. 300, 319; 159 E.R. 545, 553.

[174] 3 H. & C. 300, 319–21; 159 E.R. 545, 553–4. Cf. *Earl of Portmore* v. *Bunn* (1823) 1 B. & C. 694; 107 E.R. 255 (K.B.).

[175] (1834) 2 My. & K. 517; 39 E.R. 1042 (Ch.).

[176] Following *Whaley* v. *Laing* (1857) 2 H. & N. 476; 157 E.R. 196 (Ex.); (1858) 3 H. & N. 675, 901; 157 E.R. 639, 733 (Ex. Ch.); (1860) 5 H. & N. 480; 157 E.R. 1269 (Ex. Ch.).

obligation as a right of grant did not breach the rule in *Hill* v. *Tupper*[177] preventing mere contractual relations binding third parties, as the transfer of riparian rights was not merely a covenanted right of action, but gave a type of possession of flowing water.[178] Bramwell B, employing some creative interpretations to circumvent contrary authority, here characterized flowing water as a species of commodified property, fully capable of transfer as a property right binding third parties, and not naturally tied to ownership of riparian property.[179]

Bramwell's Commodification Experiment Rejected

In the 1866 case of *Nuttal* v. *Bracewell*[180] a mill owner sued to protect flow of water conveyed to his mill through an artificial goit, a right he had been granted and had enjoyed for over twenty years. Bramwell B again affirmed his belief that 'as a general rule, when a man has a property he may grant to others estates in and rights of enjoyment of it, and the grantees may maintain actions against those who disturb them'.[181] The majority took care to reject this reasoning, but allowed the mill owner-grantee's action on the theory that a permanent artificial channel to supply a mill merely branched or extended the riparian area, and thus was not a wrongful or unprotected abstraction by a person lacking any appurtenant estate.[182] Martin B's judgment suggests that practicalities prevented extending the *Stockport* doctrine to deny enforcement of water rights in such cases. After detailing the immense economic value of water rights in manufacture,[183] he stated the following position:

> According to the law so enunciated [in modern cases]... it would be competent for [a riparian owner] to erect a mill... and take the water from the stream to work it, provided he neither penned back the water upon his neighbour above, nor injuriously affected the volume and flow of the water of the stream to his neighbour below. And the law favours the exercise of such a right; it is at once beneficial to the owner and to the commonwealth. And if this be so, why may not the owners of two adjoining closes agree together, for their mutual benefit, to take the water through a goit from the close of the one into the close of the other, returning the water to the stream in the close of the latter, and thereby doing no injury to any one. In point of fact, very many goits

[177] (1863) 2 H. & C. 121; 159 E.R. 51 (Ex.).

[178] *Stockport Waterworks Company* v. *Potter* (1864) 3 H. & C., 300, 321–2; 11 E.R. 545, 554.

[179] For Bramwell's strongly utilitarian and libertarian convictions and their expression in his judgments, see references in Introduction, above, n. 13.

[180] (1866) L.R. 2 Exch. 1 (Ex.).

[181] Ibid., 11.

[182] Ibid., 9–10 per Martin B; 13–14 per Channell B and Pollock CB, citing *Sutcliffe* v. *Booth* (1863) 32 L.J.Q.B. 136 (Q.B.) per Wightman J. This method of extending riparian rights to assignees was expressly rejected by the same judges in the *Stockport Waterworks* case.

[183] (1866) L.R. 2 Ex. 1, 9 (Ex.); see Ch. 1, the text accompanying n. 132 above.

pass through the land of different landowners between the place where the water is taken from the stream and the mill where it works the machinery. The right to a flow of water in a goit is a well-known easement, and is an incorporeal hereditament, and although it is not competent for an owner of land to render it subject to a new species of burthen at his fancy or caprice, the burthen of one man's land being subject to the right of another to have a flow of water running through it to work his mill, is as old as the law itself, and in my opinion is the subject of property and of grant, and not merely of licence.[184]

Martin B carefully avoided choosing between the majority appurtenancy doctrine in *Stockport* and Bramwell B's dissent allowing rights in gross generally. Instead, he held that the present case could conveniently be distinguished from *Stockport* on its facts.

In the 1875 case of *Swindon Waterworks Co.* v. *Wilts and Berks Canal Co.*,[185] an appeal from Chancery, the House of Lords reaffirmed the principle that riparian rights did not permit water to be abstracted as a saleable commodity to persons unconnected with an appurtenant riparian estate. The case concerned a water company which abstracted a large portion of water from an upstream mill site in order to fill a reservoir supplying a town with domestic water. These operations denied water to the plaintiff canal company, which had been filling its canal from a mill site further downstream.

The lower courts decided the case upon an interpretation of the local canal act of 1795 (35 Geo. 3, c. 52), entitling P to abstract sufficient water to maintain its navigation. Lord Cairns's leading speech in the Lords applied the *Embrey* legal tests allowing unlimited ordinary or domestic use of water, and reasonable extraordinary use for irrigation and manufacturing:[186]

[T]he lower riparian owner is entitled to the accustomed flow of the water for the ordinary purposes for which he can use the water, that is quite consistent with the right of the upper owner also to use the water for all ordinary purposes, namely, as has been said *ad lavandum et ad potandum*, whatever portion of the water may be thereby exhausted and may cease to come down by reason of that use. But farther, there are uses no doubt to which the water may be put by the upper owner, namely, uses connected with the tenement of that upper owner. Under certain circumstances, and provided no material injury is done, the water may be used and may be diverted for a time by the upper owner for the purpose of irrigation.... [T]he exhaustion of the water which may thereby take place may be so inconsiderable as not to form a subject of complaint by the lower owner, and the water may be restored after the object of irrigation is answered, in a volume substantially equal to that in which it passed before. Again... there may be a use of the water by the upper owner for... manufacturing purposes, so reasonable that no just complaint can be made upon the subject

[184] L.R. 2 Exch. 1, 9–10.

[185] (1875) L.R. 7 H.L. 697 (H.L.), on appeal from (1874) L.R. 9 Ch. 453 per Sir R. Malins VC at first instance; per James and Mellish LJJ (Ch. Ap.).

[186] No variance between equity and law was indicated by the Lord Chancellor.

by the lower owner. Whether such a use in any particular case could be made for manufacturing purposes connected with the upper tenement would . . . depend upon whether the use was a reasonable use. Whether it was a reasonable use would depend, at all events in some degree, on the magnitude of the stream from which the deduction was made for this purpose over and above the ordinary use of the water.[187]

Lord Cairns stressed that in all cases a reasonable use of natural flow must be for 'purposes connected with the tenement of the . . . owner'. Hence a utility company owning riparian land could not pump any amount of water to supply a town, for this was 'not for the purpose of their tenement at all', but was 'a complete diversion of the stream', an 'annihilation' of the water, a 'confiscation' or 'alienation' of the rights of lower riparian owners.[188] In the result he granted an injunction restraining D's appropriations.

Lord Cairns did not provide indicia structuring the concept of reasonable use; he did not, for example, spell out that an interference with natural flow in the absence of damage could be a legal injury if it might harden into an adverse right by prescription. The reasonableness standard for permissible abstractions against common right was left to be determined on the individual facts of each case. Neither did Lord Cairns decide whether it was a reasonable or 'ordinary' form of use to consume water flow for industry in an established industrial area. In the general law of nuisance pertaining to harms to land such as pollution, the courts had allowed a form of 'zoning', allowing a higher level of harm in areas of heavy industry.[189] In the law of nuisance specific to escaping harms (*Rylands* v. *Fletcher*[190] liability), a workable distinction was drawn between 'natural' and 'non-natural' uses of land. Such line-drawing proved to be more difficult in the sphere of riparian rights. In *Ormerod* v. *Todmorton Mill Company*,[191] the judges of the Court of Appeal tended to the position that in industrial districts manufacturing was

[187] (1875) L.R. 7 H.L. 697, 704.

[188] Ibid., 704–5. See also *Owen* v. *Davies* (1878) 10 Ch. D. 707 (Ch.); *McCartney* v. *Londonderry & Lough Swill Railway Company* [1904] A.C. 301 (H.L.).

[189] *St. Helens' Smelting Company* v. *Tipping* (1865) 11 H.L.C. 642; 11 E.R. 1483 (H.L.); *Sturges* v. *Bridgeman* (1879) 11 Ch. D. 855 (C.A.). For an earlier and somewhat stricter approach see *Rex* v. *White* (1757) 1 Burrow 333; 97 E.R. 338 (K.B.). This case law has generated a quantity of secondary literature: for *St. Helens'* see J. F. Brenner, 'Nuisance Law and the Industrial Revolution' (1973) 3 Journal of Legal Studies 403; J. S. McLaren, 'Nuisance Law and the Industrial Revolution: Some Lessons From Social History' (1983) 3 Oxford Journal of Legal Studies 155; W. R. Cornish and G. de N. Clark, *Law and Society in England 1750–1950* (London, 1989) 154–8; A. W. B. Simpson, 'Victorian Judges and the Problem of Social Cost: *Tipping* v. *St. Helens' Smelting Company* (1865)', in A. W. B. Simpson, *Leading Cases*, 163–94. For *Sturges* see A. W. B. Simpson, '*Coase v. Pigou* Reexamined' (1996) 25 Journal of Legal Studies 53, which critically analyses R. H. Coase's use of the case in his celebrated article 'The Problem of Social Cost' (1960) 3 Journal of Law and Economics 1.

[190] *Rylands* v. *Fletcher* (1865–68) 3 H. & C. 774; 159 E.R. 737 (Ex.); L.R. 1 Ex. 265 (Ex. Ch.); L.R. 3 H.L. 330 (H.L.); Dalton, *Losing History*, 225–67.

[191] (1883) 11 Q.B.D. 155 (Q.B.).

an ordinary activity, and riparian manufacturers could therefore consume riparian waters without limit, though no final decision was taken on this point.[192] Earlier cases had indicated that manufacturers might use riparian waters for non-consumptive uses, as observed by Lord Cottenham LC:

In the manufacturing districts where there are as many mills along a stream as the water will supply, it would be extremely hard that a proprietor of one of such mills might not divert the stream within his own land, restoring it to its ancient channel before it entered into the lands of his neighbour without a diminution of the usual quality.[193]

This unexceptional statement did not clarify whether manufacturers who consumed water supply that would otherwise have been available to neighbours ought to be restrained as engaging in 'extraordinary use'.[194] In *Earl of Sandwich* v. *Great Northern Railway*,[195] Bacon VC suggested that the riparian manufacturer could not consume waters to the detriment of neighbours:

He may take all that is requisite for the purpose of his business, provided only that he does not take so much as injures the other persons whose rights are equal to his own, which injury he can prevent by returning the requisite quantity into the stream.

This judgment was overruled on different grounds in 1904 in *McCartney* v. *Londonderry & Lough Swill Railway Company*.[196] Lord Macnaghten did not address the issue of permissible uses of streams, stating only that the riparian owner 'may use it for ordinary or primary purposes, for domestic purposes, and the wants of his cattle'.[197] The court took Lord Cairns' uninformative doctrine from the *Swindon* case to have settled or even codified the modern law.[198] In other areas of land-use law the appellate judges left reasoned and articulate bodies of doctrine to guide the courts.[199] Water law, by contrast, was left in a state inviting intuitive, ad hoc decision-making.

[192] Ibid., at 166–7 per Brett MR; at 172 per Bowen LJ.

[193] *Elmhirst* v. *Spencer* (1849) 2 Mac. & G. 45, 50; 42 E.R. 18, 20 (Ch.) per Lord Cottenham LC.

[194] Cf. *Attorney-General* v. *Great Eastern Railway Co.* (1970) 23 L.T. 344 per Romilly MR; L.R. 6 Ch. 572 (Ch.). See further A. H. Hudson, 'Industry as a Riparian Use' (1959) 22 Modern Law Review 35.

[195] (1878) 10 Ch. D. 707, 711 (Ch.).

[196] [1904] A.C. 315 (H.L.). Cf. P. Brett, 'The Right to Take Flowing Water' (1950) 14 The Conveyancer 154, 156–7.

[197] [1904] A.C. 301, 306–7.

[198] *McCartney* v. *Londonderry & Lough Swill Railway Company* [1904] A.C. 301, 304, per Lord Halsbury LC; at 308 per Lord Macnaghten; at 315 per Lord Lindley; *Sharp* v. *Wilson* (1905) 93 L.T. 155; and see *Baily* v. *Clark* [1902] 1 Ch. 649.

[199] E.g. *Dalton* v. *Angus* (1881) 6 App. Cas. 825 (right of support); *Rylands* v. *Fletcher* (1866) L.R. 1 Ex. 265 (Ex. Ch.); (1868) L.R. 3 H.L. 330 (H.L.) (escapes); *St. Helens' Smelting Company* v. *Tipping* (1865) 11 H.L.C. 642; 11 E.R. 1483 (H.L.) (nuisance by pollution); *Webb* v. *Bird* (1863) 10 C.B.N.S. 268; 142 E.R. 455 (C.P.); 13 C.B.N.S. 841; 143 E.R. 332 (Ex. Ch.) (air); *Colls* v. *Home and Colonial Stores* [1904] A.C. 179 (H.L.) (window light); *Sturges* v. *Bridgman* (1879) 11 Ch.D. 852 (C.A.) (noise).

It was finally established that a 'reasonable' abstraction of water by a non-riparian user with licence from a riparian owner was permissible.[200] Reasonable use in this context meant that no material damage was caused to other riparian proprietors; it did not allow interferences with others' rights to the extent permitted by the *Embrey* doctrine; nor did it mean that the slightest perceptible change of flow was actionable in order to forestall prescription.[201] Thus where a railway company, with a narrow access to a river front beneath a culvert, licensed a manufacturer to lay a pipe at the culvert in order to abstract large amounts of water for a sugar-refining factory, this was a permissible abstraction by a non-appurtenant user, provided that there was no material injury to downstream owners. The abstraction could not be proscribed merely because the user owned no riparian land.[202]

Physical Interference with River Channels

A special rule was developed for cases where a user interfered physically with the river bed or channel, rather than merely affecting the water flow. In the Scottish appeal of *Bickett* v. *Morris*[203] Lord Westbury held that this rule was not an instance of *injuria sine damno*, but of a rebuttable presumption of actionable damage. For example, where a boat house was built on a stream, thereby inevitably interfering with the channel of the river, this would be actionable unless the court was satisfied that there would be no injury resulting from the structure either then or at a future time. There might be difficulties in determining whether the interference might later produce harm; if there was a reasonable prospect of damage to the opposite or lower riparian owners, then that would give a right of action, even though no actual injury was presently shown to have resulted from it.[204] Here also, an unstructured reasonableness standard was deployed to decide between competing users and conflicting property rights.

The relationship of soil and river-bed ownership to riparian rights was clarified by Lord Selborne LC in *Lyon* v. *Fishmongers' Company* in 1896:

200 *Ormerod* v. *Todmorton Mill Company* (1883) 11 Q.B.D. 155 (Q.B.); *Kensit* v. *Great Eastern Railway* (1884) 27 Ch.D. 122 (C.A.); *Owen* v. *Davies* (1878) 10 Ch.D. 707 (Ch.); *Pennington* v. *Brinsop Hall Company* (1875) 5 Ch.D. 769 (Ch.) per Fry J; *Bunting* v. *Hicks* (1894) 70 L.T. 455 (C.A.); *Roberts* v. *Gwyfrai District Council* [1899] 2 Ch. 608 (C.A.). For later English and American developments of the doctrine of 'transferability', see L. L. Butler, 'Allocating Consumptive Water Rights in a Riparian Jurisdiction: Defining the Relationship Between Public and Private Interests' (1985) 47 University of Pittsburgh Law Review 95.

201 *Kensit* v. *Great Eastern Railway* (1884) 27 Ch.D. 122 (C.A.).

202 Ibid.

203 (1866) L.R. 1 Sc. Ap. 47 (H.L.(Sc.)).

204 See *Edleston* v. *Crossley & Sons* (1868) 18 L.T. 15; 7 Bar Rep. 15 (V.C.); *Kensit* v. *Great Eastern Railway* (1884) 27 Ch.D. 122, 131 (C.A.) per Cotton LJ.

With respect to the ownership of the bed of the river, this cannot be the natural foundation of riparian rights properly so called, because the word 'riparian' is relative to the bank, and not to the bed, of the stream; and the connection, when it exists, of property on the bank with property in the bed of the stream depends not upon nature, but on grant and presumption of law.... The title to the soil constituting the bed of a river does not carry with it any exclusive right of property in the running water of the stream, which can only be appropriated by severance, and which may be lawfully so appropriated by every one having a right of access to it.[205]

Lord Blackburn and the Scots Theory of Riparianism

Scots cases furnished a sophisticated discussion of water rights in the later nineteenth century, as before in the time of Lord Kames.[206] It is well to end this study with the important 1877 decision of *Orr Ewing* v. *Colquhoun*,[207] where Lord Blackburn took the opportunity of a Scottish House of Lords appeal to elucidate the jurisprudence of water use.[208]

The facts were that D, the owner of a dye works, erected piers on the side of a river, blocking navigation and access to the public and especially affecting P, who owned a salmon fishery on the river. The non-tidal river had been a public navigable river since time out of mind. P claimed a private right to sue as riparian owner, and also as a member of the public particularly harmed by D's interferences with communal navigation and fishery rights.

The court excluded P's claim based on public right, holding that, in both Scots and English law, a public nuisance not causing temporal damage and not infringing some further right of private property could give rise to no relief by damages or injunction. Lord Blackburn put it thus:

Now the public who have acquired by user a right of way on land, or a right of navigation on an inland water, have no right of property. They have a right to pass as fully and freely, and as safely as they have been wont to do, but unless there is a present interference with that right, or it can be shewn that what is now done will interfere with that right, there is no *injuria*, and I think that if there be no *injuria*, the foundation of the right to have the thing removed, fails.[209]

[205] (1876) 1 App. Cas. 673, 683 (H.L.). Lord Selborne went on to discuss the problem of tidal rivers: see further Coulson and Forbes, *Law Relating to Waters* (1st edn., London, 1880) 100–14.

[206] Cf. *Magistrates of Linlithgow* v. *Elphinstone* (1768) 3 Kames' Decisions (S.C.S.) 331, Ch. 5, the text accompanying nn. 45–50 above.

[207] (1877) 2 App. Cas. 839 (H.L.(Sc.)).

[208] See also *Bickett* v. *Morris* (1866) L.R. 1 Sc. Ap. 47 (H.L.(Sc.)), the text accompanying nn. 203–204 above. The sophistication of earlier Scots water law is laid out in N. Whitty, 'Water Law Regimes', in K. Reid and R. Zimmermann (eds.), *A History of Private Law in Scotland*, 2 vols. (Oxford, 2000) i, 420–79.

[209] (1877) 2 App. Cas. 839, 854. On the riparian owner's right to river access for navigation, see Coulson and Forbes, *Law Relating to Waters* (6th edn. by Hobday, London, 1952) 139–44.

Turning to the claim based on private property rights, Lord Blackburn began with an analysis of the principle in *Bickett* v. *Morris* concerning physical interferences with the river channel:

[W]here any unauthorized erection is a sensible injury to the proprietary rights of an individual, there is *injurio*, for which he might in a Court of Law in *England*, recover at least nominal damages. A Court of Equity... would not order the removal of the erection if convinced that the damage was only nominal, but where there is an injury to the proprietary rights in running streams, the present injury now producing no damage may hereafter produce much....

[T]he principle of *Bickett* v. *Morris* [is] that where an erection is a present sensible *injuria* to the proprietary right of the owner of the other part of the *alveus*, or of the opposite bank [or downstream bank] of a running stream, he may have it removed on the ground that there is a present injury to the right of property, if it is impossible to predicate that it may not produce serious damage in future, though the complaining party is not yet in a position to quantify present damage.[210]

The foundations of riparian doctrine were then described:

[W]here the property in the banks of a natural stream, above the flow of the tide, is in different persons, *prima facie*, and until the contrary is shewn, the boundary between their properties is the *medium filum aquae*. In this respect there is no difference between the law of *England* and *Scotland*. And, after some diversity of opinions, it has, I think, been for many years the settled law of *England*, that the proprietor of land on the bank of such a river has, as incident to his property in the land, a proprietary right to have the stream flow in its natural state, neither increased nor diminished, and this quite independently of whether he has as yet made use of it, or, as it used to be called, appropriated the water. This can hardly be considered as settled law in *England* before the case of *Mason* v. *Hill*, in 1833. It had been the law of *Scotland* from a much earlier period. In *Bannatyne* v. *Cranston*:[211]

> 'It was not found necessary to the Pursuer [Plaintiff] to libel or qualify any use of the burn and water thereof wherein he was prejudiced by the Defenders taking in the same, seeing the lords found that the water running by his land which lay marching contiguous to one side thereof, could not be drawn from any part of the land marching thereto without his own consent. For albeit, he had no present use thereof, yet he might possibly find thereafter some use for the same.'

This was in the year 1625. Precisely the same law has been now established in *America*, *Blanchard* v. *Miller* [*Baker*], and in *England*, *Mason* v. *Hill*, without, I think, either the American or English Judges being aware that the Scotch Judges had so long before anticipated their reasoning.[212] This right is subject to the use of the water by those above him, below him, and opposite to him, either acquired by user, or such as the general law gives to riparian proprietors.[213]

[210] (1877) 2 App. Cas. 839, 853.

[211] Citing Mor. Dict. 12,769, 'Property'.

[212] Lord Blackburn did not advert to the case of *Magistrates of Linlithgow* v. *Elphinstone* (1768) 3 Kames' Decisions 331 (S.C.S.), which was usually cited in the leading modern English riparian cases.

[213] *Orr Ewing* v. *Colquhoun* (1877) 2 App. Cas. 839, 854–5 (H.L.(Sc.)) per Lord Blackburn.

Lord Blackburn referred to Parke B's *Embrey* judgment 'as containing an exposition of the English law', and then cited and approved the summary of doctrine given by Lord Kingsdown in *Miner* v. *Gilmour*. Later decisions repeat the formulae of these leading nineteenth-century cases, but develop little or no fresh doctrine.[214] The long evolution of the common law of water rights had ended.

[214] See e.g. *Crossley & Sons Ltd.* v. *Lightowler* (1866) L.R. 3 Eq. 279 (Ch.); (1867) L.R. 2 Ch. App. 478 (V.C.); *Holker* v. *Porrit* (1875) L.R. 10 Ex. 62 (Ex.); *Lyon* v. *Fishmongers' Company* (1876) 1 App. Cas. 673 (H.L.); *Pennington* v. *Brinsop Hall Company* (1877) 5 Ch. D. 769 (Ch.); *Rameshur Pershad Narain Singh* v. *Koonj Behari Pattuk* (1878) 4 App. Cas. 121 (P.C.); *Roberts* v. *Richards* (1881) 51 L.J. Ch. 944 (C.A.); *Goodman* v. *Saltash Corporation* (1882) 48 L.T. 239 (H.L.); *Frechette* v. *Compagnie Manufacturie de St. Hyacinthe* (1883) 9 A.C. 170 (P.C.); *French Hoek Commissioner* v. *Hugo* (1885) 10 App. Cas. 336 (P.C.); *Belfast Ropeworks* v. *Boyd* (1887) 21 L.R.Ir. 560; *M'Glone* v. *Smith* (1888) 22 L.R. Ir. 554; *North Shore Railway Company* v. *Pion* (1889) 14 App. Cas. 612 (P.C.); *Young & Co.* v. *Bankier Distillery Co.* [1893] A.C. 691 (H.L.); *Bunting* v. *Hicks* (1894) 70 L.T. 455 (C.A.); *Hamelin* v. *Bannerman* [1895] A.C. 237 (P.C.); *Somerset Drainage Commissioners* v. *Bridgewater Corporation* (1899) 81 L.T. 729 (H.L.); *Baily* v. *Clark* [1902] 1 Ch. 649; *Jeremiah Ambler & Sons Ltd.* v. *Mayor of Bradford* [1902] 2 Ch. 585 (C.A.); *McCartney* v. *Londonderry & Lough Swill Railway Company* [1904] A.C. 301 (H.L.); *Roberts* v. *Fellowes* (1906) 94 L.T. 279; *Edinburgh Water Trustees* v. *Sommerville* (1906) 95 L.T. 217 (H.L.(Sc.)); *White (John) & Sons* v. *White* [1906] A.C. 72 (P.C.); *Portsmouth Waterworks Co.* v. *London Brighton and South Coast Railway* (1909) 26 T.L.R. 175 (Ch.); *Stollmeyer* v. *Trinidad Lake Petroleum Company* [1918] A.C. 485; *Attwood* v. *Llay* [1926] 1 Ch. 444 (Ch.); D. A. Stroud, *The Law of Easements, Founded on Select Cases* (London, 1934) 176–206; W. Howarth, *Wisdom's Law of Watercourses* (previously entitled *The Law of Rivers and Watercourses*) (5th edn., Crayford, 1992). The most encyclopaedic modern treatment remains Coulson and Forbes, *Law Relating to Waters* (6th edn. by Hobday, 1952).

Conclusion

INTERNAL AND EXTERNAL INTERPRETATION OF THE LAW

From one perspective the history of water doctrine can be described purely in terms of the discrete development of legal concepts. The judges re-work their precedents and forms of action, searching only the legal materials for solutions in resolving conflicts over use of resources. Ideas from Roman and early common law are received, re-invented, applied, discarded, simplified, and adapted until a serviceable structure of doctrine emerges in the later nineteenth century.[1] Such a process of legal development is not entirely mindless, unselfconscious, or mechanical jurisprudence.[2] In developing the modern law of water rights, the judges brought under close scrutiny the general principles of delict and contract, the relationship of possession and property, the interplay of prescriptive and natural rights, and other problems of high doctrine. With help from civilians, English text writers, and American courts, a coherent modern law of property and property torts comes into being. The problems of rival land and water use provoked by industrialization are brought to the courts with alacrity by litigants, to have their conflicts translated into legal issues amenable to legal solutions.

This study has in the main adhered to such a formalist legal analysis, giving an 'internal view' of the lawyers' long historical debates over water entitlements. But is an internal story of hermetic doctrinal evolution finally adequate to explain the long and convoluted history of water rights?[3] Doctrinal questions easily merged into debates of an overtly political or economic nature, such as the proper legal attitude to security of property rights; the tests for balancing of rival legitimate interests; the regulation of competition and

[1] Cf. S. J. Stoljar, *A History of Contract at Common Law* (Canberra, 1975) p. vi, who advocates 'explaining complex developments and even of treating legal history almost as an extension of legal analysis'.

[2] Cf. S. F. C. Milsom, 'Reason in the Development of the Common Law', and 'Law and Fact in Legal Development', both in S. F. C. Milsom, *Studies in the History of the Common Law* (London, 1985) at 149–70 and 171–89.

[3] Compare A. Watson, 'The Transformation of American Property Law: A Comparative Law Approach' (1990) 24 Georgia Law Review 163, reprinted as 'Jurists, Judges, Custom, Legislation: Water Rights', in A. Watson, *The Evolution of Western Private Law* (2nd edn., Baltimore, Md., 2001) 138–92, which offers a strongly internalist analysis of the antecedents and nature of American water law, drawing from civilian as well as English jurisprudence. Watson concludes (at 216–21) that nineteenth-cetury water law in the eastern states was surprisingly incoherent and indifferent to practical consequences. To like effect is J. Gordley, 'The Origin of Riparian Rights', in P. Birks and A. Pretto (eds.), *Themes in Comparative Law: In Honour of Bernard Rudden* (Oxford, 2002) 107, describing riparian law as conceptually arbitrary. He contrasts this with the developed appropriation theory of the Glossators.

monopoly; and the role of discretion in law and adjudication. The lines between technical law and judicial policy and ideology could easily be blurred.

Even in the pragmatic and a-theoretic culture of the common law, philosophical ideas about property did play a role in the history of riparian law. The law of water rights was influenced at crucial points by political theories of the sanctity of ancient practice and custom; by Hobbesian social contract implying mutual obligation to create order and resolve conflict; by Lockean or Kantian concepts of appropriation or usage expressing possessive intention; and by Benthamite requirements of certainty of rights promoting allocative efficiency. Some judges even invoked a quasi-Hegelian theory of dominion involving freedom of disposal.[4] Locke, as we saw at the start of this book, used the very example of flowing water in his *Second Treatise* to help illustrate and explain his theory of title based on first appropriation of freely available public goods.[5] But water as an ephemeral and changeable element incapable of exclusive possession was hard to fit within any available legal or philosophical categories. And the problems posed by water reached back to challenge the law's basic ideas about all forms of property. Should property rights ultimately be based on productive use, as an instrumental institution promoting social welfare? Or is property rather justified as a title, belonging to persons as an expression of their identity or personality or role in society, quite apart from what they do with their property and how their ownership affects others? Should one lose property if one does not use it? Or is ownership guaranteed by virtue of one's existing title? These questions were constantly working within the common law, though not always in philosophical garb.

HARNESSING POSSESSION AND USUFRUCT

Richard Epstein has grappled with the problems of harnessing first possession theories embedded in Roman and common law to explain the patterns of private and common property, including the structure of riparian law. His approach is to restate the first possession theory as a norm well-calculated to

[4] For analysis of philosophical property theories see O. W. Holmes Jr., *The Common Law* (Boston, Mass., 1881; ed. with an introduction by M. De Wolfe Howe, 1968) lect. VI. on Possession, 163–94; A. Ryan, *Property and Political Theory* (Oxford, 1984); J. Waldron, *The Right To Private Property* (Oxford, 1988); J. W. Harris, *Property and Justice* (Oxford, 1996); J. E. Penner, *The Idea of Property in Law* (Oxford, 1997); S. R. Munzer, *A Theory of Property* (Cambridge, 1990).

[5] J. Locke, *Second Treatise of Government* s. 33, in *Two Treatises of Government* (ed. by P. Laslett, Cambridge, 1960) 333 (see epigraph to the Introduction to this book, above); cf. G. A. Cohen, 'Self-Ownership, World-Ownership, and Equality: Part II' (1986) 3 Social Philosophy and Policy 77, 83, reprinted in G. A. Cohen, *Self-ownership, Freedom, and Equality* (Cambridge, 1995) 77 ff.

promote orderly and effective use of resources for production and trade.[6] The strand of Lockean theory emphasizing the act of appropriation itself as a 'mixing of labour' creative of property is put aside as incoherent. Hence for Epstein possession cannot justify the erection of individual property rights where these would diminish effective use of a resource. He argues that the Roman approach of differentiating between types of resources when defining property concepts is the correct solution. Thus exclusive possessory rights over the waters of the high seas and navigable rivers are not permitted in Roman law for good reason: possession would not improve such goods but only raise the cost of use. Here *res communes* or open commons made best sense. As for water diversion where there were multiple rival uses, the Roman solution was in effect to allow possessory rights in water only where this raised the marginal value of the resource; the Roman jurists 'adopted an intermediate solution that left the commons dominant, but nonetheless allowed some diversion from it'. This marginal diversionary interest was modelled on usufruct, the right to use and enjoy without diminishing the underlying corpus of property. Yet usufruct was an imperfect analogy, since instream water flow is shared simultaneously by many 'usufructary' riparian owners and its use need not involve harvesting, since much water once used is recycled or returned to the pool. Moreover there is no overall owner of the water commons to compare to the *dominus* in the case of usufruct. But if the analysis was imperfect, the pragmatic stretching of well-understood concepts of *res communes*, first possession, and usufruct was perfectly sensible; these concepts supported a workable and adaptable water allocation system. For Epstein, the lawyers reach for familiar institutional tools from within their discourse to do the job; abstract principles of entitlement in themselves are not all that useful.

In a separate set of arguments, Epstein finds good reasons for the emergence of the riparian reasonable use doctrine.[7] He writes:

> Flowing water is a valuable resource for which there is no obvious single owner. Assuming, as was the case historically, that the Crown or the state does not own these

[6] R. A. Epstein, 'On the Optimal Mix of Private and Common Property' (1994) 11 Social Philosophy and Policy 17, and 'Possession as the Root of Title' (1979) 13 Georgia Law Review 1221, both extracted in R. A. Epstein (ed.), *Liberty, Property, and the Law, Vol. III, Private and Common Property* (New York, 2000) at 357 and 175; Epstein reprises his arguments in *Takings: Private Property and the Power of Eminent Domain* (Cambridge, Mass., 1985) 67–70, 216–17; see also R. A. Epstein, 'Past and Future: The Temporal Dimension in the Law of Property' (1986) 64 Washington University Law Quarterly 667 and 'Possession', in P. Newman (ed.), *The New Palgrave Dictionary of Economics and the Law* (London, 1998) (*NPDEL*) ii, 62. Cf. C. M. Rose, 'Possession as the Origin of Property' (1985) 52 University of Chicago Law Review 73 reprinted in C. M. Rose, *Property and Persuasion: Essays on the History, Theory, and Rhetoric of Ownership* (Boulder, Col., 1994) 11; D. Lueck, 'First Possession', *NPDEL*, ii, 132.

[7] R. A. Epstein, 'Why Restrain Alienation?' (1985) 85 Columbia Law Review 970, 979–82. See further S. Rose-Ackerman, 'Inalienability and the Theory of Property Rights' (1985) 85 Columbia Law Review 931 and 'Inalienability', in *NPDEL*, ii, 268.

rights . . . then there must be some natural mode of acquisition that matches claims to water with individual owners.

Epstein argues that first possession, as applied to the case of wild animals, was an unacceptable regime for instream water as it would divide and destroy the river as a 'going concern' for all participants. The solution was to allow use only to riparians, thus forming a closed common pool, and then allow each riparian a fair and reasonable use only. Alienation of water rights was possible only through alienation of riparian land. This was an efficient market for water entitlements, because a person valuing the water rights highly enough would pay for riparian land, and at the same time would be restrained from unstinted consumption by the legal norm that user should be proportionate to land ownership. 'By so providing', argues Epstein, 'the law necessarily made the river into a common pool asset owned by a group of individuals who did not stand in a consensual relationship one to another'. The reasonable use test can then be adjusted to permit a hierarchy of uses, domestic, agricultural, and commercial. Epstein's theory is a convincing articulation of some of the policy ideas implicit in riparian law; but it does not explain how the law sets reasonable use levels. This was the bedevilling detail that prompted so much litigation across the centuries. Epstein asserts blankly that legal rules of thumb are no worse than administrative solutions, which have the disadvantage of being prone to distortion by interest groups. That leads to the next account seeking to explain water law.

THE ECONOMIC IDEOLOGY ACCOUNT

Other scholars have given primacy to policy factors wholly external to formal doctrine in their interpretation of water law, to the degree that extra-legal factors are held to drive the development of riparian doctrine. T. E. Lauer found abundant economic policy-making in the case law in his benchmark study of 1969.[8] He argued that there were neat stages of doctrine reflecting changing economic needs and social mores across the centuries. Thus a 'feudal', tradition-bound concept of customary water rights, based on hallowed ancient use, gave way to theories of natural rights and rights by appropriation, as modern judges sought to promote 'active' and 'dynamic' industrial uses of property rather than 'static', 'rural' forms of ownership. During the Industrial Revolution, the courts searched for a theory of access to water that would promote productive uses without destructive competition. Judges experimented with the Blackstonian appropriation theory in

[8] T. E. Lauer, 'The Common Law Background of the Riparian Doctrine' (1963) 28 Missouri Law Review 60.

their search for solutions, before finally adopting the serviceable reasonable use test.

Lauer's trawl through nine centuries of English water law ignored the structure of the forms of action which governed much legal argument, and therefore mistook the import of the authorities dealing with damage, appropriation, and prescription as bases of actions. However, his version of the history has had few rivals in the past thirty years, and it was this version which was accepted by Morton Horwitz in his influential 1997 study of *The Transformation of American Law 1780–1860*[9] as the English common-law prelude to American developments.

Horwitz portrayed riparian law as a set of instrumentalist norms promoting capitalist interests in industrializing America, overriding settled, traditional individual rights. The development of riparian and nuisance law embodied a portentous 'transformation' of concepts of property, a sharp legal break with the pre-industrial past. Horwitz's larger claim is that the new private law doctrines expressed a judicial 'instrumentalism' and pro-industrialism, whether in contract, tort, or property law.[10] The history of water law holds centre stage in his story of a pro-capitalist judiciary.

[9] (Cambridge, Mass., 1977).

[10] For criticisms of the larger Horwitz theses of private law development see A. J. Field, 'Do Legal Systems Matter?' (1991) 28 Explorations in Economic History 1, 26–9; R. G. Bone, 'Normative Theory and Legal Doctrine in American Nuisance Law: 1850 to 1920' (1986) 59 South California Law Review 1101, 1202 ff.; R. A. Epstein, 'The Social Consequences of Common Law Rules' (1982) 95 Harvard Law Review 1717; G. Gilmore, 'From Tort to Contract: Industrialization and the Law', Review of M. J. Horwitz, *The Transformation of American Law 1780–1860* (1977) 86 Yale Law Journal 788; W. Holt, 'Morton Horwitz and the Transformation of American Legal History' (1982) 23 William and Mary Law Review 663; H. Hovenkamp, 'The Economics of Legal History' (1982–83) 67 Minnesota Law Review 645; P. Karsten, *Heart versus Head: Judge-made Law in Nineteenth-century America* (Chapel Hill, NC, 1997) esp. 298 ff; R. A. Posner, *Economic Analysis of Law* (5th edn., New York, 1998) 276–81; G. T. Schwartz, 'Tort Law and the Economy in Nineteenth-Century America: A Reinterpretation' (1981) 90 Yale Law Journal 1721 and 'The Character of Early American Tort Law' (1989) 36 University of California Los Angeles Law Review 641; S. F. Williams, 'Transforming American Law: Doubtful Economics Makes Doubtful History' (1977) 25 University of California Los Angeles Law Review 1187. For the Horwitz thesis as it touches on English legal history see R. B. Ferguson, 'The Horwitz Thesis and Common Law Discourse in England' (1983) 3 Oxford Journal of Legal Studies 34; J. Getzler, 'Theories of Property and Economic Development' (1996) 26 Journal of Interdisciplinary History 639; A. W. B. Simpson, 'The Horwitz Thesis and the History of Contracts', in A. W. B. Simpson, *Legal Theory and Legal History. Essays on the Common Law* (London, 1987) 203–72. The 'Horwitz debate' is judiciously analysed by R. W. Gordon in 'Morton Horwitz and his Critics: A Conflict of Narratives' (2002) 37 Tulsa Law Review 915. Many of Horwitz's functionalist themes were trailed by Lawrence Friedman in his *Contract Law in America: A Social and Economic Case Study* (Madison, Wis., 1965) and *A History of American Law* (New York, 1973). Friedman defends functionalism and assails Peter Karsten's formalist approach in 'Losing One's Head: Judges and the Law in Nineteenth-Century American Legal History' (1999) 24 Law and Social Inquiry 253; Karsten presses his evidence again in 'Using One's Head: Were Jurists "Unconscious" Socio-Economic Ciphers or Conscious Agents? A Response to Friedman' at (1999) 24 Law and Social Inquiry 281. The debate between functionalism and formalism is unlikely to be resolved.

Horwitz identified in American riparian law a progression closely reflecting the successive needs of capitalist industry. According to his interpretation, the law of water began with a natural-right theory of ownership inherited from eighteenth-century England, whereby water was to be enjoyed as part of the immutable natural order of things, an element of the quiet enjoyment of land which may not be exploited to the detriment of other proprietors. This 'old property' principle restrained the industrial development of water resources, reflecting the pre-capitalist, anti-industrialist orientation of the judges. Horwitz claims that 'In English water cases, ... [the] distinction between "natural" and "artificial" uses of water became an important ideological tool for preferring agrarian over industrial uses of water'. In support of this he cites the 1911 study of *Rylands* v. *Fletcher* by Bohlen, where it was claimed that:

In England, the dominant class was the landed gentry, whose opinions the judges, who either sprang from this class, or hoped to establish themselves and their families therein—naturally reflected. To such a class it was inevitable, that the right of exclusive dominion over land should appear paramount to its commercial utilization,—to them, commerce and manufacture, in which they had little or no direct interest, appeared comparatively unimportant.[11]

Bohlen's class analysis of the law was elaborated in 1952 by Morris, who wrote:

It has been suggested that most of the judges were recruited from the gentry, a class which frowned on the industrial invasion of the stately English countryside. Mills were no longer picturesque grinders of home-grown grain for kitchen-baked bread; they were unsightly, ungainly, 'non-natural' textile factories run by men 'in trade.' They should at least pay their way—which included paying for damage to neighbours.[12]

The class analysis favoured by the American commentators[13] was restated by Horwitz in his 1977 monograph and given a new and powerful extension. He argued that a pro-industrial ethos eventually did win over the elitist judiciary. One result of this was that the old natural-rights theories of water use gave way to the principle of ownership by first appropriation, a theory distinct from ancient doctrines of prescriptive title. Under this theory

[11] F. Bohlen, 'The Rule in Rylands v Fletcher' (1911) 59 University of Pennsylvania Law Review 298, 318–19, reprinted in F. Bohlen, *Studies in the Law of Torts* (Indianapolis, Ind., 1926) 344–440, at 368–70. The Bohlen thesis, which long reigned as a received wisdom in the U.S. law schools, was picked apart by R. T. Molloy in '*Fletcher* v. *Rylands*' (1941–2) 9 University of Chicago Law Review 266.

[12] C. Morris, 'Hazardous Enterprises and Risk Bearing Capacity' (1952) 61 Yale Law Journal 1172, 1175.

[13] See further C. Dalton, *Losing History: Tort Liability in the Nineteenth Century and the Case of Rylands v Fletcher* (MS., 1987) 281–302; K. Hall, *The Magic Mirror: Law in American History* (New York, 1989) 114–19.

the first occupier exploiting flowing water was given a protected title or monopoly in order to encourage innovation in the use of water resources. This 'protectionist' regime helped to establish industry, but in time was replaced by a reasonable-use doctrine which allowed no monopolization of water rights, but which provided all entrants with the opportunity to divert water 'reasonably' for the purposes of competitive development. English law is said to follow a roughly similar evolution.[14] Horwitz writes:

> Viewed retrospectively, one is tempted to see a Machiavellian hand in this process. How better to develop an economy than initially to provide the first developers with guarantees against future competitive injury? And once development has reached a certain level, can the claims of still greater efficiency through competition be denied? By changing the rules and disguising the changes in the complexities of technical legal doctrine, the facade of economic security can be maintained even as new property is allowed to sweep away the old.[15]

Horwitz argues that the tension in law between security of property rights and insecurity of possession through competition is reproduced in the plasticity of property doctrine in the hands of the judiciary; and further that the tension is resolved in favour of the strong, the active, and the entrepeneurial who are favoured by development-minded courts.[16]

Lauer's and Horwitz's accounts of riparian law reduce the multiplicity of ideas into simple categories—those of ancient right, mutual natural right, right from appropriation, and right to 'reasonable' use of nature. In their account successive 'stages' of doctrine correlate to shifts in judicial (and social) ideology. But this approach is challenged by the finding that different riparian theories coexisted and merged in the minds of the lawyers. There was often a merging of customary and natural rights in pleadings and judgments, and similarly with claims derived from implied grants and rights from appropriation. This collapsing or telescoping of theories in practice weakens the central interpretative claims of the 'developmental' school, for it cannot be claimed that a prior appropriation theory was promoted by the courts around 1800 as an instrumental doctrine, intentionally designed to encourage monopolist exploitation of water privileges without restraint from natural rights. Nor can it be demonstrated that this stage was followed in turn by a regime of competitive exploitation regulated by the reasonable use

[14] Horwitz, *Transformation*, 32–53, 274–85, especially 277–99 for English law.

[15] Ibid., 34.

[16] For recent discussions of the American history see J. S. Martin, 'Water Law and Economic Power: A Reinterpretation of Morton Horwitz's Subsidy Thesis' (1991) 77 Virginia Law Review 397; T. Steinberg, *Nature Incorporated: Industrialization and the Waters of New England* (New York, 1991); C. M. Rose, 'A Tale of Two Rivers' (1993) 91 Michigan Law Review 1623; Bone, 'American Nuisance Law'; C. M. Rose, 'Energy and Efficiency in the Realignment of Common-Law Water Rights' (1990) 19 Journal of Legal Studies 261, 277–88, reprinted in C. M. Rose, *Property and Persuasion: Essays on the History, Theory, and Rhetoric of Ownership* (Boulder, Col., 1994), 175–88; Karsten, *Heart versus Head*, 41–6; Gordley, 'Origin of Riparian Rights'.

principle. The history of water law shows that it was never entirely clear which riparian doctrines applied in England at least until *Embrey* v. *Owen* in 1851,[17] and possibly even later. This instability of doctrine was demonstrated time after time by the courts' vacillation on crucial issues such as the nature of prescriptive presumptions; or the extent of rights to drain, discharge, or divert waters above and below ground to the detriment of a neighbour; or whether injury to present uses was necessary to found an action; or whether the action on the case was primarily a damage-centred tort action defending possession, or a rights-based proprietary action defending title. Because of these complications and uncertainties, it is difficult to see any progression of clear developmental stages in riparian doctrine during the period of modern industrialization. Rather there is a marked instability of theory, with the Blackstonian appropriation doctrine surfacing in the early nineteenth-century King's Bench and Common Pleas, only to be ignored or rejected by Chancery, Exchequer, and the later King's Bench, such courts preferring a variant of natural flow theory.

Horwitz implies that the final stage of 'reasonable use' doctrines in property law after 1850 were formalistic rules consolidating capitalist development of land and its resources as commodity.[18] This view again cannot be accepted without heavy qualification. We have seen how, in the later nineteenth century, strong natural-right and praedial concepts, of Roman and Bractonian origin, prevented the ultimate commodification of water as assignable property, severable from landownership. More important still, Horwitz may have mistaken the proper characterization of the *Embrey* v. *Owen* reasonable-use doctrine. On closer scrutiny it appears not as a 'formalistic' rule, but rather as a strongly discretionary principle, giving judges as much power to restrain its industrial development of resources as 'unnatural' or 'unreasonable' as to promote such development.[19]

[17] (1851) 6 Exch. 353; 155 E.R. 579 (Ex), Ch. 5, the text accompanying nn. 48–72 above.

[18] Horwitz, *Transformation*, 31–62.

[19] For a demolition of the Horwitzian stages theory with respect to American riparian law see Martin, 'Water Law and Economic Power'; Karsten, *Heart versus Head*, 41–6; A. Watson, 'The Transformation of American Property Law: A Comparative Law Approach' (1990) 24 Georgia Law Review 163; cf. E. P. Krauss, 'The Legal Form of Liberalism: A Study of Riparian and Nuisance Law in Nineteenth Century Ohio' [1984] Akron Law Review 223. Horwitz's study of the nineteenth-century Mills Acts (*Transformation of American Law* at 47–53) as a regime of regulatory takings has generated a further rich debate that will not be broached here. See further J. Sax *et al.*, *Legal Control of Water Resources* (3rd edn., St Paul, Minn., 2000) 172–92; J. F. Hart, 'The Maryland Mill Act, 1669–1766: Economic Policy and the Confiscatory Redistribution of Private Property' (1995) 39 American Journal of Legal History 1 and 'Property Rights, Costs, and Welfare: Delaware Water Mill Legislation, 1719–1859' (1998) 27 Journal of Legal Studies 455; L. W. George, 'Public Rights in West Virginia Watercourses: A Unique Legacy of Virginia Common Lands and the Jus Publicum of the English Crown' (1998) 101 West Virgina Law Review 407; E. C. Martini, 'Wisconsin's Milldam Act: Drawing New Lessons from an Old Law' [1998] Wisconsin Law Review 1305.

THE TRANSACTION COSTS ACCOUNT

The ambiguity of the reasonableness standard is stressed by Carol Rose in her recent study of common-law riparian rights.[20] Rose explains the development of a discretionary riparian common law as a response to scarcity of partially-renewable water resources, in an environment of high transaction costs which prevent efficient private allocations. Her account of evolution of property rights in a common-pool resource (that is, riparian water) differs importantly from the conventional economic theory of property as a device to promote investment in resources through the creation of exclusive rights.[21]

According to Rose, the older riparian law in England (and New England) represented a static system of protection of natural (or ancient) uses attached to riparian lands. The rise of hydro-power led to transformation of the system, both in England and in America. Where the bulk of the instream water flow is used by a succession of riparian owners for power, the law sets rules to protect the stock of the resource (being the instream water flow) from appropriation, whilst allowing appropriation of the flow of the resource at the margin. This means that the law allows use of the water flow for power where the stock is not affected; and also abstraction for the consumptive use of riparian owners where no significant drop in the stock results. No race to appropriate through first possession can be allowed because this would interefere with the stock, being the flow of instream water available to all riparian owners for power. The final feature of this system is that entitlements are confined to riparian users and cannot be severed from riparian tenements and transferred or assigned. This is a crucial feature based on the dispersion of riparian users along the stream who all depend on each others' forbearance in use of the stock. It would be impossible for users to contract with each other to prevent predatory use degrading the stock of instream flow available to all. For example, one greedy user could hold an entire river of mill owners to ransom by interfering with their hydro-power flow, yet a clearing market bringing all affected parties into relations allowing efficient trade of entitlements would be unlikely to develop. By contrast, the standard for consumptive appropriation of flow, rather than usufructary enjoyment of stock, is typically that of first possession or prior appropriation rather than 'reasonable user'. Such a water regime emerged in the western territories of the United States in the nineteenth century, cultivated initially through the customary usage of ranchers and miners, and later ratified and adopted by courts and legislatures, displacing the riparian reasonableness standard of the eastern states. Three conditions were present for the emergence of this

[20] Rose, 'Energy and Efficiency in the Realignment of Water Rights'.

[21] Cf. H. Demsetz, 'Toward a Theory of Property Rights' (1967) 57 American Economic Review 347; Y. Barzel, *Economic Analysis of Property Rights* (2nd edn., Cambridge, 1997); T. Besley, 'Investment Incentives and Property Rights', in *NPDEL*, ii, 359.

alternative regime. Water abstraction was chiefly for consumptive use; there was no call to maintain the resource in the form of a stock of water flow for power; and flows were typically appropriated by users unconnected to riparian tenements. A race to appropriate through first possesssion can be efficient in such circumstances, because water entitlements severed from the stock of instream riparian water can then be traded on commodity markets to the highest-value users; hold-outs, free-riding, and monopoly are less likely, as players can more readily individualize their calls on water as commodity rather than integral resource stock.[22]

Rose's account may be suggestive for United States developments,[23] but it does not begin to capture the procedural and doctrinal complexity of English water law. Rose resorts to elaborate factual speculation to make sense of English developments, ignoring more obvious and accurate doctrinal explanations. For example, she assumes like Horwitz and Bohlen that pleadings of 'ancient use' in common-law actions indicated an appeal to political-jurisprudential theories of reactionary stasis and tradition.[24] We have seen that 'ancient use' was instead an extremely varied set of concepts, including ideas of prescription and implied grant proved by evidential implication. Relying too heavily on Lauer's sketch of early English water law, Rose assumes that there was no heavy industrial water use and little water litigation in the early modern period. She further assumes that entrepreneurs and their lawyers in the earlier Industrial Revolution period must have proceeded in ignorance of the legal rights to water enjoyment they owned at common law: '[e]xtensive investment in [water] improvements in itself suggested that legal doctrines placed few practical impediments in the path of private conduct'.[25] Blackstone's new natural-right theory is cited by Rose as evidence that no

[22] For elaboration of this theoretical approach see C. M. Rose, 'The Comedy of the Commons: Custom, Commerce and Inherently Public Property' (1986) University of Chicago Law Review 711 and 'Crystals and Mud in Property Law' (1988) 40 Stanford Law Review 577, both reprinted in C. M. Rose, *Property and Persuasion* at 105, 199; C. M. Rose, 'Property as the Keystone Right?' (1996) 71 Notre Dame Law Review 329, 'A Tale of Two Rivers' (1993) 91 Michigan Law Review 1623, 'Evolution of Property Rights', *NPDEL* ii, 93–8, and 'Riparian Rights', *NPDEL* iii, 344.

[23] And maybe not. Economists have shown that riparian use and prior appropriation systems of water allocation each result in distinct economic inefficiencies and waste, and that neither regime is particularly good at cultivating a market for transferable water rights. Local collectivism, public ownership, and regulation have been the most effective modern solutions for guaranteeing water access and equity in the arid western states, but this technique has inevitably politicized the water supply. See M. Gaffney, 'Economic Aspects of Water Resource Policy' (1969) 28 American Journal of Economics and Sociology 131, an enduring classic of water economics. See further J. Sax, *Water Law, Planning and Policy: Cases and Materials* (Indianapolis, Ind., 1968), esp. at 459–67; cf. B. H. Thomson, Jr., 'Water Law as a Pragmatic Exercise' (1998) 25 Ecology Law Quarterly 363.

[24] Rose, like many American writers, relies heavily on the impressionistic account of prescriptive theory supplied in J. G. A. Pocock's *The Ancient Constitution and the Feudal Law* (Cambridge, 1957, 2nd edn., 1987).

[25] Rose, 'Energy and Efficiency in the Realignment of Water Rights', 269–70.

developed riparian doctrine had emerged by the eighteenth century, since Blackstone writes without attending to or following any of the extant case law. The considerable amount of water litigation, the cultivation of elaborate Romanist and common-law doctrines before 1750, and Blackstone's obvious awareness of Bractonian, civilian, and common-law sources, are absent from Rose's account. The history of prescription and of the action of trespass on the case for nuisance is likewise passed over.

Instead of taking doctrine seriously, Rose propounds a schematized model of the history of water rights, drawing on a transaction-cost model of the evolution of property rights. Three stages of property rights are postulated: a first stage of natural entitlements to property as public goods when they are relatively plentiful; a second stage of indefinite customary and individual controls of property when scarcity encroaches; and a third stage of clear and distinct private property when competition for resources becomes acute. The puzzle she sets out to explain is why both English and Eastern American water law revert to stage two ('reasonable usage' of the public good of flowing water), after a considerable period of stage-three rights (the individualistic prior appropriation doctrine). The answer, according to Rose, lies in the transaction costs of arranging the sharing of a partially renewed resource. Her analysis merits serious attention, for it does point towards a cogent explanation of long-term trends.

According to Rose, 'ancient use' theories required that a new user of water compensate existing users for damage caused; it was therefore a doctrine of developed and stable property rights. If the predictions of Coasean transaction-cost economics can be applied, then bargaining between right-holders enjoying clearly defined rights should easily take place, thus re-allocating 'ancient rights' to the most efficient contemporary users.[26] The history of the early industrialists suggests that this type of bargained exchange of rights, from landowners to industrialists, did indeed take place. However, there are also many cases of self-help with force (such as the throwing down of dams and blocking of channels). The persistent failure of negotiation suggests that users were not always rational bargainers; or they were strategic bargainers whose individualistic rationality could be self-defeating, for example through holding out in order to extract a monopoly rent and so preventing trade and development. Despite these problems of failed trade in rights, pre-modern society continued to favour tried and true water uses over newer untried methods of allocation; hence ancient use doctrines had a long reign.

Rose next argues that in the period of earlier industrialization, plentiful supplies of water in industrial areas meant that a newcomer to a water source was the effective cause of any ensuing conflict. A newcomer might have

[26] R. H. Coase, 'The Problem of Social Cost' (1960) 3 Journal of Law and Economics 1. For a summary of the Coasean model in this context see Getzler, 'Theories of Property and Economic Development', 658–64.

found a site to occupy without disturbing those already installed, or at least without adequately compensating them for the intrusion. Where water was plentiful, established uses might be protected against the newcomer by enjoining all uncompensated intrusions and takings, without in any way diminishing overall economic activity. Four conditions were necessary for this no-change, ancient-use regime of rights to work effectively. These were: infrequent rivalries; one-on-one conflicts eliminating the danger of strategic bargaining; easy exit if negotiations failed; and stable industrial usages of water. Those four conditions all vanished around 1800, with the rise of the new textile industrialism. It was around this time (telescoping Rose's account a little) that Blackstone propounded his rule of occupancy 'which meant that the right would go to the first one to *alter* a resource from its natural state. His position implicitly shifted the balance to favour the rapidly developing new mills, which clearly altered the mill sites along the water—as against ancient uses, which were often simply passive enjoyments of the water's flow with no special marks of occupancy.'[27] The Blackstonian paradigm of occupancy now replaced ancient use. Water could be 'owned' by any established existing use, regardless of time; the new test was occupancy, allowing appropriation of hitherto public goods. This is a strong version of a stage-three right—clear, individual rights of appropriation based on initial occupation or prior appropriation.

Why, then, did English and Massachusetts law in the mid-nineteenth century move from stage three (individual appropriative rights) to a new stage-two regime of reasonable usage? After 1800, Rose argues, the English cases had redefined prescription to make it look more like rights by occupancy. By requiring something akin to adverse possession, with actual injury to another's user, a rivalrous concept of prescription replaced the idea of long use itself as the basis of a claim. The legal explanation of this progression identifies new ideas of damage and injury surfacing within the nuisance and action on the case forms of writ. Rose instead invokes economic theory to explain this progression.

Rose's primary supposition is that much of water conflict in the industrializing age must have been mediated by private contract.[28] Prior appropriation and natural-right doctrines of entitlement simply created different baselines for negotiation and different wealth effects following trades and settlements. Following Coase again, the different property regimes would have had little impact on the process of bargaining and reallocation of rights to the most desirous user. The prior appropriation doctrine of *c.*1800 made a simple assumption that new and hungry water user would be more beneficial than

[27] Rose, 'Energy and Efficiency in the Realignment of Water Rights', 273.

[28] Examples given are *Wright* v. *Howard* (1823) 1 Sim. & St. 192; 57 E.R. 76 (V.C.), and *Mason* v. *Hill* (1832) 3 B. & Ad. 304; 110 E.R. 112; (1833) 5 B. & Ad. 1; 110 E.R. 692 (K.B.), Ch. 5, the text accompanying nn. 76–80, 101–112 above.

old, so that a legal baseline based on prior appropriation would require less bargaining than any other to shift water resources to their best uses. The optimal world of Coasean bargaining could not exist, however, if there were significant obstacles to efficient transactions taking place. Apart from the costs of transacting (such as time and cost of negotiating, specifying, and enforcing contract rights), two-person bargaining could commonly fail owing to strategic behaviour, for example where each side rationally holds out for a larger share of the potentially available profits from co-operation, but through such behaviour defeats the trust necessary for co-operation and agreement.[29] The problems of strategic bargaining steeply increase with multiple players where negotiating trusting relationships is elusive or impossible. In conditions of low-density water use, much bargaining between water users would have been successful; but with heightened water use the conditions of bargaining worsened as the complexity and cost of transacting increased. Rose puts the multiple bargaining problem as follows:

> [F]irst possession doctrine was, no doubt, adequate for the typical case of mill-wheel swamping, where the damage stemmed from an immediate downstream backflow. But a new kind of case, involving large numbers of potential claimants, began to appear in Massachusetts by mid-century, and in England as well. The new cases concerned interruption of the flow and pollution from upstream sources. These upstream problems potentially affected not just one neighbour but many downstream riparian users, and hence dramatically raised the costs of bargaining. When the courts confronted these new large-number cases, they turned away from first appropriation doctrine towards reasonable use.[30]

The reasonable use doctrine allows an upstream user to interfere with the stream to a vaguely defined level, without requiring arduous bargains to be struck with all affected users downstream. New York courts led the way in developing this approach, with all the relevant cases involving upstream interference. However, where there was a backstream interference causing conflict between individuals only, the courts resorted to natural-right doctrines—a 'stage three' regime permitting exchange of clear property rights between parties bargaining for water resources. Rose's general theory, then, is that with high transaction costs and multiple bargaining problems between parties, caused especially by upstream interferences with multiple downstream users, then courts will tend to invent discretionary measures and standards to decide conflicts, rather than try to apply mechanical rules deciding who is the private owner of a precise proportion of the resource.

Rose notes that *Embrey* v. *Owen*,[31] the seed-bed English case of reasonable riparian use, was an upstream interference case. Hence the court could

[29] R. Cooter, 'The Cost of Coase' (1982) 11 Journal of Legal Studies 1, esp. at 14–24.
[30] Rose, 'Energy and Efficiency in the Realignment of Water Rights', 282.
[31] (1851) 6 Exch. 353; 155 E.R. 579 (Ex.).

readily adopt Story J's discretionary New England doctrine. The *Embrey* decision stabilized English riparian law around an equal correlative right doctrine after decades of wavering. In America, by contrast, the western states adhered to a stage three system of individualistic private rights to water by prior appropriation. The reasons for this were two-fold: water in the West was very scarce; and it was used for private consumption rather than as a public good for renewable power. In a context of consumptive use rather than usufruct of a replenished public good, tradeable private goods accruing to the highest-value consumption proved to be the most efficient system. East coast and English riparianism was different in that water streams were used chiefly for power; and streams were therefore most productive if kept intact for use by all. In these conditions, doctrines of reasonable use and natural flow were the most appropriate and workable, and were therefore recognized and adopted by the courts. It is not the case that eastern states and England were locked by their history into a sub-optimal regime of water rights; more generally, it is an over-simplification to hold that path dependencies, or the particular historical starting points of legal and social institutions, will prevent the laws from moving to efficient solutions: there can be many bargaining points struck by competing parties with unique historical endowments that may be perceived as 'efficient'.[32] In the industrial context of eastern and English water use, the riparian regime that emerged was in fact highly efficient. Rose's final conclusion is that goods which are most valuable when kept intact for the public attract an equal correlative right system of property. The story of water law thus goes against the ideological model of judicial subsidy to developers, and also contradicts the conventional economic tale of individuation of tradeable private rights.[33]

Rose's anatomy of Anglo-American water law history is a brilliantly sustained attempt to make sense of a confused story; but problems of proof undermine the case. Many or most of the leading cases of modern English riparianism concerned not upstream obstruction as Rose supposes, but rather downstream, underground, and surface waters, and often consumptive uses such as mining, irrigation, and pollutive manufacturing in addition to municipal and domestic water supply, with canal building, fisheries, and navigation also important. Whilst many of the leading cases

[32] Cf. J. M. Ramseyer, 'Water Law in Imperial Japan: Public Goods, Private Claims, and Legal Convergence' (1989) 18 Journal of Legal Studies 51, 72–7.

[33] Rose, 'Energy and Efficiency in the Realignment of Water Rights', 261–7, 294–6. Rose's later work (e.g. 'Riparian Rights, *NPDEL* iii, 344–7) acknowledges the trend of recent law towards tradeable out-of-stream water entitlements replacing the classical riparian doctrine: see further L. L. Butler, 'Allocating Consumptive Water Rights in a Riparian Jurisdiction—Defining the Relationship Between Public and Private Interests' (1984) 47 University of Pittsburgh Law Review 95.

involve a tussle over water for power use,[34] it is not clear that this factor of itself is determining the nature of the decisions; the main point is that more intensive hydro-power use together with other forms of industrialization is exacerbating levels of conflict. It is true that both *Mason* v. *Hill* and *Embrey* v. *Owen* involved upstream interferences with the water supply to downstream mill operations; but all the prior appropriation cases involve near-identical facts of upstream interference, with the sole exception of *Saunders* v. *Newman* which involved flooding of an upstream mill by a downstream weir. The facts of one King's Bench case of 1818 cannot be the basis for a theory of centuries of legal doctrinal evolution. Moreover it is hardly the case that dense mill use of water in England dated only from the 1830s and 1840s; the timing of industrialization cannot give the key to the doctrinal history. A more general criticism is that Rose assumes that common-law judges had efficiency objectives (maybe tacit) firmly in mind as they shaped English riparian doctrine. The inner history of court determinations does not support that view. Rose's theory must therefore be viewed as an imaginative model of the history based on tenuous data.

The evidential weakness and speculative quality of modern interpretations of water law suggest that historians investigating the relationship between legal and economic change have unduly neglected the internal intellectual history of the law. Historians must recognize the signal dominance of conceptualism in the thinking of common lawyers if they are to capture the meaning and significance of common-law evolution with any accuracy. The inheritance of concepts from Roman law and medieval early-modern formulary law was the major determinant in shaping modern riparian doctrine. Sophisticated extra-legal policy arguments may have exerted some pull, but policy was expressed or filtered through the ancient vocabulary of the law.[35]

[34] e.g. *Magistrates of Linlithgow* v. *Elphinstone* (1768) 3 Kames' Decisions (S.C.S.) 331; *Robinson* v. *Lord Byron* (1785) 1 Bro. C.C. 588; 28 E.R. 1315 (Ch.); *Bealey* v. *Shaw* (1805) 6 East. 208; 102 E.R. 1266 (K.B.); *Saunders* v. *Newman* (1818) 1 B. & Ad. 258; 106 E.R. 95 (K.B.); *Wright* v. *Howard* (1823) 1 Sim. & St. 192; 57 E.R. 76 (V.C.); *Liggins* v. *Inge* (1831) 7 Bing. 682; 131 E.R. 263 (C.P.); *Mason* v. *Hill* (1832) 3 B. & Ad. 304; 110 E.R. 112; (1833) 5 B. & Ad. 1; 110 E.R. 692 (K.B.); *Arkwright* v. *Gell* (1839) 5 M. & W. 203; 151 E.R. 87 (Ex.); *Embrey* v. *Owen* (1851) 6 Exch. 353; 155 E.R. 579 (Ex.); *Miner* v. *Gilmour* (1858) 12 Moo. P.C. 131; 14 E.R. 861 (P.C.); *Broadbent* v. *Ramsbotham* (1856) 11 Exch. 602; 156 E.R. 971, 25 L.J. [N.S.] 115 (Ex.); *Chasemore* v. *Richards* (1857) 2 H. & N. 168, 191; 157 E.R. 71, 80 (Ex.); (1859) 7 H.L.C. 349; 11 E.R. 140 (H.L.); *Nuttal* v. *Bracewell* (1866) L.R. 2 Ex.1 (Ex.). But as many cases did not involve power mills.

[35] For a similar argument regarding polluting nuisances see J. S. McLaren, 'Nuisance Law and the Industrial Revolution: Some Lessons From Social History' (1983) 3 Oxford Journal of Legal Studies 155.

EVIDENCE AND DOCTRINE: 'FACT' BECOMES 'LAW'

The broad, discretionary character of English riparian law in its final development remains a puzzle. Rose identified a key issue in asking why individuated rights were remodelled as mutual or correlative. The reasonable-use metric was not a part of the ancient authorities, and was only partially prefigured in the *sic utere tuo* maxim. An alternative interpretation of the origins of the modern riparian doctrine may be posited focusing on the administration of justice. The problem of transaction costs was indeed a central issue driving legal developments, but the problem in the view of the courts had little to do with the litigating parties' own transaction costs in the pre-trial phase of the conflict. The problem lay rather in the costs of court administration. As the courts moved from old customary and natural-right theories to the more modern concept of rights of grant or appropriation based on the real or presumed intentions of proprietors, the task of adjudication perforce became intensely fact-sensitive. In the older common law, formalistic legal rules left a wide power of fact-finding and fact-determination to juries and to the litigants themselves through their pleadings.[36] In more modern times, this gave way to formulation of legal rules seeking carefully to characterize and differentiate conduct so as to curb discretion both of local jurisdictions and local and central juries.[37] There were important exceptions to this general trend, notably the use of special juries to advise the court on some special area of expertise and help the court

[36] For the important role of jury discretion in the history of contract see P. S. Atiyah, *The Rise and Fall of Freedom of Contract* (Oxford, 1979) 151, 210–11, 424–31; A. W. B. Simpson, 'The Horwitz Thesis and the History of Contracts', in A. W. B. Simpson, *Legal Theory and Legal History. Essays on the Common Law* (London, 1987) 203, 270–1; cf. M. Lobban, 'Contractual Fraud in Law and Equity, c.1750–c.1850' (1997) 17 Oxford Journal of Legal Studies 441.

[37] See Sir William Blackstone, *Commentaries on the Law of England*, 4 vols. (1st edn., Oxford, 1765–9; 15th edn. by E. Christian, 1809) iii, ch. 23, 349–85, and note Blackstone's 'eulogium' to the excellence of the jury system, ibid., at 378–81; G. Worthington, *Inquiry into the Power of Juries to Decide Incidentally on Questions of Law* (London, 1825); W. Forsyth, *History of Trial By Jury* (London, 1852) 93–191, 259–98, 415–50; F. Pollock and F. W. Maitland, *The History of English Law Before the Time of Edward I* (2nd edn., Cambridge, 1898, reprinted 1968) i, 138–50; ii, 617–50; J. B. Thayer, *Preliminary Treatise on Evidence at the Common Law* (London, 1898) 47–262; J. P. Dawson, *A History of Lay Judges* (Cambridge, Mass., 1962) 118–29; S. F. C. Milsom, *Historical Foundations of the Common Law* (2nd edn., London, 1981) 33–50, 58–9, 66–81, 243–6, 410–28, 'Law and Fact in Legal Development', and 'Reason in the Development of the Common Law', both in S. F. C. Milsom, *Studies in the History of the Common Law*, (London, 1985) 171–89; and 149–70; J. H. Baker, *An Introduction to English Legal History* (4th edn., London, 2002) 71–96; J. Stone and W. A. N. Wells, *Evidence: Its History and Policies* (Sydney, 1991) 16–23, 55–9; R. M. Jackson, 'The Incidence of Jury Trial During the Past Century' (1937) 1 Modern Law Review 132; W. S. Holdsworth, *A History of English Law*, 13 vols. (London, 1922–52) i, 312–50; iii, 639–56; ix, 126–39, 167–72, 298–315; W. R. Cornish, *The Jury* (London, 1968) 10–14; J. Getzler, 'The Fate of the Civil Jury in Late Victorian England: Malicious Prosecution as a Test Case', in G. R. Rubin and K. O'Donovan, (eds.), *Human Rights and Legal History: Essays for Brian Simpson* (Oxford, 2000) 205–24, reprinted in J. W. Cairns and G. McLeod (eds.), *'The Dearest Birth Right of the People of England': The Jury in the History of the Common Law* (Oxford, 2002) 217–37.

determine which business norms and practices to absorb into legal principle. The best-known instance was Lord Mansfield's liberal use of special juries of merchants to help develop new doctrines of insurance, bills of exchange, promissory notes, and other areas of commercial law.[38] However, the traditional use of the special jury with its valued non-legal expertise did not contradict the wider swing away from the ideal of the untutored citizen jury as a sure fount of justice.[39] The common jury's strong fact-finding discretion was a black box of decision-making many shades too dark for the rationalizing judges of the Victorian Age. The Common Law Commissioners of 1852–3 may have been expressing the opinion of many judges when they reported to Parliament on the perceived inadequacies of the civil jury:

> [W]e are not at all blind to the fact that in many instances juries are not so constituted as to ensure such an average amount of intelligence as might be desired;...in the agricultural districts the common juries are sometimes composed of a class of persons whose intelligence by no means qualifies them for the due discharge of judicial functions. Such persons, unaccustomed to severe intellectual exercise or to protracted thought...sometimes pronounce verdicts which bring the institution of juries into disrespect.[40]

Driven by sentiments such as these, judges sought to replace the breadth of jury discretion with more and more elaborate adjectival and substantive law. For most of the nineteenth century, judges were forced to do this gradually by evolving new doctrinal and procedural methods limiting the jury's role. It was not until 1883 that explicit rules explicitly permitted judges to exclude the jury from civil trials at discretion, wherever matters were formerly dealt with in Chancery or Admiralty without the assistance of a jury, or in matters where a jury could not conveniently make investigation.[41] Even after that important reform, common lawyers could still assail the unintelligent and unguided populism of jury trial. Dicey, for example, wrote a celebrated attack in 1885:

> Trial by jury is open to much criticism... the habit of submitting difficult problems of fact to twelve men of not more than average education and intelligence will in the near future be considered an absurdity as patent as ordeal by battle.... Juries are often biassed against the Government. A technical question is referred for decision, from

[38] See J. C. Oldham, 'Special Juries in England: Nineteenth Century Usage and Reform' (1987) 8 Journal of Legal History 148 and *The Mansfield Manuscripts and the Growth of English Law in the Eighteenth Century*, 2 vols. (Chapel Hill, NC, 1992) i, 82–99.

[39] J. C. Oldham, 'The Origins of the Special Jury' (1983) 50 University of Chicago Law Review 137; M. Lobban, 'The Strange Life of the English Civil Jury, 1837–1914', in Cairns and McLeod (eds.), *'The Dearest Birth Right'*, 173–215.

[40] (1852–3) H. C. Parliamentary Papers, xl. 701, 708, quoted in Atiyah, *Rise and Fall of Freedom of Contract*, 390. Reform came with the Juries Acts of 1825 and 1918–1925, and the Rules of the Supreme Court (1883), Order XXXVI.

[41] Rules of the Supreme Court (1883), Order XXXVI.

persons who know something about the subject, and are impartial, to persons who are both ignorant and prejudiced.[42]

Jackson has estimated that until the 1883 reform, 90 per cent of common-law civil trials were heard before juries; after the reform, the proportion dipped to 50 per cent and then continued to decline. The Juries Acts of 1918–25 finally decreed that civil trials be conducted without juries unless ordered by the court; civil jury trials became the exception rather than the rule.[43] Before these late reforms, however, and throughout the formative period of water and land use law, juries sat on almost all civil hearings; and judges strove to find methods to hem the jury in and curb its decisional power. The chief method employed was to engage in more and more judicial fact-finding, in the guise of testing the propriety of pleadings, and then applying formal legal doctrine to the established facts. Juries were reduced to deciding narrow questions of fact as determined by the judges, with a seemingly automatic legal result following from the factual findings. Once the judges could decide which questions were relevant by means of fine-grained legal tests, they had won control of the adjudicative process.

In order to apply the more elaborate and discriminating legal tests in the sphere of water rights, the courts were required to sift through evidence of the parties' conduct to discover who had appropriated water, at which times, with whose knowledge and acquiescence. The detailed investigations of fact undertaken are evidenced by the immense statements of facts (including deeds, maps, and testimony) and elaborate pleadings recorded in the early nineteenth-century law reports.[44] For example in *Arkwright* v. *Gell*, Abinger CB began his discussion of the case by observing:

A special case was reserved on the trial, for the opinion of the Court, stating a great number of documents and facts, upon which the Court are not merely to give their judgment on matters of law, but to take the office of the jury, by determining whether any and what inferences of fact ought to be drawn from the facts stated. This course leads to one great inconvenience, as it tends to confound the rule of law with an inference of fact only, which inference may have been varied by a very slight circumstance.[45]

[42] A. V. Dicey, *An Introduction to the Study of the Law of the Constitution* (1st edn., London, 1885; 10th edn., London, 1959) 394, 398. Dicey also preferred the judge-made law of the elitist professional courts to the legislation of an untutored and short-sighted Parliament: see his *Lectures on the Relation Between Law and Public Opinion in England During the Nineteenth Century* (London, 1905) 361–98.

[43] Jackson, 'Incidence of Jury Trial'. Lobban has reinterpreted Jackson's statistics and argues that the decline is prompted not by loss of confidence in the jury but by referral of cases to single judges involving either non-contentious or complex facts, or limited discretion over damages: 'Strange Life of the English Civil Jury', 186–92. Reasons for the resilience of jury trials on the criminal side are anatomized in A. A. S. Zuckerman, *The Principles of Criminal Evidence* (Oxford, 1989) 29–46.

[44] Almost all case reports up to 1860 discussed in the last two Chapters display this feature.

[45] (1839) 5 M. & W. 227, 227–8; 151 E.R. 87, 97 (Ex.).

This was a special case where the judges sat as a fact-finding jury; but the judges' experience of adjudication was not dissimilar where a standard jury did participate. Abinger CB revealed a growing sense that the courts had bitten off more than they could chew in the field of fact-finding and evidence. Intense pressures on court time, with the heightened litigation of a burgeoning industrial and commercial economy, soon demanded a different style of adjudication and definition of rights.[46]

The pre-eminent solution to this problem was to preserve the common-law intention-based concepts, but to simplify them—even transform them—by 'objectification' of the operative intention or consent.[47] The final simplification of the law was to emphasize the objectivity of rights of user per se, independently of any actual intent or agreement—a shift exemplified by tests such as 'reasonableness' of user, 'reasonableness' in ascription of prescriptive rights. Actual or presumed intentions could then be reduced to a subsidiary role. This allowed adjudication to proceed in a more peremptory or summary mode, directly enforcing broad, discretionary policy standards; and, in tandem, discouraging parties from litigating chiefly on the basis of instance-specific, detailed factual pleading.[48] Atiyah and Gilmore have detected similar trends in contract doctrine, with Gilmore observing: 'At the height of the classical period it seemed that it was hardly possible to phrase any contract issue other than as a question of law.'[49] Much of nineteenth-century civil law—and especially riparian doctrine—can be understood in terms of social engineering and efficiency-maximization, but the efficiency inheres in the operation of the legal system, not of the productive economy at large.

INSTITUTIONAL DESIGN AND THE 'TRAGEDY OF THE COMMONS'

In Elinor Ostrom's 1990 study entitled *Governing the Commons*, she analyses the regulation of access to common-pool resources such as water by self-

[46] Cf. Atiyah, *Rise and Fall of Freedom of Contract*, 390–1.

[47] 'Objectification' of consent in English legal history is perhaps the leading theme of Holmes, *The Common Law*: see M. De W. Howe, 'Introduction', to *The Common Law*, pp. xx–xxvii; H. L. A. Hart, 'Diamonds and String: Holmes and the Common Law' in H. L. A. Hart, *Essays in Jurisprudence and Philosophy* (Oxford, 1983) 278, 279–83; M. J. Horwitz, 'The Legacy of 1776 in Legal and Economic Thought' (1976) 19 Journal of Law and Economics 621, 626 ff.

[48] A similar interpretation of the evolution of nineteenth-century contract law is propounded in Atiyah, *Rise and Fall of Freedom of Contract*, 388 ff., especially 405–8. Arguably the search for actual will is more determinate in contract than in property law since contract (largely) deals with the declared intentions of transacting parties, rather than the implied intentions of non-transacting owner-neighbours.

[49] G. Gilmore, *The Death of Contract* (Columbus, Ohio, 1974) 99.

interested individuals.[50] The classical economic problem in such cases is the 'tragedy of the commons'—the risk that rational users will take too much of the common resource and so deplete it, reducing the welfare they would collectively have enjoyed if they had disciplined their takings and cared for the resource.[51] Aristotle had identified the same problem in the *Politics*:

> That which is common to the greatest number has the least care bestowed upon it.... Everyone thinks chiefly of his own, hardly at all of the common interest, and only when he is himself concerned as an individual. For besides other considerations, everybody is more inclined to neglect the duty which he expects another to fulfil...[52]

The underlying problem can be reduced to a non-co-operative game dilemma: to act with restraint and to conserve the resource may not be a rational strategy for the individual if other competing individuals can be expected to take without regard for limits. Thus even rational, far-sighted, and restrained users will be drawn into competition to take their stake in a vanishing resource.[53] Ostrom identified three possible solutions to the tragedy of the commons. The first was to create a Leviathan, a coercive command-economy state to ration, monitor, and enforce constrained user.[54] The second was to create a private market with clearly-defined and exclusive property rights, so abolishing common resources with all of their inherent problems. There is a third technique, however, which is to create public, communal, and market agencies that can help parties to build norms of restraint and trust by

[50] E. Ostrom, *Governing the Commons. The Evolution of Institutions for Collective Action* (Cambridge, 1990) 1–57, 182–216. Much of the theoretical analysis of Ostrom's book was derived from empirical material of ground-water commons management in southern California. Recent empirical and theoretical findings are summarized in E. Ostrom, 'Self-governance of Common-Pool Resources', *NPDEL* iii, 425; P. Seabright, 'Local Common Property Rights', *NPDEL*, ii, 591; and E. G. Furobotn and R. Richter, *Institutions and Economic Theory: The Contribution of the New Institutional Economics* (Ann Arbor, Mich., 1998) 69–120; J. Boyle (ed.), *The Public Domain (Symposium)* (2003) 66 Law and Contemporary Problems 1–483.

[51] The locus classicus of the concept is G. Hardin, 'The Tragedy of the Commons' (1968) 162 Science 1243.

[52] Aristotle, *Politics and Poetics* (B. Jowett, trans., Oxford, 1885, New York, 1957) bk. II, ch. 3, sect. 1261b. Still plainer is the maxim 'everybody's property is nobody's property'.

[53] Ostrom, *Governing the Commons*, 2–8.

[54] An alternative to public ownership *tout court* is the public trust doctrine drawing from *res communes* concepts: J. Sax, 'The Public Trust Doctrine in Natural Resource Law: Effective Judicial Intervention' (1970) 68 Michigan Law Review 471, 'Liberating the Public Trust Doctrine from its Historical Shackles' (1980) 14 University of California Davis Law Review 185 and 'The Limits of Private Rights in Public Waters' (1989) 19 Environmental Law 473; P. Deveney, 'Title, Jus Publicum, and the Public Trust: An Historical Analysis' (1976) 1 Sea Grant Law Journal 13; R. Ausness, 'Water Rights, The Public Trust Doctrine and the Protection of Instream Uses' (1986) 2 University of Illinois Law Review 407; R. A. Epstein, 'The Public Trust Doctrine' (1987) 7 Cato Journal 411; C. M. Rose, 'Joseph Sax and the Idea of the Public Trust' (1998) 25 Ecology Law Quarterly 351. The law is further complicated by federal reservations of water rights for native or national use: T. A. Fisher, 'The Winter of Our Discontent: Federal Reserved Water Rights in Western States' (1984) 69 Cornell Law Review 1077; H. B. Lee, 'Forcing the Federal Hand—Reserved Water Rights v. States Rights for Instream Protection' (1990) 41 Hastings Law Journal 1271.

agreement and praxis, and then assist the parties to monitor and enforce those norms.[55] Economists have postulated that common-pool resource regimes can be governed by private contract without resorting to property regimes that can be difficult to create and enforce.[56] However, restraining norms, less formal and coercive than contract, can also be envisaged. It is well observed that informal systems of stinting and mutual forbearance succeed best where the resource is not wholly non-exclusive but open only to members of a closed and exclusive group. Stinting of a closed-pool resource will be still more effective where the participating parties are bound together in close spiritual and material community.[57] Robert Ellickson's study of ranchers' control of grazing land and herds in the American West makes this point forcefully,[58] and Eyal Benvenisti has recently highlighted the role of kinship bonds in the peasant village in facilitating water sharing and conservation, as in the traditional Arab village, contrasting this with the impersonal conflicts of neighbour-states struggling over access to common water supplies.[59] The communitarian theory of the self-regulating commons is not in tension with the conventional economic theory of property but is a special case. The conventional theory postulates that parties move out of common pooling into privatized property regimes in situations where trust and stinting cannot be generated between self-interested parties.[60] The commons theory locates instances where self-regulated pools become possible through the constraints of rational self-interest buttressed by culture or repeat transacting; privatization is then unnecessary or even sub-optimal.

Ostrom throws doubt on both the communitarian and the economistic assumptions that high levels of trust and community are required for stinted pools to function well.[61] It may be important to prevent trade or commodification of shares in a common-pool resource and restrict the class of users; but the pool can successfully be operated by self-interested or individualistic strangers, who may submit to norms of mutual forbearance and themselves

[55] Ostrom, *Governing the Commons*, 1–18.

[56] The seminal paper here is S. N. S. Cheung, 'The Structure of a Contract and the Theory of a Non-Exclusive Resource' (1970) 13 Journal of Law and Economics 49.

[57] M. Taylor, *Community, Anarchy and Liberty* (Cambridge, 1982) and S. Singleton and M. Taylor, 'Common Property, Collective Action and Community' (1992) 4 Journal of Theoretical Politics 309.

[58] R. C. Ellickson, *Order Without Law: How Neighbours Settle Disputes* (Cambridge, Mass., 1991); to similar effect is Rose, 'Comedy of the Commons'.

[59] E. Benvenisti, 'Collective Action in the Utilization of Shared Freshwater: The Challenges of International Water Resources Law' (1996) 90 American Journal of International Law 384.

[60] Cf. G. D. Libecap, *Contracting for Property Rights* (Cambridge, 1989); Barzel, *Economic Analysis of Property Rights*.

[61] E. Ostrom, 'Community and the Endogenous Solution of Commons Problems' (1992) 4 Journal of Theoretical Politics 343, criticizing the communitarian commons theory. In her 'Self-governance of Common-Pool Resources', *NPDEL* iii, 425–33, Ostrom brings game-theoretical and experimental results to demonstrate that co-operation over common pool resources can be evolved to near-optimal levels through limited repeat plays, in the absence of intimate trust.

generate such norms, especially when guided by a suitable enforcement agency. It may even be that access to the resource can freely be traded, such that the exclusive class of users permits liberal entrance and exit; and yet incoming players readily learn to submit to the collective rules of forbearance. The class can be exclusive yet porous.[62]

Riparian water use is well-explained by such models. There is a closed class of riparian proprietors who alone may extract water from a river, yet who may swap out of the class by simply selling on their riparian lands. But the key point here is to identify how stinting to reasonable-use levels operated. The answer is that the historical institutions of English riparian law provided an enforcement agency buttressing reasonable forbearance as viewed by the participants in the pool. The law acted as a third-party enforcer of norms where the norms themselves were set by the interacting parties. Under the supervision of courts and juries, each neighbour with access to the common good of riparian waters was to enjoy limited correlative rights to interfere with the public goods available to all. The procedures and doctrines of the common law paid careful attention to the agreements, understandings, and practices of the parties. The law depended on the parties' monitoring of each other's performances, their collecting of evidence, and their crafting and presentation of pleadings in litigation to make the system run. There was little risk of the system degenerating into a tragedy of the commons, because the law with its ad hoc reasonableness test founded on the parties' own conduct would restrain destructive consumption of the common good. This was not a system of adjudication where one right holder confronted another right holder seeking victory before a judge; as Lon Fuller pointed out many years ago, where such conflictual adjudication prevails, the law soon turns to administrative and governmental solutions.[63]

[62] This is the theme of H. Dagan and M. A. Heller, 'The Liberal Commons' (2001) 110 Yale Law Journal 549, 566–602. They survey the expanding literature on rational choice and collective action in control of common pool resources at 551–66. See further C. M. Rose, 'Rethinking Environmental Controls: Management Strategies for Common Resources' [1991] Duke Law Journal 1; 'Comparing Newfangled Tradable Allowance Schemes To Old-Fashioned Common Property Regimes' (1999) 10 Duke Environmental Law & Policy Forum 45, and 'Romans, Roads, and Romantic Creators: Traditions of Public Property in the Information Age' (2003) 66 Law and Contemporary Problems 89. Please note that many of the recent theoretical 'advances' of understanding common-pool resources are laid out already in Epstein's 1985 article 'Why Restrain Alienation?' at 979–82, discussed in the text accompanying n. 7 above.

[63] Lon L. Fuller in 'Irrigation and Tyranny' (1965) 17 Stanford Law Review 1021, 1041–2, uses water rights to highlight the problem of litigation with multiple parties' interests in conflict:

> The earliest decisions in England in the field we now call administrative law related to similar questions. ... We may indeed describe the law relating to the control of waters as the most ancient branch of administrative law.... When things go wrong we are more and more inclined to run to the judge. This is... an escapist solution. Problems concerned with the sharing of water supplies and the joint utilization of river systems are inherently unsuited to adjudicative solution, involving as they do a complex interplay of diverse interests. Only those who know those interests intimately, who can feel their way toward the best reciprocal adjustment of them, are competent to find a truly satisfactory solution.

The history of English riparian law is a story of the evolution of institutions and agencies able effectively to enforce the norms of commons management. Those norms and their supporting institutions evolved significantly over time, notably in the mid-nineteenth century when the old jury-based system of fact-finding and verdict began to break down. The underlying purpose of riparian law—effective commons management—remained constant notwithstanding the instability of riparian doctrine. Thus the problems of allocating common water resources in the modernizing English economy were resolved by private treaty and custom, assisted by law. This form of semi-private regulation was not always effective or available; it could be blocked by conservative landowners unwilling to allow development in their own backyard; and sensible deals could be threatened by parties exploiting vested rights, either to hold out for excessive remuneration, or to free-ride upon the investments of others and collect unearned increments to their property values. In such circumstances new institutional interventions came to the fore: first, the private bill procedures; and then, in the later nineteenth century, a new world of public planning legislation and administration.

PUBLIC POWER AND PRIVATE RIGHTS

The private bill procedures, pioneered in the cases of enclosure and canal building in the eighteenth century, were in fact the chief weapon of urban and industrial developers in the nineteenth, and in scope and sheer number they dwarfed public or general legislation. In the canal and enclosure era of the later eighteenth century the House of Lords played a prominent role in running this semi-privatized technique of legislation.[64] Contemporaries

Fuller later expanded the critique of 'polycentric' litigation into a generalized theory in his posthumous piece 'The Forms and Limits of Adjudication' (1978) 92 Harvard Law Review 353. See further E. T. Freyfogle, 'Water Rights and the Common Wealth' [1996] Environmental Law 27, and for theoretical elaboration G. D. Libecap, 'Common Property', *NPDEL* i, 317, 321–3.

[64] F. Clifford, *A History of Private Bill Legislation* 2 vols. (London, 1885–7); S. B. Bristowe, *Private Bill Legislation* (London, 1859); O. Williams, *The Historical Development of Private Bill Procedure and Standing Orders in the House of Commons* (London, 1948); J. Prest, *Liberty and Locality: Parliament, Permissive Legislation, and Ratepayers' Democracies in the Nineteenth Century* (Oxford, 1990); D. L. Rydz, *The Parliamentary Agents: A History* (London, 1979); S. Lambert, *Bills and Acts: Legislative Procedure in Eighteenth-Century England* (Cambridge, 1971); A. W. B. Simpson, 'Legal Liability for Bursting Reservoirs: The Historical Context of *Rylands v. Fletcher*' (1984) 13 Journal of Legal Studies 209, 252–64; J. Hoppit (ed.), *Failed Legislation, 1660–1800, Extracted from the Commons and Lords Journals* (introd. by J. Hoppit and J. Innes, London, 1997); R. W. Kostal, *Law and English Railway Capitalism 1825–1875* (Oxford, 1994) 110–80; J. Getzler, 'Judges and Hunters: Law and Economic Conflict in the English Countryside, 1800–1860' in C. Brooks and M. Lobban (eds.), *Communities and Courts in Britain 1150–1900* (London, 1997) 199. The full history of private bill legislation as the prime legal instrument for economic development in the eighteenth and nineteenth centuries is yet to be written. This topic lies beyond the scope of this book; a detailed study by Ron Harris and the present author is planned.

were well aware of the importance of these instruments of governance. The Victorian barrister and journalist Frederick Clifford wrote a massive *History of Private Bill Legislation* in two volumes from 1885, and published an encomium to the private act in his dedication to Queen Victoria:

During the fifty years of your Majesty's Reign, nearly Eleven thousand Local and Personal Statutes have been passed by the Imperial Parliament.... To the vast undertakings completed by Railway and other Companies, and the money expended on the faith of those Statutes, is due in large measure within this period a Social and Industrial Progress throughout the United Kingdom of which History affords hardly another example. No less remarkable during the same fifty years has been the great Sanitary and other works, together with numerous Parks, Baths, Picture Galleries, Libraries and Public Buildings, provided by Local Authorities under Local Acts, adding materially thereby to the health, comfort and enjoyment of your Majesty's subjects in the ever-growing towns, and accomplishing their ends by measures of local self-government in harmony with the best English traditions.[65]

In the forum of Parliament and in the regulatory tribunals that later developed, open arguments of utility and communal benefit and interest-group direction could replace the courtroom search for common-law entitlement. Armed with state powers, the canal companies, municipal corporations, and water companies could take land and water for waterworks, and stipulate for protection of the water supply from pollution and diversion. Parliament armed the promoters of private bill schemes with expropriative powers, and set out schemes for compensation. Also crucial were the legal protections afforded to the investors' capital, the guarantees of service and supply to the public, and the regulation of monopolist enterprises' prices and rates of return. Common-law regulation based on property, tort, and contract could not possibly have achieved the reordering of interests necessary to permit rapid industrialization and modernization.[66] To search for an economically

[65] Clifford, *Private Bill Legislation* ii, Dedication.

[66] See generally Clifford, *Private Bill Legislation* i, v–x, 1–12, 33–42, 249–55; ii, 36–198; F. B. Smith, *The People's Health, 1830–1910* (New York, 1979, Aldershot, 1993); G. M. Binnie, *Early Victorian Water Engineers* (London, 1981) 1–48; B. Rudden, *The New River: A Legal History* (Oxford, 1985) 131–89; J. Hassan, *A History of Water in Modern England and Wales* (Manchester, 1998) 1–50. Examples of utility and municipal legislation regulating water entitlements, generally narrowly interpreted in order to protect private property, are legion; see eg. *Gaby* v. *Wilts and Berks Canal Company* (1815) 3 M. & S. 580, 105 E.R. 727 (K.B.); *Rex* v. *Medley* (1834) 6 Car. & P. 292, 172 E.R. 1246 (K.B.); *Wynn* v *Shropshire Union Railways and Canal Company* (1850) 5 Exch. 420, 155 ER 183 (Ex.); *Regina* v. *Inhabitants of Kentmere* (1851) 17 Q.B. 551, 117 E.R. 1392 (Q.B.); *Mayor of Manchester* v. *Overseers of the Poor Manchester* (1852) 17 Q.B. 859, 117 E.R. 1509 (Q.B.); *Bostock* v. *North Staffordshire Railway Company* (1855) 4 El. & Bl. 798, 119 E.R. 295 (Q.B.); *Llewellyn* v. *Swansea Canal Navigation Company* (1856) 1 H. & N. 343, 156 E.R. 1235 (Ex.); *Mayor of Liverpool* v. *Overseers of West Derby* (1856) 6 El. & Bl. 704, 119 E.R. 1026 (Q.B.); *Preston* v. *Norfolk Railway Company* (1858) 2 H. & N. 735, 157 E.R. 303 (Ex.); *Hildreth* v. *Adamson* (1860) 8 C.B. N.S. 587, 141 E.R. 1296 (C.P.); *Colbran* v. *Barnes* (1861) 11 C.B.N.S. 246; 142 E.R. 791 (C.P.); *Mayor &c of Waller* v. *Manchester* (1861) 6 H. & N. 667, 158 E.R. 275 (Ex.); *R.* v. *Metropolitan Board of Works* (1863) 3 B. & S. 710, 122 E.R. 266 (Q.B.); *R.* v.

functional common law during the long span of industrialization is therefore to bark up the wrong tree; to change the metaphor, the actors in this drama largely preferred the stage of Parliament to that of the courts.

The rise of legislative, administrative, and indeed market solutions did not, however, mean that the courts were unimportant. The vast amount of litigation over water rights and property use-rights generally proves the reverse. The turn to legislation did little to extinguish lawyers' and litigants' belief in a naturalist set of legal rights to resources, rights which were embedded within the technical reasoning of the common law as it investigated the agreements, customs, and practices of the parties. This sophisticated ideal of formal legal justice articulating local norms dominates the story of riparian law. However quaint and open to demolition by sceptical modern observers, the secular common-law faith in legalism is resilient and valuable. The lesson is that in order to maintain the trust and commitment of participants within any complex system of resource allocation, a strong belief both in individual rights and the consensual justice of adjudications is essential. It is a lesson with purchase across the widest fields of the law.

Darlington Local Board of Health (1864) 5 B. & S. 515, 122 E.R. 924 (Q.B.); *R.* v. *Godmanchester Local Board of Health* (1864) 5 B. & S. 886, 122 E.R. 1060 (Q.B.); *R.* v. *Bradford Navigation Company* (1865) 6 B. & S. 631, 122 E.R. 1328 (Q.B.)

For a close description of a water bill that misfired badly for its promoters see A. W. B. Simpson, 'Victorian Law and the Industrial Spirit' (Selden Society Lecture, 1995) 21–8, and M. Taggart, *Private Property and Abuse of Rights in Victorian England: The Story of Edward Pickles and the Bradford Water Supply* (Oxford, 2002) 5–22, both describing the legislative history leading to the 'leading case' of *Bradford Corporation* v. *Pickles* [1895] 3 Ch. 53 (Ch.) per North J; [1895] A.C. 587 (H.L.).

Bibliography

I. PRIMARY SOURCES

A. Archival Papers relating to Arkwright Water Privileges

ARKWRIGHT, R., Correspondence with Sir Christopher and Sir M. M. Sykes *re* water rights, etc., at West Beck and Wansford Mills, Hull University Library, P.P. 345–6, 1789–1822

—— Deeds and papers related to mill at Bakewell, East Sussex Record Office, Cavendish private records, Ark. 1–97.

—— 'A State of Facts Respecting the Case of Mr. Richard Arkwright...Cotton Manufacturer' (1782), and J. Chippindale, 'Petition [of the Manchester Committee of Trade against the Arkwright patent]' (9 February 1782) (Seligman Folio 1782E St29, Columbia University Rare Book and Manuscript Library)

Worthington-Samuel, G., Oldknow Correspondence (Arkwright–Oldknow Collection, Columbia University Rare Book and Manuscript Library, uncatalogued)

B. State Papers relating to Cromford Canal Private Bills

House of Commons Journals, xliv (1789) 280, 376, 410, 422

House of Lords Committee Book xxxiii (1789) 175–6, 183–92, 197–34 (H.L.R.O)

House of Lords Petitions (1789) LP 281/21–4, 29, 40–1 (H.L.R.O.)

House of Lords Journals xxxviii (1789) 437, 443–59, 460, 470, 475, 497, 502–3, 514, 574, 577–86; xxxix (1790) 356–62, 392–3, 401 (H.L.R.O.)

C. Legal Treatises, Monographs, Abridgements, Collections of Laws and Other Sources Before 1800

ANON., *The Laws of Sewers* (London, 1726, 2nd edn., London, 1732)

ARISTOTLE, *Politics and Poetics* (B. Jowett (trans.), Oxford, 1885, New York, 1957)

BLACKSTONE, SIR WILLIAM, *Commentaries on the Law of England* 4 vols. (1st edn., Oxford, 1765–9; ed. E. Christian, 15th edn., Oxford, 1809)

BRACTON, H. DE, *Bracton's Note Book* 3 vols. (F. W. Maitland (ed.), London, 1887)

—— *De Legibus et Consuetudinibus Angliae* 4 vols. (G. E. Woodbine (ed.), S. E. Thorne (trans.), Cambridge, Mass., 1968–1977)

A Briefe Declaration for What Manner of Speciall Nuisance Concerning Private Dwelling Houses, A Man May Have His Remedy by Assise, or Other Action as the Case Requires, Unfolded in the Argument, and Opinions of Four Famous Sages of the Common Law (London, 1636)

Britton (F. M. Nichols (ed.), Oxford, 1865)

BROOKE, R., *La Graunde Abridgement* (London, 1573)

CALLIS, R., *The Reading of Robert Callis upon the Statute of Sewers, 23 Hen. VIII c. 5* (London, 1622; 4th edn. by W. J. Broderip, London, 1824)

Codex Justinianus (534 CE) (P. Krueger (ed.), Berlin, 1877)

COKE, SIR EDWARD, *The First Part of the Institutes of the Laws of England, or, A Commentary on Littleton* (London, 1628, ed. F. Hargrave and C. Butler, 19th edn., London, 1832) ('*Co.Litt.*')

COMYNS, J., *Digest of the Laws of England* (1st edn., London, 1767; 4th edn., London, 1793; 5th edn. by A. Hammond, London, 1822)

Corpus Juris Civilis 17 vols. (S. P. Scott (ed. and trans.), Cincinatti, Ohio, 1973)

COWELL, J., *The Institutes of the Lawes of England* (London, 1651)

CUJACIUS, J., *Opera Omnia* (Paris, 1658, Naples, 1758) vii, *Ad diversos titulos Pandectarum*

DEFOE, D., *A Tour Through the Whole Island of Great Britain* 2 vols. (1724–6, ed. G. D. H. Cole and D. C. Browning, London, 1962)

Digest of Justinian (533 CE) 4 vols. (T. Mommsen and P. Krueger (eds.), A. Watson (trans. and ed.), Philadelphia, Penn., 1985)

Dyer's Reports Vol. 1 (J. H. Baker (ed.), Selden Society, cix, London, 1993)

The Earliest English Law Reports Vol. 1 (P. A. Brand (ed.), Selden Society, cxi, London, 1996)

Early Curia Regis Rolls (C. T. Flower (ed.), Selden Society, lxii, London, 1943)

English Law Suits from William I to Richard I, Vol. I (R. C. van Caenegem (ed.), Selden Society, cvi, London, 1990)

English Law Suits from William I to Richard I, Vol. II (R. C. van Caenegem (ed.), Selden Society, cvii, London, 1991)

Early Registers of Writs (E. de Haas and G. D. G. Hall (eds.), Selden Society, lxxxvii, London, 1970)

FINCH, SIR HENRY, *Law, or, a Discourse Thereof* (*Nomotechnia*) (London, 1613, English edn., D. Pickering (ed.), London, 1729)

FITZHERBERT, A., *La Graunde Abridgement* (1st edn., London, 1514–16; London, 1577 edn.)

—— *The New Natura Brevium* (1st edn., London, 1534; 9th edn., London, 1794)

Fleta, seu commentarius Iuris Anglicani (*Fleta, A Commentary on the Laws of England*) (*c.*1290) (H. G. Richardson and G. O. Sayles (ed. and trans.), ii, Selden Society, lxxii, London, 1955; iii, Selden Society, lxxxix, London, 1972; iv, G. O. Sayles (ed.), Selden Society, xcix, London, 1984)

Fontes Iuris Romani Antiqui (G. G. Bruns (ed.), Tübingen, 1909)

FRONTINUS, *De Aquis Urbis Romae* (*c.*97 CE), in C. Herschel, *The Two Books of the Water Supply of the City of Rome of Sextus Julius Frontinus* (Boston, Mass., 1879)

GAIUS, *Institutiones Iuris Civilis, The Institutes of Gaius* (F. de Zulueta (ed. and trans.), Oxford, 1946)

GLANVILL, H. DE, *Tractatus de Legibus et Consuetudinibus regni Anglie qui Glanvilla vocatur* (*The Treatise on the Laws and Customs of the Realm of England Commonly Called Glanvill*) (c.1187–9) (G. D. G. Hall (ed. and trans.), London, 1965)

GROTIUS, H., *De Jure Belli Ac Pacis* (*On the Law of War and Peace*) (Paris, 1625, revised edition, Amsterdam, 1646; 2 vols., F. W. Kelsey (ed. and trans.), Oxford, 1925)

HALE, SIR MATTHEW, *De Jure Maris* (c.1670) in F. Hargrave (ed.), *A Collection of Tracts Relative to the Law of England* (London, 1787); reprinted in S. A. Moore, *A History of the Foreshore* (3rd edn., London, 1888)

JACOB, G., *A New Law Dictionary* (1st edn., London, 1729, 3rd edn., London, 1736)

Justinian's *Digest*, *see Digest*, *Corpus Juris Civilis*

Justinian's Institutes (P. Krueger (ed.), P. B. H. Birks and G. McLeod (trans.), London, 1987)

KAMES, LORD [HENRY], *Principles of Equity* (2nd edn., Edinburgh, 1767; 3rd edn., Edinburgh, 1778)

Leet Jurisdiction in the City of Norwich During the 13th and 14th Centuries (W. Hudson (ed.), Selden Society, v, London, 1891)

LILLY, J., 'Preface' to *Reports and Pleadings of Cases in Assise [etc.]* (London, 1719)

LITTLETON, T., *Les Tenures* (London, 1481) (E. Wambaugh (ed.), Washington D.C., 1903)

LOCKE, J., *Second Treatise of Government*, in J. Locke, *Two Treatises of Government* (P. Laslett (ed.), Cambridge, 1960)

Notebook of Sir John Port (J. H. Baker (ed.), Selden Society, cii, London, 1986)

Novae Narrationes (E. Shanks and S. F. C. Milsom (eds.), Selden Society, lxxx, London, 1963)

PLINY, *Natural History* (H. Rackham (trans.), Cambridge, Mass., 1986)

POTHIER, R., *Traité des obligations* (*Treatise on the Law of Obligations*) (Paris, 1761–4; W. D. Evans (trans.), London, 1806)

—— *Oeuvres complètes*, 25 vols. (St. A. Berville (ed.), Paris, 1821–4) xvii

Public Works in Mediaeval Law Vol. 1 (C. T. Flower (ed.), Selden Society, xxxii, London, 1915)

Public Works in Mediaeval Law Vol. 2 (C. T. Flower (ed.), Selden Society, xl, London, 1923)

PUFENDORF, S. VON, *De Jure Nature et Gentium* (Lund, 1672), *Of the Law of Nature and Nations* (with notes of J. Barbeyrac, B. Kennett (trans.), Oxford, 1710, enlarged edn., London, 1729)

Readings and Moots at the Inns of Court Vol. 2 (S. E. Thorne and J. H. Baker (eds.), Selden Society, cv, London, 1997)

Registrum Omnium Brevium (London, 1531, reprinted London, 1634 and 1687)

Reports of Cases by John Caryll Vol. 1 (J. H. Baker (ed.), Selden Society, cxv, London, 1999)

Reports of Cases by John Caryll Vol. 2 (J. H. Baker (ed.), Selden Society, cxvi, London, 2000)

ROLLE, H., *Un Abridgment des Plusieurs Cases et Resolutions del Common Ley* 2 vols. (M. Hale (ed.), London, 1668)

Royal Writs in England from the Conquest to Glanvill (R. C. van Caenegem (ed.), Selden Society, lxxvii, London, 1959)

ST. GERMAN, C., *Doctor and Student* (London, 1523–30) (T. F. T. Plucknett and J. L. Barton (eds.), Selden Society xci, London, 1974)

SELDEN, J., *Mare Clausum* (1635); *Of the Dominion or Ownership of the Sea* (translated by Marchamont Nedham, London, 1652), reprinted in S. A. Moore. *A History of the Foreshore* (3rd edn., London, 1888)

Select Cases in the Court of King's Bench Vol. 6 (G. O. Sayles (ed.), Selden Society, lxxxii, London, 1965)

Select Cases in the Court of King's Bench Vol. 7 (G. O. Sayles (ed.), Selden Society, lxxxviii, London, 1971)

Select Cases in the Exchequer Chamber Vol. 2 (M. Hemmant (ed.), Selden Society, lxiv, London, 1948)

Select Cases of Trespass from the King's Courts 1307–1399 Vol. 1 (M. S. Arnold (ed.), Selden Society, c, London, 1985)

Select Cases of Trespass from the King's Courts 1307–1399 Vol. 2 (M. S. Arnold (ed.), Selden Society, ciii, London, 1987)

Spelman's Reports Vol. 2 (J. H. Baker (ed.), Selden Society, xciv, London, 1978)

John Spelman's Reading on Quo Warranto delivered in Gray's Inn (Lent 1519) (J. H. Baker (ed.), Selden Society, cxiii, London, 1997)

VINER, C., *General Abridgement of Law and Equity* 23 vols. (Aldershot, 1741–53; 2nd edn., London, 1794, with Supplement, 1806)

VINNIUS, A., *Institutionum Imperialium Commentarius* (Amsterdam, 1642)

VITRUVIUS, *De Architectura* (*On Architecture*) 2 vols. (F. Granger (ed. and trans.), London, 1934)

'Water', in *The Rees Cyclopedia*, xxxviii (London, 1819)

WEBSTER, T., *Reports and Notes of Cases on Letters Patent for Inventions* (London, 1844)

WOOD, T., *An Institute of the Laws of England* (London, 1720)

WOODDESSON, R., *A Systematical View of the Laws of England* 3 vols. (London, 1792–3; 2nd edn. with notes by W. R. Williams, London, 1834)

Year Books of Edward II (S. J. Stoljar and L. J. Downer (eds.), Selden Society, civ, London, 1988)

Year Books of Henry VIII, 12–14 Hen. VIII 1520–1523 (J. H. Baker (ed.), Selden Society, cix, London, 2002)

Year Books of Richard II: 6 Richard II (S. E. Thorne (ed.), C. Donahue Jr. (introd.), Ames Foundation, Cambridge, Mass., 1996)

II. TREATISE LITERATURE AFTER 1800 AND OTHER SECONDARY SOURCES

A. Unpublished Papers and Dissertations

DALTON, C., *Losing History: Tort Liability in the Nineteenth Century and the Case of Rylands v Fletcher* (MS., 1987, on deposit at Bodleian Law Library)

DAVID, P. A., 'Why Are Institutions the "Carriers of History"? Notes on Path-Dependence and the Evolution of Conventions, Organizations and Institutions' (Working paper, Stanford Institute for Theoretical Economics, 1992)

FISHER, W. W. III, *The Law of the Land: An Intellectual History of American Property Doctrine, 1776–1940* (MS., Harvard Law School, 1990)

KEDAR, A. J., 'History of Anglo-American Law of Light' (Harvard LL.M thesis, MS., 1990)

B. Books and Articles

ABBOTT, L. W., *Law Reporting in England, 1485–1585* (London, 1973)

ABRAHAM, D., 'Liberty and Property: Lord Bramwell and the Political Economy of Liberal Jurisprudence, Individualism; Freedom and Utility' (1994) 38 American Journal of Legal History 288

ACKERMAN, B. A. (ed.), *Economic Foundations of Property Law* (New Haven, Conn., 1975)

ADAMS, F., 'The Economical Use of Water as Affecting the Extent of Rights under the Doctrine of Prior Appropriation' (1913–14) 2 California Law Review 367

ADAMS, J. N., and AVERLY, G. A., *A Bibliography of 18th Century Legal Literature* (London, 1982)

ALCHIAN, A., 'The Property Rights Paradigm' (1973) 33 Journal of Economic History 16

ALLEN, R. C., *Enclosure and the Yeoman: The Agricultural Development of the South Midlands, 1450–1850* (Oxford, 1992)

ALSCHULER, A. W., 'Rediscovering Blackstone' (1996) 145 University of Pennsylvania Law Review 1

ANDERSON, J. S., 'Easement and Prescription—Changing Perspectives in Classification' (1975) 38 Modern Law Review 641

—— 'Land Law Texts and the Explanation of 1925' (1984) 37 Current Legal Problems 63

ANDERSON, T. L., and HILL, P. J., 'Privatizing the Commons: An Improvement?' (1985) 37 Stanford Law Review 1373

—— and —— 'The Race for Property Rights' (1990) 33 Journal of Law and Economics 177

ANGELL, J. K., *A Treatise on the Law of Watercourses* (1st edn., Boston, Mass., 1824; 3rd edn., Boston, Mass., 1840)

ANGELL, J. K., *An Inquiry into the Rule of Law Which Creates a Right to an Incorporeal Hereditament by an Adverse Enjoyment of Twenty Years with Remarks on the Application of the Rule to Light, and in Certain Cases to a Water Privilege* (Boston, Mass., 1827)

Anon., 'Water Rights in Roman Law' (1903) 20 South African Law Journal 266

—— 'Reasonable Use of Percolating Waters in the West' (1923–4) 37 Harvard Law Review 602

Arnold, M. S., 'Law and Fact in the Medieval Jury Trial: Out of Sight, Out of Mind' (1974) 18 American Journal of Legal History 267

—— 'Introduction' to *Select Cases of Trespass from the King's Courts 1307–1399, Vol. 1* (Selden Society, c, London, 1985)

——, GREEN, T. A., SCULLY, S. A., and WHITE, S. D. (eds.), *On the Laws and Customs of England. Essays in Honour of Samuel E. Thorne* (Chapel Hill, NC, 1981)

ASHTON, T. S., *The Industrial Revolution 1760–1830* (London, 1948, reprinted 1969)

ATIYAH, P. S., *The Rise and Fall of Freedom of Contract* (Oxford, 1979)

AULT, W. O., *Private Jurisdiction in England* (New Haven, Conn., 1923)

AUSNESS, R., 'Water Rights, The Public Trust Doctrine, and the Protection of Instream Uses' (1986) 2 University of Illinois Law Review 407

BAADE, H. W., 'Springs, Creeks, and Groundwater in Nineteenth-Century German Roman-Law Jurisprudence with a Twentieth Century Postscript', in D. S. Clark (ed.), *Comparative and Private International Law. Essays in Honour of John Henry Merryman on his Seventieth Birthday* (Berlin, 1990) 61

BAGSHAW, R., 'Inducing Breach of Contract', in J. Horder (ed.), *Oxford Essays in Jurisprudence, Fourth Series* (Oxford, 2000) 131

BAINBRIDGE, W., *A Treatise on the Law of Mines and Minerals* (1st edn., London, 1841; 2nd edn., London, 1856)

BAINES, E., *History of the Cotton Manufacture* (London, 1835; 2nd edn., London, 1966)

BAKER, J. H., 'Introduction' to *Spelman's Reports, Vol. 2*, (Selden Society, xciv, London, 1978) 1–346

—— (ed.), *Legal Records and the Historian* (London, 1978)

—— *The Legal Profession and The Common Law. Historical Essays* (London, 1986)

—— 'Records, Reports and the Origins of Case-Law in England' in J. H. Baker (ed.), *Judicial Records, Law Reports and the Growth of Case-Law* (London, 1989) 15

—— 'The Third University of England: The Inns of Court and the Common-Law Tradition' (Selden Society Lecture, London, 1990)

—— *The Law's Two Bodies. Some Evidential Problems in English Legal History* (Oxford, 2001)

—— *An Introduction to English Legal History* (4th edn., London, 2002)

—— and MILSOM, S. F. C., *Sources of English Legal History. Private Law to 1750* (London, 1986)

'Baron Bramwell at the End of the Twentieth Century' (Symposium) (1994) 38 American Journal of Legal History 241–373

BARRELL, J., *The Dark Side of the Landscape* (Cambridge, 1980)

BARTON, J. L., 'Bracton as Civilian' (1968) 42 Tulane Law Review 555

—— *Roman Law in England* (1971) Ius Romanum Medii Aevi, Pars V, 13a

—— '*Animus* and *possessio nomine alieno*', in P. B. H. Birks (ed.), *New Perspectives in the Roman Law of Property* (Oxford, 1989) 43

—— 'The Action on the Case', in J. L. Barton (ed.), *Towards a General Law of Contract* (Berlin, 1990) 39

—— 'The Medieval Contract', in J. L. Barton (ed.), *Towards a General Law of Contract* (Berlin, 1990) 15

—— 'The Mystery of Bracton' (1994) 14 Journal of Legal History 1

BARZEL, Y., *Economic Analysis of Property Rights* (Cambridge, 1989; 2nd edn., Cambridge, 1997)

BASALLE, G., *The Evolution of Technology* (Cambridge, 1988)

BAUMAN, R. A., *Lawyers in Roman Republican Politics: A Study of the Roman Jurists in their Political Setting, 316–82 BC* (Munich, 1983)

BECKERMAN, J. S., 'Adding Insult to *Iniuria*: Affronts to Honor and the Origins of Trespass', in M. S. Arnold, T. A. Green, S. A. Scully, and S. D. White (eds.), *On the Laws and Customs of England* (Chapel Hill, NC, 1981) 159

—— 'Procedural Innovation and Institutional Change in Medieval English Manorial Courts' (1992) 10 Law and History Review 197

BENNETT, R., and ELTON, J., *History of Cornmilling* 4 vols. (London, 1898–1904; reprinted East Ardsley, 1973)

BENVENISTI, E., 'Collective Action in the Utilization of Shared Freshwater: The Challenges of International Water Resources Law' (1996) 90 American Journal of International Law 384

BERG, M., *The Machinery Question and the Making of Political Economy, 1815–1848* (Cambridge, 1980)

—— *The Age of Manufactures 1700–1820: Industry, Innovation, and Work in Britain* (2nd edn., London, 1994)

—— and BRULAND, K. (eds.), *Technological Revolutions in Europe: Historical Perspectives* (Cheltenham, 1998)

—— and HUDSON, P., 'Rehabilitating the Industrial Revolution' (1992) 45 Economic History Review 24

BESLEY, T., 'Investment Incentives and Property Rights', in *The New Palgrave Dictionary of Economics and the Law* 3 vols. (P. Newman (ed.), London, 1998) ii, 359

BEZANSON, A., 'The Early Uses of the Term Industrial Revolution' (1921–22) 36 Quarterly Journal of Economics 343

BIANCALANA, J., 'Medieval County Courts: A Review Essay' (1983) 52 University of Cincinnati Law Review 994

BIANCALANA, J., 'For Want of Justice: Legal Reforms of Henry II' (1988) 88 Columbia Law Review 433

—— 'Actions of Covenant 1200–1330' (2002) 20 Law and History Review 1

BINNIE, G. M., *Early Victorian Water Engineers* (London, 1981)

BIRKS, P. B. H., 'The Roman Law Concept of *Dominium* and the Idea of Absolute Ownership' [1985] Acta Juridica 1

—— (ed.), *New Perspectives in the Roman Law of Property: Essays for Barry Nicholas* (Oxford, 1989)

—— and MACCORMICK, N. (eds.), *The Legal Mind: Essays in Honour of Tony Honoré* (Oxford, 1986)

—— and MCLEOD, G., 'Introduction' to *Justinian's Institutes* (London, 1987)

BLAKE, W., *The Complete Poems* (W. H. Stevenson (ed.), London, 1972)

BLOCH, M., *Feudal Society* 2 vols. (Paris, 1940;. L. A. Manyon (trans), London, 1961)

—— 'The Advent and Triumph of the Watermill', in M. Bloch, *Land and Work in Mediaeval Europe: Selected Papers by Marc Bloch* (J. E. Anderson (trans.), London, 1967) 136

—— *Land and Work in Mediaeval Europe: Selected Papers by Marc Bloch* (J. E. Anderson (trans.), London, 1967)

—— 'Medieval "Inventions" ', in M. Bloch, *Land and Work in Mediaeval Europe: Selected Papers by Marc Bloch* (J. E. Anderson (trans.), London, 1967) 169

—— 'Technical Change as a Problem of Collective Psychology', in M. Bloch, *Land and Work in Mediaeval Europe: Selected Papers by Marc Bloch* (J. E. Anderson (trans.), London, 1967) 124

BLUM, J., *The End of the Old Order in Rural Europe* (Princeton, N.J., 1990)

BOHLEN, F., 'The Rule in Rylands v Fletcher', Parts 1–3 (1911) 59 University of Pennsylvania Law Review 298, 373, 423, reprinted in F. Bohlen, *Studies in the Law of Torts* (Indianapolis, Ind., 1926) 344

—— 'Incomplete Privilege to Inflict Intentional Invasions of Interests of Property and Personality' (1926) 39 Harvard Law Review 307, reprinted in F. Bohlen, *Studies in the Law of Torts* (Indianapolis, Ind., 1926) 614

BOND, M. F., *The Private Bill Records of the House of Lords* (H.L.R.O., London, 1957)

—— *Materials for Transport History amongst the Records of Parliament* (1959) 4 Journal of Transport History 37

—— *Guide to the Records of Parliament* (H.M.S.O., London, 1971)

BONE, R. G., 'Normative Theory and Legal Doctrine in American Nuisance Law: 1850 to 1920' (1986) 59 South California Law Review 1101

BORDWELL, P., 'Ejectment takes Over' (1970) 55 Iowa Law Review 1089

BOYLE, J. (ed.), *The Public Domain (Symposium)* (2003) 66 Law and Contemporary Problems 1–483

Brand, P., *The Making of the Common Law* (London, 1993)

—— ' "Multis Vigiliis Excogitatam et Inventam": Henry II and the Creation of the English Common Law', in P. Brand, *The Making of the Common Law* (London, 1993) 77

—— 'The Origins of English Land Law: Milsom and After', in P. Brand, *The Making of the Common Law* (London, 1993) 203

—— '"Quo Warranto" Law in the Reign of Edward I: A Hitherto Undiscovered Opinion of Chief Justice Hengham' in P. Brand, *The Making of the Common Law* (London, 1993) 393

BRENNER, J. F., 'Nuisance Law and the Industrial Revolution' (1973) 3 Journal of Legal Studies 403

BRETT, P., 'The Right to Take Flowing Water' (1950) 14 The Conveyancer 154

BREWER, J., and STAVES, S., *Early Modern Conceptions of Property* (London, 1995)

BRION, D. J., 'The Common Law of Waterpower in New England' (1980) 5 Vanderbilt Law Review 201

BRISTOWE, S. B., *Private Bill Legislation* (London, 1859)

BROWN, E. A. R., 'The Tyranny of a Construct: Feudalism and Historians of Medieval Europe' (1974) 79 American Historical Review 1063

BROWNE, J. H. B., *The Law of Usages and Customs* (London, 1875)

BRUUN, C., *The Water Supply of Ancient Rome: A Study in Imperial Administration* (Helsinki, 1991)

BRYSON, W. H., 'Law Reports in England from 1603 to 1660', in C. Stebbings (ed.), *Law Reporting in England* (London, 1995) 113

BUCKLAND, W. W., *Elementary Principles of the Roman Private Law* (Cambridge, 1912)

—— 'Interpolations in the Digest' (1923–24) 33 Yale Law Journal 343

—— 'The Conception of Servitudes in Roman Law' (1928) 44 Law Quarterly Review 426

—— 'The Protection of Servitudes in Roman Law' (1930) 46 Law Quarterly Review 447

—— *Main Institutions of Roman Private Law* (London, 1931)

—— *Manual of Roman Private Law* (2nd edn., London, 1939)

—— *A Textbook of Roman Law from Augustus to Justinian* (3rd edn., revised P. G. Stein, Cambridge, 1963)

BULLEN, E., and LEAKE, S. M., *Precedents of Pleading in the Superior Courts of Common Law* (1st edn., London, 1860; 3rd edn., London, 1868)

BURNS, R. P., 'Blackstone's Theory of the "Absolute" Rights of Property' (1985) 54 University of Cincinnati Law Review 67

BURTON, W. H., *An Elementary Compendium of the Law of Real Property* (1st edn., London, 1828)

BUTLER, L. L., 'Allocating Consumptive Water Rights in a Riparian Jurisdiction: Defining the Relationship Between Public and Private Interests' (1985) 47 University of Pittsburgh Law Review 95

BUTZER, K., *Early Hydraulic Civilization in Egypt* (Chicago, Ill., 1976)

CAENEGEM, R. C., VAN *The Birth of the English Common Law* (2nd edn., Cambridge, 1985)

CAIN, P. J., and HOPKINS, A. G., 'Gentlemanly Capitalism and British Expansion Overseas' (1986) 39 Economic History Review 501 and (1987) 40 Economic History Review 1

CAIN, P. J., and HOPKINS, A. G., *British Imperialism: Innovation and Expansion, 1688–1914* (London, 1993)

CAIRNS, J. W., 'Blackstone, An English Institutist: Legal Literature and the Rise of the Nation State' (1984) 4 Oxford Journal of Legal Studies 318

—— 'Craig, Cujas, and the Definition of *feodum*: Is a Feu a Usufruct?', in P. B. H. Birks (ed.), *New Perspectives in the Roman Law of Property* (Oxford, 1989) 76

CALABRESI, G., and MELAMED, A. D., 'Property Rules, Liability Rules, and Inalienability Rules: One View of the Cathedral' (1972) 85 Harvard Law Review 1089

CANNADINE, D., 'The Present and the Past in the English Industrial Revolution 1880–1980' (1984) 103 Past and Present 131

CARUS-WILSON, E. M., 'An Industrial Revolution of the Thirteenth Century' (1941) 11 Economic History Review 1, reprinted in E. M. Carus-Wilson, *Essays in Economic History I* (London, 1954) 41

—— (ed.), *Essays in Economic History* 3 vols. (London, 1954–1962)

Cases Relating to Railways and Canals 1835–54 7 vols. (London, 1840–55)

CHAPMAN, S. D., *The Early Factory Masters: The Transition to the Factory System in the Midlands Textile Industry* (London, 1967, reissued Aldershot, 1992)

—— 'The Cost of Power in the Industrial Revolution in England: The Case of the Textile Industry' (1971) 1 Midland History 8

—— *The Cotton Industry in the Industrial Revolution* (2nd edn., Basingstoke, 1987) reprinted in L. A. Clarkson (ed.), *The Industrial Revolution: A Compendium* (Basingstoke, 1990) 1–64

—— *Merchant Enterprise in Britain: From the Industrial Revolution to World War One* (London, 1992)

CHENEY, M., '*Possessio/proprietas* in Ecclesiastical Courts in Mid-Twelfth-Century England', in G. Garnett and J. Hudson (eds.), *Law and Government in Medieval England and Normandy. Essays in Honour of Sir James Holt* (Cambridge, 1994) 245

CHESTER, A. C., COLEMAN-NORTON, P. R., and BOURNE, F. C. (eds.), *Ancient Roman Statutes* (Austin, Texas, 1961)

CHEUNG, S. N. S., 'The Structure of a Contract and the Theory of a Non-Exclusive Resource' (1970) 13 Journal of Law and Economics 49

—— 'Common Property Rights', in *The New Palgrave: A Dictionary of Economics* 4 vols. (J. Eatwell, M. Milgate, and P. Newman (eds.), London, 1987) i, 504

CHEW, H. M., and KELLAWAY, W. (eds.), *The London Assize of Nuisance, 1301–1431* (London, 1973)

CLANCHY, M. T., *From Memory to Written Record: England 1066–1307* (2nd edn., London, 1993)

CLARK, G., 'Agriculture and the Industrial Revolution, 1700–1850' in Mokyr, J. (ed.), *The British Industrial Revolution: An Economic Perspective* (Boulder, Col., 1993) 227–66

—— 'Factory Discipline' (1994) 54 Journal of Economic History 128

CLARK, G. N., *The Later Stuarts, 1660–1714* (Oxford, 1934)

CLARKSON, L. A. (ed.), *The Industrial Revolution: A Compendium* (Basingstoke, 1990)

—— *Proto-Industrialization: The First Phase of Industrialization* (Basingstoke, 1985), reprinted in L. A. Clarkson (ed.), *The Industrial Revolution: A Compendium* (Basingstoke, 1990) 149

CLAYBERG, J. B., 'The Law of Percolating Waters' (1915–16) 14 Michigan Law Review 119

CLAYRE, A., *Nature and Industrialization* (Oxford, 1977)

CLIFFORD, F., *A History of Private Bill Legislation* 2 vols. (London, 1885–7)

COASE, R. H., 'The Problem of Social Cost' (1960) 3 Journal of Law and Economics 1

—— *The Firm, the Market and the Law* (Chicago, Ill., 1988)

—— 'The Institutional Structure of Production', in R. H. Coase, *Essays on Economics and Economists* (Chicago, Ill., 1994) 3

COBBETT, W., *The Law of Turnpikes* (London, 1824)

Code Civil, in J.-B. J. Pailliet, *Manuel de Droit Français* 2 vols. (Paris, 1837)

COHEN, G. A., 'Self-Ownership, World-Ownership, and Equality: Part II' (1986) 3 Social Philosophy and Policy 77, reprinted in G. A. Cohen, *Self-ownership, Freedom, and Equality* (Cambridge, 1995), 77

COLLINS, H., *Marxism and Law* (Oxford, 1982)

COOKE, G. W., *The Acts for Facilitating the Inclosure of Commons in England and Wales, With a Treatise on the Law of Rights of Common* (3rd edn., London, 1856)

COOTER, R., 'The Cost of Coase' (1982) 11 Journal of Legal Studies 1

COQUILLETTE, D. R., 'Mosses from an Old Manse: Another Look At Some Historic Property Cases About the Environment' (1979) 64 Cornell Law Review 761

CORNISH, W. R., *The Jury* (London, 1968)

—— and CLARK, G. DE N., *Law and Society in England 1750–1950* (London, 1989)

CORRÉ, J. I., 'The Argument, Decision, and Reports of *Darcy v. Allen*' (1996) 45 Emory Law Journal 1261

COSTELLO, L., *Profits à Prendre to Mineral Rights: The Evolution of Remedies in English Law* (Unpublished M.Phil thesis, University of Exeter, 1984)

COULSON, H. J. W., and FORBES, U. A., *The Law Relating to Waters, Sea, Tidal and Inland, and Land Drainage* (6th edn., London, by S. R. Hobday, 1952)

—— and ——, *The Law Relating to Waters, Sea, Tidal, and Inland* (1st edn., London, 1880)

CRAFTS, N. F. R., *British Economic Growth During the Industrial Revolution* (Oxford, 1985)

—— and HARLEY, C. K., 'Output Growth and the Industrial Revolution: A Restatement of the Crafts-Harley View' (1992) 45 Economic History Review 703

DAGAN, H., and HELLER, M. A., 'The Liberal Commons' (2001) 110 Yale Law Journal 549

DANIELL, E. R., *A Treatise on the Practice of the High Court of Chancery, with some Practical Observations on the Pleadings of that Court* (London, 1837)
DANIELS, G. W., *The Early English Cotton Industry* (London, 1920)
DAUBE, D., 'Slightly Different' (1961) 12 Iura 81
DAUNTON, M. J., 'Gentlemanly Capitalism and British Industry 1820–1914' (1989) 122 Past and Present 119
—— *Progress and Poverty. An Economic and Social History of Britain 1700–1850* (Oxford, 1995)
DAVIS, P. N., 'Wells and Springs: Relationship at Law' (1972) 37 Missouri Law Review 189
DAWSON, J. P., 'The Codification of the French Customs' (1940) 39 Michigan Law Review 780
—— *A History of Lay Judges* (Cambridge, Mass., 1962)
—— *The Oracles of the Law* (Ann Arbor, Mich., 1968)
DEANE, P., *The First Industrial Nation* (Cambridge, 1965)
—— and COLE, W. H., *British Economic Growth 1688–1959* (2nd edn., Cambridge, 1967)
DEMSETZ, H., 'Towards a Theory of Property Rights' (1967) 55 American Economic Review 347
—— ' Property Rights', in *The New Palgrave Dictionary of Economics and the Law* 3 vols. (P. Newman (ed.), London, 1998), iii, 144
DERHAM, D. P., 'Interference with Surface Waters by Lower Landholders' (1958) 74 Law Quarterly Review 361
DERWENT VALLEY MILLS PARTNERSHIP, *The Derwent Valley Mills and their Communities* (Derby, 2001)
DEVENEY, P., 'Title, Jus Publicum, and the Public Trust: An Historical Analysis' (1976) 1 Sea Grant Law Journal 13
DIAMOND, J., *Guns, Germs and Steel: The Fates of Human Societies* (New York, 1997)
DICEY, A. V., *An Introduction to the Study of the Law of the Constitution* (1st edn., London, 1885; 10th edn., London, 1959)
—— *Lectures on the Relation Between Law and Public Opinion in England During the Nineteenth Century* (London, 1905)
DIGBY, K. E., *An Introduction to the History of the Law of Real Property with Original Authorities* (1st edn., 1875; 5th edn., Oxford, 1897)
DIOSDI, G., *Ownership in Ancient and Preclassical Roman Law* (Budapest, 1970)
DOCKRAY, M., 'Savigny and the Squatter' (1985) 6 Journal of Legal History 109
DONAHUE C. Jr., 'Ius Commune in England' (1992) 66 Tulane Law Review 1745
—— KEEPER, T. E., and MARTIN, P. W., *Property: An Introduction to the Concept and the Institution. Cases and Materials* (3rd edn., St. Paul, Minn., 1993)
DUBOIS, A. B., *The English Business Company After the Bubble Act 1720–1800* (New York, 1938)

DUBOIS, F., 'Water Rights and the Limits of Environmental Law' (1994) 6 Journal of Environmental Law 73

DUMAN, D., *The Judicial Bench in England, 1727–1875: The Reshaping of a Professional Elite* (London, 1982)

DURKHEIM, E., 'The Nature and Origins of Property', from *Professional Ethics and Civic Morals* (C. Brookfield (trans.), London, 1957), reprinted in S. Lukes and A. T. Scull (eds.), *Durkheim and the Law (Selected Writings of Durkheim on Law)* (Oxford, 1983) 158

DUXBURY, N., *Jurists and Judges: An Essay on Influence* (Oxford, 2001)

EGGERTSSON, T., *Economic Behaviour and Institutions* (Cambridge, 1990)

ELLICKSON, R. C., *Order Without Law: How Neighbours Settle Disputes* (Cambridge, Mass., 1991)

—— 'Property in Land' (1993) 102 Yale Law Journal 1315

—— and DIARCINO-THORLAND, C. E., 'Ancient Land Law: Mesopotamia, Egypt and Israel' (1995) 71 Chicago-Kent Law Review 321

—— ROSE, C. M., and ACKERMAN, B. A., *Perspectives on Property Law* (3rd edn., New York, 2002)

EPSTEIN, R. A., 'Nuisance Law: Corrective Justice and its Utilitarian Constraints' (1979) 8 Journal of Legal Studies 49

—— 'Possession as the Root of Title' (1979) 13 Georgia Law Review 1221, reprinted in R. A. Epstein (ed.), *Liberty, Property, and the Law, Vol. III: Private and Common Property* (New York, 2000) 175

—— 'The Social Consequences of Common Law Rules' (1982) 95 Harvard Law Review 1717

—— *Takings: Private Property and the Power of Eminent Domain* (Cambridge, Mass., 1985)

—— 'Why Restrain Alienation?' (1985) 85 Columbia Law Review 970

—— 'Past and Future: The Temporal Dimension in the Law of Property' (1986) 64 Washington University Law Quarterly 667

—— 'The Public Trust Doctrine' (1987) 7 Cato Journal 411

—— 'For a Bramwell Revival' (1994) 38 American Journal of Legal History 246

—— 'On the Optimal Mix of Private and Common Property' (1994) 11 Social Philosophy and Policy 17, reprinted in R. A. Epstein (ed.), *Liberty, Property, and the Law, Vol. III: Private and Common Property* (New York, 2000) 357

—— 'Possession', in *The New Palgrave Dictionary of Economics and the Law* 3 vols. (P. Newman (ed.), London, 1998) ii, 62

—— 'Takings', in *The New Palgrave Dictionary of Economics and the Law* 3 vols. (P. Newman (ed.), London, 1998), iii, 561

EVANS-JONES, R., and MACCORMACK, G. D., '*Iusta causa traditionis*', in P. B. H. Birks (ed.), *New Perspectives in the Roman Law of Property* (Oxford, 1989) 99

FAIRFIELD, C., *Some Account of George William Wilshere Baron Bramwell of Hever and his Opinions (A Memoir of Lord Bramwell)* (London, 1898)

FAIRMAN, C., 'The So-called Granger Cases, Lord Hale, and Justice Bradley' (1953) 5 Stanford Law Review 587

FARNHAM, H., *Waters and Water Rights* (Boston, Mass., 1904)

FEENSTRA, R., '*Dominium* and *ius in re aliena*: The Origins of a Civil Law Distinction', in P. B. H. Birks (ed.), *New Perspectives in the Roman Law of Property* (Oxford, 1989) 111

FERGUSON, R. B., 'The Horwitz Thesis and Common Law Discourse in England' (1983) 3 Oxford Journal of Legal Studies 34

FIELD, A. J., 'Do Legal Systems Matter?' (1991) 28 Explorations in Economic History 1

FIFOOT, C. H. S., *Lord Mansfield* (London, 1936)

—— *History and Sources of the Common Law: Tort and Contract* (London, 1949)

—— *Judge and Jurist in the Reign of Queen Victoria* (London, 1959)

FINCH, W. C., *Watermills and Windmills, a historical survey of their rise, decline and fall as portrayed by those of Kent* (London, 1933)

FINLEY, M. I., *The Ancient Economy* (London, 1973)

—— 'Technical Innovation and Economic Progress in the Ancient World' (1965) 18 Economic History Review 29, reprinted in M. I. Finley, *Economy and Society in Ancient Greece* (London, 1981) 176

FISHER, T. A., 'The Winter of Our Discontent: Federal Reserved Water Rights in Western States' (1984) 69 Cornell Law Review 1077

FITTON, R. S., *The Arkwrights: Spinnners of Fortune* (Manchester, 1989)

—— and WADSWORTH, A. P., *The Strutts and the Arkwrights 1758–1830. A Study of the Early Factory System* (Manchester, 1958)

FLOUD, R., and JOHNSON, P., (eds.), *The Cambridge Economic History of Modern Britain* (Cambridge, 2004)

FLOUD, R., and MCCLOSKEY, D. N. (eds.), *The Economic History of Britain Since 1700, Vol. 1 1700–1860* (1st edn., Cambridge, 1981)

—— and —— (eds.), *The Economic History of Britain Since 1700, Vol. 1 1700–1860* (2nd edn., Cambridge, 1994)

FOREMAN-PECK, J., and MILLWARD, R., *Public and Private Ownership of British Industry 1820–1900)* (Oxford, 1994)

FORSYTH, W., *History of Trial By Jury* (London, 1852)

FOWLER, D. B., *The Practice of the Court of Exchequer upon Proceedings in Equity* (2nd edn., London, 1817)

French Civil Code (J. H. Crabb (trans.), South Hackensack, NJ, 1977)

FREYFOGLE, E. T., 'Water Justice' [1986] 2 University of Illinois Law Review 481

—— 'Water Rights and the Common Wealth' [1996] Environmental Law 27

FRIDMAN, G. H. L., 'Motive in the English Law of Nuisance' (1954) 40 Virginia Law Review 583

FRIEDMAN, L., *Contract Law in America: A Social and Economic Case Study* (Madison, Wis., 1965)

—— *A History of American Law* (2nd edn., New York, 1985)

—— 'Losing One's Head: Judges and the Law in Nineteenth-Century American Legal History' (1999) 24 Law and Social Inquiry 253

FRIER, B., *The Rise of the Roman Jurists* (Princeton, NJ, 1985)

FULLER, L. L., 'Irrigation and Tyranny' (1965) 17 Stanford Law Review 1021

—— 'The Forms and Limits of Adjudication' (1978) 92 Harvard Law Review 353

FUROBOTN, E. G., and RICHTER, R., *Institutions and Economic Theory: The Contribution of the New Institutional Economics* (Ann Arbor, Mich., 1998)

GAFFNEY, M., 'Economic Aspects of Water Resource Policy' (1969) 28 American Journal of Economics and Sociology 131

GALE, C. J., *A Treatise on the Law of Easements* (1st edn., with T. D. Whatley, London, 1839; 2nd edn., London, 1849; 3rd edn. by W. H. Willes, London, 1862; 4th edn. by D. Gibbons, London, 1868; 5th edn., London, 1876; 6th edn. by G. Cave, London, 1888; 7th edn. by G. Cave, London, 1899; 15th edn. by S. G. Maurice, London, 1986; 16th edn. by J. Gaunt and P. Morgan, London, 1997)

GARNETT, G., 'The Origins of the Crown', in J. Hudson (ed.), *The History of English Law: Centenary Essays on 'Pollock and Maitland'* (Proceedings of the British Academy 89, Oxford, 1996) 171

—— and HUDSON, J. (eds.), *Law and Government in Medieval England and Normandy. Essays in Honour of Sir James Holt* (Cambridge, 1994)

GELLNER, E., 'The Economic Interpretation of History', in *The New Palgrave: A Dictionary of Economics* 4 vols. (J. Eatwell, M. Milgate, and P. Newman (eds.), London, 1987) ii, 47

GEORGE, L. W., 'Public Rights in West Virginia Watercourses: A Unique Legacy of Virginia Common Lands and the Jus Publicum of the English Crown' (1998) 101 West Virginia Law Review 407

GETZLER, J., 'Theories of Property and Economic Development,' (1996) 26 Journal of Interdisciplinary History 639

—— 'Judges and Hunters: Law and Economic Conflict in the English Countryside, 1800–1860' in C. Brooks and M. Lobban (eds.), *Communities and Courts* (London, 1997) 199

—— 'Patterns of Fusion', in P. B. H. Birks (ed.), *The Classification of Obligations* (Oxford, 1997) 157

—— 'Roman Ideas of Landownership', in J. Dewar and S. Bright (eds.), *Law and Land: Themes and Perspectives* (Oxford, 1998) 81

—— 'Duty of Care', in P. B. H. Birks and A. Pretto (eds.), *Breach of Trust* (Oxford, 2002) 41

—— 'The Fate of the Civil Jury in Late Victorian England: Malicious Prosecution as a Test Case', in G. R. Rubin and K. O'Donovan (eds.), *Human Rights and Legal History: Essays for Brian Simpson* (Oxford, 2000) 205; reprinted in J. W. Cairns and G. McLeod (eds.), *'The Dearest Birth Right of the People of England': The Jury in the History of the Common Law* (Oxford, 2002) 217

GETZLER, J., 'Roman and English Prescription for Incorporeal Property', in J. Getzler (ed.), *Rationalizing Property, Equity and Trusts: Essays in Honour of Edward Burn* (London, 2003) 281

GIBBONS, D., *A Treatise on the Law of Dilapidations and Nuisances* (London, 1849)

GIES, F., and GIES, J., *Cathedral, Forge, and Waterwheel: Technology and Invention in the Middle Ages* (New York, 1994)

GILMORE, G., *The Death of Contract* (Columbus, Ohio, 1974)

—— 'From Tort to Contract: Industrialization and the Law', Review of M. J. Horwitz, *The Transformation of American Law 1780–1860*, (1977) 86 Yale Law Journal 788

GIMPEL, J., *The Medieval Machine: The Industrial Revolution in the Middle Ages* (London, 1977, reissued 1992)

GODDARD, J. L., *A Treatise on the Law of Easements* (1st edn., London, 1871, 2nd edn., 1877; 3rd edn., 1884; 4th edn., 1891; 5th edn., 1896; 9th edn., 1921)

GOODHART, A. L., 'Liability for Things Naturally on the Land' [1930–32] Cambridge Law Journal 13

GOODIN, R., 'Theories of Compensation' (1989) 9 Oxford Journal of Legal Studies 56

GOODMAN, M. J., 'Adverse Possession or Prescription? Problems of Conflict' (1968) 32 Conveyancer 270

GORDLEY, J., 'Water Rights' in J. A. R. Nafziger and S. C. Symeonides (eds.), *Law and Justice in a Multistate World: Essays in Honour of Arthur T. von Mehren* (Ardsley, NY, 2002) 683

—— 'The Origin of Riparian Rights', in P. Birks and A. Pretto (eds.), *Themes in Comparative Law in Honour of Bernard Rudden* (Oxford, 2002) 107

GORDON, R. B., 'Cost and Use of Water Power during Industrialization in New England and Great Britain: A Geological Interpretation' (1983) 36 Economic History Review, 2nd Ser., 240

—— ' "Factory Discipline" during Industrialization in New England and Great Britain: A Geological Interpretation' (1983) 36 Economic History Review 240

GORDON, R. W., 'Historicism in Legal Scholarship' (1981) 90 Yale Law Journal 1017

—— 'Critical Legal Histories' (1984) 36 Stanford Law Review 57

—— 'Paradoxical Property', in J. Brewer and S. Staves (eds.), *Early Modern Conceptions of Property* (London, 1995) 95

—— 'Morton Horwitz and his Critics: A Conflict of Narratives' (2002) 37 Tulsa Law Review 915

GORDON, W. M., 'The Importance of the *iusta causa of traditio*', in P. B. H. Birks (ed.), *New Perspectives in the Roman Law of Property* (Oxford, 1989) 123

GOUBERT, J.-P., *The Conquest of Water: The Advent of Health in the Industrial Age* (Oxford, 1989)

GOULD, G. A., 'Transfer of Water Rights' (1980) 29 Natural Resources Journal 457

GOULD, J. M., *A Treatise on the Law of Waters, including Riparian Rights* (1st edn., Chicago, Ill., 1883)

GRAZIADEI, M., 'Changing Images of the Law in XIX Century English Legal Thought (The Continental Impulse)', in M. Reimann (ed.), *The Reception of Continental Ideas in the Common Law World 1820–1920* (Berlin, 1993) 115

GREENBERG, D., 'Reassessing the Power Patterns of the Industrial Revolution: An Anglo-American Comparison' (1982) 87 American Historical Review 1237

—— 'Energy, Power, and Perceptions of Social Change in the Early Nineteenth Century' (1990) 95 American Historical Review 693

GÜTERBOCK, C., *Bracton and His Relation to English Law: a contribution to the history of the Roman law in the middle ages* (Berlin, 1862, B. Coxe (trans.), Philadelphia, Penn., 1866)

HABBAKKUK, H. J., *American and British Technology in the Nineteenth Century: The Search for Labour Saving Inventions* (Cambridge, 1962)

HALL, B., 'Lynn White's *Medieval Technology and Social Change* After Thirty Years' in R. Fox (ed.), *Technological Change: Methods and Themes in the History of Technology* (Amsterdam, 1996) 85

HALL., K., *The Magic Mirror: Law in American History* (New York, 1989)

HAMBURGER, P. A., 'Revolution and Judicial Review: Chief Justice Holt's Opinion in City of London v. Wood' (1994) 94 Columbia Law Review 2091

HARDIN, G., 'The Tragedy of the Commons' (1968) 162 Science 1243

HARLEY, C. K., 'Reassessing the Industrial Revolution: A Macro View', in J. Mokyr (ed.), *The British Industrial Revolution: An Economic Perspective* (Boulder, Col., 1993) 171

HARRIS, J. W., 'Ownership of Land in English Law', in P. B. H. Birks and N. MacCormick (eds.), *The Legal Mind: Essays in Honour of Tony Honoré* (Oxford, 1986)

—— 'Private and Non-Private Property' (1995) 111 Law Quarterly Review 421

—— *Property and Justice* (Oxford, 1996)

HARRIS, R., *Industrializing English Law: Entrepreneurship and Business Organization, 1720–1844* (Cambridge, 2000)

—— 'Government and the Economy' in R. Floud and P. Johnson (eds.), *The Cambridge Economic History of Modern Britain* (Cambridge, 2004) i, 204–37.

HART, H. L. A., 'Blackstone's Use of the Law of Nature' (1956) 3 Butterworth's South African Law Review 169

—— 'Diamonds and String: Holmes and the Common Law' in *Essays in Jurisprudence and Philosophy* (Oxford, 1983) 278

HART, J. F., 'The Maryland Mill Act, 1669–1766: Economic Policy and the Confiscatory Redistribution of Private Property' (1995) 39 American Journal of Legal History 1

—— 'Property Rights, Costs, and Welfare: Delaware Water Mill Legislation, 1719–1859' (1998) 27 Journal of Legal Studies 455

HARTWELL, R. M., *The Industrial Revolution and Economic Growth* (London, 1971)

—— 'Was There an Industrial Revolution?' (1990) 14 Social Science History 567

HARVEY, D., *The Limits to Capital* (Oxford, 1982)

HASSAN, J. A., 'The Growth and Impact of the British Water Industry in the Nineteenth Century' (1985) 38 Economic History Review 531

—— *A History of Water in Modern England and Wales* (Manchester, 1998)

HAWKE, G. R., and HIGGINS, J. P. P., 'Transport and Social Overhead Capital', in R. Floud and D. N. McCloskey (eds.), *The Economic History of Britain Since 1700, Vol. 1, 1700–1860* (Cambridge, 1981) 227

HAZELTINE, H. D., 'The Renaissance and the Laws of Europe', in G. G. Alexander (ed.), *Cambridge Legal Essays* (Cambridge, 1926) 139

HEARNSHAW, J. C., *Leet Jurisdiction in England* (Southampton, 1908)

HEDLEY, S, 'Words, Words, Words: Making Sense of Legal Judgements, 1875–1940', in C. Stebbings (ed.), *Law Reporting in Britain* (London, 1995) 169

HELMHOLZ, R. H., 'Continental Law and Common Law: Historical Strangers or Companions?' [1990] Duke Law Journal 1207

—— 'Use of the Civil Law in Post-Revolutionary American Jurisprudence' (1992) 66 Tulane Law Review 1649

—— 'Magna Carta and the Ius Commune' (1999) 66 University of Chicago Law Review 297

—— *The Ius Commune in England: Four Studies* (Oxford, 2001)

HERBERT, T. A., *The History of the Law of Prescription in England* (London, 1880)

HERSCHEL, C., *The Two Books of the Water Supply of the City of Rome of Sextus Julius Frontinus* (Boston, Mass., 1879)

HESS, C., and OSTROM, E., 'Ideas, Artifacts, and Facilities: Information as a Common-Pool Resource' (2003) 66 Law and Contemporary Problems 111

HEWISH, J., 'From Cromford to Chancery Lane: New Light on the Arkwright Patent Trials' (1987) 28 Technology and Culture 80

HILL, C., *Intellectual Origins of the English Revolution* (Oxford, 1965)

HILLS, R. L., *Power in the Industrial Revolution* (Manchester, 1970)

HOEFLICH, M. H., *Roman and Civil Law and the Development of Anglo-American Jurisprudence in the Nineteenth Century* (Athens, Ga., 1997)

HOHFELD, W. N., *Fundamental Legal Conceptions as Applied in Judicial Reasoning* (New Haven, Conn., 1919)

HOLDSWORTH, W. S., *A History of English Law* 13 vols. (London, 1922–52)

—— *An Historical Introduction to the Land Law* (Oxford, 1927)

HOLMES, O. W. Jr., 'Possession' (1878) 12 American Law Review 688, reprinted in *The Formative Essays of Justice Holmes: The Making of an American Legal Philosophy*, ed. F. R. Kellogg (Westport, Conn., 1984)

—— *The Common Law* (Boston, Mass., 1881; ed. M. De Howe, Boston, Mass., 1963)

—— 'Privilege, Malice and Intent' (1894) 8 Harvard Law Review 1

HOLT, J. C., '1086', in J. C. Holt, *Colonial England 1066–1215* (London, 1997) 31

—— 'Politics and Property in Early Medieval England', in J. C. Holt, *Colonial England 1066–1215* (London, 1997)

HOLT, R., 'Whose Were the Profits of Corn Milling? An Aspect of the Changing Relationship Between the Abbotts of Glastonbury and their Tenants 1086–1350' (1987) 116 Past and Present 3

—— *The Mills of Medieval England* (Oxford, 1988)

—— 'Medieval Technology and the Historians: The Evidence of the Mill', in R. Fox (ed.), *Technological Change: Methods and Themes in the History of Technology* (Amsterdam, 1996) 103

HOLT, W., 'Morton Horwitz and the Transformation of American Legal History' (1982) 23 William and Mary Law Review 663

HOLWAY, H., *The Story of Water Supply* (New York and London, 1929)

HONORÉ, T., 'Ownership', in A. G. Guest (ed.), *Oxford Essays in Jurisprudence* (Oxford, 1961), 107, reprinted in T. Honoré, *Making Law Bind: Essays Legal and Philosophical* (Oxford, 1987)

—— *Gaius* (London, 1962)

HOPPIT, J., 'Counting the Industrial Revolution,' (1990) 43 Economic History Review 173

—— (ed.), *Failed Legislation, 1660–1800, Extracted from the Commons and Lords Journals* (introd. by J. Hoppit and J. Innes, London, 1997)

—— and WRIGLEY, E. A. (ed.), *The Industrial Revolution in Britain* 2 vols. (Oxford, 1994)

HORAK, F., *Rationes decidendi: Entscheidungsbegründungen bei den älteren römischen Juristen bis Labeo Vol. I* (Aalen, 1969)

HORDEN, P., and PURCELL, N., *The Corrupting Sea: A Study of Mediterranean History* (Oxford, 2000)

HORWITZ, M. J., 'The Legacy of 1776 in Legal and Economic Thought' (1976) 19 Journal of Law and Economics 621

—— *The Transformation of American Law 1780–1860* (Cambridge, Mass., 1977)

—— *The Transformation of American Law 1870–1960: The Crisis of Legal Orthodoxy* (New York, 1992)

HOSKINS, W. G., *The Making of the English Landscape* (Harmondsworth, 1970)

HOVENKAMP, H., 'The Economics of Legal History' (1982–83) 67 Minnesota Law Review 645

—— 'Evolutionary Models in Jurisprudence' (1985) 64 Texas Law Review 645

HOWARTH, W., *Wisdom's Law of Watercourses* (previously entitled *The Law of Rivers and Watercourses*) (5th edn., Crayford, 1992)

HOWE, M. DE W., 'Introduction' to O. W. Holmes Jr., *The Common Law* (Boston, Mass., 1881; ed. M. De Howe, Boston, Mass., 1963)

HUDSON, A. H., 'Industry as a Riparian Use' (1959) 22 Modern Law Review 35

HUDSON, J., 'Anglo-Norman Land Law and the Origins of Property', in G. Garnett and J. Hudson (eds.), *Law and Government in Medieval England and Normandy. Essays in Honour of Sir James Holt* (Cambridge, 1994) 198

—— *Land, Law, and Lordship in Anglo-Norman England* (Oxford, 1994)

HUDSON, J. (ed.), *The History of English Law: Centenary Essays on 'Pollock and Maitland'* (Proceedings of the British Academy 89, Oxford, 1996)

HUDSON, P. (ed.), *Regions and Industries. A Perspective on the Industrial Revolution in Britain* (Cambridge, 1989)

HUFFCUT, E. W., 'Percolating Waters: The Rule of Reasonable User' (1903–04) 13 Yale Law Journal 222

HULSEBOSCH, D. J., 'Writs to Rights: "Navigability" and the Transformation of the Common Law in the Nineteenth Century' (2002) 23 Cardozo Law Review 1049

HUNT, B. C., *The Development of the Business Corporation in England 1800–1867* (Cambridge, Mass., 1936)

HUNTER, L. C., *Waterpower in the Century of the Steam Engine*, in L. C. Hunter and L. Bryant, *A History of Industrial Power in the United States, 1780–1930* 3 vols. (Charlottesville, Va., 1979) i

—— and BRYANT, L., *A History of Industrial Power in the United States, 1780–1930* 3 vols. (Charlottesville, Va., and Cambridge, Mass., 1979–1991)

HURST, J. W., *Law and Economic Growth* (Cambridge, Mass., 1964)

HYAMS, P. R., 'The Charter as a Source for the Early Common Law' (1991) 12 Journal of Legal History 173

IBBETSON, D. J., 'Sixteenth Century Contract Law: *Slade's Case* in Context' (1984) 4 Oxford Journal of Legal Studies 295

—— 'Words and Deeds: The Action of Covenant in the Reign of Edward I' (1986) 4 Law and History Review 71

—— 'Law Reporting in the 1590s', in C. Stebbings (ed.), *Law Reporting in England* (London, 1995) 73

—— *A Historical Introduction to the Law of Obligations* (Oxford, 1999)

—— ' "The Law of Business Rome": Foundations of the Anglo-American Tort of Negligence' [1999] Current Legal Problems 74

—— 'Common Law and *Ius Commune*' (Selden Society Lecture, London, 2001)

—— 'Natural Law and Common Law' (2001) 5 Edinburgh Law Review 4

JACKSON, R. M., 'The Incidence of Jury Trial During the Past Century' (1937) 1 Modern Law Review 132

JEREMY, D. J., *Transatlantic Industrial Revolution: The transfusion of textile technologies between Britain and America 1790–1830s* (Oxford, 1981)

—— (ed.), *Technology and Power in the Early American Cotton Industry: James Montgomery, the second edition of his 'Cotton Manufacture' (1840), and the 'Justitia' Controversy about Relative Power Costs* (Philadelphia, Pa., 1990)

JOHNSON, R. N., GISSER, M., and WERNER, M., 'The Definition of a Surface Water Right and Transferability' (1981) 24 Journal of Law and Economics 273

JOHNSTON, D., 'Owners and Neighbours: From Rome to Scotland', in R. Evans-Jones (ed.), *The Civil Law Tradition in Scotland* (Edinburgh, 1995) 176

—— *Prescription and Limitation* (Edinburgh, 1999)

—— *Roman Law in Context* (Cambridge, 1999)

JOLOWICZ, H. F., 'Political Implications of Roman Law' (1947) 22 Tulane Law Review 62

—— 'Some English Civilians' (1949) 2 Current Legal Problems 139

—— and NICHOLAS, B., *Historical Introduction to the Study of Roman Law* (3rd edn., Cambridge, 1972)

JONES, A. H. M., *The Roman Economy. Studies in Ancient Economic and Administrative History* (P. A. Brunt (ed.), Oxford, 1974)

Jurist, The (New Series) (1866) XII, Part 2, Notes on Water Rights, at 231, 359, 429, 443

KAGAN, K., 'The Nature of Servitudes and the Association of Usufruct with Them' (1947) 22 Tulane Law Review 94

KAHN-FREUND, O., 'Introduction,' to K. Renner, *The Institutions of Private Law and their Social Functions* (London, 1949) 1–43

KARSTEN, P., *Heart versus Head: Judge-made Law in Nineteenth-century America* (Chapel Hill, NC, 1997)

—— 'Using One's Head: Were Jurists "Unconscious" Socio-Economic Ciphers or Conscious Agents? A Response to Friedman' (1999) 24 Law and Social Inquiry 281

KASER, M., *Eigentum und Besitz im älteren römischen Recht* (2nd edn., Cologne, 1956)

—— 'The Concept of Roman Ownership' [1964] Tydskrif vir Hedendaagse Romeins-Hollandse Reg 5

—— *Roman Private Law* (R. Dannenbring (trans.), based on the tenth revised German edition, 3rd edn., Pretoria, 1980)

KEETON, P., 'Trespass, Nuisance and Strict Liability' (1959) 59 Columbia Law Review 457

KELLY, J. M., *A Short History of Western Legal Theory* (Oxford, 1992)

KENNEDY, D., 'The Structure of Blackstone's Commentaries' (1979) 28 Buffalo Law Review 205

KENT, J., *Commentaries on American Law* 4 vols. (1st edn., Boston, Mass., 1826; 2nd edn., Boston, Mass., 1832; 3rd edn., Boston, Mass., 1840)

KING, P., 'Gleaners, Farmers and the Failure of Legal Sanctions in England 1750–1850' (1989) 125 Past and Present 116

—— 'The Origins of the Gleaning Judgement of 1788, A Case Study of Legal Change, Customary Right and Social Conflict in Late Eighteenth Century England' (1992) 10 Law and History Review 1

—— *Crime, Justice, and Discretion in England, 1740–1820* (Oxford, 2000)

KIRALFY, A. K., 'The Persuasive Authority of American Rulings in England' (1948) 23 Tulane Law Review 209

—— *The Action on the Case* (London, 1951)

—— *A Source Book of English Law* (London, 1957)

KOSTAL, R. W., *Law and English Railway Capitalism 1825–1875* (Oxford, 1994)

KRAUS, E. P., 'The Legal Form of Liberalism: A Study of Riparian and Nuisance Law in Nineteenth Century Ohio' [1984] Akron Law Review 223

KREPS, D. M., 'Nash equilibrium', in *The New Palgrave: A Dictionary of Economics* 4 vols. (J. Eatwell, M. Milgate, P. Newman (eds.), London, 1987) iii, 584

—— *Game Theory and Economic Modelling* (Oxford, 1990)

KRETZMER, D., 'Transformation of Tort Liability in the Nineteenth Century: The Visible Hand' (1984) 4 Oxford Journal of Legal Studies 46

KUNKEL, W, *An Introduction to Roman Legal and Constitutional History* (J. M. Kelly (trans.), Oxford, 1966)

KURTZ, S. F., and HOVENKAMP, H., *Cases and Materials on American Property Law* (2nd edn., St Paul, Minn., 1993)

LAMBERT, S., *Bills and Acts. Legislative Procedure in Eighteenth-Century England* (Cambridge, 1971)

LAMOND, R., 'An Early Fulling Mill' (1947) 17 Economic History Review 150

LANDELS, J. G., *Engineering in the Ancient World* (London, 1978)

LANDES, D. S., *The Unbound Prometheus: Technological Change and Industrial Development in Western Europe from 1750 to the Present* (Cambridge, 1969)

—— 'What Do Bosses Really Do?' (1986) 46 Journal of Economic History 585

LANGBEIN, J. H., 'Chancellor Kent and the History of Legal Literature' (1993) 93 Columbia Law Review 547

LAUER, T. E., 'The Common Law Background of the Riparian Doctrine' (1963) 28 Missouri Law Review 60

—— 'Reflections on Riparianism' (1970) 35 Missouri Law Review 1

LAWSON, F. H., and RUDDEN, B., *The Law of Property* (2nd edn., Oxford, 1982)

LEAKE, S. M., *A Digest of the Law of Uses and Profits of Land* (London, 1888)

LEE, H. B., 'Forcing the Federal Hand—Reserved Water Rights v. States Rights for Instream Protection' (1990) 41 Hastings Law Journal 1271

LETWIN, W. L., 'The English Common Law Concerning Monopolies' (1954) 21 University of Chicago Law Review 355

LEVMORE, S., 'Rethinking Comparative Law: Variety and Uniformity in Ancient and Modern Tort Law' (1986) 61 Tulane Law Review 235

LEWIN, J. L., 'Compensated Injunctions and the Evolution of Nuisance Law' (1986) 71 Iowa Law Review 569

LEWIS, A. D. E., ' "What Marcellus says is against you": Roman Law and Common Law', in A. D. E. Lewis and D. J. Ibbetson (eds.), *The Roman Law Tradition* (Cambridge, 1994) 199–208

—— and IBBETSON, D. J. (eds.), *The Roman Law Tradition* (Cambridge, 1994)

LIBECAP, G. D., *Contracting for Property Rights* (Cambridge, 1989)

—— 'Common Property', in *The New Palgrave Dictionary of Economics and the Law* 3 vols. (P. Newman (ed.), London, 1998) i, 317

LIEBERMAN, D., 'Property, Commerce and the Common Law: Attitudes to Legal Change in the Eighteenth Century', in J. Brewer and S. Staves, *Early Modern Conceptions of Property* (London, 1995) 144

LOBBAN, M. J., 'Blackstone and the Science of Law' (1987) 30 Historical Journal 311

—— *The Common Law and English Jurisprudence 1760–1850* (Oxford, 1991)

—— 'Contractual Fraud in Law and Equity, c.1750–c.1850' (1997) 17 Oxford Journal of Legal Studies 441

—— 'The Strange Life of the English Civil Jury, 1837–1914', in J. W. Cairns and G. McLeod (eds.), *'The Dearest Birth Right of the People of England': The Jury in the History of the Common Law* (Oxford, 2002) 173

LOCKE, J., *Second Treatise of Government*, in J. Locke, *Two Treatises of Government*, ed. P. Laslett (Cambridge, 1960)

LOENGARD, J., 'Free Tenements and Bad Neighbours: The Assizes of Novel Disseisin and Nuisance in the King's Courts before the Statute of Merton (1236)' (unpublished doctoral dissertation, Columbia University, New York, 1970)

—— 'The Assize of Nuisance: Origins of an Action at Common Law' [1978] Cambridge Law Journal 144

LOUX, A. C., 'The Persistence of the Ancient Regime: Custom, Utility, and the Common Law in the Nineteenth Century' (1993) 79 Cornell Law Review 183

LÜCKE, H. K., 'Good Faith and Contractual Performance', in P. D. Finn (ed.), *Essays on Contract* (Sydney, 1987) 155

LUECK, D., 'First Possession', in *The New Palgrave Dictionary of Economics and the Law* 3 vols. (P. Newman (ed.), London, 1998) ii, 132

LUPOI, M., *The Origins of the European Legal Order* (Cambridge, 2000)

MCCOY, B. S., 'The Role of Adverse Possession in Water Law' (1986) 10 Harvard Environmental Law Review 257

MACGRADY, G. J., 'The Navigability Concept in the Civil and Common Law' (1975) 3 Florida State University Law Review 511

MCLAREN, J. S., 'Nuisance Law and the Industrial Revolution: Some Lessons From Social History' (1983) 3 Oxford Journal of Legal Studies 155

MACLEOD, C., *Inventing the Industrial Revolution: The English Patent System, 1660–1800* (Cambridge, 1988)

MACNAIR, M., 'Sir Jeffrey Gilbert and his Treatises' (1994) 15 Journal of Legal History 252

—— 'The Nature and Function of the Early Chancery Reports', in C. Stebbings (ed.), *Law Reporting in England* (London, 1995) 123

—— *The Law of Proof in Early Modern Equity* (Berlin, 1999)

—— 'Vicinage and the Antecedents of the Jury' (1999) 17 Law and History Review 537

MCNEIL, K., *Common Law Aboriginal Title* (Oxford, 1989)

MACPHERSON, C. B., *The Political Theory of Possessive Individualism. Hobbes to Locke* (Oxford, 1962)

MAGER, W., 'Proto-Industrialization and Proto-Industry; The Uses and Drawbacks of Two Concepts' (1993) 8 Continuity and Change 181

MAINE, H. S., *Early Law and Custom* (London, 1891)

MAITLAND, F. W., *Domesday Book and Beyond* (Cambridge, 1897, 2nd edn. with a foreword by J. C. Holt, Cambridge, 1987)

MAITLAND, F. W., 'The Beatitude of Seisin' (1888) 4 Law Quarterly Review 24

—— 'Introduction' to *Bracton and Azo* (Selden Society, viii, London, 1894)

—— 'Introduction' to O. Gierke, *Political Theories of the Middle Ages* (Cambridge, 1900) pp. vii–xlv

—— *English Law and the Renaissance* (Cambridge, 1901)

—— *The Forms of Action at Common Law* (1st edn., 1909), ed. A. H. Chaytor and S. J. Whittaker (Cambridge, 1965)

—— *Collected Papers* 3 vols. (H. A. L. Fisher (ed.), Cambridge, 1911)

—— 'Trust and Corporation', in F. W. Maitland, *Collected Papers* (H. A. L. Fisher (ed.), Cambridge, 1911) iii, 321

MANCHESTER, A. H., *A Modern Legal History of England and Wales 1750–1950* (London, 1980)

MANTOUX, P., *The Industrial Revolution in the Eighteenth Century* (Paris, 1905; M. Vernon (trans.), London, 1928)

MARGLIN, S. A., 'What Do Bosses Do?' (1974) 6 Review of Radical Political Economy 60, reprinted in A. Gorz (ed.), *The Division of Labour: The Labour Process and Class Struggle in Modern Capitalism* (Hassocks, 1976)

MARTIN, J. S., 'Water Law and Economic Power: A Reinterpretation of Morton Horwitz's Subsidy Thesis' (1991) 77 Virginia Law Review 397

MARTINI, E. C., 'Wisconsin's Milldam Act: Drawing New Lessons from an Old Law' [1998] Wisconsin Law Review 1305

MARX, K., *Pre-Capitalist Economic Foundations* (J. Cohen (ed. and trans.), London, 1964)

MASON, K. M., *Woolcombers, Worsteds and Watermills: Addingham's Industrial Revolution* (Addington, 1989)

MATHIAS, P., *The First Industrial Nation* (2nd edn., London, 1983)

—— 'The Industrial Revolution: Concept and Reality', in P. Mathias and J. A. Davies (eds.), *The First Industrial Revolutions* (Oxford, 1989) 4

MATTEI, U., *Basic Principles of Property Law: A Comparative Legal and Economic Introduction* (Westport, Conn., 2000)

MEGARRY, R. E., and WADE, H. W. R., *The Law of Real Property* (4th edn., London, 1984)

MELOSSI, D., and PAVARINI, M., *The Prison and the Factory: Origins of the Penitentiary System* (London, 1981)

MERRILL, T. W., 'Property Rules, Liability Rules and Adverse Possession' (1985) 79 Northwestern University Law Review 1122

—— 'Trespass, Nuisance, and the Costs of Determining Property Rights' (1985) 14 Journal of Legal Studies 13

—— 'Land Use Doctrines', in *The New Palgrave Dictionary of Economics and the Law* 3 vols. (P. Newman (ed.), London, 1998) ii, 437

MICHAEL, W. H., and WILL, J. S., *On the Law Relating to Water* (9th edn., by H. R. McDowell and C. F. Chamberlin, with supplementary volume, London, 1950)

MILSOM, S. F. C., 'Legal Introduction' to *Novae Narrationes* (E. Shanks and S. F. C. Milsom (ed.), Selden Society, lxxx, London, 1963) pp. xxx–ccxiv

—— 'Introduction' to F. Pollock, and F. W. Maitland, *The History of English Law Before the Time of Edward I* 2 vols. (1895; 2nd. edn., Cambridge, 1898, reprinted 1968) i, pp. xxiii–lxxiii

—— 'The Real Actions', introduction to F. Pollock and F. W. Maitland, *The History of English Law Before the Time of Edward I* (Cambridge, 1895, 2nd edn., Cambridge, 1898, reprinted 1968) i, pp. xxvii–xlix

—— *Legal Framework of English Feudalism* (Cambridge, 1976)

—— *Historical Foundations of the Common Law* (2nd edn., London, 1981)

—— 'F. W. Maitland', in S. F. C. Milsom, *Studies in the History of the Common Law* (London, 1985) 261

—— 'Law and Fact in Legal Development', in S. F. C. Milsom, *Studies in the History of the Common Law* (London, 1985) 171

—— 'The Nature of Blackstone's Achievment', in S. F. C. Milsom, *Studies in the History of the Common Law* (London, 1985) 197

—— 'Not Doing is No Trespass: A View of the Boundaries of Case', in S. F. C. Milsom, *Studies in the History of the Common Law* (London, 1985) 91

—— 'Reason in the Development of the Common Law', in S. F. C. Milsom, *Studies in the History of the Common Law* (London, 1985) 149

—— ' "Sale of Goods in the Fifteenth Century", in S. F. C. Milsom, *Studies in the History of the Common Law* (London, 1985) 105

—— 'Trespass from Henry III to Edward III', in S. F. C. Milsom, *Studies in the History of the Common Law* (London, 1985) 1

MOCCIA, L., 'English Law Attitudes to "Civil Law" ' (1981) 2 Journal of Legal History 157

MOKYR, J. (ed.), *The Economics of the Industrial Revolution* (London, 1985)

—— *The Lever of Riches. Technological Creativity and Economic Progress* (New York, 1990)

—— (ed.), *The British Industrial Revolution: An Economic Perspective* (Boulder, Col., 1993)

—— 'Introduction' to J. Mokyr (ed.), *The British Industrial Revolution: An Economic Perspective* (Boulder, Col., 1993) 1–131

—— 'Knowledge, Technology, and Economic Growth During the Industrial Revolution', in B. Van Ark, S. K. Kuipers, and G. Kuper (eds.), *Productivity, Technology and Economic Growth* (The Hague, 2000)

MOLLOY, R. T., '*Fletcher* v. *Rylands*' (1941–2) 9 University of Chicago Law Review 266

MOORE, S. A., *A History of the Foreshore* (3rd edn., London, 1888)

MORISON, J., *John Austin* (London, 1982)

MORRIS, C., 'Hazardous Enterprises and Risk Bearing Capacity' (1952) 61 Yale Law Journal 1172

MUENDEL, J., 'The "French" Mill in Medieval Tuscany' (1984) 10 Journal of Medieval History 215

MUNZER, S. R., *A Theory of Property* (Cambridge, 1990)

MURPHY, E. F., 'English Water Law Doctrines Before 1400' (1957) 1 American Journal of Legal History 103

MUSSON, A. E., *The Growth of British Industry* (London, 1978)

NASH, J. F., 'The Bargaining Problem' (1950) 18 Econometrica 155

NASH, M. L., '1189 and the Limit of Legal Memory' (1989) 139 New Law Journal 1763

NELSON, W., *Americanization of the Common Law. The Impact of Legal Change on Massachusetts Society, 1760–1830* (Cambridge, Mass., 1975)

The New Palgrave: A Dictionary of Economics 4 vols. (J. Eatwell, M. Milgate, and P. Newman (eds.), London, 1987)

The New Palgrave Dictionary of Economics and the Law 3 vols. (P. Newman (ed.), London, 1998)

NEWARK, F. H., 'The Boundaries of Nuisance' (1949) 65 Law Quarterly Review 480

—— 'Non-Natural User and Rylands v Fletcher' (1961) 24 Modern Law Review 557

NICHOLAS, B., *An Introduction to Roman Law* (3rd edn., Oxford, 1962)

NOEL, D. W., 'Nuisances From Land in its Natural Condition' (1943) 56 Harvard Law Review 772

NORTH, D. C., *Structure and Change in Economic History* (New York, 1981)

—— *Institutions, Institutional Change and Economic Performance* (Cambridge, 1990)

NOYES, C. R., *The Institution of Property* (New York, 1936)

O'BRIEN, P. K., 'Central Government and the Economy, 1688–1815', in R. Floud and D. N. McCloskey (eds.), *The Economic History of Britain Since 1700, Vol. 1, 1700–1860* (2nd edn., Cambridge, 1994) 205

—— GRIFFITHS T., and HUNT, P., 'Political Components of the Industrial Revolution: Parliament and the English Cotton Textile Industry, 1660–1774' (1991) 44 Economic History Review 395

—— and QUINAULT, R. (eds.), *The Industrial Revolution and British Society* (Cambridge, 1993)

O'GRADA, C., 'The Landlord and Agricultural Transformation, 1870–1900: A Comment on Richard Perren's Hypothesis' (1979) 27 Agricultural History Review 40

OFFER, A., *Property and Politics 1870–1914: Landownership, Law, Ideology and Urban Development in England* (Cambridge, 1981)

—— *The First World War: An Agrarian Interpretation* (Oxford, 1989)

OLDHAM, J. C., 'The Origins of the Special Jury' (1983) 50 University of Chicago Law Review 137

—— 'Special Juries in England: Nineteenth Century Usage and Reform' (1987) 8 Journal of Legal History 148

—— *The Mansfield Manuscripts and the Growth of English Law in the Eighteenth Century* (Chapel Hill, NC, 1992)

OLIVER, D. T., 'Roman Law in Modern Cases in English Courts', in G. G. Alexander (ed.), *Cambridge Legal Essays* (Cambridge, 1926) 243

OSTROM, E., *Governing the Commons. The Evolution of Institutions for Collective Action* (Cambridge, 1990)

—— 'Community and the Endogenous Solution of Commons Problems' (1992) 4 Journal of Theoretical Politics 343

—— 'Self-governance of Common-Pool Resources', in *The New Palgrave Dictionary of Economics and the Law* 3 vols. (P. Newman (ed.), London, 1998) iii, 425

PAILLIET, J.-B. J., *Manuel de Droit Français* 2 vols. (Paris, 1837)

PALMER, R. C., 'The Feudal Framework of English Law' (1981) 79 Michigan Law Review 1130

—— *The County Courts of Medieval England 1150–1350* (Princeton, NJ, 1982)

—— 'The Economic and Cultural Impact of the Origins of Property: 1180–1220' (1985) 3 Law and History Review 375

—— 'The Origins of Property in England' (1985) 3 Law and History Review 1

—— 'Covenant, Justicies Writs, and Reasonable Showings' (1987) 31 American Journal of Legal History 97

—— *English Law in the Age of the Black Death* (Chapel Hill, NC, 1993)

PARRY, D. H., 'Economic Theories in English Case Law' (1931) 47 Law Quarterly Review 183

PAWSON, E., *The Early Industrial Revolution: Britain in the Eighteenth Century* (London, 1979)

PENNER, J. E., *The Idea of Property in Law* (Oxford, 1997)

PENNINGTON, R. R., *Stannary Law* (London, 1973)

PENNOCK, J. R., and CHAPMAN, J. W. (eds.), *Ethics, Economics, and the Law* (1982) 24 Nomos

PERRUSO, R., 'The Development of the Doctrine of *Res Communes* in Medieval and Early Modern Europe' (2002) 70 Tijdschrift voor rechtsgeschiedenis (Legal History Review) 69

PIKE, L. O., 'Feoffment and Livery of Incorporeal Hereditaments' (1889) 5 Law Quarterly Review 29

PHEAR, J. B., *A Treatise on Rights of Water, including Public and Private Rights to the Sea and Sea-Shore* (London, 1859)

[PHILBIN, P.], 'Proving the Will of Another: The Specialty Requirement in Covenant' (1992) 105 Harvard Law Review 2001

PISANI, D. J., *From the Family Farm to Agribusiness: The Irrigation Crusade in California and the West 1850–1931* (Berkeley, Calif., 1984)

—— 'Enterprise and Equity: A Critique of Western Water Law in the Nineteenth Century' (1987) Western Historical Quarterly 18

—— *To Reclaim a Divided West: Water, Law, and Public Policy, 1848–1902* (Albuquerque, N. Mex., 1992)

—— *Water, Land, and Law in the West: The Limits of Public Policy, 1850–1920* (Lawrence, Kan., 1996)

PLESCIA, J., 'The Roman Law of Waters' (1993) 21 Index—International Survey of Roman Law 433
PLUCKNETT, T. F. T., 'The Relations Between Roman Law and English Common Law Down to the Sixteenth Century: A General Survey' (1939) 3 University of Toronto Law Journal 24, 351
—— *A Concise History of the Common Law* (5th edn., London, 1956)
POCOCK, J. C. A., *The Ancient Constitution and the Feudal Law* (Cambridge, 1957, 2nd edn., 1987)
POLLARD, S., 'Fixed Capital in the Industrial Revolution in Britain' (1964) 24 Journal of Economic History 299
—— *The Genesis of Modern Management. A Study of the Industrial Revolution in Great Britain* (London, 1965; reissued Aldershot, 1993)
POLLOCK, F., and MAITLAND, F. W., *The History of English Law Before the Time of Edward I* 2 vols. (Cambridge, 1895, 2nd edn., Cambridge, 1898, reprinted 1968)
POSNER, R. A., *Tort Law: Cases and Economic Analysis* (Boston, Mass., 1982)
—— *Economic Analysis of Law* (4th edn., Boston, Mass., 1992; 5th edn., New York, 1998)
—— 'The Material Basis of Jurisprudence', in R. A. Posner, *Overcoming Law* (Cambridge, Mass., 1995) 33
POSTAN, M. M., 'Why Was Science Backward in the Middle Ages', in M. M. Postan, *Essays on Medieval Agriculture and General Problems of Medieval Economy* (Cambridge, 1973) 81
POSTGATE, J. N., *Early Mesopotamia: Society and Economy at the Dawn of History* (London, 1992, 1994)
POUND, R., 'Law in Books and Law in Action' (1910) 44 American Law Review 12
POWELL, R., 'Roman Law in Common Law Courts' (1958) 11 Current Legal Problems 19
PREST, J., *Liberty and Locality: Parliament, Permissive Legislation, and Ratepayers' Democracies in the Nineteenth Century* (Oxford, 1990)
PRICHARD, M. J., 'Trespass, Case and the Rule in Williams v Holland' [1964] Cambridge Law Journal 234
—— '*Auctoritas* in Early Roman Law' (1974) 90 Law Quarterly Review 378
—— 'Early Usucapio' (1974) 90 Law Quarterly Review 234
—— *Scott v Shepherd (1773) and the Emergence of the Tort of Negligence* (Selden Society Lecture, London, 1976)
PRINGSHEIM, F., 'The Inner Relationship Between English and Roman Law' (1933–5) 5 Cambridge Law Journal 347
PROUDHON, M., *Traite des Droits d'Usufruit, d'Usage, d'Habitation, et de Superficie*, 9 vols. (Dijon, 1824–1827)
PROVINE, D. M., 'Balancing Pollution and Property Rights: A Comparison of the Development of English and American Nuisance Law' (1978) 7 Anglo-American Law Review 31

RAMASASTRY, A., 'The Parameters, Progressions, and Paradoxes of Baron Bramwell' (1994) 38 American Journal of Legal History 322.

RAMSEYER, J. M., 'Water Law in Imperial Japan: Public Goods, Private Claims, and Legal Convergence' (1989) 18 Journal of Legal Studies 51

RENNER, K., *The Institutions of Private Law and their Social Functions* (O. Kahn-Freund (ed.), London, 1949)

RENNISON, R. W., *Water to Tyneside. A History of the Newcastle Water Company* (London, 1979)

REYNOLDS, S. M. G., *Fiefs and Vassals: The Medieval Evidence Reinterpreted* (Oxford, 1994)

REYNOLDS, T. S., *Stronger than One Hundred Men: A History of the Vertical Water Wheel* (London, 1983)

RICHARDSON, H. G., and SAYLES, G. O., 'The Writ of Trespass' (Selden Society, lx, London, 1941) pp. cviii–cxxxiv

—— and —— *Law and Legislation* (London, 1966)

ROBINSON, O. F., *Ancient Rome: City Planning and Administration* (London, 1992)

ROBINSON, R. B., 'The Two Institutes of Thomas Wood: A Study in 18th Century Legal Scholarship' (1999) 35 American Journal of Legal History 432

RODGER, A., *Owners and Neighbours in Roman Law* (Oxford, 1972)

—— 'Concealing a Servitude', in P. G. Stein and A. D. E. Lewis (eds.), *Studies in Justinian's Institutes in Memory of J. A. C. Thomas* (London, 1983) 134

—— 'The Position of *aquae ductus* in the Praetor's Edict', in P. B. H. Birks (ed.), *New Perspectives in the Roman Law of Property. Essays for Barry Nicholas* (Oxford, 1989) 177

ROSE, C. M., 'Possession as the Origin of Property' (1985) 52 University of Chicago Law Review 73, reprinted in C. M. Rose, *Property and Persuasion* (Boulder, Col., 1994) 11

—— 'The Comedy of the Commons: Custom, Commerce and Inherently Public Property' (1986) University of Chicago Law Review 711, reprinted in C. M. Rose, *Property and Persuasion* (Boulder, Col., 1994) 105

—— 'Crystals and Mud in Property Law' (1988) 40 Stanford Law Review 577, reprinted in C. M. Rose, *Property and Persuasion* (Boulder, Col., 1994) 199

—— 'Energy and Efficiency in the Realignment of Common Law Water Rights' (1990) 19 Journal of Legal Studies 261, reprinted in C. M. Rose, *Property and Persuasion* (Boulder, Col., 1994) 163

—— 'Rethinking Environmental Controls: Management Strategies for Common Resources' [1991] Duke Law Journal 1

—— 'A Tale of Two Rivers' (1993) 91 Michigan Law Review 1623

—— *Property and Persuasion: Essays on the History, Theory, and Rhetoric of Ownership* (Boulder, Col., 1994)

—— 'Property as the Keystone Right?' (1996) 71 Notre Dame Law Review 329

—— 'The Shadow of the Cathedral' (1997) 106 Yale Law Journal 2175

Rose, C. M., 'Canons of Property Talk, or, Blackstone's Anxiety' (1998) 108 Yale Law Journal 601

—— 'Evolution of Property Rights', in *The New Palgrave Dictionary of Economics and the Law* 3 vols. (P. Newman (ed.), London, 1998) ii, 93

—— 'Joseph Sax and the Idea of the Public Trust' (1998) 25 Ecology Law Quarterly 351

—— 'Riparian Rights', in *The New Palgrave Dictionary of Economics and the Law* 3 vols. (P. Newman (ed.), London, 1998) iii, 344

—— 'Comparing Newfangled Tradable Allowance Schemes To Old-Fashioned Common Property Regimes' (1999) 10 Duke Environmental Law & Policy Forum 45

—— 'Romans, Roads, and Romantic Creators: Traditions of Public Property in the Information Age' (2003) 66 Law and Contemporary Problems 89

Rose-Ackerman, S., 'Inalienability and the Theory of Property Rights' (1985) 85 Columbia Law Review 931

—— 'Inalienability', in *The New Palgrave Dictionary of Economics and the Law* 3 vols. (P. Newman (ed.), London, 1998) ii, 268

Rosenberg, N., *Perspectives on Technology* (Cambridge, 1976)

—— *Inside the Black Box. Technology and Economics* (Cambridge, 1982)

—— 'Marx as a Student of Technology', in N. Rosenberg, *Inside the Black Box. Technology and Economics* (Cambridge, 1982) 34–51

Rosenthal, J.-L., *The Fruits of Revolution. Property Rights, Litigation, and French Agriculture, 1700–1860* (Cambridge, 1992)

Round, O. S., *Riparian Rights, Being a Concise Review of the Law Relating to Running Streams, Angling, and the Sea Shore* (London, 1859)

Routledge, R. A., 'Statutory Control of Land Use on Environmental Grounds in England 1485–1945' (1981) 2 Journal of Legal History 77

Rubin, G. R., and Sugarman, D., 'Towards a New History of Law and Material Society in England, 1750–1914', in G. R. Rubin and D. Sugarman (eds.), *Law, Economy and Society in England, 1750–1914: Essays in the History of the English Law* (Abingdon, 1984) 1

Rubinstein, W. D., 'Gentlemanly Capitalism and British Industry 1820–1914' (1991) 132 Past and Present 150

—— *Capitalism, Culture and Decline in Britain, 1750–1990* (London, 1993)

Rudden, B., *The New River: A Legal History* (Oxford, 1985)

—— 'Equity as Alibi', in S. Goldstein (ed.), *Equity and Contemporary Legal Developments* (Jerusalem, 1992) 30

Runnington, C., *The History, Principles and Practice of the Legal Remedy by Ejectment, and the Resulting Action for Mesne Profits* (2nd edn., London, 1820)

Ryan, A., *Property and Political Theory* (Oxford, 1984)

Rydz, D. L., *The Parliamentary Agents: A History* (London, 1979)

Sackville and Neaves' Property Law: Cases and Materials (4th edn., by M. A. Neave, C. J. Rossiter and M. A. Stone, Sydney, 1988)

SALMOND, J. W., 'The History of the Law of Prescription', in J. W. Salmond, *Essays in Jurisprudence and Legal History* (London, 1891) 73

SALT, H. E., 'The Local Ambit of a Custom', in G. G. Alexander (ed.), *Cambridge Legal Essays* (Cambridge, 1926) 279

SAMUEL, G., 'Roman Law and Modern Capitalism' (1984) 4 Legal Studies 185

SAMUEL, R., 'Workshop of the World: Steampower and Hand-Technology in Mid-Victorian Britain' (1977) 3 History Workshop 6

SAX, J., *Water Law, Planning and Policy: Cases and Materials* (Indianapolis, Ind., 1968)

—— 'The Public Trust Doctrine in Natural Resource Law: Effective Judicial Intervention' (1970) 68 Michigan Law Review 471

—— 'Liberating the Public Trust Doctrine from its Historical Shackles' (1980) 14 University of California Davis Law Review 185

—— 'The Limits of Private Rights in Public Waters' (1989) 19 Environmental Law 473

—— *et al.*, *Legal Control of Water Resources* (3rd edn., St Paul, Minn., 2000)

SCHAMA, S., *Landscape and Memory* (London, 1995)

SCHEIBER, H. N., 'The Road to *Munn*: Eminent Domain and the Concept of Public Purpose in the State Courts', in D. Fleming and B. Bailyn (eds.), *Law in American History* (*Perspectives in American History*, v) (Boston, Mass., 1971) 329

—— 'Law and the Imperatives of Progress: Private Rights and Public Values in American Legal History', in J. R. Pennock and J. W. Chapman (eds.), *Ethics, Economics, and the Law* (1982) 24 Nomos 303

—— (ed.), *The State and Freedom of Contract* (Stanford, 1998)

SCHILLER, A. A., *Roman Law: Mechanisms of Development* (New York, 1978)

SCHULZ, F., *Principles of Roman Law* (M. Wolff (trans.), Oxford, 1936)

—— *History of Roman Legal Science* (Oxford, 1946)

—— *Classical Roman Law* (London, 1951)

SCHWARTZ, G. T., 'Tort Law and the Economy in Nineteenth-Century America: A Reinterpretation' (1981) 90 Yale Law Journal 1721

—— 'The Character of Early American Tort Law' (1989) 36 University of California Los Angeles Law Review 641

SCHWARTZ, P., 'John Stuart Mill and Laissez Faire: London Water' (1966) 33 Economica 71

SCOTT, A., and COUSTALIN, G., 'The Evolution of Water Rights' (1995) 35 Natural Resources Journal 821

SCRUTTON, T. E., *The Influence of Roman Law on the Law of England* (Cambridge, 1885)

—— *Commons and Common Fields or the History and Policy of the Laws Relating to Commons and Enclosure in England* (Cambridge, 1887)

SEABRIGHT, P., 'Local Common Property Rights', in *The New Palgrave Dictionary of Economics and the Law* 3 vols. (P. Newman (ed.), London, 1998) ii, 591

SEIPP, D. J., 'Bracton, the Year Books, and the "Transformation of Elementary Legal Ideas" in the Early Common Law' (1989) 7 Law and History Review 175

—— 'Roman Legal Categories in the Early Common Law', in T. G. Watkin (ed.), *Legal Record and Historical Reality* (London, 1989) 9

—— 'The Structure of English Common Law in the Seventeenth Century', in W. M. Gordon and T. D. Fergus (eds.), *Legal History in the Making* (London, 1989) 61

—— 'The Reception of Roman and Civil Law in the Common Law Courts Before 1600' (1993) 13 Oxford Journal of Legal Studies 388

—— 'The Concept of Property in Early Common Law' (1994) 12 Law and History Review 29

SHAW, J., *Water Power in Scotland, 1550–1870* (Edinburgh, 1984)

SILVER, M., *Economic Structures of the Ancient Near East* (London, 1983)

SIMPSON, A. W. B., *History of the Common Law of Contract: The Rise of the Action of Assumpsit* (Oxford, 1975)

—— 'Introduction' to Blackstone's *Commentaries* ii (Chicago, 1979)

—— (ed.), *Biographical Dictionary of the Common Law* (London, 1984)

—— 'Legal Liability for Bursting Reservoirs: The Historical Context of *Rylands v. Fletcher*' (1984) 13 Journal of Legal Studies 209, revised and reprinted as 'Bursting Reservoirs and Victorian Tort Law: *Rylands and Horrocks v. Fletcher* (1868)' in A. W. B. Simpson, *Leading Cases in the Common Law* (Oxford, 1995) 195

—— *A History of the Land Law* (2nd edn., Oxford, 1986)

—— 'The Horwitz Thesis and the History of Contracts', in A. W. B. Simpson, *Legal Theory and Legal History. Essays on the Common Law* (London, 1987) 203

—— 'Innovation in Nineteenth Century Contract Law', in A. W. B. Simpson, *Legal Theory and Legal History. Essays on the Common Law* (London, 1987) 171

—— *Legal Theory and Legal History. Essays on the Common Law* (London, 1987)

—— 'The Rise and Fall of the Legal Treatise: Legal Principles and the Forms of Legal Literature', in A. W. B. Simpson, *Legal Theory and Legal History: Essays on the Common Law* (London, 1987) 273

—— 'The Rule in Wheeldon v. Burrows and the Code Civil', in A. W. B. Simpson, *Legal Theory and Legal History: Essays on the Common Law* (London, 1987) 163

—— *Leading Cases in the Common Law* (Oxford, 1995)

—— 'The Study of Cases', in A. W. B. Simpson, *Leading Cases in the Common Law* (Oxford, 1995) 1

—— 'The Timeless Principles of the Common Law: *Keeble* v. *Hickeringill* (1707)', in A. W. B. Simpson, *Leading Cases in the Common Law* (Oxford, 1995) 45

—— 'Victorian Judges and the Problem of Social Cost: *Tipping* v. *St. Helens' Smelting Company* (1865)', in A. W. B. Simpson, *Leading Cases in the Common Law* (Oxford, 1995) 163

—— 'Victorian Law and the Industrial Spirit' (Selden Society Lecture, London, 1995)

—— '*Coase v. Pigou* Reexamined' (1996) 25 Journal of Legal Studies 53

—— 'Land Ownership and Economic Freedom', in H. N. Scheiber (ed.), *The State and Freedom of Contract* (Stanford, 1998) 13

SINGLETON, S., and TAYLOR, M., 'Common Property, Collective Action and Community' (1992) 4 Journal of Theoretical Politics 309

SINGER, J. W., 'The Legal Rights Debate in Analytical Jurisprudence from Bentham to Hohfeld' [1982] Wisconsin Law Review 975

—— *Entitlement: The Paradoxes of Property* (New Haven, Conn., 2000)

SMITH, F. B., *The People's Health, 1830–1910* (corrected edn. 1990; reissued edn., Aldershot, 1993)

SMITH, L. D., 'The Motive Not the Deed', in J. Getzler (ed.), *Rationalizing Property, Equity and Trusts. Essays in Private Law in Honour of Edward Burn* (London, 2003) 53

SMITH, N., *A History of Dams* (1st edn., London, 1971; U.S. edn., Secaucus, NJ, 1972)

SOKOL, M., 'Bentham and Blackstone on Incorporeal Hereditaments' (1994) 15 Journal of Legal History 287

SOKOLOFF, K. L., and DOLLAR, D., 'Agricultural Seasonality and the Organization of Manufacturing in Early Industrial Economies: The Contrast between England and the United States' (1997) 57 Journal of Economic History 288

SPENCER, J. R., 'Public Nuisance—A Critical Examination' (1989) 48 Cambridge Law Journal 55

STARKIE, T., *A Practical Treatise of the Law of Evidence* 3 vols. (3rd edn., London, 1842)

STEIN, P. G., *Regulae Iuris: From Juristic Rules to Legal Maxims* (Edinburgh, 1966)

—— *Law and English Jurisprudence Yesterday and Today* (Cambridge, 1969)

—— *Legal Evolution* (Cambridge, 1980)

—— 'The Development of the Institutional System', in P. G. Stein and A. D. E. Lewis (eds.), *Studies in Justinian's Institutes in Memory of J. A. C. Thomas* (London, 1983)

—— *Legal Institutions. The Development of Dispute Settlement* (London, 1984)

—— 'The Attraction of the Civil Law in Post-Revolutionary America', in P. G. Stein, *The Character and Influence of the Roman Civil Law. Historical Essays* (London, 1988) 411

—— *The Character and Influence of the Roman Civil Law. Historical Essays* (London, 1988)

—— 'Continental Influences in English Legal Thought, 1600–1900', in P. G. Stein, *The Character and Influence of the Roman Civil Law. Historical Essays* (London, 1988) 209

—— 'The Fate of the Institutional System', in P. G. Stein, *The Character and Influence of the Roman Civil Law. Historical Essays* (London, 1988) 73

STEIN, P. G., 'The Four Stage Theory of the Development of Societies', in P. G. Stein, *The Character and Influence of the Roman Civil Law. Historical Essays* (London, 1988) 395

—— 'Donellus and the Origins of the Modern Civil Law', in J. A. Ankum (ed.), *Mélanges Felix Wubbe* (Fribourg, 1993) 439

—— *Roman Law in European History* (Cambridge, 1999)

STEINBERG, T., *Nature Incorporated: Industrialization and the Waters of New England* (New York, 1991)

STOLJAR, S. J., *A History of Contract at Common Law* (Canberra, 1975)

STOLJAR, S. J., 'Concerning Strict Liability' in P. D. Finn (ed.), *Essays on Tort* (Sydney, 1989) 267–93

STONE, J., and WELLS, W. A. N., *Evidence: Its History and Policies* (Sydney, 1991)

STRETTON, H., *Capitalism, Socialism and the Environment* (Cambridge, 1976)

STROUD, D. A., *The Law of Easements, Founded on Select Cases* (London, 1934)

STURLEY, M. F., 'Easements in Gross' (1980) 96 Law Quarterly Review 557

SUGARMAN, D., 'Legal Theory, the Common Law Mind and the Making of the Textbook Tradition', in W. Twining (ed.), *Legal Theory and Common Law* (Oxford, 1986) 26

SUTCLIFFE, J., *Treatise on Canals and Reservoirs, and the Best Mode of Designing and Executing Them* (Rochdale, 1816)

SUTHERLAND, D. W., *Quo Warranto Proceedings during the Reign of Edward I* (Oxford, 1963)

—— *The Assize of Novel Disseisin* (Oxford, 1973)

TAGGART, M, *Private Property and Abuse of Rights in Victorian England: The Story of Edward Pickles and the Bradford Water Supply* (Oxford, 2002)

TARLOCK, A. D., 'The Changing Meaning of Water Conservation in the West' (1987) 66 Nebraska Law Review 145

TAYLOR, M., *Community, Anarchy and Liberty* (Cambridge, 1982)

TECLAFF, L. A., *Water Law in Historical Perspective* (Buffalo, Col., 1985)

THAYER, J. B., *Preliminary Treatise on Evidence at the Common Law* (London, 1898)

THOMAS, J. A. C., *Institutes of Justinian. Text and Commentary* (London, 1975)

—— *Textbook of Roman Law* (Amsterdam, 1976)

THOMAS, J. H., *A Systematic Arrangement of Lord Coke's First Institutes of the Laws of England* 3 vols. (London, 1818)

THOMAS, K., *Man and the Natural World. Changing Attitudes in England 1500–1800* (Harmondsworth, 1984)

THOMPSON, F. M. L., *English Landed Society in the Nineteenth Century* (London, 1963)

THOMSON, B. H. Jr., 'Water Law as a Pragmatic Exercise' (1998) 25 Ecology Law Quarterly 363

THORNE, S. E., 'Introduction' to Henry de Bracton, *De Legibus et Consuetudinibus Angliae* 4 vols. (G. E. Woodbine (ed.), S. E. Thorne (trans.), Cambridge, Mass., 1977) i

—— 'Introduction' to Henry de Bracton, *De Legibus et Consuetudinibus Angliae* 4 vols. (G. E. Woodbine (ed.), S. E. Thorne (trans.), Cambridge, Mass., 1977) iii, pp. xiii–lii

—— *Essays in English Legal History* (London, 1985)

—— 'Henry de Bracton, 1268–1968', in S. E. Thorne, *Essays in English Legal History* (London, 1985) 75

—— 'The Text of Bracton's *De Legibus Angliae*', in S. E. Thorne, *Essays in English Legal History* (London, 1985) 93

TILLOTSON, J. H. (ed.), *Monastery and Society in the Late Middle Ages. Selected Account Rolls from Selby Abbey, Yorkshire, 1398–1537* (Woodbridge, 1988)

TREVOR-HODGE, A., *Roman Aqueducts and Water Supply* (London, 1992)

TUNZELMANN, G. N. von, *Steam Power and British Industrialization to 1860* (Oxford, 1978)

—— 'Technology in the Early Nineteenth Century' in R. Floud and D. N. McCloskey (eds.), *The Economic History of Britain Since 1700, Vol. 1, 1700–1860* (Cambridge, 2nd edn., 1994) 271–99

—— *Technology and Industrial Progress: The Foundations of Economic Growth* (Aldershot, 1995)

TURNBULL, G., 'Canals, Coal and Regional Growth during the Industrial Revolution' (1987) 40 Economic History Review 537

UELMEN, D. L., 'The Law of Underground Water: A Half-Century of Huber v. Merkel' [1953] Wisconsin Law Review 491

ULLMANN, W., 'Medieval Principles of Evidence' (1946) 62 Law Quarterly Review 77, reprinted in *Law and Jurisdiction in the Middle Ages (Collected Studies)* (G. Garnett (ed.), London, 1988)

UNWIN, G., *Samuel Oldknow and the Arkwrights* (London, 1924, reprint edn., Manchester, 1968)

URE, A., *The Philosophy of Manufactures; or, An Exposition of the Scientific, Moral and Commercial Economy of the Factory System of Great Britain* (London, 1835)

—— *An Historical Introduction to Private Law* (D. Johnston (trans.), Cambridge, 1992)

VANDEVELDE, K. J., 'The New Property of the 19th Century: The Development of the Modern Concept of Property' (1980) 29 Buffalo Law Review 325

VILLIERS, M. DE, 'Nuisances in Roman Law' (1897) 13 Law Quarterly Review 387

VINOGRADOFF, P., 'The Problem of Customary Law', in P. Vinogradoff, *Collected Papers* ii (H. A. L. Fisher (ed.), Oxford, 1928) ii, 410

—— 'Some Considerations on the Methods of Ascertaining Legal Customs', in P. Vinogradoff, *Collected Papers* (H. A. L. Fisher (ed.), Oxford, 1928) ii, 402

VRIES, J. DE, 'The Industrial Revolution and the Industrious Revolution' (1994) 54 Journal of Economic History 249

WADE MARTINS, S., *A Great Estate at Work: The Holken Estate and Its Inhabitants in the Nineteenth Century* (Cambridge, 1980)

WAGNER, D. O.. 'Coke and the Rise of Economic Liberalism' (1935–6) 6 Economic History Review Ser. 1, 30

—— 'The Common Law and Free Enterprise: An Early Case of Monopoly' (1936–7) 7 Economic History Review Ser. 1, 217

WALDRON, J., 'What is Private Property?' (1985) 5 Oxford Journal of Legal Studies 313

—— *The Right To Private Property* (Oxford, 1988)

WALLACE, J. W., *The Reporters, Arranged and Characterized with Incidental Remarks* (4th edn., Boston, Mass., 1882)

WARD, J. R., *The Finance of Canal Building in Eighteenth-Century England* (Oxford, 1974)

WARE, E. F., *Roman Water Law, Translated from the Pandects of Justinian* (St Paul, Minn., 1905, reprinted Littleton, Col., 1985)

WATKIN, T. G., *An Historical Introduction to Modern Civil Law* (Aldershot, 1999)

WATSON, A., 'The Structure of Blackstone's Commentaries' (1988) 97 Yale Law Journal 795

—— 'Chancellor Kent's Use of Foreign Law', in M. Reimann (ed.), *The Reception of Continental Ideas in the Common Law World 1820–1920* (Berlin, 1993) 45

—— 'The Transformation of American Property Law: A Comparative Law Approach' (1990) 24 Georgia Law Review 163, reprinted as 'Jurists, Judges, Custom, Legislation: Water Rights', in A. Watson, *The Evolution of Western Private Law* (2nd edn., Baltimore, Mld., 2001) 138

WEBER, M., *Economy and Society: An Outline of Interpretive Sociology*, 3 vols. (*Wirtschaft und Gesellschaft*, Tübingen, 1921–2; G. Roth and C. Wittich (eds.), New York, 1968, Berkeley, Calif., 1978)

—— 'The Development of Bureaucracy and its Relation to Law', from *Wirtschaft und Gesellschaft (Economy and Society)* (1922), reprinted in *Max Weber: Selections in Translation* (W. R. Runciman (ed.), Cambridge, 1978) 341

WEBSTER, R. G., *The Law Relating to Canals, Comprising a Treatise on Navigable Rivers and Canals* (London, 1885)

WEIR, T., *Economic Torts* (Oxford, 1997)

WELLINGTON, C., 'Sir Richard Arkwright—Premier Crook in the Industrial Revolution' (1993) 20 International Journal of Social Economics 37

WESTCOAT, J. L., 'Toward a Modern Map of Roman Water Law' (1997) 18 Urban Geography 100

WHELAN, F. G., 'Property as Artifice: Hume and Blackstone', in J. R. Pennock and J. W. Chapman, eds., *Property*, Nomos XXII (New York, 1980) 101

WHITE, G. E., *The American Judicial Tradition. Profiles of Leading American Judges* (2nd edn., New York, 1988)

WHITE, K. D., *Greek and Roman Technology* (Ithaca, 1984)

WHITE, L., Jr., *Medieval Technology and Social Change* (Oxford, 1962)

WHITMAN, J. Q., *The Legacy of Roman Law in the German Romantic Era: Historical Vision and Legal Change* (Princeton, NJ, 1990)

—— 'Why Did the Revolutionary Lawyers Confuse Custom and Reason?' (1991) 58 University of Chicago Law Review 1321

—— 'The Seigneurs Descend to the Rank of Creditors' (1994) 6 Yale Journal of Law and the Humanities 249

WHITTY, N., 'Water Law Regimes', in K. Reid and R. Zimmermann (eds.), *A History of Private Law in Scotland* 2 vols. (Oxford, 2000) i, 420–79

WIEACKER, F., *Römische Rechtsgeschichte* 3 vols. (Munich, 1988) i

—— *A History of Private Law In Europe: With Particular Reference to Germany* (T. Weir (trans.), R. Zimmermann (introd.), Oxford, 1995)

WIEL, S. C., 'Running Water' (1909) 22 Harvard Law Review 190

—— 'Determination of Water Titles and the Water Commission Bill' (1913–14) 2 California Law Review 435

—— 'A Short Code of Underground Water' (1913–14) 2 California Law Review 367

—— 'Theories of Water Law' (1913–14) 27 Harvard Law Review 530

—— 'Mingling of Waters' (1915–16) 29 Harvard Law Review 137

—— 'Origin and Comparative Development of the Law of Watercourses in the Common Law and in the Civil Law' (1917–18) 6 California Law Review 245, 342

—— 'Waters: American Law and French Authority' (1919) 33 Harvard Law Review 133

—— 'Fifty Years of Water Law' (1936) 50 Harvard Law Review 252

WILLIAMS, E. N., *The Eighteenth Century Constitution 1688–1815: Documents and Commentary* (Cambridge, 1960)

WILLIAMS, J., *Principles of the Law of Real Property* (1st edn., London, 1845)

—— *Rights of Common and other Prescriptive Rights* (London, 1880)

WILLIAMS, O., *The Historical Development of Private Bill Procedure and Standing Orders in the House of Commons* (London, 1948)

WILLIAMS, R., *The Country and the City* (London, 1973)

WILLIAMS, S. F., 'Transforming American Law: Doubtful Economics Makes Doubtful History' (1977) 25 University of California Los Angeles Law Review 1187

WILSON, P. N., 'Water Power and the Industrial Revolution' (1954) 6 Water Power 8

WINELD, P. H., 'Nuisance as a Tort' [1930–32] Cambridge Law Journal 189

—— and GOODHART, A. L., 'Trespass and Negligence' (1933) 49 Law Quarterly Review 359

WITTFOGEL, K. A., 'The Theory of Oriental Society', reprinted in M. H. Fried (ed.), *Readings in Anthropology* (2nd edn., New York, 1968) ii, 180

WITTFOGEL, K. A., *Oriental Despotism. A Comparative Study of Total Power* (New Haven, Conn., 1957; New York, 1981)

WOOLRYCH, H. W., *A Treatise on the Law of Waters* (1st. edn., London, 1830; 2nd edn., 1851)

WORDSWORTH, W., *Poetical Works* (T. Hutchinson (ed.), E. de Selincourt (rev. edn.), Oxford, 1936)

WORSTER, D., *Rivers of Empire: Water, Aridity, and the Growth of the American West* (New York, 1985)

WORTHINGTON, G., *Inquiry into the Power of Juries to Decide Incidentally on Questions of Law* (London, 1825)

WRIGLEY, E. A., *People, Cities and Wealth. The Transformation of Traditional Society* (Oxford, 1987)

—— *Continuity, Chance and Change. The Character of the Industrial Revolution in England* (Cambridge, 1988)

YALE, D. E. C., ' "Of No Mean Authority": Some Later Uses of Bracton', in M. S. Arnold, T. A. Green, S. A. Scully, and S. D. White (eds.), *On the Laws and Customs of England* (Chapel Hill, NC, 1981) 383

YOOL, G. V., *An Essay on Waste, Nuisance, and Trespass, Chiefly with Reference to Remedies in Equity* (London, 1863)

ZUCKERMAN, A. A. S., *The Principles of Criminal Evidence* (Oxford, 1989)

ZULUETA, F. de, *The Institutes of Gaius*, Part 2, Commentary (Oxford, 1953)

Index